Environmental Philosophy

FROM ANIMAL RIGHTS TO RADICAL ECOLOGY

General Editor

Michael E. Zimmerman
Tulane University

Associate Editors

J. Baird Callicott
University of Wisconsin–Stevens Point

George Sessions
Sierra College

Karen J. Warren
Macalester College

John Clark
Loyola University of the South

Prentice Hall, Englewood Cliffs, New Jersey 07632

Library of Congress Cataloging-in-Publication Data

Environmental philosophy : from animal rights to radical ecology /
   general editor, Michael E. Zimmerman : associate editors, J. Baird
   Callicott . . . [et al.].
      p.   cm.
   Includes bibliographical references.
   ISBN 0–13–666959–X
      1. Human ecology—Philosophy. 2. Human ecology—Moral and ethical
   aspects. I. Zimmerman, Michael E., (date)
   GF21.E56 1993
      179'.1—dc20   92–32188
                                                           CIP

Acquisitions editor: Ted Bolen
Editorial/production: Bridget Mooney
Interior design: Peggy Gordon
Copy editor: Durrae Johanek
Cover design: Bruce Kenselaar
Cover art: Kinuko Y. Craft
Prepress buyer: Herb Klein
Manufacturing buyer: Patrice Fraccio

 © 1993 by Prentice-Hall, Inc.
A Paramount Communications Company
Englewood Cliffs, New Jersey 07632

Printed in the United States of America
10 9 8 7 6 5

ISBN 0-13-666959-X

Prentice-Hall International (UK) Limited, *London*
Prentice-Hall of Australia Pty. Limited, *Sydney*
Prentice-Hall Canada Inc., *Toronto*
Prentice-Hall Hispanoamericana, S.A., *Mexico*
Prentice-Hall of India Private Limited, *New Delhi*
Prentice-Hall of Japan, Inc., *Tokyo*
Simon & Schuster Asia Pte. Ltd., *Singapore*
Editora Prentice-Hall do Brasil, Ltda., *Rio de Janeiro*

 Contents

General Introduction

Michael E. Zimmerman

Michael E. Zimmerman is professor and chair of philosophy at Tulane University. Author of many essays in environmental philosophy and two books, including Heidegger's Confrontation with Modernity, *he is completing a new book on radical ecology in the postmodern age.*

In the past two decades, a growing number of philosophers have become concerned about the potentially disastrous ecological problems of modern industrial civilization, ranging from depletion of atmospheric ozone to the loss of species diversity. Many 'ecophilosophers' argue that one major source of these problems is Western society's concept of endless material 'progress.' This concept was promoted by Enlightenment thinkers who were so inspired by developments in modern science, technology, and market economies that they believed humankind could eventually control nature, thereby eliminating poverty, sickness, and social disorders, including political oppression. In the nineteenth century, industrial expansion and technological innovation encouraged widespread optimism about future social and material progress. Although two brutal world wars and the alienating effects of industrial technology weakened this optimism during the twentieth century, the postwar years saw most people remaining committed to the model of infinite growth, neglecting to consider its potentially devastating ecological consequences.

During the late 1960s, however, members of the youthful 'counter-cultural' movement began calling for a radical transformation of Western society in order to save humankind and the planet from the social and ecological consequences of endless material progress. Counterculturalists argued that the same technological expertise that brought about extraordinary improvements in medicine, transportation, manufacturing, and communication also enabled people to build nuclear-tipped ICBMs capable of destroying life on the planet. Moreover, the same economic systems that increased the wealth of many Western people helped to impoverish the Third World, simultaneously generating ecological problems that threatened the stability of the biosphere. Despite disagreements about means, counterculturists agreed about many goals: halting the suicidal and wasteful arms race, developing ecologically sound and egalitarian economic practices, freeing people from oppression, dismantling the one-dimensional technological system that repressed alternative ways of thinking and behaving, liberating humanity's spiritual and creative capacities, and emancipating nonhuman beings from abuse. Although critical of many aspects of technological modernity, counterculturists often employed modernity's emancipatory rhetoric.

Thirty years ago, most philosophers were preoccupied with specialized topics of interest geared primarily toward other philosophers: epistemology, philosophy of language, and ethical metatheory. Some philosophers were so affected by the countercultural, civil rights, anti-war, environmental, and women's movements, however, that they initiated what has come to be known as 'applied philosophy,' which addresses a wide variety of issues, ranging from feminism to business ethics. At times, environmental philosophers may be said to engage in such applied philosophy. At other times, they go further: They question the foundations of Western metaphysics, epistemology, ethics, and politics. They ask: Why do we consider nature as nothing but raw material, whose value lies only in its use for some human end? Are humans the most important thing in the universe? If so, how do we know this? To what extent do ecological problems stem from humanity-nature dualism? How do we know that history has any 'direction' at all, much less a 'progressive' one? If there is a progressive trend in history, on what basis do we assume that progress consists in having humans dominate nonhumans? Do humans have any ethical obligations to nonhumans? When we are told that industrial technology furthers 'man's progress,' who is meant by 'man'? Why do wealthy groups seem to gain the most from technological innovation, often at the expense of poor or dispossessed people? Why are waste incinerators and polluting factories most often built near the homes of the poor and powerless? In speaking of 'man's progress,' do we mean the attempt by groups of male humans to gain control over nature in a way analogous to how they have gained control over women in patriarchy? Do technological innovations really contribute to the goal of freeing people, or do those innovations give rise to serious social and ecological problems, as well as new forms of enslavement? How can industrial technology 'free' humanity, if that same technology is employed in economic systems which are poisoning the planet? To what extent is human freedom compatible with the disappearance of everything wild and free in nature?

One may roughly divide environmental philosophy into three major fields. The first field, 'radical' ecophilosophy, often associated with the countercultural movement, includes deep ecology, ecofeminism, and social ecology. Radical ecophilosophers regard themselves as radical for two reasons. First, they claim that their analyses disclose the conceptual, attitudinal, and social origins of the ecological crisis. Second, they argue that only a revolution or a cultural paradigm shift can save the planet from further destruction. While acknowledging that reforming current practices (e.g., demanding tighter controls on industrial pollution, or encouraging recycling) may help matters in the short run, radical ecologists maintain that reforms will be insufficient in the long run because they only address the symptoms, not the roots of the ecological crisis.

While agreeing about the limitations of reformism, radical ecophilosophers have different ideas about what constitutes the roots of the ecological crisis. Deep ecologists think that one of its roots involves anthropocentrism: the view that humans are the origin and measure of all value. Such a view breeds an arrogance that leads people to treat nature as nothing but raw material for satisfying human desires. Many ecofeminists think that its major root is patriarchy: an oppressive social structure which justifies its exploitation of women and nature, because it regards both as somehow 'inferior' to men. Social ecologists argue that the principal root of the ecological crisis involves social hierarchy: Authoritarian social structures allow some people not only to dominate other people, but also to waste, despoil, and destroy nonhuman beings.

The second field of environmental philosophy, environmental ethics, maintains that progress could be made in ending the ecological crisis if we changed our anthropocentric ethical attitudes and granted 'moral considerability' to nonhuman beings. Environmental ethicists hope that just as today one is morally and legally obligated to refrain from abusing or killing people, so tomorrow one may be morally and legally obligated to refrain from abusing or killing many kinds of living beings—except for nontrivial reasons. Some environmental ethicists are so critical of the atomistic, anthropocentric, and dualistic categories of Western society that they verge on being radical ecophilosophers. Other environmental ethicists, however, adhere to a less radical position, sometimes known as 'weak' anthropocentrism. This position affirms that human beings are intrinsically more valuable than nonhumans, but also holds that at least some nonhuman beings cannot be treated merely instrumentally, for they have a worth of their own. Hence, a 'weak' anthropocentric environmental philosopher would justify protecting an unspoiled natural area from development, or defending an endangered species, *not* simply because doing so might benefit some group of humans, but also because the natural area and the species are somehow good in themselves. Just what this 'good' might be has been the subject of extensive debate.

Something like a 'weak' anthropocentric viewpoint is discernible in social ecology, according to which humans are so valuable in part because only they can disclose and measure the worth of nonhuman beings. It is misleading, then, to conclude that all radical ecologists share deep ecology's critique of anthropocentrism. What social ecology *does* share with deep ecology, and what differentiates social ecology from most versions of 'weak' anthropocentrism, is the belief that only a radical transformation of existing social and economic arrangements can end the practices generating the ecological crisis.

The third field in environmental philosophy, anthropocentric reformism, argues that the root of our environmental problems is neither anthropocentric attitudes about humanity's place in nature, nor the political-economic structures that embody those attitudes. Rather, air and water pollution, wasteful use of natural resources, and the like, stem from ignorance, greed, and shortsightedness. Such factors may be addressed by enacting legislation, changing public policy, increasing education, altering tax laws, returning 'public lands' to private ownership, emphasizing moral obligations to future generations of humans, promoting wise 'stewardship' of nature, and otherwise encouraging more prudent use and more equitable allocation of natural resources. According to these reformists, while nature has value only as an instrument for human ends, those ends range from the food provided by plants and animals to the aesthetic pleasure provided by a beautiful wild landscape. Anthropocentric reformists regard radical ecologists as naive about the prospects of introducing drastic changes in the social attitudes and institutions allegedly responsible for ecological problems.

Despite such reservations, I believe that the radical ecophilosophy's analyses of the social and conceptual origins of ecological problems offer an important alternative to the approach recommended by reform-minded anthropocentric ecophilosophers. Increasingly, the views of radical ecophilosophers are being taken more seriously by people from mainstream groups. A few years ago, for example, a *Time* cover story called for major social changes to forestall ecological disaster. Reflecting this growing interest, this anthology covers radical ecophilosophy, as well as environmental ethics. Because of the crucial role played by environmental ethics in legitimizing ecophilosophy in professional circles, we devote the first section of this anthology to environmental ethics. Although some people *equate* environmental philosophy with environmental ethics, I believe this equation is misleading for the following reason.

Deep ecologists, arguing that environmental ethicists often draw on categories that are part of the anthropocentric and atomistic worldview that has led to the ecological crisis, maintain that we need an ontological shift in our currently anthropocentric understanding of what it means 'to be' human. By virtue of such a shift, we are told, ecologically-sensitive moral attitudes would arise spontaneously. Similarly, ecofeminists maintain that existing ethical systems usually presuppose the universal validity of conceptions of selfhood that are in fact grounded primarily in the experience of certain classes of men. From a masculinist social ontology which conceives of people as being isolated egos competing for survival with other egos, one can imagine how a rights-based ethics of justice and fairness could be derived. By challenging such 'gendered' conceptions of what it means 'to be' a self or a person, ecofeminists hope to promote alternative ethical norms, including norms pertaining to treatment of non-human beings. Hence, while ethical issues are of concern to radical ecologists, they often maintain that important ontological issues must be clarified before attempting to 'extend' to non-human beings ethical norms that originally applied only to humans—and perhaps then only to certain groups.

While including essays on environmental ethics and radical ecophilosophy, this anthology omits coverage of reformist anthropocentric ecophilosophy. This omission is *not* meant as a slight to people who have done such important work in that area. Environmental philosophy has become such a large field that any anthology trying to represent all its many facets would not do justice to any one of them. Hence, it was necessary to make a strategic decision regarding areas to be covered. While reformist anthropocentric environmental philosophy is well-represented in other anthologies, they generally omit coverage of radical environmental philosophy. The present anthology makes up for that omission. While doing our best to adequately represent trends within the areas we *do* cover, we regret that many valuable essays had to be omitted for reasons of space.

In recent years, serious conflicts have occurred among radical ecophilosophers. While not wishing to discount the intellectual and political differences which sparked some of these debates, I feel that these philosophers share the same ultimate concern: to further the well-being of all life on Earth. Moreover, they agree that the predominant attitudes and socio-economic structures of Western society must be dramatically changed in order to save the planet. Whether such shared concerns and convictions can transcend important differences remains to be seen. In any event, for people to learn from one another, genuine dialogue is needed. In my own essays, I have encouraged such a dialogue.[1] All the editors of the present anthology hope that it will contribute to productive discussions about eco-philosophy among teachers and students in courses for which the anthology is adopted. The vision of my associate editors, each of whom has made significant scholarly contributions to their field, has made this anthology much stronger than it would have been otherwise. I thank them for their participation, encouragement, and support.

I would like to acknowledge the inspiration of my students over the years, especially those in my Humanity's Place in Nature course. Thanks also go to three anonymous reviewers for their sound criticisms, and to Ted Bolen at Prentice Hall, whose faith in our project kept it alive at a crucial moment.

NOTE

1. Cf. Michael E. Zimmerman, "Toward a Heideggerean *Ethos* for Radical Environmentalism," *Environmental Ethics*, 5 (Summer, 1983), 99-131; "Feminism, Deep Ecology, and Environmental Ethics," *Environmental Ethics*, 9 (Spring, 1987), 21-44; "Deep Ecology and Ecofeminism: The Emerging Dialogue," in *Reweaving the World*, ed. Irene Diamond and Gloria Feman Orenstein (San Francisco: Sierra Club Books, 1990); "Quantum Theory, Intrinsic Value, and Non-Dualism," *Environmental Ethics*, X (Spring, 1988), 3-30.

PART ONE

Environmental Ethics

Introduction

J. Baird Callicott

J. Baird Callicott is professor of philosophy and natural resources at the University of Wisconsin–Stevens Point. He is the author of In Defense of the Land Ethic: Essays in Envirnonmental Philosophy *and editor of* Companion to a Sand County Almanac: Interpretative and Critical Essays.

In 1973, with the publication of three seminal papers, environmental ethics made its formal debut on the staid and conservative stage of professional philosophy. That spring, the young Australian philosopher Peter Singer published "Animal Liberation" in *The New York Review of Books.* That summer, "The Shallow and the Deep, Long Range Ecology Movement: A Summary" by the distinguished Norwegian philosopher and mountaineer Arne Naess appeared in the international philosophy journal, *Inquiry.* That fall, another young Australian philosopher, Richard Sylvan (then Routley), addressed his colleagues at the Fifteenth World Congress of Philosophy in Varna, Bulgaria, with a question: "Is There a Need for a New, an Environmental, Ethic?"

Over the next several years, a few more papers in this novel and exciting area of research appeared in such professional journals as *Ethics* and the *Journal of Philosophy.* Then, in 1979, Eugene C. Hargrove established a new quarterly, *Environmental Ethics,* and the floodgates opened. Articles in environmental ethics poured forth. College courses began to be offered in the subject. By the middle of the next decade a number of book-length discussions had appeared. Thus a whole new field of philosophy has come into being.

The three seminal papers of 1973 stand at the fountainhead not of one but of three increasingly divergent streams of thought. Deep ecology, flowing from the paper by Naess, has now solidified into an eight-point "platform," which has been adopted by members of the radical green movement, including its covert operatives, the "eco-warriors" of Earth First!. Moreover, deep ecology has become a "practice" aimed at directly *experiencing* connectedness with nature. Deep ecology seems, accordingly, vaguely anti-intellectual and overtly hostile to the impersonal (as the deep ecologists think of it) "ethical reduction" of what they believe should be a more intimate relationship to the natural world than that typical of morality. The ethical theory of animal liberation/animal rights has become the philosophical wing of an even more visible and increasingly militant movement. The goals of that movement, however, have been not only different from but also often in conflict with the goals of the environmental movement. And as moral philosophies, animal liberation/rights and environmental ethics are now recognized as separate fields of study each with its own agenda.

Accordingly, in this anthology, deep ecology has its own section, while this first part is divided into two distinct groups of essays: Individualistic Approaches and Holistic Approaches. Since the conflict between animal liberation/rights and environmental ethics has been more profound or at least longer standing than the internecine disputes among ecofeminism, deep ecology, and social ecology, one might suppose that essays in animal welfare ethics might be excluded from this anthology. But there are good reasons for including some of those essays here. Those reasons follow.

Historically, animal liberation/rights and environmental ethics were conflated. Even today, though the schism between the two occurred in the early 1980s, most philosophers, let alone laypeople, regard them as being pretty much the same thing. Because we are large vertebrates ourselves, thoughts of other large vertebrates understandably come to mind when we consider the natural environment. Wild animals *are* a significant part of the natural environment, but domestic animals—who get the lion's share of attention from animal welfare ethicists—are not. And the natural environment comprises much, much more than just our furry friends.

Practically, animal liberation/rights and environmental ethics often overlap and, as just noted, often conflict. For example, domestic cattle and sheep, feral rabbits, goats, pigs, and the like often threaten to destroy delicate ecosystems and to extinguish endangered plant species. The ethics of most environmentalists would require preserving ecosystems and certainly plant species at all costs, even if that should mean assassinating the commonplace herbivorous mammals, while the ethics of animal liberationists and animal rights activists would favor the mammals, even if that should mean further ecological degradation and the erosion of biodiversity.

Methodologically, however, animal liberation/rights and environmental ethicists are united by a resolute commitment to the methods of traditional Western philosophy. Both spin their theories out of the strands of thought found in the history of European and Euro-American thought. Both develop moral philosophies that ground ethical theories, which in turn imply practical precepts. Both believe in the power of reason to persuade and to engender consensus. And both believe in the power of ideas to direct individual action, to change social values, and to forge new cultural ideals.

Theoretically, and most important for our purposes here, animal liberation/rights broke new ground in moral philosophy by taking a step beyond the species barrier. The very able and persuasive articulation of animal liberation by Singer and animal rights by Tom Regan—both decidedly non-anthropocentic (nonhuman centered) moral philosophies—blazed a path followed by a second wave of philosophers with wider concerns. Thus while animal liberation/rights is an end-point in support of the agenda of the very popular animal welfare movement, animal liberation/rights can be regarded, as it is here, as but the first step toward a more encompassing environmental ethic oriented to all living things severally or individually.

We begin part one of this anthology with Sylvan's summons to the global community of philosophers to focus philosophy's formidable powers of conceptual analysis and cognitive creativity on the environmental problematique. In 1973, an adequate, nonanthropocentric environmental ethic simply did not exist in Western intellectual traditions, Sylvan argues, although one had been prophetically envisioned by the great American conservationist, Aldo Leopold, at midcentury. So he urged contemporary philosophers to take up Leopold's mantle and make it their business to provide one.

The principal deficiency, as Sylvan's arresting "last people" and "last man" ethical thought experiments at the heart of his paper are intended to drive home, is that the "base class" of traditional Western ethics is coextensive with the class of human beings. Adapting a term from liberal feminism (ecofeminism by then had not emerged as such), traditional Western ethical theory has been guilty of "human [as well as male] chauvinism." Hence the principal theoretical problem that Sylvan sets out for the philosophers who would respond to his challenge is how to enlarge the ethical base class so that it will include nonhuman as well as human beings.

Notice that Sylvan mentions, among the large class of ethically disenfranchised beings that an eventual environmental ethic might embrace, both individual plants (trees) and animals (dingoes), on the one hand, and environmental collectives or wholes such as species (*the* blue whale) and ecosystems, on the other. As he is simply sketching the problem, not attempting to solve it, he is rather casual about what nonhuman beings ought and ought not to be included in the moral base class of an adequate environmental ethic or how theoretically to go about expanding the base class.

We may regard Peter Singer's paper as a first attempt to address the philosophical problem as Sylvan has set it out, though Singer was of course not deliberately responding to Sylvan's plea. In traditional Western moral philosophy, human chauvinism or what Singer and Richard Ryder (also drawing on the rhetoric of contemporaneous feminism) call "speciesism" (on analogy with sexism) is not simply asserted without defense. Moral philosophers from Plato to Rawls have spent considerable energy explaining what makes human beings so special and what makes us and us alone worthy of moral treatment. Singer exploits this ubiquitous feature of classic Western moral philosophy and poses the following dilemma for any human chauvinist ethics.

If what entitles a human being to be a member of the moral base class (call it the philosopher's preferred "criterion for moral standing") is pitched high enough to exclude other animals, then it will also exclude the human "marginal cases"—human infants, the severely retarded, and abjectly senile people. If we are serious about the possession of a certain capacity—say the capacity to reason or to speak—demarcating the difference between those who do deserve moral consideration and those who don't, and if we are self-consistent, then we should permit treating the marginal cases just as we treat other morally disenfranchised beings: without qualms, researchers might perform painful medical experiments and test products on unwanted babies, state fish and game departments might open a hunting season on the retarded, and Purina might make dog food out of the senile.

Outrageous! To be sure. That's just the point. But in order to bring the marginal cases into the moral base class, we shall have to lower the entry requirement. To what level? Singer turns for an answer to the criterion proposed by Jeremy Bentham: sentience, the capacity to experience pleasure and pain. Sentience is arguably a more relevant criterion for moral treatment than some more exclusive alternative, since the minimum consideration one asks of others is not to be harmed by them. And one may suppose that to be harmed, in the last analysis, means to be hurt, to be caused to suffer. Where exactly the "insuperable line," as Bentham calls it, falls between those animals who are and those who are not sentient is far from clear, but it *is* entirely clear that at the very least all vertebrates ought to be included in the moral base class as so delineated.

The enormous appeal of Singer's animal liberation ethic stems, ironically, from the fact that he has really put forth nothing new. Rather, he has simply demanded that the value theory—pleasure is good and pain is evil—of classical utilitarianism be consistently applied. Classical utilitarianism insisted upon the *impartial* accounting of pleasures and pains, but arbitrarily limited that accounting to the pleasures and pains of human beings. Remove this *ad hoc* limitation, and voilà!, one has animal liberation.

That, however, exposed Singer's animal liberation ethic to all the problems that classical utilitarianism's ingenious critics had worked out over two centuries. Singer is an advocate of vegetarianism for purely moral reasons, but even this basic practical implication of the ethical enfranchisement of animals is suspect on purely utilitarian grounds. We might raise animals in comfort, slaughter them painlessly, and still enjoy our steaks, chops, and bacon and eggs.

Such considerations as these led Tom Regan to counter Singer's animal liberation ethic with the equally familiar and classical antidote—rights, animal rights in this case. According to Regan, those animals who are subjects of a life, which from their own point of view may be better or worse, have "inherent value" and therefore rights, which "trump" the "principle of utility," that, roughly, directs us to do whatever would produce a greater balance on average of pleasure over pain among all the sentient creatures whom one's actions affect.

For Singer and Regan, the ethical entitlement of "animals" is a philosophical goal in and of itself. If, on the other hand, our goal is to develop the more inclusive environmental ethic originally envisioned by Sylvan, animal liberation and animal rights are at best a way station.

Obviously, plants are left totally out of account by animal liberation/rights, to say nothing of the nonliving parts of ecosystems about which we environmentalists are concerned, such as the soil, water, and air. Moreover, despite the title, "All Animals Are Equal," of the first chapter of Singer's book, *Animal Liberation,* not even *all* animals are included in Singer's charmed circle of moral patients, since many kinds of animals may not be sentient. The animals to which Regan's theory would extend rights are even more narrowly restricted, indeed much more so.

In a 1978 paper, "On Being Morally Considerable," Kenneth E. Goodpaster tentatively took moral philosophy beyond animal liberation/rights into environmental ethics proper. He agreed with Bentham and Singer that withholding ethical entitlement from entities that fail to meet the more restrictive of historically proposed criteria (such as being rational) for "moral considerability" was neither intellectually honest nor ultimately warranted. But he disagreed with them that the insuperable line should be drawn by the sentience criterion. From a biological point of view, sentience is a means, not an end—a means to life. Hence, not sentience, but "being alive" should be the criterion for moral considerability. Further, such a criterion is arguably more relevant to the benefit for which it selects, since nonsentient living things may also intelligibly be said to have interests and, if so, they may be directly benefited or harmed—even though harming them may not hurt them, may not cause them consciously to suffer. But Goodpaster's reasoning clearly follows the form classically established by Bentham and recently elaborated by Singer.

Goodpaster's "life-principle" ethic is minimalistic. He expressly avoids the issue of how much weight we ought to give the interests of plants and other barely living beings. And he even admits that while technically they may be morally considerable, practically they may fall well below the human "threshold" of moral sensitivity. Thus we may forever be unable actually to take the interests of all the living things that our actions affect into account as we make our day-to-day practical decisions.

Three years later, the distinguished American philosopher Paul W. Taylor proffered a much stronger version of biocentrism (literally, a "life-centered" ethical theory). According to Taylor, all living things are "teleo-logical centers of life." An organism's *telos* (Greek for "end, goal") is to reach a state of maturity and to reproduce. Our actions can interdict the fulfillment of an organism's telos; and to do just that is to harm it. Taylor agrees with Goodpaster that all living things have interests and thus a good of their own, quite irrespective of the uses to which we might put them and quite independently of whether they are sentient or care. While Taylor withholds rights from nonhuman natural entities, he argues that *all* wild organisms have *equal* inherent worth. (Taylor's limiting moral con-siderability to *wild* telelogical centers of life appears to be theoretically unjustified, however.)

The idea that all wild organisms (from fruit flies to sperm whales) are of equal moral worth runs counter to our considered ethical intuitions accord-ing to which long-lived, conscious beings are intrinsically more valuable than ephemeral, insentient beings. However, even if we were persuaded by Taylor's bioegalitarianism, the resulting environmental ethic would be be-side the point, not to mention diabolically difficult to practice. The welfare of grubs, bugs, and shrubs is simply not the focus of environmental concern. As Sylvan's programmatic paper suggests, environmental concern focuses less on individual living things (though their well-being is not ignored entirely) than on species and other "holistic" entities, on biotic communi-ties, ecosystems, wilderness, and the planetary biosphere as a whole.

In "Animal Liberation and Environmental Ethics: Bad Marriage, Quick Divorce," Mark Sagoff highlights many of the differences between the individualistic and holistic approaches to nonanthropocentric moral philosophy. His discussion is confined to the individualistic animal wel-fare ethics, but appropriately generalized, it applies with equal force to the exclusively individualistic life-principle or respect-for-life ethics.

It's not just that the animal welfare ethics do not go far enough, rather they run in a different and often contrary direction to environmental concerns, Sagoff argues. In addition to conflicts between the welfare of domestic or feral sentient animals and endangered plant species or overall ecosystem health, there also exist conflicts of interest between domestic and feral animals, on the one hand, and wild animals on the other. In "Animal Rights, Human Wrongs," Regan expresses a concern for both whales and gibbon apes. But most of the concern of animal liberation/rights has been lavished on animals like cattle (especially veal calves or "bobby calves" as Regan refers to them), chickens, and the like that are factory farmed. While factory farming is environmentally destructive because of the irrechargable aquifers depleted, soil eroded, and polluting chemicals applied, the well-being of domestic creatures themselves—plants included, certainly, as well as animals—is just not an environmental issue. Environmentally speaking, wild animal and plant *populations* are the important issue, and they are often severely impacted adversely by competition from domestic and feral types.

In sum, as Sagoff forcefully points out, environmental concerns are predominantly holistic, not individualistic. Thus the exclusively individualistic approach to environmental ethics inadequately addresses these concerns. Environmental concerns and exclusively individualistic environmental ethics pass one another by, like the proverbial ships in the night, without meeting or making contact.

Well, what to do? Perhaps we can get a clue by diagnosing the problem. Singer, Regan, Goodpaster, and Taylor all provide variations on a common theoretical theme that could be called the standard paradigm of traditional moral philosophy. The standard paradigm identifies and justifies a property or characteristic that entitles the possessor to moral considerability. The principal difference between the theories of Singer, Regan, Goodpaster, and Taylor and those of their anthropocentric predecessors lies in the choice of the ethically enfranchising property or characteristic. Most traditional exponents of the standard paradigm carefully select a property or characteristic that they believe only human beings possess. Singer, Regan, Goodpaster, and Taylor have deliberately chosen theirs to include not only all human beings but also a wide range of nonhuman beings. All vertebrates possess Singer's; all mammals possess Regan's; and all living things possess Goodpaster's and Taylor's.

Attempts have been made to attribute unconscious interests—similar to those attributed to plants and insentient animals by Goodpaster and Taylor—to environmental wholes, such as species and ecosystems. And attempts have been made to argue that mere existence is a property warranting moral consideration. But such attempts have not been taken seriously. Biocentrism thus represents the end point of this simple line of argument. It stretches this familiar pattern of moral reasoning to its limit. Like a rubber band asked to encircle too big a bundle, attempts to stretch it further have snapped its credibility.

The holistic approach to environmental ethics would seem, therefore, to require either a different theoretical paradigm or some theoretical means of cogently augmenting biocentrism. Basing his theory on hints and suggestions offered by Aldo Leopold, J. Baird Callicott has pursued the former alternative, while Holmes Rolston, III has pursued the latter. Leopold claims that "a land ethic changes the role of *Homo sapiens* from conqueror of the land community to plain member and citizen of it. It implies respect for his fellow-members and also respect for the *community as such*." Indeed, as "The Land Ethic" progresses, "fellow-members" recede farther and farther from the author's attention and concern for the "community as such" looms ever larger in importance. When Leopold finally comes to write the summary moral maxim or golden rule of the land ethic, he seems to have forgotten about individual plants and animals altogether, and only the ecosystem as a whole remains as the object of moral considerability: "A thing is right when it tends to preserve the integrity, stability, and beauty of the biotic community. It is wrong when it tends otherwise."

Because of the perfect fit of the land ethic with their holistic concerns, contemporary environmentalists have made it their ethic of choice. But Leopold was a forester by training and wildlife ecologist by profession, not a philosopher. Hence his brief but suggestive foray into ethics is not theoretically well formed or fully argued. In "The Conceptual Foundations of the Land Ethic," J. Baird Callicott attempts explicitly to construct the theoretical superstructure that occasionally shows through the informal texture of Leopold's prose.

The standard paradigm requires us to grant moral considerability to whatever the philosopher's preferred (and justified) criterion of moral considerability identifies as morally considerable—no matter how we may *feel* about such beings. Callicott argues that Leopold's land ethic belongs to the tradition of moral philosophy classically articulated in the eighteenth century by David Hume and Adam Smith, in which ethics are rooted precisely in altruistic feelings like benevolence, sympathy, and loyalty. According to Callicott, Charles Darwin suggested that such feelings were naturally selected in many species, including our prehuman ancestors, because without them individuals could not bond together into mutually beneficial societies and communities. Rudimentary ethics emerged as human beings evolved to the point that they could articulate codes of conduct conforming to their social sentiments. As human societies grew in scope and complexity, so did our ethics. By now, we have reached the point that the enlightened among us regard all human persons as members of one world community, the "global village," subject to a common ethics of humanity, the "human rights" ethic.

Leopold envisions the land ethic to be the next stage of human moral evolution, for presently ecology portrays terrestrial nature to be a biotic community composed of plants and animals, soils and waters. A universal ecological literacy would trigger sympathy and fellow-feeling for *fellow-members* of the biotic community *and* feelings of loyalty and patriotic regard for the *community as a whole*, Callicott suggests. How to balance human interests against those of nonhuman natural entities and nature as a whole is as big a problem for the feeling-based land ethic as for any other environmental ethic. Callicott defends the land ethic against the charge that it amounts to an "environmental fascism," which some of its exclusively individualistic critics have, in retaliation for his very generous critique of their views, leveled against it.

If the biocentrism of Goodpaster and Taylor errs in being exclusively individualistic, the ecocentrism (short for ecosystem-centered ethic) of Leopold and Callicott may err in being excessively—though by no means exclusively—holistic. Rolston has attempted a different synthesis of individualism and holism. At the foundation of his theory lies the core claim of biocentrism—that any and every living thing is intrinsically valuable and thus morally considerable. But for his approach to be more plausible than that of Goodpaster and Taylor, he must somehow reconcile the moral considerability of individual plants (from the lowliest shrub to the most magnificent sequoia) and animals (from gnats to mountain gorillas) with common sense, and he must also somehow make his theory reach environmental wholes. Rolston has been working at this project since the publication of his 1975 essay, "Is There an Ecological Ethic?" which was as seminal as the slightly earlier paper by Sylvan reprinted here. His "Challenges in Environmental Ethics" summarizes the fruits of nearly two decades of inquiry.

To the equal baseline intrinsic value of living things, each with a good of its own, Rolston adds a value premium, so to speak, for sentience and an additional value premium for self-consciousness. Thus sentient animals possess more intrinsic value than plants and insentient animals; and we self-conscious rational animals possess the most intrinsic value of all individual natural entities. Therefore, in cases of conflict, human interests take precedence over those of individual animals and plants, as most sensible people believe; and, by the same token, the interests of sentient animals take precedence over those of insentient animals and plants. Rolston then awards a value dividend, as it were, to species, the perpetuation of which is the reproductive end of specimens, and to ecosystems as the matrix in which baseline intrinsically valuable living things evolved and upon which they remain dependent for their flourishing. In Rolston's essentially biocentric system, like the moon that shines by a borrowed light, natural wholes, such as species and ecosystems, possess an intrinsic value derived from the baseline intrinsic value of living organisms and thus enjoy only derivative moral considerability. Further, it is not clear how applying Rolston's system might adjudicate conflicts of interest between wholes and individuals. That problem, however, is endemic to all ethics that go beyond traditional anthropocentrism, and so it would be unfair to suggest that Rolston's environmental ethic is any less decisive, in respect to such practical conundrums, than are any of its competitors.

Is There a Need for a New, an Environmental, Ethic?

Richard Sylvan (Routley)

Richard Sylvan (formerly Routley) is a fellow with the Research School of Social Sciences at the Australian National University in Canberra. With Don Mannison and Michael McRobbie, he edited Environmental Philosophy.

1

It is increasingly said that civilization, Western civilization at least, stands in need of a new ethic (and derivatively of a new economics) setting out people's relations to the natural environment, in Leopold's words "an ethic dealing with man's relation to land and to the animals and plants which grow upon it."[1] It is not of course that old and prevailing ethics do not deal with man's relation to nature; they do, and on the prevailing view man is free to deal with nature as he pleases, i.e., his relations with nature, insofar at least as they do not affect others, are not subject to moral censure. Thus assertions such as "Crusoe ought not to be mutilating those trees" are significant and morally determinate but, inasmuch at least as Crusoe's actions do not interfere with others, they are false or do not hold—and trees are not, in a good sense, moral objects.[2] It is to this, to the values and evaluations of the prevailing ethics, that Leopold and others in fact take exception. Leopold regards as subject to moral criticism, as wrong, behavior that on prevailing views is morally permissible. But it is not, as Leopold

This essay was originally published in *Proceedings of the XV World Congress of Philosophy*, No. 1. Varna, Bulgaria, 1973, pp. 205–210. Reprinted with permission of author.

seems to think, that such behavior is beyond the scope of the prevailing ethics and that an *extension* of traditional morality is required to cover such cases, to fill a moral void. If Leopold is right in his criticism of prevailing conduct what is required is a *change* in the ethics, in attitudes, values and evaluations. For as matters stand, as he himself explains, men do not feel morally ashamed if they interfere with a wilderness, if they maltreat the land, extract from it whatever it will yield, and then move on; and such conduct is not taken to interfere with and does not rouse the moral indignation of others. "A farmer who clears the woods off a 75% slope, turns his cows into the clearing, and dumps its rainfall, rocks, and soil into the community creek, is still (if otherwise decent) a respected member of society."[3] Under what we shall call *an environmental ethic* such traditionally permissible conduct would be accounted morally wrong, and the farmer subject to proper moral criticism.

Let us grant such evaluations for the purpose of the argument. What is not so clear is that a *new* ethic is required even for such radical judgments. For one thing it is none too clear what is going to count as a new ethic, much as it is often unclear whether a new development in physics counts as a new physics or just as a modification or extension of the old. For, notoriously, ethics are not clearly articulated or at all well worked out, so that the application of identity criteria for ethics may remain obscure.[4] Furthermore we tend to cluster a family of ethical systems which do not differ on core or fundamental principles together as one ethic; e.g. the Christian ethic, which is an umbrella notion covering a cluster of differing and even competing systems. In fact then there are two other possibilities, apart from a new environmental ethic, which might cater for the evaluations, namely that of an extension or modification of the prevailing ethics or that of the development of principles that are already encompassed or latent within the prevailing ethic. The second possibility, that environmental evaluations can be incorporated within (and ecological problems solved within) the framework of prevailing Western ethics, is open because there isn't a single ethical system uniquely assumed in Western civilization: on many issues, and especially on controversial issues such as infanticide, women's rights, and drugs, there are competing sets of principles. Talk of a new ethic and prevailing ethics tends to suggest a sort of monolithic structure, a uniformity, that prevailing ethics, and even a single ethic, need not have.

Indeed Passmore has mapped out three important traditions in Western ethical views concerning man's relation to nature; a dominant tradition, the despotic position, with man as despot (or tyrant), and two lesser traditions, the stewardship position, with man as custodian, and the co-operative position with man as perfecter.[5] Nor are these the only traditions; primitivism is another, and both romanticism and mysticism have influenced Western views.

The dominant Western view is simply inconsistent with an environmental ethic; for according to it nature is the dominion of man and he is free to deal with it as he pleases (since—at least on the mainstream Stoic-Augustine view—it exists only for his sake), whereas on an environmental ethic man is not so free to do as he pleases. But it is not quite so obvious that an environmental ethic cannot be coupled with one of the lesser traditions. Part of the problem is that the lesser traditions are by no means adequately characterized anywhere, especially when the religious backdrop is removed, e.g. *who* is man steward for and responsible to? However both traditions are inconsistent with an environmental ethic because they imply policies of complete interference, whereas on an environmental ethic some worthwhile parts of the earth's surface should be preserved from substantial human interference, whether of the "improving" sort or not. Both traditions would in fact prefer to see the earth's land surfaces reshaped along the lines of the tame and comfortable north-European small farm and village landscape. According to the co-operative position man's proper role is to develop, cultivate and perfect nature—all nature eventually—by bringing out its potentialities, the test of perfection being primarily usefulness for human purposes; while on the stewardship view man's role, like that of a farm manager, is to make nature productive by his efforts though not by means that will deliberately degrade its resources. Although these positions both depart from the dominant position in a way which enables the incorporation of some evaluations of an environmental ethic, e.g. some of those concerning the irresponsible farmer, they do not go far enough: for in the present situation of expanding populations confined to finite natural areas, they will lead to, and enjoin, the perfecting, farming and utilizing of all natural areas. Indeed these lesser traditions lead to, what a thoroughgoing environmental ethic would reject, a principle of total use, implying that every natural area should be cultivated or otherwise used for human ends, "humanized."[6]

As the important Western traditions exclude an environmental ethic, it would appear that such an ethic, not primitive, mystical or romantic, would be new alright. The matter is not so straightforward; for the dominant ethic has been substantially qualified by the rider that one is not always entitled to do as one pleases where this physically interferes with others. Maybe some such proviso was implicit all along (despite evidence to the contrary), and it was simply assumed that doing what one pleased with natural items would not affect others (the non-interference assumption). Be this as it may, the *modified* dominant position appears, at least for many thinkers, to have supplanted the dominant position; and the modified position can undoubtedly go much further towards an environmental ethic. For example, the farmer's polluting of a community stream may be ruled immoral on the grounds that it physically interferes with others who use or would use the streams. Likewise business enterprises which destroy the natural environment for no satisfactory returns or which cause pollution deleterious to the health of future humans, can be criticized on the sort of welfare basis (e.g. that of Barkley and Seckler) that blends with the modified position; and so on.[7] The position may even serve to restrict the sort of family size one is entitled to have since in a finite situation excessive population levels will interfere with future people. Nonetheless neither the modified dominant position nor its Western variants, obtained by combining it with the lesser traditions, is adequate as an environmental ethic, as I shall try to show. A new ethic *is* wanted.

2

As we noticed (an) *ethic* is ambiguous, as between a specific ethical system, a *specific* ethic, and a more generic notion, a super ethic, under which specific ethics cluster.[8] An ethical system S is, near enough, a propositional system (i.e. a structured set of propositions) or theory which includes (like individuals of a theory) a set of values and (like postulates of a theory) a set of general evaluative judgments concerning conduct, typically of what is obligatory, permissible and wrong, of what are rights, what is valued, and so forth. A general or lawlike proposition of a system is a principle; and certainly if systems S_1 and S_2 contain different principles, then they are different systems. It follows that any environmental ethic differs from the important traditional ethics outlined. Moreover if environmental ethics differ from Western ethical systems on some *core* principle embedded in Western systems, then these systems differ from the Western super ethic (assuming, what seems to be so, that it can be uniquely characterized)—in which case if an environmental ethic *is* needed then a new ethic is wanted. It suffices then to locate a core principle and to provide environmental counter examples to it.

It is commonly assumed that there are, what amount to, core principles of Western ethical systems, principles that will accordingly belong to the super ethic. The fairness principle inscribed in the Golden Rule provides one example. Directly relevant here, as a good stab at a core principle, is the commonly formulated liberal principle of the modified dominance position. A recent formulation runs as follows:

"The liberal philosophy of the Western world holds that one should be able to do what he wishes, providing (1) that he does not harm others and (2) that he is not likely to harm himself irreparably."[9]

Let us call this principle *basic (human) chauvinism*—because under it humans, or people, come first and everything else a bad last—though sometimes the principle is hailed as a *freedom* principle because it gives permission to perform a wide range of actions (including actions which mess up the environment and natural things) providing they do not harm others. In fact it tends to cunningly shift the onus of proof to others. It is worth remarking that *harming others* in the restriction is narrower than a restriction to the (usual) interests of others; it is not enough that it is in my interests, because I detest you, that you stop breathing; you are free to breathe, for the time being anyway, because it does not harm me. There remains a problem however as to exactly what counts as harm or interference. Moreover the width of the principle is so far obscure because "other" may be filled out in significantly different ways: it makes a difference to the extent, and privilege, of the chauvinism whether "other" expands to "other human"—which is too restrictive—or to "other person" or to "other sentient being"; and it makes a difference to the adequacy of the principle, and inversely to its economic applicability, to which class of others it is intended to apply, whether to future as well as to present others, whether to remote future others or only to non-discountable future others and whether to possible others. The latter would make the principle completely unworkable, and it is generally assumed that it applies at most to present and future others.

It is taken for granted in designing counter examples to basic chauvinist principles, that a semantical analysis of permissibility and obligation statements stretches out over ideal situations (which may be incomplete or even inconsistent), so that what is permissible holds in some ideal situation, what is obligatory in every ideal situation, and what is wrong is excluded in every ideal situation. But the main point to grasp for the counter examples that follow, is that ethical principles if correct are universal and are assessed over the class of ideal situations.

(i) The *last man* example. The last man (or person) surviving the collapse of the world system lays about him, eliminating, as far as he can, every living thing, animal or plant (but painlessly if you like, as at the best abattoirs). What he does is quite permissible according to basic chauvinism, but on environmental grounds what he does is wrong. Moreover one does not have to be committed to esoteric values to regard Mr. Last Man as behaving badly (the reason being perhaps that radical thinking and values have shifted in an environmental direction in advance of corresponding shifts in the formulation of fundamental evaluative principles).

(ii) The *last people* example. The last man example can be broadened to the last people example. We can assume that they know they are the last people, e.g. because they are aware that radiation effects have blocked any chance of reproduction. One considers the last people in order to rule out the possibility that what these people do harms or somehow physically interferes with later people. Otherwise one could as well consider science fiction cases where people arrive at a new planet and destroy its ecosystems, whether with good intentions such as perfecting the planet for their ends and making it more fruitful or, forgetting the lesser traditions, just for the hell of it.

Let us assume that the last people are very numerous. They humanely exterminate every wild animal and they eliminate the fish of the seas, they put all arable land under intensive cultivation, and all remaining forests disappear in favor of quarries or plantations, and so on. They may give various familiar reasons for this, e.g. they believe it is the way to salvation or to perfection, or they are simply satisfying reasonable needs, or even that it is needed to keep the last people employed or occupied so that they do not worry too much about their impending extinction. On an environmental ethic the last people have behaved badly; they have simplified and largely destroyed all the natural ecosystems, and with their demise the world will soon be an ugly and largely wrecked place. But this conduct may conform with the basic chauvinist principle, and as well with the principles enjoined by the lesser traditions. Indeed the main point of elaborating this example is because, as the last man example reveals, basic chauvinism may conflict with stewardship or co-operation principles. The conflict may be removed it seems by conjoining a further proviso to the basic principle, the effect (3) that he does not willfully destroy natural resources. But as the last people do not destroy resources willfully, but perhaps "for the best of reasons," the variant is still environmentally inadequate.

(iii) The *great entrepreneur* example. The last man example can be adjusted so as to not fall foul of clause (3). The last man is an industrialist; he runs a giant complex of automated factories and farms which he proceeds to extend. He produces automobiles among other things, from renewable and recyclable resources of course, only he dumps and recycles these shortly after manufacture and sale to a dummy buyer instead of putting them on the road for a short time as we do. Of course he has the best of reasons for his activity, e.g. he is increasing gross world product, or he is improving output to fulfill some plan, and he will be increasing his own and general welfare since he much prefers increased output and productivity. The entrepreneur's behavior is on the Western ethic quite permissible; indeed his conduct is commonly thought to be quite fine and may even meet Pareto optimality requirements given prevailing notions of being "better off."

Just as we can extend the last man example to a class of last people, so we can extend this example to the *industrial society* example: the society looks rather like ours.

(iv) The *vanishing species* example. Consider the blue whale, a mixed good on the economic picture. The blue whale is on the verge of extinction because of his qualities as a private good, as a source of valuable oil and meat. The catching and marketing of blue whales does not harm the whalers; it does not harm or physically interfere with others in any good sense, though it may upset them and they may be prepared to compensate the whalers if they desist; nor need whale hunting be willful destruction. (Slightly different examples which eliminate the hunting aspect of the blue whale example are provided by cases where a species is eliminated or threatened through destruction of its habitat by man's activity or the activities of animals he has introduced, e.g. many plains-dwelling Australian marsupials and the Arabian oryx.) The behavior of the whalers in eliminating this magnificent species of whale is accordingly quite permissible—at least according to basic chauvinism. But on an environmental ethic it is not. However, the free-market mechanism will not cease allocating whales to commercial uses, as a satisfactory environmental economics would; instead the market model will grind inexorably along the private demand curve until the blue whale population is no longer viable—if that point has not already been passed.[10]

In sum, the class of permissible actions that rebound on the environment is more narrowly circumscribed on an environmental ethic than it is in the Western super ethic. But aren't environmentalists going too far in claiming that these people, those of the examples and respected industrialists, fishermen and farmers are behaving, when engaging in environmentally degrading activities of the sort described, in a morally impermissible way? No, what these people do is to a greater or lesser extent evil, and hence in serious cases morally impermissible. For example, insofar as the killing or forced displacement of primitive peoples who stand in the way of an industrial development is morally indefensible and impermissible, so also is the slaughter of the last remaining blue whales for private profit. But how to reformulate basic chauvinism as a satisfactory freedom principle is a more difficult matter. A tentative, but none too adequate beginning might be made by extending (2) to include harm to or interference with others who would be so affected by the action in question were they placed in the environment and (3) to exclude speciecide. It may be preferable, in view of the way the freedom principle sets the onus of proof, simply to scrap it altogether, and instead to specify classes of rights and permissible conduct, as in a bill of rights.

3

A radical change in a theory sometimes forces changes in the meta-theory; e.g. a logic which rejects the Reference Theory in a thoroughgoing way requires a modification of the usual meta-theory which also accepts the Reference Theory and indeed which is tailored to cater only for logics which do conform. A somewhat similar phenomenon seems to occur in the case of a meta-ethic adequate for an environmental ethic. Quite apart from introducing several environmentally important notions, such as *conservation, pollution, growth* and *preservation*, for meta-ethical analysis, an environmental ethic compels re-examination and modified analyses of such characteristic actions as *natural right, ground* of right, and of the relations of obligation and permissibility to rights; it may well require re-assessment of traditional analyses of such notions as *value* and *right*, especially where these are based on chauvinist assumptions; and it forces the rejection of many of the more prominent meta-ethical positions. These points are illustrated by a very brief examination of accounts of *natural right* and then by a sketch of the species bias of some major positions.[11]

Hart accepts, subject to defeating conditions which are here irrelevant, the classical doctrine of natural rights according to which, among other things, "any adult human. . .capable of choice is at liberty to do (i.e. is under no obligation to abstain from) any action which is not one coercing or restraining or designed to injure other persons."[12] But this sufficient condition for a human natural right depends on accepting the very human chauvinist principle an environmental ethic rejects, since if a person has a natural right he has a right; so too the *definition* of a natural right adopted by classical theorists and accepted with minor qualifications by Hart presupposes the same defective principle. Accordingly an environmental ethic would have to amend the classical notion of a natural right, a far from straightforward matter now that human rights with respect to animals and the natural environment are, like those with respect to slaves not all that long ago, undergoing major re-evaluation.

An environmental ethic does not commit one to the view that natural objects such as trees have rights (though such a view is occasionally held, e.g. by pantheists. But pantheism is false since artefacts are not alive). For moral prohibitions forbidding certain actions with respect to an object do not award that object a correlative right. That it would be wrong to mutilate a given tree or piece of property does not entail that the tree or piece of property has a correlative right not to be mutilated (without seriously stretching the notion of a right). Environmental views can stick with mainstream theses according to which rights are coupled with corresponding responsibilities and so with bearing obligations, and with corresponding interests and concern; i.e. at least, whatever has a right also has responsibilities and therefore obligations, and whatever has a right has interests. Thus although any person may have a right by no means every living thing can (significantly) have rights, and arguably most sentient objects other than persons cannot have rights. But persons can relate morally, through obligations, prohibitions and so forth, to practically anything at all.

The species bias of certain ethical and economic positions which aim to make principles of conduct or reasonable economic behavior calculable is easily brought out. These positions typically employ a single criterion p, such as preference or happiness, as a *summum bonum;* characteristically each individual of some *base* class, almost always humans, but perhaps including future humans, is supposed to have an ordinal p ranking of the states in question (e.g. of affairs, of the economy); then some principle is supplied to determine a collective p ranking of these states in terms of individual p rankings, and what is best or ought to be done is determined either directly, as in act-utilitarianism under the Greatest Happiness principle, or indirectly, as in rule-utilitarianism, in terms of some optimization principle applied to the collective ranking. The species bias is transparent from the selection of the base class. And even if the base class is extended to embrace persons, or even some animals (at the cost, like that of including remotely future humans, of losing testability), the positions are open to familiar criticism, namely that the whole of the base class may be prejudiced in a way which leads to unjust principles. For example if every member of the base class detests dingoes, on the basis of mistaken data as to dingoes' behavior, then by the Pareto ranking test the collective ranking will rank states where dingoes are exterminated very highly, from which it will generally be concluded that dingoes ought to be exterminated (the evaluation of most Australian farmers anyway). Likewise it would just be a happy accident, it seems, if collective demand (horizontally summed from individual demand) for a state of the economy with blue whales as a mixed good, were to succeed in outweighing private whaling demands; for if no one in the base class happened to know that blue whales exist or cared a jot that they do then "rational" economic decision-making would do nothing to prevent their extinction. Whether the blue whale survives should not have to depend on what humans know or what they see on television. Human interests and preferences are far too parochial to provide a satisfactory basis for deciding on what is environmentally desirable.

These ethical and economic theories are not alone in their species chauvinism; much the same applies to most going meta-ethical theories which, unlike intuitionistic theories, try to offer some rationale for their basic principles. For instance, on social contract positions obligations are a matter of mutual agreements between individuals of the base class; on a social justice picture rights and obligations spring from the application of symmetrical fairness principles to members of the base class, usually a rather special class of persons, while on a Kantian position which has some vague obligations somehow arise from respect for members of the base class persons. In each case if members of the base class happen to be ill-disposed to items outside the base class then that is too bad for them: that is (rough) justice.

NOTES

1. Aldo Leopold, *A Sand Country Almanac with Essays on Conservation from Round River* (New York: Ballantine, 1966), p. 238.
2. A view occasionally tempered by the idea that trees house spirits.
3. Leopold, *Sand County*, p. 245.

4. To the consternation no doubt of Quineans. But the fact is that we can talk perfectly well about inchoate and fragmentary systems the identity of which may be indeterminate.

5. John Passmore, *Man's Responsibility for Nature: Ecological Problems and Western Traditions* (New York: Scribner's, 1974).

6. If 'use' is extended, somewhat illicitly, to include use for preservation, this total use principle is rendered innocuous at least as regards its actual effects. Note that the total use principle is tied to the resource view of nature.

7. P. W. Barkley and D. W. Seckler, *Economic Growth and Environmental Decay: The Solution Becomes the Problem* (New York: Harcourt, Brace, Jovanovich, 1972).

8. A *meta-ethic* is, as usual, a theory about ethics, super ethics, their features and fundamental notions.

9. Barkley and Seckler, *Economic Growth and Environmental Decay*, p. 58. A related principle is that (modified) free enterprise can operate within similar limits.

10. For the tragedy of the commons type reasons well explained in Barkley and Seckler, *Economic Growth and Environmental Decay*.

11. Some of these points are developed by those protesting about human mal-treatment of animals; see especially the essays collected in S. and R. Godlovitch and J. Harris, eds., *Animals, Men and Morals: An Enquiry into the Maltreatment of Non-humans* (New York: Grove Press, 1971).

12. H. L. A. Hart, "Are There any Natural Rights?" reprinted in A. Quinton, ed., *Political Philosophy* (London: Oxford University Press, 1967).

Animal Liberation

Peter Singer

Peter Singer is professor of philosophy and director of the Centre for Human Bioethics at Monash University in Melbourne, Australia. He is the author of Animal Liberation: A New Ethics for Our Treatment of Animals *and* Practical Ethics.

I

We are familiar with Black Liberation, Gay Liberation, and a variety of other movements. With Women's Liberation some thought we had come to the end of the road. Discrimination on the basis of sex, it has been said, is the last form of discrimination that is universally accepted and practiced without pretense, even in those liberal circles which have long prided themselves on their freedom from racial discrimination. But one should always be wary of talking of "the last remaining form of discrimination." If we have learned anything from the liberation movements, we should have learned how difficult it is to be aware of the ways in which we discriminate until they are forcefully pointed out to us. A liberation movement demands an expansion of our moral horizons, so that practices that were previously regarded as natural and inevitable are now seen as intolerable.

Animals, Men and Morals is a manifesto for an Animal Liberation movement. The contributors to the book may not all see the issue this way. They are a varied group. Philosophers, ranging from professors to graduate students, make up the largest contingent. There are five of them, including the three editors, and there is also an extract from the unjustly neglected German philosopher with an English name, Leonard Nelson, who died in 1927. There are essays by two novelist/critics, Brigid Brophy and Maureen

Reprinted from *The New York Review of Books*, April 5, 1973, by permission of the author. Copyright Peter Singer, 1973.

Duffy, and another by Muriel the Lady Dowding, widow of Dowding of Battle of Britain fame and the founder of "Beauty without Cruelty," a movement that campaigns against the use of animals for furs and cosmetics. The other pieces are by a psychologist, a botanist, a sociologist, and Ruth Harrison, who is probably best described as a professional campaigner for animal welfare.

Whether or not these people, as individuals, would all agree that they are launching a liberation movement for animals, the book as a whole amounts to no less. It is a demand for a complete change in our attitudes to nonhumans. It is a demand that we cease to regard the exploitation of other species as natural and inevitable, and that, instead, we see it as a continuing moral outrage. Patrick Corbett, Professor of Philosophy at Sussex University, captures the spirit of the book in his closing words:

> . . . we require now to extend the great principles of liberty, equality and fraternity over the lives of animals. Let animal slavery join human slavery in the graveyard of the past.

The reader is likely to be skeptical. "Animal Liberation" sounds more like a parody of liberation movements than a serious objective. The reader may think: We support the claims of blacks and women for equality because blacks and women really are equal to whites and males—equal in intelligence and in abilities, capacity for leadership, rationality, and so on. Humans and nonhumans obviously are not equal in these respects. Since justice demands only that we treat equals equally, unequal treatment of humans and nonhumans cannot be an injustice.

This is a tempting reply, but a dangerous one. It commits the non-racist and non-sexist to a dogmatic belief that blacks and women really are just as intelligent, able, etc., as whites and males—and no more. Quite possibly this happened to be the case. Certainly attempts to prove that racial or sexual differences in these respects have a genetic origin have not been conclusive. But do we really want to stake our demand for equality on the assumption that there are no genetic differences of this kind between the different races or sexes? Surely the appropriate response to those who claim to have found evidence for such genetic differences is not to stick to the belief that there are no differences, whatever the evidence to the contrary; rather one should be clear that the claim to equality does not depend on IQ. Moral equality is distinct from factual equality. Otherwise it would be nonsense to talk of the equality of human beings, since humans, as individuals, obviously differ in intelligence and almost any ability one cares to name. If possessing greater intelligence does not entitle one human to exploit another, why should it entitle humans to exploit nonhumans?

Jeremy Bentham expressed the essential basis of equality in his famous formula: "Each to count for one and none for more than one." In other words, the interests of every being that has interests are to be taken into account and treated equally with the like interests of any other being. Other moral philosophers, before and after Bentham, have made the same point in different ways. Our concern for others must not depend on whether they possess certain characteristics, though just what that concern involves may, of course, vary according to such characteristics.

Bentham, incidentally, was well aware that the logic of the demand for racial equality did not stop at the equality of humans. He wrote:

> The day *may* come when the rest of the animal creation may acquire those rights which never could have been withholden from them but by the hand of tyranny. The French have already discovered that the blackness of the skin is no reason why a human being should be abandoned without redress to the caprice of a tormentor. It may one day come to be recognized that the number of the legs, the villosity of the skin, or the termination of the *os sacrum*, are reasons equally insufficient for abandoning a sensitive being to the same fate. What else is it that should trace the insuperable line? Is it the faculty of reason, or perhaps the faculty of discourse? But a full-grown horse or dog is beyond comparison a more rational, as well as a more conversable animal, than an infant of a day, or a week, or even a month old. But suppose they were otherwise, what would it avail? The question is not, Can they *reason?* nor Can they *talk?* but, Can they *suffer?*[1]

Surely Bentham was right. If a being suffers, there can be no moral justification for refusing to take that suffering into consideration, and, indeed, to count it equally with the like suffering (if rough comparisons can be made) of any other being.

So the only question is: do animals other than man suffer? Most people agree unhesitatingly that animals like cats and dogs can and do suffer, and this seems also to be assumed by those laws that prohibit wanton cruelty to such animals. Personally, I have no doubt at all about this and find it hard to take seriously the doubts that a few people apparently do have. The editors and contributors of *Animals, Men and Morals* seem to feel the same way, for although the question is raised more than once, doubts are quickly dismissed each time. Nevertheless, because this is such a fundamental point, it is worth asking what grounds we have for attributing suffering to other animals.

It is best to begin by asking what grounds any individual human has for supposing that other humans feel pain. Since pain is a state of consciousness, a "mental event," it can never be directly observed. No observations, whether behavioral signs such as writhing or screaming or physiological or neurological recordings, are observations of pain itself. Pain is something one feels, and one can only infer that others are feeling it from various external indications. The fact that only philosophers are ever skeptical about whether other humans feel pain shows that we regard such inference as justifiable in the case of humans.

Is there any reason why the same inference should be unjustifiable for other animals? Nearly all the external signs which lead us to infer pain in other humans can be seen in other species, especially "higher" animals such as mammals and birds. Behavioral signs—writhing, yelping, or other forms of calling, attempts to avoid the source of pain, and many others—are present. We know, too, that these animals are biologically similar in the relevant respects, having nervous systems like ours which can be observed to function as ours do.

So the grounds for inferring that these animals can feel pain are nearly as good as the grounds for inferring other humans do. Only nearly, for there is one behavioral sign that humans have but nonhumans, with the exception of one or two specially raised chimpanzees, do not have. This, of course, is a developed language. As the quotation from Bentham indicates, this has long been regarded as an important distinction between man and other animals. Other animals may communicate with each other, but not in the way we do. Following Chomsky, many people now mark this distinction by saying that only humans communicate in a form that is governed by rules of syntax. (For the purposes of this argument, linguists allow those chimpanzees who have learned a syntactic sign language to rank as honorary humans.) Nevertheless, as Bentham pointed out, this distinction is not relevant to the question of how animals ought to be treated, unless it can be linked to the issue of whether animals suffer.

This link may be attempted in two ways. First, there is a hazy line of philosophical thought, stemming perhaps from some doctrines associated with Wittgenstein, which maintains that we cannot meaningfully attribute states of consciousness to beings without language. I have not seen this argument made explicit in print, though I have come across it in conversation. This position seems to me very implausible, and I doubt that it would be held at all if it were not thought to be a consequence of a broader view of the significance of language. It may be that the use of a public, rule-governed language is a precondition of conceptual thought. It may even be, although personally I doubt it, that we cannot meaningfully speak of a creature having an intention unless that creature can use a language. But states like pain, surely, are more primitive than either of these, and seem to have nothing to do with language.

Indeed, as Jane Goodall points out in her study of chimpanzees, when it comes to the expression of feelings and emotions, humans tend to fall back on nonlinguistic modes of communication which are often found among apes, such as a cheering pat on the back, an exuberant embrace, a clasp of hands, and so on.[2] Michael Peters makes a similar point in his contribution to *Animals, Men and Morals* when he notes that the basic signals we use to convey pain, fear, sexual arousal, and so on are not specific to our species. So there seems to be no reason at all to believe that a creature without language cannot suffer.

The second, and more easily appreciated way of linking language and the existence of pain is to say that the best evidence that we can have that another creature is in pain is when he tells us that he is. This is a distinct line of argument, for it is not being denied that a non-language-user conceivably could suffer, but only that we could know that he is suffering. Still, this line of argument seems to me to fail, and for reasons similar to those just given. "I am in pain" is not the best possible evidence that the speaker is in pain (he might be lying) and it is certainly not the only possible evidence. Behavioral signs and knowledge of the animals' biological similarity to ourselves together provide adequate evidence that animals do suffer. After all, we would not accept linguistic evidence if it contradicted the rest of the evidence. If a man was severely burned, and behaved as if he were in pain, writhing, groaning, being very careful not to let his burned skin touch anything, and so on, but later said he had not been in pain at all, we would be more likely to conclude that he was lying or suffering from amnesia than that he had not been in pain.

Even if there were stronger grounds for refusing to attribute pain to those who do not have a language, the consequences of this refusal might lead us to examine these grounds unusually critically. Human infants, as well as some adults, are unable to use language. Are we to deny that a year-old infant can suffer? If not, how can language be crucial? Of course, most parents can understand the responses of even very young infants better than they understand the responses of other animals, and sometimes infant responses can be understood in the light of later development.

This, however, is just a fact about the relative knowledge we have of our own species and other species, and most of this knowledge is simply derived from closer contact. Those who have studied the behavior of other animals soon learn to understand their responses at least as well as we understand those of an infant. (I am not just referring to Jane Goodall's and other well-known studies of apes. Consider, for example, the degree of understanding achieved by Tinbergen from watching herring gulls.)[3] Just as we can understand infant human behavior in the light of adult human behavior, so we can understand the behavior of other species in the light of our own behavior (and sometimes we can understand our own behavior better in the light of the behavior of other species).

The grounds we have for believing that other mammals and birds suffer are, then, closely analogous to the grounds we have for believing that other humans suffer. It remains to consider how far down the evolutionary scale this analogy holds. Obviously it becomes poorer when we get further away from man. To be more precise would require a detailed examination of all that we know about other forms of life. With fish, reptiles, and other vertebrates the analogy still seems strong, with molluscs like oysters it is much weaker. Insects are more difficult, and it may be that in our present state of knowledge we must be agnostic about whether they are capable of suffering.

If there is no moral justification for ignoring suffering when it occurs, and it does occur in other species, what are we to say of our attitudes toward these other species? Richard Ryder, one of the contributors to *Animals, Men and Morals,* uses the term "speciesism" to describe the belief that we are entitled to treat members of other species in a way in which it would be wrong to treat members of our own species. The term is not euphonious, but it neatly makes the analogy with racism. The non-racist would do well to bear the analogy in mind when he is inclined to defend human behavior toward nonhumans. "Shouldn't we worry about improving the lot of our own species before we concern ourselves with other species?" he may ask. If we substitute "race" for "species" we shall see that the question is better not asked. "Is a vegetarian diet nutritionally adequate?" resembles the slave-owner's claim that he and the whole economy of the South would be ruined without slave labor. There is even a parallel with skeptical doubts about whether animals suffer, for some defenders of slavery professed to doubt whether blacks really suffer in the way that whites do.

I do not want to give the impression, however, that the case for Animal Liberation is based on the analogy with racism and no more. On the contrary, *Animals, Men and Morals* describes the various ways in which humans exploit nonhumans, and several contributors consider the defenses that have been offered, including the defense of meat-eating mentioned in the last paragraph. Sometimes the rebuttals are scornfully dismissive, rather than carefully designed to convince the detached critic. This may be a fault, but it is a fault that is inevitable, given the kind of book this is. The issue is not one on which one can remain detached. As the editors state in their Introduction:

> Once the full force of moral assessment has been made explicit there can be no rational excuse left for killing animals, be they killed for food, science, or sheer personal indulgence. We have not assembled this book to provide the reader with yet another manual on how to make brutalities less brutal. Compromise, in the traditional sense of the term, is simple unthinking weakness when one considers the actual reasons for our crude relationships with the other animals.

The point is that on this issue there are few critics who are genuinely detached. People who eat pieces of slaughtered nonhumans every day find it hard to believe that they are doing wrong; and they also find it hard to imagine what else they could eat. So for those who do not place nonhumans beyond the pale of morality, there comes a stage when further argument seems pointless, a stage at which one can only accuse one's opponent of hypocrisy and reach for the sort of sociological account of our practices and the way we defend them that is attempted by David Wood in his contribution to this book. On the other hand, to those unconvinced by the arguments, and unable to accept that they are rationalizing their dietary preferences and their fear of being thought peculiar, such sociological explanations can only seem insultingly arrogant.

II

The logic of speciesism is most apparent in the practice of experimenting on nonhumans in order to benefit humans. This is because the issue is rarely obscured by allegations that nonhumans are so different from humans that we cannot know anything about whether they suffer. The defender of vivisection cannot use this argument because he needs to stress the similarities between man and other animals in order to justify the usefulness to the former of experiments on the latter. The researcher who makes rats choose between starvation and electric shocks to see if they develop ulcers (they do) does so because he knows that the rat has a nervous system very similar to man's, and presumably feels an electric shock in a similar way. . . .

There is nothing secret about these experiments. One has only to open any recent volume of a learned journal, such as the *Journal of Comparative and Physiological Psychology,* to find full descriptions of experiments of this sort, together with the results obtained—results that are frequently trivial and obvious. The experiments are often supported by public funds.

It is a significant indication of the level of acceptability of these practices that, although these experiments are taking place at this moment on university campuses throughout the country, there has, so far as I know, not been the slightest protest from the student movement. Students have been rightly concerned that their universities should not discriminate on grounds of race or sex, and that they should not serve the purposes of the military or big business. Speciesism continues undisturbed, and many students participate in it. There may be a few qualms at first, but since everyone regards it as normal, and it may even be a required part of a course, the student soon becomes hardened and, dismissing his earlier feelings as "mere sentiment," comes to regard animals as statistics rather than sentient beings with interests that warrant consideration.

Argument about vivisection has often missed the point because it has been put in absolutist terms: would the abolitionist be prepared to let thousands die if they could be saved by experimenting on a single animal? The way to reply to this purely hypothetical question is to pose another: Would the experimenter be prepared to experiment on a human orphan under six months old, if it were the only way to save many lives? (I say "orphan" to avoid the complication of parental feelings, although in doing so I am being overfair to the experimenter, since the nonhuman subjects of experiments are not orphans.) A negative answer to this question indicates that the experimenter's readiness to use nonhumans is simple discrimination, for adult apes, cats, mice, and other mammals are more conscious of what is happening to them, more self-directing, and, so far as we can tell, just as sensitive to pain as a human infant. There is no characteristic that human infants possess that adult mammals do not have to the same or a higher degree.

(It might be possible to hold that what makes it wrong to experiment on a human infant is that the infant will in time develop into more than the nonhuman, but one would then, to be consistent, have to oppose abortion, and perhaps contraception, too, for the fetus and the egg and sperm have the same potential as the infant. Moreover, one would still have no reason for experimenting on a nonhuman rather than a human with brain damage severe enough to make it impossible for him to rise above infant level.)

The experimenter, then, shows a bias for his own species whenever he carries out an experiment on a nonhuman for a purpose that he would not think justified him in using a human being at an equal or lower level of sentience, awareness, ability to be self-directing, etc. No one familiar with the kind of results yielded by these experiments can have the slightest doubt that if this bias were eliminated the number of experiments performed would be zero or very close to it.

III

If it is vivisection that shows the logic of speciesism most clearly, it is the use of other species for food that is at the heart of our attitudes toward them. Most of *Animals, Men and Morals* is an attack on meat-eating—an attack which is based solely on concern for nonhumans, without reference to arguments derived from considerations of ecology, macrobiotics, health, or religion.

The idea that nonhumans are utilities, means to our ends, pervades our thought. Even conservationists who are concerned about the slaughter of wild fowl but not about the vastly greater slaughter of chickens for our tables are thinking in this way—they are worried about what we would lose if there were less wildlife. Stanley Godlovitch, pursuing the Marxist idea that our thinking is formed by the activities we undertake in satisfying our needs, suggests that man's first classification of his environment was into Edibles and Inedibles. Most animals came into the first category, and there they have remained.

Man may always have killed other species for food, but he has never exploited them so ruthlessly as he does today. Farming has succumbed to business methods, the objective being to get the highest possible ratio of output (meat, eggs, milk) to input (fodder, labor costs, etc.). Ruth Harrison's essay "On Factory Farming" gives an account of some aspects of modern methods, and of the unsuccessful British campaign for effective controls, a campaign which was sparked off by her *Animal Machines* (Stuart: London, 1964).

Her article is in no way a substitute for her earlier book. This is a pity since, as she says, "Farm produce is still associated with mental pictures of animals browsing in the fields. . . .of hens having a last forage before going to roost. . . ." Yet neither in her article nor elsewhere in *Animals, Men and Morals* is this false image replaced by a clear idea of the nature and extent of factory farming. . . .

How many of those who support factory farming by buying its produce know anything about the way it is produced? How many have heard something about it, but are reluctant to check up for fear that it will make them uncomfortable? To nonspeciesists, the typical consumer's mixture of ignorance, reluctance to find out the truth, and vague belief that nothing really bad could be allowed seems analogous to the attitudes of "decent Germans" to the death camps.

There are, of course, some defenders of factory farming. Their arguments are considered, though again rather sketchily, by John Harris. Among the most common: "Since they have never known anything else, they don't suffer." This argument will not be put by anyone who knows anything about animal behavior, since he will know that not all behavior has to be learned. Chickens attempt to stretch wings, walk around, scratch, and even dust-bathe or build a nest, even though they have never lived under conditions that allowed these activities. Calves can suffer from maternal deprivation no matter at what age they were taken from their mothers. "We need these intensive methods to provide protein for a growing population." As ecologists and famine relief organizations know, we can produce far more protein per acre if we grow the right vegetable crop, soy beans for instance, than if we use the land to grow crops to be converted into protein by animals who use nearly 90 percent of the protein themselves, even when unable to exercise.

There will be many readers of this book who will agree that factory farming involves an unjustifiable degree of exploitation of sentient creatures, and yet will want to say that there is nothing wrong with rearing animals for food, provided it is done "humanely." These people are saying, in effect, that although we should not cause animals to suffer, there is nothing wrong with killing them.

There are two possible replies to this view. One is to attempt to show that this combination of attitudes is absurd. Roslind Godlovitch takes this course in her essay, which is an examination of some common attitudes to animals. She argues that from the combination of "animal suffering is to be avoided" and "there is nothing wrong with killing animals" it follows that all animal life ought to be exterminated (since all sentient creatures will suffer to some degree at some point in their lives). Euthanasia is a contentious issue only because we place some value on living. If we did not, the least amount of suffering would justify it. Accordingly, if we deny that we have a duty to exterminate all animal life, we must concede that we are placing some value on animal life.

This argument seems to me valid, although one could still reply that the value of animal life is to be derived from the pleasures that life can have for them, so that, provided their lives have a balance of pleasure over pain, we are justified in rearing them. But this would imply that we ought to produce animals and let them live as pleasantly as possible, without suffering.

At this point, one can make the second of the two possible replies to the view that rearing and killing animals for food is all right so long as it is done humanely. This second reply is that so long as we think that a nonhuman may be killed simply so that a human can satisfy his taste for meat, we are still thinking of nonhumans as means rather than as ends in themselves. The factory farm is nothing more than the application of technology to this concept. Even traditional methods involve castration, the separation of mothers and their young, the breaking up of herds, branding or ear-punching, and of course transportation to the abattoirs and the final moments of terror when the animal smells blood and senses danger. If we were to try rearing animals so that they lived and died without suffering, we should find that to do so on anything like the scale of today's meat industry would be a sheer impossibility. Meat would become the prerogative of the rich.

I have been able to discuss only some of the contributions to this book, saying nothing about, for instance, the essays on killing for furs and for sport. Nor have I considered all the detailed questions that need to be asked once we start thinking about other species in the radically different way presented by this book. What, for instance, are we to do about genuine conflicts of interest like rats biting slum children? I am not sure of the answer, but the essential point is just that we *do* see this as a conflict of interests, that we recognize that rats have interests too. Then we may begin to think about other ways of resolving the conflict—perhaps by leaving out rat baits that sterilize the rats instead of killing them.

I have not discussed such problems because they are side issues compared with the exploitation of other species for food and for experimental purposes. On these central matters, I hope that I have said enough to show that this book, despite its flaws, is a challenge to every human to recognize his attitudes to nonhumans as a form of prejudice no less objectionable than racism or sexism. It is a challenge that demands not just a change of attitudes, but a change in our way of life, for it requires us to become vegetarians.

Can a purely moral demand of this kind succeed? The odds are certainly against it. The book holds out no inducements. It does not tell us that we will become healthier, or enjoy life more, if we cease exploiting animals. Animal Liberation will require greater altruism on the part of mankind than any other liberation movement, since animals are incapable of demanding it for themselves, or of protesting against their exploitation by votes, demonstrations, or bombs. Is man capable of such genuine altruism? Who knows? If this book does have a significant effect, however, it will be a vindication of all those who have believed that man has within himself the potential for more than cruelty and selfishness.

NOTES

1. *The Principles of Morals and Legislation,* Ch. XVII, Sec. 1, footnote to paragraph 4. (Italics in original.)
2. Jane van Lawick-Goodall, *In the Shadow of Man* (Houghton Mifflin, 1971), p. 225.
3. N. Tinbergen, *The Herring Gull's World* (Basic Books, 1961).

Animal Rights, Human Wrongs

Tom Regan

Tom Regan is professor of philosophy and university alumni distin-guished professor at the North Carolina State University. He is the author of The Case for Animal Rights *and, with Peter Singer, he edited* Animal Rights and Human Obligations.

THE KANTIAN ACCOUNT

It is a commonplace to say that morality places some limits on how animals may be treated. We are not to kick dogs, set fire to cats' tails, torment hamsters or parakeets. Philosophically, the issue is not so much *whether* but *why* these acts are wrong.

An answer favored by many philosophers, including Thomas Aquinas and Immanuel Kant, is that people who treat animals in these ways develop a habit which, in time, inclines them to treat humans similarly.[1] People who torment animals will, or are likely to, torment people. It is this spillover effect that makes mistreating animals wrong. We are not concerned directly with the ill-treatment that the animals themselves receive. Rather, our concern is that this bodes ill for humankind. So, on this Kantian account, the moral principle runs something like this: don't treat animals in ways that will lead you to mistreat human beings.

One need have no quarrel with this principle itself. The real quarrel lies with the grounds on which this principle is allegedly based. Peter Singer argues that there is a close parallel between this view and those of the racist and sexist, a view which, following Richard Ryder, he denomi-

This essay originally appeared in *Environmental Ethics*, Vol. 2, No. 2 (Summer 1980), 99–120. Reprinted with permission.

nates speciesism.[2] The racist believes that the interests of others matter only if they happen to be members of his own race. The speciesist believes that the interests of others matter only if they happen to be members of his own species. Racism has been unmasked for the prejudice that it is. The color of one's skin cannot be used to determine the relevance of an individual's interests. Singer and Ryder both argue that neither can the number of one's legs, whether one walks upright or on all fours, lives in the trees, the sea or the suburbs. Here they recall Bentham.[3] There is, they argue forcefully, no rational, unprejudiced way to exclude the interests of nonhuman animals just because they are not the interests of human beings. Because the Kantian account would have us think otherwise, we are right to reject it.

THE CRUELTY ACCOUNT

A second view about constraints on how animals may be treated involves the idea of cruelty. The reason we are not to kick dogs is that we are not to be cruel to animals and kicking dogs is cruel. It is the prohibition against cruelty which covers and conveniently sums up our negative duties to animals, duties concerning how animals are *not* to be treated.

The prohibition against cruelty can be given a distinctively Kantian twist. This happens when the grounds given are that cruelty to animals leads people to be cruel to other people. John Locke suggests, but does not clearly endorse, this view:

> One thing I have frequently observed in Children, that when they have got possession of any poor Creature, they are apt to use it ill: They often *torment*, and treat very roughly, young Birds, Butterflies, and such other poor Animals, which fall into their Hands, and that with a seeming kind of Pleasure. This I think should be watched in them, and if they incline to any such *Cruelty*, they should be taught the contrary Usage. For the Custom of Tormenting and Killing of Beasts, will, by Degrees, harden their Minds even towards Men; and they who delight in the Suffering and Destruction of Inferior Creatures, will not be apt to be very compassionate, or benign to those of their own kind.[4]

Locke's position suggests the speciesism which characterizes the Kantian account and will not do for the same reasons. However, Locke's understanding of what cruelty is—tormenting a sentient creature or causing it to suffer, "with a seeming kind of Pleasure"—seems correct and has important implications. Many thinkers, including many persons active in the humane movement, champion the prohibition against cruelty to animals because it is wrong to be cruel to the animals themselves. This way of grounding the prohibition against cruelty, which I call "the cruelty account," deserves our critical attention.

It is difficult to overestimate the importance the idea of preventing cruelty has played, and continues to play, in the movement to secure better treatment for animals. Entire societies are devoted to this cause, the Society for the Prevention of Cruelty to Animals (SPCA) in the United States and the Royal Society for the Prevention of Cruelty to Animals (RSPCA) in Great Britain being perhaps the best known examples. I do not wish to deny the importance of preventing cruelty nor to deprecate the crusading work done by these organizations, but I must conclude that to stake so much on the prevention of cruelty both clouds the fundamental moral issues and runs a serious risk of being counterproductive.

Cruel is a term of moral appraisal used to refer either to the character of a person or to an individual action. Persons are cruel who are inclined to delight in or, in Locke's phrase, to take "a seeming kind of Pleasure" in causing pain. An individual action is cruel if one takes pleasure in making another suffer. It is clear that someone's being cruel is distinct from someone's causing pain. Surgeons cause pain. Dentists cause pain. Wrestlers, boxers, football players cause pain. But it does not follow that they are cruel people or that their individual actions are cruel. To establish cruelty we need to know more than that someone caused pain; we also need to know the state of mind of the agent, whether he/she took "a seeming kind of Pleasure" in the pain inflicted. It is faulty to reason in this way:

> Those who cause pain are cruel. Surgeons (football players, etc.) cause pain. Therefore, surgeons (football players, etc.) are cruel.

But just as clearly, it is faulty to reason in the following way:

> Those who cause pain are cruel. Those who experiment on animals (or kill whales, or raise veal calves in isolation, etc.) cause pain. Therefore those who treat animals in these ways are cruel.

Those who are inclined to march under the banner of anti-cruelty must soon recognize the speciousness of this line of reasoning, if their thought, however well intentioned, is not to cloud the issues.

Once cruelty is understood in the way Locke saw that it should be, we can understand why more is needed. Take the case of the use of animals in the Draize test. Increasingly people want to object morally to this, to say it is wrong. However, if this required establishing cruelty, the weight of the evidence would be on the side of the experimenters and against the objectors, for there is no adequate evidence for believing that people who administer the Draize test are cruel people or that they are cruel when they administer this test. Do they take "a seeming kind of Pleasure" in causing the animals pain? That they cause *pain* to the animals is certain. But causing pain does not establish cruelty. Except for a few sadists in the scientific community, there is good reason to believe that researchers are no more cruel than are most persons.

Does this mean that using animals in the Draize test is right? Precisely not. Rather, to ask whether this is right is logically distinct from, and should not be confused with, asking whether someone is cruel. Cruelty has to do with a person's state of mind. The moral rightness or wrongness of a person's actions is different. Persons can do what is right or wrong whatever their state of mind. Researchers using the Draize test can be doing what is wrong, whether or not they enjoy causing animals to suffer. If they do enjoy this, we shall certainly think less of them as persons. But even if they enjoy the pain it will not follow that the pain is unjustified, any more than it will follow that the pain is justified if they feel sorry for the animals or feel nothing at all. The more we are able to keep in view how the morality of what a person does is distinct from his/her state of mind, distinct from the presence or absence of taking pleasure in pain, the better the chances will be for significant dialogue between vivisectors and anti-vivisectionists.

To charge vivisectors with cruelty *can* only serve to call forth all their defenses, because the charge will be taken as a denunciation of *what they are* (evil people) rather than of *what they do*. It will also give them an easy way out. After all, *they* are in privileged position to know their own mental states; *they* can take a sober moment and see whether in fact they do take a "seeming kind of Pleasure" in causing pain. If, as will usually be the case, they find that they honestly do not, then they can reply that they are not cruel (evil) people. So we see now where the well-intentioned efforts of those defending animals can be and often are counterproductive. If it's cruelty they are charged with, and they are not cruel, then they can come away with a feeling that their hands are clean. They win, and the litany of accusations about cruelty is so much water off their backs. It is no good trying to improve the lot of animals by trying to convince persons who are not cruel that they are.

Some will complain that my argument is "too picky." They might say that cruelty has been interpreted too narrowly: what is meant is treating animals badly in ways they don't deserve, harming or wronging them. In practice this is what anti-cruelty charges often come to. But then this is the way the charges should be made, lest they be misunderstood or be counterproductive. To ask for more care in the charges leveled is not to strain at gnats. It is to begin to make the charges more difficult to answer. Perhaps a name like "The Society for the Prevention of Maltreatment of Animals" is not as euphonious as "The Anti-Cruelty Society," but a lack of euphony is a price those laboring for animal welfare should gladly pay.

THE UTILITARIAN ACCOUNT

Utilitarians give a different account of the constraints regarding how animals ought to be treated. The utilitarian account, or one version of it, involves two principles.[5] The first is a principle of equality. This principle declares that the desires, needs, hopes, etc. of different individuals, when these are of equal importance *to* these individuals, *are* of equal importance or value no matter who the individuals are, prince or pauper, genius or moron, white or black, male or female, *human or animal.* This equality of interests principle seems to provide a philosophical basis for avoiding the grossest forms of prejudice, including racism, sexism and, following Ryder and Singer, speciesism. Whether it succeeds is an issue which we shall take up below.

The second principle is that of utility itself. Roughly speaking, according to this principle, we are to act so as to bring about the greatest possible balance of good over evil, for example, the greatest possible balance of satisfaction over dissatisfaction, taking the interests of everyone affected into account *and* counting equal interests equally. Now, since animals have interests, *their* interests must be taken into account, and because their interests are frequently as important to them as comparable interests are to human beings, *their* interests must be given the same weight as comparable human interests. It is because kicking dogs and setting fire to cats' tails run counter to the principles of equality and utility that, on this utilitarian account, they are wrong.

Granted, this is a very rough sketch; nonetheless, it enables us to understand the main features of the utilitarian account, and also to find points of resemblance and contrast between it and the other accounts so far described. Like the Kantian account, but unlike the cruelty account, the utilitarian account emphasizes results or consequences, but unlike the Kantian account, and resembling the cruelty account, the utilitarian account recognizes the moral status of animals in their own right. We are not to measure morality by the speciesist yardstick of human interest alone. Finally, unlike the cruelty account, but in concert with the Kantian, the utilitarian does not conflate the morality of an act with the mental state of the agent. The utilitarian can be as opposed to cruelty as anyone else, but within the utilitarian theory right and wrong are determined by consequences, not feelings and intentions: the ordinary moral constraints placed on how we may treat animals are accounted for because they are necessary if we are not to violate the equality of interests principle *or* if we are to succeed in bringing about the greatest possible balance of good over bad.

The utilitarian account has much to recommend it. How far can it take us in challenging the way in which animals are routinely treated, for example, as subjects in scientific research? Peter Singer, a utilitarian whose work has well deserved influence, holds that utilitarianism leads to far-reaching consequences here. Singer argues that we become vegetarians *and* that we oppose much (even if not quite all) research involving animal subjects. Singer's main argument is that the intensive rearing of animals as well as their routine use in experimentation violates the equality of interests principle. The animals involved, we have reason to believe, have an interest in not being made to suffer, and this interest, we have further reason to believe, is as important to them as is the comparable interest in the case of human beings. This being so, Singer contends, it is wrong to do to animals what we would not do to humans. It cannot be right to raise animals intensively or use them in research if we would morally oppose doing these things to human beings. We do condemn cannibalism and the coerced use of humans in research and we must, Singer argues, morally condemn the comparable treatment of animals. We have a moral obligation to become vegetarians and oppose much, if not quite all, vivisection.

As clear and powerful as this argument is, I do not believe that Singer succeeds in making a fully convincing case. He shows that animals are treated differently than human beings, but not that this differential treatment violates either the equality of interests principle or the principle of utility. Consider the equality of interests principle first. We can count equal interests equally, no matter whose interests they are, and still treat individuals quite differently. For example, I might correctly regard my son's and my neighbor's son's interests in receiving a medical education as being equal and yet help only my son. I treat them differently but I do *not* necessarily count their equal interests differently, and neither do I thereby do anything that is in any obvious sense morally reprehensible. I have duties to my son which I do not have to the children of others.

The general point is this: the differential treatment of individuals with equal interests does not by itself violate the equality of interests principle. Singer has to give an *argument* which shows *more* than that they are treated differently. What argument does he give and how adequate is it? Singer proceeds by asking whether we would do to humans what we allow to be done to animals.[6] For example, would a researcher use an orphaned, profoundly retarded human baby in the sort of painful experiment in which he is willing to use a more intellectually and emotionally developed animal? If the researcher says no, Singer charges him with speciesism, with violating the equality of interests principle. The animal's interest in avoiding pain is just as important to it as is the infant's interest to him/her.

This argument begs the question. It assumes that by treating the involved individuals differently, we count their equal interests differently. As I have explained, however, this is not always true. Whether it is true in any particular case, therefore, is something which must be established, not simply assumed on the basis of differential treatment. Singer, I believe, assumes just this, and thus begs the question.

Singer's argument has a further deficiency, which involves the principle of utility. First, Singer does not show that the differential treatment of animals runs counter to the utilitarian objective of bringing about the greatest possible balance of good over evil. To show this Singer would have to give an elaborate, detailed description, not only of how animals are treated, a part of the task which he does complete with great skill, but an analysis of what, all considered, are the consequences for everyone involved. He would have to inquire how the world's economy depends on present levels of productivity in the animal industry, how many people's lives are directly and indirectly involved with the maintenance or growth of this industry, etc. Even more, he would have to show in detail what would probably be the consequences of a collapse or slowdown of the animal industry's productivity.

Secondly, Singer needs to make a compelling case for the view that *not* raising animals intensively or *not* using them routinely in research leads to better consequences, all considered, than those which now result from treating animals in these ways. Singer is required to show that better consequences *would* result, or at last that it is *very probable* that they would. Showing that it is possible or conceivable that they might is insufficient. It comes as a disappointment, therefore, that we do not find anything approaching this kind of required empirical data. What we find, instead, are passages where he bemoans (rightly, I believe) the fact that animals are fed protein-rich grains which could be fed to malnourished human beings.[7] The point, however, is not whether these grains *could* be fed to the malnourished; it is whether we have solid empirical grounds for believing that they *would* be made available to and eaten by these people, if they were not fed to animals, *and* that the consequences resulting from this shift would be better, all considered. I hope I am not unfair to Singer in observing that these calculations are missing, not only here, but, to my knowledge, throughout the body of his published writings.

This, then, is the first thing to note regarding Singer and the principle of utility: *he fails to show, with reference to this principle, that it is wrong* to treat animals as they are now being treated in modern farming and scientific research. The second thing to note is that, for all we know and so long as we rely on the principle of utility, the present treatment of animals might actually be justified. The grounds for thinking so are as follows.

On the face of it, utilitarianism seems to be the fairest, least prejudicial view available. Everyone's interests count, and no one's counts for more or less than the equal interests of anyone else. The trouble is, as we have seen, that there is no necessary connection, no preestablished harmony between respect for the equality of interests principle *and* promoting the utilitarian objective of maximizing the balance of good over bad. On the contrary, the principle of utility might be used to justify the most radical kinds of differential treatment between individuals or groups of individuals, and thus it might justify forms of racism and sexism, for these prejudices can take different forms and find expression in different ways. One form consists in not even taking the interests of a given race or sex into account at all; another takes these interests into account but does not count them equally with those of the equal interests of the favored group. Another does take their interests into account equally, but adopts laws and policies, engages in practices and customs which give greater opportunities to the members of the favored group, because doing so promotes the greatest balance of good over evil, all considered.

Thus, forms of racism or sexism, which seem to be eliminated by the utilitarian principle of equality of interests, could well be resurrected and justified by the principle of utility. If a utilitarian here replies that denying certain humans an equal opportunity to satisfy or promote their equal interests on racial or sexual grounds must violate the equality of interests principle and so, on his position, is wrong, we must remind him that differential treatment is not the same as, and does not entail, violating the equality of interests principle. It is quite possible, for example, to count the equal interests of blacks and whites the same (and thus to honor the equality principle) and still discriminate between races when it comes to what members of each race are permitted to do to pursue those interests, on the grounds that such discrimination promotes the utilitarian objective. So, utilitarianism, despite initial appearances, does not provide us with solid grounds on which to exclude all forms of racism or sexism.

Similarly with speciesism. The same kind of argument can show a possible utilitarian justification of an analogous speciesism. We count the equal interests of animals and humans equally; it just so happens that the consequences of treating animals in ways that humans are not treated, such as intensively raising animals, but not humans, are better, all considered, than are other arrangements. Thus, utilitarianism might provide a basis for speciesist practices. Whether it *actually* does depends on whether the consequences are better, all considered, if animals continue to be treated as they are. Since Singer fails to provide us with empirical data showing that the consequences would be better if we changed, it follows that, for all we know, the present speciesist way of treating animals might actually be justified, given his version of utilitarianism.

ANIMAL RIGHTS

Our results to this point are mainly negative. I have thus far argued (1) that the moral principles we seek cannot refer to the agent's state of mind, to whether the agent takes a "seeming kind of Pleasure" in causing animal suffering. (2) These principles cannot refer only to consequences that harm or benefit human beings, since this prejudicially leaves out of account the harms and benefits to the animals themselves. (3) These principles cannot refer only to the utilitarian objective of maximizing the balance of good over evil, even if animal harms and benefits are taken into account. What is wanted, then, is an account which avoids each of these shortcomings. This account is to be found, I believe, by postulation the existence of animal rights. Indeed, I believe that only if we postulate human rights can we provide a theory which adequately guards humans against the abuses which utilitarianism might permit.

Various analyses of the concept of a right have been proposed. We will bypass the nooks and crannies of these competing analyses so as to focus attention on the role that moral rights play in our thinking about the status of the individual, relative to the interests of the group. Here the truth seems to lie where Ronald Dworkin sees it: the rights of the individual trump the goals of the group.[8]

What does this mean? It means that the moral rights of the individual place a justifiable limit on what the group can do to the individual. Suppose a group of people stand to gain enjoyment by arranging for others to be harmed. Imagine, for example, the Romans enjoying how the Christians go up against lions. Such a group does wrong because they allow their interests to override the individual's moral rights. This does not mean that there are no circumstances in which an individual's rights must give way to the collective interest. Imagine that Bert has inadvertently swallowed the microfilmed code which we must have in order to prevent a massive nuclear explosion in New Zealand. Bert sits safely in Tucson, Arizona. We explain the situation but Bert refuses to consent to our request that we operate, retrieve the code, and prevent the explosion. He cites his right to determine what is to be done to his body. In such a case it is not implausible to say that Bert's right must give way to the collective interests of others.

Individual rights then normally, but not always, trump collective interests. To give a precise statement of the conditions which determine which ought to prevail is very difficult indeed, but the following conditions, which deal only with the right not to be harmed, at least seem to incorporate necessary conditions for overriding this right.[9]

An individual's right not to be harmed can justifiably be overridden only if—

a) we have very good reason to believe that overriding the individual's right by itself will prevent, and is the only realistic way to prevent, vastly greater harm to other innocent individuals; or

b) we have very good reason to believe that allowing the individual to be harmed is a necessary link in a chain of events which collectively will prevent vastly greater harm to innocent individuals, *and* we have very good reason to believe that this chain of events is the only realistic way to prevent this vastly greater harm; or

c) we have very good reason to believe that it is only if we override the individual's right that we can have a reasonable hope of preventing vastly greater harm to other innocent individuals.

There is much that is vague in these conditions, e.g., "vastly greater harm," "innocent individuals," "reasonable hope." At present, however, we will have to make do with them as they stand. Even so we can see that these conditions attempt to do justice to the complexity of conflicts of interest. In particular, they attempt to explain how, in a principled way, we might justify overriding an individual's right not to be harmed even though *just* doing this will not guarantee the prevention of vastly greater harm. Condition (b) brings this out—harming an individual is only one part of a more complex series of events which we have very good reason to believe will prevent vastly greater harm, or because—as (c) brings out—we simply do not know how things will turn out, but do have very good reason to believe that we have no reasonable hope of preventing some catastrophe unless we allow an individual to be harmed. Possibly some will find these conditions too liberal. Condition (c) in particular might seem too lenient. Even (b) might go too far. I am not certain what to say here and beg to leave this issue unresolved, except to say that the case for not harming animals is proportionately greater the more one is inclined to restrict the above set just to condition (a). For reasons that will become clearer, however, even the more liberal view, that harm can not be justified unless one of the three conditions is met, is sufficient to make a strong case against our routine abuse of animals.

These conditions share an extremely important feature. Each specifies what we must know or have good reason to believe if we are justified in overriding an individual's right not to be harmed. Each requires anyone who would harm an individual to show that this does not involve violating the individual's right. Part of the importance of the question, whether animals have rights, specifically, the right not to be harmed, now comes into clear focus. *If* they have this right, then it will be violated whenever animals are harmed and condition (a), (b), or (c) is not satisfied. Moreover, the onus of justification is always on those who harm animals to explain how they are not violating the right of animals not to be harmed, if animals have this right. So, the question continues to press itself upon us. Do animals have the right not to be harmed?

This is not an easy question to answer. One is reminded of Bentham's observation that the idea of moral rights is "nonsense on stilts." Bentham meant this in the case of *human* moral rights. One can only speculate regarding what he might have thought concerning the moral rights of *animals*! So, how is one to procede? The circuitous path we must cautiously travel, I think, is in broad outline as follows.[10]

We begin by asking about our reasons for thinking that human beings have the moral right not to be harmed; then we go on to ask whether, given these reasons, a case can be made for saying that animals have this right as well. Let us go back to the idea that individual human beings have this right and that, except in extreme cases, this right trumps collective interest. Why? What is there about being a human being to which we can point and say, "*That's* why you must not harm the individual even if the group benefits" ?

The heart of the answer lies, I believe, in thinking that human beings have a certain kind of value, inherent value. By this I mean that each human being has value logically independently of whether he/she is valued by anyone else (or, what perhaps comes to the same thing, whether he/she is the object of anyone else's interest).[11] The view that human beings have inherent value implies that the kind of value properly attributable to them is not exclusively instrumental. Humans have value not just because, and not just so long as, they are good for something. They have value distinct from their utility and skill.

If this is true, we can explain, in general terms reminiscent of Kant, what is involved in mistreating human beings. Humans are mistreated if they are treated as valuable only if they forward the interests of other beings. To treat a human being thus is to show a lack of proper respect for the sort of value humans have. In Kant's terms, what has value in itself must always be treated as an end, never merely as a means. However, this is precisely what we are doing if we harm an individual so that others might gain pleasure or profit; we are treating the individual merely as a means, as valuable only to the extent he/she contributes to the collective interest.

Now, *if* we accept the postulate that human beings have inherent value, we can press on and ask how rights enter the picture. They enter in being grounded in inherent value. In other words, it is individuals who have inherent value who have moral rights, and it is *because* they have value of this kind that they have a moral right not to be treated in ways that deny their having this kind of value. Rather than rights being connected with *the value of consequences* which affect individuals for good or ill, rather than rights being justified by the utility of recognizing them, rights are based on *the value of individuals.* In the case of the right not to be harmed, then, what we can say is that individuals who have inherent value have the right not to be harmed, which precludes treating them merely as a means. This would fail to treat these individuals with that respect to which, because of the kind of value they have, they are entitled.

Now, certainly the foregoing is not a definitive account of the view that individuals having inherent value have basic moral rights, in particular the right not to be harmed. One omission is especially conspicuous. What is there about being a human being that underlies this inherent value? Any answer is controversial, and a sustained defense of the answer proposed here is not possible.[12] But here is the answer I would give: human beings not only are alive; *they have a life.*[13] What is more, we are the subjects of a life that is better or worse for us, logically independently of anyone else's valuing us or finding us useful.

I do not mean that others cannot contribute to or detract from the value of our lives. On the contrary, the great goods of life (love, friendship, and, in general, fellow feeling) and its great evils (hatred, enmity, loneliness, alienation) all involve our relationships with other persons. What I mean, rather, is that our being *the subject* of a life that is better or worse for us does not depend logically on what others do or do not do. This fact, I believe, provides the illumination we seek. Humans have inherent value because we are ourselves the subjects of a life that is more or less valuable to us. In sum:

> Human beings have inherent value because, logically independently of the interest of others, each individual is the subject of a life that is better or worse for that individual. Because of the type of value that human beings have, it is wrong (a sign of disrespect and a violation of rights) to treat humans as if they had value merely as a means (e.g., to use humans merely to advance the pleasures of the group). In particular, to harm human beings for the sake of the profit or pleasure of any group is to violate their right not to be harmed.

The question now arises whether this same line of argument can be developed in the case of animals. It can, at least in the case of those animals who are the subjects of a life that is better or worse for them, logically independently of whether they are valued by anyone else. And there can be no rational doubt that there *are* numerous species of animals of which this is true. . . . They too have a distinctive kind of value in their own right, if we do; therefore, they too have a right not to be treated in ways that fail to respect this value, if we do. And, like humans, this right of theirs will be overridden unjustifiably if they are harmed merely to advance the profits or pleasures of others.

CONCLUSION

Two final philosophical points are in order, before I bring the results of my argument to bear on how animals are treated in the world at large. First, it is important to realize that I have not *proven* that animals have rights, or even that *human* beings have rights. Rather, I have argued that if humans have rights, so do many animals. More particularly, I have argued for what appears to be the most promising line of argument for explaining human rights, the view that we have inherent value, and that this can rationally be extended to animals of some kinds. So, while I admit that I have not proven that animals (or humans) have rights, I hope at least to have made clear the direction in which future argument ought to proceed. Erecting pointers, to be sure, is not the same as constructing proofs, but pointers are the best I can do here.

Second, the history of moral philosophy teaches us that utilitarianism dies hard. Just when one thinks it has been forced off the stage for good, one finds it loitering in the wings, awaiting yet another curtain call. The utilitarian can be counted on to say that there is nothing introduced by the idea of rights for which he cannot account.[14] One has only to see that the utilitarian objective is promoted if we recognize a strict obligation not to harm individuals except in extreme cases, *and* that, furthermore, utility is promoted by saying that individuals have the right not to be harmed, this invocation of a right functioning as an especially forceful way of conveying the idea that we ought not to harm individuals.

I am not convinced by this attempt to resurrect utilitarianism, and here I raise my final and most fundamental objection to it. The utilitarian is in no position to say that he knows that the utilitarian objective is promoted by talk of individuals having rights. But even if it is true that talk of rights helps promote the utilitarian objective, and for this reason such talk ought to be encouraged and honored, there can only be a *contingent* connection between any right, such as the right not to be harmed, and the fact that respecting this right forwards the utilitarian objective. The most that the utilitarian can say is that recognizing the right not to be harmed *as a matter of fact* fits in with forwarding his goal of maximizing the balance of good over evil.[15] The utilitarian must also accept that things could have been (and could become) otherwise. He must accept the possibility that it could have been or might become all right to harm individuals if this ever happened to forward the utilitarian objective. But neither the wrongness of harming individuals nor the right not to be harmed can change in the ways utilitarian theory implies they can. They are not contingent upon *utility*. Neither depends on the value of consequences. Instead, each depends on *the value of individuals.*

Let us put this in perspective before applying it. . . . Making an informed judgment about the morality of whaling or the use of the Draize test we must know both facts and moral principles. Otherwise, we cannot know which facts are morally relevant; and without this preliminary knowledge, we do not know what moral judgments to make. To determine what these principles are. . .is one of the distinctive tasks of moral philosophy. Three positions were examined and found wanting: the Kantian account, the cruelty account, and the utilitarian account. We then considered an account ascribing rights to animals, a position which meets the objections which were fatal to the views examined earlier. Unlike the Kantian account, the rights account insists upon the moral status of animals in their own right; unlike the cruelty account, the rights account does not confuse the morality of acts with the mental states of agents; and unlike utilitarianism, this account closes the door to the justification of prejudices which merely happen to bring about the best consequences. This emphasis on the value of individuals becomes prominent now as we turn at last to the task of applying the rights account to the whale, the veal calf, and the others.

It would be grotesque to suggest that the whale, the rabbit, the gibbon, the bobbie calf, the millions of animals brought so much pain and death at the hands of humans are not harmed, for harm is not restricted to human beings. They are harmed, harmed in a literal, not a metaphorical sense.

They are made to endure what is detrimental to their welfare, even death.
Those who would harm them, therefore, must justify doing so. Thus, members of the whaling industry, the cosmetics industry, the farming industry,
the network of hunters-exporters-importers must justify the harm they
bring animals in a way that is consistent with recognizing the animals' right
not to be harmed. To produce such a justification it is not enough to argue
that people profit, satisfy their curiosity, or derive pleasure from allowing
animals to be treated in these ways. These facts are not the morally relevant
ones. Rather, what must be shown is that overriding the right of animals not
to be harmed is justified because of further facts. For example, because we
have very good reason to believe that overriding the individual's right
prevents, and is the only realistic way to prevent, vastly greater harm to
other innocent individuals.

Let us ask the whaling industry whether they have so justified their
trade. Have they made their case in terms of the morally relevant facts? Our
answer must be: no! And the cosmetic industry? No! The farmers who raise
veal calves? No! The retailer of exotic animals? No! A thousand times we
must say: no! I do not say that they cannot possibly justify what they do. The
individual's right not to be harmed, we have argued, almost always trumps
the interests of the group, but it is possible that such a right must sometimes
give way. Possibly the rights of animals must sometimes give way to human
interests. It would be a mistake to rule this possibility out. Nevertheless, the
onus of justification must be borne by those who cause the harm to show
that they do not violate the rights of the individuals involved.

We allow then that it is *possible* that harming animals might be
justified; but we also maintain that those harming animals typically fail to
show that the harm caused is *actually* justified. A further question we must
ask ourselves is what, morally speaking, we ought to do in such a situation?
Reflection on comparable situations involving human beings will help
make the answer clear.

Consider racism and sexism. Imagine that slavery is an institution of
the day and that it is built on racist or sexist lines. Blacks or women are
assigned the rank of slave. Suppose we are told that in extreme circumstances even slavery might conceivably be justified, and that we ought not
to object to it or try to bring it down, even though no one has shown that it
is actually justified in the present case. Well, I do not believe for a moment
that we would accept such an attempt to dissuade us from toppling the
institution of slavery. Not for a moment would we accept the general
principle involved here, that an institution actually is justified because it
might conceivably be justified. We would accept the quite different principle that we are morally obligated to oppose any practice which appears to
violate rights unless we are shown that it really does not do so. To be
satisfied with anything less is to cheapen the value attributable to the
victims of the practice.

Exactly the same line of reasoning applies in the case where animals are regarded as so many dispensable commodities, models, subjects, etc. We ought not to back away from bringing these industries and related practices to a halt just because it is *possible* that the harm caused to the animals *might* be justified. If we do, we fail to mean it when we say that animals are not mere things, that they are the subjects of a life that is better or worse for them, that they have inherent value. As in the comparable case involving harm to human beings, our duty is to act, to do all that we can to put an end to the harm animals are made to endure. The fact that the animals themselves cannot speak out on their own behalf, the fact that they cannot organize, petition, march, exert political pressure, or raise our level of consciousness—all this does not weaken our obligation to act on their behalf. If anything, their impotence makes our obligation the greater.[23] . . .

NOTES

1. Relevant selections from both St. Thomas and Kant are included in Regan and Singer, *Animal Rights and Human Obligations.* What I call the Kantian account is critized further in my "Exploring the Idea of Animal Rights" in D. Paterson and R. Ryder, eds., *Animal Rights: A Symposium* (London: Centaur Press, 1979). Kant's views are criticized at length by Elizabeth Pybus and Alexander Broadie, "Kant's Treatment of Animals," *Philosophy* 49 (1974): 375–83. I defend Kant against their objections in my "Broadie and Pybus on Kant," *Philosophy* 51 (1976): 471–72. Broadie and Pybus reply in their "Kant on the Maltreatment of Animals," *Philosophy* 53 (1978): 560–61. At present I am persuaded that Broadie and Pybus are correct in arguing that Kant cannot account for the idea that animals themselves can be maltreated.
2. Singer, *Animal Liberation,* and Ryder, *Victims of Science.*
3. The famous passage from Bentham reads as follows (from *The Principles of Morals and Legislation* (1789), chap. 17, Sect. 1, reprinted in Regan and Singer, *Animal Rights and Human Obligations*): "The day has been, I grieve to say in many places it is not yet past, in which the greater part of the species, under the denomination of slaves, have been treated by the law exactly upon the same footing as, in England for example, the inferior races of animals are still. The day may come, when the rest of the animal creation may acquire those rights which never could have been withholden from them but by the hand of tyranny. The French have already discovered that the blackness of the skin is no reason why a human being should be abandoned without redress to the caprice of a tormentor. It may come one day to be recognized, that the number of the legs, the villosity of the skin, or the termination of the os sacrum, are reasons equally insufficient for abandoning a sensitive being to the same fate. What else is it that should trace the insuperable line? Is it the faculty of reason, or, perhaps, the faculty of discourse? But a full-grown horse or dog is beyond comparison a more rational, as well as a more conversable animal, than an infant of a day, or a week, or even a month, old. But suppose the case were otherwise, what would it avail? The question is not, Can they reason? nor, Can they talk? but, Can they suffer?"
4. John Locke, *Some Thoughts Concerning Education,* 5th ed. (London, 1905).

See also James Axtell, ed., *The Educational Writings of John Locke* (Cambridge: Cambridge University Press, 1968), sec. 116, pp. 225–26.

5. The utilitarian position I consider is the one associated with Bentham and forcefully presented by Peter Singer. That Singer is a utilitarian is made unmistakably clear in his "The Fable of the Fox and the Unliberated Animals" *Ethics* 88 (1978): 119–25.

6. See Singer, *Animal Liberation,* especially pp. 78–83.

7. Ibid., chap. 4.

8. Ronald Dworkin, *Taking Rights Seriously* (Cambridge: Harvard University Press, 1977).

9. The present statement of these conditions deviates somewhat from my earlier effort in "The Moral Basis of Vegetarianism," *Canadian Journal of Philosophy* 5 (1975): 181–214. I believe the inclusion of conditions (b) and (c) marks an improvement over the earlier formulation. However, a fuller statement has to include more than simply the idea of *preventing* vastly greater harm; for example, *reducing* already existing harm also has a place.

10. See my "An Examination and Defense of One Argument Concerning Animal Rights," *Inquiry* 22 (1979): 189–219.

11. Whether sense can be made of including irreversibly comatose human beings in the class of beings having inherent value is a troublesome question indeed. I consider this issue, perhaps not very adequately, in the essay referred to in footnote 17.

12. I do not believe it is absurd to think of natural objects which lack consciousness, or collections of such objects, as having inherent value, in the sense in which I use this expression. An X has inherent value if it has value logically independently of anyone's valuing X. I do not say this is easy to clarify or to defend, and it may be wrongheaded. At present, however, I believe it is a view that must be held, if we are to develop an environmental ethic, as distinct from an ethic for the use of the environment.

13. The distinction between being alive and having a life is one James Rachels frequently makes. See, for example, his "Euthanasia" in Tom Regan, ed., *Matters of Life and Death* (New York: Random House, 1980). Rachels does not, so far as I am aware, relate this distinction to the idea of inherent value.

14. It is possible that Mill meant to give rights a utilitarian basis. On this see David Lyons, "Human Rights and the General Welfare," *Philosophy and Public Affairs* 6 (1977): 113–29, reprinted in David Lyons, ed., *Rights* (Belmont, California: Wadsworth Publishing Co., 1979). The principal objection to this enterprise is the third objection I raise against utilitarianism here.

15. I do not believe utilitarianism is alone in implying that the duty not to harm an individual (or the individual's right not to be harmed) are *contingent* moral truths, which *might* have been otherwise (or *might* become otherwise). Certain aspects of Kant's theory as well as ethical egoism arguably imply this as well. This is absolutely fatal to these theories, a point I argue in my "Utilitarianism, Vegetarianism, and Animal Rights," in *Philosophy and Public Affairs.*

16. For a more complete list of recent philosophical work relating to the topics discussed in the present essay, see Charles Magel and Tom Regan, "Animal Rights and Human Obligations: A Select Bibliography," *Inquiry* 22 (1979): 243–47.

On Being Morally Considerable

Kenneth E. Goodpaster

Kenneth E. Goodpaster holds the David and Barbara Koch chair in business ethics at the University of St. Thomas, St. Paul, Minnesota. With Kenneth M. Sayre, he edited Ethics and Problems of the 21st Century.

A thing is right when it tends to preserve the integrity, stability, and beauty of the biotic community. It is wrong when it tends otherwise.

—*Aldo Leopold*

What follows is a preliminary inquiry into a question which needs more elaborate treatment than an essay can provide. The question can be and has been addressed in different rhetorical formats, but perhaps G. J. Warnock's formulation of it[1] is the best to start with:

> Let us consider the question to whom principles of morality apply from, so to speak, the other end—from the standpoint not of the agent, but of the "patient." What, we may ask here, is the condition of moral *relevance?* What is the condition of having a claim to be *considered*, by rational agents to whom moral principles apply? (148)

In the terminology of R. M. Hare (or even Kant), the same question might be put thus: In universalizing our putative moral maxims, what is the scope of the variable over which universalization is to range? A more legalistic idiom, employed recently by Christopher D. Stone,[2] might ask:

This essay originally appeared in *The Journal of Philosophy*, LXXV, 6 (June 1978), 308–25. Reprinted with permission.

What are the requirements for "having standing" in the moral sphere? However the question gets formulated, the thrust is in the direction of necessary and sufficient conditions on X in

(1) For all A, X deserves moral consideration from A. where A ranges over rational moral agents and moral 'consideration' is construed broadly to include the most basic forms of practical respect (and so is not restricted to "possession of rights" by X).

I

The motivation for addressing such a question stems from several sources. The last decade has seen a significant increase in the concern felt by most persons about "the environment." This new awareness manifests itself in many ways. One is a quest for methods of "technology assessment," for criteria for social choice that capture the relevant costs and benefits (be they quantifiable or not). On another front, heated controversies have arisen over endangered species and our treatment of animals generally (both as sources of food and as sources of experimental knowledge). The morality of abortion and, in general, the proper uses of medical technology have also tried our ethical sensitivities about the scope and nature of moral considerability.

These developments emphasize the importance of clarity about the *framework* of moral consideration as much as about the *application* of that framework. We need to understand better, for example, the scope of moral respect, the sorts of entities that can and should receive moral attention, and the nature of the "good" which morality (since it at least *includes* beneficence) is supposed to promote. In addition, we need principles for weighing or adjudicating conflicting claims to moral consideration.

The question focused on here is therefore only a first step toward the larger task. It is a framework question more than an application question— though its practical relevance is not so remote as to be purely a matter of logical speculation. My convictions about the proper answer to the question are sketched in another place,[8] but they can be summarized more explicitly as follows.

Modern moral philosophy has taken ethical egoism as its principal foil for developing what can fairly be called a *humanistic* perspective on value and obligation. That is, both Kantian and Humean approaches to ethics tend to view the philosophical challenge as that of providing an epistemological and motivational generalization of an agent's natural self-interested concern. Because of this preoccupation with moral "take-off," however, too little critical thought has been devoted to the flight and its destination. One result might be a certain feeling of impotence in the minds of many moral philosophers when faced with the sorts of issues mentioned earlier, issues that question the breadth of the moral enterprise more than its departure point. To be sure, questions of conservation, preservation of the environment, and technology assessment *can* be approached simply as application questions, e.g., "How shall we evaluate the alternatives available to us instrumentally in relation to humanistic satisfactions?" But there is something distressingly uncritical in this way of framing such issues—distressingly uncritical in the way that deciding foreign policy solely in terms of "the national interest" is uncritical. Or at least, so I think.

It seems to me that we should not only wonder about, but actually follow "the road not taken into the wood." Neither rationality nor the capacity to experience pleasure and pain seem to me necessary (even though they may be sufficient) conditions on moral considerability. And only our hedonistic and concentric forms of ethical reflection keep us from acknowledging this fact. Nothing short of the condition of *being alive* seems to me to be a plausible and nonarbitrary criterion. What is more, this criterion, if taken seriously, could admit of application to entities and systems of entities heretofore unimagined as claimants on our moral attention (such as the biosystem itself). Some may be inclined to take such implications as a *reductio* of the move "beyond humanism." I am beginning to be persuaded, however, that such implications may provide both a meaningful ethical vision and the hope of a more adequate action guide for the long-term future. Paradigms are crucial components in knowledge—but they can conceal as much as they reveal. Our paradigms of moral considerability are individual persons and their joys and sorrows. I want to venture the belief that the universe of moral consideration is more complex than these paradigms allow.

II

My strategy, now that my cards are on the table, will be to spell out a few rules of the game (in this section) and then to examine the "hands" of several respected philosophers whose arguments seem to count against casting the moral net as widely as I am inclined to (sections III, IV, and V). In the concluding section (VI), I will discuss several objections and touch on further questions needing attention.

The first (of four) distinctions that must be kept clear in addressing our question has already been alluded to. It is that between moral *rights* and moral *considerability*. My inclination is to construe the notion of rights as more specific than that of considerability, largely to avoid what seem to be unnecessary complications over the requirements for something's being an appropriate "bearer of rights." The concept of rights is used in wider and narrower senses, of course. Some authors (indeed, one whom we shall consider later in this paper) use it as roughly synonymous with Warnock's notion of "moral relevance." Others believe that being a bearer of rights involves the satisfaction of much more demanding requirements. The sentiments of John Passmore[4] are probably typical of this narrower view:

> The idea of "rights" is simply not applicable to what is non-human. . .It is one thing to say that it is wrong to treat animals cruelly, quite another to say that animals have rights (116/7).

I doubt whether it is so clear that the class of rights-bearers is or ought to be restricted to human beings, but I propose to suspend this question entirely by framing the discussion in terms of the notion of moral considerability (following Warnock), except in contexts where there is reason to think the widest sense of 'rights' is at work. Whether beings who deserve moral consideration in themselves, not simply by reason of their utility to human beings, also possess moral *rights* in some narrow sense is a question which will, therefore, remain open here—and it is a question the answer to which need not be determined in advance.

A second distinction is that between what might be called a *criterion of moral considerability* and a *criterion of moral significance*. The former represents the central quarry here, while the latter, which might easily get confused with the former, aims at governing *comparative* judgments of moral "weight" in cases of conflict. Whether a tree, say, deserves any moral consideration is a question that must be kept separate from the question of whether trees deserve more or less consideration than dogs, or dogs than human persons. We should not expect that the criterion for having "moral standing" at all will be the same as the criterion for adjudicating competing claims to priority among beings that merit that standing. In fact, it may well be an insufficient appreciation of this distinction which leads some to a preoccupation with rights in dealing with morality. I suspect that the real force of attributions of "rights" derives from comparative contexts, contexts in which moral considerability is presupposed and the issue of strength is crucial. Eventually, of course, the priority issues have to be dealt with for an operational ethical account—this much I have already acknowledged—but in the interests of clarity, I set them aside for now.

Another important distinction, the third, turns on the difference between questions of intelligibility and questions of normative substance. An adequate treatment of this difficult and complicated division would take us far afield,[5] but a few remarks are in order. It is tempting to assume, with Joel Feinberg,[6] that we can neatly separate such questions as

(2) What sorts of being can (logically) be *said* to deserve moral consideration?

from questions like

(3) What sorts of beings do, as a matter of "ethical fact" deserve moral consideration?

But our confidence in the separation here wanes (perhaps more quickly than in other philosophical contexts where the conceptual/substantive distinction arises) when we reflect upon the apparent *flexibility* of our metamoral beliefs. One might argue plausibly, for example, that there were times and societies in which the moral standing of blacks was, as a matter of *conceptual analysis,* deniable. Examples could be multiplied to include women, children, fetuses, and various other instances of what might be called "metamoral disenfranchisement." I suspect that the lesson to be learned here is that, as William Frankena has pointed out,[7] metaethics is, and has always been, a partially normative discipline. Whether we are to take this to mean that it is really impossible ever to engage in morally neutral conceptual analysis in ethics is, of course, another question. In any case, it appears that, with respect to the issue at hand, keeping (2) and (3) apart will be difficult. At the very least, I think, we must be wary of arguments that purport to answer (3) *solely* on the basis of "ordinary language" –style answers to (2).

Though the focus of the present inquiry is more normative than conceptual [hence aimed more at (3) than at (2)], it remains what I called a "framework" inquiry nonetheless, since it prescinds from the question of relative weights (moral significance) of moral considerability claims.

Moreover—and this brings us to the fourth and last distinction—there is another respect in which the present inquiry involves framework questions rather than questions of application. There is clearly a sense in which we are subject to *thresholds* of moral sensitivity just as we are subject to thresholds of cognitive or perceptual sensitivity. Beyond such thresholds we are "morally blind" or suffer disintegrative consequences analogous to "information overload" in a computer. In the face of our conative limitations, we often will distinguish between moral demands that are relative to those limitations and moral demands that are not. The latter demands represent claims on our consideration or respect which we acknowledge as in some sense ideally determinative if not practically determinative. We might mark this distinction by borrowing Ross's categories of "prima facie vs. actual duty" except that (A) these categories tend to map more naturally onto the distinction mentioned earlier between considerability and significance, and (B) these categories tend to evoke conditionality and lack thereof of a sort which is rooted more in a plurality of "external" moral pressures than in an agent's "internal" capacities for practical response. Let us, then, say that the moral considerability of X is *operative* for an agent A if and only if the thorough acknowledgement of X by A is psychologically (and in general, causally) possible for A. If the moral considerability of X is defensible on all grounds independent of operativity, we shall say that it is *regulative.* An

agent may, for example, have an obligation to grant regulative considerability to all living things, but be able psychologically and in terms
of his own nutrition to grand operative consideration to a much smaller
class of things (though note that capacities in this regard differ among
persons and change over time).

Using all these distinctions, and the rough and ready terminology that
they yield, we can now state the issue in (1) as a concern for a relatively
substantive (vs. purely logical) criterion of moral considerability (vs. moral
significance) of a regulative (vs. operative) sort. As far as I can see, X's being
a living thing is both necessary and sufficient for moral considerability so
understood, whatever may be the case for the moral *rights* that rational
agents should acknowledge.

III

Let us begin with Warnock's own answer to the question, now that the
question has been clarified somewhat. In setting out his answer, Warnock
argues (in my view, persuasively) against two more restrictive candidates.
The first, what might be called the *Kantian principle,* amounts to little more
than a reflection of the requirements of moral *agency* onto those of moral
considerability:

(4) For X to deserve moral consideration from A, X must be a rational
human person.

Observing that such a criterion of considerability eliminates children
and mentally handicapped adults, among others, Warnock dismisses it as
intolerably narrow.

The second candidate, actually a more generous variant of the first,
sets the limits of moral considerability by disjoining "potentiality":

(5) For all A, X deserves moral consideration from A if and only if X
is a rational human person or is a potential rational human person.

Warnock's reply to this suggestion is also persuasive. Infants and
imbeciles are no doubt potentially rational, but this does not appear to be
the reason why we should not maltreat them. And we would not say that
an imbecile reasonably judged to be incurable would thereby reasonably
be taken to have no moral claims (151). In short, it seems arbitrary to draw
the boundary of moral *considerability* around rational human beings (actual or potential), however plausible it might be to draw the boundary of
moral *responsibility* there.[8]

Warnock then settles upon his own solution. The basis of moral
claims, he says, may be put as follows:

> . . .just as liability to be judged as a moral agent follows from one's general
> capability of alleviating, by moral action, the ills of the predicament, and is

for that reason confined to rational beings, so the condition of being a proper "beneficiary" of moral action is the capability of *suffering* the ills of the predicament—and for that reason is not confined to rational beings, nor even to potential members of that class (151).

The criterion of moral considerability then, is located in the *capacity to suffer:*

(6) For all *A*, *X* deserves moral consideration from *A* if and only if *X* is capable of suffering pain (or experiencing enjoyment).

And the defense involves appeal to what Warnock considers to be (analytically) the *object* of the moral enterprise: Amelioration of "the predicament."

Now two issues arise immediately in the wake of this sort of appeal. The first has to do with Warnock's own over-all strategy in the context of the quoted passage. Earlier on in his book, he insists that the appropriate analysis of the concept of morality will lead us to an "object" whose pursuit provides the framework for ethics. But the "object" seems to be more restrictive:

> . . .the general object of moral evaluation must be to contribute in some respects, by way of the actions of rational beings, to the amelioration of the human predicament—that is, of the conditions in which *these* rational beings, humans, actually find themselves (16; emphasis in the original).

It appears that, by the time moral considerability comes up later in the book, Warnock has changed his mind about the object of morality by enlarging the "predicament" to include nonhumans.

The second issue turns on the question of analysis itself. As I suggested earlier, it is difficult to keep conceptual and substantive questions apart in the present context. We can, of course, stipulatively *define* 'morality' as both having an object and having the object of mitigating suffering. But, in the absence of more argument, such definition is itself in need of a warrant. Twentieth-century preoccupation with the naturalistic or definist fallacy should have taught us at least this much.

Neither of these two observations shows that Warnock's suggested criterion is wrong, of course. But they do, I think, put us in a rather more demanding mood. And the mood is aggravated when we look to two other writers on the subject who appear to hold similar views.

W. K. Frankena, in a recent paper,[9] joins forces:

> Like Warnock, I believe that there are right and wrong ways to treat infants, animals, imbeciles, and idiots even if or even though (as the case may be) they are not persons or human beings—just because they are capable of pleasure and suffering, and not just because their lives happen to have some value to or for those who clearly are persons or human beings.

And Peter Singer[10] writes:

> If a being is not capable of suffering, or of experiencing enjoyment or happiness, there is nothing to be taken into account. This is why the limit of sentience (using the term as a convenient, if not strictly accurate, shorthand for the capacity to suffer or experience enjoyment or happiness) is the only defensible boundary of concern for the interests of others (154).

I say that the mood is aggravated because, although I acknowledge and even applaud the conviction expressed by these philosophers that the capacity to suffer (or perhaps better, *sentience*) is sufficient for moral considerability, I fail to understand their reasons for thinking such a criterion necessary. To be sure, there are hints at reasons in each case. Warnock implies that nonsentient beings could not be proper "beneficiaries" of moral action. Singer seems to think that beyond sentience "there is nothing to take into account." And Frankena suggests that nonsentient beings simply do not provide us with moral reasons for respecting them unless it be potentiality for sentience.[11] Yet it is so clear that there *is* something to take into account, something that is not merely "potential sentience" and which surely does qualify beings as beneficiaries and capable of harm—namely, *life*—that the hints provided seem to me to fall short of good reasons.

Biologically, it appears that sentience is an adaptive characteristic of living organisms that provides them with a better capacity to anticipate, and so avoid, threats to life. This at least suggests, though of course it does not prove, that the capacities to suffer and to enjoy are ancillary to something more important rather than tickets to considerability in their own right. In the words of one perceptive scientific observer:

> If we view pleasure as rooted in our sensory physiology, it is not difficult to see that our neurophysiological equipment must have evolved via variation and selective retention in such a way as to record a positive signal to adaptationally satisfactory conditions and a negative signal to adaptationally unsatisfactory conditions. . .The pleasure signal is only an evolutionarily derived indicator, not the goal itself. It is the applause which signals a job well done, but not the actual completion of the job.[12]

Nor is it absurd to imagine that evolution might have resulted (indeed might still result?) in beings whose capacities to maintain, protect, and advance their lives did not depend upon mechanisms of pain and pleasure at all.

So far, then, we can see that the search for a criterion of moral considerability takes one quickly and plausibly beyond humanism. But there is a tendency, exhibited in the remarks of Warnock, Frankena, and Singer, to draw up the wagons around the notion of sentience. I have suggested that there is reason to go further and not very much in the way of argument not to. But perhaps there is a stronger and more explicit case that can be made for sentience. I think there is, in a way, and I propose to discuss it in detail in the section that follows.

IV

Joel Feinberg offers (51) what may be the clearest and most explicit case for a restrictive criterion on moral considerability (restrictive with respect to life). I should mention at the outset, however, that the context for his remarks is

(I) the concept of "rights," which, we have seen, is sometimes taken to be narrower than the concept of "considerability"; and

(II) the *intelligibility* of rights-attributions, which, we have seen, is problematically related to the more substantive issue of what beings deserve moral consideration.

These two features of Feinberg's discussion might be thought sufficient to invalidate my use of that discussion here. But the context of his remarks is clearly such that 'rights' is taken very broadly, much closer to what I am calling moral considerability than to what Passmore calls "rights." And the thrust of the arguments, since they are directed against the *intelligibility* of certain rights attributions, is *a fortiori* relevant to the more substantive issue set out in (1). So I propose to treat Feinberg's arguments as if they were addressed to the considerability issue in its more substantive form, whether or not they were or would be intended to have such general application. I do so with due notice to the possible need for scare-quotes around Feinberg's name, but with the conviction that it is really in Feinberg's discussion that we discover that the clearest line of argument in favor of something like sentience, an argument which was only hinted at in the remarks of Warnock, Frankena, and Singer.

The central thesis defended by Feinberg is that a being cannot intelligibly be said to possess moral rights (read: deserve moral consideration) unless that being satisfies the "interest principle," and that only the subclass of humans and higher animals among living beings satisfies this principle:

> . . .the sorts of beings who can have rights are precisely those who have (or can have) interests. I have come to this tentative conclusion for two reasons: (1) because a right holder must be capable of being represented and it is impossible to represent a being that has no interests, and (2) because a right holder must be capable of being a beneficiary in his own person, and a being without interests is a being that is incapable of being harmed or benefited, having no good or "sake" of its own (51).

Implicit in this passage are the following two arguments, interpreted in terms of moral considerability:

(A1) Only beings who can be represented can deserve moral consideration.

Only beings who have (or can have) interests can be represented.

Therefore, only beings who have (or can have) interests can deserve moral consideration.

(A2) Only beings capable of being beneficiaries can deserve moral consideration.

Only beings who have (or can have) interests are capable of being beneficiaries.

Therefore, only beings who have (or can have) interests can deserve moral consideration.

I suspect that these two arguments are at work between the lines in Warnock, Frankena, and Singer, though of course one can never be sure. In any case, I propose to consider them as the best defense of the sentience criterion in recent literature.

I am prepared to grant, with some reservations, the first premises in each of these obviously valid arguments. The second premises, though, are *both* importantly equivocal. To claim that only beings who have (or can have) interests can be represented might mean that "mere things" cannot be represented because they have nothing to represent, no "interests" as opposed to "usefulness" to defend or protect. Similarly, to claim that only beings who have (or can have) interests are capable of being beneficiaries might mean that "mere things" are incapable of being benefited or harmed—they have no "well-being" to be sought or acknowledged by rational moral agents. So construed, Feinberg seems to be right; but he also seems to be committed to allowing any *living* thing the status of moral considerability. For as he himself admits, even plants

> . . .are not "mere things"; they are vital objects with inherited biological propensities determining their natural growth. Moreover we do say that certain conditions are "good" or "bad" for plants, thereby suggesting that plants, unlike rocks, are capable of having a "good" (51).

But Feinberg pretty clearly wants to draw the nets tighter than this—and he does so by interpreting the notion of "interests" in the two second premises more narrowly. The contrast term he favors is not 'mere things' but 'mindless creatures'. And he makes this move by insisting that "interests" logically presuppose *desires* or *wants* or *aims,* the equipment for which is not possessed by plants (nor, we might add, by many animals or even some humans?).

But why should we accept this shift in strength of the criterion? In doing so, we clearly abandon one sense in which living organisms like plants do have interests that can be represented. There is no absurdity in imagining the representation of the needs of a tree for sun and water in the face of a proposal to cut it down or pave its immediate radius for a parking lot. We might of course, on reflection, decide to go ahead and cut it down or do the paving, but there is hardly an intelligibility problem about representing the tree's interest in our deciding not to. In the face of their obvious tendencies to maintain and heal themselves, it is very difficult to reject the idea of interests on the part of trees (and plants generally) in remaining alive.[13]

Nor will it do to suggest, as Feinberg does, that the needs (interests) of living things like trees are not really their own but implicitly *ours:* "Plants may need things in order to discharge their functions, but their functions are assigned by human interests, not their own" (54). As if it were human interests that assigned to trees the tasks of growth or maintenance! The interests at stake are clearly those of the living things themselves, not simply those of the owners or users or other human persons involved. Indeed, there is a suggestion in this passage that, to be capable of being represented, an organism must *matter* to human beings somehow—a suggestion whose implications for human rights (disenfranchisement) let alone the rights of animals (inconsistently for Feinberg, I think)— are grim.

The truth seems to be that the "interests" that nonsentient beings share with sentient beings (over and against "mere things") are far more plausible as criteria of *considerability* than the "interests" that sentient beings share (over and against "mindless creatures"). This is not to say that interests construed in the latter way are morally irrelevant—for they may play a role as criteria of moral *significance*—but it is to say that psychological or hedonic capacities seem unnecessarily sophisticated when it comes to locating the minimal conditions for something's deserving to be valued for its own sake. Surprisingly, Feinberg's own reflections on "mere things" appear to support this very point:

> ...mere things have no conative life: no conscious wishes, desires, and hopes; or urges and impulses; or unconscious drives, aims, and goals; or latent tendencies, direction of growth, and natural fulfillments. Interests must be compounded somehow out of conations; hence mere things have no interests (49).

Together with the acknowledgment, quoted earlier, that plants, for example, are not "mere things," such observations seem to undermine the interest principle in its more restrictive form. I conclude, with appropriate caution, that the interest principle either grows to fit what we might call a "life principle" or requires an arbitrary stipulation of psychological capacities (for desires, wants, etc.) which are neither warranted by (A1) and (A2) nor independently plausible.

V

Thus far, I have examined the views of four philosophers on the necessity of sentience or interests (narrowly conceived) as a condition on moral considerability. I have maintained that these views are not plausibly supported, when they are supported at all, because of a reluctance to acknowledge in nonsentient living beings the presence of independent needs, capacities for benefit and harm, etc. I should like, briefly, to reflect on a more general level about the roots of this reluctance before proceeding to a consideration of objections against the "life" criterion which I have been defending. In the course of this reflection, we might gain some insight into the sources of our collective hesitation in viewing environmental ethics in a "nonchauvinistic" way.[14]

When we consider the reluctance to go beyond sentience in the context of moral consideration—and look for both explanations and justifications—two thoughts come to mind. The first is that, given the connection between beneficence (or nonmaleficence) and morality, it is natural that limits on moral considerability will come directly from limits on the range of beneficiaries (or "maleficiaries"). This is implicit in Warnock and explicit in Feinberg. The second thought is that, if one's conception of the good is *hedonistic* in character, one's conception of a beneficiary will quite naturally be restricted to beings who are capable of pleasure and pain. If pleasure or satisfaction is the only ultimate gift we have to give, morally, then it is to be expected that only those equipped to receive such a gift will enter into our moral deliberation. And if pain or dissatisfaction is the only ultimate harm we can cause, then it is to be expected that only those equipped for it will deserve our consideration. There seems, therefore, to be a noncontingent connection between a hedonistic or quasi-hedonistic[15] theory of value and a response to the moral-considerability question which favors sentience of interest possession (narrowly conceived).

One must, of course, avoid drawing too strong a conclusion about this connection. It does not follow from the fact that hedonism leads naturally to the sentience criterion either that it entails that criterion or that one who holds that criterion must be a hedonist in his theory of value. For one might be a hedonist with respect to the good and yet think that moral consideration was, on other grounds, restricted to a subclass of the beings capable of enjoyment or pain. And one might hold to the sentience criterion for considerability while denying that pleasure, for example, was the only intrinsically good thing in the life of a human (or nonhuman) being. So hedonism about value and the sentience criterion of moral considerability are not logically equivalent. Nor does either entail the other. But there is some sense, I think, in which they mutually support each other—both in terms of "rendering plausible" and in terms of "helping to explain." As

Derek Parfit is fond of putting it, "there are not entailments, but then there seldom are in moral reasoning."[16]

Let me hazard the hypothesis, then, that there is a nonaccidental affinity between a person's or a society's conception of value and its conception of moral considerability. More specifically, there is an affinity between hedonism or some variation on hedonism and a predilection for the sentience criterion of considerability or some variation on it. The implications one might draw from this are many. In the context of a quest for a richer moral framework to deal with a new awareness of the environment, one might be led to expect significant resistance from a hedonistic society unless one forced one's imperatives into an instrumental form. One might also be led to an appreciation of how technology aimed at largely hedonistic goals could gradually "harden the hearts" of a civilization to the biotic community in which it lives—at least until crisis or upheaval raised some questions.[17]

VI

Let us now turn to several objections that might be thought to render a "life principle" of moral considerability untenable quite independently of the adequacy or inadequacy of the sentience or interest principle.

(O1) A principle of moral respect or consideration for life in all its forms is mere Schweitzerian romanticism, even if it does not involve, as it probably does, the projection of mental or psychological categories beyond their responsible boundaries into the realms of plants, insects, and microbes.

(R1) This objection misses the central thrust of my discussion, which is *not* that the sentience criterion is necessary, but applicable to all life forms—rather the point is that the possession of sentience is not necessary for moral considerability. Schweitzer himself may have held the former view—and so have been "romantic"—but this is beside the point.

(O2) To suggest seriously that moral considerability is coextensive with life is to suggest that conscious, feeling beings have no more central role in the moral life than vegetables, which is downright absurd—if not perverse.

(R2) This objection misses the central thrust of my discussion as well, for a different reason. It is consistent with acknowledging the moral considerability of all life forms to go on to point out differences of moral significance among these life forms. And as far as perversion is concerned, history will perhaps be a better judge of our civilization's treatment of animals and the living environment on that score.

(O3) Consideration of life can serve as a criterion only to the degree that life itself can be given a precise definition; and it can't.

(R3) I fail to see why a criterion of moral considerability must be strictly decidable in order to be tenable. Surely rationality, potential rationality, sentience, and the capacity for or possession of interests fare no better here. Moreover, there do seem to be empirically respectable accounts of the nature of living beings available which are not intolerably vague or open-textured:

> The typifying mark of a living system. . .appears to be its persistent state of low entropy, sustained by metabolic processes for accumulating energy, and maintained in equilibrium with its environment by homeostatic feedback processes.[18]

Granting the need for certain further qualifications, a definition such as this strikes me as not only plausible in its own right, but ethically illuminating, since it suggests that the core of moral concern lies in respect for self-sustaining organization and integration in the face of pressures toward high entropy.

(O4) If life, as understood in the previous response, is really taken as the key to moral considerability, then it is possible that larger systems besides our ordinarily understood "linear" extrapolations from human beings (e.g., animals, plants, etc.) might satisfy the conditions, such as the biosystem as a whole. This surely would be a *reductio* of the life principle.

(R4) At best, it would be a *reductio* of the life principle in this form or without qualification. But it seems to me that such (perhaps surprising) implications, if true, should be taken seriously. There is some evidence that the biosystem as a whole exhibits behavior approximating to the definition sketched above,[19] and I see no reason to deny it moral considerability on that account. Why should the universe of moral considerability map neatly onto our medium-sized framework of organisms?

(O5) There are severe epistemological problems about imputing interests, benefits, harms, etc. to nonsentient beings. What is it for a tree to have needs?

(R5) I am not convinced that the epistemological problems are more severe in this context than they would be in numerous others which the objector would probably not find problematic. Christopher Stone has put this point nicely:

> I am sure I can judge with more certainty and meaningfulness whether and when my lawn wants (needs) water than the Attorney General can judge whether and when the United States wants (needs) to take an appeal from an adverse judgment by a lower court. The lawn tells me that it wants water by a certain dryness of the blades and soil—immediately obvious to the touch—the appearance of bald spots, yellowing, and a lack of springiness after being walked on; how does "the United States" communicate to the Attorney General? (24).

We make decisions in the interests of others or on behalf of others every day—"others" whose wants are far less verifiable than those of most living creatures.

(O6) Whatever the force of the previous objections, the clearest and most decisive refutation of the principle of respect for life is that one cannot *live* according to it, nor is there any indication in nature that we were intended to. We must eat, experiment to gain knowledge, protect ourselves from predation (macroscopic and microscopic), and in general deal with the overwhelming complexities of the moral life while remaining psychologically intact. To take seriously the criterion of considerability being defended, all these things must be seen as somehow morally wrong.

(R6) This objection, if it is not met by implication in (R2), can be met, I think, by recalling the distinction made earlier between regulative and operative moral consideration. It seems to me that there clearly are limits to the operational character of respect for living things. We must eat, and usually this involves killing (though not always). We must have knowledge, and sometimes this involves experimentation with living things and killing (though not always). We must protect ourselves from predation and disease, and sometimes this involves killing (though not always). The regulative character of the moral consideration due to all living things asks, as far as I can see, for sensitivity and awareness, not for suicide (psychic or otherwise). But it is not vacuous, in that it does provide a *ceteris paribus* encouragement in the direction of nutritional, scientific, and medical practices of a genuinely life-respecting sort.

As for the implicit claim, in the objection, that since nature doesn't respect life, we needn't, there are two rejoinders. The first is that the premise is not so clearly true. Gratuitous killing in nature is rare indeed. The second, and more important, response is that the issue at hand has to do with the appropriate moral demands to be made on rational moral agents, not on beings who are not rational moral agents. Besides, this objection would tell equally against *any* criterion of moral considerability so far as I can see, if the suggestion is that nature is amoral.

I have been discussing the necessary and sufficient conditions that should regulate moral consideration. As indicated earlier, however, numerous other questions are waiting in the wings. Central among them are questions dealing with how to balance competing claims to consideration in a world in which such competing claims seem pervasive. Related to these questions would be problems about the relevance of developing or declining status in life (the very young and the very old) and the relevance of the part-whole relation (leaves to a tree; species to an ecosystem). And there are many others.

Perhaps enough has been said, however, to clarify an important project for contemporary ethics, if not to defend a full-blown account of moral considerability and moral significance. Leopold's ethical vision and its implications for modern society in the form of an environmental ethic are important—so we should proceed with care in assessing it.

NOTES

1. *The Object of Morality* (New York: Methuen, 1971); parenthetical page references to Warnock will be to this book.
2. *Should Trees Have Standing?* (Los Altos, Calif.: William Kaufmann, 1974); parenthetical page references to Stone will be to this book.
3. "From Egoism to Environmentalism," in Goodpaster and K. M. Sayre, eds., *Ethics and Problems of the 21st Century* (Notre Dame, Ind.: University Press, 1978).
4. *Man's Responsibility for Nature* (New York: Scribner's, 1974).
5. Cf. R. M. Hare, "The Argument from Received Opinion," in *Essays on Philosophical Method* (New York: Macmillan, 1971), p. 117.
6. "The Rights of Animals and Unborn Generations," in Blackstone, *Philosophy and Environmental Crisis* (University of Georgia, 1974), p. 43; parenthetical page references to Feinberg will be to this paper.
7. "On Saying the Ethical Thing," in Goodpaster, ed., *Perspectives on Morality* (Notre Dame, Ind.: University Press, 1976), pp. 107–124.
8. Actually, it seems to me that we ought not to draw the boundary of moral responsibility just here. See my "Morality and Organizations," in *Proceedings of the Second National Conference on Business Ethics* (Waltham, Mass.: Bentley College, 1978).
9. "Ethics and the Environment," in Goodpaster and Sayre, *op. cit.*
10. "All Animals Are Equal," in Tom Regan and Peter Singer, *Animal Rights and Human Obligations* (Englewood Cliffs, N.J.: Prentice-Hall, 1976). See p. 316.
11. "I can see no reason, from the moral point of view, why we should respect something that is alive but has no conscious sentiency and so can experience no pleasure or pain, joy or suffering, unless perhaps it is potentially a consciously sentient being, as in the case of a fetus. Why, if leaves and trees have no capacity to feel pleasure or to suffer, should I tear no leaf from a tree? Why should I respect its location any more than that of a stone in my driveway, if no benefit or harm comes to any person or sentient being by my moving it?" ("Ethics and the Environment").
12. Mark W. Lipsey, "Value Science and Developing Society," paper delivered to the Society for Religion in Higher Education, Institute on Society, Technology and Values (July 15–Aug. 4, 1973), p. 11.
13. See Albert Szent-Gyorgyi, *The Living State* (New York: Academic Press, 1972), esp. ch. VI, "Vegetable Defense Systems."
14. Cf. R. and V. Routley, "Not for Humans Only," in Goodpaster and Sayre, note 3. R. Routley is, I think, the originator of the phrase "human chauvinism".
15. Frankena uses the phrase "quasi-hedonist" in *Ethics* (Englewood Cliffs, N.J.: Prentice-Hall, 1973), p. 90.
16. "Later Selves and Moral Principles," in A. Montefiori, ed., *Philosophy and Personal Relations* (Boston: Routledge & Kegan Paul, 1973), p. 147.
17. There is more, but much depends, I think, on defending claims about the value theory at work in our society and about the need for noninstrumental approaches to value change. Value theory, like scientific theory, tends to evolve

by trying to accommodate to the conventional pattern any new suggestions about what is good or should be respected. I suspect that the analogy holds true for the explanations to be given of ethical revolutions—a new and simpler way of dealing with our moral sense emerges to take the place of the old contrivances—be they egoistic, utilitarian, or in the present case hedonistic (if not humanistic). Such topics are, of course, not the topics of this essay. Perhaps I can be excused for raising them here by the contention that a line of argument in ethics (indeed, in philosophy generally) needs not only to be criticized—it needs to be *understood*.

18. K. M. Sayre, *Cybernetics and the Philosophy of Mind* (New York: Humanities, 1976), p. 91.
19. See J. Lovelock and S. Epton, "The Quest for Gaia," *The New Scientist*, LXV, 935 (Feb. 6, 1975): 304–309.

The Ethics of Respect for Nature

Paul W. Taylor

Paul W. Taylor is professor emeritus of philosophy at Brooklyn College, City University of New York. He is the author of Respect for Nature: A Theory of Environmental Ethics.

HUMAN-CENTERED AND LIFE-CENTERED SYSTEMS OF ENVIRONMENTAL ETHICS

When the basic characteristics of the attitude of respect for nature are made clear, it will be seen that a life-centered system of environmental ethics need not be holistic or organicist in its conception of the kinds of entities that are deemed the appropriate objects of moral concern and consideration. Nor does such a system require that the concepts of ecological homeostasis, equilibrium, and integrity provide us with normative principles from which could be derived (with the addition of factual knowledge) our obligations with regard to natural ecosystems. The "balance of nature" is not itself a moral norm, however important may be the role it plays in our general outlook on the natural world that underlies the attitude of respect for nature. I argue that finally it is the good (well-being, welfare) of individual organisms, considered as entities having inherent worth, that determines our moral relations with the Earth's wild communities of life.

In designating the theory to be set forth as life-centered, I intend to contrast it with all anthropocentric views. According to the latter, human actions affecting the natural environment and its nonhuman inhabitants are right (or wrong) by either of two criteria: they have consequences which

This essay originally appeared in *Environmental Ethics*, Vol. 3, No. 3 (Fall 1981), pp. 197–218. Reprinted with permission.

are favorable (or unfavorable) to human well-being, or they are consistent (or inconsistent) with the system of norms that protect and implement human rights. From this human-centered standpoint it is to humans and only to humans that all duties are ultimately owed. We may have responsibilities *with regard to* the natural ecosystems and biotic communities of our planet, but these responsibilities are in every case based on the contingent fact that our treatment of those ecosystems and communities of life can further the realization of human values and/or human rights. We have no obligation to promote or protect the good of nonhuman living things, independently of this contingent fact.

A life-centered system of environmental ethics is opposed to human-centered ones precisely on this point. From the perspective of a life-centered theory, we have prima facie moral obligations that are owed to wild plants and animals themselves as members of the Earth's biotic community. We are morally bound (other things being equal) to protect or promote their good for *their* sake. Our duties to respect the integrity of natural ecosystems, to preserve endangered species, and to avoid environmental pollution stem from the fact that these are ways in which we can help make it possible for wild species populations to achieve and maintain a healthy existence in a natural state. Such obligations are due those living things out of recognition of their inherent worth. They are entirely additional to and independent of the obligations we owe to our fellow humans. Although many of the actions that fulfill one set of obligations will also fulfill the other, two different grounds of obligation are involved. Their well-being, as well as human well-being, is something to be realized *as an end in itself*.

If we were to accept a life-centered theory of environmental ethics, a profound reordering of our moral universe would take place. We would begin to look at the whole of the Earth's biosphere in a new light. Our duties with respect to the "world" of nature would be seen as making prima facie claims upon us to be balanced against our duties with respect to the "world" of human civilization. We could no longer simply take the human point of view and consider the effects of our actions exclusively from the perspective of our own good. . . .

We can think of the good of an individual nonhuman organism as consisting in the full development of its biological powers. Its good is realized to the extent that it is strong and healthy. It possesses whatever capacities it needs for successfully coping with its environment and so preserving its existence throughout the various stages of the normal life cycle of its species. The good of a population or community of such individuals consists in the population or community maintaining itself from generation to generation as a coherent system of genetically and ecologically related organisms whose average good is at an optimum level for the given environment. (Here *average good* means that the degree of realization of the good of *individual organisms* in the population or community is, on average, greater than would be the case under any other ecologically functioning order of interrelations among those species populations in the given ecosystem.)

The idea of a being having a good of its own, as I understand it, does not entail that the being must. . .take an interest in what affects its life for better or for worse. We can act in a being's interest or contrary to its interest without its being interested in what we are doing to it in the sense of wanting or not wanting us to do it. It may, indeed, be wholly unaware that favorable and unfavorable events are taking place in its life. I take it that trees, for example, have no knowledge or desires or feelings. Yet is is undoubtedly the case that trees can be harmed or benefited by our actions. We can crush their roots by running a bulldozer too close to them. We can see to it that they get adequate nourishment and moisture by fertilizing and watering the soil around them. Thus we can help or hinder them in the realization of their good. It is the good of trees themselves that is thereby affected. . . .

When construed in this way, the concept of a being's good is not coextensive with sentience or the capacity for feeling pain. William Frankena has argued for a general theory of environmental ethics in which the ground of a creature's being worthy of moral consideration is its sentience. I have offered some criticisms of this view elsewhere, but the full refutation of such a position, it seems to me, finally depends on the positive reasons for accepting a life-centered theory of the kind I am defending in this essay. . . .[1]

Since I am concerned only with human treatment of wild organisms, species populations, and communities of life as they occur in our planet's natural ecosystems, it is to those entities alone that the concept "having a good of its own" will here be applied. I am not denying that other living things, whose genetic origin and environmental conditions have been produced, controlled, and manipulated by humans for human ends, do have a good of their own in the same sense as do wild plants and animals. It is not my purpose in this essay, however, to set out or defend the principles that should guide our conduct with regard to their good. It is only insofar as their production and use by humans have good or ill effects upon natural ecosystems and their wild inhabitants that the ethics of respect for nature comes into play. . . .

THE BIOCENTRIC OUTLOOK ON NATURE

[The] belief system underlying the attitude of respect for nature I call (for want of a better name) "the biocentric outlook on nature." Since it is not wholly analyzable into empirically confirmable assertions, it should not be thought of as simply a compendium of the biological sciences concerning our planet's ecosystems. It might best be described as a philosophical world view, to distinguish it from a scientific theory or explanatory system. However, one of its major tenets is the great lesson we have learned from the science of ecology: the interdependence of all living things in an organically unified order whose balance and stability are necessary conditions for the realization of the good of its constituent biotic communities.

Before turning to an account of the main components of the biocentric outlook, it is convenient here to set forth the overall structure of my theory of environmental ethics as it has now emerged. The ethics of respect for nature is made up of three basic elements: a belief system, an ultimate moral attitude, and a set of rules of duty and standards of character. These elements are connected with each other in the following manner. The belief system provides a certain outlook on nature which supports and makes intelligible an autonomous agent's adopting, as an ultimate moral attitude, the attitude of respect for nature. It supports and makes intelligible the attitude in the sense that, when an autonomous agent understands its moral relations to the natural world in terms of this outlook, it recognizes the attitude of respect to be the only *suitable* or *fitting* attitude to take toward all wild forms of life in the Earth's biosphere. Living things are now viewed as *the appropriate objects of the attitude of respect* and are accordingly regarded as entities possessing inherent worth. One then places intrinsic value on the promotion and protection of their good. As a consequence of this, one makes a moral commitment to abide by a set of rules of duty and to fulfill (as far as one can by one's own efforts) certain standards of good character. Given one's adoption of the attitude of respect, one makes that moral commitment because one considers those rules and standards to be validly binding on all moral agents. They are seen as embodying forms of conduct and character structures in which the attitude of respect for nature is manifested.

This three-part complex which internally orders the ethics of respect for nature is symmetrical with a theory of human ethics grounded on respect for persons. Such a theory includes, first, a conception of oneself and others as persons, that is, as centers of autonomous choice. Second, there is the attitude of respect for persons as persons. When this is adopted as an ultimate moral attitude it involves the disposition to treat every person as having inherent worth or "human dignity." Every human being, just in virtue of her or his humanity, is understood to be worthy of moral consideration, and intrinsic value is placed on the autonomy and well-being of each. This is what Kant meant by conceiving of persons as ends in themselves. Third, there is an ethical system of duties which are acknowledged to be owed by everyone to everyone. These duties are forms of conduct in which public recognition is given to each individual's inherent worth as a person.

This structural framework for a theory of human ethics is meant to leave open the issue of consequentialism (utilitarianism) versus non-consequentialism (deontology). That issue concerns the particular kind of system of rules defining the duties of moral agents toward persons. Similarly, I am leaving open in this paper the question of what particular kind of system of rules defines our duties with respect to the natural world.

The biocentric outlook on nature has four main components. (1) Humans are thought of as members of the Earth's community of life, holding that membership on the same terms as apply to all the nonhuman members. (2) The Earth's natural ecosystems as a totality are seen as a complex web of interconnected elements, with the sound biological functioning of each being dependent on the sound biological functioning of the others. (This is the component referred to above as the great lesson that the science of ecology has taught us.) (3) Each individual organism is conceived of as a teleological center of life, pursuing its own good in its own way. (4) Whether we are concerned with standards of merit or with the concept of inherent worth, the claim that humans by their very nature are superior to other species is a groundless claim and, in the light of elements (1), (2), and (3) above, must be rejected as nothing more than an irrational bias in our own favor.

The conjunction of these four ideas constitutes the biocentric outlook on nature. In the remainder of this paper I give a brief account of the first three components, followed by a more detailed analysis of the fourth. I then conclude by indicating how this outlook provides a way of justifying the attitude of respect for nature.

HUMANS AS MEMBERS OF THE EARTH'S COMMUNITY OF LIFE

We share with other species a common relationship to the Earth. In accepting the biocentric outlook we take the fact of our being an animal species to be a fundamental feature of our existence. We consider it an essential aspect of "the human condition." We do not deny the differences between ourselves and other species, but we keep in the forefront of our consciousness the fact that in relation to our planet's natural ecosystems we are but one species population among many. Thus we acknowledge our origin in the very same evolutionary process that gave rise to all other species and we recognize ourselves to be confronted with similar environmental challenges to those that confront them. The laws of genetics, of natural selection, and of adaptation apply equally to all of us as biological creatures. In this light we consider ourselves as one with them, not set apart from them. We, as well as they, must face certain basic conditions of existence that impose requirements on us for our survival and well-being.

Each animal and plant is like us in having a good of its own. Although our human good (what is of true value in human life, including the exercise of individual autonomy in choosing our own particular value systems) is not like the good of a nonhuman animal or plant, it can no more be realized than their good can without the biological necessities for survival and physical health.

When we look at ourselves from the evolutionary point of view, we see that not only are we very recent arrivals on Earth, but that our emergence as a new species on the planet was originally an event of no particular importance to the entire scheme of things. The Earth was teeming with life long before we appeared. Putting the point metaphorically, we are relative newcomers, entering a home that has been the residence of others for hundreds of millions of years, a home that must now be shared by all of us together.

The comparative brevity of human life on Earth may be vividly depicted by imagining the geological time scale in spatial terms. Suppose we start with algae, which have been around for at least 600 million years. (The earliest protozoa actually predated this by several *billion* years.) If the time that algae have been here were represented by the length of a football field (300 feet), then the period during which sharks have been swimming in the world's oceans and spiders have been spinning their webs would occupy three quarters of the length of the field; reptiles would show up at about the center of the field; mammals would cover the last third of the field; hominids (mammals of the family *Hominidae*) the last two feet; and the species *Homo sapiens* the last six inches.

Whether this newcomer is able to survive as long as other species remains to be seen. But there is surely something presumptuous about the way humans look down on the "lower" animals, especially those that have become extinct. We consider the dinosaurs, for example, to be biological failures, though they existed on our planet for 65 million years. One writer has made the point with beautiful simplicity:

> We sometimes speak of the dinosaurs as failures; there will be time enough for that judgment when we have lasted even for one tenth as long. . . .[2]

The possibility of the extinction of the human species, a possibility which starkly confronts us in the contemporary world, makes us aware of another respect in which we should not consider ourselves privileged beings in relation to other species. This is the fact that the well-being of humans is dependent upon the ecological soundness and health of many plant and animal communities, while their soundness and health does not in the least depend upon human well-being. Indeed, from their standpoint the very existence of humans is quite unnecessary. Every last man, woman, and child could disappear from the face of the Earth without any significant detrimental consequence for the good of wild animals and plants. On the contrary, many of them would be greatly benefited. The destruction of their habitats by human "developments" would cease. The poisoning and polluting of their environment would come to an end. The Earth's land, air, and water would no longer be subject to the degradation they are now undergoing as the result of large-scale technology and uncontrolled population growth. Life communities in natural ecosystems would gradually return to their former healthy state. Tropical forests, for example, would again be able to make their full contribution to a life-sustaining atmosphere for the whole planet. The rivers, lakes, and oceans of the world would (perhaps) eventually become clean again. Spilled oil, plastic trash, and even radioactive waste might finally, after many centuries, cease doing their terrible work. Ecosystems would return to their proper balance, suffering only the disruptions of natural events such as volcanic eruptions and glaciation. From these the community of life could recover, as it has so often done in the past. But the ecological disasters now perpetrated on it by humans—disasters from which it might never recover—these it would no longer have to endure.

If, then, the total, final, absolute extermination of our species (by our own hands?) should take place and if we should not carry all the others with us into oblivion, not only would the Earth's community of life continue to exist, but in all probability its well-being would be enhanced. Our presence, in short, is not needed. If we were to take the standpoint of the community and give voice to its true interest, the ending of our six-inch epoch would most likely be greeted with a hearty "Good riddance!"

THE NATURAL WORLD AS AN ORGANIC SYSTEM

To accept the biocentric outlook and regard ourselves and our place in the world from its perspective is to see the whole natural order of the Earth's biosphere as a complex but unified web of interconnected organisms, objects, and events. The ecological relationships between any community of living things and their environment form an organic whole of functionally interdependent parts. Each ecosystem is a small universe itself in which the interactions of its various species populations comprise an intricately woven network of cause-effect relations. Such dynamic but at the same time relatively stable structures as food chains, predator-prey relations, and plant succession in a forest are self-regulating, energy-recycling mechanisms that preserve the equilibrium of the whole.

As far as the well-being of wild animals and plants is concerned, this ecological equilibrium must not be destroyed. The same holds true of the well-being of humans. When one views the realm of nature from the perspective of the biocentric outlook, one never forgets that in the long run the integrity of the entire biosphere of our planet is essential to the realization of the good of its constituent communities of life, both human and nonhuman.

Although the importance of this idea cannot be overemphasized, it is by now so familiar and so widely acknowledged that I shall not further elaborate on it here. However, I do wish to point out that this "holistic" view of the Earth's ecological systems does not itself constitute a moral norm. It is a factual aspect of biological reality, to be understood as a set of causal connections in ordinary empirical terms. Its significance for humans is the same as its significance for nonhumans, namely, in setting basic conditions for the realization of the good of living things. Its ethical implications for our treatment of the natural environment lie entirely in the fact that our *knowledge* of these causal connections is an essential *means* to fulfilling the aims we set for ourselves in adopting the attitude of respect for nature. In addition, its theoretical implications for the ethics of respect for nature lie in the fact that it (along with the other elements of the biocentric outlook) makes the adopting of that attitude a rational and intelligible thing to do.

INDIVIDUAL ORGANISMS AS TELEOLOGICAL CENTERS OF LIFE

As our knowledge of living things increases, as we come to a deeper understanding of their life cycles, their interactions with other organisms, and the manifold ways in which they adjust to the environment, we become more fully aware of how each of them is carrying out its biological functions according to the laws of its species-specific nature. But besides this, our increasing knowledge and understanding also develop in us a sharpened awareness of the uniqueness of each individual organism. Scientists who have made careful studies of particular plants and animals, whether in the field or in laboratories, have often acquired a knowledge of their subjects as identifiable individuals. Close observation over extended periods of time has led them to an appreciation of the unique "personalities" of their subjects. Sometimes a scientist may come to take a special interest in a particular animal or plant, all the while remaining strictly objective in the gathering and recording of data. Nonscientists may likewise experience this development of interest when, as amateur naturalists, they make accurate observations over sustained periods of close acquaintance with an individual organism. As one becomes more and more familiar with the organism and its behavior, one becomes fully sensitive to the particular way it is living out its life cycle. One may become fascinated by it and even experience some involvement with its good and bad fortunes (that is, with the occurrence of environmental conditions favorable or unfavorable to the realization of its good). The organism comes to mean something to one as a unique, irreplaceable individual. The final culmination of this process is the achievement of a genuine understanding of its point of view and, with that understanding, an ability to "take" that point of view. *Conceiving of it as a center of life, one is able to look at the world from its perspective.*

This development from objective knowledge to the recognition of individuality, and from the recognition of individuality to full awareness of an organism's standpoint, is a process of heightening our consciousness of what it means to be an individual living thing. We grasp the particularity of the organism as a teleological center of life, striving to preserve itself and to realize its own good in its own unique way.

It is to be noted that we need not be falsely anthropomorphizing when we conceive of individual plants and animals in this manner. Understanding them as teleological centers of life does not necessitate "reading into" them human characteristics. We need not, for example, consider them to have consciousness. Some of them may be aware of the world around them and other may not. Nor need we deny that different kinds and levels of awareness are exemplified when consciousness in some form is present. But conscious or not, all are equally teleological centers of life in the sense that each is a unified system of goal-oriented activities directed toward their preservation and well-being.

When considered from an ethical point of view, a teleological center of life is an entity whose "world" can be viewed from the perspective of *its* life. In looking at the world from that perspective we recognize objects and events occurring in its life as being beneficent, maleficent, or indifferent. The first are occurrences which increase its powers to preserve its existence and realize its good. The second decrease or destroy those powers. The third have neither of these effects on the entity. With regard to our human role as moral agents, we can conceive of a teleological center of life as a being whose standpoint we can take in making judgments about what events in the world are good or evil, desirable or undesirable. In making those judgments it is what promotes or protects the being's own good, not what benefits moral agents themselves, that sets the standard of evaluation. Such judgments can be made about anything that happens to the entity which is favorable or unfavorable in relation to its good. As was pointed out earlier, the entity itself need not have any (conscious) *interest* in what is happening to it for such judgments to be meaningful and true.

It is precisely judgments of this sort that we are disposed to make when we take the attitude of respect for nature. In adopting that attitude those judgments are given weight as reasons for action in our practical deliberation. They become morally relevant facts in the guidance of our conduct.

THE DENIAL OF HUMAN SUPERIORITY

This fourth component of the biocentric outlook on nature is the single most important idea in establishing the justifiability of the attitude of respect for nature. Its central role is due to the special relationship it bears to the first three components of the outlook. This relationship will be brought out after the concept of human superiority is examined and analyzed.[3]

In what sense are humans alleged to be superior to other animals? We are different from them in having certain capacities that they lack. But why should these capacities be a mark of superiority? From what point of view are they judged to be signs of superiority and what sense of superiority is meant? After all, various nonhuman species have capacities that humans lack. There is the speed of a cheetah, the vision of an eagle, the agility of a monkey. Why should not these be taken as signs of *their* superiority over humans?

One answer that comes immediately to mind is that these capacities are not as *valuable* as the human capacities that are claimed to make us superior. Such uniquely human characteristics as rational thought, aesthetic creativity, autonomy and self-determination, and moral freedom, it might be held, have a higher value than the capacities found in other species. Yet we must ask: valuable to whom, and on what grounds?

The human characteristics mentioned are all valuable to humans. They are essential to the preservation and enrichment of our civilization and culture. Clearly it is from the human standpoint that they are being judged to be desirable and good. It is not difficult here to recognize a begging of the question. Humans are claiming human superiority from a strictly human point of view, that is, from a point of view in which the good of humans is taken as the standard of judgment. All we need to do is to look at the capacities of nonhuman animals (or plants, for that matter) from the standpoint of *their* good to find a contrary judgment of superiority. The speed of the cheetah, for example, is a sign of its superiority to humans when considered from the standpoint of the good of its species. If it were as slow a runner as a human, it would not be able to survive. And so for all the other abilities of nonhumans which further their good but which are lacking in humans. In each case the claim to human superiority would be rejected from a nonhuman standpoint.

When superiority assertions are interpreted in this way, they are based on judgments of *merit*. To judge the merits of a person or an organism one must apply grading or ranking standards to it. (As I show below, this distinguishes judgments of merit from judgments of inherent worth.) Empirical investigation then determines whether it has the "good-making properties" (merits) in virtue of which it fulfills the standards being applied. In the case of humans, merits may be either moral or nonmoral. We can judge one person to be better than (superior to) another from the moral point of view by applying certain standards to their character and conduct. Similarly, we can appeal to nonmoral criteria in judging someone to be an excellent piano player, a fair cook, a poor tennis player, and so on. Different social purposes and roles are implicit in the making of such judgments, providing the frame of reference for the choice of standards by which the nonmoral merits of people are determined. Ultimately such purposes and roles stem from a society's way of life as a whole. Now a society's way of life may be thought of as the cultural form given to the realization of human values. Whether moral or nonmoral standards are being applied, then, all judgments of people's merits finally depend on human values. All are made from an exclusively human standpoint.

The question that naturally arises at this juncture is: why should standards that are based on human values be assumed to be the only valid criteria of merit and hence the only true signs of superiority? This question is especially pressing when humans are being judged superior in merit to nonhumans. It is true that a human being may be a better mathematician than a monkey, but the monkey may be a better tree climber than a human being. If we humans value mathematics more than tree climbing, that is because our conception of civilized life makes the development of mathematical ability more desirable than the ability to climb trees. But is it not unreasonable to judge nonhumans by the values of human civilization, rather than by values connected with what it is for a member of *that* species to live a good life? If all living things have a good of their own, it at least makes sense to judge the merits of nonhumans by standards derived from *their* good. To use only standards based on human values is already to commit oneself to holding that humans are superior to nonhumans, which is the point in question.

A further logical flaw arises in connection with the widely held conviction that humans are *morally* superior beings because they possess, while others lack, the capacities of a moral agent (free will, accountability, deliberation, judgment, practical reason). This view rests on a conceptual confusion. As far as moral standards are concerned, only beings that have the capacities of a moral agent can properly be judged to be *either* moral (morally good) *or* immoral (morally deficient). Moral standards are simply not applicable to beings that lack such capacities. Animals and plants cannot therefore be said to be morally inferior in merit to humans. Since the only beings that can have moral merits *or be deficient in such merits* are moral agents, it is conceptually incoherent to judge humans as superior to nonhumans on the ground that humans have moral capacities while nonhumans don't.

Up to this point I have been interpreting the claim that humans are superior to other living things as a grading or ranking judgment regarding their comparative merits. There is, however, another way of understanding the idea of human superiority. According to this interpretation, humans are superior to nonhumans not as regards their merits but as regards their inherent worth. Thus the claim of human superiority is to be understood as asserting that all humans, simply in virtue of their humanity, have *a greater inherent worth* than other living things.

The inherent worth of an entity does not depend on its merits.[4] To consider something as possessing inherent worth, we have seen, is to place intrinsic value on the realization of its good. This is done regardless of whatever particular merits it might have or might lack, as judged by a set of grading or ranking standards. In human affairs, we are all familiar with the principle that one's worth as a person does not vary with one's merits or lack of merits. The same can hold true of animals and plants. To regard such entities as possessing inherent worth entails disregarding their merits and deficiencies, whether they are being judged from a human standpoint or from the standpoint of their own species.

The idea of one entity having more merit than another, and so being superior to it in merit, makes perfectly good sense. Merit is a grading or ranking concept, and judgments of comparative merit are based on the different degrees to which things satisfy a given standard. But what can it mean to talk about one thing being superior to another in inherent worth? In order to get at what is being asserted in such a claim it is helpful first to look at the social origin of the concept of degrees of inherent worth.

The idea that humans can possess different degrees of inherent worth originated in societies having rigid class structures. Before the rise of modern democracies with their egalitarian outlook, one's membership in a hereditary class determined one's social status. People in the upper classes were looked up to, while those in the lower classes were looked down upon. In such a society one's social superiors and social inferiors were clearly defined and easily recognized.

Two aspects of these class-structured societies are especially relevant to the idea of degrees of inherent worth. First, those born into the upper classes were deemed more worthy of respect than those born into the lower orders. Second, the superior worth of upper class people had nothing to do with their merits nor did the inferior worth of those in the lower classes rest on their lack of merits. One's superiority or inferiority entirely derived from a social position one was born into. The modern concept of a meritocracy simply did not apply. One could not advance into a higher class by any sort of moral or nonmoral achievement. Similarly, an aristocrat held his title and all the privileges that went with it just because he was the eldest son of a titled nobleman. Unlike the bestowing of knighthood in contemporary Great Britain, one did not earn membership in the nobility by meritorious conduct.

We who live in modern democracies no longer believe in such hereditary social distinctions. Indeed, we would wholeheartedly condemn them on moral grounds as being fundamentally unjust. We have come to think of class systems as a paradigm of social injustice, it being a central principle of the democratic way of life that among humans there are no superiors and no inferiors. Thus we have rejected the whole conceptual framework in which people are judged to have different degrees of inherent worth. That idea is incompatible with our notion of human equality based on the doctrine that all humans, simply in virtue of their humanity, have the same inherent worth. (The belief in universal human rights is one form that this egalitarianism takes.)

The vast majority of people in modern democracies, however, do not maintain an egalitarian outlook when it comes to comparing human beings with other living things. Most people consider our own species to be superior to all other species and this superiority is understood to be a matter of inherent worth, not merit. There may exist thoroughly vicious and depraved humans who lack all merit. Yet because they are human they are thought to belong to a higher class of entities than any plant or animal. That one is born into the species *Homo sapiens* entitles one to have lordship over those who are one's inferiors, namely, those born into other species. The parallel with hereditary social classes is very close. Implicit in this view is a hierarchical conception of nature according to which an organism has a position of superiority or inferiority in the Earth's community of life simply on the basis of its genetic background. The "lower" orders of life are looked down upon and it is considered perfectly proper that they serve the interests of those belonging to the highest order, namely humans. The intrinsic value we place on the well-being of our fellow humans reflects our recognition of their rightful position as our equals. No such intrinsic value is to be placed on the good of other animals, unless we choose to do so out of fondness or affection for them. But their well-being imposes no moral requirement on us. In this respect there is an absolute difference in moral status between ourselves and them.

This is the structure of concepts and beliefs that people are committed to insofar as they regard humans to be superior in inherent worth to all other species. I now wish to argue that this structure of concepts and beliefs is completely groundless. If we accept the first three components of the biocentric outlook and from that perspective look at the major philosophical traditions which have supported that structure, we find it to be at bottom nothing more than the expression of an irrational bias in our own favor. The philosophical traditions themselves rest on very questionable assumptions or else simply beg the question. I briefly consider three of the main traditions to substantiate the point. These are classical Greek humanism, Cartesian dualism, and the Judeo-Christian concept of the Great Chain of Being.

The inherent superiority of humans over other species was implicit in the Greek definition of man as a rational animal. Our animal nature was identified with "brute" desires that need the order and restraint of reason to rule them (just as reason is the special virtue of those who rule in the ideal state). Rationality was then seen to be the key to our superiority over animals. It enables us to live on a higher plane and endows us with a nobility and worth that other creatures lack. This familiar way of comparing humans with other species is deeply ingrained in our Western philosophical outlook. The point to consider here is that this view does not actually provide an argument *for* human superiority but rather makes explicit the framework of thought that is implicitly used by those who think of humans as inherently superior to nonhumans. The Greeks who held that humans, in virtue of their rational capacities, have a kind of worth greater than that of any nonrational being, never looked at rationality as but one capacity of living things among many others. But when we consider rationality from the standpoint of the first three elements of the ecological outlook, we see that its value lies in its importance for *human* life. Other creatures achieve their species-specific good without the need of rationality, although they often make use of capacities that humans lack. So the humanistic outlook of classical Greek thought does not give us a neutral (nonquestion-begging) ground on which to construct a scale of degrees of inherent worth possessed by different species of living things.

The second tradition, centering on the Cartesian dualism of soul and body, also fails to justify the claim to human superiority. That superiority is supposed to derive from the fact that we have souls while animals do not. Animals are mere automata and lack the divine element that makes us spiritual beings. I won't go into the now familiar criticisms of this two-substance view. I only add the point that, even if humans are composed of an immaterial, unextended soul and a material, extended body, this in itself is not a reason to deem them of greater worth than entities that are only bodies. Why is a soul substance a thing that adds value to its possessor? Unless some theological reasoning is offered here (which many, including myself, would find unacceptable on epistemological grounds), no logical connection is evident. An immaterial something which thinks is better than a material something which does not think only if thinking itself has value, either intrinsically or instrumentally. Now it is intrinsically valuable to humans alone, who value it as an end in itself, and it is instrumentally valuable to those who benefit from it, namely humans.

For animals that neither enjoy thinking for its own sake nor need it for living the kind of life for which they are best adapted, it has no value. Even if "thinking" is broadened to include all forms of consciousness, there are still many living things that can do without it and yet live what is for their species a good life. The anthropocentricity underlying the claim to human superiority runs throughout Cartesian dualism.

A third major source of the idea of human superiority is the Judeo-Christian concept of the Great Chain of Being. Humans are superior to animals and plants because their Creator has given them a higher place on the chain. It begins with God at the top, and then moves to the angels, who are lower than God but higher than humans, then to humans, positioned between the angels and the beasts (partaking of the nature of both), and then on down to the lower levels occupied by nonhuman animals, plants, and finally inanimate objects. Humans, being "made in God's image," are inherently superior to animals and plants by virtue of their being closer (in their essential nature) to God.

The metaphysical and epistemological difficulties with this conception of a hierarchy of entities are, in my mind, insuperable. Without entering into this matter here, I only point out that if we are unwilling to accept the metaphysics of traditional Judaism and Christianity, we are again left without good reasons for holding to the claim of inherent human superiority.

The foregoing considerations (and others like them) leave us with but one ground for the assertion that a human being, regardless of merit, is a higher kind of entity than any other living thing. This is the mere fact of the genetic makeup of the species *Homo sapiens*. But this is surely irrational and arbitrary. Why should the arrangement of genes of a certain type be a mark of superior value, especially when this fact about an organism is taken by itself, unrelated to any other aspect of its life? We might just as well refer to any other genetic makeup as a ground of superior value. Clearly we are confronted here with a wholly arbitrary claim that can only be explained as an irrational bias in our own favor.

That the claim is nothing more than a deep-seated prejudice is brought home to us when we look at our relation to other species in the light of the first three elements of the biocentric outlook. Those elements taken conjointly give us a certain overall view of the natural world and of the place of humans in it. When we take this view we come to understand other living things, their environmental conditions, and their ecological relationships in such a way as to awake in us a deep sense of our kinship with them as fellow members of the Earth's community of life. Humans and nonhumans alike are viewed together as integral parts of one unified whole in which all living things are functionally interrelated. Finally, when our awareness focuses on the individual lives of plants and animals, each is seen to share with us the characteristic of being a teleological center of life striving to realize its own good in its own unique way.

As this entire belief system becomes part of the conceptual framework through which we understand and perceive the world, we come to see ourselves as bearing a certain moral relation to nonhuman forms of life. Our ethical role in nature takes on a new significance. We begin to look at other species as we look at ourselves, seeing them as beings which have a good they are striving to realize just as we have a good we are striving to realize. We accordingly develop the disposition to view the world from the standpoint of their good as well as from the standpoint of our own good. Now if the groundlessness of the claim that humans are inherently superior to other species were brought clearly before our minds, we would not remain intellectually neutral toward that claim but would reject it as being fundamentally at variance with our total world outlook. In the absence of any good reasons for holding it, the assertion of human superiority would then appear simply as the expression of an irrational and self-serving prejudice that favors one particular species over several million others.

Rejecting the notion of human superiority entails its positive counterpart: the doctrine of species impartiality. One who accepts that doctrine regards all living things as possessing inherent worth—the *same* inherent worth, since no one species has been shown to be either "higher" or "lower" than any other. Now we saw earlier that, insofar as one thinks of a living thing as possessing inherent worth, one considers it to be the appropriate object of the attitude of respect and believes that attitude to be the only fitting or suitable one for all moral agents to take toward it.

Here, then, is the key to understanding how the attitude of respect is rooted in the biocentric outlook on nature. The basic connection is made through the denial of human superiority. Once we reject the claim that humans are superior either in merit or in worth to other living things, we are ready to adopt the attitude of respect. The denial of human superiority is itself the result of taking the perspective on nature built into the first three elements of the biocentric outlook.

Now the first three elements of the biocentric outlook, it seems clear, would be found acceptable to any rational and scientifically informed thinker who is fully "open" to the reality of the lives of nonhuman organisms. Without denying our distinctively human characteristics, such a thinker can acknowledge the fundamental respects in which we are members of the Earth's community of life and in which the biological conditions necessary for the realization of our human values are inextricably linked with the whole system of nature. In addition, the conception of individual living things as teleological centers of life simply articulates how a scientifically informed thinker comes to understand them as the result of increasingly careful and detailed observations. Thus, the biocentric outlook recommends itself as an acceptable system of concepts and beliefs to anyone who is clear-minded, unbiased, and factually enlightened, and who has a developed capacity of reality awareness with regard to the lives of individual organisms. This, I submit, is as good a reason for making the moral commitment involved in adopting the attitude of respect for nature as any theory of environmental ethics could possibly have.

MORAL RIGHTS AND THE MATTER
OF COMPETING CLAIMS

I have not asserted anywhere in the foregoing account that animals or plants have moral rights. This omission was deliberate. I do not think that the reference class of the concept, bearer of moral rights, should be extended to include nonhuman living things. My reasons for taking this position, however, go beyond the scope of this paper. I believe I have been able to accomplish many of the same ends which those who ascribe rights to animals or plants wish to accomplish. There is no reason, moreover, why plants and animals, including whole species populations and life communities, cannot be accorded *legal* rights under my theory. To grant them legal protection could be interpreted as giving them legal entitlement to be protected, and this, in fact, would be a means by which a society that subscribed to the ethics of respect for nature could give public recognition to their inherent worth.

There remains the problem of competing claims, even when wild plants and animals are not thought of as bearers of moral rights. If we accept the biocentric outlook and accordingly adopt the attitude of respect for nature as our ultimate moral attitude, how do we resolve conflicts that arise from our respect for persons in the domain of human ethics and our respect for nature in the domain of environmental ethics? This is a question that cannot adequately be dealt with here. My main purpose in this paper has been to try to establish a base point from which we can start working toward a solution to the problem. I have shown why we cannot just begin with an initial presumption in favor of the interests of our own species. It is after all within our power as moral beings to place limits on human population and technology with the deliberate intention of sharing the Earth's bounty with other species. That such sharing is an ideal difficult to realize even in an approximate way does not take away its claim to our deepest moral commitment.

NOTES

1. See W. K. Frankena, "Ethics and the Environment," in K. E. Goodpaster and K. M. Sayre, eds., *Ethics and Problems of the 21st Century* (Notre Dame, University of Notre Dame Press, 1979), pp. 3–20. I critically examine Frankena's views in "Frankena on Environmental Ethics," *Monist*, Vol. 64, No. 3 (July 1981), pp. 313–324.
2. Stephen R. L. Clark, *The Moral Status of Animals* (Oxford: Clarendon Press, 1977), p. 112.
3. My criticisms of the dogma of human superiority gain independent support from a carefully reasoned essay by R. and V. Routley showing the many logical weaknesses in arguments for human-centered theories of environmental

ethics. R. and V. Routley, "Against the Inevitability of Human Chauvinism," in K. E. Goodpaster and K. M. Sayre, eds., *Ethics and Problems of the 21st Century* (Notre Dame: University of Notre Dame Press, 1979), pp. 36–59.

4. For this way of distinguishing between merit and inherent worth, I am indebted to Gregory Vlastos, "Justice and Equality," in R. Brandt, ed., *Social Justice* (Englewood Cliffs, N.J.: Prentice-Hall, 1962), pp. 31–72.

Animal Liberation and Environmental Ethics: Bad Marriage, Quick Divorce

Mark Sagoff

Mark Sagoff is director and senior research scholar at the Institute for Philosophy and Public Policy at the University of Maryland. He is the author of The Economy of the Earth: Philosophy, Law, and the Environment.

I

"The land ethic," Aldo Leopold wrote in *A Sand County Almanac*, "simply enlarges the boundaries of the community to include soils, waters, plants, and animals, or collectively, the land."[1] What kind of community does Leopold refer to? He might mean a *moral* community, for example, a group of individuals who respect each other's right to treatment as equals or who regard one another's interests with equal respect and concern. He may also mean an *ecological* community, that is, a community tied together by biological relationships in interdependent webs or systems of life.[2]

    Let us suppose, for a moment, that Leopold has a *moral* community in mind; he would expand our *moral* boundaries to include not only human beings, but also soils, waters, plants and animals. Leopold's view, then, might not differ in principle from that of Christopher Stone, who has sug-

This essay originally appeared in *Law Journal*, Vol. 22, No. 2, 297–307. Reprinted by permission.

gested that animals and even trees be given legal standing, so that their interests may be represented in court.[3] Stone sees the expansion of our moral consciousness in this way as part of a historical progress by which societies have recognized the equality of groups of oppressed people, notably blacks, women and children.[4] Laurence Tribe eloquently makes the same point:

> What is crucial to recognize is that the human capacity for empathy and identification is not static; the very process of recognizing rights in those higher vertebrates with whom we can already empathize could well pave the way for still further extensions as we move upward along the spiral of moral evolution. It is not only the human liberation movements—involving first blacks, then women, and now children—that advance in waves of increased consciousness.[5]

Peter Singer, perhaps more than any other writer, has emphasized the analogy between human liberation movements (for example, abolitionism and suffragism) and "animal liberation" or the "expansion of our moral horizons" to include members of other species in the "basic principle of equality."[6] Singer differs from Stone and Tribe, however, in two respects. First, he argues that the capacity of animals to suffer pain or to enjoy pleasure or happiness places people under a moral obligation which does not need to be enhanced by a doctrine about rights. Second, while Stone is willing to speak of the interests of his lawn in being watered,[7] Singer argues that "only a being with subjective experiences, such as the experience of pleasure or the experience of pain, can have interests in the full sense of the term."[8] A tree, as Singer explains, may be said to have an "interest" in being watered, but all this means is that it needs water to grow properly as an automobile needs oil to function properly.[9] Thus, Singer would not include rocks, trees, lakes, rivers or mountains in the moral community or the community of morally equal beings.

Singer's thesis, then, is not necessarily that animals have rights which we are to respect. Instead, he argues that they have utilities that ought to be treated on an equal basis with those of human beings. Whether Tribe and Stone argue a weaker or a different thesis depends upon the rights they believe animals and other natural things to have. They may believe that all animals have a right to be treated as equals, in effect, they may agree with Singer that the interests of *all* animals should receive equal respect and concern. On the other hand, Tribe, Stone or both may believe that animals have a right only to life or only to those very minimal and basic rights without which they could not conceivably enjoy any other right.[10] I will, for the moment, assume that Tribe and Stone agree that animals have basic rights, for example, a right to live or a right not to be killed for their meat. I will consider later the possibility that environmental law might protect the rights of animals without necessarily improving their welfare or protecting their lives.

Moral obligations to animals, to their well-being or to their rights, may arise in either of two ways. First, duties to non-human animals may be based on the principle that cruelty to animals is obnoxious, a principle nobody denies. Muckraking journalists (thank God for them) who depict the horrors which all too often occur in laboratories and on farms, appeal quite properly to the conviction and intuition that people should never inflict needless pain on animals and especially not for the sake of profit. When television documentaries or newspaper articles report the horrid ways in which domestic animals are often treated, the response is, as it should be, moral revulsion. This anger is directed at human responsibility for the callous, wanton and needless cruelty human beings inflict on domestic animals. It is not simply the pain but the way it is caused which justified moral outrage.

Moral obligations, however, might rest instead on a stronger contention, which is that human beings are obliged to prevent and to relieve animal suffering however it is caused. Now, insofar as the animal equality or animal liberation movement makes a philosophically interesting claim, it insists on the stronger thesis, that there is an obligation to serve the interests, or at least to protect the lives, of *all* animals who suffer or are killed, whether on the farm or in the wild. Singer, for example, does not stop with the stultifying platitude that human beings ought not to be cruel to animals. No; he argues the controversial thesis that society has an obligation to prevent the killing of animals and even to relieve their suffering wherever, however, and as much as it is able, at a reasonable cost to itself.

II

I began by supposing that Aldo Leopold viewed the community of nature as a *moral* community—one in which human beings, as members, have obligations to all other animals, presumably to minimize their pain. I suggested that Leopold, like Singer, may be committed to the idea that the natural environment should be preserved and protected only insofar as, and because, its protection satisfies the needs or promotes the welfare of individual animals and perhaps other living things. I believe, however, that this is plainly not Leopold's view. The principle of natural selection is not obviously a humanitarian principle; the predator-prey relation does not depend on moral empathy. Nature ruthlessly limits animal populations by doing violence to virtually every individual before it reaches maturity; these conditions respect animal equality only in the darkest sense. Yet these are precisely the ecological relationships which Leopold admires; they are the conditions which he would not interfere with, but protect. Apparently, Leopold does not think that an ecological system has to be an egalitarian moral system in order to deserve love and admiration. An ecological system has a beauty and an authenticity that demands respect—but plainly not on humanitarian grounds.

In a persuasive essay, J. Baird Callicott describes a number of differences between the ideas of Leopold and those of Singer—differences which suggest that Leopold's environmental ethic and Singer's humane utilitarianism lead in opposite directions. First, while Singer and other animal liberationists deplore the suffering of domestic animals, "Leopold manifests an attitude that can only be described as indifference."[11] Second, while Leopold expresses an urgent concern about the disappearance of species, Singer, consistently with his premises, is concerned with the welfare of individual animals, without special regard to their status as endangered species. Third, the preservation of wilderness, according to Leopold, provides "a means of perpetuating, in sport form, the more virile and primitive skills. . . ."[12] He had hunting in mind. Leopold recognized that since top predators are gone, hunters may serve an important ecological function. Leopold was himself an enthusiastic hunter and wrote unabashedly about his exploits pursuing game. The term "game" as applied to animals, Callicott wryly comments, "appears to be morally equivalent to referring to a sexually appealing young woman as a "piece" or to a strong, young black man as a "buck"—if animal rights, that is, are to be considered on par with women's rights and the rights of formerly enslaved races."[13]

Singer expresses disdain and chagrin at what he calls " 'environmentalist' " organizations such as the Sierra Club and the Wildlife Fund, which actively support or refuse to oppose hunting. I can appreciate Singer's aversion to hunting, but why does he place the word "environmentalist" in shudder quotes when he refers to organizations like the Sierra Club? Environmentalist and conservationist organizations traditionally have been concerned with ecological, not humanitarian issues. They make no pretense of acting for the sake of individual animals; rather, they attempt to maintain the diversity, integrity, beauty and authenticity of the natural environment. These goals are ecological, not eleemosynary. Their goals are entirely consistent, then, with licensing hunters to shoot animals whose populations exceed the carrying capacity of their habitats. Perhaps hunting is immoral; if so, environmentalism is consistent with an immoral practice, but it is environmentalism without quotes nonetheless. The policies environmentalists recommend are informed by the concepts of population biology, not the concepts of animal equality. The S.P.C.A. does not set the agenda for the Sierra Club.

I do not in any way mean to support the practice of hunting; nor am I advocating environmentalism at this time. I merely want to point out that groups like the Sierra Club, the Wilderness Society and the World Wildlife Fund do not fail in their mission insofar as they devote themselves to causes other than the happiness or welfare of individual creatures; that never was their mission. These organizations, which promote a love and respect for the functioning of natural ecosystems, differ ideologically from organizations that make the suffering of animals their primary concern—groups like the Fund for Animals, the Animal Protection Institute, Friends of Animals, the American Humane Association, and various single issue groups such as Friends of the Sea Otter, Beaver Defenders, Friends of the Earthworm, and Worldwide Fair Play for Frogs.[14]

D. G. Ritchie, writing in 1916, posed a difficulty for those who argue that animals have rights or that we have obligations to them created simply by their capacity to suffer. If the suffering of animals creates a human obligation to mitigate it, is there not as much an obligation to prevent a cat from killing a mouse as to prevent a hunter from killing a deer? "Are we not to vindicate the rights of the persecuted prey of the stronger?" Ritchie asks. "Or is our declaration of the rights of every creeping thing to remain a mere hypocritical formula to gratify pug-loving sentimentalists?"[15]

If the animal liberation or animal equality movement is not to deteriorate into "a hypocritical formula to gratify pug-loving sentimentalists," it must insist, as Singer does, that moral obligations to animals are justified, in the first place, by their distress, and, in the second place, by human ability to relieve that distress. The liberationist must morally require society to relieve animal suffering wherever it can and at a lesser cost to itself, whether in the chicken coop or in the wild. Otherwise, the animal liberationist thesis becomes interchangeable with the platitude one learns along with how to tie shoestrings: people ought not to be cruel to animals. I do not deny that human beings are cruel to animals, that they ought not to be, that this cruelty should be stopped and that sermons to this effect are entirely appropriate and necessary. I deny only that these sermons have anything to do with environmentalism or provide a basis for an environmental ethic.

III

In discussing the rights of human beings, Henry Shue describes two that are basic in the sense that "the enjoyment of them is essential to the enjoyment of all other rights."[16] These are the right to physical security and the right to minimum subsistence. These are positive, not merely negative rights. In other words, these rights require governments to provide security and subsistence, not merely to refrain from invading security and denying subsistence. These basic rights require society, where possible, to rescue individuals from starvation; this is more than the merely negative obligation not to cause starvation. No; if people have basic rights—and I have no doubt they do—then society has a positive obligation to satisfy those rights. It is not enough for society simply to refrain from violating them.

This, surely, is true of the basic rights of animals as well, if we are to give the conception of "right" the same meaning for both people and animals. For example, to allow animals to be killed for food or to permit them to die of disease or starvation when it is within human power to prevent it, does not seem to balance fairly the interests of animals with those of human beings. To speak of the rights of animals, of treating them as equals, of liberating them, and at the same time to let nearly all of them perish unnecessarily in the most brutal and horrible ways is not to display humanity but hypocrisy in the extreme.

Where should society concentrate its efforts to provide for the basic welfare—the security and subsistence—of animals? Plainly, where animals most lack this security, when their basic rights, needs, or interests are most thwarted and where their suffering is most intense. Alas, this is in nature. Ever since Darwin, we have been aware that few organisms survive to reach sexual maturity; most are quickly annihilated in the struggle for existence. Consider as a rough but reasonable statement of the facts the following:

> All species reproduce in excess, way past the carrying capacity of their niche. In her lifetime a lioness might have 20 cubs; a pigeon, 150 chicks; a mouse, 1,000 kits; a trout, 20,000 fry, a tuna or cod, a million fry or more; an elm tree, several million seeds; and an oyster, perhaps a hundred million spat. If one assumes that the population of each of these species is, from generation to generation, roughly equal, then on the average only one offspring will survive to replace each parent. All the other thousands and millions will die, one way or another.[17]

The ways in which creatures in nature die are typically violent: predation, starvation, disease, parasitism, cold. The dying animal in the wild does not understand the vast ocean of misery into which it and billions of other animals are born only to drown. If the wild animal understood the conditions into which it is born, what would it think? It might reasonably prefer to be raised on a farm, where the chances of survival for a year or more would be good, and to escape from the wild, where they are negligible. Either way, the animal will be eaten: few die of old age. The path from birth to slaughter, however, is often longer and less painful in the barnyard than in the woods. Comparisons, sad as they are, must be made to recognize where a great opportunity lies to prevent or mitigate suffering. The misery of animals in nature—which humans can do much to relieve—makes every other form of suffering pale in comparison. Mother Nature is so cruel to her children she makes Frank Perdue look like a saint.

What is the practical course society should take once it climbs the spiral of moral evolution high enough to recognize its obligation to value the basic rights of animals equally with that of human beings? I do not know how animal liberationists, such as Singer, propose to relieve animal suffering in nature (where most of it occurs), but there are many ways to do so at little cost. Singer has suggested, with respect to pest control, that animals might be fed contraceptive chemicals rather than poisons.[18] It may not be beyond the reach of science to attempt a broad program of contraceptive care for animals in nature so that fewer will fall victim to an early and horrible death. The government is spending hundreds of millions of dollars to store millions of tons of grain. Why not lay out this food, laced with contraceptives, for wild creatures to feed upon? Farms which so overproduce for human needs might then satisfy the needs of animals. The day may come when entitlement programs which now extend only to human beings are offered to animals as well.

One may modestly propose the conversion of national wilderness areas, especially national parks, into farms in order to replace violent wild areas with more humane and managed environments. Starving deer in the woods might be adopted as pets. They might be fed in kennels; animals that once wandered the wilds in misery might get fat in feedlots instead. Birds that now kill earthworms may repair instead to birdhouses stocked with food, including textured soybean protein that looks and smells like worms. And to protect the brutes from cold, their dens could be heated, or shelters provided for the all too many who will otherwise freeze. The list of obligations is long, but for that reason it is more, not less, compelling. The welfare of all animals is in human hands. Society must attend not solely to the needs of domestic animals, for they are in a privileged class, but to the needs of all animals, especially those which, without help, would die miserably in the wild.

Now, whether you believe that this harangue is a *reductio* of Singer's position, and thus that it agrees in principle with Ritchie, or whether you think it should be taken seriously as an ideal is of no concern to me. I merely wish to point out that an environmentalist must take what I have said as a *reductio,* whereas an animal liberationist must regard it as stating a serious position, at least if the liberationist shares Singer's commitment to utilitarianism. Environmentalists cannot be animal liberationists. Animal liberationists cannot be environmentalists. The environmentalist would sacrifice the lives of individual creatures to preserve the authenticity, integrity and complexity of ecological systems. The liberationist—if the reduction of animal misery is taken seriously as a goal—must be willing, in principle, to sacrifice the authenticity, integrity and complexity of ecosystems to protect the rights, or guard the lives, of animals.

IV

A defender of the rights of animals may answer that my argument applies only to someone like Singer who is strongly committed to a utilitarian ethic. Those who emphasize the rights of animals, however, need not argue that society should enter the interests of animals equitably into the felicific calculus on which policy is based. For example, Laurence Tribe appeals to the rights of animals not to broaden the class of wants to be included in a Benthamite calculus but to "move beyond wants" and thus to affirm duties "ultimately independent of a desire-satisfying conception."[19] Tribe writes:

> To speak of "rights" rather than "wants", after all, is to acknowledge the possibility that want-maximizing or utility-maximizing actions will be ruled out in particular cases as inconsistent with a structure of agreed-upon obligations. It is Kant, not Bentham, whose thought suggests the first step toward making us "different persons from the manipulators and subjugators we are in danger of becoming."[20]

It is difficult to see how an appeal to rights helps society to "move beyond wants" or to affirm duties "ultimately independent of a desire-satisfying conception." Most writers in the Kantian tradition analyze rights as claims to something in which the claimant has an interest.[21] Thus, rights-theorists oppose utilitarianism not to go beyond wants but because they believe that some wants or interests are moral "trumps" over other wants and interests.[22] To say innocent people have a right not to be hanged for crimes they have not committed, even when hanging them would serve the general welfare, is to say that the interest of innocent people not to be hanged should outweigh the general interest in deterring crime. To take rights seriously, then, is simply to take some interests, or the general interest, more seriously than other interests for moral reasons. The appeal to rights simply is a variation on utilitarianism, in that it accepts the general framework of interests, but presupposes that there are certain interests that should not be traded off against others.[23]

A second problem with Tribe's reply is more damaging than the first. Only *individuals* may have rights, but environmentalists think in terms of protecting *collections, systems* and *communities.* Consider Aldo Leopold's oft-quoted remark: "A thing is right when it tends to preserve the integrity, stability, and beauty of the biotic community. It is wrong when it tends to do otherwise."[24] The obligation to preserve the "integrity, stability, and beauty of the biotic community," whatever those words mean, implies no duties whatever to individual animals in the community, except in the rare instance in which an individual is important to functioning of that community. For the most part, individual animals are completely expendable. An environmentalist is concerned only with maintaining a population. Accordingly, the moral obligation Leopold describes cannot be grounded in or derived from the rights of individuals. Therefore, it has no basis in rights at all.[25]

Consider another example: the protection of endangered species.[26] An individual whale may be said to have rights, but the species cannot; a whale does not suddenly have rights when its kind becomes endangered.[27] No; the moral obligation to preserve species is not an obligation to individual creatures. It cannot, then, be an obligation that rests on rights. This is not to say that there is no moral obligation with regard to endangered species, animals or the environment. It is only to say that moral obligations to nature cannot be enlightened or explained—one cannot even take the first step— by appealing to the rights of animals and other natural things.

V

Garrett Hardin, in his "Foreword" to *Should Trees Have Standing?*, suggests that Stone's essay answers Leopold's call for a "new ethic to protect land and other natural amenities. . . ."[28] But as one reviewer has pointed out,

> Stone himself never refers to Leopold, and with good reason: he comes from a different place, and his proposal to grant rights to natural objects has emerged not from an ecological sensibility but as an extension of the philosophy of the humane movement.[29]

A humanitarian ethic—an appreciation not of nature, but of the welfare of animals—will not help us to understand or to justify an environmental ethic. It will not provide necessary or valid foundations for environmental law.

NOTES

1. Leopold, *A Sand County Almanac* (1949) at 204.
2. For discussion, see Heffernan, *The Land Ethic: A Critical Appraisal* (1982), 4 Envt'l Ethics 235. Heffernan notes that "when Leopold talks of preserving the 'integrity, stability and beauty of the biotic community' he is referring to preserving the characteristic structure of an ecosystem and its capacity to withstand change or stress." *Id.* at 237.
3. Stone, *Should Trees Have Standing?* (1974).
4. *Id.* at 44.
5. Tribe, *Ways Not to Think About Plastic Trees: New Foundations in Environmental Law* (1973), 83 Yale L. J. 1315 at 1345.
6. Singer, *All Animals Are Equal* (1974), 1 Phil. Exchange 103.
7. Stone, *supra* note 3, at 24.
8. Singer, "Not For Humans Only: The Place of Nonhumans in Environmental Issues," in Goodpaster and Sayre, eds., *Ethics and the Problems of the Twenty-first Century* (1979) at 194.
9. *Id.* at 195.
10. For a discussion of basic rights, see Shue, *Basic Rights* (1980).

11. Callicott, *Animal Liberation: A Triangular Affair* (1980), 2 Envt'l Ethics 311 at 315.
12. Leopold, *supra* note 1, at 269.
13. Callicott, *supra* note 11, at 314–15.
14. Singer, *supra* note 8, at 201.
15. Ritchie, *Natural Rights* (3rd ed., 1916) at 107. For an excellent discussion of this passage, see Clark, *The Rights of Wild Things* (1979), 22 Inquiry 171.
16. Shue, *supra* note 10, at 18–29.
17. Hapgood, *Why Males Exist* (1979) at 34.
18. Singer, *supra* note 8, at 198.
19. Tribe, *From Environmental Foundations to Constitutional Structures: Learning From Nature's Future* (1974), 84 Yale L. J. 545 at 551, 552.
20. *Id.* at 552.
21. For discussion, see Feinberg, *Duties, Rights, and Claims* (1966), 3 Amer. Phil. Q. 137.
22. See Dworkin, "Liberalism," in Hampshire, ed., *Public and Private Morality* (1978) at 113–43. Rights "function as trump cards held by individuals." *Id.* at 136.
23. Barry observes:

> On the surface, rights theories stand in opposition to utilitarianism, for rights, whatever their foundation (or lack thereof), are supposed to trump claims that might be made on behalf of the general welfare. The point here is, however, that the whole notion of rights is simply a variation on utilitarianism in that it accepts the definition of the ethical problem as conterminous with the problem of conflicting interests, and replaces the felicific calculus (in which the interests are simply added) with one which does not permit certain interests to be traded off against others.

Barry, "Self-government Revisited," in Miller and Siedentop, eds., *The Nature of Political Theory* (1983) at 125; see generally 121–54.
24. Leopold, *supra* note 1, at 262.
25. For discussion of this point, see Katz, *Is There a Place For Animals in the Moral Consideration of Nature* (1983), 4 *Ethics and Animals* 74; Norton, "Environmental Ethics and Nonhuman Rights" (1982), 4 *Envt'l Ethics* 17; Rodman, "The Liberation of Nature?" (1977), 20 *Inquiry* 83; Goodpaster, "On Being Morally Considerable" (1978), 75 *J. Phil.* 308. Tom Regan discusses this issue in "The Case for Animal Liberation" (1983):

> Because paradigmatic rights-holders are individuals, and because the dominant thrust of contemporary environmental efforts (*e.g.,* wilderness preservation) is to focus on the whole rather than on the part (*i.e.,* the individual), there is an understandable reluctance on the part of environmentalists to "take rights seriously," or at least a reluctance to take them as seriously as the rights view contends we should. . . .A rights-based environmental ethic. . .ought not to be dismissed out of hand by environmentalists as being in principle antagonistic to the goals for which they work. It isn't. Were we to show proper respect for the rights of individuals who make up the biotic community, would not the *community* be preserved?

(*Id.* at 362.) I believe this is an empirical question, the answer to which is "no." The environmentalist is concerned about preserving evolutionary processes; whether these processes, *e.g.,* natural selection, have deep enough respect for the rights of individuals to be preserved on those grounds, is a question that might best left be addressed by an evolutionary biologist.

26. *The Endangered Species Act of 1973*, 16 U.S.C. § 1531 (1976 & Supp. I 1977 & Supp. II 1978 & Supp. III 1979).
27. Feinberg, "The Rights of Animals and Unborn Generations," in Blackstone, ed., *Philosophy and the Environmental Crisis* (1974) 43 at 55–56.
28. Hardin, "Foreward," in Stone, *supra* note 3, at xii.
29. Rodman, *supra* note 25, at 110.

The Land Ethic

Aldo Leopold

Aldo Leopold (1887–1949) was professor of wildlife management at the University of Wisconsin from 1933 until his death. He is the author of A Sand County Almanac, *often called the bible of the contemporary environmental movement.*

When god-like Odysseus returned from the wars in Troy, he hanged all on one rope a dozen slave-girls of his household whom he suspected of misbehavior during his absence.

This hanging involved no question of propriety. The girls were property. The disposal of property was then, as now, a matter of expediency, not of right and wrong.

Concepts of right and wrong were not lacking from Odysseus' Greece: witness the fidelity of his wife through the long years before at last his black-prowed galleys clove the wine-dark seas for home. The ethical structure of that day covered wives, but had not yet been extended to human chattels. During the three thousand years which have since elapsed, ethical criteria have been extended to many fields of conduct, with corresponding shrinkages in those judged by expediency only.

THE ETHICAL SEQUENCE

This extension of ethics, so far studied only by philosophers, is actually a process in ecological evolution. Its sequences may be described in ecological as well as in philosophical terms. An ethic, ecologically, is a limitation on freedom of action in the struggle for existence. An ethic, philosophically, is a differentiation of social from anti-social conduct. These are two definitions of one thing. The thing has its origin in the tendency of interdependent individuals or groups to evolve modes of co-operation. The ecologist calls these symbioses. Politics and economics are advanced symbioses in which the original free-for-all competition has been replaced, in part, by co-operative mechanisms with an ethical content.

The complexity of co-operative mechanisms has increased with population density, and with the efficiency of tools. It was simpler, for example, to define the anti-social uses of sticks and stones in the days of the mastodons than of bullets and billboards in the age of motors.

The first ethics dealt with the relation between individuals; the Mosaic Decalogue is an example. Later accretions dealt with the relation between the individual and society. The Golden Rule tries to integrate the individual to society; democracy to integrate social organization to the individual.

There is as yet no ethic dealing with man's relation to land and to the animals and plants which grow upon it. Land, like Odysseus' slave-girls, is still property. The land-relation is still strictly economic, entailing privileges but not obligations.

The extension of ethics to this third element in human environment is, if I read the evidence correctly, an evolutionary possibility and an ecological necessity. It is the third step in a sequence. The first two have already been taken. Individual thinkers since the days of Ezekiel and Isaiah have asserted that the despoliation of land is not only inexpedient but wrong. Society, however, has not yet affirmed their belief. I regard the present conservation movement as the embryo of such an affirmation.

An ethic may be regarded as a mode of guidance for meeting ecological situations so new or intricate, or involving such deferred reactions, that the path of social expediency is not discernible to the average individual. Animal instincts are modes of guidance for the individual in meeting such situations. Ethics are possibly a kind of community instinct in-the-making.

THE COMMUNITY CONCEPT

All ethics so far evolved rest upon a single premise: that the individual is a member of a community of interdependant parts. His instincts prompt him to compete for his place in that community, but his ethics prompt him also to co-operate (perhaps in order that there may be a place to compete for).

The land ethic simply enlarges the boundaries of the community to include soils, waters, plants, and animals, or collectively: the land.

This sounds simple: do we not already sing our love for and obligation to the land of the free and the home of the brave? Yes, but just what and whom do we love? Certainly not the soil, which we are sending helter-skelter downriver. Certainly not the waters, which we assume have no function except to turn turbines, float barges, and carry off sewage. Certainly not the plants, of which we exterminate whole communities without batting an eye. Certainly not the animals, of which we have already extirpated many of the largest and most beautiful species. A land ethic of course cannot prevent the alteration, management, and use of these "resources," but it does affirm their right to continued existence, and, at least in spots, their continued existence in a natural state.

In short, a land ethic changes the role of *Homo sapiens* from conqueror of the land-community to plain member and citizen of it. It implies respect for his fellow-members, and also respect for the community as such.

In human history, we have learned (I hope) that the conqueror role is eventually self-defeating. Why? Because it is implicit in such a role that the conqueror knows, *ex cathedra,* just what makes the community clock tick, and just what and who is valuable, and what and who is worthless, in community life. It always turns out that he knows neither, and this is why his conquests eventually defeat themselves.

In the biotic community, a parallel situation exists. Abraham knew exactly what the land was for: it was to drip milk and honey into Abraham's mouth. At the present moment, the assurance with which we regard this assumption is inverse to the degree of our education.

The ordinary citizen today assumes that science knows what makes the community clock tick; the scientist is equally sure that he does not. He knows that the biotic mechanism is so complex that its workings may never be fully understood.

That man is, in fact, only a member of a biotic team is shown by an ecological interpretation of history. Many historical events, hitherto explained solely in terms of human enterprise, were actually biotic interactions between people and land. The characteristics of the land determined the facts quite as potently as the characteristics of the men who lived on it.

Consider, for example, the settlement of the Mississippi valley. In the years following the Revolution, three groups were contending for its control: the native Indian, the French and English traders, and the American settlers. Historians wonder what would have happened if the English at Detroit had thrown a little more weight into the Indian side of those tipsy scales which decided the outcome of the colonial migration into the cane-lands of Kentucky. It is time now to ponder the fact that the cane-lands, when subjected to the particular mixture of forces represented by the cow, plow, fire, and axe of the pioneer, became bluegrass. What if the plant succession inherent in this dark and bloody ground had, under the impact of these forces, given us some worthless sedge, shrub, or weed? Would Boone and Kenton have held out? Would there have been any overflow into Ohio, Indiana, Illinois, and Missouri? Any Louisiana Purchase? Any transcontinental union of new states? Any Civil War?

Kentucky was one sentence in the drama of history. We are commonly told what the human actors in this drama tried to do, but we are seldom told that their success, or the lack of it, hung in large degree on the reaction of particular soils to the impact of the particular forces exerted by their occupancy. In the case of Kentucky, we do not even know where the bluegrass came from—whether it is a native species, or a stowaway from Europe.

Contrast the cane-lands with what hindsight tells us about the Southwest, where the pioneers were equally brave, resourceful, and persevering. The impact of occupancy here brought no bluegrass, or other plant fitted to withstand the bumps and buffetings of hard use. This region, when grazed by livestock, reverted through a series of more and more worthless grasses, shrubs, and weeds to a condition of unstable equilibrium. Each recession of plant types bred erosion; each increment to erosion bred a further recession of plants. The result today is a progressive and mutual deterioration, not only of plants and soils, but of the animal community subsisting thereon. The early settlers did not expect this: on the ciénegas of New Mexico some even cut ditches to hasten it. So subtle has been its progress that few residents of the region are aware of it. It is quite invisible to the tourist who finds this wrecked landscape colorful and charming (as indeed it is, but it bears scant resemblance to what it was in 1848).

This same landscape was "developed" once before, but with quite different results. The Pueblo Indians settled the Southwest in pre-Columbian times, but they happened *not* to be equipped with range livestock. Their civilization expired, but not because their land expired.

In India, regions devoid of any sod-forming grass have been settled, apparently without wrecking the land, by the simple expedient of carrying the grass to the cow, rather than vice versa. (Was this the result of some deep wisdom, or was it just good luck? I do not know.)

In short, the plant succession steered the course of history; the pioneer simply demonstrated, for good or ill, what successions inhered in the land. Is history taught in this spirit? It will be, once the concept of land as a community really penetrates our intellectual life.

THE ECOLOGICAL CONSCIENCE

Conservation is a state of harmony between men and land. Despite nearly a century of propaganda, conservation still proceeds at a snail's pace; progress still consists largely of letterhead pieties and convention oratory. On the back forty we still slip two steps backward for each forward stride.

The usual answer to this dilemma is "more conservation education." No one will debate this, but is it certain that only the *volume* of education needs stepping up? Is something lacking in the *content* as well?

It is difficult to give a fair summary of its content in brief form, but, as I understand it, the content is substantially this: obey the law, vote right, join some organizations, and practice what conservation is profitable on your own land; the government will do the rest.

Is not this formula too easy to accomplish anything worth-while? It defines no right or wrong, assigns no obligation, calls for no sacrifice, implies no change in the current philosophy of values. In respect of land-use, it urges only enlightened self-interest. Just how far will such education take us? An example will perhaps yield a partial answer.

By 1930 it had become clear to all except the ecologically blind that southwestern Wisconsin's topsoil was slipping seaward. In 1933 the farmers were told that if they would adopt certain remedial practices for five years, the public would donate CCC labor to install them, plus the necessary machinery and materials. The offer was widely accepted, but the practices were widely forgotten when the five-year contract period was up. The farmers continued only those practices that yielded an immediate and visible economic gain for themselves.

This led to the idea that maybe farmers would learn more quickly if they themselves wrote the rules. Accordingly the Wisconsin Legislature in 1937 passed the Soil Conservation District Law. This said to farmers, in effect: *We, the public, will furnish you free technical service and loan you specialized machinery, if you will write your own rules for land-use. Each county may write its own rules, and these will have the force of law.* Nearly all the counties promptly organized to accept the proffered help, but after a decade of operation, *no county has yet written a single rule.* There has been visible progress in such practices as strip-cropping, pasture renovation, and soil liming, but none in fencing woodlots against grazing, and none in excluding plow and cow from steep slopes. The farmers, in short, have selected those remedial practices which were profitable anyhow, and ignored those which were profitable to the community, but not clearly profitable to themselves.

When one asks why no rules have been written, one is told that the community is not yet ready to support them; education must precede rules. But the education actually in progress makes no mention of obligations to land over and above those dictated by self-interest. The net result is that we have more education but less soil, fewer healthy woods, and as many floods as in 1937.

The puzzling aspect of such situations is that the existence of obligations over and above self-interest is taken for granted in such rural community enterprises as the betterment of roads, schools, churches, and baseball teams. Their existence is not taken for granted, nor as yet seriously discussed, in bettering the behavior of the water that falls on the land, or in the preserving of the beauty or diversity of the farm landscape. Land-use ethics are still governed wholly by economic self-interest, just as social ethics were a century ago.

To sum up: we asked the farmer to do what he conveniently could to save his soil, and he has done just that, and only that. The farmer who clears the woods off a 75 per cent slope, turns his cows into the clearing, and dumps its rainfall, rocks, and soil into the community creek, is still (if otherwise decent) a respected member of society. If he puts lime on his fields and plants his crops on contour, he is still entitled to all the privileges and emoluments of his Soil Conservation District. The District is a beautiful piece of social machinery, but it is coughing along on two cylinders because we have been too timid, and too anxious for quick success, to tell the farmer the true magnitude of his obligations. Obligations have no meaning without conscience, and the problem we face is the extension without conscience, and the problem we face is the extension of the social conscience from people to land.

No important change in ethics was ever accomplished without an internal change in our intellectual emphasis, loyalties, affections, and convictions. The proof that conservation has not yet touched these foundations of conduct lies in the fact that philosophy and religion have not yet heard of it. In our attempt to make conservation easy, we have made it trivial.

SUBSTITUTES FOR A LAND ETHIC

When the logic of history hungers for bread and we hand out a stone, we are at pains to explain how much the stone resembles bread. I now describe some of the stones which serve in lieu of a land ethic.

One basic weakness in a conservation system based wholly on economic motives is that most members of the land community have no economic value. Wildflowers and songbirds are examples. Of the 22,000 higher plants and animals native to Wisconsin, it is doubtful whether more than 5 per cent can be sold, fed, eaten, or otherwise put to economic use. Yet these creatures are members of the biotic community, and if (as I believe) its stability depends on its integrity, they are entitled to continuance.

When one of these non-economic categories is threatened, and if we happen to love it, we invent subterfuges to give it economic importance. At the beginning of the century songbirds were supposed to be disappearing. Ornithologists jumped to the rescue with some distinctly shaky evidence to the effect that insects would eat us up if birds failed to control them. The evidence had to be economic in order to be valid.

It is painful to read these circumlocutions today. We have no land ethic yet, but we have at least drawn nearer the point of admitting that birds should continue as a matter of biotic right, regardless of the presence or absence of economic advantage to us.

A parallel situation exists in respect of predatory mammals, raptorial birds, and fish-eating birds. Time was when biologists somewhat overworked the evidence that these creatures preserve the health of game by killing weaklings, or that they control rodents for the farmer, or that they prey only on 'worthless' species. Here again, the evidence had to be economic in order to be valid. It is only in recent years that we hear the more honest argument that predators are members of the community, and that no special interest has the right to exterminate them for the sake of a benefit, real or fancied, to itself. Unfortunately this enlightened view is still in the talk stage. In the field the extermination of predators goes merrily on: witness the impending erasure of the timber wolf by fiat of Congress, the Conservation Bureaus, and many state legislatures.

Some species of trees have been 'read out of the party' by economics-minded foresters because they grow too slowly, or have too low a sale value to pay as timber crops: white cedar, tamarack, cypress, beech, and hemlock are examples. In Europe, where forestry is ecologically more advanced, the non-commercial tree species are recognized as members of the native forest community, to be preserved as such, within reason. Moreover some (like beech) have been found to have a valuable function in building up soil fertility. The interdependence of the forest and its constituent tree species, ground flora, and fauna is taken for granted.

Lack of economic value is sometimes a character not only of species or groups, but of entire biotic communities: marshes, bogs, dunes, and 'deserts' are examples. Our formula in such cases is to relegate their conservation to government as refuges, monuments, or parks. The difficulty is that these communities are usually interspersed with more valuable private lands; the government cannot possibly own or control such scattered parcels. The net effect is that we have relegated some of them to ultimate extinction over large areas. If the private owner were ecologically minded, he would be proud to be the custodian of a reasonable proportion of such areas, which add diversity and beauty to his farm and to his community.

In some instances, the assumed lack of profit in these 'waste' areas has proved to be wrong, but only after most of them had been done away with. The present scramble to reflood muskrat marshes is a case in point.

There is a clear tendency in American conservation to relegate to government all necessary jobs that private landowners fail to perform. Government ownership, operation, subsidy, or regulation is now widely prevalent in forestry, range management, soil and watershed management, park and wilderness conservation, fisheries management, and migratory bird management, with more to come. Most of this growth in governmental conservation is proper and logical, some of it is inevitable. That I imply no disapproval of it is implicit in the fact that I have spent most of my life working for it. Nevertheless the question arises: What is the ultimate magnitude of the enterprise? Will the tax base carry its eventual ramifications? At what point will governmental conservation, like the mastodon, become handicapped by its own dimensions? The answer, if there is any, seems to be in a land ethic, or some other force which assigns more obligation to the private landowner.

Industrial landowners and users, especially lumbermen and stockmen, are inclined to wail long and loudly about the extension of government ownership and regulation to land, but (with notable exceptions) they show little disposition to develop the only visible alternative: the voluntary practice of conservation on their own lands.

When the private landowner is asked to perform some unprofitable act for the good of the community, he today assents only with outstretched palm. If the act costs him cash this is fair and proper, but when it costs only forethought, open-mindedness, or time, the issue is at least debatable. The overwhelming growth of land-use subsidises in recent years must be ascribed, in large part, to the government's own agencies for conservation education: the land bureaus, the agricultural colleges, and the extension services. As far as I can detect, no ethical obligation toward land is taught in these institutions.

To sum up: a system of conservation based solely on economic self-interest is hopelessly lopsided. It tends to ignore, and thus eventually to eliminate, many elements in the land community that lack commercial value, but that are (as far as we know) essential to its healthy functioning. It assumes, falsely, I think, that the economic parts of the biotic clock will function without the uneconomic parts. It tends to relegate to government many functions eventually too large, too complex, or too widely dispersed to be performed by government.

An ethical obligation on the part of the private owner is the only visible remedy for these situations.

THE LAND PYRAMID

An ethic to supplement and guide the economic relation to land presupposes the existence of some mental image of land as a biotic mechanism. We can be ethical only in relation to something we can see, feel, understand, love, or otherwise have faith in.

The image commonly employed in conservation education is 'the balance of nature.' For reasons too lengthy to detail here, this figure of speech fails to describe accurately what little we know about the land mechanism. A much truer image is the one employed in ecology: the biotic pyramid. I shall first sketch the pyramid as a symbol of land, and later develop some of its implications in terms of land-use.

Plants absorb energy from the sun. This energy flows through a circuit called the biota, which may be represented by a pyramid consisting of layers. The bottom layer is the soil. A plant layer rests on the soil, an insect layer on the plants, a bird and rodent layer on the insects, and so on up through various animal groups to the apex layer, which consists of the larger carnivores.

The species of a layer are alike not in where they came from, or in what they look like, but rather in what they eat. Each successive layer depends on those below it for food and often for other services, and each in turn furnishes food and services to those above. Proceeding upward, each successive layer decreases in numerical abundance. Thus, for every carnivore there are hundreds of his prey, thousands of their prey, millions of insects, uncountable plants. The pyramidal form of the system reflects this numerical progression from apex to base. Man shares an intermediate layer with the bears, raccoons, and squirrels which eat both meat and vegetables.

The lines of dependency for food and other services are called food chains. Thus soil-oak-deer-Indian is a chain that has now been largely converted to soil-corn-cow-farmer. Each species, including ourselves, is a link in many chains. The deer eats a hundred plants other than oak, and the cow a hundred plants other than corn. Both, then, are links in a hundred chains. The pyramid is a tangle of chains so complex as to seem disorderly, yet the stability of the system proves it to be a highly organized structure. Its functioning depends on the co-operation and competition of its diverse parts.

In the beginning, the pyramid of life was low and squat; the food chains short and simple. Evolution has added layer after layer, link after link. Man is one of thousands of accretions to the height and complexity of the pyramid. Science has given us many doubts, but it has given us at least one certainty: the trend of evolution is to elaborate and diversify the biota.

Land, then, is not merely soil; it is a fountain of energy flowing through a circuit of soils, plants, and animals. Food chains are the living channels which conduct energy upward; death and decay return it to the soil. The circuit is not closed; some energy is dissipated in decay, some is added by absorption from the air, some is stored in soils, peats, and long-lived forests; but it is a sustained circuit, like a slowly augmented revolving fund of life. There is always a net loss by downhill wash, but this is normally small and offset by the decay of rocks. It is deposited in the ocean and, in the course of geological time, raised to form new lands and new pyramids.

The velocity and character of the upward flow of energy depend on the complex structure of the plant and animal community, much as the upward flow of sap in a tree depends on its complex cellular organization. Without this complexity, normal circulation would presumably not occur. Structure means the characteristic numbers, as well as the characteristic kinds and functions, of the component species. This interdependence between the complex structure of the land and its smooth functioning as an energy unit is one of its basic attributes.

When a change occurs in one part of the circuit, many other parts must adjust themselves to it. Change does not necessarily obstruct or divert the flow of energy; evolution is a long series of self-induced changes, the net result of which has been to elaborate the flow mechanism and to lengthen the circuit. Evolutionary changes, however, are usually slow and local. Man's invention of tools has enabled him to make changes of unprecedented violence, rapidity, and scope.

One change is in the composition of floras and faunas. The larger predators are lopped off the apex of the pyramid; food chains, for the first time in history, become shorter rather than longer. Domesticated species from other lands are substituted for wild ones, and wild ones are moved to new habitats. In this world-wide pooling of faunas and floras, some species get out of bounds as pests and diseases, others are extinguished. Such effects are seldom intended or foreseen; they represent unpredicted and often untraceable readjustments in the structure. Agricultural science is largely a race between the emergence of new pests and the emergence of new techniques for their control.

Another change touches the flow of energy through plants and animals and its return to the soil. Fertility is the ability of soil to receive, store, and release energy. Agriculture, by overdrafts on the soil, or by too radical a substitution of domestic for native species in the superstructure, may derange the channels of flow or deplete storage. Soils depleted of their storage, or of the organic matter which anchors it, wash away faster than they form. This is erosion.

Waters, like soil, are part of the energy circuit. Industry, by polluting waters or obstructing them with dams, may exclude the plants and animals necessary to keep energy in circulation.

Transportation brings about another basic change: the plants or animals grown in one region are now consumed and returned to the soil in another. Transportation taps the energy stored in rocks, and in the air, and uses it elsewhere; thus we fertilize the garden with nitrogen gleaned by the guano birds from the fishes of seas on the other side of the Equator. Thus the formerly localized and self-contained circuits are pooled on a world-wide scale.

The process of altering the pyramid for human occupation releases stored energy, and this often gives rise, during the pioneering period, to a deceptive exuberance of plant and animal life, both wild and tame. These releases of biotic capital tend to becloud or postpone the penalties of violence.

This thumbnail sketch of land as an energy circuit conveys three basic ideas:

(1) That land is not merely soil.

(2) That the native plants and animals kept the energy circuit open; others may or may not.

(3) That man-made changes are of a different order than evolutionary changes, and have effects more comprehensive than is intended or foreseen.

These ideas, collectively, raise two basic issues: Can the land adjust itself to the new order? Can the desired alterations be accomplished with less violence?

Biotas seem to differ in their capacity to sustain violent conversion. Western Europe, for example, carries a far different pyramid than Caesar found there. Some large animals are lost; swampy forests have become meadows or plow-land; many new plants and animals are introduced, some of which escape as pests; the remaining natives are greatly changed in distribution and abundance. Yet the soil is still there and, with the help of imported nutrients, still fertile; the waters flow normally; the new structure seems to function and to persist. There is no visible stoppage or derangement of the circuit.

Western Europe, then, has a resistant biota. Its inner processes are tough, elastic, resistant to strain. No matter how violent the alterations, the pyramid, so far, has developed some new *modus vivendi* which preserves its habitability for man, and for most of the other natives.

Japan seems to present another instance of radical conversion without disorganization.

Most other civilized regions, and some as yet barely touched by civilization, display various stages of disorganization, varying from initial symptoms to advanced wastage. In Asia Minor and North Africa diagnosis is confused by climatic changes, which may have been either the cause or the effect of advanced wastage. In the United States the degree of disorganization varies locally; it is worst in the Southwest, the Ozarks, and parts of the South, and least in New England and the Northwest. Better land-uses may still arrest it in the less advanced regions. In parts of Mexico, South America, South Africa, and Australia a violent and accelerating wastage is in progress, but I cannot assess the prospects.

This almost world-wide display of disorganization in the land seems to be similar to disease in an animal, except that it never culminates in complete disorganization or death. The land recovers, but at some reduced level of complexity, and with a reduced carrying capacity for people, plants, and animals. Many biotas currently regarded as 'lands of opportunity' are in fact already subsisting on exploitative agriculture, i.e. they have already exceeded their sustained carrying capacity. Most of South America is overpopulated in this sense.

In arid regions we attempt to offset the process of wastage by reclamation, but it is only too evident that the prospective longevity of reclamation projects is often short. In our own West, the best of them may not last a century.

The combined evidence of history and ecology seems to support one general deduction: the less violent the manmade changes, the greater the probability of successful readjustment in the pyramid. Violence, in turn, varies with human population density; a dense population requires a more violent conversion. In this respect, North America has a better chance for permanence than Europe, if she can contrive to limit her density.

This deduction runs counter to our current philosophy which assumes that because a small increase in density enriched human life, that an indefinite increase will enrich it indefinitely. Ecology knows of no density relationship that holds for indefinitely wide limits. All gains from density are subject to a law of diminishing returns.

Whatever may be the equation for men and land, it is improbable that we as yet know all its terms. Recent discoveries in mineral and vitamin nutrition reveal unsuspected dependencies in the up-circuit: incredibly minute quantities of certain substances determine the value of soils to plants, of plants to animals. What of the down-circuit? What of the vanishing species, the preservation of which we now regard as an esthetic luxury? They helped build the soil; in what unsuspected ways may they be essential to its maintenance? Professor Weaver proposes that we use prairie flowers to reflocculate the wasting soils of the dust bowl; who knows for what purpose cranes and condors, otters and grizzlies may some day be used?

LAND HEALTH AND THE A-B CLEAVAGE

A land ethic, then, reflects the existence of an ecological conscience, and this in turn reflects a conviction of individual responsibility for the health of the land. Health is the capacity of the land for self-renewal. Conservation is our effort to understand and preserve this capacity.

Conservationists are notorious for their dissensions. Superficially these seem to add up to mere confusion, but a more careful scrutiny reveals a single plane of cleavage common to many specialized fields. In each field one group (A) regards the land as soil, and its function as commodity-production; another group (B) regards the land as a biota, and its function as something broader. How much broader is admittedly in a state of doubt and confusion.

In my own field, forestry, group A is quite content to grow trees like cabbages, with cellulose as the basic forest commodity. It feels no inhibition against violence; its ideology is agronomic. Group B, on the other hand, sees forestry as fundamentally different from agronomy because it employs natural species, and manages a natural environment rather than creating an artificial one. Group B prefers natural reproduction on principle. It worries on biotic as well as economic grounds about the loss of species like chestnut, and the threatened loss of the white pines. It worries about a whole series of secondary forest functions: wildlife, recreation, watersheds, wilderness areas. To my mind, Group B feels the stirrings of an ecological conscience.

In the wildlife field, a parallel cleavage exists. For Group A the basic commodities are sport and meat; the yardsticks of production are ciphers of take in pheasants and trout. Artificial propagation is acceptable as a permanent as well as a temporary recourse—if its unit costs permit. Group B, on the other hand, worries about a whole series of biotic side-issues. What is the cost in predators of producing a game crop? Should we have further recourse to exotics? How can management restore the shrinking species, like prairie grouse, already hopeless as shootable game? How can management restore the threatened rarities, like trumpeter swan and whooping crane? Can management principles be extended to wildflowers? Here again it is clear to me that we have the same A-B cleavage as in forestry.

In the larger field of agriculture I am less competent to speak, but there seem to be somewhat parallel cleavages. Scientific agriculture was actively developing before ecology was born, hence a slower penetration of ecological concepts might be expected. Moreover the farmer, by the very nature of his techniques, must modify the biota more radically than the forester or the wildlife manager. Nevertheless, there are many discontents in agriculture which seem to add up to a new vision of 'biotic farming.'

Perhaps the most important of these is the new evidence that poundage or tonnage is no measure of the food-value of farm crops; the products of fertile soil may be qualitatively as well as quantitatively superior. We can bolster poundage from depleted soils by pouring on imported fertility, but we are not necessarily bolstering food-value. The possible ultimate ramifications of this idea are so immense that I must leave their exposition to abler pens.

The discontent that labels itself 'organic farming,' while bearing some of the earmarks of a cult, is nevertheless biotic in its direction, particularly in its insistence on the importance of soil flora and fauna.

The ecological fundamentals of agriculture are just as poorly known to the public as in other fields of land-use. For example, few educated people realize that the marvelous advances in technique made during recent decades are improvements in the pump, rather than the well. Acre for acre, they have barely sufficed to offset the sinking level of fertility.

In all of these cleavages, we see repeated the same basic paradoxes: man the conqueror *versus* man the biotic citizen; science the sharpener of his sword *versus* science the search-light on his universe; land the slave and servant *versus* land the collective organism. Robinson's injunction to Tristram may well be applied, at this juncture, to *Homo sapiens* as a species in geological time:

> Whether you will or not
> You are a King, Tristram, for you are one

Of the time-tested few that leave the world,
When they are gone, not the same place it was.
Mark what you leave.

THE OUTLOOK

It is inconceivable to me that an ethical relation to land can exist without love, respect, and admiration for land, and a high regard for its value. By value, I of course mean something far broader than mere economic value; I mean value in the philosophical sense.

Perhaps the most serious obstacle impeding the evolution of a land ethic is the fact that our educational and economic system is headed away from, rather than toward, an intense consciousness of land. Your true modern is separated from the land by many middlemen, and by innumerable physical gadgets. He had no vital relation to it; to him it is the space between cities on which crops grow. Turn him loose for a day on the land, and if the spot does not happen to be a golf links or a 'scenic' area, he is bored stiff. If crops could be raised by hydroponics instead of farming, it would suit him very well. Synthetic substitutes for wood, leather, wool, and other natural land products suit him better than the originals. In short, land is something he has 'outgrown.'

Almost equally serious as an obstacle to a land ethic is the attitude of the farmer for whom the land is still and adversary, or a taskmaster that keeps him in slavery. Theoretically, the mechanization of farming ought to cut the farmer's chains, but whether it really does is debatable.

One of the requisites for an ecological comprehension of land is an understanding of ecology, and this is by no means co-extensive with 'education'; in fact, much higher education seems deliberately to avoid ecological concepts. An understanding of ecology does not necessarily originate in courses bearing ecological labels; it is quite as likely to be labeled geography, botany, agronomy, history, or economics. This is as it should be, but whatever the label, ecological training is scarce.

The case for a land ethic would appear hopeless but for the minority which is in obvious revolt against these 'modern' trends.

The 'key-log' which must be moved to release the evolutionary process for an ethic is simply this: quit thinking about decent land-use as solely an economic problem. Examine each question in terms of what is ethically and esthetically right, as well as what is economically expedient. A thing is right when it tends to preserve the integrity, stability, and beauty of the biotic community. It is wrong when it tends otherwise.

It of course goes without saying that economic feasibility limits the tether of what can or cannot be done for land. It always has and it always will. The fallacy the economic determinists have tied around our collective neck, and which we now need to cast off, is the belief that economics determines *all* land-use. This is simply not true. An innumerable host of actions and attitudes, comprising perhaps the bulk of all land relations, is determined by the land-users' tastes and predilections, rather than by his purse. The bulk of all land relations hinges on investments of time, forethought, skill, and faith rather than on investments of cash. As a land-user thinketh, so is he.

I have purposely presented the land ethic as a product of social evolution because nothing so important as an ethic is ever 'written.' Only the most superficial student of history supposes that Moses 'wrote' the Decalogue; it evolved in the minds of a thinking community, and Moses wrote a tentative summary of it for a 'seminar.' I say tentative because evolution never stops.

The evolution of a land ethic is an intellectual as well as emotional process. Conservation is paved with good intentions which prove to be futile, or even dangerous, because they are devoid of critical understanding either of the land, or of economic land-use. I think it is a truism that as the ethical frontier advances from the individual to the community, its intellectual content increases.

The mechanism of operation is the same for any ethic: social approbation for right actions: social disapproval for wrong actions.

By and large, our present problem is one of attitudes and implements. We are remodeling the Alhambra with a steamshovel, and we are proud of our yardage. We shall hardly relinquish the shovel, which after all has many good points, but we are in need of gentler and more objective criteria for its successful use.

The Conceptual Foundations of the Land Ethic

J. Baird Callicott

J. Baird Callicott is professor of philosophy and natural resources at the University of Wisconsin–Stevens Point. He is the author of In Defense of the Land Ethic: Essays in Environmental Philosophy *and editor of* Companion to a Sand County Almanac: Interpretative and Critical Essays.

The two great cultural advances of the past century were the Darwinian theory and the development of geology. . . .Just as important, however, as the origin of plants, animals, and soil is the question of how they operate as a community. That task has fallen to the new science of ecology, which is daily uncovering a web of interdependencies so intricate as to amaze—were he here—even Darwin himself, who, of all men, should have least cause to tremble before the veil.

—Aldo Leopold, *fragment 6B16, no. 36, Leopold Papers,*
University of Wisconsin—Madison Archives

As Wallace Stegner observes, *A Sand County Almanac* is considered "almost a holy book in conservation circles," and Aldo Leopold a prophet, "an American Isaiah." And as Curt Meine points out, "The Land Ethic" is the climactic essay of *Sand County*, "the upshot of 'The Upshot.'"[1] One might, therefore, fairly say that the recommendation and justification of

This essay originally appeared in *Companion to a Sand County Almanac*. Reprinted with permission from the University of Wisconsin Press.

moral obligations on the part of people to nature is what the prophetic *A Sand County Almanac* is all about.

But, with few exceptions, "The Land Ethic" has not been favorably received by contemporary academic philosophers. Most have ignored it. Of those who have not, most have been either nonplussed or hostile. Distinguished Australian philosopher John Passmore dismissed it out of hand, in the first book-length academic discussion of the new philosophical subdiscipline called "environmental ethics."[2] In a more recent and more deliberate discussion, the equally distinguished Australian philosopher H. J. McCloskey patronized Aldo Leopold and saddled "The Land Ethic" with various far-fetched "interpretations." He concludes that "there is a real problem in attributing a coherent meaning to Leopold's statements, one that exhibits his land ethic as representing a major advance in ethics rather than a retrogression to a morality of a kind held by various primitive peoples."[3] Echoing McCloskey, English philosopher Robin Attfield went out of his way to impugn the philosophical respectability of "The Land Ethic." And Canadian philosopher L. W. Sumner has called it "dangerous nonsense."[4] Among those philosophers more favorably disposed, "The Land Ethic" has usually been simply quoted, as if it were little more than a noble, but naive, moral plea, altogether lacking a supporting theoretical framework—i.e., foundational principles and premises which lead, by compelling argument, to ethical precepts.

The professional neglect, confusion, and (in some cases) contempt for "The Land Ethic" may, in my judgment, be attributed to three things: (1) Leopold's extremely condensed prose style in which an entire conceptual complex may be conveyed in a few sentences, or even in a phrase or two; (2) his departure from the assumptions and paradigms of contemporary philosophical ethics; and (3) the unsettling practical implications to which a land ethic appears to lead. "The Land Ethic," in short, is, from a philosophical point of view, abbreviated, unfamiliar, and radical.

Here I first examine and elaborate the compactly expressed abstract elements of the land ethic and expose the "logic" which binds them into a proper, but revolutionary, moral theory. I then discuss the controversial features of the land ethic and defend them against actual and potential criticism. I hope to show that the land ethic cannot be ignored as merely the groundless emotive exhortations of a moonstruck conservationist or dismissed as entailing wildly untoward practical consequences. It poses, rather, a serious intellectual challenge to business-as-usual moral philosophy.

"The Land Ethic" opens with a charming and poetic evocation of Homer's Greece, the point of which is to suggest that today land is just as routinely and remorsely enslaved as human beings then were. A panoramic glance backward to our most distant cultural origins, Leopold suggests, reveals a slow but steady moral development over three millennia. More of our relationships and activities ("fields of conduct") have fallen under the aegis of moral principles ("ethical criteria") as civilization has grown and matured. If moral growth and development continue, as not only a synoptic review of history, but recent past experience suggest that it will, future generations will censure today's casual and universal environmental bondage as today we censure the casual and universal human bondage of three thousand years ago.

A cynically inclined critic might scoff at Leopold's sanguine portrayal of human history. Slavery survived as an institution in the "civilized" West, more particularly in the morally self-congratulatory United States, until a mere generation before Leopold's own birth. And Western history from imperial Athens and Rome to the Spanish Inquisition and the Third Reich has been a disgraceful series of wars, persecutions, tyrannies, pogroms, and other atrocities.

The history of moral practice, however, is not identical with the history of moral consciousness. Morality is not descriptive; it is prescriptive or normative. In light of this distinction, it is clear that today, despite rising rates of violent crime in the United States and institutional abuses of human rights in Iran, Chile, Ethiopia, Guatemala, South Africa, and many other places, and despite persistent organized social injustice and oppression in still others, moral consciousness is expanding more rapidly now than ever before. Civil rights, human rights, women's liberation, children's liberation, animal liberation, etc., all indicate, as expressions of newly emergent moral ideals, that ethical consciousness (as distinct from practice) has if anything recently accelerated—thus confirming Leopold's historical observation.

Leopold next points out that "this extension of ethics, so far studied only by philosophers"—and therefore, the implication is clear, not very satisfactorily studied—"is actually a process in ecological evolution" (202). What Leopold is saying here, simply, is that we may understand the history of ethics, fancifully alluded to by means of the Odysseus vignette, in biological as well as philosophical terms. From a biological point of view, an ethic is "a limitation on freedom of action in the struggle for existence" (202).

I had this passage in mind when I remarked that Leopold manages to convey a whole network of ideas in a couple of phrases. The phrase "struggle for existence" unmistakably calls to mind Darwinian evolution as the conceptual context in which a biological account of the origin and development of ethics must ultimately be located. And at once it points up a paradox: Given the unremitting competitive "struggle for existence" how could "limitations on freedom of action" ever have been conserved and spread through a population of *Homo sapiens* or their evolutionary progenitors?

For a biological account of ethics, as Harvard social entomologist

Edward O. Wilson has recently written, "the central theoretical problem. . .[is] how can altruism [elaborately articulated as morality or ethics in the human species], which by definition reduces personal fitness, possibly evolve by natural selection?"[5] According to modern sociobiology, the answer lies in kinship. But according to Darwin—who had tackled this problem himself "exclusively from the side of natural history" in *The Descent of Man*—the answer lies in society.[6] And it was Darwin's classical account (and its divers variations), from the side of natural history, which informed Leopold's thinking in the late 1940s.

Let me put the problem in perspective. How, we are asking, did ethics originate and, once in existence, grow in scope and complexity?

The oldest answer in living human memory is theological. God (or the gods) imposes morality on people. And God (or the gods) sanctions it. A most vivid and graphic example of this kind of account occurs in the Bible when Moses goes up on Mount Sinai to receive the Ten Commandments directly from God. That text also clearly illustrates the divine sanctions (plagues, pestilences, droughts, military defeats, etc.) for moral disobedience. Ongoing revelation of the divine will, of course, as handily and as simply explains subsequent moral growth and development.

Western philosophy, on the other hand, is almost unanimous in the opinion that the origin of ethics in human experience has somehow to do with human reason. Reason figures centrally and pivotally in the "social contract theory" of the origin and nature of morals in all its ancient, modern, and contemporary expressions from Protagoras, to Hobbes, to Rawls. Reason is the wellspring of virtue, according to both Plato and Aristotle, and of categorical imperatives, according to Kant. In short, the weight of Western philosophy inclines to the view that we are moral beings because we are rational beings. The ongoing sophistication of reason and the progressive illumination it sheds upon the good and the right explain "the ethical sequence," the historical growth and development of morality, noticed by Leopold.

An evolutionary natural historian, however, cannot be satisfied with either of these general accounts of the origin and development of ethics. The idea that God gave morals to man is ruled out in principle—as any supernatural explanation of a natural phenomenon is ruled out in principle in natural science. And while morality might *in principle* be a function of human reason (as, say, mathematical calculation clearly is), to suppose that it is so *in fact* would be to put the cart before the horse. Reason appears to be a delicate, variable, and recently emerged faculty. It cannot, under any circumstances, be supposed to have evolved in the absence of complex linguistic capabilities which depend, in turn, for their evolution upon a highly developed social matrix. But we cannot have become social beings unless we assumed limitations on freedom of action in the struggle for existence. Hence we must have become ethical before we became rational.

Darwin, probably in consequence of reflections somewhat like these, turned to a minority tradition of modern philosophy for a moral psychology consistent with and useful to a general evolutionary account of ethical phenomena. A century earlier, Scottish philosophers David Hume and Adam Smith had argued that ethics rest upon feelings or "sentiments"— which, to be sure, may be both amplified and informed by reason.[7] And since in the animal kingdom feelings or sentiments are arguably far more common or widespread than reason, they would be a far more likely starting point for an evolutionary account of the origin and growth of ethics.

Darwin's account, to which Leopold unmistakably (if elliptically) alludes in "The Land Ethic," begins with the parental and filial affections common, perhaps, to all mammals.[8] Bonds of affection and sympathy between parents and offspring permitted the formation of small, closely kin social groups, Darwin argued. Should the parental and filial affections bonding family members chance to extend to less closely related individuals, that would permit an enlargement of the family group. And should the newly extended community more successfully defend itself and/or more efficiently provision itself, the inclusive fitness of its members severally would be increased, Darwin reasoned. Thus, the more diffuse familial affections, which Darwin (echoing Hume and Smith) calls the "social sentiments," would be spread throughout a population.[9]

Morality, properly speaking—i.e., morality as opposed to mere altruistic instinct—requires, in Darwin's terms, "intellectual powers" sufficient to recall the past and imagine the future, "the power of language" sufficient to express "common opinion," and "habituation" to patterns of behavior deemed, by common opinion, to be socially acceptable and beneficial.[10] Even so, ethics proper, in Darwin's account, remains firmly rooted in moral feelings or social sentiments which were—no less than physical faculties, he expressly avers—naturally selected, by the advantages for survival and especially for successful reproduction, afforded by society.[11]

The protosociobiological perspective on ethical phenomena, to which Leopold as a natural historian was heir, leads him to a generalization which is remarkably explicit in his condensed and often merely resonant rendering of Darwin's more deliberate and extended paradigm: Since "the thing [ethics] has its origin in the tendency of interdependent individuals or groups to evolve modes of co-operation,. . .all ethics so far evolved rest upon a single premise: that the individual is a member of a community of interdependent parts" (202–3).

Hence, we may expect to find that the scope and specific content of ethics will reflect both the perceived boundaries and actual structure or organization of a cooperative community or society. *Ethics and society or community are correlative.* This single, simple principle constitutes a powerful tool for the analysis of moral natural history, for the anticipation of future moral development (including, ultimately, the land ethic), and for

systematically deriving the specific precepts, the prescriptions and pro-
scriptions, of an emergent and culturally unprecedented ethic like a land
or environmental ethic.

Anthropological studies of ethics reveal that in fact the boundaries of the
moral community are generally coextensive with the perceived boundaries
of society.[12] And the peculiar (and, from the urbane point of view, sometimes inverted) representation of virtue and vice in tribal society—the
virtue, for example, of sharing to the point of personal destitution and the
vice of privacy and private property—reflects and fosters the life way of
tribal peoples.[13] Darwin, in his leisurely, anecdotal discussion, paints a
vivid picture of the intensity, peculiarity, and sharp circumscription of
"savage" mores: "A savage will risk his life to save that of a member of the
same community, but will be wholly indifferent about a stranger."[14] As
Darwin portrays them, tribes people are at once paragons of virtue "within
the limits of the same tribe" and enthusiastic thieves, manslaughterers, and
torturers without.[15]

For purposes of more effective defense against common enemies, or
because of increased population density, or in response to innovations in
subsistence methods and technologies, or for some mix of these or other
forces, human societies have grown in extent or scope and changed in form
or structure. Nations—like the Iroquois nation or the Sioux nation—came
into being upon the merger of previously separate and mutually hostile
tribes. Animals and plants were domesticated and erstwhile hunter-gath-
erers became herders and farmers. Permanent habitations were established.
Trade, craft, and (later) industry flourished. With each change in society
came corresponding and correlative changes in ethics. The moral community expanded to become coextensive with the newly drawn boundaries of
societies and the representation of virtue and vice, right and wrong, good
and evil, changed to accommodate, foster, and preserve the economic and
institutional organization of emergent social orders.

Today we are witnessing the painful birth of a human super-commu-
nity, global in scope. Modern transportation and communication technologies, international economic interdependencies, international economic
entities, and nuclear arms have brought into being a "global village." It has
not yet become fully formed and it is at tension—a very dangerous tension—with its predecessor, the nation-state. Its eventual institutional structure, a global federalism or whatever it may turn out to be, is, at this point,
completely unpredictable. Interestingly, however, a corresponding global
human ethic—the "human rights" ethic, as it is popularly called—has been
more definitely articulated.

Most educated people today pay lip service at least to the ethical
precept that all members of the human species, regardless of race, creed,
or national origin, are endowed with certain fundamental rights which it

is wrong not to respect. According to the evolutionary scenario set out by Darwin, the contemporary moral ideal of human rights is a response to a perception—however vague and indefinite—that mankind worldwide is united into one society, one community—however indeterminate or yet institutionally unorganized. As Darwin presciently wrote:

> As man advances in civilization, and small tribes are united into larger communities, the simplest reason would tell each individual that he ought to extend his social instincts and sympathies to all the members of the same nation, though personally unknown to him. This point being once reached, there is only an artificial barrier to prevent his sympathies extending to the men of all nations and races. If, indeed, such men are separated from him by great differences of appearance or habits, experience unfortunately shows us how long it is, before we look at them as our fellow-creatures.[16]

According to Leopold, the next step in this sequence beyond the still incomplete ethic of universal humanity, a step that is clearly discernible on the horizon, is the land ethic. The "community concept" has, so far, propelled the development of ethics from the savage clan to the family of man. "The land ethic simply enlarges the boundary of the community to include soils, waters, plants, and animals, or collectively: the land" (204).

As the foreword to *Sand County* makes plain, the overarching thematic principle of the book is the inculcation of the idea—through narrative description, discursive exposition, abstractive generalization, and occasional preachment—"that land is a community" (viii). The community concept is "the basic concept of ecology" (viii). Once land is popularly perceived a biotic community—as it is professionally perceived in ecology—a correlative land ethic will emerge in the collective cultural consciousness.

Although anticipated as far back as the mid-eighteenth century—in the notion of an "economy of nature"—the concept of the biotic community was more fully and deliberately developed as a working model or paradigm for ecology by Charles Elton in the 1920s.[17] The natural world is organized as an intricate corporate society in which plants and animals occupy "niches," or as Elton alternatively called them, "roles" or "professions," in the economy of nature.[18] As in a feudal community, little or no socioeconomic mobility (upward or otherwise) exists in the biotic community. One is born to one's trade.

Human society, Leopold argues, is founded, in large part, upon mutual security and economic interdependency and preserved only by limitations on freedom of action in the struggle for existence—that is, by ethical constraints. Since the biotic community exhibits, as modern ecology reveals, an analogous structure, it too can be preserved, given the newly amplified impact of "mechanized man," only by analogous limitations on freedom of action—that is, by a land ethic (viii). A land ethic, furthermore, is not only "an ecological necessity," but an "evolutionary possibility" because a moral response to the natural environment—Darwin's social sympathies, sentiments, and instincts translated and codified into a body of principles and precepts—would be automatically triggered in human beings by ecology's social representation of nature (203).

Therefore, the key to the emergence of a land ethic is, simply, universal ecological literacy.

The land ethic rests upon three scientific cornerstones: (1) evolutionary and (2) ecological biology set in a background of (3) Copernican astronomy. Evolutionary theory provides the conceptual link between ethics and social organization and development. It provides a sense of "kinship with fellow-creatures" as well, "fellow-voyagers" with us in the "odyssey of evolution" (109). It establishes a diachronic link between people and nonhuman nature.

Ecological theory provides a synchronic link—the community concept—a sense of social integration of human and nonhuman nature. Human beings, plants, animals, soils, and waters are "all interlocked in one humming community of cooperations and competitions, one biota."[19] The simplest reason, to paraphrase Darwin, should, therefore, tell each individual that he or she ought to extend his or her social instincts and sympathies to all the members of the biotic community though different from him or her in appearance or habits.

And although Leopold never directly mentions it in *A Sand County Almanac,* the Copernican perspective, the perception of the Earth as "a small planet" in an immense and utterly hostile universe beyond, contributes, perhaps subconsciously, but nevertheless very powerfully, to our sense of kinship, community, and interdependence with fellow denizens of the Earth household. It scales the Earth down to something like a cozy island paradise in a desert ocean.

Here in outline, then, are the conceptual and logical foundations of the land ethic: Its conceptual elements are a Copernican cosmology, a Darwinian protosociobiological natural history of ethics, Darwinian ties of kinship among all forms of life on Earth, and an Eltonian model of the structure of biocenoses all overlaid on a Humean-Smithian moral psychology. Its logic is that natural selection has endowed human beings with an affective moral response to perceived bonds of kinship and community membership and identity; that today the natural environment, the land, is represented as a community, the biotic community; and that, therefore, an environmental or land ethic is both possible—the biopsychological and cognitive conditions are in place—and necessary, since human beings collectively have acquired the power to destroy the integrity, diversity, and stability of the environing and supporting economy of nature. In the remainder of this essay I discuss special features and problems of the land ethic germane to moral philosophy.

The most salient feature of Leopold's land ethic is its provision of what Kenneth Goodpaster has carefully called "moral considerability" for the biotic community per se, not just for fellow members of the biotic community:[20]

> In short, a land ethic changes the role of *Homo sapiens* from conqueror of the land-community to plain member and citizen of it. It implies respect for his fellow-members, *and also respect for the community as such.* (204, emphasis added)

The land ethic, thus, has a holistic as well as an individualistic cast.

Indeed, as "The Land Ethic" develops, the focus of moral concern shifts gradually away from plants, animals, soils, and waters severally to the biotic community collectively. Toward the middle, in the subsection called Substitutes for a Land Ethic, Leopold invokes the "biotic rights" of *species*—as the context indicates—of wildflowers, songbirds, and predators. In The Outlook, the climactic section of "The Land Ethic," nonhuman natural entities, first appearing as fellow members, then considered in profile as species, are not so much as mentioned in what might be called the "summary moral maxim" of the land ethic: "A thing is right when it tends to preserve the integrity, stability, and beauty of the biotic community. It is wrong when it tends otherwise" (224–25).

By this measure of right and wrong, not only would it be wrong for a farmer, in the interest of higher profits, to clear the woods off a 75 percent slope, turn his cows into the clearing, and dump its rainfall, rocks, and soil into the community creek, it would also be wrong for the federal fish and wildlife agency, in the interest of individual animal welfare, to permit populations of deer, rabbits, feral burros, or whatever to increase unchecked and thus to threaten the integrity, stability, and beauty of the biotic communities of which they are members. The land ethic not only provides moral considerability for the biotic community per se, but ethical consideration of its individual members is preempted by concern for the preservation of the integrity, stability, and beauty of the biotic community. The land ethic, thus, not only has a holistic aspect; it is holistic with a vengeance.

The holism of the land ethic, more than any other feature, sets it apart from the predominant paradigm of modern moral philosophy. It is, therefore, the feature of the land ethic which requires the most patient theoretical analysis and the most sensitive practical interpretation.

As Kenneth Goodpaster pointed out, mainstream modern ethical philosophy has taken egoism as its point of departure and reached a wider circle of moral entitlement by a process of generalization:[21] I am sure that *I*, the enveloped ego, am intrinsically or inherently valuable and thus that *my* interests ought to be considered, taken into account, by "others" when their actions may substantively affect *me.* My own claim to moral consideration, according to the conventional wisdom, ultimately rests upon a psychological capacity—rationality or sentiency were the classical candidates of Kant and Bentham, respectively—which is arguably valuable in itself and which thus qualifies *me* for moral standing.[22] However, then I am forced grudgingly to grant the same moral consideration I demand from others, on this basis, to those others who can also claim to possess the same general psychological characteristic.

A *criterion* of moral value and consideration is thus identified. Goodpaster convincingly argues that mainstream modern moral theory is based, when all the learned dust has settled, on this simple paradigm of ethical justification and logic exemplified by the Benthamic and Kantian prototypes.[23] If the criterion of moral values and consideration is pitched low enough—as it is in Bentham's criterion of sentiency—a wide variety of animals are admitted to moral entitlement.[24] If the criterion of moral value and consideration is pushed lower still—as it is in Albert Schweitzer's reverence-for-life ethic—all minimally conative things (plants as well as animals) would be extended moral considerability.[25] The contemporary animal liberation/rights, and reverence-for-life/life-principle ethics are, at bottom, simply direct applications of the modern classical paradigm of moral argument. But this standard modern model of ethical theory provides no possibility whatever for the moral consideration of wholes—of threatened *populations* of animals and plants, or of endemic, rare, or endangered *species*, or of biotic *communities*, or most expansively, of the *biosphere* in its totality—since wholes per se have no psychological experience of any kind.[26] Because mainstream modern moral theory has been "psychocentric," it has been radically and intractably individualistic or "atomistic" in its fundamental theoretical orientation.

Hume, Smith, and Darwin diverged from the prevailing theoretical model by recognizing that altruism is as fundamental and autochthonous in human nature as is egoism. According to their analysis, moral value is not identified with a natural quality objectively present in morally considerable beings—as reason and/or sentiency is objectively present in people and/or animals—it is, as it were, projected by valuing subjects.[27]

Hume and Darwin, furthermore, recognize inborn moral sentiments which have society as such as their natural object. Hume insists that "we must renounce the theory which accounts for every moral sentiment by the principle of self-love. We must adopt a more *public affection* and allow that the *interests of society* are not, *even on their own account,* entirely indifferent to us."[28] And Darwin, somewhat ironically (since "Darwinian evolution" very often means natural selection operating exclusively with respect to individuals), sometimes writes as if morality had no other object than the commonweal, the welfare of the community as a corporate entity:

> We have now seen that actions are regarded by savages, and were probably so regarded by primeval man, as good or bad, solely as they obviously affect the welfare of the tribe,—not that of the species, nor that of the individual member of the tribe. This conclusion agrees well with the belief that the so-called moral sense is aboriginally derived from social instincts, for both relate at first exclusively to the community.[29]

Theoretically then, the biotic community owns what Leopold, in the lead paragraph of The Outlook, calls "value in the philosophical sense"—i.e., direct moral considerability—because it is a newly discovered proper object of a specially evolved "public affection" or "moral sense" which all psychologically normal human beings have inherited from a long line of ancestral social primates.[30]

In the land ethic, as in all earlier stages of social-ethical evolution, there exists a tension between the good of the community as a whole and the "rights" of its individual members considered severally. While The Ethical Sequence section of "The Land Ethic" clearly evokes Darwin's classical biosocial account of the origin and extension of morals, Leopold is actually more explicitly concerned, in that section, with the interplay between the holistic and individualistic moral sentiments—between sympathy and fellow-feeling on the one hand, and public affection for the commonweal on the other:

> The first ethics dealt with the relation between individuals; the Mosaic Decalogue is an example. Later accretions dealt with the relation between the individual and society. The Golden Rule tries to integrate the individual to society; democracy to integrate social organization to the individual. (202–3)

Actually, it is doubtful that the first ethics dealt with the relation between individuals and not at all with the relation between the individual and society. (This, along with the remark that ethics replaced an "original free-for-all competition," suggests that Leopold's Darwinian line of thought has been uncritically tainted with Hobbesean elements. [202]. Of course, Hobbes's "state of nature," in which there prevailed a war of each against all, is absurd from an evolutionary point of view.) A century of ethnographic studies seems to confirm, rather, Darwin's conjecture that the relative weight of the holistic component is greater in tribal ethics—the tribal ethic of the Hebrews recorded in the Old Testament constitutes a vivid case in point—than in more recent accretions. The Golden Rule, on the other hand, does not mention, in any of its formulations, society per se. Rather, its primary concern seems to be "others," i.e., other human individuals.

Democracy, with its stress on individual liberties and rights, seems to further rather than countervail the individualistic thrust of the Golden Rule.

In any case, the conceptual foundations of the land ethic provide a well-formed, self-consistent theoretical basis for including both fellow members of the biotic community and the biotic community itself (considered as a corporate entity) within the purview of morals. The preemptive emphasis, however, on the welfare of the community as a whole, in Leopold's articulation of the land ethic, while certainly *consistent* with its Humean-Darwinian theoretical foundations, is not *determined* by them alone. The overriding holism of the land ethic results, rather, more from the way our moral sensibilities are informed by ecology.

Ecological thought, historically, has tended to be holistic in outlook.[31] Ecology is the study of the *relationships* of organisms to one another and to the elemental environment. These relationships bind the *relata*—plants, animals, soils, and waters—into a seamless fabric. The ontological primary of objects and the ontological subordination of relationships, characteristic of classical Western science, is, in fact, reversed in ecology.[32] Ecological relationships determine the nature of organisms rather than the other way around. A species is what it is because it has adapted to a niche in the ecosystem. The whole, the system itself, thus, literally and quite straightforwardly shapes and forms its component parts.

Antedating Charles Elton's community model of ecology was F. E. Clements' and S. A. Forbes's organism model.[33] Plants and animals, soils and waters, according to this paradigm, are integrated into one superorganism. Species are, as it were, its organs; specimens its cells. Although Elton's community paradigm (later modified, as we shall see, by Arthur Tansley's ecosystem idea) is the principal and morally fertile ecological concept of "The Land Ethic," the more radically holistic superorganism paradigm of Clements and Forbes resonates in "The Land Ethic" as an audible overtone. In the peroration of Land Health and the A-B Cleavage, for example, which immediately precedes The Outlook, Leopold insists that

> in all of these cleavages, we see repeated the same basic paradoxes: man the conqueror *versus* man the biotic citizen; science the sharpener of his sword *versus* science the searchlight on his universe; land the slave and servant *versus* land the collective organism. (223)

And on more than one occasion Leopold, in the latter quarter of "The Land Ethic," talks about the "health" and "disease" of the land—terms which are at once descriptive and normative and which, taken literally, characterize only organisms proper.

In an early essay, "Some Fundamentals of Conservation in the Southwest," Leopold speculatively flirted with the intensely holistic superorganism model of the environment as a paradigm pregnant with moral implications:

> It is at least not impossible to regard the earth's parts—soil, mountains, rivers, atmosphere, etc.—as organs or parts of organs, of *a co-ordinated whole,* each part with a definite function. And if we could see *this whole, as a whole,* through a great period of time, we might perceive not only organs with coordinated functions, but possibly also that process of consumption and replacement which in biology we call metabolism, or growth. In such a case we would have all the visible attributes of a living thing, which we do not realize to be such because it is too big, and its life processes too slow. And there would also follow that invisible attribute—a soul or consciousness—which. . .many philosophers of all ages ascribe to all living things and aggregates thereof, including the "dead" earth.
> Possibly in our intuitive perceptions, which may be truer than our science and less impeded by words than our philosophies, we realize the indivisibility of the earth—its soil, mountains, rivers, forests, climate, plants, and animals—and *respect it collectively* not only as a useful servant but as a living being, vastly less alive than ourselves, but vastly greater than ourselves in time and space. . . .Philosophy, then, suggests one reason why we cannot destroy the earth with moral impunity; namely, that the "dead" earth is an organism possessing a certain kind and degree of life, which we intuitively respect as such.[34]

Had Leopold retained this overall theoretical approach in "The Land Ethic," the land ethic would doubtless have enjoyed more critical attention from philosophers. The moral foundations of a land or, as he might then have called it, "earth" ethic, would rest upon the hypothesis that the Earth is alive and ensouled—possessing inherent psychological characteristics, logically parallel to reason and sentiency. This notion of a conative whole Earth could plausibly have served as a general criterion of intrinsic worth and moral considerability, in the familiar format of mainstream moral thought.

Part of the reason, therefore, that "The Land Ethic" emphasizes more and more the integrity, stability, and beauty of the environment as a whole, and less and less the "biotic right" of individual plants and animals to life, liberty, and the pursuit of happiness, is that the superorganism ecological paradigm invites one, much more than does the community paradigm, to hypostatize, to reify the whole, and to subordinate its individual members.

In any case, as we see, rereading "The Land Ethic" in light of "Some Fundamentals," the whole Earth organism image of nature is vestigially present in Leopold's later thinking. Leopold may have abandoned the "earth ethic" because ecology had abandoned the organism analogy, in favor of the community analogy, as a working theoretical paradigm. And the community model was more suitably given moral implications by the social/sentimental ethical natural history of Hume and Darwin.

Meanwhile, the biotic community ecological paradigm itself had acquired, by the late thirties and forties, a more holistic cast of its own. In 1935 British ecologist Arthur Tansley pointed out that from the perspective of physics the "currency" of the "economy of nature" is energy.[35] Tansley suggested that Elton's qualitative and descriptive food chains, food webs, trophic niches, and biosocial professions could be quantitatively expressed by means of a thermodynamic flow model. It is Tansley's state-of-the-art thermodynamic paradigm of the environment that Leopold explicitly sets out as a "mental image of land" in relation to which "we can be ethical" (214). And it is the ecosystemic model of land which informs the cardinal practical precepts of the land ethic.

The Land Pyramid is the pivotal section of "The Land Ethic"—the section which effects a complete transition from concern for "fellow-members" to the "community as such." It is also its longest and most technical section. A description of the "ecosystem" (Tansley's deliberately non-metaphorical term) begins with the sun. Solar energy "flows through a circuit called the biota" (215). It enters the biota through the leaves of green plants and courses through plant-eating animals, and then on to omnivores and carnivores. At last the tiny fraction of solar energy converted to biomass by green plants remaining in the corpse of a predator, animal feces, plant detritus, or other dead organic material is garnered by decomposers—worms, fungi, and bacteria. They recycle the participating elements and degrade into entropic equilibrium any remaining energy. According to this paradigm

> land, then, is not merely soil; it is a fountain of energy flowing through a circuit of soils, plants, and animals. Food chains are the living channels which conduct energy upward; death and decay return it to the soil. The circuit is not closed;. . .but it is a sustained circuit, like a slowly augmented revolving fund of life. (216)

In this exceedingly abstract (albeit poetically expressed) model of nature, process precedes substance and energy is more fundamental than matter. Individual plants and animals become less autonomous beings than ephemeral structures in a patterned flux of energy. According to Yale biophysicist Harold Morowitz,

> viewed from the point of view of modern [ecology], each living thing. . .is a dissipative structure, that is it does not endure in and of itself but only as a result of the continual flow of energy in the system. An example might be instructive. Consider a vortex in a stream of flowing water. The vortex is a structure made of an ever-changing group of water molecules. It does not exist as an entity in the classical Western sense; it exists only because of the flow of water through the stream. In the same sense, the structures out of which biological entities are made are transient, unstable entities with constantly changing molecules, dependent on a constant flow of energy from food in

order to maintain form and structure. . . .From this point of view the reality of individuals is problematic because they do not exist per se but only as local perturbations in this universal energy flow.[36]

Though less bluntly stated and made more palatable by the unfailing charm of his prose, Leopold's proffered mental image of land is just as expansive, systemic, and distanced as Morowitz's. The maintenance of "the complex structure of the land and its smooth functioning as an energy unit" emerges in The Land Pyramid as the *summum bonum* of the land ethic (216).

From this good Leopold derives several practical principles slightly less general, and therefore more substantive, than the summary moral maxim of the land ethic distilled in The Outlook. "The trend of evolution [not its "goal," since evolution is ateleological] is to elaborate and diversify the biota" (216). Hence, among our cardinal duties is the duty to preserve what species we can, especially those at the apex of the pyramid—the top carnivores. "In the beginning, the pyramid of life was low and squat; the food chains short and simple. Evolution has added layer after layer, link after link" (215–16). Human activities today, especially those, like systematic deforestation in the tropics, resulting in abrupt massive extinctions of species, are in effect "devolutionary"; they flatten the biotic pyramid; they choke off some of the channels and gorge others (those which terminate in our own species).[37]

The land ethic does not enshrine the ecological status quo and devalue the dynamic dimension of nature. Leopold explains that "evolution is a long series of self-induced changes, the net result of which has been to elaborate the flow mechanism and to lengthen the circuit. Evolutionary changes, however, are usually slow and local. Man's invention of tools has enabled him to make changes of unprecedented violence, rapidity, and scope" (216–17). "Natural" species extinction, i.e., species extinction in the normal course of evolution, occurs when a species is replaced by competitive exclusion or evolves into another form.[38] Normally speciation outpaces extinction. Mankind inherited a richer, more diverse world than had ever existed before in the 3.5 billion-year odyssey of life on Earth.[39] What is wrong with anthropogenic species extirpation and extinction is the *rate* at which it is occurring and the *result:* biological impoverishment instead of enrichment.

Leopold goes on here to condemn, in terms of its impact on the ecosystem, "the world-wide pooling of faunas and floras," i.e., the indiscriminate introduction of exotic and domestic species and the dislocation of native and endemic species; mining the soil for its stored biotic energy, leading ultimately to diminished fertility and to erosion; and polluting and damming water courses (217).

According to the land ethic, therefore: Thou shalt not extirpate or render species extinct; thou shalt exercise great caution in introducing exotic and domestic species into local ecosystems, in extracting energy from the soil and releasing it into the biota, and in damming or polluting water courses; and thou shalt be especially solicitous of predatory birds and mammals. Here in brief are the express moral precepts of the land ethic. They are all explicitly informed—not to say derived—from the energy circuit model of the environment.

The living channels—"food chains"—through which energy courses are composed of individual plants and animals. A central, stark fact lies at the heart of ecological processes: Energy, the currency of the economy nature, passes from one organism to another, not from hand to hand, like coined money, but so to speak, from stomach to stomach. Eating *and being eaten,* living *and dying* are what make the biotic community hum.

The precepts of the land ethic, like those of all previous accretions, reflect and reinforce the structure of the community to which it is correlative. Trophic asymmetries constitute the kernel of the biotic community. It seems unjust, unfair. But that is how the economy of nature is organized (and has been for thousands of millions of years). The land ethic, thus, affirms as good, and strives to preserve, the very inequities in nature whose social counterparts in human communities are condemned as bad and would be eradicated by familiar social ethics, especially by the more recent Christian and secular egalitarian exemplars. A "right to life" for individual members is not consistent with the structure of the biotic community and hence is not mandated by the land ethic. This disparity between the land ethic and its more familiar social precedents contributes to the apparent devaluation of individual *members* of the biotic community and augments and reinforces the tendency of the land ethic, driven by the systemic vision of ecology, toward a more holistic or community-per-se orientation.

Of the few moral philosophers who have given the land ethic a moment's serious thought, most have regarded it with horror because of its emphasis on the good of the community and its deemphasis on the welfare of individual members of the community. Not only are other sentient creatures members of the biotic community and subordinate to its integrity, beauty, and stability; so are *we.* Thus, if it is not only morally permissible, from the point of view of the land ethic, but morally required, that members of certain species be abandoned to predation and other vicissitudes of wild life or even deliberately culled (as in the case of alert and sentient whitetail deer) for the sake of the integrity, stability, and beauty of the biotic community, how can we consistently exempt ourselves from a similar draconian regime? We too are only "plain members and citizens" of the biotic community. And our global population is growing unchecked. According to William Aiken, from the point of view of the land ethic, therefore, "massive human diebacks would be good. It is our duty to cause them. It is our species' duty, relative to the whole, to eliminate 90 percent of our numbers." Thus, according to Tom Regan, the land ethic is a clear case of "environmental fascism."[40]

Of course Leopold never intended the land ethic to have either inhumane or antihumanitarian implications or consequences. But whether he intended them or not, a logically consistent deduction from the theoretical premises of the land ethic might force such untoward conclusions. And given their magnitude and monstrosity, these derivations would constitute a *reductio ad absurdum* of the whole land ethic enterprise and entrench and reinforce our current human chauvinism and moral alienation from nature. If this is what membership in the biotic community entails, then all but the most radical misanthropes would surely want to opt out.

The land ethic, happily, implies neither inhumane nor inhuman consequences. That some philosophers think it must follows more from their own theoretical presuppositions than from the theoretical elements of the land ethic itself. Conventional modern ethical theory rests moral entitlement, as I earlier pointed out, on a criterion or qualification. If a candidate meets the criterion—rationality or sentiency are the most commonly posited—he, she, or it is entitled to equal moral standing with others who possess the same qualification in equal degree. Hence, reasoning in this philosophically orthodox way, and forcing Leopold's theory to conform: if human beings are, with other animals, plants, soils, and waters, equally members of the biotic community, and if community membership is the criterion of equal moral consideration, then not only do animals, plants, soils, and waters have equal (highly attenuated) "rights," but human beings are equally subject to the same subordination of individual welfare and rights in respect to the good of the community as a whole.

But the land ethic, as I have been at pains to point out, is heir to a line of moral analysis different from that institutionalized in contemporary moral philosophy. From the biosocial evolutionary analysis of ethics upon which Leopold builds the land ethic, it (the land ethic) neither replaces nor overrides previous accretions. Prior moral sensibilities and obligations attendant upon and correlative to prior strata of social involvement remain operative and preemptive.

Being citizens of the United States, or the United Kingdom, or the Soviet Union, or Venezuela, or some other nation-state, and therefore having national obligations and patriotic duties, does not mean that we are not also members of smaller communities or social groups—cities or townships, neighborhoods, and families—or that we are relieved of the peculiar moral responsibilities attendant upon and correlative to these memberships as well. Similarly, our recognition of the biotic community and our immersion in it does not imply that we do not also remain members of the human community—the "family of man" or "global village"—or that we are relieved of the attendant and correlative moral responsibilities of that membership, among them to respect universal human rights and uphold the principles of individual human worth and dignity. The biosocial development of morality does not grow in extent like an expanding balloon, leaving no trace of its previous boundaries, so much as like the circumference of a tree.[41] Each emergent, and larger, social unit is layered over the more primitive, and intimate, ones.

Moreover, as a general rule, the duties correlative to the inner social circles to which we belong eclipse those correlative to the rings farther from the heartwood when conflicts arise. Consider our moral revulsion when zealous ideological nationalists encourage children to turn their parents in to the authorities if their parents should dissent from the political or economic doctrines of the ruling party. A zealous environmentalist who advocated visiting war, famine, or pestilence on human populations (those existing somewhere else, of course) in the name of the integrity, beauty, and stability of the biotic community would be similarly perverse. Family obligations in general come before nationalistic duties and humanitarian obligations in general come before environmental duties. The land ethic, therefore, is not draconian or fascist. It does not cancel human morality. The land ethic may, however, as with any new accretion, demand choices which affect, in turn, the demands of the more interior social-ethical circles. Taxes and the military draft may conflict with family-level obligations. While the land ethic, certainly, does not cancel human morality, neither does it leave it unaffected.

Nor is the land ethic inhumane. Nonhuman fellow members of the biotic community have no "human rights," because they are not, by definition, members of the human community. As fellow members of the biotic community, however, they deserve respect.

How exactly to express or manifest respect, while at the same time abandoning our fellow members of the biotic community to their several fates or even actively consuming them for our own needs (and wants), or deliberately making them casualties of wildlife management for ecological integrity, is a difficult and delicate question.

Fortunately, American Indian and other traditional patterns of human-nature interaction provide rich and detailed models. Algonkian woodland peoples, for instance, represented animals, plants, birds, waters, and minerals as other-than-human persons engaged in reciprocal, mutually beneficial socioeconomic intercourse with human beings.[42] Tokens of payment, together with expressions of apology, were routinely offered to the beings whom it was necessary for these Indians to exploit. Care not to waste the usable parts, and care in the disposal of unusable animal and plant remains, were also an aspect of the respectful, albeit necessarily consumptive, Algonkian relationship with fellow members of the land community. As I have more fully argued elsewhere, the Algonkian portrayal of human-nature relationships is, indeed, although certainly different in specifics, identical in abstract form to that recommended by Leopold in the land ethic.[43]

Ernest Partridge has turned the existence of an American Indian land ethic, however, against the historicity of the biosocial theoretical foundations of the land ethic:

> Anthropologists will find much to criticize in [Leopold's] account. . . .The anthropologist will point out that in many primitive cultures, far greater moral concern may be given to animals or even to trees, rocks, and mountains, than are given to persons in other tribes. . . .Thus we find not an "extension of ethics," but a "leap-frogging" of ethics, over and beyond persons to natural beings and objects. Worse still for Leopold's view, a primitive culture's moral concern for nature often appears to "draw back" to a human centered perspective as that culture evolves toward a civilized condition.[44]

Actually, the apparent historical anomalies, which Partridge points out, confirm, rather than confute, Leopold's ethical sequence. At the tribal stage of human social evolution, a member of another tribe was a member of a separate and independent social organization, and hence of a separate and alien moral community; thus, "[human] persons in other tribes" were not extended moral consideration, just as the biosocial model predicts. However, at least among those tribal people whose world view I have studied in detail, the animals, trees, rocks, and mountains of a tribe's territory were portrayed as working members and trading partners of the local community. Totem representation of clan units within tribal communities facilitated this view. Groups of people were identified as cranes, bears, turtles, and so on; similarly, populations of deer, beaver, fox, etc., were clans of "people"—people who liked going about in outlandish get-ups. Frequent episodes in tribal mythologies of "metamorphosis"—the change from animal to human form and vice versa—further cemented the tribal integration of local nonhuman natural entities. It would be very interesting to know if the flora and fauna living in another tribe's territory would be regarded, like its human members, as beyond the moral pale.

Neither does the " 'draw-back' to a human centered [ethical] perspective as [a] culture evolves toward a civilized condition," noticed by Partridge, undermine the biosocial theoretical foundations of the land ethic. Rather, the biosocial theoretical foundations of the land ethic elucidate this historical phenomenon as well. As a culture evolves toward civilization, it increasingly distances itself from the biotic community. "*Civil*ization" means "cityfication"—inhabitation of and participation in an artificial, humanized environment and a corresponding perception of isolation and alienation from nature. Nonhuman natural entities, thus, are divested of their status as members in good standing of the moral community as civilization develops. Today, two processes internal to civilization are bringing us to a recognition that our renunciation of our biotic citizenship was a mistaken self-deception. Evolutionary science and ecological science, which certainly are products of modern civilization now supplanting the anthropomorphic and anthropocentric myths of earlier civilized generations, have rediscovered our integration with the biotic community. And the negative feedback received from modern civilization's technological impact upon nature—pollution, biological impoverishment, etc.—forcefully reminds us that mankind never really has, despite past assumptions to the contrary, existed apart from the environing biotic community.

This reminder of our recent rediscovery of our biotic citizenship brings us face to face with the paradox posed by Peter Fritzell.[45] Either we are plain members and citizens of the biotic community, on a par with other creatures, or we are not. If we are, then we have no moral obligations to our fellow members or to the community per se because, as understood from a modern scientific perspective, nature and natural phenomena are amoral. Wolves and alligators do no wrong in killing and eating deer and dogs (respectively). Elephants cannot be blamed for bulldozing acacia trees and generally wreaking havoc in their natural habitats. If human beings are natural beings, then human behavior, however destructive, is natural behavior and is as blameless, from a natural point of view, as any other behavioral phenomenon exhibited by other natural beings. On the other hand, we are moral beings, the implication seems clear, precisely to the extent that we are civilized, that we have removed ourselves from nature. We are more than natural beings; we are metanatural—not to say, "supernatural"—beings. But then our moral community is limited to only those beings who share our transcendence of nature, i.e., to human beings (and perhaps to pets who have joined our civilized community as surrogate persons) and to the human community. Hence, have it either way—we are members of the biotic community or we are not—a land or environmental ethic is aborted by either choice.

But nature is *not* amoral. The tacit assumption that we are deliberating, choice-making ethical beings only to the extent that we are metanatural, civilized beings, generates this dilemma. The biosocial analysis of human moral behavior, in which the land ethic is grounded, is designed precisely to show that in fact intelligent moral behavior *is* natural behavior. Hence, we are moral beings not in spite of, but in accordance with, nature. To the extent that nature has produced at least one ethical species, *Homo sapiens*, nature is not amoral.

Alligators, wolves, and elephants are not subject to reciprocal interspecies duties or land ethical obligations themselves because they are incapable of conceiving and/or assuming them. Alligators, as mostly solitary, entrepreneurial reptiles, have no apparent moral sentiments or social instincts whenever. And while wolves and elephants certainly do have social instincts and at least protomoral sentiments, as their social behavior amply indicates, their conception or imagination of community appears to be less culturally plastic than ours and less amenable to cognitive information. Thus, while we might regard them as ethical beings, they are not able, as we are, to form the concept of a universal biotic community, and hence conceive an all-inclusive, holistic land ethic.

The paradox of the land ethic, elaborately noticed by Fritzell, may be cast more generally still in more conventional philosophical terms: Is the land ethic prudential or deontological? Is the land ethic, in other words, a matter of enlightened (collective, human) self-interest, or does it genuinely admit nonhuman natural entities and nature as a whole to true moral standing?

The conceptual foundations of the land ethic, as I have here set them out, and much of Leopold's hortatory rhetoric, would certainly indicate that the land ethic is deontological (or duty oriented) rather than prudential. In the section significantly titled The Ecological Conscience, Leopold complains that the then-current conservation philosophy is inadequate because "it defines no right or wrong, assigns no obligation, calls for no sacrifice, implies no change in the current philosophy of values. In respect of land-use, it urges *only* enlightened self-interest" (207–8, emphasis added). Clearly, Leopold himself thinks that the land ethic goes beyond prudence. In this section he disparages mere "self-interest" two more times, and concludes that "obligations have no meaning without conscience, and the problem we face is the extension of the social conscience from people to land" (209).

In the next section, Substitutes for a Land Ethic, he mentions rights twice—the "biotic right" of birds to continuance and the absence of a right on the part of human special interest to exterminate predators.

Finally, the first sentences of The Outlook read: "It is inconceivable to me that an ethical relation to land can exist without love, respect, and admiration for land, and a high regard for its value. By value, I of course mean something far broader than mere economic value; I mean value in the philosophical sense" (223). By "value in the philosophical sense," Leopold can only mean what philosophers more technically call "intrinsic value" or "inherent worth."[46] Something that has intrinsic value or inherent worth is valuable in and of itself, not because of what it can do for us. "Obligation," "sacrifice," "conscience," "respect," the ascription of rights, and intrinsic value—all of these are consistently opposed to self-interest and seem to indicate decisively that the land ethic is of the deontological type.

Some philosophers, however, have seen it differently. Scott Lehmann, for example, writes,

> Although Leopold claims for communities of plants and animals a "right to continued existence," his argument is homocentric, appealing to the human stake in preservation. Basically it is an argument from enlightened self-interest, where the self in question is not an individual human being but humanity—present and future—as a whole. . . .[47]

Lehmann's claim has some merits, even though it flies in the face of Leopold's express commitments. Leopold does frequently lapse into the language of (collective, long-range, human) self-interest. Early on, for example, he remarks, "in human history, we have learned (I hope) that the conqueror role is eventually *self*-defeating" (204, emphasis added). And later, of the 95 percent of Wisconsin's species which cannot be "sold, fed, eaten, or otherwise put to economic use," Leopold reminds us that "these creatures are members of the biotic community, and if (as I believe) its stability depends on its integrity, they are entitled to continuance" (210). The implication is 'clear: the economic 5 percent cannot survive if a significant portion of the uneconomic 95 percent are extirpated; nor may *we*, it goes without saying, survive without these "resources."

Leopold, in fact, seems to be consciously aware of this moral paradox. Consistent with the biosocial foundations of his theory, he expresses it in sociobiological terms:

> An ethic may be regarded as a mode of guidance for meeting ecological situations so new or intricate, or involving such deferred reactions, that the path of social expediency is not discernible to the average individual. Animal instincts are modes of guidance for the individual in meeting such situations. Ethics are possibly a kind of community instinct in-the-making. (203)

From an objective, descriptive sociobiological point of view, ethics evolve because they contribute to the inclusive fitness of their carriers (or, more reductively still, to the multiplication of their carriers' genes); they are expedient. However, the path to self-interest (or to the self-interest of the selfish gene) is not discernible to the participating individuals (nor, certainly, to their genes). Hence, ethics are grounded in instinctive feeling—love, sympathy, respect—not in self-conscious calculating intelligence. Somewhat like the paradox of hedonism—the notion that one cannot achieve happiness if one directly pursues happiness per se and not other things—one can only secure self-interest by putting the interests of others on a par with one's own (in this case long-range collective human self-interest and the interest of other forms of life and of the biotic community per se).

So, is the land ethic deontological or prudential, after all? It is both—self-consistently both—depending upon point of view. From the inside, from the lived, felt point of view of the community member with evolved moral sensibilities, it is deontological. It involves an affective-cognitive posture of genuine love, respect, admiration, obligation, self-sacrifice, conscience, duty, and the ascription of intrinsic value and biotic rights. From the outside, from the objective and analytic scientific point of view, it is prudential. "There is no other way for land to survive the impact of mechanized man," nor, therefore, for mechanized man to survive his own impact upon the land (viii).

NOTES

1. Wallace Stegner, "The Legacy of Aldo Leopold"; Curt Meine, "Building 'The Land Ethic' "; both in J. Baird Callicott, ed., *Companion to A Sand County Almanac: Interpretive and Critical Essays* (Madison: University of Wisconsin Press, 1987), 233–245, 172–185, respectively. The oft-repeated characterization of Leopold as a prophet appears traceable to Roberts Mann, "Aldo Leopold: Priest and Prophet," *American Forests* 60, no. 8 (August 1954): 23, 42–43; it was picked up, apparently, by Ernest Swift, "Aldo Leopold: Wisconsin's Conservationist Prophet," *Wisconsin Tales and Trails* 2, no. 2 (September 1961): 2–5; Roderick Nash institutionalized it in his chapter, "Aldo Leopold: Prophet," in *Wilderness and the American Mind* (New Haven: Yale University Press, 1967; revised edition, 1982).
2. John Passmore, *Man's Responsibility for* [significantly not "to"] *Nature: Ecological Problems and Western Traditions* (New York: Charles Scribner's Sons, 1974).
3. H. J. McCloskey, *Ecological Ethics and Politics* (Totowa, N.J.: Rowman and Littlefield, 1983), 46.
4. Robin Attfield, in "Value in the Wilderness," *Metaphilosophy* 15 (1984), writes, "Leopold the philosopher is something of a disaster, and I dread the thought of the student whose concept of philosophy is modeled principally on these extracts. (Can value 'in the philosophical sense' be contrasted with instrumental value? If concepts of right and wrong did not apply to slaves in Homeric Greece, how could Odysseus suspect the slavegirls of 'misbehavior'? If all ethics rest on interdependence how are obligations to infants and small children possible? And how can 'obligations have no meaning without conscience,' granted that the notion of conscience is conceptually dependent on that of obligation?)" (294). L. W. Sumner, "Review of Robin Attfield, *The Ethics of Environmental Concern*," *Environmental Ethics* 8 (1986): 77.
5. Edward O. Wilson, *Sociobiology: The New Synthesis* (Cambridge: Harvard University Press, 1975), 3. See also W.D. Hamilton, "The Genetical Theory of Social Behavior," *Journal of Theoretical Biology* 7 (1964): 1–52.
6. Charles R. Darwin, *The Descent of Man and Selection in Relation to Sex* (New York: J. A. Hill and Company, 1904). The quoted phrase occurs on p. 97.
7. See Adam Smith, *Theory of the Moral Sentiments* (London and Edinburgh: A. Millar, A. Kinkaid, and J. Bell, 1759) and David Hume, *An Enquiry Concerning the Principles of Morals* (Oxford: The Clarendon Press, 1777; first published in 1751). Darwin cites both works in the key fourth chapter of *Descent* (pp. 106 and 109, respectively).
8. Darwin, *Descent*, 98ff.
9. Ibid., 105f.
10. Ibid., 113ff.
11. Ibid., 105.

12. See, for example, Elman R. Service, *Primitive Social Organization: An Evolutionary Perspective* (New York: Random House, 1962).
13. See Marshall Sahlins, *Stone Age Economics* (Chicago: Aldine Atherton, 1972).
14. Darwin, *Descent*, 111.
15. Ibid., 117ff. The quoted phrase occurs on p. 118.
16. Ibid., 124.
17. See Donald Worster, *Nature's Economy: The Roots of Ecology* (San Francisco: Sierra Club Books, 1977).
18. Charles Elton, *Animal Ecology* (New York: Macmillan, 1927).
19. Aldo Leopold, *Round River* (New York: Oxford University Press, 1953), 148.
20. Kenneth Goodpaster, "On Being Morally Considerable," *Journal of Philosophy* 22 (1978): 308–25. Goodpaster wisely avoids the term *rights*, defined so strictly albeit so variously by philosophers, and used so loosely by non-philosophers.
21. Kenneth Goodpaster, "From Egoism to Environmentalism" in *Ethics and Problems of the 21st Century*, ed. K. E. Goodpaster and K. M. Sayre (Notre Dame, Ind.: University of Notre Dame Press, 1979), 21–35.
22. See Immanuel Kant, *Foundations of the Metaphysics of Morals* (New York: Bobbs-Merrill, 1959; first published in 1785); and Jeremy Bentham, *An Introduction to the Principles of Morals and Legislation*, new edition (Oxford: The Clarendon Press, 1823).
23. Goodpaster, "Egoism to Environmentalism." Actually Goodpaster regards Hume and Kant as the cofountainheads of this sort of moral philosophy. But Hume does not reason in this way. For Hume, the other-oriented sentiments are as primitive as self-love.
24. See Peter Singer, *Animal Liberation: A New Ethics for Our Treatment of Animals* (New York: Avon Books, 1975) for animal liberation; and see Tom Regan, *All That Dwell Therein: Animal Rights and Environmental Ethics* (Berkeley: University of California Press, 1982) for animal rights.
25. See Albert Schweitzer, *Philosophy of Civilization: Civilization and Ethics*, trans. John Naish (London: A. & C. Black, 1923). For a fuller discussion see J. Baird Callicott, "On the Intrinsic Value of Non-human Species," in *The Preservation of Species*, ed Bryan Norton (Princeton: Princeton University Press, 1986), 138–72.
26. Peter Singer and Tom Regan are both proud of this circumstance and consider it a virtue. See Peter Singer, "Not for Humans Only: The Place of Nonhumans in Environmental Issues" in *Ethics and Problems of the 21st Century*, 191–206; and Tom Regan, "Ethical Vegetarianism and Commercial Animal Farming" in *Contemporary Moral Problems*, ed. James E. White (St. Paul, Minn.: West Publishing Co., 1985), 279–94.
27. See J. Baird Callicott, "Hume's Is/Ought Dichotomy and the Relation of Ecology to Leopold's Land Ethic," *Environmental Ethics* 4 (1982): 163–74, and "Non-anthropocentric Value Theory and Environmental Ethics," *American Philosophical Quarterly* 21 (1984): 299–309, for an elaboration.
28. Hume, *Enquiry*, 219.
29. Darwin, *Descent*, 120.
30. I have elsewhere argued that "value in the philosophical sense" means "intrinsic" or "inherent" value. See J. Baird Callicott, "The Philosophical Value of Wildlife," in *Valuing Wildlife: Economic and Social Values of Wildlife*, ed. Daniel J. Decker and Gary Goff (Boulder, Col.: Westview Press, 1986), 214–221.
31. See Worster, *Nature's Economy*.

32. See J. Baird Callicott, "The Metaphysical Implications of Ecology," *Environmental Ethics* 8 (1986): 300–315, for an elaboration of this point.
33. Robert P. McIntosh, *The Background of Ecology: Concept and Theory* (Cambridge: Cambridge University Press, 1985).
34. Aldo Leopold, "Some Fundamentals of Conservation in the Southwest," *Environmental Ethics* 1 (1979): 139–40, emphasis added.
35. Arthur Tansley, "The Use and Abuse of Vegetational Concepts and Terms," *Ecology* 16 (1935): 292–303.
36. Harold J. Morowitz, "Biology as a Cosmological Science," *Main Currents in Modern Thought* 28 (1972): 156.
37. I borrow the term "devolution" from Austin Meredith, "Devolution," *Journal of Theoretical Biology* 96 (1982): 49–65.
38. Holmes Rolston, III, "Duties to Endangered Species," *Bioscience* 35 (1985): 718–26. See also Geerat Vermeij, "The Biology of Human-Caused Extinction," in Norton, *Preservation of Species*, 28–49.
39. See D. M. Raup and J. J. Sepkoski, Jr., "Mass Extinctions in the Marine Fossil Record," *Science* 215 (1982): 1501–3.
40. William Aiken, "Ethical Issues in Agriculture," in *Earthbound: New Introductory Essays in Environmental Ethics*, ed. Tom Regan (New York: Random House, 1984), 269. Tom Regan, *The Case for Animal Rights* (Berkeley: University of California Press, 1983) 262, and "Ethical Vegetarianism," 291. See also Eliott Sober, "Philosophical Problems for Environmentalism," in Norton, *Preservation of Species*, 173–94.
41. I owe the tree-ring analogy to Richard and Val Routley (now Sylvan and Plumwood, respectively), "Human Chauvinism and Environmental Ethics," in *Environmental Philosophy*, ed. D. Mannison, M. McRobbie, and R. Routley (Canberra: Department of Philosophy, Research School of the Social Sciences, Australian National University, 1980), 96–189. A good illustration of the balloon analogy may be found in Peter Singer, *The Expanding Circle: Ethics and Sociobiology* (New York: Farrar, Straus and Giroux, 1983).
42. For an elaboration see Thomas W. Overholt and J. Baird Callicott, *Clothed-in-Fur and Other Tales: An Introduction to an Ojibwa World View* (Washington, D.C.: University Press of America, 1982).
43. J. Baird Callicott, "Traditional American Indian and Western European Attitudes Toward Nature: An Overview," *Environmental Ethics* 4 (1982): 163–74.
44. Ernest Partridge, "Are We Ready for an Ecological Morality?" *Environmental Ethics* 4 (1982): 177.
45. Peter Fritzell, "The Conflicts of Ecological Conscience," *Companion to A Sand County Almanac*, 128–153.
46. See Worster, *Nature's Economy*.
47. Scott Lehmann, "Do Wildernesses Have Rights?" *Environmental Ethics* 3 (1981): 131.

Challenges in Environmental Ethics

Holmes Rolston, III

Holmes Rolston, III, is professor of philosophy at Colorado State University. He is the author of Philosophy Gone Wild: Essays in Environmental Ethics *and* Environmental Ethics: Duties to and Values in the Natural World.

Ethicists had settled on at least one conclusion as ethics became modern in Darwin's century: that the moral has nothing to do with the natural. To argue otherwise commits the naturalistic fallacy, moving without justification from what *is* in nature to what *ought to be* in culture. Science describes natural history, natural law; ethics prescribes human conduct, moral law; and to confuse the two makes a category mistake. Nature simply *is,* without objective value; the preferences of human subjects establish value; and these human values, appropriately considered, generate human duties. Only humans are ethical subjects and only humans are ethical objects. Nature is amoral; the moral community is interhuman.

In the last third of this century, unsettled as we enter the next millennium, there is foreboding revolution. Only the human species contains moral agents, but perhaps conscience on such an earth ought not be used to exempt every other form of life from consideration, with the resulting paradox that the sole moral species acts only in its collective self-interest toward all the rest. There is something overspecialized about

This essay was originally prepared for an American Philosophical Association symposium on Rolston's book, *Environmental Ethics.* A revised version appears in *Ecology, Economics, Ethics: The Broken Circle,* Yale University Press (New Haven, London, 1991).

an ethic, held by the dominant class of *Homo sapiens,* that regards the welfare of only one of several million species as an object and beneficiary of duty. We need an interspecific ethics. Whatever ought to be in culture, this biological world that *is* also *ought to be;* we must argue from the natural to the moral.

If this requires a paradigm change about the sorts of things to which duty can attach, so much the worse for those humanistic ethics no longer functioning in, nor suited to, their changing environment. The anthropocentrism associated with them was fiction anyway. There is something Newtonian, not yet Einsteinian, besides something morally naive, about living in a reference frame where one species takes itself as absolute and values everything else relative to its utility. If true to their specific epithet, ought not *Homo sapiens* value this host of life as something with a claim to care in its own right? Man may be the only measurer of things, but is man the only measure of things? The challenge of environmental ethics is a principled attempt to redefine the boundaries of ethical obligation.

Still there is the sense of anomaly that forebodes paradigm overthrow. An ecological conscience? Sometimes this seems to be a category mistake, joining a scientific adjective with an ethical noun, rather like Christian biochemistry mismatches a religious adjective and a scientific noun. With analysis, we suspect that the relation is three-place. Person A has a duty to person B concerning the environment C, and no one has ever denied that natural things have instrumental value to humans. Humans are helped or hurt by the condition of their environment, and we have duties to humans that concern their valuable environment, an environment they are able to value. So conservatives may shrink back into the persistent refusal of philosophers to think biologically, to naturalize ethics in the deep sense. They will fear that it is logically incoherent to suppose there is a non-anthropogenic value, or that this is too metaphysically speculative ever to be operational and that it does not make any pragmatic difference anyway, claiming that an adequate environmental ethic can be anthropogenic, even anthropocentric.

When we face up to the crisis, however, we undergo a more direct moral encounter. Environmental ethics is not a muddle; it is an invitation to moral development. All ethics seeks an appropriate respect for life, but respect for human life is only a subset of respect for all life. What ethics is about, in the end, is seeing outside your own sector of self-interest, of class interest. A comprehensive ethic will find values in and duties to the natural world. The vitality of ethics depends on our knowing what is really vital, and there will be found the intersection of value and duty. An ecological conscience requires an unprecedented mix of science and conscience, of biology and ethics.

1. HIGHER ANIMALS

We have direct encounters with life that has eyes, at least where our gaze is returned by something that itself has a concerned outlook. The relation is two-place: I–thou, subject to subject. Compared with concern about soil and water, which are instrumentally vital but blind, when we meet the higher animals there is somebody there behind the fur and feathers. "The environment" is external to us all, but where there is inwardness in this environment, perhaps we ought to be conscious of other consciousness. Whatever matters to animals, matters morally.

Wild animals defend their own lives, because they have a good of their own. Animals hunt and howl, seek shelter, build nests and sing, care for their young, flee from threats, grow hungry, thirsty, hot, tired, excited, sleepy, seek out their habitats and mates. They suffer injury and lick their wounds. They can know security and fear, endurance and fatigue, comfort and pain. When they figure out their helps and hurts in the environment, they do not make man the measure of things at all; more, man is not the only measurer of things.

Still, man is the only moral measurer of things, and how should he count these wild, nonmoral things? One might expect classical ethics to have sifted well an ethics for animals. Our ancestors did not think about endangered species, ecosystems, acid rain, or the ozone layer, but they lived in closer association with wild and domestic animals than do we. Nevertheless, until recently, the scientific, humanistic centuries since the so-called Enlightenment have not been sensitive ones for animals. Animals were mindless, living matter; biology was mechanistic. Even psychology, rather than defending animal experience, was behaviorist. Philosophy, as we have already said, thought man the measure of things. Across several centuries of hard science and humanist ethics there has been little compassion for animals. We eat millions of them every year and we use many millions more in industry and research, as though little matters unless it matters to humans.

So far as we got ethically, we rather oddly said that we should be humane toward nonhuman animals. "The question is not," said Bentham, "Can they reason, nor Can they talk? but, Can they suffer?" These nonhumans do not share with humans the capacity to reason or talk, but they do share the capacity to suffer, and human ethics can be extended so far forth to our animal cousins. We may be unsure about insects and fish, but at least we will need an avian and a mammal ethics.

The progress of recent science itself has increasingly smeared the human-nonhuman boundary line. Animal anatomy, biochemistry, perception, cognition, experience, behavior, and evolutionary history are kin to our own. Animals have no immortal souls, but then persons may not either, or beings with souls may not be the only kind that count morally. Ethical progress further smeared the boundary. Sensual pleasures are a good thing, ethics should be egalitarian nonarbitrary, nondiscriminatory. There are ample scientific grounds that animals enjoy pleasures and suffer pains; and ethically no grounds to value these in humans and not in animals. The *is* in nature and the *ought* in ethics are not so far apart after all. We should treat animals humanely, that is, treat animals equally with ourselves where they have equal interests.

Recently, then, there has been a vigorous reassessment of human duties to sentient life. More has been written on this subject in the past fifteen years than in the previous fifteen centuries. The world cheered in the fall of 1988 when humans rescued two whales from the winter ice. A sign in Rocky Mountain National Park enjoins humans not to harass bighorn sheep: "Respect their right to life." We have passed animal welfare legislation and set up animal care committees in our universities. We have made a vital breakthrough past humans, and the first lesson in environmental ethics has been learned.

But the risk of ethical inadequacy here lies in a moral extension that expands rights as far as mammals and not much further, a psychologically based ethic that counts only felt experience. We respect life in our nonhuman but near-human animal cousins, a semi-anthropic and still quite subjective ethics. Justice remains a concern for just-us subjects. Extending our human ethics, we say that the sheep, too, have rights and that we should be humane to the whales. There has, in fact, not been much theoretical breakthrough, no paradigm shift. We do not yet have a biologically based ethics.

We certainly need an ethic for animals, but that is only one level of concern in a comprehensive environmental ethics. When we try to use culturally extended rights and psychologically based utilities to protect the flora or even the insentient fauna, to protect endangered species or ecosystems, we can only stammer. Indeed, we get lost trying to protect bighorns, because in the wild the cougar is not respecting the rights or utilities of the sheep she slays. There are no rights in the wild, and nature is indifferent to the welfare of particular animals. Further, in culture, humans slay sheep and eat them regularly, while humans have every right not to be eaten by either humans or cougars.

A bison fell through the ice into a river in Yellowstone Park; the environmental ethic there, letting nature take its course, forbade would-be rescuers from either saving or mercy killing the suffering animal. A drowning human would have been saved at once. It was as vital to the struggling bison as to any human to get out; the poor thing froze to death that night. Was the Yellowstone ethic callous to life, inhumane? Or had it other vitalities to consider? This ethic seems rather to have concluded that a moral extension is too nondiscriminating; we are unable to separate an ethics for humans from an ethics for wildlife. To treat wild animals with compassion learned in culture does not appreciate their wildness.

Man, said Socrates, is the political animal; humans maximally are what they are in culture, where the natural selection pressures (impressively productive in ecosystems) are relaxed without detriment to the species *Homo sapiens,* and indeed with great benefit to its member persons. Wild and even domestic animals cannot enter culture; they do not have that capacity. They cannot acquire language at sufficient levels to take part in culture; they cannot make their clothing, or build fires, much less read books or receive an education.

Worse, cultural protection can work to their detriment; with too much human or humane care their wildness is made over into a human artifact. A cow does not have the integrity of a deer, a poodle that of a wolf. Culture is a good thing for humans, often a bad thing for animals. Culture does make a relevant ethical difference, and environmental ethics has different criteria from interhuman ethics.

Can they talk? and, Can they reason?, indicating cultural capacities, are relevant questions, not just, Can they suffer? Compassionate respect for life in its suffering is only part of the analysis. Sometimes in an environmental ethic we do need to follow nature, and not so much to treat animals humanely, like we do humans, as to treat animals naturally, for what they are by themselves. Even when we treat them humanely within culture, part of the ethic may also involve treating them naturally.

"Equality" is a positive word in ethics, "discriminatory" a pejorative one. On the other hand, simplistic reduction is a failing in the philosophy of science and epistemology; to be "discriminating" is desirable in logic and value theory. Something about treating humans as equals with bighorns and cougars seems to "reduce" humans to merely animal levels of value, a "no more" counterpart in ethics of the "nothing but" fallacy often met in science. Humans are "nothing but" naked apes. Something about treating sheep and cougars as the equals of humans seems to elevate them unnaturally, unable to value them for what they are. There is something insufficiently discriminating in such judgments—species blind in a bad sense, blind to the real differences between species, valuational differences that do count morally. To the contrary, a discriminating ethicist will insist on preserving the differing richness of valuational complexity, wherever found.

Two tests of discrimination are pain and diet. It might be thought that pain is a bad thing, whether in nature or culture. Perhaps when dealing with humans in culture, additional levels of value and utility must be protected by conferring rights that do not exist in the wild, but meanwhile at least we should minimize animal suffering. That is indeed a worthy imperative in culture where animals are removed from nature and bred, but it may be misguided where animals remain in ecosystems. When the bighorn sheep of Yellowstone caught pinkeye—blinded, injured, and starving in result—300 bighorns, over half the herd, perished. Wildlife veterinarians wanted to treat the disease, as they would have in any domestic herd, and as they did with Colorado bighorns infected with an introduced lungworm, but the Yellowstone ethicists left them to suffer, seemingly not respecting their life. Had they no mercy? Was this again inhumane?

They knew rather that, while intrinsic pain is a bad thing whether in humans or in sheep, pain in ecosystems is instrumental pain, through which the sheep are naturally selected for a more satisfactory adaptive fit. Pain in a medically skilled culture is pointless, once the alarm to health is sounded, but pain operates functionally in bighorns in their niche, even after it becomes no longer in the interests of the pained individuals. To have interfered in the interests of the blinded sheep would have weakened the species. The question, Can they suffer? is not as simple as Bentham thought. What we *ought* to do depends on what *is*. The *is* of nature differs significantly from the *is* of culture, even when similar suffering is present in both.

Some ethicists will insist that at least in culture we can minimize animal pain, and that will constrain our diet. There is predation in nature; humans evolved as omnivores. But humans, the only moral animals, should refuse to participate in the meat-eating phase of their ecology, just as they refuse to live merely by the rules of natural selection. Humans do not look to the behavior of wild animals as an ethical guide in other matters (marriage, truth telling, promise keeping, justice, charity). There they do not follow nature. Why should they justify their dietary habits by watching what animals do?

But the difference is that these other matters are affairs of culture; these are person-to-person events, not events at all in spontaneous nature. By contrast, eating is omnipresent in wild nature; humans eat because they are in nature, not because they are in culture. Eating animals is not an event between persons, but is a human-to-animal event; and the rules for this come from the ecosystems in which humans evolved and which they have no duty to remake. We must eat to live; nature absolutely requires that. We evolved to eat as omnivores; that animal nature underruns over human nature. Even in culture meat eating is still relatively natural; there is nothing immoral about fitting into one's ecology. We follow nature, treat animals naturally, capture nutritional values, and learn our place in the scheme of life and death. This respects life, profoundly so. Humans, then, can model their dietary habits from their ecosystems, though they cannot and should not so model their interpersonal justice or charity. When eating they ought to minimize animal suffering, and they also may gladly affirm their ecology. The boundary between animals and humans has not been rubbed out after all; only what was a boundary line has been smeared into a boundary zone. We have discovered that animals count morally, though we are only beginning to solve the challenge of how to count them.

2. ORGANISMS

In college zoology I did an experiment on nutrition in rats, to see how they grew with and without vitamins. When the experiment was completed, I was told to take the rats out and drown them. I felt squeamish but did it. In college botany I did an experiment on seedlings to test how they grew with this or that fertilizer. The experiment over, I threw out the seedlings without a second thought. While there can be ethics about sentient animals, after that perhaps ethics is over. Respect for life ends somewhere in zoology; it is not part of botany. No consciousness, no conscience. Without sentience, ethics is nonsense.

Or do we want an ethic that is more objective about life? In Yosemite National Park for almost a century humans entertained themselves by driving through a tunnel cut in a giant sequoia. Two decades ago the Wawona tree, weakened by the cut, blew down in a storm. People said: Cut us another drive-through sequoia. The Yosemite environmental ethic, deepening over the years, said no! You ought not to mutilate majestic sequoias for amusement. Respect their life! Indeed, some ethicists count the value of redwoods so highly that they will spike redwoods, lest they be cut. In the Rawah Wilderness in alpine Colorado, old signs read, "Please leave the flowers for others to enjoy." When they rotted out, the new signs urged a less humanist ethic: "Let the flowers live!"

But trees and flowers cannot care, so why should we? We are not considering animals that are close kin, nor can they suffer or experience anything. There are no humane societies for plants. Plants are not valuers with preferences that can be satisfied or frustrated. It seems odd to claim that plants need our sympathy, odd to ask that we should consider their point of view. They have no subjective life, only objective life.

Fishermen in Atlantic coastal estuaries and bays toss beer bottles overboard, a convenient way to dispose of trash. On the bottom, small crabs, attracted by the residual beer, make their way inside the bottles and become trapped, unable to get enough foothold on the slick glass neck to work their way out. They starve slowly. Then one dead crab becomes bait for the next victim, an indefinitely resetting trap! Are those bottle traps of ethical concern, after fishermen have been warned about this effect? Or is the whole thing out of sight, out of mind, with crabs too mindless to care about? Should sensitive fishermen pack their bottle trash back to shore—whether or not crabs have much, or any, felt experience?

Flowers and sequoias live; they ought to live. Crabs have value out of sight, out of mind. Afraid of the naturalistic fallacy, conservative ethicists will say that people should enjoy letting flowers live or that it is silly to cut drive-through sequoias, aesthetically more excellent for humans to appreciate both for what they are. The crabs are out of sight, but not really out of mind; humans value them at a distance. But these ethically conservative reasons really do not understand what biological conservation is in the deepest sense. Nothing matters to a tree, but much is *vital.*

An organism is a spontaneous, self-maintaining system, sustaining and reproducing itself, executing its program, making a way through the world, checking against performance by means of responsive capacities with which to measure success. It can reckon with vicissitudes, opportunities, and adversities that the world presents. Something more than physical causes, even when less than sentience, is operating within every organism. There is *information* superintending the causes; without it the organism would collapse into a sand heap. This information is a modern equivalent of what Aristotle called formal and final causes; it gives the organism a *telos,* "end," a kind of (nonfelt) goal. Organisms have ends, although not always ends-in-view.

All this cargo is carried by the DNA, essentially a *linguistic* molecule. By a serial "reading" of the DNA, a polypeptide chain is synthesized, such that its sequential structure determines the bioform into which it will fold. Ever-lengthening chains (like ever-longer sentences), are organized into genes (like paragraphs and chapters). Diverse proteins, lipids, carbohydrates, enzymes—all the life structures are "written into" the genetic library. The DNA is thus a *logical set,* not less than a biological set, informed as well as formed. Organisms use a sort of symbolic logic, use these molecular shapes as symbols of life. The novel resourcefulness lies in the epistemic content conserved, developed, and thrown forward to make biological resources out of the physicochemical sources. This executive steering core is cybernetic—partly a special kind of cause and effect system, and partly something more: partly a historical information system discovering and evaluating ends so as to map and make a way through the world, partly a system of significances attached to operations, pursuits, resources. In this sense, the genome is a set of *conservation* molecules.

The genetic set is really a *propositional* set—to choose a provocative term—recalling how the Latin *propositum* is an assertion, a set task, a theme, a plan, a proposal, a project, as well as a cognitive statement. From this it is also a motivational set, unlike human books, since these life motifs are set to drive the movement from genotypic potential to phenotypic expression. Given a chance, these molecules seek organic self-expression. They thus proclaim a life way, and with this an organism, unlike an inert rock, claims the environment as source and sink, from which to abstract energy and materials and into which to excrete them. It "takes advantage" of its environment. Life thus arises out of earthen sources (as do rocks), but life turns back on its sources to make resources out of them (unlike rocks). An acorn becomes an oak; the oak stands on its own.

So far we have only description. We begin to pass to value when we recognize that the genetic set is a *normative set;* it distinguishes between what *is* and what *ought to be.* This does not mean that the organism is a moral system, for there are no moral agents in nature; but the organism is an axiological, evaluative system. So the oak grows, reproduces, repairs its wounds, and resists death. The physical state that the organism seeks, idealized in its programmatic form, is a valued state. *Value* is present in this achievement. *Vital* seems a better word for it than *biological.* We are not dealing simply with an individual defending its solitary life but with an individual having situated fitness in an ecosystem. Still, we want to affirm that the living individual, taken as a "point experience" in the web of interconnected life, is *per se* an intrinsic value.

A life is defended for what it is in itself, without necessary further contributory reference, although, given the structure of all ecosystems, such lives necessarily do have further reference. The organism has something it is conserving, something for which it is standing: its life. Organisms have their own standards, fit into their niche though they must. They promote their own realization, at the same time that they track an environment. They have a technique, a know-how. Every organism has a *good-of-its-kind;* it defends its own kind as a *good kind.* In that sense, as soon as one knows what a giant sequoia tree is, one knows the biological identity that is sought and conserved. Man is neither the measurer nor the measure of things; value is not anthropogenic, it is biogenic.

There seems no reason why such own-standing normative organisms are not morally significant. A moral agent deciding his or her behavior, ought to take account of the consequences for other evaluative systems. This does not follow nature, if we mean by that to imitate ethical agents there, for nature is amoral. But it does follow nature, if we mean by that we respect these amoral organic norms as we shape our conduct. Such an ethic will be teleological, I suppose, since it values the *telos* in organisms, but it seems equally deontological, since it owes (Gk: *deont-*) respect for life in itself, intrinsically, and not just instrumentally, consequentially. (Frankly, the classical teleological/deontological distinction seems as troublesome as helpful in moral analysis here.)

Within the community of moral agents one has not merely to ask whether *x* is a normative system, but, since the norms are at personal option, to judge the norm and the consequences. But within the biotic community organisms are amoral normative systems, and there are no cases where an organism seeks a good of its own that is morally reprehensible. The distinction between having a good of its kind and being a good kind vanishes, so far as any faulting of the organism is concerned. To this extent, everything with a good of its kind is a good kind and thereby has intrinsic value.

One might say that an organism is a bad organism if, during the course of pressing its normative expression, it upsets the ecosystem or causes widespread disease, bad consequences. Remember though, that an organism cannot be a good kind without situated environmental fitness. By natural selection the kind of goods to which it is genetically programmed must mesh with its ecosystemic role. Despite the ecosystem as a perpetual contest of goods in dialectic and exchange, it is difficult to say that any organism is a bad kind in this instrumental sense either. The misfits are extinct, or soon will be. In spontaneous nature any species that preys upon, parasitizes, competes with, or crowds another will be a bad kind from the narrow perspective of its victim or competitor.

But if we enlarge that perspective it typically becomes difficult to say that any species is a bad kind overall in the ecosystem. An "enemy" may even be good for the "victimized" species, though harmful to individual members of it, as when predation keeps the deer herd healthy. Beyond this, the "bad kinds" typically play useful roles in population control, in symbiotic relationships, or in providing opportunities for other species. The *Chlamydia* microbe is a bad kind from the perspective of the bighorns, but when one thing dies, something else lives. After the pinkeye outbreak, the golden eagle population in Yellowstone flourished, preying on the bighorn carcasses. For them *Chlamydia* is a good kind instrumentally.

Some biologist-philosophers will say that, even though an organism evolves to have a situated environmental fitness, not all such situations are good arrangements; some can be clumsy or bad. True, the vicissitudes of historical evolution do sometimes result in ecological webs that are sub-optimal solutions, within the biologically limited possibilities and powers of interacting organisms. Still, such systems have been selected over millennia for functional stability; and at least the burden of proof is on a human evaluator to say why any natural kind is a bad kind and ought not to call forth admiring respect. Something may be a good kind intrinsically but a bad kind instrumentally in the system; these will be anomalous cases, however, with selection pressures against them. These claims about good kinds do not say that things are perfect kinds, or that there can be no better ones, only that natural kinds are good kinds until proven otherwise.

What is almost invariably meant by a "bad" kind is that an organism is instrumentally bad when judged from the viewpoint of human interests, of humane interests. "Bad" so used is an anthropocentric word; there is nothing at all biological or ecological about it, and so it has no force evaluating objective nature, however much humanist force it may sometimes have.

A really *vital* ethic respects all life, not just animal pains and pleasures, much less just human preferences. In the Rawahs, the old signs, "Leave the flowers for others to enjoy," were application signs using an old, ethically conservative, humanistic ethic. The new ones invite a change of reference frame—a wilder, more logical because more biological ethic, a radical ethic that goes down to the roots of life, that really is conservative because it understands biological conservation at depths. What the injunction, "Let the flowers live!" means is: "Daisies, marsh-marigolds, geraniums, larkspurs are evaluative systems that conserve goods of their kind, and, in the absence of evidence to the contrary, are good kinds. There are trails here by which you may enjoy these flowers. Is there any reason why your human interests should not also conserve these good kinds?" A drive-through sequoia causes no suffering; it is not cruel. but it is callous and insensitive to the wonder of life. The ethically conservative will complain that we have committed the naturalistic fallacy; rather, we invite a radical commitment to respect all life.

3. SPECIES

Certain rare species of butterflies occur in hummocks (slightly elevated forested ground) on the African grasslands. It was formerly the practice of unscrupulous collectors to go in, collect a few hundred specimens, and then burn out the hummock with the intention of destroying the species, thereby driving up the price of their collections. I find myself persuaded that they morally ought not do this. Nor will the reason resolve into the evil of greed, but it remains the needless destruction of a butterfly species.

This conviction remains even when the human goods are more worthy. Coloradans are considering whether to build the Two Forks Dam to supply urban Denver with water. This would require destroying a canyon and altering the Platte River flow, with many negative environmental consequences, including endangering a butterfly, the Pawnee montane skipper, *Hesperia leonardus montana,* as well as endangering the whooping crane downstream. I doubt whether the good of humans who wish more water for development, both for industry and for bluegrass lawns, warrants endangering species of butterflies and cranes.

Sometimes the stakes are alleged to rise even higher. The Bay checkerspot, *Euphydryas editha bayensis,* proposed to be listed as an endangered species, inhabits peripheral tracts of a large facility on which United Technologies Corporation, a missile contractor, builds and tests Minuteman and Tomahawk propulsion systems. The giant defense contractor has challenged the proposed listing and thinks it airy and frivolous that a butterfly should slow the delivery of warhead missile propulsion systems, and so went ahead and dug a water pipeline through a butterfly patch. They operated out of the classical ethics that says that butterflies do not count but that the defense of humans does.

But a more radical, environmental ethics demurs. The good of humans might override the good of butterfly species but the case must be argued. Lest this seem the foolishness of a maverick philosopher, I point out that such conviction has been written into national law. The Endangered Species Act requires that the case must be argued before a high level "God" committee.

A species exists; a species ought to exist. Environmental ethics must make both claims and move from biology to ethics with care. Species exist only instantiated in individuals, yet are as real as individual plants or animals. The claim that there are specific forms of life historically maintained in their environments over time seems as certain as anything else we believe about the empirical world. At times biologists revise the theories and taxa with which they map these forms, but species are not so much like lines of latitude and longitude as like mountains and rivers, phenomena objectively there to be mapped. The edges of these natural kinds will sometimes be fuzzy, to some extent discretionary. One species will slide into another over evolutionary time. But it does not follow from the fact that speciation is sometimes in progress that species are merely made up, not found as evolutionary lines with identity in time as well as space.

A consideration of species is revealing and challenging because it offers a biologically based counterexample to the focus on individuals—typically sentient and usually persons—so characteristic in classical ethics. In an evolutionary ecosystem, it is not mere individuality that counts, but the species is also significant because it is a dynamic life form maintained over time. The individual represents (re-presents) a species in each new generation. It is a token of a type, and the type is more important than the token.

A species lacks moral agency, reflective self-awareness, sentience, or organic individuality. The older, conservative ethic will be tempted to say that specific-level processes cannot count morally. Duties must attach to singular lives, most evidently those with a psychological self, or some analogue to this. In an individual organism, the organs report to a center; the good of a whole is defended. The members of a species report to no center. A species has no self. It is not a bounded singular. There is no analogue to the nervous hookups or circulatory flows that characterize the organism.

But singularity, centeredness, selfhood, individuality, are not the only processes to which duty attaches. A more radically conservative ethic knows that having a biological identity reasserted genetically over time is as true of the species as of the individual. Identity need not attach solely to the centered organism; it can persist as a discrete pattern over time. Thinking this way, the life that the individual has is something passing through the individual as much as something it intrinsically possesses. The individual is subordinate to the species, not the other way around. The genetic set, in which is coded the *telos,* is as evidently the property of the species as of the individual through which it passes. A consideration of species strains any ethic fixed on individual organisms, much less on sentience or persons. But the result can be biologically sounder, though it revises what was formerly thought logically permissible or ethically binding. This is a higher teleological ethic, finding now the specific *telos,* and concerned about consequences at that level; again, it is deontological, duty bound to the dynamic form of life for what it is in itself.

The species line is the *vital* living system, the whole, of which individual organisms are the essential parts. The species too has its integrity, its individuality, its "right to life" (if we must use the rhetoric of rights); and it is more important to protect this vitality than to protect individual integrity. The right to life, biologically speaking, is an adaptive fit that is right for life, that survives over millennia, and this generates at least a presumption that species in niche are good right where they are, and therefore that it is right for humans to let them be, to let them evolve.

Processes of value that we earlier found in an organic individual reappear at the specific level: defending a particular form of life, pursuing a pathway through the world, resisting death (extinction), regeneration maintaining a normative identity over time, creative resilience discovering survival skills. It is as logical to say that the individual is the species' way of propagating itself as to say that the embryo or egg is the individual's way of propagating itself. The dignity resides in the dynamic form; the individual inherits this, exemplifies it, and passes it on. If, at the specific level, these processes are just as evident, or even more so, what prevents duties arising at that level? The appropriate survival unit is the appropriate level of moral concern. This would be following nature specifically.

Sensitivity to this level, however, can sometimes make an environmental ethicist seem callous. On San Clemente Island, the U.S. Fish and Wildlife Service and the California Department of Fish and Game planned to shoot 2,000 feral goats to save three endangered plant species, *Malacothamnus clementinus, Castilleja grisea, Delphinium kinkiense*, of which the surviving individuals numbered only a few dozens. After a protest, some goats were trapped and relocated. But trapping all was impossible and many hundreds were killed. Is it inhumane to count plant species more than mammal lives, a few plants more than a thousand goats?

Those who wish to restore rare species of big cats to the wilds have asked about killing genetically inbred, inferior cats, presently held in zoos, in order to make space available for the cats needed to reconstruct and maintain a population genetically more likely to survive upon release. All the Siberian tigers in zoos in North America are descendants of seven animals; if these were replaced by others nearer to the wild type and with more genetic variability, the species could be saved in the wild. When we move to the level of species, we may kill individuals for the good of their kind.

Or we may now refuse to let nature take its course. The Yellowstone ethicists let the bison drown, callous to its suffering; they let the blinded bighorns die. But in the spring of 1984 a sow grizzly and her three cubs walked across the ice of Yellowstone Lake to Frank Island, two miles from shore. They stayed several days to feast on two elk carcasses, when the ice bridge melted. Soon afterward, they were starving on an island too small to support them. This time the Yellowstone ethicists promptly rescued the grizzlies and released them on the mainland, in order to protect an endangered species. They were not rescuing individual bears so much as saving the species. They thought that humans had already and elsewhere imperiled the grizzly, and that they ought to save this form of life.

Humans have more understanding than ever of the natural world they inhabit, of the speciating processes, more predictive power to foresee the intended and unintended results of their actions, and more power to reverse the undesirable consequences. The duties that such power and vision generate no longer attach simply to individuals or persons but are emerging duties to specific forms of life. The wrong that humans are doing, or allowing to happen through carelessness, is stopping the historical vitality of life, the flow of natural kinds.

Every extinction is an incremental decay in this stopping life, no small thing. Every extinction is a kind of superkilling. It kills forms (*species*), beyond individuals. It kills "essences" beyond "existences," the "soul" as well as the "body." It kills collectively, not just distributively. It kills birth as well as death. Afterward nothing of that kind either lives or dies. A shutdown of the life stream is the most destructive event possible. Never before has this level of question—superkilling by a superkiller—been deliberately faced. What is ethically callous is the maelstrom of killing and insensitivity to forms of life and the sources producing them. What is required is principled responsibility to the biospheric earth.

Several billion years' worth of creative toil, several million species of teeming life, have been handed over to the care of this late-coming species in which mind has flowered and morals have emerged. Life on earth is a many splendored thing; extinction dims its luster. If, in this world of uncertain moral convictions, it makes any sense to claim that one ought not to kill individuals, without justification, it makes more sense to claim that one ought not to superkill the species, without superjustification. That moves from what *is* to what *ought to be;* and the fallacy is not committed by naturalists who so argue but by humanists who cannot draw these conclusions.

4. ECOSYSTEMS

"A thing is right," urged Aldo Leopold, concluding his land ethic, "when it tends to preserve the integrity, stability, and integrity of the biotic community; it is wrong when it tends otherwise." Again, we have two parts to the ethic: first that ecosystems exist, both in the wild and in support of culture; secondly that ecosystems ought to exist, both for what they are in themselves and as modified by culture. Again, we must move with care from the biological claims to the ethical claims.

Classical, humanistic ethics finds ecosystems unfamiliar territory. It is difficult to get the biology right, and, superimposed on the biology, to get the ethics right. Fortunately, it is often evident that human welfare depends on ecosystemic support, and in this sense all our legislation about clean air, clean water, soil conservation, national and state forest policy, pollution controls, oil spills, renewable resources, and so forth is concerned about ecosystem level processes. Further, humans find much of value for themselves in preserving wild ecosystems and our wilderness and park system is accordingly ecosystem oriented.

Still, a comprehensive environmental ethics needs the best, naturalistic reasons, as well as the good, humanistic ones, for respecting ecosystems. The ecosystem is the community of life; in it the fauna and flora, the species have entwined destinies. Ecosystems generate and support life, keep selection pressures high, enrich situated fitness, evolve congruent kinds in their places with sufficient containment. The ecologist finds that ecosystems are objectively satisfactory communities in the sense that organismic needs are sufficiently met for species long to survive, and the critical ethicist finds (in a subjective judgment matching the objective process) that such ecosystems are satisfactory communities to which to attach duty. Our concern must be for the fundamental unit of survival.

Giant forest fires raged over Yellowstone National Park in the summer of 1988, consuming nearly a million acres, despite the efforts of a thousand firefighters. By far the largest fires ever known in the park, the fires seemed a disaster. But the Yellowstone land ethic enjoins: Let nature take its course. Let it burn! So the fires were not fought at first, but in midsummer national authorities overrode that policy and ordered the fires put out. Even then, weeks later, fires continued to burn, partly because they were too big to control, but partly, too, because Yellowstone personnel did not altogether want the fires put out. Despite the evident destruction of trees, shrubs, and wildlife, they believe that fires are a good thing. Fires reset succession, release nutrients, recycle materials, renew the biotic community. (Nearby, in the Teton wilderness, a storm blew down 15,000 acres of trees, and some proposed that the area be declassified as wilderness for commercial salvage of the timber. But a similar environmental ethics said: No, let it rot.)

Aspen are important in the Yellowstone ecosystem. While some aspen stands are climax and self-renewing, many are serial and give way to conifers. Aspen groves support many birds and much wildlife, especially the beavers, whose activities maintain the riparian zones. Aspen are rejuvenated after fires, and the Yellowstone land ethic wants the aspen for its critical role in the biotic community. Elk browse the young aspen stems. To a degree this is a good thing, since it gives elk critical nitrogen, but in excess it is a bad thing. The elk have no predators, since the wolves are gone, and as a result they overpopulate. Excess elk also destroy the willows and this in turn destroys the beavers. Rejuvenating the aspen might require managers to cull hundreds of elk—all for the sake of a healthy ecosystem.

The Yellowstone ethic wishes to restore wolves to the greater Yellowstone ecosystem. At the level of species, this is partly for what the wolf is in itself, but it is partly because the greater Yellowstone ecosystem does not have its full integrity, stability, and beauty without this majestic animal at the top of the trophic pyramid. Restoring the wolf as a top predator would mean suffering and death for many elk, but that would be a good thing for the aspen and willows, for the beavers and riparian habitat, with mixed benefits for the bighorns and mule deer, whose food the overpopulating elk consume, but who would also be consumed by the wolves. The Yellowstone ethic demands wolves, as it does fires, in appropriate respect for life in its ecosystem.

Letting nature take its ecosystemic course is why the Yellowstone ethic forbade rescuing the drowning bison, but rescued the sow grizzly with her cubs, the latter to insure that the big predators remain. After the bison drowned, coyotes and magpies, foxes and ravens fed on the carcass. Later, even a grizzly bear fed on it. All this is a good thing because the system cycles on. On that account rescuing the whales trapped in the winter ice seems less of a good thing, when we note that rescuers had to drive away polar bears that attempted to eat the dying whales.

An ecosystem, the conservative ethicist will say, is too low a level of organization to be respected intrinsically. Ecosystems can seem little more than random, statistical processes. A forest can seem a loose collection of externally related parts, the collection of fauna and flora a jumble, hardly a community. The plants and animals within an ecosystem have needs, but their interplay can seem simply a matter of distribution and abundance, birth rates and death rates, population densities, parasitism and predation, dispersion, checks and balances, stochastic process. Much is not organic at all (rain, groundwater, rocks, soil particles, air), while some organic material is dead and decaying debris (fallen trees, scat, humus). These things have no organized needs. There is only catch-as-catch-can scrimmage for nutrients and energy, a game played with loaded dice, not really enough integrated process to call the whole a community.

Unlike higher animals, ecosystems have no experiences; they do not and cannot care. Unlike plants, an ecosystem has no organized center, no genome. It does not defend itself against injury or death. Unlike a species, there is no ongoing *telos*, no biological identity reinstantiated over time. The organismic parts are more complex than the community whole. More troublesome still, an ecosystem can seem a jungle where the fittest survive, a place of contest and conflict, beside which the organism is a model of cooperation. In animals, the heart, liver, muscles and brain are tightly integrated, as are the leaves, cambium, and roots in plants. But the ecosystem community is pushing and shoving between rivals, each aggrandizing itself, or else indifference and haphazard juxtaposition, nothing to call forth our admiration.

Environmental ethics must break through the boundary posted by disoriented ontological conservatives, who hold that only organisms are "real," actually existing as entities, whereas ecosystems are nominal—just interacting individuals. Oak trees are real but forests are nothing but collections of trees. But any level is real if it shapes behavior on the level below it. Thus the cell is real because that pattern shapes the behavior of amino acids; the organism because that pattern coordinates the behavior of hearts and lungs. The biotic community is real because the niche shapes the morphology of the oak trees within it. Being real at the level of community only requires an organization that shapes the behavior of its members.

The challenge is to find a clear model of community and to discover an ethics for it—better biology for better ethics. Even before the rise of ecology, biologists began to conclude that the combative survival of the fittest distorts the truth. The more perceptive model is coaction in adapted fit. Predator and prey, parasite and host, grazer and grazed are contending forces in dynamic process where the well-being of each is bound up with the other—coordinated (orders that couple together) as much as heart and liver are coordinated organically. The ecosystem supplies the coordinates through which each organism moves, outside which the species cannot really be located. A species is what it is where it is.

The community connections are looser than the organism's internal interconnections—but not less significant. Admiring organic unity in organisms and stumbling over environmental looseness is like valuing mountains and despising valleys. The matrix the organism requires in order to survive is the open, pluralistic ecology. Internal complexity—heart, liver, muscles, brain—arises as a way of dealing with a complex, tricky environment. The skin-out processes are not just the support, they are the subtle source of the skin-in processes. In the complete picture, the outside is as *vital* as the inside. Had there been either simplicity or lock-step concentrated unity in the environment, no organismic unity could have evolved. Nor would it remain. There would be less elegance in life.

To look at one level for what is appropriate at another makes a categorical mistake. One should not look for a single center or program in ecosystems, much less for subjective experiences. Instead, one should look for a matrix, for interconnections between centers (individual plants and animals, dynamic lines of speciation), for creative stimulus and open-ended potential. Everything will be connected to many other things, sometimes by obligate associations, more often by partial and pliable dependencies and, among other things, there will be no significant interactions. There will be functions in a communal sense: shunts and criss-crossing pathways, cybernetic subsystems, and feedback loops. An order arises spontaneously and systematically when many self-concerned units jostle and seek their own programs, each doing their own thing and forced into informed interaction.

An ecosystem is a productive, projective system. Organisms defend only their selves, with individuals defending their continuing survival and species increasing the numbers of kinds. But the evolutionary ecosystem spins a bigger story, limiting each kind, locking it into the welfare of others, promoting new arrivals, bringing forth kinds and the integration of kinds. Species *increase their kind;* but ecosystems *increase kinds*, superimposing the latter increase onto the former. *Ecosystems are selective systems, as surely as organisms are selective systems.* The natural selection comes out of the system and is imposed on the individual. The individual is programmed to make more of its kind, but more is going on systemically than that; the system is making more kinds.

This extends natural selection theory beyond the merely tautological formulation that the system selects the best adapted to survive. Ecosystems select for those features that appear over the long ranges, for individuality, for diversification, for sufficient containment, for quality supervening on quantity of life. They do this, appropriately to the community level, by employing conflict, decenteredness, probability, succession, spontaneous generation of order, and historicity. Communal processes— the competition between organisms, more or less probable events, plant and animal successions, speciation over historical time—generate an ever-richer community.

Hence the evolutionary toil, elaborating and diversifying the biota, that once began with no species and results today in five million species, increasing over time the quality of lives in the upper rungs of the tropic pyramids. One-celled organisms evolved into many-celled, highly integrated organisms. Photosynthesis evolved and came to support locomotion—swimming, walking, running, flight. Stimulus-response mechanisms became complex instinctive acts. Warm-blooded animals followed cold-blooded ones. Complex nervous systems, conditioned behavior and learning emerged. Sentience appeared—sight, hearing, smell, tastes, pleasure, pain. Brains coupled with hands. Consciousness and self-consciousness arose. Culture was superimposed on nature.

These developments do not take place in all ecosystems or at every level. Microbes, plants, and lower animals remain, good of their kinds, and serving continuing roles, good for other kinds. The understories remain occupied. As a result, the quantity of life and its diverse qualities continue—from protozoans to primates to people. There is a push-up, lock-up, ratchet effect that conserves the upstrokes and the outreaches. The later we go in time the more accelerated are the forms at the top of the tropic pyramids, the more elaborated are the multiple tropic pyramids of earth. There are upward arrows over evolutionary time.

The system is a game with loaded dice, but the loading is a prolife tendency, not mere stochastic process. Though there is no *nature* in the singular, the system has a nature, a loading that pluralizes, putting *natures* into diverse kinds, $nature_1$, $nature_2$, $nature_3$. . .$nature_n$. It does so using random elements (in both organisms and communities), but this is a secret of its fertility, producing steadily intensified interdependencies and options. An ecosystem has no head, but it has a "heading" for species diversification, support, and richness. Though not a superorganism, it is a kind of vital field.

Instrumental value uses something as a means to an end; *intrinsic value* is worthwhile in itself. No warbler eats insects to become food for a falcon; the warbler defends its own life as an end in itself and makes more warblers as it can. A life is defended intrinsically, without further contributory reference. But neither of these traditional terms is satisfactory at the level of the ecosystem. Though it has value *in* itself, the system does not have any value *for* itself. Though a value producer, it is not a value owner. We are no longer confronting instrumental value, as though the system were of value instrumentally as a fountain of life. Nor is the question one of intrinsic value, as though the system defended some unified form of life for itself. We have reached something for which we need a third term: *systemic value*. Duties arise in an encounter with the system that projects and protects these member components in biotic community. If you like, that is an ethic that is teleological again, but since we are respecting both processes and products, perhaps a better word for it now is communitarian. We follow nature, this time ecologically.

Ethical conservatives, in the humanist sense, will say that ecosystems are of value only because they contribute to human experiences. But that mistakes the last chapter for the whole story, one fruit for the whole plant. Humans count enough to have the right to flourish there, but not so much that they have the right to degrade or shut down ecosystems, not at least without a burden of proof that there is an overriding cultural gain. Earlier, environmental ethics will say that ecosystems are of value because they contribute to animal experiences or to organismic life. Later, the deeper, more conservative and more radical view sees that the stability, integrity, and beauty of biotic communities are what are most fundamentally to be conserved.

5. VALUE THEORY

In practice the ultimate challenge of environmental ethics is the conservation of life on earth. In principle the ultimate challenge is a value theory profound enough to support that ethic. We need an account of how nature carries value, and an ethics that appropriately respects those values. For subjectivists both the theory and the ethics will be nothing but human constructs; but objectivists in environmental ethics will use such theory to discover facts, how nature carries values, and from this sometimes there will follow what humans ought to do. The values that nature carries belong as much to the biology of natural history as to the psychology of human experience. Some of the values that nature carries are up to us, our assignment. But fundamentally there are powers in nature that move to us and through us. The splendors of earth do not simply lie in their roles as human resources, supports of culture, or stimulators of experience.

There is no value without an evaluator. So runs a well-entrenched dogma. Humans clearly evaluate their world; sentient animals may also. But plants cannot evaluate their environment; they have no options and make no choices. *A fortiori*, species and ecosystems, earth and nature cannot be bona fide evaluators. Value, like a tickle or remorse, must be felt to be there. Its *esse* is *percipi*. Nonsensed value is nonsense. There are no thoughts without a thinker, no percepts without a perceiver, no deeds without a doer, no targets without an aimer. Valuing is felt preferring; value is the product of this process.

If value arrives only with consciousness, experiences where humans find value there have to be dealt with as appearances of various sorts. The value has to be relocated in the valuing subject's creativity as a person meets a valueless world, or even a valuable one—one *able* to be *valued*—but which before the human bringing of value ability contains only possibility and not any actual value. Value can only be extrinsic to nature, never intrinsic to it. Nature offers but the standing possibility of valuation; value is not generated until humans appear with their valuing ability.

But the valuing subject in an otherwise valueless world is an insufficient premise for the experienced conclusions of those who respect all life. Conversion to a biological view seems truer to world experience and more logically compelling. Here the order of knowing reverses—and also enhances—the order of being. This, too, is a perspective, but ecologically better informed. Science has been steadily showing how the consequents (life, mind) are built on their precedents (energy, matter), however much they overleap them. Life and mind appear where they did not before exist, and with this levels of value emerge that did not before exist. But that gives no reason to say that all value is an irreducible emergent at the human (or upper animal) level. Nature does, of course, offer possibilities for human valuation, but the vitality of the system is not something that goes on in the human mind, nor is its value. The possibility of valuation is carried to us by evolutionary and ecological natural history, and such nature is already valuable before humans arrive to evaluate what is taking place.

How do we humans come to be charged up with values, if there was and is nothing in nature charging us up so? Some value is anthropogenic, generated by humans, but some is biogenic, in the natural genesis. A comprehensive environmental ethics reallocates value across the whole continuum. Value increases in the emergent climax, but is continuously present in the composing precedents. The system is *value-able, able* to produce *value*. Human evaluators are among its products. But when we value we must not forget our communal bonds. Sometimes we need to evaluate (appraise the worth of) what we ourselves may not value (personally prefer). Against the standard view that all value requires a beholder, some value requires only a holder, and some value is held within the historic system that carries value to and through individuals.

Here we do not want a subjective morality but an objective one, even though we find that subjectivity is the most valuable output of the objective system. Is there any reason for ethical subjects to discount the vital systemic processes unless and until accompanied by sentience? Perhaps to evaluate the entire biological world on the basis of sentience is as much a categorical mistake as to judge it according to whether justice and charity are found there. The one mistake judges biological places by extension from psychology, the other from culture. What is "right" about the biological world is not just the production of pleasures and positive experiences. What is "right" includes ecosystemic patterns, organisms in their generating, sustaining environments.

Some value depends on subjectivity, yet all value is generated within the geosystemic and ecosystemic community. Systemically, value fades from subjective to objective value, but also fans out from the individual to its role and matrix. Things do not have their separate natures merely in and for themselves, but they face outward and co-fit into broader natures. Value-in-itself is smeared out to become value-in-togetherness. Value seeps out into the system, and we lose our capacity to identify the individual as the sole locus of value.

Intrinsic value, that of an individual "for what it is in itself," becomes problematic in a holistic web. True, the system produces such values more and more with its evolution of individuality and freedom. Yet to decouple this from the biotic, communal system is to make value too internal and elementary; this forgets relatedness and externality. Every intrinsic value has leading and trailing *ands* pointing to value from which it comes and toward which it moves. Adapted fitness makes individualistic value too system independent. Intrinsic value is a part in a whole, not to be fragmented by valuing it in isolation. An isolated *telos* is biologically impossible; the ethic cannot be teleological in that sense, nor can we term it deontological either, if this requires respect for an intrinsic value regardless of ecosystemic consequences. (The classical distinction fails again.)

Everything is good in a role, in a whole, although we can speak of objective intrinsic goodness wherever a good kind defends itself. We can speak of subjective intrinsic goodness when such an event registers as a point experience, at which point humans pronounce both their experience and what it is of good without need to enlarge their focus. The system is a value transformer where form and being, process and reality, fact and value are inseparably joined. Intrinsic and instrumental values shuttle back and forth, parts-in-wholes and wholes-in-parts, local details of value embedded in global structures, gems in their settings, and their setting-situation a corporation where value cannot stand alone. Every good is in community.

This is what is radically wrong with anthropocentric or merely anthropogenic value. It arrogates to humans what permeates the community. Subjective self-satisfactions are, and ought to be, sufficiently contained within the objectively satisfactory system. The system creates life, selects for adaptive fit, constructs increasingly richer life in quantity and quality, supports myriads of species, escalates individually, autonomy, and even subjectivity, within the limits of decentralized community. When persons appraise this natural history, if such land is not a valuable, satisfactory biotic community, why not? Does earth and its community of life not claim their concern and care?

In environmental ethics one's beliefs about nature, which are based upon but exceed science, have everything to do with beliefs about duty. The way the world *is* informs the way it *ought* to be. We always shape our values in significant measure in accord with our notion of the kind of universe that we live in, and this drives our sense of duty. Our model of reality implies a model of conduct. Perhaps we can leave open what metaphysics ultimately underlies our cosmos, but for an environmental ethics at least we will need an earthbound metaphysics, a metaecology. Differing models sometimes imply similar conduct, but often they do not. A model in which nature has no value apart from human preferences will imply different conduct from one where nature projects fundamental values, some objective and others that further require human subjectivity superposed on objective nature.

This evaluation is not scientific description; hence not ecology per se, but we do move to metaecology. No amount of research can verify that, environmentally, the right is the optimum biotic community. Yet ecological description generates this valuing of nature, endorsing the systemic rightness. The transition from *is* to *good* and thence to *ought* occurs here; we leave science to enter the domain of evaluation, from which an ethic follows.

What is ethically puzzling and exciting is that an *ought* is not so much *derived* from an *is* as discovered simultaneously with it. As we progress from descriptions of fauna and flora, of cycles and pyramids, of autotrophs coordinated with heterotrophs, of stability and dynamism, on to intricacy, planetary opulence and interdependence, to unity and harmony with oppositions in counterpoint and synthesis, organisms evolved within and satisfactorily fitting their communities, arriving at length at beauty and goodness, it is difficult to say where the natural facts leave off and where the natural values appear. For some at least, the sharp *is/ought* dichotomy is gone; the values seem to be there as soon as the facts are fully in, and both alike properties of the system. This conviction, and the conscience that follows from it, can yield our best adaptive fit on earth.

PART TWO

Deep Ecology

Introduction

George Sessions

George Sessions teaches philosophy at Sierra College in Rocklin, California. He has written extensively in the area of ecophilosophy and deep ecology and is the co-author, with Bill Devall, of Deep Ecology *(1985).*

The deep ecology movement is a direct outgrowth of the ecological concerns of the 1960s. Modern environmentalism began with Rachel Carson's 1962 book, *Silent Spring,* which attacked DDT and other pesticides, thereby focusing public attention on the extent of chemical pollution, human overpopulation, disappearance of wilderness and wild species habitat, and overall environmental destruction that had occurred since World War II. This eventually led to the tremendous outpouring of concern for the earth, expressed in the celebration of Earth Day I, 1970. But as a biologist and lover of birds and the earth's wild places, Rachel Carson's indictment went deeper. Not only did she question the human competence and right to manage the planet; in the closing pages of her book she posed a philosophical challenge to the *anthropocentrism* of Western culture. She claimed that "the 'control of nature' is a phrase conceived in arrogance, born of the Neanderthal age of biology and philosophy, when it was supposed that nature exists for the convenience of man."

And as an ecological understanding of the place of humans in nature began to dawn, a reevaluation of the ecocentric nature-oriented religions and ways of life of primal peoples also began to take place. For example, then-Secretary of the Interior Stewart Udall, in his book on the environmental crisis (*The Quiet Crisis,* 1963), referred to the "land wisdom" and reverence for the land of the traditional American Indians, calling them the "first ecologists."

The whole question of the environmental crisis as fundamentally a crisis of the West's anthropocentric philosophical and religious orientations and values was raised even more forcefully a few years later by Lynn

White, Jr, in *Science* ("Historical Roots of Our Ecologic Crisis," 1967). White argued that Christianity—having desacralized Nature, having encouraged its exploitation, and having promoted an anthropocentric world view that portrays humans as the central actors in the cosmic drama, and as separate from, and superior to, the rest of Nature—is largely responsible for the ecological crisis. White also claimed that modern science and technology, having developed within a Christian matrix, are "permeated with Christian arrogance toward nature." In an effort to reform Christianity ecologically, he proposed a return to the ecological egalitarian views of Saint Francis. White's paper precipitated a major debate among theologians, philosophers, and scientists that reverberates to this day.

But White was far from the first to link our anthropocentric religious and philosophical traditions to the destructive exploitation of nature. In their quest for ecological consciousness in the nineteenth century, Henry David Thoreau and John Muir made those connections; Muir referred to modern Western humans as "Lord Man." In the early twentieth century, the critique of Western anthropocentrism continued in the writings of Harvard philosopher George Santayana, Albert Schweitzer, D. H. Lawrence, Robinson Jeffers, and Aldous Huxley. With the writings of the ecologist Aldo Leopold, culminating in his famous ecocentric "land ethic" (*A Sand County Almanac*, 1949), the full weight of the newly emerging science of ecology was brought to bear on the critique of anthropocentrism.

The prominent Norwegian academic philosopher, Arne Naess, was greatly influenced by Rachel Carson and the rapidly emerging American environmental movement, as well as by ecological developments in Norway and in other parts of Europe. As a longtime admirer and scholar of Spinoza and Gandhi, as well as an international mountaineer and dweller in wild places, it was quite natural for Naess to see the revolutionary philosophical and social implications of the emerging ecological critique of anthropocentrism. At a Third World Future conference held in Bucharest in 1972, he described the chief features of what he called the *shallow* and the *deep long-range* ecology movements ("The Shallow and the Deep, Long-Range Ecology Movements: A Summary," *Inquiry*, 1973).

He portrayed the shallow movement as a short-term anthropocentric reform approach preoccupied with pollution and resource depletion, and concerned mainly with "the health and affluence of people in the developed countries." The shallow movement was not challenging the philosophical presuppositions and fundamental correctness of the industrial social paradigm of reality. The deep ecology movement, however, was proposing a major realignment of our philosophical worldview, culture, and lifestyles, consistent with the new ecological perspective. Naess claimed that the experiences of field ecologists and others associated with wild nature gave rise to scientific conclusions and deep ecological intuitions that were amazingly similar all over the world during the 1960s.

These included an awareness of the internal interrelatedness of ecosystems and the individuals comprising them; ecological egalitarianism (ecocentrism as opposed to anthropocentrism); an appreciation of diversity, symbiosis, and ecological complexity; a "deep-seated respect, or even veneration, for ways and forms of life"; an anti-social–class posture; and an appreciation of the principles of local autonomy and decentralization. Naess also pointed out that, to deal effectively with the environmental crisis, it would be necessary to move beyond the supposedly value-neutral theories and facts of the science of ecology, to the wider philosophical perspective of ecosophy (earth wisdom together with norms for action).

Over the past twenty years, Arne Naess has, through his many papers and books, developed a sophisticated philosophic basis for deep ecology; as well as leading an exemplary spiritual/ecological lifestyle. Naess, together with the California poet and essayist, Gary Snyder, are the two most influential international exponents of the deep ecology movement. In the 1960s, Snyder began to develop his unique deep ecological synthesis of Zen Buddhism, the "old ways" of traditional American Indians and other primal peoples, and the basic principles and findings of the science of ecology. In 1975, Gary Snyder received the Pulitzer Prize in Poetry for his book *Turtle Island;* through his many writings and bioregional living in the Sierra foothills, he has helped forge the theoretical and practical basis for reinhabitation and bioregionalism.

During the 1980s, the influence of the deep ecology movement became global in scope. Deep ecology is being discussed in universities throughout the world, as well as providing inspiration for direct action groups, including those trying to live bioregionally. In his new interpretation of the history of Western civilization, the ecophilosopher Max Oelschlaeger (*The Idea of Wilderness,* 1991) sees the intellectual development from Darwin, Thoreau, Muir, Leopold, and Robinson Jeffers, to Arne Naess and Gary Snyder as providing an alternative ecological vision to the development of modern Western industrial/consumerist society. He argues that this vision provides a basis for a new philosophical/cultural paradigm for postmodern societies. And drawing upon the reevaluation of primal cultures, he calls for the recultivation of Paleolithic consciousness.

Space limitations prevent the inclusion of many key writings on deep ecology, such as selections from Gary Snyder's extraordinary new book (*The Practice of the Wild,* 1990); Snyder's brilliant ecotopian manifesto "Four Changes" (1969) in *Turtle Island* (1975); Snyder's early papers on bioregionalism and reinhabitation (Snyder, *The Old Ways,* 1977); Arne Naess's fine papers on "Deep Ecology and Lifestyle" (1983) and on the "ecological self": ("Self-Realization: An Ecological Approach to Being in the World," 1986); writings by the Australian deep ecology theorists Robyn Eckersley, Patsy Hallen, Freya Matthews, and John Seed; papers by Bill Devall and Joanna Macy, and the important paper by Michael Zimmerman on feminism and deep ecology. It is hoped that, despite these limitations, the following papers present a well-rounded view of the philosophy and concerns of the long-range deep ecology movement.

In the first paper ("The Viable Human"), Thomas Berry, one of the world's leading Christian ecotheologians, provides a succinct overview of the contemporary environmental situation. While Father Berry does not specifically identify with the deep ecology movement, the overall orientation expressed here is one with which many supporters of deep ecology would feel at home. To begin with, Berry claims that the crucial shift from an anthropocentric to a biocentric (or ecocentric) sense of reality and value requires a cosmological and planetary frame of reference; and further, that "the community of all living species is the greater reality and the greater value."

Berry vividly portrays the pervasive influence in our lives of global industrial establishments. They are the primary shapers of our contemporary social paradigm of reality and value. These establishments destroy the earth, largely through promoting an anthropocentric consumerist vision of reality. But in attempting to create a technological/consumerist "wonderworld" for humans, the industrial establishments are, in fact, creating a "wasteworld." Berry sees the conflict between the industrial entrepreneur and the ecologist as "both the central human issue and the central earth issue of this late twentieth century."

Berry's ecocentrism is expressed in his claim that "the earth belongs to itself and to all the component members of the community. . .[it is] a gorgeous celebration of existence in all its forms." His earth spirituality (and ultimate indictment of the industrial/consumerist vision) is particularly discernible in the claim that the reduction of the planet "to a resource base for consumer use. . .is already a spiritual and psychic degradation. . .the world of the sacred has been diminished as money and utility values have taken precedence [over more important human and ecological values]."

Arguing that contemporary language has been degraded to support the industrial/consumerist vision, Berry urges ecologists to "rectify" this situation. Despite raising many important issues, Berry's essay lacks a discussion of the crucial role of human overpopulation in the environmental crisis equation. Elsewhere he has agreed that population stabilization and reduction is ecologically necessary.

The charming interview with Arne Naess ("Simple in Means, Rich in Ends"), conducted by Stephen Bodian at a gathering of deep ecology theorists at the Los Angeles Zen Center in 1982, remains the best short informal introduction to the ideas, attitudes, and values of the deep ecology movement. Naess claims that the essence of deep ecology is to ask deeper questions, which, as in the traditional Socratic quest, leads us to the level of ultimate values and commitments, and to the articulation of a total worldview. He discusses the deep ecological norms of ecological equality or democracy; self-realization (or the "ecological self") as, in part, the identification with other life forms; Self-realization (with a capital *S*) as the universe (including the earth) or the Tao realizing itself; and the norms of maximum diversity and symbiosis. He argues that science, technology, and narrow rationality, alone, cannot solve our environmental problems. And so, people must cultivate and trust their basic philosophical and ecological intuitions as a basis for action. Ultimately, cultivation of an ecological self and a deep ecological lifestyle involves a materially simple life, and values that maximize the *quality* and *richness* of our experience.

In a more technical exposition of deep ecology ("The Deep Ecology Movement"), Arne Naess begins with one of his favorite themes: that ecologists and other environmental professionals have an obligation to go beyond the "facts" and to express publicly their ecological philosophies and value commitments. A discussion of "why a 'deep' ecology?" introduces the eight points of the "deep ecology platform." Naess provides illuminating contrasts between shallow and deep ecological positions on such issues as pollution, resources, human overpopulation, cultural diversity and appropriate technology, land and sea ethics, and education and the scientific enterprise.

And reinforcing his idea of philosophical deep ecology as a total worldview and as a deep questioning process, he shows how deep ecology can be portrayed as a logical derivational system, using the apron diagram. Widely differing ultimate premises, philosophies, and religious systems will, he claims, lead through the generally agreed upon "deep ecology platform," to normative (value) and factual hypothesis, and to concrete ecological decisions, which again may differ depending upon particular circumstances.

Finally, Naess discusses his personal version of ecosophy (ecosophy T) as a derivational system, which has been inspired by the philosophical and religious systems of Spinoza and Gandhi. This begins with the ultimate norm "Self-realization" from which he derives various factual and normative hypotheses. In connection with Kant's conception of a "beautiful act," Naess briefly mentions one of the distinguishing features of philosophical deep ecology: the "wider identification" thesis, which is a factual claim about *psychological* maturity in human beings; i.e., the fully mature human has progressed from an identification with narrow ego, through identification with other humans, to a more all-encompassing identification of self with other species, with ecosystems, and with the ecosphere itself. This spiritual/psychological growth process (the transformation from ego state to "ecological self") results in a radically different *perception* of the world, which provides the basis for "right action." Thus, in philosophical deep ecology, there is a decisive shift away from *ethics* (including "environmental ethics") and morality and duty, to *ontology* (a transformed mature self with its corresponding change of perception and understanding) as a basis for right action. Throughout the paper, Naess also forcefully exhibits his philosophical commitment to *diversity* (whether biological, cultural, individual, scientific, or technological, among others).

Ecology is, of course, a biological science concerned with studying the relations of organisms and species to their environment. This has prompted Thomas Berry to assert that if we are to fully understand and deal effectively with the environmental crisis, we must "reinvent the human at the species level." From Thoreau and Muir in the nineteenth century to modern ecologists beginning with Aldo Leopold and Rachel Carson, the development of the contemporary ecological perspective has resulted largely from the efforts of various individuals who, philosophically and experientially, have "stepped back" from human society (usually by spending considerable time observing ecological processes in wild nature) and have overcome anthropocentrism by taking an interspecies vantage point; what Leopold referred to as "thinking like a mountain." The experiences in wild nature of ecologists and others throughout the world provided the main impetus for the rise of the deep ecology movement during the 1960s.

Beginning in the mid-1980s, polemic attacks were directed toward deep ecology philosophy (and the statements of individual ecological activists) by Murray Bookchin and other social ecologists, and by some ecofeminists. Whereas the generalizations and findings of the science of ecology have inspired the perspectives of the deep ecology movement, Bookchin tends to argue that the science of ecology is largely irrelevant to humans and human societies while, oddly enough, referring to his position as a social "ecology." Further, he has rejected the ecocentrism and ecological egalitarianism of deep ecology, as well as the claim that anthropocentrism is the root cause of the ecological crisis. For social ecologists, the root cause is not basically philosophical, psychological, or spiritual; it is essentially *political* (an issue of human social power relations): specifically capitalism and the problem of social class domination (what is now referred to as the "left-green" position). Some of these issues are illuminated in *Defending the Earth: A Dialogue Between Murray Bookchin and Dave Foreman* (Boston: 1991).

Ecofeminists also tend to reject anthropocentrism as the root cause of the environmental crisis, pointing instead to long-standing Western cultural patriarchal attitudes of dominance over both women and nature. Thus, the root cause or causes of the environmental crisis are seen by social ecologists and ecofeminists to be essentially social justice and gender related, respectively; that is intraspecies, rather than interspecies.

In "The Deep Ecology-Ecofeminism Debate and Its Parallels," the Australian deep ecology theorist, Warwick Fox, critically examines some of the charges raised by ecofeminists and social ecologists against deep ecology philosophy. To begin with, Fox points out that deep ecology's ecocentrism encourages and logically requires an egalitarian attitude toward *all* entities; thus it *subsumes* under its theoretical framework the egalitarian interests of the various human social movements (e.g., feminism, social justice).

Ecofeminists generally agree with the positive ecocentric position of deep ecology; their criticism is directed at the claim that anthropocentrism is the basis for the ecological crisis. But why, Fox asks, should we focus on androcentrism (male-centeredness) as the root cause, rather than race, Westernization, or social hierarchy (as in the case of Bookchin)? For it is possible to imagine a society in which social, racial, and gender equality has been realized, but which is still highly exploitive ecologically. And this point holds as well for Bookchin's social ecology analysis. This leads Fox to argue that singling out androcentrism (or social hierarchy) as the root cause of the environmental crisis actually results in overly simplistic social and political analyses. At the same time, such critics tend to remain anthropocentric: they continue to focus on their respective human social and political agendas while the major *ecological* crises and issues receive a low priority, or are ignored.

Fox points out that both ecofeminists and social ecologists miss the point of deep ecology's critique of anthropocentrism by interpreting it to mean that *humans* are the root cause of the ecological crisis. This view is then often equated by critics with misanthropy. Admittedly, confusion has arisen as the result of apparently misanthropic statements made by various ecological activists. But deep ecology philosophy's critique of anthropocentrism is directed against *human-centeredness* (a legitimating ideology), not humans per se; a logical mistake, which Fox refers to as "the fallacy of misplaced misanthropy." He further argues that anthropocentrism has been the legitimating ideology used throughout history as the main justification for ecological domination and destruction. Thus deep ecology is justified in focusing on anthropocentrism as the root cause of the environmental crisis while at the same time appreciating and learning from the social analyses of other perspectives.

The paper by Sessions is both theoretical and practical, as it attempts to clarify global environmental problems and to apply deep ecological solutions to them. In "Deep Ecology and Global Ecosystem Protection," I discuss some of the recent historical background in the shift from ecocentrism to anthropocentrism and back again to ecocentrism ("from Muir to Pinchot to Muir"). Under the guidance of Gifford Pinchot's anthropocentrism, the U.S. Forest Service has been destroying the last of the temperate zone old-growth forests. In addition, anthropocentric utilitarian land-use practices throughout the world are destroying biodiversity and wild ecosystems at an accelerating rate.

The rise of the science of conservation biology in the 1980s may be crucial in the efforts to protect biodiversity and wild ecosystems. Research by conservation biologists demonstrates that existing designated wilderness areas and wildlife refuges throughout the world are ecologically inadequate to protect wild species and allow for continued speciation. Given the present situation, ecologist Michael Soulé has claimed that "vertebrate evolution may be at an end."

Since the late 1960s, environmentalists and ecologists have been proposing systems of global ecosystem zoning as a way of protecting biodiversity and wild ecosystems. There are discussions of the zoning proposals by Dave Brower, Eugene Odum, and Paul Shepard, the Biosphere Reserve concept, and the World Heritage Site system, as well as the need for ecosystem restoration. Important refinements to these proposals have been made with Arne Naess's concept of *free nature,* and Paul Taylor's concept of the *bioculture.* Further, it is claimed that animal rights theorizing fails to distinguish between the different situations of domestic animals in the bioculture, and wild animals in their natural habitats. And, following a proposal by Arne Naess, and the findings of conservation biology, there is an exploration of the question "How much wilderness and 'free nature' needs to be protected?" Finally, it is argued that our environmental problems are increasingly global in scope. Accordingly, the United Nations needs to consolidate its environmental programs and greatly increase its efforts to help stabilize human population growth and encourage the protection of wildness and biodiversity.

In "The Third World, Wilderness and Deep Ecology," which was originally intended for publication in this anthology, Arne Naess responds to the critique by Ramachandra Guha, a social ecologist from India ("Radical American Environmentalism and Wilderness Preservation: A Third World Critique," *Environmental Ethics* 11, 1 (1989): 71–83), who feels that the deep ecology movement, with its strong emphasis on the protection of biodiversity and the earth's wild ecosystems, is not relevant to Third World concerns. Mr. Guha shares social ecology's view that deep ecology's distinction between anthropocentric and ecocentric positions is not only bogus, but is irrelevant to what he sees as "the two fundamental ecological problems facing the globe: (i) overconsumption by the industrialized world and urban elites in the Third World and (ii) growing militarization. . . ." His analysis ignores what the vast majority of professional ecologists throughout the world consider to be the most serious global ecological problems: the exponentially rising rates of global human overpopulation, ozone layer depletion, the greenhouse effect, and current rates of habitat loss and species extinction—estimated at 140 per day. Hence, Guha sees the establishment of wildlife preserves in India for the protection of tigers (and other endangered species) as a form of elite ecological imperialism and "a direct transfer of resources from the poor to the rich."

Guha implies that the Third World's poor are not interested in the "intrinsic value" of nature and other species; he claims that for the poor "it is a question of sheer survival, not of enhancing the quality of life." Third world environmentalism, he says, should place primary emphasis on the human issues of "equity and social justice" and on how pollution and land ownership patterns negatively affect the poor. The deep ecology movement, he erroneously asserts, has little or no interest in the issues of restructuring society to achieve ecological sustainability and social justice, steady-state economics, and a "radical shift in consumption and production patterns." And, totally ignoring the central ecological issue of protecting the biological integrity and processes of the planet, Guha suggests that the deep ecology movement is not relevant even to First World environmentalism: "A truly radical ecology in the American context," he claims, "ought to work toward a synthesis of the appropriate technology, alternate lifestyle, and peace movements."

In reply, Arne Naess refers to Gary Snyder's point that, throughout human history, people have lived in wilderness in *moderate* numbers without appreciably reducing biological richness and diversity. Although this situation still occurs in various places in Third World countries, this is not possible in First World countries where high-consumption lifestyles and other destructive practices require, at present, the establishment of large designated wilderness areas (with no human habitation) to protect biodiversity and wildlife habitat.

While Third World people must progress economically, excessive consumption of people in the rich countries must be curtailed. But subsistence agriculture, which destroys tropical forests, cannot be considered long-term economic progress for the poor. The severe overpopulation in Third World countries requires that most of the poor will live in urban areas in the near future, and these urban areas will need massive improvements in living conditions.

But apart from the desperately poor, Naess points out that, contrary to the claims of Guha, most people in the Third World *are* concerned about the protection of wildness, biodiversity, and "free nature." He provides examples of Third World peoples, such as the Sami, the people of Beding in Nepal, and the Masai in Africa, who appear to view nonhuman nature as having "intrinsic value," and who, in some cases, *identify* with wild nature. Using an example of the fishing situation in Norway, Naess argues that the ecological situation of the poor in the Third World is, in many respects, not that different from the poor in richer countries. But protection of wildness and biodiversity in the Third World will, to a large extent, take the form of living traditionally in ecologically benign ways in "free nature," as do the Masai in Africa, and the primal societies and rubber-tappers of the Amazon.

Naess discusses the green movement, and the attempt to establish sustainable green societies. The green movement, he claims, is composed of four movements: (1) the antipoverty movement; (2) the social justice movement; (3) the alternative technology movement; and (4) the ecological movement (elsewhere he adds the peace movement to this list). It promotes confusion to identify the green movement (and all of its component movements) with the ecology movement. The deep ecology movement strongly supports sustainability for all countries and societies, but sustainability in the ecologically "wide" sense of protecting "the full richness and diversity of life forms on the planet"; it is beneath human dignity, Naess claims, to aspire to less.

Elsewhere, he argues that even though societies will not have reached full sustainability until significant progress has been made toward attaining *all* the goals of the the green movement, nevertheless a very high priority must be placed on ecological issues: "Considering the accelerating rate of irreversible ecological destruction worldwide, I find it acceptable to continue fighting *ecological* unsustainability whatever the state of affairs may be concerning the other goals of green societies." Supporters of the deep ecology movement, Naess holds, "should concentrate on specific issues relating to the *ecological* crisis (including its social and political consequences)." (For a further critique of Guha's position, see David Johns, "The Relevance of Deep Ecology to the Third World," *Environmental Ethics,* Vol. 12, No. 3 [Fall, 1990], 233–252.)

The Viable Human

Thomas Berry

Thomas Berry is director of the Riverdale Center for Religious Research in New York and is widely regarded as one of the world's leading ecotheologians. He is the author of The Dream of the Earth *(1988) and many papers in ecotheology.*

To be viable, the human community must move from its present anthropocentric norm to a geocentric norm of reality and value. Within the solar system, the earth is the immediate context of human existence. And we recognize the sun as the primary source of earth's energies. Beyond the sun, however, is our own galaxy, and beyond that is the universal galactic system that emerged some 15 billion years ago through some ineffable mystery.

To establish this comprehensive context is important; it is the only satisfactory referent in our quest for a viable presence of the human within the larger dynamics of the universe. We suppose that the universe itself is *the* enduring reality and *the* enduring value even while it finds expression in a continuing sequence of transformations. In creating the planet Earth, its living forms, and its human intelligence, the universe has found, so far as we know, the most elaborate manifestation of its deepest mystery. Here, in its human form, the universe is able to reflect on and celebrate itself in a unique mode of conscious self-awareness.

Our earliest human documents reveal a special sensitivity in human intellectual, emotional, and aesthetic responses to the natural world. These responses reveal cosmic and biologic realms of thought as well as anthropocentric life attitudes. These realms were all centered in each other, the

Originally published in *Revision*, Vol. 9, No. 2 (Winter/Spring 1987). Reprinted with permission of the Helen Dwight Reid Education Foundation. Published by Heldref Publications, 1319 Eighteenth St., N.W., Washington, D.C. 20036–1802.

later dependent on the earlier for survival, the earlier dependent on the later for their manifestation.

Instinctively, humans have always perceived themselves as a mode of being *of* the universe as well as distinctive beings *in* the universe. This was the beginning. The emergence of the human was a transformative moment for the earth as well as for the human. As with every species, the human being needed to establish its niche, a sustainable position in the larger community of life, to fulfill its need for food, shelter, and clothing, for security, for family and community. The need for community was special because of the unique human capacity for thought and speech, aesthetic appreciation, emotional sensitivities, and moral judgment. The fulfilling of these needs resulted in a cultural shaping that established the specific identifying qualities of the human being.

Whatever the cultural elaboration of the human, its basic physical as well as psychic nourishment and support came from the surrounding natural environment. In its beginnings, human society was integrated with the larger life society and the larger earth community composed of all the geological as well as biological and human elements. Just how long this primordial harmony endured we do not know beyond the last hundred thousand years of the Paleolithic period. Some ten thousand years ago, the Neolithic and then the Classical civilizations came into being. It must suffice to say that with the classical and generally literate civilizations of the past five thousand years, the great cultural worlds of the human developed, along with vast and powerful social establishments whereby humans became oppressive and even destructive of other life forms. Alienation from the natural world increased, and new ideals of human well-being neglected the needs of other living species. Because of this human dysfunctional relation with the earth, some of these earlier human cultures became nonsustainable. We can observe this especially in the classical Mediterranean civilizations of Greece and Rome. Even so, the human species as a whole was not seriously endangered; these experiences were regional and limited in their consequences. In recent times, however, this has changed.

A deep cultural pathology has developed in Western society and has now spread throughout the planet. A savage plundering of the entire earth is taking place through industrial exploitation. Thousands of poisons unknown in former times are saturating the air, the water, and the soil. The habitat of a vast number of living species is being irreversibly damaged. In this universal disturbance of the biosphere by human agents, the human being now finds that the harm done to the natural world is returning to threaten the human species itself.

The question of the viability of the human species is intimately connected with the question of the viability of the earth. These questions ultimately arise because at the present time the human community has such an exaggerated, even pathological, fixation on its own comfort and convenience that it is willing to exhaust any and all of the earth's resources to satisfy its own cravings. The sense of reality and of value is strictly directed toward the indulgences of a consumer economy. This nonsustainable situation can be clearly seen in the damage done to major elements necessary for the continued well-being of the planet. When the soil, the air, and the water have been extensively poisoned, human needs cannot be fulfilled. Strangely, this situation is the consequence of a human-centered norm of reality and value.

Once we grant that a change from an anthropocentric to a biocentric sense of reality and value is needed, we must ask how this can be achieved and how it would work. We must begin by accepting the fact that the life community, the community of all living species, is the greater reality and the greater value, and that the primary concern of the human must be the preservation and enhancement of this larger community. The human does have its own distinctive reality and its own distinctive value, but this distinctiveness must be articulated within the more comprehensive context. The human ultimately must discover the larger dimensions of its own being within this community context. That the value of the human being is enhanced by diminishing the value of the larger community is an illusion, the great illusion of the present industrial age, which seeks to advance the human by plundering the planet's geological structure and all its biological species.

This plundering is being perpetrated mainly by the great industrial establishments that have dominated the entire planetary process for the past one hundred years, during the period when modern science and technology took control not only of our natural resources but also of human affairs. If the viability of the human species is now in question, it is a direct consequence of these massive ventures, which have gained extensive control not only of our economies but also of our whole cultural development, whether it be economics, politics, law, education, medicine, or moral values. Even our language is heavily nuanced in favor of the consumer values fostered by our commercial industrial establishment.

Opposed to the industrial establishment is the ecological movement which seeks to create a more viable context for the human within the framework of the larger community. There must, however, be a clear understanding that this question of viability is not an issue that can be resolved in any permanent manner. It will be a continuing issue for the indefinite future.

The planet that ruled itself directly for the past millennia is now determining its future through human decision. Such has been the responsibility assumed by humans when we ventured into the study of the empirical sciences and their associated technologies. In this process, whatever the benefits, we endangered ourselves and every living organism on this planet.

If we look back over the total course of planetary development, we find that there was a consistent fluorescence of the life process in the larger arc of its development over some billions of years. There were innumerable catastrophic events in both the geological and biological realms, but none of these had the distinguishing characteristics or could cause such foreboding as Earth experiences at present.

The total extinction of life is not imminent, though the elaborate forms of life expression in the earth's ecosystems may be shattered in an irreversible manner. What is absolutely threatened is the degradation of the planet's more brilliant and satisfying forms of life expression. This degradation involves extensive distortion and a pervasive weakening of the life system, its comprehensive integrity as well as its particular manifestations.

While there are pathologies that wipe out whole populations of life forms and must be considered pernicious to the life process on an extensive scale, the human species has, for some thousands of years, shown itself to be a pernicious presence in the world of the living on a unique and universal scale. Nowhere has this been more evident than in the Western phase of development of the human species. There is scarcely any geological or biological reality or function that has not experienced the deleterious influence of the human. The survival of hundreds of thousands of species is presently threatened. But since the human survives only within this larger complex of ecosystems, any damage done to other species, or to the other ecosystems, or to the planet itself, eventually affects the human not only in terms of physical well-being but also in every other phase of human intellectual understanding, aesthetic expression, and spiritual development.

Because such deterioration results from a rejection of the inherent limitation of earthly existence and from an effort to alter the natural functioning of the planet in favor of a humanly constructed wonderworld for its human occupants, the human resistance to this destructive process has turned its efforts toward an emphasis on living creatively within the functioning of the natural world. The earth as a bio-spiritual planet must become, for the human, the basic reference in identifying what is real and what is worthwhile.

Thus we have the ecologist standing against industrial enterprise in defense of a viable mode of human functioning within the context of a viable planetary process. This opposition between the industrial entrepreneur and the ecologist has been both the central human issue and the central earth issue of this late 20th century. My position is that the efforts of the entrepreneur to create a wonderworld are, in fact, creating a wasteworld, a nonviable environment for the human species. The ecologist is offering a way of moving toward a new expression of the true wounderworld of nature as the context for a viable human situation. The current difficulty is that the industrial enterprise has such extensive control over the planet that we must certainly be anxious about the future.

But we are tempted to diminish our assessment of the danger lest we be overwhelmed with the difficulty, for indeed, we are caught in a profound cultural pathology. We might even say that, at present, our dominant institutions, professions, programs, and activities are counterproductive in their consequences, addictive to a consumer society; and we are paralyzed by our inability to respond effectively. Such a description is well merited if we consider the extent to which we have poisoned our environment, the air we breathe, the water we drink, and the soil that grows our food.

Having identified the magnitude of the difficulty before us, we need to establish a more specific analysis of the problems themselves. Then we need to provide specific programs leading toward a viable human situation on a viable planet.

The industrial entrepreneur is in possession of the natural resources of the planet, either directly, by corporate control, or indirectly, through governments subservient to the industrial enterprise. This possession is, of course, within limits. Fragmentary regions of the planet have been set aside as areas to be preserved in their natural state or to be exploited at a later time. These regions survive at the tolerance of the industrial establishment. Some controls now exist through governmental and private protection. These must be expanded.

Ecologists recognize that reducing the planet to a resource base for consumer use in an industrial society is already a spiritual and psychic degradation. Our main experience of the divine, the world of the sacred, has been diminished as money and utility values have taken precedence over spiritual, aesthetic, emotional, and religious values in our attitude toward the natural world. Any recovery of the natural world will require not only extensive financial funding but a conversion experience deep in the psychic structure of the human. Our present dilemma is the consequence of a disturbed psychic situation, a mental imbalance, an emotional insensitivity, none of which can be remedied by any quickly contrived adjustment. Nature has been severely, and in many cases irreversibly, damaged. Healing can occur and new life can sometimes be evoked, but only with the same intensity of concern and sustained vigor of action as that which brought about the damage in the first place. Yet, without this healing, the viability of the human is severely limited.

The basic orientation of the common law tradition is toward personal rights and toward the natural world as existing for human use. There is no provision for recognition of nonhuman beings as subjects having legal rights. To the ecologists, the entire question of possession and use of the earth, either by individuals or by establishments, needs to be profoundly reconsidered. The naive assumption that the natural world exists solely to be possessed and used by humans for their unlimited advantage cannot be accepted. The earth belongs to itself and to all the component members of the community. The entire earth is a gorgeous celebration of existence in all its forms. Each living thing participates in the celebration as the proper fulfillment of its powers of expression. The reduction of the earth to an object simply for human possession and use is unthinkable in most traditional cultures. To Peter Drucker, the entrepreneur creates resources and values. Before it is possessed and used, "every plant is a weed and every mineral is just another rock" (*Innovation and Entrepreneurship,* 1985, p. 30). To the industrial entrepreneur, human possession and use is what activates the true value of any natural object.

The Western legal tradition, with its insistence on personal rights and the freedom of the human to occupy and use the land and all its component forms, is the greatest support for the entrepreneur. There is no question of other natural beings having rights over the human. Human use is not limited by any legally recognized rights of other natural beings but only by human determination of the limits that humans are willing to accept.

To achieve a viable human-earth community, a new legal system must take as its primary task to articulate the conditions for the integral functioning of the earth process, with special reference to a mutually enhancing human-earth relationship. Within this context, each component of the earth would be a separate community and together they would constitute the integral expression of the great community of the planet Earth.

In this context, each individual being is also supported by every other being in the earth community. In turn, each contributes to the well-being of every other. Justice would consist in carrying out this sequence of creative relationships. Within the human community there would, of course, be a need for articulating patterns of social relationships, in which individual and group rights would be recognized and defended and the basic elements of personal security and personal property would be protected. The entire complex of political and social institutions would be needed. Economic organizations would also be needed. But these would be so integral with the larger earth economy that they would enhance rather than obstruct each other.

Another significant aspect of contemporary life, wherein the industrial entrepreneur has a dominant position, is language. Since we are enclosed in an industrial culture, the words we use have their significance and validation defined within this industrial framework. A central value word used by our society is "progress." This word has great significance for increasing our scientific understanding of the universe, our personal and social development, our better health and longer life. Through modern technology, we can manufacture great quantities of products with greater facility. Human technology also enables us to travel faster and with greater ease. So on and on, endlessly, we see our increasing human advantage over the natural world.

But then we see that human progress has been carried out by desolating the natural world. This degradation of the earth is the very condition of the "progress" presently being made by humans. It is a kind of sacrificial offering. Within the human community, however, there is little awareness of the misunderstanding of this word. The feeling that even the most trivial modes of human progress are preferable to the survival of the most sublime and even the most sacred aspects of the natural world is so pervasive that the ecologist is at a loss as to how to proceed. The language in which our values are expressed has been co-opted by the industrial establishments and is used with the most extravagant modes of commercial advertising to create the illusory world in which the human community is now living.

One of the most essential roles of the ecologist is to create the language in which a true sense of reality, of value, and of progress can be communicated to our society. This need for rectification of language was recognized very early by the Chinese as a first task for any acceptable guidance of the society. Just now, a rectification is needed for the term "progress." As presently used, this word might be understood more properly to mean "retardation" or "destruction." The meaning of the term "profit" also needs to be rectified. Profit according to what norms and for whom? The profit of the corporation is the deficit of the earth. The profit of the industrial enterprise can also be considered the deficit of the quality of life, even for human society.

Gender has wide implications for our conception of the universe, the earth, and the life process, as well as for the relation of human individuals toward each other and for identifying social roles. The industrial establishment is the extreme expression of a non-viable patriarchal tradition. Only with enormous psychic and social effort and revolutionary processes has this control been mitigated with regard to the rights of serfs, slaves, women and children, ethnic groups, and the impoverished classes of our society. The rights of the natural world of living beings other than humans is still at the mercy of the modern industrial corporation as the ultimate expression of patriarchal dominance over the entire planetary process. The four basic patriarchal oppressions are rulers over people, men over women, possessors over nonpossessors, and humans over nature.

For the ecologist, the great model of all existence is the natural ecosystem, which is self-ruled as a community wherein each component has its unique and comprehensive influence. The ecologist, with a greater understanding of the human as a nurturing presence within the larger community of the geological and biological modes of earth, is closer to the feminine than to the masculine modality of being and of activity.

The purpose of education, as presently envisaged, is to enable humans to be "productive" within the context of the industrial society. A person needs to become literate in order to fulfill some function within the system, whether in the acquisition or processing of raw materials, manufacturing, distributing the product in a commercially profitable manner, managing the process or the finances, or finally, spending the net earnings in acquisition and enjoyment of possessions. A total life process is envisaged within this industrial process. All professional careers now tend toward the industrial-commercial model, especially medicine, law, and the engineering sciences.

In a new context, the primary educator as well as the primary lawgiver and the primary healer would be the natural world itself. The integral earth community would be a self-educating community within the context of a self-educating universe. Education at the human level would be the conscious sensitizing of the human to those profound communications made by the universe about us, by the sun and moon and stars, the clouds and rain, the contours of the earth and all its living forms. All the music and poetry of the universe would flow into the student, the revelatory presence of the divine, as well as insight into the architectural structures of the continents and the engineering skills whereby the great hydrological cycle functions in moderating the temperature of the earth, in providing habitat for aquatic life, in nourishing the multitudes of living creatures. The earth would also be our primary teacher of sciences, especially the biological sciences, and of industry and economics. It would teach us a system in which we would create a minimum of entropy, a system in which there is no unusable or unfruitful junk. Only in such an integral system is the future viability of the human assured.

Much more could be said about the function of the natural world as educator, but this may be sufficient to suggest the context for an education that would be available to everyone from the beginning to the end of life, when the earth that brought us into being draws us back into itself to experience the deepest of all mysteries.

In this ecological context, we see that the problems of human illness are not only increasing but also are being considerably altered in their very nature by the industrial context of life. In prior centuries, human illness was experienced within the well-being of the natural world with its abundance of air and water and foods grown in a fertile soil. Even city dwellers in their deteriorated natural surroundings could depend on the purifying processes of the natural elements. The polluting materials themselves were subject to natural composition and reabsorption into the ever-renewing cycles of the life process.

But this is no longer true. The purifying processes have been overwhelmed by the volume, the composition, and the universal extent of the toxic or non-biodegradable materials. Beyond all this, the biorhythms of the natural world are suppressed by the imposition of mechanistic patterns on natural processes.

The profession of medicine must now consider its role, not only within the context of human society, but in the context of the earth process. A healing of the earth is now a prerequisite for the healing of the human. Adjustment of the human to the conditions and restraints of the natural world constitutes the primary medical prescription for human well-being. Nothing else will suffice.

Behind the long disruption of the earth process is the refusal of our Western industrial society to accept any restraints upon its quest for release—not simply from the normal ills to which we are subject but release from the human condition itself. There exists in our tradition a hidden rage against those inner as well as outer forces that create a challenge or impose a limitation on our activities.

Some ancient force in the Western psyche seems to perceive limitation as the demonic obstacle to be eliminated rather than as a discipline to evoke creativity. Acceptance of the shadow aspect of the natural world is a primary condition for creative intimacy with the natural world. Without this opaque or even threatening aspect of the universe we would lose our greatest source of creative energy. This opposing element is as necessary for us as is the weight of the atmosphere that surrounds us. This containing element, even the gravitation that binds us to the earth, should be experienced as liberating and energizing rather than confining.

Strangely enough, it is our efforts to establish a thoroughly sanitized world that have led to our toxic world. Our quest for wonderworld is making wasteworld. Our quest for energy is creating entropy on a scale never before witnessed in the historical process. We have invented a counterproductive society that is now caught in the loop that feeds back into itself in what can presently be considered a runaway situation. This includes all our present human activities, although it is most evident in the industrial-commercial aspects of contemporary life.

The communications media are particularly responsible for placing the entire life process of the human in an uncontrolled situation. Producer and consumer feed each other in an ever-accelerating process until we experience an enormous glut of basic products. But we see unmatched deprivation for the growing numbers of people living in the shantytowns of the world.

There are no prominent newspapers, magazines, and periodicals that have consistently designated space for commentary on the ecological situation. There are sections for politics, economics, sports, arts, science, education, food, entertainment, and a number of other areas of life, including religion; but only on rare occasions are there references to what is happening to the planet. Of course, these periodicals are supported by the great industrial establishment, and the ecological situation is considered threatening or limiting to the industrial enterprise. In reality, industrial control of the media is among the most devastating forces threatening the viability of the human.

Efforts are made to mitigate the evils consequent to this industrial-commercial process by modifying the manner in which these establishments function, reducing the amount of toxic waste produced as well as developing more efficient modes of storing or detoxifying waste. Yet all of this is trivial in relation to the magnitude of the problem. So, too, are the regulatory efforts of the government; these are microphase solutions for macrophase problems.

We also witness the pathos of present efforts to preserve habitats for wildlife in some areas while elsewhere the tropical rain forests of the earth are being destroyed. Other efforts to alter present destructive activities are made by confrontational groups such as Greenpeace, Earth First!, and People for the Ethical Treatment of Animals. These are daring ventures that dramatize the stark reality of the situation. That such tactics (to save the whales at sea, the wilderness life on the land, and the millions of animals being tortured in laboratories under the guise of scientific research) are needed to force humans to examine and question our behavior is itself evidence of how deep a change is needed in human consciousness.

Beyond the mitigating efforts and confrontational tactics is the clarification of more creative modes of functioning in all our institutions and professions, especially through movements associated with reinhabiting the various bioregions of the world such as the Regeneration Project of the Rodale Institute, The Land Institute in Salina, Kansas, and the two North American Bioregional Congresses. These new and mutually enhancing patterns of human-earth relationships are being developed on a functional as well as a critical-intellectual basis. Among these organizations, the Green movement may be one of the most creative and effective in its overall impact as the years pass. This movement is finding expression in politics, in economics, in education, in healing, and in spiritual reorientation. These recent movements, oriented toward a more benign human relationship with the environment, indicate a pervasive change in consciousness that is presently our best hope for developing a sustainable future.

We might also now recover our sense of the maternal aspect of the universe in the symbol of the Great Mother, especially the Earth as the maternal principle out of which we are born. Once this symbol is recovered, the dominion of the patriarchal system that has brought such aggressive attitudes into our activities will be eliminated. If this is achieved, our relationship with the natural world should undergo its most radical readjustment since the origins of our civilization in classical antiquity.

We might also recover our archetypal sense of the cosmic tree and the tree of life. The tree symbol gives expression to the organic unity of the universe but especially of the earth in its integral reality. Obviously, any damage done to the tree will be experienced through the entire organism. This could be one of our most effective ways of creating not simply conscious decisions against industrial devastation of the earth but a deep instinctive repulsion to any such activity. This instinct should be as immediate as the instinct for survival itself.

In the United States, the educational and religious professionals should be especially sensitive in discerning what is happening to the planet. These professions present themselves as guides for the establishment of our values and interpretors of the significance of our lives. The study of education and religion should awaken an awareness of the world in which we live, how it functions, how the human fits into the larger community of life, and the role that the human fulfills in the great story of the universe, the historical sequence of developments that have shaped our physical and cultural landscape. Along with an awareness of the past and present, education and religion should guide the future.

The pathos of these times, however, is precisely the impasse we witness in our educational and religious programs. Both are living in a past fundamentalist tradition or venturing into New Age programs that are often trivial in their consequences, unable to support or to guide the transformation that is needed in its proper order of magnitude. We must recognize that the only effective program available is the program offered by the earth itself as our primary guide toward a viable human mode of being.

Both education and religion need to ground themselves within the story of the universe as we now understand this story through empirical knowledge. Within this functional cosmology we can overcome our alienation and begin the renewal of life on a sustainable basis. This story is a numinous revelatory story that could evoke the vision and the energy required to bring not only ourselves but the entire planet into a new order of magnificence.

Meanwhile, in the obscure regions of the human unconsciousness, where the primordial archetypal symbols function as ultimate controlling factors in human thought, emotion, and in practical decision making, a profound reorientation toward this integral human-earth relationship is gradually taking place. This archetypal journey must be experienced as the journey of each individual, since the entire universe has been involved in shaping our psyche as well as our physical being from that first awesome moment when the universe began. In the creation of a viable human, the universe reflects on and celebrates itself in conscious self-awareness, and finds a unique fulfillment.

"Simple in Means, Rich in Ends"

An Interview with Arne Naess by Stephan Bodian

S.B.: Arne, how did you become involved in deep ecology?

Naess: When I was four or five years old, I had the opportunity to explore the shoreline of fjords in Norway, and I was intrigued by the fantastic variety of life forms, especially the tiny fishes and crabs and shrimps which would gather around me in a very friendly way. I lived with these other beings throughout the summer. When I was nine or ten, I learned to enjoy the high mountains where my mother had a cottage. Because I had no father, the mountain somehow became my father, as a friendly, immensely powerful being, perfect and extremely tranquil. Later, pressures from school, from society, from the man-made world, made me happy to be where nothing pressured me into behaving or evaluating in any particular way. For example, clouds talk to us, but they don't pressure us into believing anything. Even a work of art somehow intends something, informs us about something. But nature is overwhelmingly rich and good and does not impose anything upon us. We are completely free, our imagination is free. Of course, if we are careless, an avalanche might bury us or we might drown, but in nature, there are always warnings. I never have had the feeling that nature is something to be dominated or conquered; it is something with which we coexist.

Modern astronomy, which I have followed since the 1930's, indicates that the universe is growing, and I feel that I am growing with the universe; I identify with the universe—the greater the universe, the greater I am. Some people feel threatened when they realize that the cosmos is so immense and we are so small. But we can be just as big as the cosmos, in a sense. We

This interview was originally published in 1982 by *The Ten Directions*, Los Angeles Zen Center. Reprinted with permission.

ourselves, as human beings, are capable of *identifying* with the whole of existence.

These feelings then led me into ecology when there was an international movement developing. I did not do it for fun. I think social movements are actually boring. I would rather be in nature, but I think we must all contribute to saving a little of what is left of this planet—this is the last century in which we will have the chance. That is why I am in Los Angeles today and not in the mountains or the desert.

S.B.: From the beginning, then, your interest as a philosopher involved nature in some way.

Naess: Because people found my interests so strange, I had somehow to label and rationalize them. This prompted me to ask deeper questions about the meaning of life. In this way, philosophy was my focus very early. A philosopher, in contrast to a professor of philosophy, is one whose philosophy is expressed in his or her life. I have tried to be both in the last ten years.

S.B.: You coined the term *deep ecology*. What do you mean by deep ecology exactly, and how is it different from shallow ecology?

Naess: The essence of deep ecology—as compared with the science of ecology, and with what I call the shallow ecological movement—is to ask deeper questions. The adjective "deep" stresses that we ask why and how, where others do not. For instance, ecology as a science does not ask what kind of a society would be the best for maintaining a particular ecosystem— that is considered a question for value theory, for politics, for ethics. As long as ecologists keep narrowly to their science, they do not ask such questions. What we need today is a tremendous expansion of ecological thinking in what I call ecosophy. *Sophy* comes form the Greek term *sophia*, "wisdom," which relates to ethics, norms, rules, and practice. Ecosophy, or deep ecology, then, involves a shift from science to wisdom.

For example, we need to ask questions like, Why do we think that economic growth and high levels of consumption are so important? The conventional answer would be to point to the economic consequences of not having economic growth. But in deep ecology, we ask whether the present society fulfills basic human needs like love and security and access to nature, and, in so doing, we question our society's underlying assumptions. We ask which society, which education, which form of religion, is beneficial to all life on the planet as a whole, and then we ask further what we need to do in order to make the necessary changes. We are not limited to a scientific approach; we have an obligation to verbalize a total view.

Of course, total views may differ. Buddhism, for example, provides a fitting background or context for deep ecology, certain Christian groups have formed platforms of action in favor of deep ecology, and I myself have worked out my own philosophy, which I call ecosophy T. In general, however, people do not question deeply enough to explicate or make clear a total view. If they did, most would agree with saving the planet from the destruction that's in progress. The differing ecosophies can provide a motivating force for all the activities and movements aimed at saving the planet from human domination and exploitation.

S.B.: It seems that, if we ask deeply enough, our questions will require us to make a radical shift in the way we see the world, what some people have called a paradigm shift.

Naess: Yes. I think it's a shift from being dominated by means, instruments, gadgets, all the many things we think will give us pleasure or make us happy or perfect. The shift comes about when we seriously ask ourselves, "In what situations do I experience the maximum satisfaction of my whole being?" and find that we need practically nothing of what we are supposed to need for a rich and fulfilling life. And if we make that shift toward a life simple in means but rich in goals, we are not threatened by plans for saving the planet elaborated by environmentalists. For instance, we can see that, instead of an energy crisis, we have a crisis of consumption—we have more than enough energy. There is no reason to continue increasing our consumption of energy or of any of the other material aspects of life. In countries like the United States, the crisis is rather one of lifestyle, of our traditions of thoughtlessness and confusion, or our inability to question deeply what is and is not worthwhile in life. Within fifty years, either we will need a dictatorship to save what is left of the diversity of life forms, or we will have a shift of values, a shift of our total view such that no dictatorship will be needed. It is thoroughly natural to stop dominating, exploiting, and destroying the planet. A "smooth" way, involving harmonious living with nature, or a "rough" way, involving a dictatorship and coercion—those are the options.

S.B.: What then would you consider the fundamental characteristics or attributes of deep ecology, and how do they differ from those of shallow ecology?

Naess: One of the basic norms of deep ecology is that every life form has in principle a right to live and blossom. As the world is made, of course, we have to kill in order to eat, but there is a basic intuition in deep ecology that we have no right to destroy other living beings without sufficient reason. Another norm is that, with maturity, human beings will experience joy when other life forms experience joy, and sorrow when other life forms experience sorrow. Not only do we feel sad when our brother or a dog or a cat feels sad, but we will grieve when living beings, including landscapes, are destroyed. In our civilization, we have vast means of destruction at our disposal but extremely little maturity in our feelings. Only a very narrow range of feelings have interested most human beings until now.

For deep ecology, there is a core democracy in the biosphere. The shallow ecology movement tends to talk only about resources for humans, whereas in deep ecology we talk about resources for each species. Shallow ecology is concerned about overpopulation in developing countries but not about overpopulation in industrial countries—countries which may destroy one hundred times more per capita than a country like Bangladesh. In deep ecology, we have the goal not only of stabilizing the human population but also of reducing it to a sustainable minimum by humane means which do not require a revolution or a dictatorship. I should think that we would not need more than one billion people in order to have the variety of human cultures we had one hundred years ago. We need the conservation of human cultures, just as we need the conservation of animal species. We need diversity of both human and non-human life!

S.B.: So diversity is of great value at the human level as well as at the level of plants and animals.

Naess: Yes. Personally, I think that, to maximize self-realization—and I don't mean self as ego but self in a broader sense—we need maximum diversity and maximum symbiosis. Diversity, then, is a fundamental norm and a common delight. As supporters of the deep ecology movement, we take a natural delight in diversity, as long as it does not include crude intrusive forms, such as Nazi culture, that are destructive to others.

A long-range view is characteristic of deep ecology—we feel responsible for future generations, not just the first, but the second, third, and fourth generation as well. Our perspective in time and space is very long. By contrast, the shallow ecological movement tends to repair only some of the worst consequences of our lifestyle and social structure—it does not address itself to fundamental questions.

S.B.: What do you mean when you say that maximum self-realization and maximum diversity are closely related?

Naess: Self-realization is the realization of the potentialities of life. Organisms that differ from each other in three ways give us less diversity than organisms that differ from each other in one hundred ways. Therefore, the self-realization we experience when we identify with the universe is heightened by an increase in the number of ways in which individuals, societies, and even species and life forms realize themselves. The greater the diversity then, the greater the Self-realization. This seeming duality between individuals and the totality is encompassed by what I call the Self, and what the Chinese call the Tao. Most people in deep ecology have had the feeling—usually, but not always, in nature—that they are connected with something greater than their ego, greater than their name, their family, their special attributes as an individual—a feeling that is often called oceanic because many have had this feeling on the ocean. Without that identification, one is not so easily drawn to become involved in deep ecology.

Many people have had this feeling when they see a death struggle—for instance when they see tiny animals like flies or mosquitoes fighting for their lives. When they see animals suffering, they may identify with a life form they usually don't identify with. Such situations offer us an opportunity to develop a more mature point of view. Insofar as this conversion, these deep feelings, are religious, then deep ecology has a religious component. People who have done the most to make societies aware of the destructive way in which we live in relation to nature have had such religious feelings. Rachel Carson, for example, said that we *cannot* do what we have been doing, that we have no religious or ethical justification for behaving as we have toward nature. Her argument was not calculated or "reasonable" in the usual sense of saying that if we continue poisoning nature, we will be less healthy, or will have fewer resources, and so on. She said that we cannot permit ourselves to behave in that way. Some will say that nature is not man's property, it's the property of God: others will say it in other ways. Deep ecology may be said to have a religious component, fundamental intuitions that everyone must cultivate if he or she is to have a life based on values and not function like a computer. Shallow ecology, if taken to its logical extreme, is like a computerized cost-benefit analysis designed to benefit only humans.

S.B.: You mention a long time frame. On the other hand, of course, the situation is critical right now—species are becoming extinct at a very rapid rate, ecosystems are being destroyed. How do you balance the need for a long time frame with the very urgent need for immediate action?

Naess: It is very natural to combine the two, because the long perspective in time and space motivates one to act in a profound and consistent way. That is to say, being concerned with the whole, with the religious and philosophical background, one learns, for example, that there are practically no more rain forests on far away Sumatra, and only six percent left on Sri Lanka, and one is motivated immediately by some deep evaluation that says, "This cannot go on, this must be changed." So the long time frame—absolutely necessary in questions of population reduction, for instance—is necessary both because of certain facts and because of the motivation we derive from eternal concerns like Self-realization, identification with the universe, and other religious notions that involve millennia or even eternity, rather than five or ten years.

S.B.: Deep ecology, then, is a fundamental view of the world that at the same time calls for immediate action. In addition to contrasting it with shallow ecology, can you suggest ways in which the two might work together? Can deep ecology inform movements which may be anthropocentric and may not articulate a fundamental world view yet are also large and effective?

Naess: I think that the deep ecology movement must cooperate with various movements, including what we call narrow or shallow environmental organizations. The Sierra Club, for example, cannot have deep ecological principles in its statutes but must include people who are very anthropocentric and think only about the maximum benefit for human beings within a ten or twenty year time frame. We need to work with movements whose members do not know anything about deep ecology and may not have contact with wilderness or personal relationships with animals other than cats and dogs. And of course we can cooperate with movements that deal with related issues, such as the antinuclear movement and certain Christian movements for the dignity of life, at the same time trying to expand and deepen their views in a new direction.

However, we must also have programs that may not be meaningful to those who are not supporters of deep ecology—the reduction of human population, for instance. We must be flexible but never forget fundamental principles, because, like Buddhism and certain other philosophies in the Western and Eastern traditions, deep ecology involves basic views of man and the world.

S.B.: Some people, particularly in this country, have great faith that, once we've perfected our computer technology and can process all the available information, we'll be able to make informed decisions. You, on the other hand, have spoken about the importance of admitting that we don't know, admitting our ignorance in the face of the complexity of nature, and at the same time be willing to trust our intuition and stand up and say, "I know in my heart that this is what we need to do."

Naess: I think that, one hundred and fifty years ago, in government decision making in America and in Europe, more information was available in proprotion to the amount needed than is available today. Today, we are using thousands of new chemicals, and we don't know their combined long-range effects. We interfere a million times more deeply in nature than we did one hundred years ago, and our ignorance is increasing in proportion to the information that is required.

S.B.: In other words, many more questions are being raised, but fewer answers are being provided.

Naess: Exactly. One indication is that, if you take the number of scientific articles published each year with neat, authoritative conclusions and divide it by the number of questions posed to scientists by responsible people concerned with the consequences of our interventions in nature, you will find that the quotient approaches zero. That is, the number of questions is becoming indefinitely large very quickly, whereas the number of answers is increasing very slowly indeed. And, in any case, within a hundred years, we'll run out of paper to print the billion articles that supply the relevant answers needed each year.

S.B.: So you don't think that, if we just perfect our science and technology, our answers will somehow catch up with the number of questions being raised?

Naess: On the contrary, technology is more helpless than ever before because the technology being produced doesn't fulfill basic human needs, such as meaningful work in a meaningful environment. Technical progress is sham progress because the term *technical progress* is a cultural, not a technical term. Our culture is the only one in the history of mankind in which the culture has adjusted itself to the technology, rather than vice versa. In traditional Chinese culture, the bureaucracy opposed the use of inventions that were not in harmony with the general cultural aims of the nation. A vast number of technical inventions were not used by the populace because it was simply not permitted. Whereas here we have the motto, "You can't stop progress," you can't interfere with technology, and so we allow technology to dictate cultural forms.

S.B.: In connection with that, it has been pointed out that the hazardous nature of the materials used to generate nuclear power will have unforeseen political consequences.

Naess: Yes. Security, for instance, is a major problem. And even more importantly, such technology presupposes a tremendous, centralized society, whereas, in more ecologically defensible societies, energy creation and energy sources would be decentralized and widely distributed, with small groups in local communities in control of their own resources. As it is now, we have increasing centralization, which fosters diminished self-determination for individuals and local cultures, and diminished freedom of action. The more centralized our energy sources, the more dependent we are on centralized institutions hundreds of miles away.

There's no reason to believe there won't be another war. On the contrary, the statistics give us every reason to believe we will continue to have wars in the future. During World War II, people were highly self-sufficient—they could raise pigs, they could burn wood—whereas, in a war today some nations could be conquered almost immediately because all resources are centralized. We don't know how to grow food, we don't have anything to burn. In the year 2000, we will be so dependent that, if an aggressor were to take over the energy sources and the political institutions, ninety-nine percent of the population would have to surrender, whereas in the last war we were able to continue our culture. Deep ecology is concerned with these long-range problems, particularly with the question of war and peace, because, of all man-made ecological catastrophes, nuclear war would be the most devastating.

S.B.: This brings us back to the question of information versus intuition. Your feeling is that we can't expect to have an ideal amount of information but must somehow act on what we already know.

Naess: Yes. It's easier for people in deep ecology than for others because we have certain fundamental values, a fundamental view of what's meaningful in life, what's worth maintaining, which makes it completely clear that we in the rich countries are opposed to further development for the sake of increased domination and an increased standard of living. The material standard of living should be reduced and the quality of life, in the sense of basic satisfaction in the depths of one's heart or soul, should be maintained or increased. This view is intuitive, as are all important views, in the sense that it can't be proven. As Aristotle said, it shows a lack of education to try to prove everything, because you have to have a starting point. You can't prove the methodology of science, you can't prove logic, because logic presupposes fundamental premises.

All the sciences are fragmentary and incomplete in relation to basic rules and norms, so it's very shallow to think that science can solve our problems. Without basic norms, there is no science. Of course, we need science—in fact, a thousand times more than we have—if we are to answer scientifically the questions politicians ask about the consequences of our actions. As it is now, we have to say, for the most part, that we don't know although we can make informed guesses. And since politicians give priority to increased growth and consumption, their reply is, "If you can't tell us authoritatively what the bad consequences will be from this project, then we'll go ahead with it." For example, they may give researchers so many dollars to discover the effects of oil spills on plankton. And after a year, we may have to say as scientists that we don't really know, we are just beginning to understand. But common sense and intuition tell us that, if we continue to dump more oil into the sea, we will cause the destruction of life forms on a vast scale.

S.B.: Nowadays, people have been trained to defer taking a stand on an issue until all the facts are in. As an example, some experts say that nuclear reactors are unsafe, others say that they are safe, and people are bewildered.

Naess: I tell people that if they make clear their fundamental assumptions about what is needed for a life simple in means and rich in ends, they will necessarily come to the conclusion that it is not a lack of energy consumption that makes them unhappy. They can then oppose nuclear power without having read thick books and without knowing the myriad facts that are used in newspapers and periodicals. And they must also find others who feel the same way and form circles of friends who give one another confidence and support in living in a way that the majority finds ridiculous, naive, stupid, and unnecessarily simplistic. But in order to do that, one must already have enough self-confidence to follow one's intuitions—a quality very much lacking in broad sections of the populace. Many people follow the trends and advertisements and tend to become philosophical and ethical cripples.

S.B.: What do you consider the priorities for action in the deep ecology movement over the next twenty-five years?

Naess: Each of us has to act on a different part of a very broad frontier. One of the most important activities for the next five to ten years will be to dissseminate the knowledge we have—regarding the destruction of the tropical rain forests, for example, or the climatic changes and other global factors that are now getting out of hand. Communication is crucial, and all of us can do something. In deep ecology, another major question is how to get along with the various religious populations—Christians, Buddhists, and others—in which a minority, especially the young, is completely aware of the destruction of the planet and believes that it must not be permitted. We must cooperate with these religious movements because, as I've mentioned, the motivation for strong action must come from deep sources in philosophy and ethics.

In the matter of political action, I am very much inspired by the Gandhian approach of maximizing the communication on a friendly footing—that is, even if people don't want to talk with you at a certain moment, try to be personally helpful and to make personal contact. Another way to make contact is to canvass from house to house. I think the personal approach has not been sufficiently explored, especially with labor organizations. Many actions in Norway have been unsuccessful because the intellectuals and the middle class have not communicated with the working classes. laborers are concerned about unemployment and think ecology is a kind of fad among the upper classes, whereas, in an ecological crisis, laborers and others with limited economic means will actually be the hardest hit. The credibility and effectiveness of the ecological movement will remain low as long as we don't make contact with working people. We must learn to talk with them in language they are familiar with. Canvassing should not mean that we talk only with people who think like us.

S.B.: The head of the machinists' union at an aerospace company involved in a great deal of defense contracting recently made a similar point. He stressed that, if the disarmament movement wanted to join with workers in the arms industry, it would have to emphasize the conversion of weapons manufacturing to peace-time industry. Otherwise, it would be threatening their livelihood and would never win their support.

Naess: That relates also to what we are doing now in Norway. In trying to compete with Japan, Singapore, and various other countries, we have had to build large, centralized, automated factories. Instead, what we need to do is to reduce our imports and therefore our exports, convert our big factories into small-scale, labor-intensive industry that makes products we need, and continue to sustain our culture as it has been, rather than try to compete on the world market. Then we will have very little unemployment, and work will be much more meaningful. If we come to the workers with this kind of program, they will be more receptive than if we come from our middle or upper-class residences and talk to them in our own language about our rather abstract concerns.

S.B.: How important do you feel it is for individuals to practice deep ecology in their own lives? And I was wondering how you practice it in yours?

Naess: I think that, in the long run, in order to participate joyfully and wholeheartedly in the deep ecology movement, you have to take your own life very seriously. People who successfully maintain a low material standard of living and successfully cultivate a deep, intense sense of life are much better able to consistently maintain a deep ecological view and to act on behalf of it. As I sit down and breathe deeply and just feel where I am, I can ask myself where and when I really enjoy my life and what would be the minimum means necessary to maintain these enjoyable feelings and situations. For example, I myself have been too eager to go climbing in the Himalayas, whereas the peculiar satisfaction I have as a mountaineer could be had in Norway. If you concentrate on what gives you satisfaction, you will find that it can be obtained much more easily and simply than we are educated to believe in our society, where the bigger, the more elaborate, and the more expensive are considered better.

S.B.: I like what you said recently about spending an hour or two just looking at a little patch of ground.

Naess: Yes. Look at this (holding up a tiny flower). If you took the forms and the symmetries and made them into a painting, you might win first prize in any competition.

S.B.: I have relatives in England who take endless delight in climbing the same mountains in Wales and the same hills near their home.

Naess: That's right. A hill is never the same in a repetitious way! The development of sensitivity toward the good things of which there are enough is the true goal of education. Not that we need to limit our goals. I'm not for the simple life, except in the sense of a life simple in means but rich in goals and values. I have tremendous ambition. Only the best is good enough for me. I like richness, and I feel richer than the richest person when I'm in my cottage in the country with water I've carried from a certain well and with wood I've gathered. When you take a helicopter to the summit of a mountain, the view looks like a postcard, and, if there's a restaurant on top, you might complain that the food is not properly made. But if you struggle up from the bottom, you have this deep feeling of satisfaction, and even the sandwiches mixed with ski wax and sand taste fantastic.

The Deep Ecological Movement: Some Philosophical Aspects

Arne Naess

Arne Naess is professor emeritus at the University of Oslo, Norway, where he was chairman of the philosophy department for many years. Naess coined the term and developed the basic concepts of "deep ecology" in 1972. Widely regarded as one of the leading scholars in Europe, he is the author of Ecology, Community and Lifestyle *(English trans. 1989) and many books and papers on empirical linguistics, Spinoza, Gandhi, and ecosophy.*

1. DEEP ECOLOGY ON THE DEFENSIVE

Increasing pressures for continued growth and development have placed the vast majority of environmental professionals on the defensive. By way of illustration:

The field ecologist Ivar Mysterud, who both professionally and vigorously advocated deep ecological principles in the late 1960's, encountered considerable resistance. Colleagues at his university said he should keep to his science and not meddle in philosophical and political matters. He should resist the temptation to become a prominent "popularizer" through mass media exposure. Nevertheless, he persisted and influenced thousands of people (including myself).

Mysterud became a well-known professional "expert" at assessing the damage done when bears killed or maimed sheep and other domestic

This essay originally appeared in *Philosophical Inquiry,* Vol. VIII, No. 1–2, 1986, pp. 10–31. Reprinted with permission.

animals in Norway. According to the law, their owners are paid damages. And licensed hunters receive permission to shoot bears if their misdeeds become considerable.[1] Continued growth and development required that the sheep industry consolidate, and sheepowners became fewer, richer, and tended to live in cities. As a result of wage increases, they could not afford to hire shepherds to watch the flocks, so the sheep were left on their own even more than before. Continued growth also required moving sheep to what was traditionally considered "bear territory." In spite of this invasion, bear populations grew and troubles multiplied.

How did Mysterud react to these new problems? Did he set limits to the amount of human/sheep encroachment on bear territory? Did he attempt a direct application of his deep ecological perspective to these issues? Quite the contrary. He adopted what appeared to be a shallow wildlife management perspective, and defended the sheepowners: more money to compensate for losses, quicker compensation, and the immediate hiring of hunters who killed mostly "juvenile delinquent" bears accused of killing many sheep.

Protectors of big carnivores noted with concern the change of Mysterud's public "image"; had he really abandoned his former value priorities? Privately he insisted that he hadn't. But in public he tended to remain silent.

The reason for M.'s unexpected actions was not difficult to find: the force of economic growth was so strong that the laws protecting bears would be changed in a highly unfavorable direction if the sheepowners were not soon pacified by accepting some of their not unreasonable demands. After all, it did cost a lot of money to hire and equip people to locate a flock of sheep which had been harassed by a bear and, further, to prove the bear's guilt. And the bureaucratic procedures involved were time consuming. M. had not changed his basic value priorities at all. Rather, he had adopted a purely defensive compromise. He stopped promoting his deep ecology philosophy publicly in order to retain credibility and standing among opponents of his principles and to retain his friendships with sheepowners.

And what is true of Mysterud is also true of thousands of other professional ecologists and environmentalists. These people often hold responsible positions in society where they might strengthen responsible environmental policy, but, given the exponential forces of growth, their publications, if any, are limited to narrowly professional and specialized concerns. Their writings are surely competent, but lack a deeper and more comprehensive perspective (although I admit that there are some brilliant exceptions to this).

If professional ecologists persist in voicing their value priorities, their jobs are often in danger, or they tend to lose influence and status among those who are in charge of overall policies.[2] Privately, they admit the necessity for deep and far-ranging changes, but they no longer speak out in public. As a result, people deeply concerned about ecology and the environment feel abandoned and even betrayed by the "experts" who work within the "establishment."

In ecological debates, many participants know a lot about particular conservation policies in particular places, and many others have strong views concerning fundamental philosophical questions of environmental ethics, but only a few have both qualities. When these people are silent, the loss is formidable.

For example, the complicated question concerning how industrial societies can increase energy production with the least undesirable consequences is largely a waste of time if this increase is pointless in relation to ultimate human ends. Thousands of experts hired by the government and other big institutions devote their time to this complicated problem, yet it is difficult for the public to find out or realize that many of these same experts consider the problem to be pointless and irrelevant. What these experts consider relevant are the problems of how to stabilize and eventually decrease consumption without losing genuine quality of life for humans. But they continue to work on the irrelevant problems assigned to them while, at the same time, failing to speak out, because the ultimate power is not in their hands.

2. A CALL TO SPEAK OUT

What I am arguing for is this: even those who completely subsume ecological policies under the narrow ends of human health and well-being cannot attain their modest aims, at least not fully, without being joined by the supporters of deep ecology. They need what these people have to contribute, and this will work in their favor more often than it will work against them. Those in charge of environmental policies, even if they are resource-oriented (and growth tolerating?) decision makers, will increasingly welcome, if only for tactical and not fundamental reasons, what deep ecology supporters have to say. Even though the more radical ethic may seem nonsensical or untenable to them, they know that its advocates are, in practice, doing conservation work that sooner or later must be done. They concur with the practice even though they operate from diverging theories. The time is ripe for professional ecologists to break their silence and express their deepest concerns more freely. A bolder advocacy of deep ecological concerns by those working within the shallow, resource-oriented environmental sphere is the best strategy for regaining some of the strength of this movement among the general public, thereby contributing, however modestly, to a turning of the tide.

What do I mean by saying that even the more modest aims of shallow environmentalism have a need for deep ecology? We can see this by considering the World Conservation Strategy—prepared by the International Union for the Conservation of Nature and Natural Resources (IUCN) in cooperation with the United Nations Environmental Programme (UNEP) and the World Wildlife Fund (WWF). The argument in this important document is thoroughly anthropocentric in the sense that all its recommendations are justified exclusively in terms of their effects upon human health and basic well-being.[3]

A more ecocentric environmental ethic is also recommended apparently for tactical reasons: "A new ethic, embracing plants and animals as well as people, is required for human societies to live in harmony with the natural world on which they depend for survival and well-being." But such an ethic would surely be more effective it it were acted upon by people who believe in its validity, rather than merely its usefulness. This, I think, will come to be understood more and more by those in charge of educational policies. Quite simply, it is indecent for a teacher to proclaim an ethic for tactical reasons only.

Furthermore, this point applies to all aspects of a world conservation strategy. Conservation strategies are more eagerly implemented by people who love what they are conserving, and who are convinced that what they love is intrinsically lovable. Such lovers will not want to hide their attitudes and values, rather they will increasingly give voice to them in public. They possess a genuine ethics of conservation, not merely a tactically useful instrument for human survival.

In short, environmental education campaigns can fortunately combine human-centered arguments with a practical environmental ethic based on either a deeper and more fundamental philosophic or religious perspective, and on a set of norms resting on intrinsic values. But the inherent strength of this overall position will be lost if those who work professionally on environmental problems do not freely give testimony to fundamental norms.

The above is hortatory in the positive etymological sense of that word. I seek "to urge, incite, instigate, encourage, cheer" (Latin: *hortari*). This may seem unacademic but I consider it justifiable because of an intimate relationship between hortatory sentences and basic philosophical views which I formulate in section 8. To trace what follows from fundamental norms and hypotheses is eminently philosophical.

3. WHAT IS DEEP ECOLOGY?

The phrase "deep ecology movement" has been used up to this point without trying to define it. One should not expect too much from definitions of movements; think, for example, of terms like "conservatism," "liberalism," or the "feminist movement." And there is no reason why supporters of movements should adhere exactly to the same definition, or to any definition, for that matter. It is the same with characterizations, criteria, or a set of proposed necessary conditions for application of the term or phrase. In what follows, a set of principles or key terms and phrases (or a platform), agreed upon by George Sessions and myself, are tentatively proposed as basic to deep ecology.[4] More accurately, the sentences have a double function. They are meant to express important points which the great majority of supporters accept, implicitly or explicitly, at a high level of generality. Furthermore, they express a proposal to the effect that those who solidly reject one or more of these points should not be viewed as supporters of deep ecology. This might result because they are supporters of a shallow (or reform) environmental movement or rather they may simply dislike one or more of the 8 points for semantical or other reasons. But they may well accept a different set of points which, to me, has roughly the same meaning, in which case I shall call them supporters of the deep ecology movement, but add that they *think* they disagree (maybe Henryk Skolimowski is an example of the latter). The 8 points are:

(1) The well-being and flourishing of human and non-human life on Earth have value in themselves (synonyms: intrinsic value, inherent worth). These values are independent of the usefulness of the non-human world for human purposes.

(2) Richness and diversity of life forms contribute to the realization of these values and are also values in themselves.

(3) Humans have no right to reduce this richness and diversity except to satisfy vital needs.

(4) The flourishing of human life and cultures is compatible with a substantially smaller human population. The flourishing of non-human life *requires* a smaller human population.

(5) Present human interference with the non-human world is excessive, and the situation is rapidly worsening.

(6) Policies must therefore be changed. These policies affect basic economic, technological, and ideological structures. The resulting state of affairs will be deeply different from the present.

(7) The ideological change will be mainly that of appreciating life quality (dwelling in situations of inherent value) rather than adhering to an increasingly higher standard of living. There will be a profound awareness of the difference between bigness and greatness.

(8) Those who subscribe to the foregoing points have an obligation directly or indirectly to try to implement the necessary changes.

Comments on the Basic Principles:

RE (1): This formulation refers to the biosphere, or more professionally, to the ecosphere as a whole (this is also referred to as "ecocentrism"). This includes individuals, species, populations, habitat, as well as human and non-human cultures. Given our current knowledge of all-pervasive intimate relationships, this implies a fundamental concern and respect.

The term "life" is used here in a more comprehensive non-technical way also to refer to what biologists classify as "non-living": rivers (watersheds), landscapes, ecosystems. For supporters of deep ecology, slogans such as "let the river live" illustrate this broader useage so common in many cultures.

Inherent value, as used in (1), is common in deep ecology literature (e.g., "The presence of inherent value in a natural object is independent of any awareness, interest, or appreciation of it by any conscious being").[5]

RE (2): The so-called simple, lower, or primitive species of plants and animals contribute essentially to the richness and diversity of life. They have value in themselves and are not merely steps toward the so-called higher or rational life forms. The second principle presupposes that life itself, as a process over evolutionary time, implies an increase of diversity and richness.

Complexity, as referred to here, is different from complication. For example, urban life may be more complicated than life in a natural setting without being more complex in the sense of multifaceted quality.

RE (3): The term "vital need" is deliberately left vague to allow for considerable latitude in judgment. Differences in climate and related factors, together with differences in the structures of societies as they now exist, need to be taken into consideration.

RE (4): People in the materially richest countries cannot be expected to reduce their excessive interference with the non-human world overnight. The stabilization and reduction of the human population will take time. Hundreds of years! Interim strategies need to be developed. But in no way does this excuse the present complacency. The extreme seriousness of our current situation must first be realized. And the longer we wait to make the necessary changes, the more drastic will be the measures needed. Until deep changes are made, substantial decreases in richness and diversity are liable to occur: the rate of extinction of species will be 10 to 100 or more times greater than in any other short period of earth history.

RE (5): This formulation is mild. For a realistic assessment, see the annual reports of the World Watch Institute in Washington, D.C.

The slogan of "non-interference" does not imply that humans should not modify some ecosystems, as do other species. Humans have modified the earth over their entire history and will probably continue to do so. At issue is the *nature and extent* of such interference. The per capita destruction of wild (ancient) forests and other wild ecosystems has been excessive in rich countries; it is essential that the poor do not imitate the rich in this regard.

The fight to preserve and extend areas of wilderness and near-wilderness ("free Nature") should continue. The rationale for such preservation should focus mainly on the ecological functions of these areas (one such function: large wilderness areas are required in the biosphere for the continued evolutionary speciation of plants and animals). Most of the present designated wilderness areas and game reserves are not large enough to allow for such speciation.

RE (6): Economic growth as it is conceived of and implemented today by the industrial states is incompatible with points (1) through (5). There is only a faint resemblance between ideal sustainable forms of economic growth and the present policies of industrial societies.

Present ideology tends to value things because they are scarce and because they have a commodity value. There is prestige in vast consumption and waste (to mention only several relevant factors).

Whereas "self-determination," "local community," and "think globally, act locally," will remain key terms in the ecology of human societies, nevertheless the implementation of deep changes requires increasingly global action: Action across borders.

Governments in Third World countries are mostly uninterested in deep ecological issues. When institutions in the industrial societies try to promote ecological measures through Third World governments, practically nothing is accomplished (e.g., with problems of desertification). Given this situation, support for global action through non-governmental international organizations becomes increasingly important. Many of these organizations are able to act globally "from grassroots to grassroots" thus avoiding negative governmental interference.

Cultural diversity today requires advanced technology, that is, techniques that advance the basic goals of each culture. So-called soft, intermediate, and alternative technologies are steps in this direction.

RE (7): Some economists criticize the term "quality of life" because it is supposedly vague. But, on closer inspection, what they consider to be vague is actually the non-quantifiable nature of the term. One cannot quantify adequately what is important for the quality of life as discussed here, and there is no need to do so.

RE (8): There is ample room for different opinions about priorities: what should be done first; what next? What is the most urgent? What is clearly necessary to be done, as opposed to what is highly desirable but not absolutely pressing? The frontier of the environmental crisis is long and varied, and there is a place for everyone.

The above formulations of the 8 points may be useful to many supporters of the deep ecology movement. But some will certainly feel that they are imperfect, even misleading. If they need to formulate in a few words what is basic to deep ecology, then they will propose an alternative set of sentences. I shall of course be glad to refer to them as alternatives. There ought to be a measure of diversity in what is considered basic and common.

Why should we call the movement "the deep ecological movement"?[6] There are at least six other designations which cover most of the same issues: "Ecological Resistance," used by John Rodman in important discussions; "The New Natural Philosophy" coined by Joseph Meeker; "Eco-phi-losophy," used by Sigmund Kvaloy and others to emphasize (1) a highly critical assessment of the industrial growth societies form a general ecological point of view, and (2) the ecology of the human species; "Green Philosophy and Politics" (while the term "green" is often used in Europe, in the United States "green" has a misleading association with the rather "blue" Green agricultural revolution); "Sustainable Earth Ethics," as used by G. Tyler Miller; and "Ecosophy" (eco-wisdom), which is my own favorite term. Others could be mentioned as well.

And so, why use the adjective "deep"? This question will be easier to answer after the contrast is made between shallow and deep ecological concerns. "Deep ecology" is not a philosophy in any proper academic sense, nor is it institutionalized as a religion or an ideology. Rather, what happens is that various persons come together in campaigns and direct actions. They form a circle of friends supporting the same kind of lifestyle which others may think to be "simple," but which they themselves see as rich and many-sided. They agree on a vast array of political issues, although they may otherwise support different political parties. As in all social movements, slogans and rhetoric are indispensable for in-group coherence. They react together against the same threats in a predominantly nonviolent way. Perhaps the most influential participants are artists and writers who do not articulate their insights in terms of professional philosophy, expressing themselves rather in art or poetry. For these reasons, I use the term "movement" rather than "philosophy." But it is essential that fundamental attitudes and beliefs are involved as part of the motivation for action.

4. DEEP VERSUS SHALLOW ECOLOGY

A number of key terms and slogans from the environmental debate will clarify the contrast between the shallow and the deep ecology movements.[7]

A. Pollution

Shallow Approach: Technology seeks to purify the air and water and to spread pollution more evenly. Laws limit permissible pollution. Polluting industries are preferably exported to developing countries.

Deep Approach: Pollution is evaluated from a biospheric point of view, not focusing exclusively on its effects on human health, but rather on life as a whole, including the life conditions of every species and system. The shallow reaction to acid rain, for example, is to tend to avoid action by demanding more research, and the attempt to find species of trees which will tolerate high acidity, etc. The deep approach concentrates on what is going on in the total ecosystem and calls for a high priority fight against the economic conditions and the technology responsible for producing the acid rain. The long-range concerns are 100 years, at least.

The priority is to fight the deep causes of pollution, not merely the superficial, short-range effects. The Third and Fourth World countries cannot afford to pay the total costs of the war against pollution in their regions; consequently they require the assistance of the First and Second World countries. Exporting pollution is not only a crime against humanity, it is a crime against life in general.

B. Resources

Shallow Approach: The emphasis is upon resources for humans, especially for the present generation in affluent societies. On this view, the resources of the earth belong to those who have the technology to exploit them. There is confidence that resources will not be depleted because, as they get rarer, a high market price will conserve them, and substitutes will be found through technological progress. Further, plants, animals, and natural objects are valuable only as resources for humans. If no human use is known, or seems likely ever to be found, it does not matter if they are destroyed.

Deep Approach: The concern here is with resources and habitats for all life forms for their own sake. No natural object is conceived of solely as a resource. This leads, then, to a critical evaluation of human modes of production and consumption. The question arises: to what extent does an increase in production and consumption foster ultimate human values? To what extent does it satisfy vital needs, locally or globally? How can economic, legal, and educational institutions be changed to counteract destructive increases? How can resource use serve the quality of life rather than the economic standard of living as generally promoted by consumerism? From a deep perspective, there is an emphasis upon an ecosystem approach rather than the consideration merely of isolated life forms or local situations. There is a long-range maximal perspective of time and place.

C. Population

Shallow Approach: The threat of (human) "overpopulation" is seen mainly as a problem for developing countries. One condones or even applauds population increases in one's own country for short-sighted economic, military, or other reasons; an increase in the number of humans is considered as valuable in itself or as economically profitable. The issue of an "optimum population" for humans is discussed without reference to the question of an "optimum population" for other life forms. The destruction of wild habitats caused by increasing human population is accepted as an inevitable evil, and drastic decreases of wildlife forms tend to be accepted insofar as species are not driven to extinction. Further, the social relations of animals are ignored. A long-term substantial reduction of the global human population is not seen to be a desirable goal. In addition, the right is claimed to defend one's borders against "illegal aliens," regardless of what the population pressures are elsewhere.

Deep Approach: It is recognized that excessive pressures on planetary life stem from the human population explosion. The pressure stemming from the industrial societies is a major factor, and population reduction must have the highest priority in those societies.

D. Cultural Diversity and Appropriate Technology

Shallow Approach: Industrialization of the Western industrial type is held to be the goal of developing countries. The universal adoption of Western technology is held to be compatible with cultural diversity, together with the conservation of the positive elements (from a Western perspective) of present non-industrial societies. There is a low estimate of deep cultural differences in non-industrial societies which deviate significantly from contemporary Western standards.

Deep Approach: Protection of non-industrial cultures from invasion by industrial societies. The goals of the former should not be seen as promoting lifestyles similar to those in the rich countries. Deep cultural diversity is an analogue on the human level to the biological richness an diversity of life forms. A high priority should be given to cultural anthropology in general education programs in industrial societies.

There should be limits on the impact of Western technology upon present existing non-industrial countries and the Fourth World should be defended against foreign domination. Political and economic policies should favor subcultures within industrial societies. Local, soft technologies should allow for a basic cultural assessment of any technical innovations, together with freely expressed criticism of so-called advanced technology when this has the potential to be culturally destructive.

E. Land and Sea Ethics

Shallow Approach: Landscapes, ecosystems, rivers, and other whole entities of nature are conceptually cut into fragments, thus disregarding larger units and comprehensive gestalts. These fragments are regarded as the properties and resources of individuals, organizations or states. Conservation is argued in terms of "multiple use" and "cost/benefit analysis." The social costs and long-term global ecological costs of resource extraction and use are usually not considered. Wildlife management is conceived of as conserving nature for "future generations of humans." Soil erosion or the deterioration of ground water quality, for example, is noted as a human loss, but a strong belief in future technological progress makes deep changes seem unnecessary.

Deep Approach: The earth does not belong to humans. For example, the Norwegian landscapes, rivers, flora and fauna, and the neighboring sea are not the property of Norwegians. Similarly, the oil under the North Sea or anywhere else does not belong to any state or to humanity. And the "free nature" surrounding a local community does not belong to the local community.

Humans only inhabit the lands, using resources to satisfy vital needs. And if their non-vital needs come in conflict with the vital needs of nonhumans, then humans should defer to the latter. The ecological destruction now going on will not be cured by a technological fix. Current arrogant notions in industrial (and other) societies must be resisted.

F. Education and the Scientific Enterprise

Shallow Approach: The degradation of the environment and resource depletion requires the training of more and more "experts" who can provide advice concerning how to continue combining economic growth with maintaining a healthy environment. We are likely to need an increasingly more dominating and manipulative technology to "manage the planet" when global economic growth makes further environmental degradation inevitable. The scientific enterprise must continue giving priority to the "hard sciences" (physics and chemistry). High educational standards with intense competition in the relevant "tough" areas of learning will be required.

Deep Approach: If sane ecological policies are adopted, then education should concentrate on an increased sensitivity to non-consumptive goods, and on such consumables where there is enough for all. Education should therefore counteract the excessive emphasis upon things with a price tag. There should be a shift in concentration from the "hard" to the "soft" sciences which stress the importance of the local and global cultures. The educational objective of the World Conservation Strategy ("building support for conservation") should be given a high priority, but within the deeper framework of respect for the biosphere.

In the future, there will be no shallow environmental movement if deep policies are increasingly adopted by governments, and thus no need for a special deep ecological social movement.

5. BUT WHY A "DEEP" ECOLOGY?

The decisive difference between a shallow and a deep ecology, in practice, concerns the willingness to question, and an appreciation of the importance of questioning, every economic and political policy in public. This questioning is both "deep" and public. It asks "why" insistently and consistently, taking nothing for granted!

Deep ecology can readily admit to the practical effectiveness of homocentric arguments:

> It is essential for conservation to be seen as central to human interests and aspirations. At the same time, people—from heads of state to the members of rural communities—will most readily be brought to demand conservation if they themselves recognize the contribution of conservation to the achievement of their needs as perceived by them, and the solution of their problems, as perceived by them.[8]

There are several dangers in arguing solely from the point of view of narrow human interests. Some policies based upon successful homocentric arguments turn out to violate or unduly compromise the objectives of deeper argumentation. Further, homocentric arguments tend to weaken the motivation to fight for necessary social change, together with the willingness to serve a great cause. In addition, the complicated arguments in human-centered conservation documents such as the World Conservation Strategy go beyond the time and ability of many people to assimilate and understand. They also tend to provoke interminable technical disagreements among experts. Special interest groups with narrow short-term exploitive objectives, which run counter to saner ecological policies, often exploit these disagreements and thereby stall the debate and steps toward effective action.

When arguing from deep ecological premises, most of the complicated proposed technological fixes need not be discussed at all. The relative merits of alternative technological proposals are pointless if our vital needs have already been met. A focus on vital issues activates mental energy and strengthens motivation. On the other hand, the shallow environmental approach, by focusing almost exclusively on the technical aspects of environmental problems, tends to make the public more passive and uninterested in the more crucial non-technical, lifestyle-related, environmental issues.

Writers with the deep ecology movement try to articulate the fundamental presuppositions underlying the dominant economic approach in terms of value priorities, philosophy, and religion. In the shallow movement, questioning and argumentation comes to a halt long before this. The deep ecology movement is therefore "the ecology movement which questions deeper." A realization of the deep changes which are required, as outlined in the deep ecology 8 point platform (discussed in #3 above) makes us realize the necessity of "questioning everything."

The terms "egalitarianism," "homocentrism," "anthropocentrism," and "human chauvinism" are often used to characterize points of view on the shallow-deep spectrum. But these terms usually function as slogans which are often open to misinterpretation. They can properly imply that man is in some respects only a "plain citizen" (Aldo Leopold) of the planet on a par with all other species, but they are sometimes interpreted as denying that humans have any "extraordinary" traits, or that, in situations involving vital interests, humans have no overriding obligations towards their own kind. But this would be a mistake: they have!

In any social movement, rhetoric has an essential function in keeping members fighting together under the same banner. Rhetorical formulations also serve to provoke interest among outsiders. Of the many excellent slogans, one might mention "nature knows best," "small is beautiful," and "all things hang together." But sometimes one may safely say that nature does not always know best, that small is sometimes dreadful, and that fortunately things hang together sometimes only loosely, or not at all.

Only a minority of deep ecology supporters are academic philosophers, such as myself. And while deep ecology cannot be a finished philosophical system, this does not mean that its philosophers should not try to be as clear as possible. So a discussion of deep ecology as a derivational system may be of value to clarify the many important premise/conclusion relations.

6. DEEP ECOLOGY ILLUSTRATED AS A DERIVATIONAL SYSTEM

Underlying the 8 tenets or principles presented in section 3, there are even more basic positions and norms which reside in philosophical systems and in various world religions. Schematically we may represent the total views logically implied in the deep ecology movement by streams of derivations from the most fundamental norms and descriptive assumptions (level 1) to the particular decisions in actual life situations (level 4).

The pyramidal model has some features in common with hypothetico-deductive systems. The main difference, however, is that some sentences at the top (= deepest) level are normative, and preferably are expressed by imperatives. This makes it possible to arrive at imperatives at the lowest derivational level: the crucial level in terms of decisions. Thus, there are "oughts" in our premises as well as in our conclusions. We never move from an "is" to an "ought," or vice versa. From a logical standpoint, this is decisive!

The above premise/conclusion structure (or diagram) of a total view must not be taken too seriously. It is not meant in any restrictive way to characterize creative thinking within the deep ecology movement. Creative thinking moves freely in any direction. But many of us with a professional background in science and analytical philosophy find such a diagram helpful.

As we dig deeper into the premises of our thinking, we eventually stop.

APRON DIAGRAM

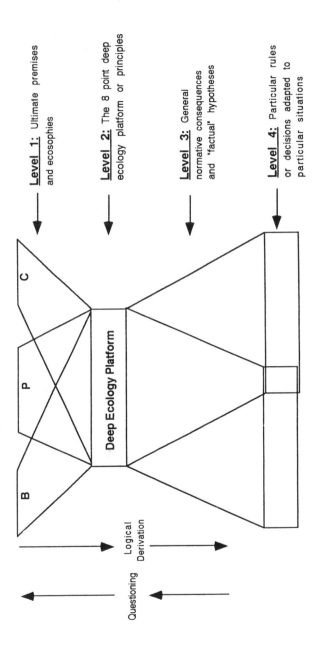

Level 1: Ultimate premises and ecosophies

Level 2: The 8 point deep ecology platform or principles

Level 3: General normative consequences and "factual" hypotheses

Level 4: Particular rules or decisions adapted to particular situations

Examples of kinds of fundamental premises:

B = Buddhist
C = Christian
P = Philosophical (e.g. Spinozist or Whiteheadian)

Logical Derivation

Questioning

Deep Ecology Platform

Those premises we stop at are our ultimates. When we philosophize, we all stop at different places. But we all use premises which, for us, are ultimate. They belong to level 1 in the diagram. Some will use a sentence like "Every life form has intrinsic value" as an ultimate premise, and therefore place it at level 1. Others try, as I do, to conceive of it as a conclusion based on a set of premises. For these people, this sentence does not belong to level 1. There will be different ecosophies corresponding to such differences.

Obviously, point 6 of the 8 point deep ecology tenets (see section 3) cannot belong to level 1 of the diagram. The statement "there must be new policies affecting basic economic structures" needs to be justified. If no logical justification is forthcoming, why not just assert instead that ecologically destructive "business as usual" economic policies should continue? In the diagram I have had ecosophies as ultimate premises in mind at level 1. None of the 8 points of the deep ecology principles belong at the ultimate level; they are derived as conclusions from premises at level 1.

Different supporters of the deep ecology movement may have different ultimates (level 1), but will nevertheless agree about level 2 (the 8 points). Level 4 will comprise concrete decisions in concrete situations which appear as conclusions from deliberations involving premises at levels 1 to 3. An important point: supporters of the deep ecology movement act from deep premises. They are motivated, in part, from a philosophical or religious position.

7. MULTIPLE ROOTS OF THE DEEP ECOLOGY PRINCIPLES

The deep ecology movement seriously questions the presuppositions of shallow argumentation. Even what counts as a rational decision is challenged, because what is "rational" is always defined in relation to specific aims and goals. If a decision is rational in relation to the lower level aims and goals of our pyramid, but not in relation to the highest level, then this decision should not be judged to be rational. This is an important point! If an environmentally oriented policy decision is not linked to intrinsic values or ultimates, then its rationality has yet to be determined. The deep ecology movement connects rationality with a set of philosophical or religious foundations. But one cannot expect the ultimate premises to constitute rational conclusions. There are no "deeper" premises available.

Deep ecological questioning thus reveals the fundamental normative orientations of differing positions. Shallow argumentation stops before reaching fundamentals, or it jumps from the ultimate to the particular; that is, from level 1 to level 4.

But it is not only normative claims that are at issue. Most (perhaps all) norms presuppose ideas about how the world functions. Typically the vast majority of assertions needed in normative systems are descriptive (or factual). This holds at all the levels.

As mentioned before, it does not follow that supporters of deep ecology must have identical beliefs about ultimate issues. They do have common attitudes about intrinsic values in nature, but these can, in turn (at a still deeper level), be derived from different, mutually incompatible sets of ultimate beliefs.

Thus, while a specific decision may be judged as rational from within the derivational system (if there is such) of shallow ecology, it might be judged as irrational from within the derivational system of deep ecology. Again, it should be emphasized that what is rational from within the deep ecology derivational pyramid does not require unanimity in ontology and fundamental ethics. Deep ecology as a conviction, with its subsequently derived practical recommendations, can follow from a number of more comprehensive world views, from differing ecosophies.

Those engaged in the deep ecology movement have so far revealed their philosophical or religious homes to be mainly in Christianity, Buddhism, Taoism, Baha'i, or in various philosophies. The top level of the derivational pyramid can, in such cases, be made up of normative and descriptive principles which belong to these religions and philosophies.

Since the late 70's, numerous Christians in Europe and America, including some theologians, have actively taken part in the deep ecology movement. Their interpretations of the Bible, and their theological positions in general, have been reformed from what was, until recently, a crude dominating anthropocentric emphasis.

There is an intimate relationship between some forms of Buddhism and the deep ecology movement. The history of Buddhist thought and practice, especially the principles of non-violence, non-injury, and reverence for life, sometimes makes it easier for Buddhists to understand and appreciate deep ecology than it is for Christians, despite a (sometimes overlooked) blessedness which Jesus recommended in peace-making. I mention Taoism chiefly because there is some basis for calling John Muir a Taoist, for instance, and Baha'i because of Lawrence Arturo.

Ecosophies are not religions in the classical sense. They are better characterized as *general* philosophies, in the sense of total views, inspired in part by the science of ecology. At level 1, a traditional religion may enter the derivational pyramid through a set of normative and descriptive assumptions which would be characteristic of contemporary interpretations (hermeneutical efforts) of that religion.

Supporters of the deep ecology movement act in contemporary conflicts on the basis of their fundamental beliefs and attitudes. This gives them a particular strength and a joyful expectation or hope for a greener future. But, naturally, few of them are actively engaged in a systematic verbal articulation of where they stand.

8. ECOSOPHY T AS AN EXAMPLE OF A DEEP ECOLOGICAL DERIVATIONAL SYSTEM

I call the ecosophy I feel at home with "Ecosophy T." My main purpose in announcing that I feel at home with Ecosophy T is didactic and dialectic. I hope to get others to announce their philosophy. If they say they have none, I maintain that they have, but perhaps don't know their own views, or are too modest or inhibited to proclaim what they believe. Following Socrates, I want to provoke questioning until others know where they stand on basic matters of life and death. This is done using ecological issues, and also by using Ecosophy T as a foil. But Socrates pretended in debate that he knew nothing. My posture seems to be the opposite. I may seem to know everything and to derive it magically from a small set of hypotheses about the world. But both interpretations are misleading! Socrates did not consistently claim to know nothing, nor do I in my Ecosophy T pretend to have comprehensive knowledge. Socrates claimed to know, for instance, about the fallibility of human claims to have knowledge.

Ecosophy T has only one ultimate norm: "Self-realization!" I do not use this expression in any narrow, individualistic sense. I want to give it an expanded meaning based on the distinction between a large comprehensive Self and a narrow egoistic self as conceived of in certain Eastern traditions of *atman*.[9] This large comprehensive Self (with a capital "S") embraces all the life forms on the planet (and elsewhere?) together with their individual selves (jivas). If I were to express this ultimate norm in a few words, I would say: "Maximize (long-range, universal) Self-realization!" Another more colloquial way to express this ultimate norm would be to say "Live and let live!" (referring to all of the life forms and natural processes on the planet). If I had to give up the term fearing its inevitable misunderstanding, I would use the term "universal symbiosis." "Maximize Self-realization!" could, of course, be misinterpreted in the direction of colossal ego trips. But "Maximize symbiosis!" could be misinterpreted in the opposite direction of eliminating individuality in favor of collectivity.

Viewed systematically, not individually, maximum Self-realization implies maximizing the manifestations of all life. So next I derive the second term, "Maximize (long-range, universal) diversity!" A corollary is that the higher the levels of Self-realization attained by any person, the more any further increase depends upon the Self-realization of others. Increased self-identity involves increased identification with others. "Altruism" is a natural consequence of this identification.

This leads to a hypothesis concerning an inescapable increase of identification with other beings when one's own self-realization increases. As a result, we increasingly see ourselves in other beings, and other see themselves in us. In this way, the self is extended and deepened as a natural process of the realization of its potentialities in others.

By universalizing the above, we can derive the norm, "Self-realization for every being!" From the norm, "Maximize diversity!" and a hypothesis that maximum diversity implies a maximum of symbiosis, we can derive the norm "Maximize symbiosis!" Further, we work for life conditions such that there is a minimum of coercion in the lives of others. And so on![10] The 8 points of the deep ecology platform are derived in a fairly simple way.

A philosophy as a world view inevitably has implications for practical situations. Like other ecosophies, Ecosophy T therefore moves on, without apologies, to the concrete questions of lifestyles. These will obviously show great variation because of differences in hypotheses about the world in which each of us lives, and in the "factual" statements about the concrete situations in which we make decisions.

I shall limit myself to a discussion of a couple of areas in which my "style" of thinking and behaving seem somewhat strange to friends and others who know a little about my philosophy.

First, I have a somewhat extreme appreciation of diversity; a positive appreciation of the existence of styles and behavior which I personally detest or find nonsensical (but which are not clearly incompatible with symbiosis); an enthusiasm for the "mere" diversity of species, or varieties within a genus of plants or animals; I support, as the head of a philosophy department, doctrinal theses completely at odds with my own inclinations, with the requirement only that the authors are able to understand fairly adequately some basic features of the kind of philosophy I myself feel at home with; an appreciation of combinations of *seemingly* incompatible interests and behaviors, which makes for an increase of subcultures within industrial states and which might to some extent help future cultural diversity. So much for "diversity!"

Second, I have a somewhat extreme appreciation of what Kant calls "beautiful actions" (good actions based on inclination), in contrast with actions which are performed out of a sense of duty or obligation. The choice of the formulation "Self-realization!" is in part motivated by the belief that maturity in humans can be measured along a scale from selfishness to an increased realization of Self, that is, by broadening and deepening the self, rather than being measured by degrees of dutiful altruism. I see joyful sharing and caring as a natural process of growth in humans.

Third, I believe that multifaceted high-level Self-realization is more easily reached through a lifestyle which is "simple in means but rich in ends" rather than through the material standard of living of the average citizens of industrial states.

The simple formulations of the deep ecology platform and Ecosophy T are not meant primarily to be used among philosophers, but also in dialogues with the "experts." When I wrote to the "experts" and environmental professionals personally, asking whether they accept the 8 points of the platform, many answered positively in relation to most or all of the points. And this includes top people in the ministries of oil and energy! Nearly all were willing to let their written answers be widely published. It is an open question, however, as to what extent they will try to influence their colleagues who use only shallow argumentation. But the main conclusion to be drawn is moderately encouraging: there are views of the human/nature relationship, widely accepted among established experts responsible for environmental decisions, which require a pervasive, substantial change of present policies in favor of our "living" planet, and these views are held not only on the basis of shortsighted human interests.

NOTES

1. For more about interspecific community relationships, see Arne Naess, "Self-realization in Mixed Communities of Humans, Bears, Sheep, and Wolves," *Inquiry* 22 (1979): 321–41; Naess and Ivar Mysterud, "Philosophy of Wolf Policies I: General Principles and Preliminary Exploration of Selected Norms," *Conservation Biology* 1, 1 (1987): 22–34.
2. These problems are discussed further in Naess's keynote address to the second international Conference on Conservation Biology held at the University of Michigan in May 1985; published as "Intrinsic Value: Will the Defenders of Nature Please Rise?" *Conservation Biology* (1986): 504–15.
3. IUCN. *World Conservation Strategy: Living Resource Conservation for Sustainable Development* (Gland, Switzerland, 1980) section 13 ("Building Support for Conversation").
4. The deep ecology principles (or platform) were agreed upon during a camping trip in Death Valley, California (April, 1984) and first published in George Sessions (ed.), *Ecophilosophy VI* newsletter (May, 1984). They have subsequently appeared in a number of publications.
5. Tom Regan, "The Nature and Possibility of an Environmental Ethics," *Environmental Ethics* 3 (1981): 19–34, citation on p. 30.
6. I proposed the name "Deep, Long-Range Ecology Movement" in a lecture at the Third World Future Research conference in Bucharest in September 1972. A summary of that lecture ("The Shallow and the Deep, Long-Range Ecology Movement") was published in *Inquiry* 16 (1973): 95–100. Within the deep ecology movement it is fairly common to use the term "deep ecologist," whereas "shallow ecologist," I am glad to say, is rather uncommon. Both terms may be considered arrogant and slightly misleading. I prefer to use the awkward, but more egalitarian expression "supporter of the deep (or shallow) ecology movement," avoiding personification. Also, it is common to call deep ecology consistently anti-anthropocentric. This has led to misconceptions: see my "A Defense of the Deep Ecology Movement," *Environmental Ethics* 5 (1983).
7. The "shallow/deep" dichotomy is rough. Richard Sylvan has proposed a much more subtle classification; see his "A Critique of Deep Ecology," *Discussion Papers in Environmental Philosophy*, RSSS, Australian National University, No. 12 (1985).
8. *World Conservation Strategy*, section 13 (concluding paragraph).
9. The term *atman* is not taken in its absolutistic senses (not as a permanent indestructible "soul"). This makes it consistent with those Buddhist denials

(the *avatman doctrine*) that the *atman* is to be taken in absolutist senses. Within the Christian tradition some theologians distinguish "ego" and "true self" in ways similar to these distinctions in Eastern religions. See the ecophilosophical interpretation of the gospel of Luke in Stephen Verney's *Onto the New Age* (Glasgow: Collins, 1976) pp. 33–41.

10. Many authors take some steps toward derivational structures, offering mild systematizations. The chapter "Environmental Ethics and Hope" (in G. Tyler Miller, *Living in the Environment,* 3rd ed. [Belmont: Wadsworth, 1983]) is a valuable start, but the derivational relations are unclear. The logic and semantics of simple models of normative systems are briefly discussed in my "Notes on the Methodology of Normative Systems," *Methodology and Science* 10 (1977): 64–79. For a defense of the thesis that as soon as people assert anything at all, they assume a total view, implicitly involving an ontology, methodology, epistemology, and ethics, see my "Reflections about Total Views," *Philosophy and Phenomenological Research* 25 (1964–65): 16–29. The best and wittiest warning against taking systematizations too seriously is to be found in Soren Kierkegaard, *Concluding Unscientific Postscript.*

    For criticism and defense of my fundamental norm ("Self-realization"), together with my answer, see *In Sceptical Wonder: Essays in Honor of Arne Naess* (Oslo: University Press, 1982). My main exposition of Ecosophy T was originally offered in the Norwegian work, *Okologi, samfunn og livsstil* (Oslo: University Press, 5th ed., 1976). Even there, the exposition is sketchy. (Editor's note: Naess's Norwegian book has been revised and reissued as Arne Naess (translated and edited by David Rothenberg), *Ecology, Community and Lifestyle* [Cambridge: Cambridge University Press, 1989].)

The Deep Ecology–Ecofeminism Debate and Its Parallels

Warwick Fox

Warwick Fox is a fellow at the Center for Environmental Studies, University of Tasmania, Australia. He is the author of Toward a Transpersonal Ecology *(1990), which focuses on the psychological dimensions of deep ecology and ecosophy.*

DEEP ECOLOGY'S ECOCENTRIC EGALITARIANISM

The question of the relative merits of deep ecology and ecofeminism has recently received considerable attention, primarily from an ecofeminist perspective. This question has an obvious significance to anyone concerned with ecophilosophy and ecopolitics since it contrasts two of the most philosophically and socially influential approaches that have developed in response to ecological concerns. For deep ecologists in particular, the ecofeminist critique of deep ecology is of interest for at least two reasons in addition to the direct challenge that it presents to deep ecological theorizing. First, as I argue throughout this paper, the same criticism that can be made of simplistic forms of ecofeminism can be applied with equal force to critiques of deep ecology that proceed from simplistic versions of a broad range of social and political perspectives—the "parallels" of my title. Second, addressing the ecofeminist critique of deep ecology provides

This essay originally appeared (in a somewhat longer version) in *Environmental Ethics*, **11**, No.1 (Spring 1989): 5–25. Reprinted with permission.

an opportunity to further elucidate the nature of deep ecology's concern with anthropocentrism.

Before examining the ecofeminist critique of deep ecology, which centers on deep ecology's negative or critical focus on anthropocentrism, it is important to outline deep ecology's positive or constructive focus. Deep ecology is concerned with encouraging an egalitarian attitude on the part of humans not only toward all *members* of the ecosphere, but even toward all identifiable *entities* or *forms* in the ecosphere. Thus, this attitude is intended to extend, for example, to such entities (or forms) as rivers, landscapes, and even species and social systems considered in their own right. If deep ecologists sometimes write as if they consider these entities to be living entities, they do so on the basis of an extremely broad sense of the term *life*—a sense as broad as that implied in such expressions as "Let the river live!" It is ultimately of little consequence to deep ecologists, however, whether one wishes to consider the kind of egalitarianism they advocate as one that extends only toward living entities (in this extremely broad sense) or as one that extends toward both living and nonliving entities. Either way, the kind of egalitarian attitude they advocate is simply meant to indicate an attitude that, within obvious kinds of practical limits, allows all entities (including humans) *the freedom to unfold in their own way unhindered by the various forms of human domination.*

There are, of course, all sorts of problems involved in defining such things as how far these practical limits should extend or, in many cases, even where one entity ends and another begins. But, against this, it must be remembered that deep ecologists are not *intending* to advocate a specific set of guidelines for action; they are only intending to advocate a *general orientation*. Deep ecologists not only accept but welcome cultural diversity when it comes to effecting the specifics of this general orientation. After all, "the freedom to unfold in their own way unhindered by the various forms of human domination" applies to the unfolding of human cultures too. As Arne Naess puts it, where we draw the limit between justifiable and unjustifiable interference with respect to this general orientation "is a question that must be related to local, regional, and national particularities. Even then a certain area of disagreement must be taken as normal."[1] For deep ecologists, the only overriding consideration is that such limits should always be worked out *in the light of* the general orientation they advocate. Naess captures the sense of this general orientation while also conveying a sense of the cultural (and personal) diversity it allows for: "A rich variety of acceptable motives can be formulated for being *more reluctant* to injure or kill a living being of kind A than a being of kind B. The cultural setting is different for each being in each culture."[2] It is this general attitude of being reluctant, *prima facie,* to interfere with the unfolding of A *or* B—indeed, to desire that both should flourish—that characterizes the general orientation that is advocated by deep ecologists.

Deep ecologists have generally referred to this general orientation or attitude as one of "biospherical egalitarianism" or, more often (in order to suggest the intended comparison with an anthropo*centric* perspective more directly), "biocentric egalitarianism." However, because the prefix *bio-* refers, etymologically, to life or living organisms, it has sometimes been assumed that deep ecology's concerns *are* restricted to entities that are (in some sense) biologically alive. To correct this impression, Arne Naess and George Sessions have, in line with my preceding remarks, often pointed out that their sense of the term *life* is so broad, that it takes in "individuals, species, populations, habitat, as well as human and nonhuman cultures."[3] To avoid the possibility of confusion, however, I prefer to describe the kind of egalitarian attitude subscribed to by deep ecologists as *ecocentric* rather than *biocentric*. While there seems to be little reason for choosing between these terms on the basis of their ecological connotations, there are other grounds for preferring the term *ecocentric* to describe the kind of egalitarianism advocated by deep ecologists.[4] First, the term *ecocentric,* which etymologically means *oikos-*, home, or, by implication, Earth-centered, is more immediately informative than the term *biocentric,* which etymologically means life-centered and so requires an appended explanation of the broad sense in which the term *life* should be understood. Second, the term *ecocentric* seems closer to the spirit of deep ecology than the term *biocentric,* because, notwithstanding their broad usage of the term *life,* the motivation of deep ecologists depends more upon a profound sense that the Earth or ecosphere is *home* than it does upon a sense that the Earth or ecosphere is necessarily alive (you don't have to subscribe to some ecological form of *hylozoism* to be a supporter of deep ecology).

In accordance with this extremely broad, ecocentric egalitarianism, supporters of deep ecology hold that their concerns well and truly subsume the concerns of those movements that have restricted their focus to the attainment of a more egalitarian *human* society. Deep ecologists, in other words, consider their concerns to subsume the egalitarian concerns associated, for example, with feminism (as distinct from *eco*feminism), Marxism, anti-racism, and anti-imperialism.[5] In the eyes of deep ecologists, the emergence of a distinct *eco*feminism, a distinct "green" socialism, and so on, are—at least in their best forms—attempts by feminists, Marxists-cum-socialists, and so on, to redress the human-centeredness of their respective perspectives.[6] Needless to say, deep ecologists welcome these developments and they recognize that ecofeminism, green socialism, and so on have their own distinctive theoretical flavors and emphases because of the different theoretical histories that inform them. Nevertheless, they see no *essential* disagreement between deep ecology and these perspectives, *providing* that the latter are genuinely able to overcome their anthropocentric legacies.

THE ECOFEMINIST CRITIQUE OF DEEP ECOLOGY

With respect to ecofeminism and deep ecology in particular, many observers agree that the two perspectives have much in common—notwithstanding their different theoretical histories.[7] However, some ecofeminist writers have begun to perceive a significant tension between their perspective and that of deep ecology. In an evenhanded examination of ecofeminist criticisms of deep ecology, Michael Zimmerman has presented what is probably the clearest formulation of what I take to be the essential ecofeminist charge against deep ecology: "Feminist critics of deep ecology assert that [deep ecology] speaks of a gender-neutral 'anthropocentrism' [i.e., human-centeredness] as the root of the domination of nature, when in fact *androcentrism* [i.e., male-centeredness] is the real root."[8] There seems to be wide support for the view that this represents the essential ecofeminist criticism of deep ecology. For example, one of the main criticism made by Janet Biehl in her critique of deep ecology is that, "For ecofeminists the concept of anthropocentrism is profoundly, even "deeply" problematical. . . .By not excluding women from anthropocentrism, deep ecologists implicitly condemn women for being as anthropocentric as they condemn men for being—that is, for presuming to be above nature, for mastering it." Marti Kheel also notes at the outset of her critique of deep ecology that deep ecologists are concerned to "challenge the anthropocentric world view" whereas for ecofeminists "it is the androcentric world view that is the focal point of the needed shift." Likewise, the first difference in emphasis that Charlene Spretnak refers to in her comparison of deep ecology and ecofeminism is that of anthropocentrism versus androcentrism.[9]

Jim Cheney has claimed, nevertheless, in response to an earlier version of this paper, that it is wrong to regard Zimmerman's formulation as representing the essential ecofeminist charge against deep ecology. For Cheney, "The 'essential' [ecofeminist] charge is not that deep ecologists focus on *anthropo*centrism whereas the problem is really with *andro*centrism; rather, the central concern is. . .that deep ecology is *itself* in some sense androcentric."[10] In comparison to what I take to be the essential ecofeminist charge against deep ecology (as formulated concisely by Zimmerman), Cheney's formulation of the essential ecofeminist charge seems to represent a significant (if somewhat confusing) concession to deep ecology, since it suggests that ecofeminists are not overly concerned about deep ecologists' critical focus on anthropocentrism so long as deep ecologists do not formulate their critique of anthropocentrism in a way that is "itself in some sense androcentric." But whether Cheney's formulation represents a significant concession to deep ecology or not, my response to his charge is simple. The charge that I propose to address (as taken from Zimmerman's analysis) is clear-cut and serious—deep ecologists cannot deny that their *negative* focus is concerned, first and foremost, with anthropocentrism and ecofeminists cannot deny that their *negative* focus is concerned, first and foremost, with androcentrism. In contrast, the best that can be said about Cheney's claim that deep ecology is androcentric in its very formulation is that such a claim is entirely contentious.[11] Cheney's own recent attempt in *Environmental Ethics* to establish this claim is essentially based upon a misinterpretation of deep ecology as resting upon a "rights-based foundation."[12] Referring to a brief paper of my own, Cheney even acknowledges in his paper (albeit in a footnote) that if (as Fox claims) deep ecology does not rest upon "the language of intrinsic value and correlated concepts of rights,. . .then deep ecology is not subject to some of the criticisms I have offered."[13]

More recently, Cheney has abandoned his previous view of deep ecology and accepted that deep ecologists are primarily concerned with the development of a state of being of wider *identification* and, hence, with the realization of a more expansive (sense of) Self.[14] This understanding of deep ecology appears to have much in common with Cheney's characterization of ecofeminism as being concerned with an ethics of love, care, and friendship as opposed to a theory of rights, justice, and obligation.[15] However, Cheney argues instead that the deep ecological emphasis on the realization of a more expansive (sense of) Self is a "totalizing view" that represents "the desperate endgame of masculine alienation from nature."[16] What Cheney means by his highly abstract and potentially obfuscating reference to a "totalizing view" is that deep ecologists identify "with particulars only in the derivative sense that the logos of the cosmos threads its way through the cosmos, binds it together as a totality, a cosmos. Identification, for the deep ecologist, does not involve seeing or hearing the other or seeing oneself in the other, but rather involves seeing the other *sub specie aeternitas.*"[17]

What Cheney seems to object to in deep ecology, then, is not the emphasis on identification *per se* but rather the fact that deep ecologists emphasize identification within a cosmological context—that is, within the context of an awareness that all entities in the universe are part of a single, unfolding process. There is, however, a fundamental problem with arguing, as Cheney seems to want to, for a purely *personal* basis for identification (as opposed to a cosmological and, hence, *transpersonal* basis). Specifically, emphasizing a purely personal basis for identification—one that "leave[s] selves intact"[18]—necessarily implies an emphasis upon identification with entities with which one has considerable personal contact. In practice, this tends to mean that one identifies with *my* self first, *my* family next, *my* friends and more distant relations next, *my* ethnic grouping next, *my* species next, and so on—more or less what the sociobiologists say we are genetically predisposed to do. The problem with this is that, while extending love, care, and friendship to one's nearest and dearest is laudable in and of itself, the *other* side of the coin, emphasizing a purely personal basis for identification (*my*self first, *my* family next, and so on), looks more like the cause of possessiveness, war, and ecological destruction than the solution to these seemingly intractable problems. In contrast, to argue for a cosmological basis for identification is to attempt to convey a lived sense that all entities (including ourselves) are relatively autonomous modes of a single, unfolding process, that all entities are leaves on the tree of life. A lived sense of this understanding means that we strive, insofar as it is within our power to do so, not to identify ourselves exclusively with our leaf (our personal biographical self), our twig (our family), our minor subbranch (our community), our major subbranch (our race/gender), our branch (our species), and so on, but rather to identify ourselves with the tree. This necessarily leads, at the limit, to impartial identification with *all* particulars (all leaves on the tree).[19]

This distinction between personally based identification and cosmologically based identification certainly represents a difference in *theoretical* stance between Cheney's conception of ecofeminism on the one hand and deep ecology on the other. But whether this difference also reflects a basic difference between feminine and masculine modes of approaching the world (as Cheney wants to suggest) is a separate issue. On my reading of the literature, I do not see how anyone can—or why they would want to—deny that many women are *vitally* interested in cultivating a cosmological/transpersonal based sense of identification.[20] The cosmological/transpersonal voice *is* a "different voice" from the personal voice, but it does not seem to respect gender boundaries. Moreover, as the above discussion suggests, whatever one's view of the relationship or lack of relationship between these approaches and gender, a personally based approach to identification is vulnerable to criticism from an ecocentric perspective in a way in which a cosmological/transpersonal approach is not.

Because this brief examination of Cheney's critique of deep ecology suggests that there are major weaknesses with his claim that the essential ecofeminist charge against deep ecology is actually "that deep ecology is *itself*, in some sense androcentric," in what follows I, therefore, consider the essential ecofeminist charge against deep ecology to be the far more clear-cut and potentially far more serious charge (vis-à-vis Cheney's charge) that deep ecology "speaks of a gender-neutral 'anthropocentrism' as the root of the domination of nature, when in fact *androcentrism* is the real root."[21]

PROBLEMS WITH THE ECOFEMINIST AND OTHER CRITIQUES

Having established the nature of the ecofeminist charge that I am concerned to address in what follows, it is important to note that this charge is *not* directed at deep ecology's positive or constructive task of encouraging an egalitarian attitude on the part of humans toward all entities in the ecosphere, but rather at deep ecology's negative or critical task of dismantling anthropocentrism. This distinction often seems to be overlooked by ecofeminist critics of deep ecology, who, presumably, are in general agreement with the constructive task of deep ecology.[22] But with respect to the critical task of these two perspectives, the fact remains that in the absence of a good answer to the ecofeminist charge, there is no reason—other than intellectual blindness or outright chauvinism in regard to issues concerning gender—why deep ecologists should not make androcentrism the focus of their critique rather than anthropocentrism. In addressing this challenge to the critical focus of deep ecology, I first make some general remarks about a certain style of social and political theorizing and then proceed to the essential deep ecological response to this ecofeminist charge.

To begin with, deep ecologists completely agree with ecofeminists that men have been far more implicated in the history of ecological destruction than women. However, deep ecologists also agree with similar charges derived from other social perspectives: for example, that capitalists, whites, and Westerners have been far more implicated in the history of ecological destruction than pre-capitalist peoples, blacks, and non-Westerners.[23] If ecofeminists also agree with these points, then the question arises as to why they do not also criticize deep ecology for being neutral with respect to issues concerning such significant social variables as socioeconomic class, race, and Westernization. There appears to be two reasons for this. First, to do so would detract from the priority that ecofeminists wish to give to their own concern with androcentrism. Second, and more significantly, these charges could also be applied with equal force to the ecofeminist focus on androcentrism itself.[24] How does one defend the ecofeminist charge against deep ecology (i.e., that androcentrism is "the real root" of ecological destruction) in the face of these charges?[25] For deep ecologists, it is simplistic on both empirical and logical grounds to think that one particular perspective on human society identifies *the* real root of ecological destruction. Empirically, such thinking is simplistic (and thus descriptively poor) because it fails to give due consideration to the multitude of interacting factors at work in any given situation. (While on a *practical* level it can be perfectly reasonable to devote most of one's energy to one particular cause—if only for straightforward reasons to do with time and energy—that, of course, is no excuse for simplistic social *theorizing*.) Such thinking fails, in other words, to adopt an ecological perspective with respect to the workings of human society itself. Logically, such thinking is simplistic (and thus facile) because it implies that the solution to our ecological problems is close at hand—all we have to do is remove "the real root" of the problem—when it is actually perfectly possible to conceive of a society that is nonandrocentric, socioeconomically egalitarian, nonracist, and nonimperialistic with respect to other human societies, but whose members nevertheless remain aggressively anthropocentric in collectively agreeing to exploit their environment for their collective benefit in ways that nonanthropocentrists would find thoroughly objectionable. Indeed, the "green" critique of socialism proceeds from *precisely* this recognition that a socially egalitarian society does not necessarily imply an ecologically benign society.

An interesting example of the failure to recognize this point is provided by Murray Bookchin's anarcho-socialist inspired "social ecology" (I describe this approach as "anarcho-socialist" in inspiration because it advocates decentralism and cooperativeness and stands opposed to all forms of hierarchy). Bookchin is interesting in this context because, on the one hand, he correctly observes in the course of a highly polemical attack upon deep ecology that it is possible for a relatively ecologically benign human society also to be extremely oppressive internally (he offers the example of ancient Egyptian society), and yet, on the other hand, he fails to see that the reverse can also apply—that is, that it is possible for a relatively egalitarian human society to be extremely exploitative ecologically.[26] For Bookchin, to accept this latter point would be to argue against the basis of his own social ecology, since in his view a nonhierarchical, decentralist, and cooperative society is "a society that will live in harmony with nature *because* its members live in harmony with each other."[27] Bookchin's presentation of social ecology thus conveys no real appreciation of the fact that the relationships between the internal organization of human societies and their treatment of the nonhuman world can be as many and varied as the outcomes of any other evolutionary process. One may certainly speak in terms of certain forms of human social organization being more *conducive* to certain kinds of relationships with the nonhuman world than others. Bookchin, however, insists far too much that there is a straightforward, necessary relationship between the internal organization of human societies and their treatment of the nonhuman world. To this extent, his social ecology is constructed upon a logically facile basis. Moreover, it serves to reinforce anthropocentrism, since the assumption that the internal organization of human societies determines their treatment of the nonhuman world carries with it the implication that we need only concentrate on *interhuman* egalitarian concerns for all to become ecologically well with the world—a point I take up again later.[28]

In doing violence to the complexities of social interaction, simplistic social and political analyses of ecological destruction are not merely descriptively poor and logically facile, they are also morally objectionable on two grounds, scapegoating and inauthenticity. Scapegoating can be thought of in terms of overinclusiveness. Simplistic analyses target all men, all capitalists, all whites, and all Westerners, for example, to an equal degree when in fact certain subclasses of these identified classes are far more responsible for ecological destruction than others. Not only that but significant minorities of these classes can be actively engaged in *opposing* the interests of both the dominant culture of their class and those members of their class most responsible for ecological destruction. Inauthenticity, on the other hand, can be thought of in terms of underinclusiveness. Simplistic analyses are inauthentic in that they lead to a complete denial of responsibility when at least partial responsibility for ecological destruction should be accepted. Such theorizing conveniently disguises the extent to which (at least a subset of) the simplistically identified oppressed group (e.g., women or the working class) also benefits from, and colludes with, those most responsible for ecological destruction (e.g., consider the case of animal destruction for furs and cosmetics consumed by Western and Westernized women, or the case of capitalists and unionists united in opposition to the antidevelopment stance of "greenies"). It can, of course, be argued in response that the hegemony of androcentrism or capitalism, for example, is such that women or unionists effectively have *no* power to choose in our society and so should not be burdened with *any* responsibility for ecological destruction. But this surely overplays the role of social determination and to that extent only serves to highlight the charge of inauthenticity. Moreover, attempting to escape the charge of inauthenticity in this way directly contradicts the view of feminists or Marxists, to continue with the same examples, that women or the working class *are* capable of self-conscious direction—of being a class *for* themselves, a revolutionary class.

Yet another kind of objection to simplistic analyses of the kind to which I have been referring is that while claiming to be "ecological" or "green," some of these critics in fact remain anthropocentric—albeit in the passive sense of serving to legitimize our continued preoccupation with interhuman affairs rather than in the aggressive sense of overtly discriminating against the nonhuman world. Advocates of these approaches say in essence: "Since the real root of our problems is androcentrism or capitalism, for example, we must *first* get our interactions between humans right (with respect to gender issues, with respect to the redistribution of wealth, and so on) and then everything else (including our ecological problems) will fall into place." Any form of direct concern with the question of the relationship between humans and the *nonhuman* world is thus trumped by concerns about the resolution of specific interhuman problems. The nonhuman world retains its traditional status as the background against which the significant action—human action—takes place.

Not surprisingly, deep ecologists find it particularly frustrating to witness representatives of simplistic social and political perspectives waving the banner of ecology while in fact continuing to promote, whether wittingly or unwittingly, the interhuman and, hence, human-centered agenda of their respective theoretical legacies. I have already commented on Bookchin's social ecology in regard to this point. Some ecofeminist writing is also relevant here. For example, the focus of Ariel Kay Salleh's critique of deep ecology is thoroughly interhuman. "To make a better world," she concludes, men have to be "brave enough to rediscover and to love the woman inside themselves," while women simply have to "be allowed to love what we are."[29] This conclusion follows from the fact that, in Salleh's version of feminism, women already "flow with the system of nature" by virtue of their essential nature.[30] Karen Warren and Michael Zimmerman have referred to this kind of approach to ecofeminism, according to which women are supposed to be "closer to nature" than men by virtue of their essential nature, as "radical feminism" (in contrast to liberal, traditional Marxist, and socialist feminism) and "essentialist feminism" respectively.[31] Warren correctly notes that "Radical feminists have had the most to say about eco-feminism," and both she and Zimmerman have made telling criticisms of this approach.[32] All I am drawing attention to here is the fact that this kind of "radical" approach simply serves to legitimize and, hence, to perpetuate our entirely *traditional* preoccupation with interhuman affairs. In accordance with the approach adopted by essentialist feminists, there is no need to give any serious consideration whatsoever to the possibility that women might, for example, discriminate against men, accumulate rather than distribute private wealth, be racist, support imperialism, or be ecologically destructive if the conditions of their historical subjugation were undone and the possibility of exercising genuine social and political power were available to them.[33] The upshot is that there is no need to worry about any form of human domination other than that of androcentrism. For deep ecologists, it's just another variation on the same old song—the song that reassures us that all will become ecologically well with the world if we just put this or that interhuman concern first.

I have objected to simplistic (and, hence, unecologically conceived) social and political analyses on the grounds that they are descriptively poor and logically facile, that they lend themselves to scapegoating on the one hand and are inauthentic on the other, and that even in their ecological guises, they are passively anthropocentric. Many who align themselves with the perspectives to which I have referred might well personally agree with the points I have made so far and consider that in virtue of this agreement, these objections do not really apply to their perspective. Thus, this kind of reaction can be quite common in the face of the sorts of objections I have made: "How could anyone be so stupid as to think that we ecofeminists (for example) are not also concerned about issues concerning socioeconomic class, race, and imperialism?" The problem is, however, that there is often a large gap between the alleged and often genuine personal concerns of members of a social and political movement and the theoretical articulation of the perspective that informs their movement. The fact that individual members of a social and political movement agree with the points I have made provides no guarantee whatsoever that the theoretical articulation of the perspective that informs their movement does not itself fall foul of these objections—and it is with this theoretical articulation that I have been concerned. By way of qualification, however, I do not in any way wish to assert that any of the objections I have made are necessarily fatal to the theoretical prospects of the social and political perspectives to which I have referred, since it is possible, at least in principle, for each of these perspectives to be revised or, at a minimum, suitably qualified so as not to fall foul of these objections.[34] But, that said, one must nevertheless be careful not to underestimate the significance of these objections, since presentations of the social and political perspectives to which I have referred continue to fall foul of them on an all too regular basis.

Variations on some (but not all) of the objections I have outlined would apply just as much to deep ecology if it were the case that deep ecologists were simply saying that humans as a whole have been far more implicated in the history of ecological destruction than nonhumans. (The ecofeminist charge against deep ecology implies that deep ecologists are saying precisely this: it turns on the contention that deep ecologists have been overinclusive in criticizing humanity *in general* for the destruction of the nonhuman world when the target of their critical attack should properly be the class of men and, of course, masculine culture in general.) However, this is *not* the essential point that deep ecologists are making, and it is here that we enter into the essential response by deep ecologists to the essential criticism made of their perspective by ecofeminists.

THE ESSENTIAL DEEP ECOLOGICAL RESPONSE TO THE ECOFEMINIST CRITIQUE

The target of the deep ecologists' critique is not humans *per se* (i.e., a general class of social actors) but rather human-*centeredness* (i.e., a legitimating ideology).[35] It is not just ecofeminist critics who miss this point. Some other critics also miss it in an even bigger way by attacking deep ecologists not simply on the grounds that they *criticize* humanity in general for its ecological destructiveness, but rather on the grounds that deep ecologists are actually *opposed* to humanity in general—that is, that they are essentially misanthropic. According to Murray Bookchin, for example, in deep ecology " '*Humanity*' is essentially seen as an ugly 'anthropocentric' thing—presumably, a malignant product of natural evolution."[36] Henryk Skolimowski also suggests (albeit rather indirectly) that deep ecologists are misanthropic. "I find it rather morbid," he writes in *The Trumpeter*, "when some human beings [and the context suggests that he means deep ecologists] think that the human lot is the bottom of the pit. There is something pathological in the contention that humans are a cancer among the species. This kind of thinking is not sane and it does not promote the sense of wholeness which we need nowadays." In line with my remarks here, Alan Drengson, *The Trumpeter*'s editor and a prominent deep ecology philosopher, intervenes immediately at this point by adding parenthetically: "And it is certainly not the thinking of deep ecologists. Ed."37

The extent to which people in general are ready to equate opposition to human-centeredness with opposition to humans per se can be viewed as a function of the dominance of the anthropocentric frame of reference in our society. Just as those who criticize capitalism, for example, are often labeled as "Communists" and, by implication, "the enemy," when, in reality, they may be concerned with such things as a more equitable distribution of wealth in society, so those who criticize anthropocentrism are liable to be labeled as *mis*anthropists when, in reality, they may be (and, in the context of environmentalism, generally are) concerned with encouraging a more egalitarian attitude on the part of humans toward all entities in the ecosphere. In failing to notice the fact that being opposed to human-*centeredness* (deep ecology's critical task) is logically distinct from being opposed to humans per se (or, in other words, that being opposed to anthropo*centrism* is logically distinct from being *mis*anthropic), and in equating the former with the latter, Bookchin and Skolimowski commit what I refer to as *the fallacy of misplaced misanthropy*.38 Committing this fallacy in the context of criticizing deep ecology involves not just a crucial misreading of deep ecology's critical task, but also the oversight of two other considerations that contradict such a misreading. The first is that deep ecology's *constructive* task is to encourage an egalitarian attitude on the part of humans toward all entities in the ecosphere—including *humans*. The second is that deep ecologists are among the first to highlight and draw inspiration from the fact that not all humans have been human-centered either within the Western tradition or outside it. Far from being misanthropic, deep ecologists celebrate the existence of these human beings.

In making human-*centeredness* (rather than humans per se) the target of their critique, deep ecologists have contended that the assumption of human self-importance in the larger scheme of things has, to all intents and purposes, been the single deepest and most persistent assumption of (at least) all the *dominant* Western philosophical, social, and political traditions since the time of the classical Greeks—notwithstanding the fact that the dominant classes representing these traditions have typically adjudged themselves *more* human than others—and that, for a variety of reasons, this assumption is unwarranted and should be abandoned in favor of an ecocentric outlook.39 Thus, what deep ecologists are drawing critical attention to is the fact that *whatever* class of social actors one identifies as having been most responsible for social domination and ecological destruction (e.g., men, capitalists, whites, Westerners), one tends at the most fundamental level to find a common kind of legitimation for the alleged superiority of these classes over others and, hence, for the assumed rightfulness of their domination of these others. Specifically, these classes of social actors have not sought to legitimate their position on the grounds that they are, for example, men, capitalists, white, or Western per se, but rather on the grounds that they have most exemplified whatever it is that has been taken to constitute the *essence of humanness* (e.g., being favored by God or possessing rationality). These classes of social actors have, in other words, habitually assumed themselves to be somehow *more fully human* than others, such as women ("the weaker vessel"), the "lower" classes, blacks, and non-Westerners ("savages," "primitives," "heathens"). The cultural spell of anthropocentrism has been considered sufficient to justify not only moral superiority (which, in itself, might be construed as carrying with it an obligation to help rather than dominate those who are less blessed), but also all kinds of domination within human society—let alone domination of the obviously nonhuman world.

That anthropocentrism has served as the most fundamental kind of legitimation employed by *whatever* powerful class of social actors one wishes to focus on can also be seen by considering the fundamental kind of legitimation that has habitually been employed with regard to large-scale or high-cost social enterprises such as war, scientific and technological development, or environmental exploitation. Such enterprises have habitually been undertaken not simply in the name of men, capitalists, whites, or Westerners, for example, but rather in the name of God (and thus our essential humanity—or our anthropocentric projection upon the cosmos, depending upon one's perspective) or simply in the name of humanity in general. (This applies notwithstanding the often sexist expression of these sentiments in terms of "man," "mankind," and so on, and notwithstanding the fact that certain classes of social actors benefit disproportionately from these enterprises.) Thus, to take some favorite examples, Francis Bacon and Descartes ushered in the development of modern science by promising, respectively, that it would lead to "enlarging the bounds of Human Empire" and that it would render humanity the "masters and possessors of nature."[40] Approximately three and a half centuries later, Neil Armstrong's moon walk—the culmination of a massive, politically directed, scientific and technological development effort—epitomized both the literal acting out of this vision of "enlarging the bounds of Human Empire" and the literal expression of its anthropocentric spirit: Armstrong's moon walk was, in his own words at the time, a "small step" for him, but a "giant leap for mankind." Here on Earth, not only do examples abound of environmental *exploitation* being undertaken in the name of humanity, but this also constitutes the fundamental kind of legitimation that is still most often employed for environmental *conservation and preservation*—it is implicit in every argument for the conservation or preservation of the nonhuman world on account of its use value to humans (e.g., its scientific, recreational, or aesthetic value) rather than for its own sake or its use value to *nonhuman* beings.

The cultural pervasiveness of anthropocentrism in general and anthropocentric legitimations in particular are further illustrated when one turns to consider those social movements that have *opposed* the dominant classes of social actors to which I have been referring. With respect to the pervasiveness of anthropocentrism in general, it can be seen that those countermovements that have been most concerned with exposing discriminatory assumptions and undoing their effects have typically confined their interests to the human realm (i.e., to such issues as imperialism, race, socioeconomic class, and gender). With respect to the pervasiveness of anthropocentric legitimations in particular, it can equally be seen that these countermovements have not sought to legitimate their own claims on the basis that they are, for example, women, workers, black, or non-Western per se, but rather on the grounds that they too have exemplified—at least equally with those to whom they have been opposed—either whatever it is that *has* been taken to constitute the essence of humanness or else some redefined essence of humanness. While it would, in any case, be contrary to the (human-centered) egalitarian concerns of these countermovements to seek to legitimate their own claims by the former kind of approach (i.e., on the basis that they are, for example, women, workers, black, or non-Western per se), the pity is (from a deep ecological perspective) that these countermovements have not been egalitarian enough. Rather than attempting to replace the ideology of anthropocentrism with some broader, ecocentrically inclined perspective, these countermovements have only served to reinforce it.

It should be clear from this brief survey that the history of anthropocentrism takes in not only the assumption of the centrality and superiority of humans *in general,* but also the various claims and counterclaims that various classes of humans have made with regard to the exemplification of whatever attributes have been considered to be quintessentially human. Deep ecologists recognize that the actual historical reasons for the domination of one class by another (and here I also refer to the domination that humans as a class now exert over the nonhuman world) cannot be identified in any simplistic manner; they can be as complex as any ecological web or the evolutionary path of any organism. However, deep ecologists also recognize that claims to some form of human exclusiveness have typically been employed to *legitimate* the bringing about and perpetuation of historical and evolutionary outcomes involving unwarranted domination. In consequence, deep ecologists have been attempting to get people to see that historical and evolutionary outcomes simply represent "the way things happen to have turned out"—nothing more—and that self-serving anthropocentric legitimations for these outcomes are just that.

What the ecofeminist criticism of deep ecology's focus on anthropocentrism overlooks, then, is the fact that deep ecologists are not primarily concerned with exposing the *classes of social actors* historically most responsible for social domination and ecological destruction, but rather with the task of sweeping the rug out from under the feet of these classes of social actors by exposing the most fundamental kind of *legitima-tion* that they have habitually employed in justifying their position. (This distinction between a concern with classes of social actors on the one hand and the most fundamental kind of legitimation they employ on the other hand should be apparent from the fact that deep ecology has been elabo-rated within a philosophical context rather than a sociological or political context—which is not to suggest that deep ecology does not have profound social and political implications.) Of course, ecofeminists, green socialists, and so on are also concerned with questions of legitimation, but they are generally concerned with these questions in a different sense than deep ecologists are concerned with them. The primary emphasis of ecofeminists, green socialists, and the other social and political analysts to whom I have referred is on the distribution of power in society and the ways in which that distribution is reinforced and reproduced. In this context, references to legitimation tend not to be to the "bottom line" rationale employed by these powerful classes (i.e., to legitimation in the fundamental or philo-sophical sense), but rather to the ways in which existing power structures utilize their sources of power to back up existing states of affairs (from overtly physical forms of power such as the police and the military to less tangible forms such as economic power and the manipulation of social status). To the extent that ecofeminists, green socialists, and so on *are* concerned to expose the fundamental, philosophical legitimation em-ployed by the classes of social actors whose unwarranted degree of power is the focus of their critique, and to the extent that this concern extends out into a genuinely ecocentric perspective, it becomes difficult to see any significant difference between what they call ecofeminism, green social-ism, and so on and what others call deep ecology (such differences as remain are simply differences of theoretical flavor and emphasis rather than differences of substance).

Deep ecologists want to unmask the ideology of anthropocentrism so that it can no longer be used as the "bottom line" legitimation for social domination and ecological destruction by *any* class of social actors (men, capitalists, whites, Westerners, humans generally—or even essentialist feminists!).[41] Thus, those who align themselves with certain perspectives on the distribution of power in human society (e.g., feminism, Marxism, anti-racism, or anti-imperialism) misunderstand the essential nature of deep ecology if they see it in terms of their perspective *versus* deep ecology (e.g., in the case of ecofeminism and deep ecology, androcentrism *versus* anthropocentrism)—or if they criticize deep ecology on the basis that it has "no analysis of power." Rather, just as deep ecologists have learned and incorporated much from, and should be open to, a range of perspectives on the distribution of power in human society, so those who align themselves with these social and political perspectives can learn and incorporate much from, and should be open to, the deep ecologists' critique of the most fundamental kind of legitimation that has habitually been employed by those most responsible for social domination and ecological destruction.

NOTES

1. Arne Naess, "Sustainable Development and the Deep Long-Range Ecological Movement," unpublished manuscript.
2. Arne Naess, "Intuition, Intrinsic Value, and Deep Ecology," *The Ecologist* 14 (1984): 202 (emphasis added). Naess fully accepts that "any realistic praxis necessitates some killing, exploitation, and suppression" ("The Shallow and the Deep, Long-Range Ecology Movement: A Summary." *Inquiry* 16 [1973]: 95). For more on the relevance of tradition and culture, see Naess's paper "Self-realization in Mixed Communities of Humans, Bears, Sheep, and Wolves," *Inquiry* 22 (1979): 231–41.
3. See the eight point list of "basic principles" of deep ecology proposed by Arne Naess and George Sessions and published in numerous places including Bill Devall and George Sessions, *Deep Ecology: Living as if Nature Mattered* (Layton, Utah: Gibbs M. Smith, 1985), chap. 5; and Arne Naess, "The Deep Ecological Movement: Some Philosophical Aspects," *Philosophical Inquiry* 8 (1986): 10–31.
4. *Biocentric* and *ecocentric* are equally useful in connoting the biosphere and the ecosphere respectively and these latter terms are themselves generally used interchangeably. However, where a distinction *is* made between the terms *biosphere* and *ecosphere,* it is the latter term that is taken as the more inclusive.
5. I am, of course, speaking here of the full realization of deep ecology's concerns, i.e., of the breadth of deep ecology's concerns *in principle.* In practice, however, deep ecologists, like everyone else, can fail to realize the full implications of their own principles.
6. In referring to *green socialism* and to *socialists.* I am aware that the term *socialism,* considered in its own right, is today popularly construed as referring to virtually the whole range of (human) social egalitarian concerns and that the concerns of socialism and green socialism might therefore be considered as subsuming the concerns of feminism and ecofeminism respectively. But there are nevertheless significant differences between these approaches at the level of their theoretical flavors and emphases.
7. There is nothing to suggest that there is any incompatibility between deep ecology and an ecologically informed feminism in any of the works by the following authors, all of whom make explicit reference to both perspectives: Fritjof Capra, *The Turning Point: Science, Society, and the Rising Culture* (New York: Bantam Books, 1983), chap. 12; Don E. Marietta, Jr, "Environmentalism, Feminism, and the Future of American Society," *The Humanist,* May–June 1984, pp. 15–18 and 30; Bill Devall and George Sessions, *Deep Ecology,* chap. 6; Charlene Spretnak, "The Spiritual Dimension of Green Politics," appendix C in Charlene Spretnak and Fritjof Capra, *Green Politics: The Global Promise* (London: Paladin, Grafton Books, 1986); and Patsy Hallen, "Making Peace with Nature: Why Ecology Needs Feminism," *The Trumpeter* 4. No. 3 (1987): 3–14. Even those authors who do see a tension between these perspectives generally acknowledge that these perspectives at least bear a strong apparent similarity to each other. For example, Jim Cheney

writes: "On the face of it, that *branch* of environmentalism called the 'deep ecology movement' seems to have answered the [ecofeminist] call for a nonhierarchical, nondomineering attitude toward nature ("Eco-Feminism and Deep Ecology, *"Environmental Ethics* 9 [1987]: 115–45).

8. Zimmerman, "Feminism, Deep Ecology, and Environmental Ethics," *Environmental Ethics* 9 (1987): 21–44.
9. Janet Biehl "It's Deep, But is it Broad? An Eco-feminist Looks at Deep Ecology" *Kick it Over,* Winter 1987, p. 2A; Marti Kheel, "Ecofeminism and Deep Ecology," and Charlene Spretnak, "Ecofeminism: Our Roots and Flowering." *The Elmwood Newsletter,* Winter 1988, p. 7.
10. Personal communication, 21 April 1988.
11. Zimmerman ("Feminism, Deep Ecology, and Environmental Ethics," pp. 38–42) provides a thoughtful consideration of the various problems associated with the kind of claim that Cheney makes.
12. Cheney, "Eco-Feminism and Deep Ecology," p. 129.
13. Ibid., p. 133. The brief paper of mine that Cheney refers to is "A Postscript on Deep Ecology and Intrinsic Value," *The Trumpeter* 2, no. 4 (1985): 20–23. For a far more extensive critique of the view that deep ecology rests upon what Cheney refers to as "the language of intrinsic value and correlated concepts of rights," see my monograph *Approaching Deep Ecology: A Response to Richard Sylvan's Critique of Deep Ecology,* Environmental Studies Occasional Paper, no. 20 (Hobart: Centre for Environmental Studies, University of Tasmania, 1986).
14. Jim Cheney, "The Neo-Stoicism of Radical Environmentalism," unpublished early draft. This version of Cheney's critique of deep ecology follows his reading of my *Approaching Deep Ecology* and is, in large measure, a response to it.
15. See Cheney, "Eco-Feminism and Deep Ecology," p. 128.
16. Cheney, "Neo-Stoicism."
17. Ibid., p. 16.
18. Ibid., p. 15.
19. The fact that cosmologically based identification tends to be more *impartial* than personally based identification does not mean that it need be any less deeply felt. Consider Robinson Jeffers! For Jeffers, "This whole [the universe] is in *all its parts* so beautiful, and is felt by me to be so intensely in earnest, that I am *compelled* to love it" (quoted in Devall and Sessions, *Deep Ecology,* p. 101; emphasis added).
20. See, for example, Dolores LaChapelle *Earth Wisdom* (Los Angeles: Guild of Tutors Press, 1978); Joanna Macy, "Deep Ecology and the Council of All Beings," and "Gaia Meditations (Adapted from John Seed)," *Awakening in the Nuclear Age,* Summer/Fall 1986, pp. 6–10 (both reprinted in *Revision,* Winter/Spring 1987, pp. 53–57); Freya Matthews, "Conservation and Self-Realization: A Deep Ecology Perspective," *Environmental Ethics* 10 (1988): 347–55; and Frances Vaughan, "Discovering Transpersonal Identity," *Journal of Humanistic Psychology* 25 (1985): 13–38.
21. Zimmerman, "Feminism, Deep Ecology, and Environmental Ethics," p. 37.
22. In a thoughtful analysis of the strengths and shortcomings of several varieties of feminism (liberal, traditional Marxist, radical, and socialist) for the development of a genuinely ecofeminist perspective, Karen J. Warren concurs that an ecologically informed feminism—"a transformative feminism"—would tie "the liberation of women to the elimination of all systems of oppression" ("Feminism and Ecology: Making Connections," *Environmental Ethics* 9

[1987]: 18). Unfortunately, however, many feminists who claim to be ecofeminists do not make their (presumed) commitment to an *ecocentric* egalitarianism particularly explicit, with the result that ecofeminist analyses can sometimes serve to reinforce anthropocentrism rather than overcome it. As for those ecofeminists, such as Warren, who are explicit about their commitment to an ecocentric egalitarianism, it becomes difficult to see any essential difference between their approach and that of deep ecology. As one ecofeminist-cum-deep ecologist said to me after reading Warren's article: "Why doesn't she just call it [i.e., Warren's vision of a transformative feminism] deep ecology? Why specifically attach the label *feminism* to it if she's advocating a genuinely nonprioritizing, biocentric egalitarianism?"

23. When I refer to any class of social actors, I expressly mean also to refer to the culture(s) associated with that class. However, I omit writing "men and their associated cultures," "non-Westerners and their associated cultures," and so on simply for ease of comprehension. In referring to capitalists and, hence, the culture of capitalism, I also mean to refer to "state capitalism" as found in the industrialized communist countries.

24. Indeed, even as I wrote this paper, a significant real-life example of such criticisms was being played out between the women of Greenham Common in the form of a "bitter dispute" over allegations of racism at the camp. Reports suggested that this dispute "threatens the world's most renowned peace camp after six years" (Deborah Smith, "Showdown at Greenham Common," *The Times on Sunday*, 25 October 1987, p. 27). Karen J. Warren similarly criticizes radical feminists—that group of feminists who "have had the most to say about ecofeminism"—for paying "little attention to the historical and material features of women's oppression (including the relevance of race, class, ethnic, and national background)" ("Feminism and Ecology," pp. 14–15).

25. Note that I am borrowing the phrase "the real root" from Michael Zimmerman's previously quoted formulation of what I consider to be the essential ecofeminist charge against deep ecology. I employ this phrase several times in the argument that follows.

26. Murray Bookchin, "Social Ecology Versus 'Deep Ecology,'" *Green Perspectives: Newsletter of the Green Program Project*, Summer 1987.

27. Ibid., p. 2 (emphasis added). This view is central to Bookchin's major statement of social ecology: *The Ecology of Freedom: The Emergence and Dissolution of Hierarchy* (Palo Alto: Cheshire Books, 1982).

28. This observation is in keeping with the anthropocentric flavor than many deep ecologists detect in Bookchin's work notwithstanding his avowed ecological orientation.

29. Salleh, "Deeper than Deep Ecology," p. 345. In another presentation of the ecofeminist sensibility, Don Davis also concludes by reiterating this conclusion of Salleh's ("Ecosophy: The Seduction of Sophia?" *Environmental Ethics* 8 [1986]: 151–62).

30. Salleh, "Deeper than Deep Ecology," p. 340.

31. Warren, "Feminism and Ecology," pp. 13–15, and Zimmerman, "Feminism, Deep Ecology," p. 40.

32. Warren, "Feminism and Ecology," p. 14. See also Alan E. Wittbecker, "Deep Anthropology: Ecology and Human Order," *Environmental Ethics* 8 (1986): 261–70, which provides a number of counterinstances to Salleh's essentialist feminist claim that the suppression of the feminine is "universal."

33. Stunningly obvious instances of these kinds of examples, such as the Prime Minister of England, Margaret Thatcher (the "Iron Lady"), sending warships

to the Falklands, are typically explained in terms of the hegemony of androcentrism being such as to have overpowered the offending woman's essential nature. The implication is that if, as Salleh says, women could just "be allowed to love what we are," then it would no longer be possible to find such examples.

34. Where revised, such perspectives would no doubt continue to differ from deep ecology in terms of their theoretical flavors and emphases, but they would not differ from deep ecology in terms of their essential concerns. Whether these revised perspectives would be recognizable or acceptable to their earlier supporters is of course an interesting question.

35. Ecofeminists, green socialists, and so on are also concerned with questions of legitimation, but generally in a different sense than deep ecologists are.

36. Bookchin, "Social Ecology," p. 3 (emphasis added).

37. Henryk Skolimowski, "To Continue the Dialogue with Deep Ecology," *The Trumpeter* 4, no. 4 (1987): 31. Skolimowski has previously been taken to task for the anthropocentrism inherent in his own approach: see George Sessions' review of Skolimowski's *Eco-Philosophy* in *Environmental Ethics* 6 (1984): 167–74. Since then Skolimowski has become a regular critic of deep ecology: see his articles "The dogma of Anti-Anthropocentrism and Ecophilosophy," *Environmental Ethics* 6 (1984): 283–88 (Skolimowski's response to Sessions' review); "In Defence of Ecophilosophy and of Intrinsic Value: A Call for Conceptual Clarity," *The Trumpeter* 3, no. 4 (1986): 9–12 (this issue of *The Trumpeter* also carried replies from Bill Devall, Arne Naess, and myself); "To Continue the Dialogue with Deep Ecology"; and "Eco-Philosophy and Deep Ecology," *The Ecologist* 18 (1988): 124–27. I defend Sessions' reading of Skolimowski in my "Further Notes in Response to Skolimowski," *The Trumpeter* 4, no. 4 (1987): 32–34.

38. Much of Bookchin's case for his (mistaken) contention that deep ecology is essentially a misanthropic enterprise rests on certain statements by one or two significant figures in Earth First!—especially Dave Foreman and his personal, unhistorical, and abhorrently simplistic views on population control. However, Bookchin overlooks the surely obvious fact that Foreman says elsewhere in the same interview (p. 42), "I am speaking for myself, not for Earth First!," and both he and Foreman overlook the equally obvious fact that such a view runs contrary to the deep-ecological principle of encouraging an egalitarian attitude on the part of humans toward all entities in the ecosphere. In contrast to Foreman, Arne Naess says in a recent paper: "Sustainable development today means development along the lines of each culture, not development along a common, centralized line. But faced with hungry children humanitarian action is a priority, whatever its relation to developmental plans and cultural invasion" ("Sustainable Development and the Deep-Long-Range Ecological Movement").

39. There are two significant qualifications to be noted in this statement. First, I say "to all intents and purposes" because where these traditions have supposedly been primarily theocentric rather than anthropocentric, it has of course still been humans who have, by divine decree, had "dominion. . .over all the earth [which they are enjoined to 'fill and subdue']. . .and over every living thing that moves upon the earth" (Genesis 1:26 and 1:28). From a deep ecological perspective, personalistic theocentrisms, in which humans are made in the image of a god to whom they have a privileged personal relationship, are simply anthropocentric projections upon the cosmos. Second, I say "since the time of the *classical* Greeks" (i.e., the Sophists, Socrates,

Plato, and Aristotle) as distinct from the *early* Greeks, who initiated Western philosophy (i.e., the early and later Ionians, the Pythagoreans, the Eleatics, and the Atomists—often collectively referred to as the pre-Socratics), because, as Bertrand Russell has pointed out, "What is amiss, even in the best philosophy after Democritus [i.e., after the pre-Socratics], is an undue emphasis on man as compared with the universe" (Bertrand Russell, *History of Western Philosophy* [London: Unwin Paperbacks, 1979], p. 90). Russell's statement is meant to refer to humanity in general, although it also applies, of course, if its sexist expression is read as representing its intended meaning (i.e., if "man" is read as "men"). It should be noted in this regard, however, that the reason why Russell's statement is true in the gender specific sense is, as I argue below, precisely because men have seen themselves as essentially *more* human than women—an observation that returns us to Russell's intended meaning in a dialectical manner. For excellent discussions of the anthropocentric nature of Western philosophy since the time of the pre-Socratics, see George Sessions, "Anthropocentrism and the Environmental Crisis," *Humboldt Journal of Social Relations* 2 (1974): 71–81 and George Sessions, "Spinoza and Jeffers on Man in Nature," *Inquiry* 20 (1977): 481–528.

40. Both quotes are from Brain Easlea's erudite and inspiring book *Liberation and the Aims of Science: An Essay on Obstacles to the Building of a Beautiful World* (London: Chatto and Windus, 1973), p. 253.

41. I include a reference to essentialist feminists here because, as Michael Zimmerman points out ("Feminism, Deep Ecology," p. 40), "In recent years, a number of feminists have favoured. . .an essentialist view [that women are essentially more attuned to nature than men] and have concluded that woman is *better* than man" (my emphasis). Karen Warren criticizes this point of view sharply ("Feminism and Ecology," p. 15): "The truth is that women, like men, are both connected to nature and separate from it, natural and cultural beings....locating women either on the nature or on the culture side. . .mistakenly perpetuates the sort of oppositional, dualistic thinking for which patriarchal conceptual frameworks are criticized." But, even more fundamentally (since this is the end that such oppositional, dualistic thinks *serves*), essentialist feminism perpetuates the anthropocentric assumption that some humans are more equal than others by virtue of their essential nature.

Deep Ecology and Global Ecosystem Protection

George Sessions

George Sessions teaches philosophy at Sierra College in Rocklin, California. He has written extensively in the area of ecophilosophy and deep ecology and is the co-author, with Bill Devall, of Deep Ecology *(1985).*

I. WILDERNESS: FROM MUIR TO PINCHOT TO MUIR

The ecophilosopher Holmes Rolston quotes disapprovingly from a 1978 U.S. Forest Service document on "wilderness management," which asserts:

> Wilderness is for people. . . .The preservation goals established for such areas are designed to provide values and benefits to society. . . .Wilderness is not set aside for the sake of its flora or fauna, but for people.[1]

It is disappointing to find Forest Service theorists in the late 1970s still promoting narrowly human-centered views of the function and values of wilderness. In so doing, they follow in the footsteps of the U.S. Forest Service founder, Gifford Pinchot. As the ideological arch-rival of John Muir at the turn of the century, Pinchot promoted the anthropocentrism that has pervaded conservationist and land-use agency policy since the turn of the century that, in Pinchot's words, "there are just people and resources."[2]

It is ironic that these Forest Service theorists continue in this un-ecological vein when we consider that Aldo Leopold (the founder of the Forest Service wilderness concept in the 1920s) published his justly famous ecocentric "land ethic" over forty years ago. It fact, it was Aldo Leopold

A longer version of this paper appears in Max Oelschlaeger (ed.), *The Wilderness Condition* (Sierra Club Books, San Francisco, 1991).

who (together with Rachel Carson) deserves the main credit for initiating the wave of holistic ecological thinking, which resulted in the ecological revolution (the "Age of Ecology") of the 1960s and 70s.[3]

In the nineteenth century, Henry David Thoreau and John Muir developed what we call today an ecocentric or deep ecological consciousness. At the time of his famous 1851 Concord speech, Thoreau had seen through the anthropocentric illusions of the modern world when he claimed that "in wildness is the preservation of the world [and]. . .in short, all good things are wild and free." Muir carried the ecocentric/wilderness philosophy to even greater heights and was primarily responsible for spearheading the drive for wilderness preservation in the late nineteenth century, eventually serving as the first president of the Sierra Club. As Max Oelschlaeger demonstrates in his remarkable new reinterpretation of the history of Western culture (*The Idea of Wilderness*), ecocentric consciousness and the Age of Ecology involve a radical departure from traditional and modern Western modes of thought. The search for a postmodern ecological cultural paradigm has its roots in Darwin, Thoreau, Muir, and Leopold, and leads to the recultivation of Paleolithic consciousness.[4]

The ecological revolution of the 1960s (which overturned Pinchot's anthropocentrism and resurrected the ecocentrism of Thoreau, Muir, and Leopold) actually began shortly after World War II with the rise to prominence of the science of ecology. It also surfaced as an ideological battle within the conservation organizations, primarily the Sierra Club. After Muir's death in 1914, the club's vision had narrowed to that of a "hiking organization" concerned primarily with the protection of wilderness seen as providing high-quality recreation and aesthetic experience for its members. For conservationists of this period, the rest of the planet was implicitly handed over to developers as an arena for exploitation or for resource conservation and development.

This explosive anthropocentric orientation began to change when the Sierra Club-sponsored Wilderness Conferences (beginning in 1949 and continuing over the next twenty years) provided a public forum for ecologists to broach issues much wider than the value of wilderness as mere aesthetics or recreation. As executive director of the club during these years, David Brower (referred to by historian Stephen Fox as "Muir reincarnate") in effect began to "ecologize" the club and the general public by encouraging professional ecologists to speak out at these conferences on the *ecological* importance of wilderness and wild places; the importance of protecting old-growth forest ecosystems; and the dangers of human overpopulation. Through his newly found ecological approach to conservation, and his aggressive campaign tactics, Brower turned the Sierra Club into what *The New York Times* called (in 1967) "the gangbusters of the conservation movement."[5]

When Congress passed the Forest Reserve Act in 1891 enabling

President Harrison to set aside 13 million acres in "forest reserves," John Muir had reason to believe they would be protected as wilderness. But the "forest reserves" later became national forests, and Pinchot and the U.S. Forest Service had other plans for them.

Many recent environmental battles have involved the U.S. Forest Service, which, as a branch of the Department of Agriculture, has seen its primary function as a handmaiden of industrial "resource" exploitation. Ecologically destructive activities such as mining, domestic animal grazing, and sport hunting are allowed even within national forest designated wilderness areas. And just as the pioneers cleared wild forests to make way for agriculture, the Forest Service has facilitated and promoted the destruction of the last unprotected old-growth (ancient) forest ecosystems in America to make way for agriculture in the form of monocultural "tree farms." As early as 1976, the ecophilosopher John Rodman pointed out:

> The charges frequently made in recent years by Preservationists and others—e.g., that the Forest Service is a captive (or willing) agent of corporate interests, that it allows ecologically disruptive clear-cutting as well as cutting in excess of official quotas, while permitting grazing corporations to overgraze the land while paying fees far less than they would have to pay for the use of private land, etc.,—represent less the latter-day capture of an agency by one or more of its constituents than a maturation of the basic principles of the founder [Pinchot]. The Forest Service is, in effect, a perennial government subsidy, in exchange for certain regulatory controls, to certain types of corporations.[6]

The massive clearcutting of the last of the old-growth coniferous forests along the West Coast of America from California to Washington and into the Tongass National Forest in southeast Alaska, is surpassed in unbridled destruction only by the unrestricted Canadian clear-cutting of British Columbia. At the present rate of clear-cutting along the British Columbia coast, this world's largest remaining temperate rainforest will be gone in fifteen years.[7] Surely, the loss of these last great temperate zone forest ecosystems in North America will go down as one of the great ecological crimes and blunders of this century; comparable to present rainforest destruction in the Amazon and the rest of Central and South America, Africa, Australia, and Southeast Asia.

Actually, the destruction of the biodiversity of wild forest ecosystems and their replacement with unstable even-age tree plantations is now occurring all over the world at an increasingly rapid rate. Those who advocate just "planting trees" to help stem the greenhouse effect are proposing an ecologically simple-minded solution. Destruction of wild forests must cease, and a massive global effort should be made to try to *restore* diverse wild forest ecosystems. Fortunately, widescale public pressure is now being applied to modern forestry ideology to bring about major ecological reform. And even Pinchot-trained foresters are beginning to undergo a change of heart. As Canadian forester Bob Nixon recently remarked:

> As a forester, I learned to view forests as a source of industrial fibre. Now, I know that forests are much more than vertical assemblages of lumber, so very much more important than just a source of consumer products.. . .Natural forests, the new research tells us, are no longer something to move through, in the economic sense, in our quest for higher gains, but indeed a key element in the balanced functioning of planetary life.

And how has wildness fared in Muir's national parks under the anthropocentric orientation of twentieth century America? The parks, based on the "preservationist" ideal (although still preservation of the wildlife and the natural beauty primarily for the enjoyment of this and future generations of *humans*), does not allow resource extraction within its boundaries, including its newly designated wilderness areas. But many of the parks have been damaged by NPS policies over the years, which have catered to dominant American values and lifestyles, which see the parks as essentially natural "scenery" and recreational escapes for city-dwellers. This has encouraged a Disneyland atmosphere of excessive tourism and overdeveloped facilities, upgraded high-speed roads ("scenic drives"), mechanized recreation such as snowmobiling, which disturbs the serenity and the wildlife, and human overcrowding: what Edward Abbey called "industrial tourism."[9] In short, there has been a constant push from the commercially motivated to turn the parks into resorts and international "roadside attractions." And the adequacy of presently designated wilderness areas, conceived of as ecosystem habitat for wildlife, both in the national forests and parks, has received a serious jolt from the findings of the new science of conservation biology.

II. THE IMPLICATIONS OF CONSERVATION BIOLOGY FOR THE EARTH'S EVOLUTIONARY PROCESSES

During the 1970s and 80s, ecophilosophers have concentrated their efforts on such issues as (a) whether modern humanistic ethical theory can be "extended" to cover the concerns raised by ecology, or whether a "new" environmental ethic will be required; (b) whether nonhuman individuals, species, and ecosystems have inherent worth and, if so, how much; (c) the cataloging and evaluation of the various arguments for the protection of wild species and wilderness, and (d) whether the existing anthropocentric technological/industrial society can be "reformed" in properly ecological ways, or whether ecological realities will require a new "postmodern" society based on an ecological worldview.

It now appears that an overall broad consensus is now emerging on these issues among ecophilosphers and professional ecologists to the effect that modern moral theory *cannot* be extended to cover adequately ecological situations; that nonhuman individuals, species, and ecosystems have *equal inherent value or worth* along with humans; and that a new postmodern nonconsumerist sustainable society *is required* based on an ecocentric worldview.

Arne Naess has recognized various functions and activities as existing within the long-range deep ecological movement. There is a philosophical component (both in terms of pure theory such as developing ecosophies, and the "intellectual activism" involved in proposing and criticizing environmental strategies), together with the activism involved in ecological lifestyle changes, bioregional living, and nonviolent "direct action" to resist further environmental destruction.

In the 1960s, professional biologists (beginning with Rachel Carson, and continuing with Lamont Cole, Raymond Dasmann, Barry Commoner, Garrett Hardin, and Paul Ehrlich) stepped outside their narrow areas of scientific expertise and warned the public of the impending ecological disaster. They also proposed various public strategies to cope with these problems. The "intellectual activism" begun by these ecologists has been institutionalized into a new branch of ecology called "conservation biology." According to Mitch Friedman:

> Conservation biology considers the application of ecological theory and knowledge to conservation efforts. The development and utilization of this new discipline is a welcome advance in conservation, where ecological considerations tend to be overshadowed by political and economic forces, in part due to poor understanding of the effects of land-use decisions.[10]

Conservation biology has been spearheaded largely by Michael Soule (an ecologist and former student of Paul Ehrlich). Soule has also recently worked closely with Arne Naess. Soule refers to conservation biology as a "crisis discipline," which has to apply its findings in the absence of certainty. This new field integrates ethical norms with the latest findings of ecological science.[11]

Soule has provided scientific definitions for the terms "conservation" and "preservation." In his usage, preservation means "the maintenance of individuals or groups, but not for their evolutionary change." He proposes that conservation be taken to denote "policies and programs for the long-term retention of natural communities under conditions that provide for the potential for continuing evolution." Mitch Friedman carries this a step further by introducing the concept of "ecosystem conservation," which

> ...involves the preservation of ecosystem wilderness: enough of the land area and functional components—the creatures *and* their habitat—to insure the continuation of processes which have co-evolved over immeasurable time.[12]

One can quibble over the choice of terms. "Conservation" has negative associations with Pinchot and the Resource Conservation and Development position. And "preservation" does not necessarily mean trying to maintain something in a static state such as "preserving jam" or "deep freezing" a wilderness. Perhaps "protection" would be a more neutral term. However, the term "ecosystem conservation" means protecting the ongoing dynamic continuum of evolutionary processes that constitutes the overall healthy ecological planetary condition (in the Leopoldian sense).

It is thus clear that the *primary purpose* in setting aside and evaluating wilderness areas (and nature reserves), from the standpoint of conservation biology and the ecological crisis, is the conservation and protection of wild plants, animals, and ecosystems (biotic diversity) and the possibilities for the continuation of natural evolutionary processes.

Based on these objectives, we need to look at present global ecological realities. As Friedman points out:

> An element of panic is present within the literature of conservation biology, as well as among the conservation community at large. This panic originates predominantly from the present rate of species extinction, and the forecasts for impending mass extinction. We presently have scarcely a clue of even the total number of species on the planet, with estimates ranging between three and thirty-seven million. Yet, some researchers are predicting that anthropogenic extinctions, at current rates (which do not consider military disasters or other unpredictable events), may eliminate as many as a third of the planet's species over the next several decades (Meyers, 1987). This is shocking to anyone who treasures the intrinsic values of Earth's natural diversity and fecundity, or who fears for the fate of humanity and the planet as a whole. While most of these extinctions are occurring as a result of tropical rainforest deforestation, the same processes are occurring in temperate areas, including the United States (Wilcove et al. 1986).[13]

A further crisis brought to public attention by conservation biology (as the result of ecological research in the 1980s) is that existing nature reserves (e.g., national park and forest wilderness areas) do not meet realistic ecological criteria: they are too small and disconnected to protect adequately biodiversity and ecological/evolutionary processes:

> It is not enough to preserve some habitat for each species if we want to conserve ecosystems; the habitat must remain in the conditions under which the resident species evolved. For this reason, national forests, under present "multiple-use" management, may not be effective nature reserves for many species.
> Historically, national parks and other reserves have been established according to political, or other nonbiological considerations.. . .To conserve species diversity, the legal boundaries of nature reserves should be congruent with natural criteria (Newmark 1985). For instance, a reserve may be large [e.g., Everglades National Park] while still not protecting the ecological integrity of the area.

Newmark (1985) suggests that reserves contain not only entire watersheds, but at least the minimum area necessary to maintain viable populations of those species which have the largest home ranges. Others have stated that complete, intact ecosystems should be preserved (Terbourgh and Winter, 1980; Noss, 1985).[14]

In the 1970's Michael Soule examined twenty wildlife reserves in East Africa, including the massive Tsavo and Serengeti National Parks. He and his fellow researchers projected that:

all of the reserves will suffer extinctions in the near future. Their study predicts that a typical reserve, if it becomes a habitat island, will lose almost half of its large mammal species over the next 500 years. . .when a habitat island, for instance a national park surrounded by national forest, is reduced in size (i.e., clearcutting along the park boundaries), the number of species in that island will decrease. The empirical evidence for the relaxation effect is alarming, and reflects the urgency with which we must re-evaluate our conservation strategies and remedy the situation.[15]

Edward Grumbine further points out that:

Newmark (1985) investigated eight parks and park assemblages and found that even the largest reserve was six times too small to support minimum viable populations of species such as grizzly bear, mountain lion, black bear, wolverine, and gray wolf. A recent study by Salwasser et al. (1987) looked beyond park boundaries and included adjacent public lands as part of conservation networks. The results were the same. Only the largest areas (81,000 square km) were sufficient to protect large vertebrate species over the long term. . . .Virtually every study of this type has reached similar conclusions: No park in the coterminus U.S. is capable of supporting minimum viable populations of large mammals over the long term. And the situation is worsening.[16]

Frankel and Soule claim that "an area on the order of 600,000 square km (approximately equal to all of Washington and Oregon) is necessary for speciation of birds and large mammals."[17]

Christopher Manes has quoted Soule as saying that "for the first time in hundreds of millions of years significant evolutionary change in most higher organisms is coming to a screeching halt. . . .Vertebrate evolution may be at an end." Manes claims that Soule's remarks may be as significant as the findings of Copernicus or Darwin, for "only a hundred or so years after Darwin "discovered" our fundamental relationship to nature in terms of evolution, we are, according to Soule, putting an end to it." In addition, this means that wild nature and civilization will have ceased to be distinct.[18]

The inescapable conclusion is this: for those people around the world (including ecophilosophers, ecologists, and environmentalists) committed to wilderness, wild species, and the protection ("conservation") of the ongoing evolutionary processes of nature, there must be a recognition that current global wilderness/nature reserve protection policies are failing miserably. Past policies and strategies have been based on inadequate ecological understanding. Humans have effectively clogged the evolution-ary arteries of Mother Gaia. Along with protecting the ozone layer, mini-mizing the severity of the greenhouse effect, and stabilizing (and then reducing) the growth of the human population, one of the most crucial ecological tasks facing humanity at this time is to devise and implement realistic nature reserve protection strategies, and to help bring about ap-propriate reorganization of human societies and goals consistent with these strategies.

III. APPROACHES TO GLOBAL ECOSYSTEM PROTECTION ZONING

Even before conservation biologists were demonstrating the necessity for greatly expanded nature preserves throughout the world, ecologist and environmentalists (over twenty years ago) had called for worldwide zoning to protect wild nature. The first worldwide zoning proposal to protect wilderness ecosystems and wild species was made by David Brower in 1967. Claiming that less than 10 per cent of the earth had, at that time, escaped the technological exploitation of humans, he proposed protecting the remaining wilderness and "granting other life forms the right to coexist" in what Jerry Mander called an Earth International Park. Brower's increas-ingly radical ecological ideas were a major factor in his forced ouster as executive director of the Sierra Club, whereupon he formed the more ecologically radical Friends of the Earth in 1969.[19]

Another major zoning proposal was put forth by the noted ecologist, Eugene Odum, in 1971. The ecophilosopher, John Phillips, developed an argument (which has an uncanny resemblence to Naess's Ecosophy T) to support Odum's proposal:

> Being is good. Increase of diversity is increase of being. Integration of diver-sities into systems is increase of being. Therefore diversity is good and integration of diversities is good. What is good should be protected. Therefore, Protect Diversity! Protect integrated systems of diversity!

The Odum/Phillips zoning recommendation is that:

> *The biosphere as a whole should be zoned,* in order to protect it from the human impact. We must strictly confine the Urban-Industrial Zone and the Production Zone (agriculture, grazing, fishing), enlarge the Compromise Zone, and drastically expand the Protection Zone, i.e., wilderness, wild rivers. Great expanses of seacoasts and estuaries must be included in the Protection Zone, along with forests, prairies and various habitat types. We

must learn that the multiple-use Compromise Zone is no substitute, with its mining, lumbering, grazing, and recreation in the national forests, for the scientific, aesthetic, and genetic pool values of the Protection Zone. Such zoning, if carried out in time, may be the only way to limit the destructive impact of our technological—industrial—agri-business complex on earth.

Phillips concluded by saying that "to go so far as to zone the biosphere and set aside an adequate Protection Zone would be a supreme act of rationality by which the rational animal could protect the rest of life on earth, and himself, from his own irrational temptations."[20]

Paul Shepard made a daring proposal for global ecosystem protection in 1973. To allow for the huge expanses of unmanaged wilderness needed "for ecological and evolutionary systems on a scale essential to their own requirements," he proposed allowing the interiors of continents and islands to return to the wild. Based on the assumption that human population would stabilize by the year 2020 at 8 billion people, he proposed that humans would live in cities strung in narrow ribbons along the edges of the continents. Hunting/gathering forays would range into the central wilderness, but there would be no permanent habitation.[21]

Based on his ecocentric orientation, Shepard foresaw the huge amounts of wilderness necessary for the healthy ecological and evolutionary functioning of Gaia. But his proposal has a number of practical problems, not the least of which would be (1) the physical problems involved in relocating humans to the edges of the continents, and (2) the pressures exerted by these concentrated human populations on the ocean shoreline ecosystems and estuaries.

Two other strategies devised for protecting wild ecosystems are the Biosphere Reserve concept (part of UNESCO's Man and the Biosphere Program) and the World Heritage Site system. According to Edward Grumbine:

> A model biosphere reserve consists of four integrated zones: A large protected core; a buffer zone; a restoration zone; and a stable cultural area where "indigenous people live in harmony with the environment.". . .The National Park Service has informally adopted the biosphere reserve model as a guide to regional land planning [and] after eighteen years, 41 biosphere reserves exist in the U. S. many of which occupy both national park and forest lands.[22]

Grumbine sees some possibilities with World Heritage Site designations, but claims that there are serious problems with the Biosphere Reserve concept; the zones are not properly related, and the "self-sustaining" core is not large enough to allow for speciation. He suggests that the Biosphere Reserve model be replaced by a national system of biological reserves. And this needs to be further supplemented by a major program of *ecological restoration:*

Restoration of damaged lands must be married to the goal of native diversity. This follows the *wilderness recovery* strategy of Noss (1986) and would include large scale restoration of natural fire cycles, recovery of threatened, endangered, and extirpated species, road closures and reforestation projects, stream rehabilitation to increase native anadromous fisheries, and much more (see Berger, 1985). Once an area was restored, nature would take its course with minimal interference from managers. The amount of work to be done would likely offset the loss of jobs in exploitive industries.[23]

The concept of *ecological restoration* is a crucial one for all of the zones, but there is a potential danger when developers try to use it as a justification for "mitigation" procedures: in this case claiming that we can continue to develop (i.e., destroy) wild ecosystems and then compensate these losses by "restoring" an equivalent area elsewhere. This is a short-sighted foolhardy approach (part of the overall "Disneyland syndrome") that neglects the difficult and expensive process of restoration, together with the probability that restoration projects will be only partially successful and will not duplicate the incredibly complicated and diverse wild ecosystems that were destroyed. The politics of "mitigation" of wildlife habitat painfully resemble the similar process of tribal people "resettlement." In the latter case, Europeans dispossessed native peoples of their best tribal lands and moved them to the marginal edges only to find, to their chagrin, that these "useless lands" were sitting on huge deposits of coal, oil, and uranium!

Arne Naess adds an important refinement to zoning proposals and ecosystem protection strategies by distinguishing between *wilderness* protection zones (where people do not live and resource extraction is prohibited) and what he calls *"free nature."* Free nature constitutes areas of relatively sparse human habitation (e.g., the foothills of the Sierra, parts of northern Europe, and much of the Third World) where the natural processes are still essentially intact and dominant. These areas should be zoned to protect natural processes and wildlife while encouraging basically nonexploitive bioregional living. The remaining tribal peoples, such as the Bushman of the Kalahari Desert, and tribes at the headwaters of the Amazon, who are still following traditional ways with minimal impact on wild ecosystems, would be living in protection/free nature zones.

One of the central features of thinking about the "new ecological sustainable society" is the move toward decentralization and bioregional ways of life, which involves reinhabiting and restoring damaged ecosystems. But Roderick Nash (a major theorist and proponent of wilderness protection) has worried that a total movement toward bioregional reinhabitation of the earth at this point (what he calls the "garden scenario") would be ecologically disastrous. He says:

The problem, of course, is numbers. There are simply too many people on the planet to decentralize into garden environments and still have significant amounts of wilderness.[24]

Elsewhere, Nash characterizes bioregionalism as "the contemporary attempt to 'reinhabit' wilderness areas."[25]

Nash is entirely justified in calling attention to the limitations of an overly ambitious bioregional program at this point in history. It is not clear, however, that the intent of contemporary bioregionalists is to reinhabit wilderness areas. Certainly leading bioregional theorists such as Peter Berg, Gary Snyder, Raymond Dasmann, Thomas Berry, and Kirkpatrick Sale, are fully aware of the importance of establishing greatly expanded wilderness/protection zones. Bioregional ways of life are appropriate and necessary for "free nature" and for ecologically restructured cities (suggested in such projects as Peter Berg's "green cities.")[26] It is hoped that redesigned ecological cities would contain wild and semiwild areas interspersed with human inhabited areas, either by protecting and expanding upon wild or near-wild areas that now exist near the cities, or by restoring such areas.

Other ecologists and ecophilosophers have taken philosophical stands on the need for protecting wilderness and wild species. Roderick Nash points out that, "in 1982 [Edward] Abbey expressed his basic belief that humans had no right to use more than a portion of the planet and they had already passed that limit. Wild places must be left wild." In 1985, Stanford's outstanding world ecologist Paul Ehrlich claimed that "in a country like the United States, there is not the slightest excuse for developing one more square inch of undisturbed land." And in their 1987 survey of world environmental problems, Anne and Paul Ehrlich proposed that:

The prime step [is] *to permit no development of any more virgin lands. . . .* Whatever remaining relatively undisturbed land exists that supports a biotic community of any significance should be set aside and fiercely defended against encroachment.[27]

Paul Taylor also promotes the idea of wilderness protection as species habitat. He claims that we must:

. . .constantly place constraints on ourselves so as to cause the least possible interference in natural ecosystems and their biota. . . .If [humans] have a sufficient concern for the natural world, they can control their own population growth, change their habits of consumption, and regulate their technology so as to save at least part of the Earth's surface as habitat for wild animals and plants.[28]

Taylor also finds it necessary to distinguish between "basic" and "nonbasic" interests of humans. To allow for sufficient amounts of species habitat, humans must curb their population growth and reduce their nonbasic wants and consumption habits when these come into conflict with the basic needs of other species for survival and well-being. Taylor's analysis coincides with Naess's distinction between "vital" and "nonvital" needs and wants (which is incorporated into the deep ecology platform).[29]

Another important contribution that Paul Taylor makes is his concept of the *bioculture*. He defines "bioculture" as "that aspect of any human culture in which humans create and regulate the environment of living things and systematically exploit them for human benefit."[30] Agriculture, pets, domestic animal and plant breeding, and tree plantations all belong to the human bioculture. Establishing wilderness/protection zones would, in effect, separate the world of the wild from the exploitive human activities of the bioculture. "Free nature" would be a sort of hybrid buffer zone between protection zones and the bioculture where natural ecological processes predominate.

Many important groups that consider themselves to be ecological are, in effect, primarily involved with an ecological reform of the bioculture. The organic farm movement (inspired, for example, by Wendell Berry and Wes Jackson) appears largely to be an example of this. The concern of the animal rights movement with the "rights" of *all* animals, has, until recently, often failed to distinguish between the conditions of domestic animals in the bioculture and the very different conditions of wild animals in natural ecosystems, with sometimes alarming anti-ecological results.

The present unecological goals of the Forest Service, and similar efforts worldwide, to clear-cut wild forest ecosystems and replace them with "tree plantations," can now be seen as an attempt to extend the bioculture at the expense of the wild. As Taylor points out, the "ethics" of the bioculture differs fundamentally from the basically "noninterference" ethics appropriate to the wilderness/protection zones. Perhaps some ecologically enlightened version of the "stewardship" model is appropriate for the bioculture, but not for the wilderness/protection areas. Different kinds of problems arise when wild animals stray from the protection zones into biocultural zones, and when there are "mixed communities" of wild and domestic as in "free nature."[31]

It is important for those primarily concerned with biocultural ecological reform to expand their outlook to encompass an ecocentric perspective to help ensure that their policies and programs are compatible with, and supportive of, the protection of wild ecosystems and species, and the overall long-range ecological health of the earth.

But the question still remains: how much of the earth should be protected in wilderness/protection zones? The basic answer to this question has essentially been given by the recent research of the conservation biologists: enough wildlife habitat to protect species diversity and the ecological health of Gaia, and to allow for continued speciation and evolutionary change. Along these lines, Arne Naess has provided a future ecological vision toward which we can progress:

> I am not saying that we should have preserved the primordial forest as a whole, but looking back we can imagine a development such that, let us say, one third was preserved as wilderness, one third as free nature with mixed communities, which leaves one third for cities, paved roads, etc. [bioculture]. This would probably be enough, and I guess most people with influence in matters of the environment would agree. But of course, it is a wild fantasy, which is, incidentally, an important kind of wilderness![32]

To realize how out of balance we are ecologically in the United States, based upon Naess's suggestion, we have to consider Thomas Fleischner's point that "over 95% of the contiguous United States has been altered from its original state. Only 2% is legally protected from exploitive uses."[33] And even that 2 percent lacks adequate ecological protection. For example, Forest Service legally designated wilderness areas allow mining, sport hunting, and domestic animal grazing. Legislative efforts are now being made to revise existing mining laws, which have been the cause of much public land abuse. But some have claimed that, apart from ancient forest destruction, the greatest cause of ecological destruction on public lands (both wilderness and nonwilderness areas) is cattle and sheep grazing. Domestic animal grazing destroys the natural plant and grass communities, causes erosion, damages streams and other water supplies, competes with wildlife, results in federal programs to kill large numbers of large predators (including the poisoning and trapping of huge numbers of "nontarget" wildlife), and should therefore be phased out.[34]

To begin to achieve an ecological land-use balance, once the ecologically destructive uses of now-existing Forest Service wilderness have been eliminated, the additional 3 percent of de facto wilderness should be placed in protection zones. This would bring the contiguous United States total to 5 percent protected habitat. That still leaves the contiguous United States approximately 30 percent short of a one-third wilderness, one-third free nature, one-third bioculture ratio (disregarding, for the present, the zoning of free nature).

Under the provisions of the Wilderness Act of 1964, the congressional battles over legal classification of wilderness in the national parks and national forests have already been fought, and mainline reform environmentalists have compromised severely in both cases, particularly the latter. Now the battle to zone land as wilderness is occurring over the 250 million acres administered by the Bureau of Land Management (BLM). The BLM is studying only 10 percent of its land (25 million acres) for possible wilderness designation (most BLM land is contracted out to private corporations and individuals for mining and domestic animal grazing). The projections are that, after the political wrangling and compromise is concluded, only

10 to 15 million acres will be legally protected. This decision is to be made in 1991. It must be remembered that the lands being discussed here (Park Service, Forest Service, and BLM) are *public* lands!

The Wilderness Act of 1964 (while framed and successfully lobbied by dedicated conservationists) is nevertheless a pre-ecological document and, accordingly, its stated purposes and provisions do not reflect the huge tracts of wilderness protection zones (and the degree of protection) required for species and wild ecosystem protection, and for large mammal speciation. A recent newsmagazine article discussing the Wilderness Act and the upcoming BLM wilderness fight still couches the issues largely in terms of anthropocentric special interest compromise politics: of wilderness recreation versus "motorized-recreation and commercial interests." The ecological issues are all but ignored.[35]

In order to boost the wilderness protection zone percentages toward the 30 percent figure, it would probably be necessary to place almost all Forest Service and BLM lands in protection zones and restore them to wildlife habitat. The recent proposal by Deborah and Frank Popper of Rutgers University to return the Great Plains to buffalo habitat would also greatly increase ecosystem protection areas. Earth First! has been carefully studying the American land situation for some time and has developed detailed plans for greatly increasing wild ecosystem protection areas in the United States.[36]

IV. AN INTERNATIONAL PERSPECTIVE

Increasingly, our environmental problems are being recognized as global in scope and, as such, require effective international cooperation. Noel Brown, director of the U.N. Environment Program, indicated that an "ecological council" (comparable to the "Security Council") could soon be a reality.[37] With the world human population predicted to soar to 10 to 14 billion people by the end of the next century (when population ecologists argue that 1 to 2 billion people worldwide, living comfortably at a "basic needs" consumption level, would be maximum for "wide" ecological sustainability, as Naess uses the term), the United Nations also needs to reorganize its population control agencies and environmental protection programs to reflect a unified integrated ecosystem protection approach. The United Nations General Assembly has already adopted a basically ecocentric approach when it approved the World Charter for Nature in 1982. The charter asserts that:

> Every form of life is unique, warranting respect regardless of its worth to man, and, to accord other organisms such recognition, man must be guided by a

moral code of action....Nature shall be respected and its essential processes shall not be disrupted.[38]

The urgency of our current environmental situation suggests that the United Nations should greatly step up efforts to encourage stabilization of the human population in the shortest time possible while, at the same time, help protect human dignity, ideals of justice, and the freedom of individual choice. The United Nations must continue to help feed the hungry and improve basic living conditions in Third World countries; to help and encourage nations in establishing ecosystem protection zones, to protect wildlife; and to discourage consumerism as part of an overall program of ecological and economic sustainability. Major educational programs should be instituted to "ecologize" the peoples of the world.

In pursuing these goals and strategies, it should be recognized that the situations of First and Third World countries are very different. Unlike First World countries, which are already overdeveloped and ecologically unsustainable, Third World countries will need to continue to develop, although hopefully along ecologically sustainable paths. It is unrealistic and unjust to expect Third World countries to turn to the protection of their natural ecosystems *at the expense* of the vital needs of their human populations. At the same time, the magnitude and severity of the global environmental crisis must be fully appreciated. Third World countries should be encouraged to place as high a priority as possible on the expansion of ecosystem protection zones, and the protection of large areas of free nature.

The shift from an economically dominated, exploitive worldview and society, to a deep ecological green society expressing deeply satisfying human goals and values, should be seen as a joyous positive gain for humanity and the earth rather than as self-denial for individuals and humanity as a whole. To experience the transition in this way no doubt requires a conversion to an ecocentric consciousness, to what Arne Naess calls an "ecological self," or to what Paul Taylor refers to as an "inner change." While this inner change is occurring among people at an increasing rate throughout the world, and while people are adopting ecologically compatible bioregional ways of living, ecological destruction and species extinction is accelerating at a terrifying rate. Interim legalistic strategies such as ecosystem protection zoning seem indispensable at this point. Ultimately, we must work simultaneously at all levels of ecological protection and restoration, social justice, and human spiritual renewal and ecological sanity.

NOTES

1. John Hendee, George Stankey, and Robert Lucas, *Wilderness Management* (Washington: USDA Forest Service Misc. Publication No. 1365, 1978) pp. 140–41; quoted in Holmes Rolston, III, "Values Gone Wild", in Rolston,

Philosophy Gone Wild: Essays in Environmental Ethics (Buffalo: Prometheus Books, 1986), p. 119.

2. For the ideological split between Muir and Pinchot, see Stephen Fox, *John Muir and His Legacy: The American Conservation Movement* (Boston: Little, Brown, 1981), pp. 109–30.

3. For introductions to Leopold's thought, see Roderick Nash, *Wilderness and the American Mind* (New Haven: Yale University Press, 1982), 3rd ed., pp. 182–99; J. Baird Callicott (ed.), *Companion to a Sand County Almanac* (Madison: University of Wisconsin Press, 1987); Max Oelschlaeger, *The Idea of Wilderness: From Prehistory to the Age of Ecology* (New Haven: Yale University Press, 1991), pp. 205–42. For discussions of the rise of the Age of Ecology, see George Sessions, "The Deep Ecology Movement: A Review," *Environmental Review* 11, 2 (1987): 105–25; Roderick Nash, *The Rights of Nature: A History of Environmental Ethics* (Madison: University of Wisconsin Press, 1989); Warwick Fox, *Toward a Transpersonal Ecology: Developing New Foundations for Environmentalism* (Boston: Shambhala Press, 1990); Frederick Turner, *Beyond Geography: The Western Spirit Against the Wilderness* (New York: Viking Press, 1980); Morgan Sherwood, "The End of American Wilderness," *Environmental Review* 9 (1985): 197–209.

4. For recent discussions of the ecocentric philosophy of Thoreau and Muir, see Max Oelschlaeger, *The Idea of Wilderness*, pp. 133–204; Stephen Fox, *John Muir and His Legacy*, pp. 43–53, 59, 79–81, 289–91, 350–55, 361; Michael Cohen, *The Pathless Way: John Muir and American Wilderness* (Madison: University of Wisconsin Press, 1984).

5. For a discussion of the development of the Sierra Club from a hiking club to an ecologically oriented organization, see Michael Cohen, *The History of the Sierra Club: 1892–1970* (San Francisco: Sierra Club Books, 1988) esp. pp. 187–322; Stephen Fox, *John Muir and His Legacy*, esp. pp. 250–90.

6. John Rodman, "Resource Conservation—Economics and After," (1976) Pitzer College, Calif. Unpublished manuscript.

7. Joel Connelly, "British Columbia's Big Cut: Who Owns the Ancient Forests?" *Sierra* 76, 3 (1991): 42–53; see also Gary Snyder, *The Practice of the Wild* (San Francisco: North Point Press, 1990), pp. 116–43.

8. Bob Nixon, "Focus on Forests and Forestry," *The Trumpeter* 6, 2 (1989): 38; see also Chris Maser, *The Redesigned Forest* (San Pedro, Calif.: R&E Miles Publisher, 1988).

9. Edward Abbey, *Desert Solitaire: A Season in the Wilderness* (New York: McGraw-Hill, 1968); see also Joseph Sax, *Mountains Without Handrails* (Ann Arbor: University of Michigan Press, 1980).

10. Mitch Friedman, "How Much is Enough?: Lessons from Conservation Biology," in Mitch Friedman (ed.), *Forever Wild: Conserving the Greater North Cascades Ecosystem* (Mountain Hemlock Press, P.O. Box 2962, Bellingham, WA 98227, 1988), p. 34. I have drawn much of the following material on conservation biology from Friedman and from Edward Grumbine, "Ecosystem Management for Native Diversity," also in *Forever Wild*.

11. Michael Soule, "What is Conservation Biology?" *Bioscience* 35 (1985): 727–34; quoted in Friedman, ibid.; for further discussions of the importance of conservation biology for environmentalism in the 90s, see James R. Udall, "Launching the Natural Ark," *Sierra* 76, 5 (1991): 80–89.

12. Friedman, *Forever Wild*, pp. 1–2; see also O. H. Frankel and Michael Soule, *Conservation and Evolution* (Cambridge: Cambridge University Press, 1981); Michael Soule and D. Simberloff, "What do Genetics and Ecology Tell Us

About the Design of Nature Reserves?" *Biological Conservation* 35 (1986): 19–40.

13. Friedman, "How Much is Enough?": 39; Norman Myers, "The Extinction Spasm Impending: Synergisms at Work," *Conservation Biology* 1 (1987): 14–21; A. P. Dobson, C. H. McLellan, and D. S. Wilcove, "Habitat Fragmentation in the Temporate Zone," in M. Soule (ed.), *Conservation Biology: The Science of Scarcity and Diversity* (Mass.: Sinauer Press, 1986), pp. 237–56.

14. Friedman, ibid.; A. Runte, *National Parks: The American Experience* (Lincoln: University of Nebraska Press, 1987); W. D. Newmark, "Legal and Biotic Boundaries of Western North American National Parks: A Problem of Congruence," *Biological Conservation* 33 (1985): 197–208; R. M. May and D. S. Wilcove, "National Park Boundaries and Ecological Realities," *Nature* 324 (1986): 206–7; R. F. Noss, "Wilderness Recovery and Ecological Restoration," *Earth First!* 5, 8 (1985): 18–19; R. F. Noss, "Recipe for Wilderness Recovery," *Earth First!* 6 (1986): 22, 25.

15. Friedman, "How Much is Enough?": 37; C. Holtby, B. A. Wilcox, and Michael Soule, "Benign Neglect: A Model of Faunal Collapse in the Game Reserves of East Africa," *Biological Conservation* 15 (1979): 259–70.

16. Grumbine, "Ecosystem Management": 46; W. D. Newmark, "Legal and Biotic Boundaries."

17. Friedman, "How Much is Enough?": 43; Frankel and Soule, *Conservation and Evolution*, 1981.

18. Michael Soule, "Conservation Biology: Its Scope and Challenge," in M. Soule and B. Wilcox (eds.), *Conservation Biology*, p. 166; quoted in Christopher Manes, *Green Rage: Radical Environmentalism and the Unmaking of Civilization* (Boston: Little, Brown, 1990), pp. 34–5.

19. David Brower, "Toward an Earth International Park," *Sierra Club Bulletin* 52, 9 (1967): 20.

20. Eugene P. Odum, *Fundamentals of Ecology* (Philadelphia: W. B. Saunders, 1971), p. 269; John Phillips ideas, developed in 1974, were presented in "On Environmental Ethics," American Philosophical Association, San Francisco, 1978.

21. Paul Shepard, *The Tender Carnivore and the Sacred Game* (New York: Scribner's, 1973), pp. 260–73.

22. Edward Grumbine, "Ecosystem Management for Native Diversity": 48, 52–3.

23. Grumbine, ibid.; R. F. Noss, "Recipe for Wilderness Recovery"; J. J. Berger, *Restoring the Earth: How Americans are Working to Renew Damaged Environments* (New York: Knopf, 1985).

24. Roderick Nash, *Wilderness and the American Mind*, pp. 380–84.

25. Roderick Nash, *The Rights of Nature*, pp. 270–71 (footnote 28).

26. For bioregionalism, see Peter Berg, Beryl Magilavy, Seth Zuckerman, *A Green City Program* (San Francisco: Planet Drum Books, 1989); Peter Berg (ed.), *Reinhabiting a Separate Country: A Bioregional Anthology of Northern California* (San Francisco: Planet Drum Foundation, 1978); Gary Snyder, "Re-inhabitation," in Snyder, *The Old Ways* (San Francisco: City Light Books, 1977), pp. 57–66; Snyder, *Practice of the Wild;* Thomas Berry, "Bioregions: The Context for Reinhabiting the Earth," in Berry, *The Dream of the Earth* (San Francisco: Sierra Club Books, 1988), pp. 163–70; Kirkpatrick Sale, *Dwellers in the Land: The Bioregional Vision* (San Francisco: Sierra Club Books, 1985); Donald Alexander, "Bioregionalism: Science or Sensibility?" *Environmental Ethics* 12, 2 (1990): 161–73.

27. Roderick Nash, *The Rights of Nature,* 168–9; Paul Ehrlich, "Comments," *Defenders of Wildlife,* Nov/Dec, (1985); Anne and Paul Ehrlich, *Earth* (New York: Franklin Watts, 1987), p. 242.

28. Paul Taylor, *Respect for Nature: A Theory of Environmental Ethics* (Princeton: Princeton University Press, 1986), pp. 288, 310.

29. Taylor, ibid., pp. 269–77.

30. Taylor, ibid., pp. 53–58.

31. For a critique of the stewardship model as applied to agriculture, see Sara Ebenreck, "A Partnership Farmland Ethic," *Environmental Ethics* 5, 1 (1983): 33–45; Arne Naess, "Self-Realization in Mixed Communities of Humans, Bears, Sheep and Wolves," *Inquiry* 22 (1979): 231–42.

32. Arne Naess, "Ecosophy, Population, and Free Nature," *The Trumpeter* 5, 3 (1988): 118.

33. Thomas Fleischner, "Keeping It Wild: Toward a Deeper Wilderness Management," in Friedman, *Forever Wild:* 79.

34. For proposals to eliminate domestic grazing on public lands, see Denzel and Nancy Ferguson, *Sacred Cows at the Public Trough* (Bend, Ore.: Maverick Publications, 1983); Edward Abbey, "Free Speech: The Cowboy and His Cow," in Abbey, *One Life at a Time, Please* (New York: Henry Holt and Co., 1988), pp. 9–19.

35. "The Battle for the Wilderness," *U.S. News & World Report:* 107, 1 (July, 1989): 16–21, 24–5.

36. For the Earth First! wilderness proposals, see Dave Foreman and Howie Wolke, *The Big Outside* (Tucson, Ariz.: Ned Ludd Books, 1988); D. Foreman, H. Wolke, and Bart Koehler, "The Earth First! Wilderness Preserve System," *Wild Earth* 1, 1 (1991): 33–38.

37. See W. R. Prescott, "The Rights of Earth: An Interview with Dr. Noel J. Brown," *In Context* 22 (1989): 29–34.

38. *World Charter for Nature. United Nations General Assembly* (New York: United Nations, A/RES/37/7, Nov. 9, 1982); Harold W. Wood, Jr., "The United Nations World Charter for Nature," *Ecology Law Quarterly* 12 (1985): 977–96.

PART THREE

Ecofeminism

Introduction

Karen J. Warren

Karen J. Warren is a feminist philosopher who has published essays on ecofeminism and edited several special issues on ecofeminism for Hypatia: A Journal of Feminist Philosophy *and the* American Philosophical Association *Newsletter on Feminism and Philosophy. Warren is completing three books on ecological feminism, one co-authored with Jim Cheney and entitled* Ecological Feminism, *and two anthologies on ecofeminism. Warren also conducts workshops on environmental ethics and critical thinking for elementary and secondary school teachers and students, and is co-creator of an environmental ethics simulation game.*

The past few decades have witnessed an enormous interest in both the women's movement and the ecology (environmental) movement. Many feminists have argued that the goals of these two movements are mutually reinforcing; ultimately they involve the development of worldviews and practices that are not based on male-biased models of domination. As Rosemary Radford Ruether wrote in 1975 in her book, *New Woman/New Earth:*

> Women must see that there can be no liberation for them and no solution to the ecological crisis within a society whose fundamental model of relationships continues to be one of domination. They must unite the demands of the women's movement with those of the ecological movement to envision a radical reshaping of the basic socioeconomic relations and the underlying values of this [modern industrial] society. (204)

Since the early 1970s, many feminists, especially ecological feminists ("ecofeminists"), have defended Ruether's basic point: the environment is a feminist issue.

An earlier version of this essay appeared in the American Philosophical Association *Newsletter on Feminism and Philosophy* (Fall 1991).

Just what makes the environment (ecology) a feminist issue? What are some of the alleged connections between the domination of women and the domination of nature? How and why is recognition of these connections important to feminism, environmentalism, and environmental philosophy? Answering these questions is largely what ecofeminism is about.

In this essay I offer an introduction to the literature and issues of ecofeminism. I begin with a characterization of ecofeminism. Then I identify eight sorts of connections—what I call "woman-nature connections"—that ecofeminists claim link the twin dominations of women and nature. Discussion of these alleged connections provides an overview of the scholarly literature in ecofeminism and the sorts of reasons ecofeminists have given for the centrality of ecofeminist insights to environmental philosophy and feminism. It also helps to situate the four essays included in this section (essays by Merchant, Plumwood, Salleh, and Warren) within that range of scholarly positions. I conclude by suggesting that the philosophical significance of ecofeminism is that it challenges feminism to take environmental issues seriously, environmental philosophy to take feminism seriously, and philosophy to take both seriously.

A CHARACTERIZATION OF ECOFEMINISM

Just as there is not one feminism, there is not one ecofeminism. "Ecological feminism" is the name given to a variety of positions that have roots in different feminist practices and philosophies. These different perspectives reflect not only different feminist perspectives (e.g., liberal, traditional Marxist, radical, socialist, black and Third World), they also reflect different understandings of the nature of and solution to pressing environmental problems (see Warren 1987). So, it is an open question how many, which, and on what grounds any of the various positions in environmental philosophy that acknowledge feminist concerns or claim to be feminist are properly identified as ecofeminist positions. What one takes to be a genuine ecofeminist position will depend largely on how one conceptualizes *both* feminism and ecofeminism.

For instance, suppose by "feminism" one means "liberal feminism." Liberal feminism builds on a Western liberal political and philosophical framework that idealizes a society in which autonomous individuals are provided maximal freedom to pursue their own interests. There are two main ecological implications of liberal feminism: the first draws the line of moral considerability at humans, separating humans from nonhumans and basing any claims to moral consideration of nonhumans either on the alleged rights or interests of humans, or on the consequences of such consideration for human well-being. The second extends the line of moral considerability to qualified nonhumans on the grounds that they are deserving of moral consideration in their own right: they, too, are rational, sentient, interest-carriers, right-holders.

Is either liberal feminist ecological implication acceptable from an ecofeminist perspective? It depends, in part, on what one means by "ecofeminism." Many ecofeminists have argued that insofar as liberal feminism keeps intact oppressive and patriarchal ways of conceptualizing nature, including problematic human-nature dichotomies of the sort discussed by all four authors in this section, it will be inadequate from an ecofeminist perspective.

Take another construal of feminism: traditional Marxist feminism. Traditional Marxist feminism views the oppression of women as a kind of class oppression, a direct result of the institution of class society and, under capitalism, private property. Since *praxis* (i.e., conscious physical labor of humans directed at transforming the material world to meet human needs) is the distinguishing characteristic of humans, traditional Marxist feminism, following traditional Marxism, would seem to suggest that the primary value of nature is its instrumental value in the production of economic goods to meet human needs.

Is traditional Marxism fertile soil for ecofeminism? Again, it depends, in part, on what one means by ecofeminism. If ecofeminism is a position that recognizes that nature has value in addition to its use value to humans, or if ecofeminism asserts that more than gender-sensitive class analyses are needed to explain the interwoven dominations of women and nature, then traditional Marxist feminism will be inadequate from an ecofeminist perspective.

Consider one last example. A radical feminist construal of feminism departs from both liberal feminism and traditional Marxist feminism by rooting women's oppression in reproductive biology and sex-gender systems. According to radical feminists, patriarchy (i.e., the systematic oppression of women by men) subordinates women in sex-specific ways by defining women as beings whose primary functions are either to bear and raise children or to satisfy male sexual desires. The liberation of women requires the dismantling of patriarchy, particularly male control of women's bodies.

Is radical feminism ecofeminist? While radical feminists historically have had the most to say about ecofeminism, sometimes claiming that "women are closer to nature than men," some ecofeminists have worried about the extent to which radical feminism both mystifies women's experiences by locating women closer to nature than men, and offers ahistorically essentialist accounts of "women's experiences." Furthermore, some ecofeminists worry that any view that makes any group of humans closer to nature than any other is conceptually flawed and methodologically suspect: it maintains just the sort of value dualistic and hierarchical thinking that is critiqued by ecofeminism (see Griscom 1981; Roach 1991; Warren 1987). Hence the extent to which radical feminism is an adequate theoretical basis for ecofeminism will depend partly on what one takes to be the defining characteristics of ecofeminism.

What, then, can one say about ecofeminism? What characterizes ecofeminism as a theoretical position and political movement? Despite important differences among ecofeminists and the feminisms from which they gain their inspiration, there is something all ecofeminists agree about; such agreement provides a minimal condition account of ecofeminism: there are important connections between the domination of women and the domination of nature, an understanding of which is crucial to feminism, environmentalism, and environmental philosophy (Warren 1987). A main project of ecofeminism is to make visible these "woman-nature connections" and, where harmful to women and nature, to dismantle them.

If woman-nature connections are the backbone of ecofeminism, just what are they? And why is the alleged existence of these connections claimed to be so significant?

WOMAN-NATURE CONNECTIONS

There are at least eight sorts of connections that ecofeminists have identified. These alleged connections provide sometimes competing, sometimes mutually complementary or supportive, analyses of the nature of the twin dominations of women and nature. A casual, albeit philosophically uncritical, perusal of these eight alleged connections helps to identify the range and variety of ecofeminist positions on woman-nature connections.

1. *Historical, Typically Causal, Connections.* One alleged connection between women and nature is historical. When historical data are used to generate theories concerning the sources of the dominations of women and nature, it is also causal. So pervasive is the historical-causal theme in ecofeminist writings that Ariel Salleh practically defines ecofeminism in terms of it: "Eco-feminism is a recent development in feminist thought which argues that the current global environmental crisis is a predictable outcome of patriarchal culture" (Salleh 1988).

What are these alleged historical-causal connections? Some ecofeminists (e.g., Spretnak 1990; Eisler 1988, 1990) trace these connections to prototypical patterns of domination begun with the invasion of Indo-European societies by nomadic tribes from Eurasia about 4500 B.C. (see Lahar 1991, 33). Riane Eisler describes the time before these invasions as a "matrifocal, matrilineal, peaceful agrarian era." Others (e.g., Griffin 1978; Plumwood 1991, this section; Ruether 1974) trace historical connections to patriarchal dualisms and conceptions of rationality in classical Greek philosophy and the rationalist tradition. Still other feminists (e.g., Merchant 1980, this section) focus on cultural and scientific changes that occurred more recently—during the scientific revolution of the sixteenth

and seventeenth centuries: it was then that an older world order characterized by cooperation between humans and nature was replaced by a reductionist, "mechanistic world view of modern science," which sanctioned the
exploitation of nature, unchecked commercial and industrial expansion,
and the subordination of women.

What prompts and explains these alleged historical and causal
woman-nature connections? What *else* was in place to permit and sanction
these twin dominations? To answer these questions, ecofeminists have
turned to the conceptual props that they claim keep these historical
dominations in place.

2. *Conceptual Connections.* Many authors have argued that, ultimately, historical and causal links between the dominations of women and
nature are located in conceptual structures of domination that construct
women and nature in male-biased ways. Basically three such conceptual
links have been offered.

One account locates a conceptual basis of the twin dominations of
women and nature in *value dualisms,* i.e., in disjunctive pairs in which the
disjuncts are seen as oppositional (rather than as complementary) and as
exclusive (rather than as inclusive), and *value hierarchies,* i.e., perceptions
of diversity organized by a spatial Up-Down metaphor, which attributes
higher value (status, prestige) to that which is higher ("Up") (see Gray 1981;
Griffin 1978; Plumwood 1991, this section; Ruether 1974). Frequently cited
examples of these hierarchically organized value dualisms include rea-
son/emotion, mind/body, culture/nature, human/nature, and man/woman
dichotomies. These theorists argue that whatever is historically associated
with emotion, body, nature, and women is regarded as inferior to that which
is (historically) associated with reason, mind, culture, human (i.e., male)
and men.

A second account expands upon the first by housing the problematic
value dualisms and value hierarchies in larger, oppressive conceptual
frameworks—ones that are common to all social "isms of domination" (e.g.,
sexism, racism, classism, heterosexism as well as "naturism," i.e., the
unjustified domination of nonhuman nature (see Warren 1987, 1988, 1990,
this section). A conceptual framework is a socially constructed set of basic
beliefs, values, attitudes and assumptions that shapes and reflects how one
views oneself and others. It is oppressive when it explains, justifies, and
maintains relationships of domination and subordination. An oppressive
conceptual framework is *patriarchal* when it explains, justifies, and maintains the subordination of women by men.

Oppressive and patriarchal conceptual frameworks are characterized
not only by value dualisms and hierarchies but also by *"power-over"*
conceptions of power and relationships of domination (Warren 1991b) and
a *logic of domination,* i.e., a structure of argumentation that provides the
moral premise that superiority justifies subordination (Warren 1987, 1990,

this section). On this view, it is oppressive and patriarchal conceptual frameworks, and the behaviors that they give rise to, that sanction, maintain, and perpetuate the twin dominations of women and nature.

A third account locates a conceptual basis in sex-gender differences, particularly in differentiated personality formation or consciousness (see Cheney 1987; Gray 1981; Salleh, 1984). The claim is that female bodily experiences (e.g., of reproduction and childbearing), not female biology *per se,* situate women differently with respect to nature than men. This sex-gender difference is (allegedly) revealed in a different consciousness in women than men toward nature; it is rooted conceptually in "paradigms that are uncritically oriented to the dominant western masculine forms of experiencing the world: the analytic, non-related, delightfully called 'objective' or 'scientific' approaches" (Salleh 1988, 130)—just those value dualisms that are claimed to separate and inferiorize what is historically female-gender identified. These sociopsychological factors provide a conceptual link insofar as they are embedded in different conceptualization structures and strategies ("different ways of knowing"), coping strategies, and ways of relating to nature for women and men. A goal of ecofeminism, then, is to develop gender-sensitive language, theory, and practices that do not further the exploitative experiences and habits of dissociated, male-gender identified culture toward women and nature.

One project of ecofeminism is to expose and dismantle the conceptual structures of domination which have kept various "isms of domination," particularly the dominations of women and nature, in place. If ecofeminists who allege various conceptual woman-nature connections are correct, this will involve reconceiving those mainstay philosophical notions which rely on them (e.g., notions of reason and rationality, knowledge, objectivity, ethics, and the knowing, moral self).

3. *Empirical and Experiential Connections.* Many ecofeminists have focused on uncovering empirical evidence linking women (and children, people of color, the underclass) with environmental destruction. Some point to various health and risk factors borne disproportionately by women, children, racial minorities and the poor caused by the presence of low-level radiation, pesticides, toxics, and other pollutants (e.g., Caldecott and Leland 1983; Salleh 1990, this section; Shiva 1988; Warren 1991a). Others provide data to show that First World development policies result in policies and practices regarding food, forest, and water, which directly contribute to the inability of women to provide adequately for themselves and their families (e.g., Mies 1986; Shiva 1988; Warren 1988, 1989, 1991a). Feminist animal rights scholars argue that factory farming, animal experimentation, hunting, and meat eating are tied to patriarchal concepts and practices (e.g., Adams 1990, 1991; Kheel 1985; Slicer 1991). Some connect rape and pornography with male-gender identified abuse of both women and nature (e.g., Collard with Contrucci 1988; Griffin 1981). Appeal to such

empirical data is intended both to document the very real, felt, lived "experiential" connections between the dominations of women and nature and to motivate the need for joining together feminist critical analysis and environmental concerns.

Sometimes, however, the empirical and experiential connections between women and nature are intended to reveal important cultural and spiritual ties to the earth honored and celebrated by (some) women and indigenous peoples. This suggests that some woman-nature connections are features of important symbol systems.

4. *Symbolic Connections.* Some ecofeminists have explored the symbolic association and devaluation of women and nature that appears in religion, theology, art, and literature. Documenting such connections and making them integral to the project of ecofeminism is often heralded as ecofeminism's most promising contribution to the creation of liberating, life-affirming, and postpatriarchal worldviews and earth-based spiritualities or theologies. Ecofeminism is then presented as offering alternative spiritual symbols (e.g., Gaia and goddess symbols), spiritualities or theologies, and even utopian societies (e.g., see Gearhart). Appreciating such symbolic woman-nature connections involves understanding "the politics of women's spirituality" (Spretnak 1981).

Some ecofeminist theorists draw on literature, particularly "nature writing," to unpack the nature of the woman-nature linguistic symbolic connections (see Bell 1988; Kolodny 1975; Murphy 1988, 1991). Literary criticism of the sort offered by Patrick Murphy claims that patriarchal conceptions of nature and women have justified "a two-pronged rape and domination of the earth and the women who live on it" (Murphy 1988, 87), often using this as background for developing an ecofeminist literary theory (Murphy 1991).

Some theorists focus on language, particularly the symbolic connections between sexist and naturist language, i.e., language that inferiorizes women and nonhuman nature by naturalizing women and feminizing nature. For example, there are concerns about whether sex-gendered language used to describe "Mother Nature" is, in Ynestra King's words, "potentially liberating or simply a rationale for the continued subordination of women" (Y. King 1981). There are concerns about connections between the languages used to describe women, nature, and nuclear weaponry (see Cahn 1989; Strange 1989). Women are often described in animal terms (e.g., as cows, foxes, chicks, serpents, bitches, beavers, old bats, pussycats, cats, bird-brains, hare-brains). Nature is often described in female and sexual terms: nature is raped, mastered, conquered, controlled, mined. Her "secrets" are "penetrated" and her "womb" is put into the services of the "man of science." "Virgin timber" is felled, cut down. "Fertile soil" is tilled and land that lies "fallow" is "barren," useless. The claim is that language that so feminizes nature and naturalizes women describes, reflects, and perpetuates the domination and inferiorization of both by failing to see the extent to which the twin dominations of women and nature (including animals) are, in fact, culturally (and not merely figuratively) analogous. The development of theory and praxis in feminism and environmental philosophy that does not perpetuate such sexist-naturist language and the power over systems of domination they reinforce is, therefore, a goal of ecofeminism.

5. *Epistemological Connections.* The various alleged historical, causal, conceptual, empirical, and symbolic woman-nature connections (discussed above) have also motivated the need for new, ecofeminist epistemologies. Typically these emerging epistemologies build on scholarship currently under way in feminist philosophy, which challenges mainstream views of reason, rationality, knowledge, and the nature of the knower (see APA *Newsletter on Feminism and Philosophy* 1989). As Val Plumwood suggests in this section, if one mistakenly construes environmental philosophy as only or primarily concerned with ethics, one will neglect "a key aspect of the overall problem, which is concerned with the definition of the human self as separate from nature, the connection between this and the instrumental view of nature, and broader *political* aspects of the critique of instrumentalism" (1991, this section). For Plumwood, ecofeminist epistemologies must critique rationalism in the Western philosophical tradition and develop views of the ethical, knowing self that do not maintain and perpetuate harmful value dualisms and hierarchies, particularly human-nature ones.

Some feminists (e.g., Mills 1987, 1991) appeal to the critical theory of Horkheimer, Adorno, Balbus, and the Frankfurt circle, claiming that "their epistemology and substantive analysis both point to a convergence of feminist and ecological concerns, anticipating the more recent arrival of eco-feminism" (Salleh 1988, 131). For these feminists, "critical theory" provides a critique of the "nature versus culture" dichotomy and an epistemological structure for critiquing the relationships between the domination of women and the domination of nature.

6. *Political (Praxis) Connections.* Francoise d'Eaubonne introduced the term "ecofeminisme" in 1974 to bring attention to women's potential for bringing about an ecological revolution (1974, 213–52). Ecofeminism has always been a grassroots political movement motivated by pressing pragmatic concerns (see Lahar 1991). These range from issues of women's and environmental health, to science, development and technology, the treatment of animals, and peace, antinuclear, antimilitarist activism. The varieties of ecofeminist perspectives on the environment are properly seen as an attempt to take seriously such grassroots activism and political concerns by developing analyses of domination that explain, clarify, and guide that praxis.

7. *Ethical Connections.* To date, most of the philosophical literature on woman-nature connections has appeared in the area of environmental

philosophy known as "environmental ethics." The claim is that the interconnections among the conceptualizations and treatment of women, animals, and (the rest of) nature require a feminist ethical analysis and response. Minimally, the goal of ecofeminist environmental ethics is to develop theories and practices concerning humans and the natural environment that are not male-biased and provide a guide to action in the prefeminist present (Warren 1990). This may involve developing an ecofeminist ethic of care and appropriate reciprocity (Cheney 1987, 1989; Curtin 1991; Warren 1988, 1990, this section), ecofeminist kinship ethics (Plumwood 1991, this section), ecofeminist animal rights positions (Adams 1991; Slicer 1991), an ecofeminist social ecology (Y. King 1981, 1983, 1989, 1990) or ecofeminist bioregionalism (Plant 1990). As Plumwood and Warren claim in their essays in this section, mainstream environmental ethics are inadequate to the extent that they are problematically anthropocentric or hopelessly androcentric.

8. *Theoretical Connections.* The varieties of alleged woman-nature connections discussed above have generated different, sometimes competing, theoretical positions in all areas of feminist and environmental philosophy. Nowhere is this more evident than in the field of environmental ethics. Primarily because of space limitations, the discussion of "theoretical connections" offered here is restricted to environmental ethics.

In many respects, contemporary environmental ethics reflects the range of positions in contemporary philosophical ethics. The latter includes traditional consequentialist (e.g., ethical egoist, utilitarian) and nonconsequentialist or deontological (e.g., Kantian, rights-based, virtue-based) positions, as well as challenges to them by nontraditional (e.g., some feminist, existentialist, Marxist, Afrocentric, non-Western) approaches. Such is also the case in environmental ethics. There are consequentialist (e.g., ethical egoist, eco-utilitarian, utilitarian-based animal liberation ethics) and nonconsequentailist (e.g., rights-based animal liberation, stewardship ethics) approaches that extend traditional ethical considerations to include animals and the nonhuman environment. (Some would argue that these are not *bona fide* environmental ethics, since they do not make the natural environment itself deserving of moral consideration.) There also are nontraditional approaches (e.g., holistic Leopoldian land ethics, social ecology, deep ecology, ecological feminism) that raise considerations underplayed or omitted entirely from mainstream philosophical ethics. Feminists who address environmental issues can be found advocating positions within this broad philosophical range. So where do ecological feminists fit in?

Where one thinks ecological feminists fit in will depend largely on what one means by "ecological feminism." If ecological feminism is an umbrella term for any feminism that raises feminist concerns about the environment, then presumably ecofeminists can be found along the continuum of feminist-inspired and advocated environmental ethics (or, environmental philosophy). If, however, the term "ecological feminism" is used as I am using the term and as it is used by the authors in this section, viz., as the name for a variety of positions expressly committed to exploring woman-nature connections (of the sort identified above) and to developing feminist and environmental philosophies based on these insights, then ecological feminism is best viewed as one of several nontraditional approaches to environmental ethics and philosophy. We are back to where we began: "ecological feminism" is the name of a variety of positions that make visible different sorts of woman-nature connections, claiming that an understanding of these connections is necessary for any adequate feminism, environmentalism, or environmental philosophy. Whether the connections alleged and the arguments advanced in support of them are accepted on feminist and philosophical grounds is a question the friendly critic must answer.

THE ESSAYS INCLUDED IN THIS SECTION

As review of the literature overview given above reveals, the four essays included in this section provide only a glimpse of the positions advocated by ecofeminists. Still, together they raise issues across all eight categories of woman-nature connections that were identified above. Their inclusion here provides a sample of the philosophically relevant contributions ecofeminist historians, sociologists, and philosophers have made to ecofeminist and environmental philosophy.

Historian of environmental science Carolyn Merchant published her highly influential book *The Death of Nature: Women, Ecology and the Scientific Revolution* in 1980. In it she argues that prior to the seventeenth century, nature was conceived on an organic model as a benevolent female and a nurturing mother; after the scientific revolution, nature was conceived on a mechanistic model as (mere) machine, inert, dead. On both models, nature was female. Merchant argues that the move from the organic to the mechanistic model permitted the justified exploitation of the (female) earth, by removing the sorts of barriers to such treatment that the metaphor of nature as alive previously prevented; the mechanistic worldview of modern science sanctioned the exploitation of nature, unrestrained commercial expansion, and socioeconomic conditions that perpetuated the subordination of women. *The Death of Nature* wove together scholarly material from politics, art, literature, physics, technology, philosophy and popular culture to show how this mechanistic worldview replaced an older, organic worldview, which provided gendered moral restraints on how one treated nature.

The essay by Merchant which appears in this section, "The Death of Nature," is culled from *The Death of Nature*. This essay represents an edited version of the philosophically significant aspects of Merchant's main argument in *The Death of Nature;* it sidesteps some of the more technical, literary, or scientific specifics that receive extensive attention in the book. Inclusion of the Merchant essay in this section ensures representation of an early and classic, although not universally accepted (see Plumwood 1986), historical ecofeminist position on the patriarchal source of the domination of nature.

In "Nature, Self, and Gender: Feminism, Environmental Philosophy, and the Critique of Rationalism," Val Plumwood argues that the key to woman-nature connections in the Western world is found in "rationalism," that long-standing philosophical tradition that affirms the human/nature dichotomy and a network of other related dualisms (e.g., masculine/feminine, reason/emotion, spirit/body) and offers an account of the human self as masculine and centered around rationality to the exclusion of its contrasts (especially characteristics regarded as feminine, animal, or natural). Plumwood criticizes both deep ecology and environmental philosophy generally for missing entirely the ecofeminist critique that "anthropocentrism and androcentrism are linked." She claims,

> The failure to observe such connections is the result of an inadequate historical analysis and understanding of the way in which the inferiorization of both women and nature is grounded in rationalism, and the connections of both to the inferiorizing of the body, hierarchical concepts of labor, and disembedded and individualist accounts of the self.

Plumwood concludes that "the effect of ecofeminism is not to absorb or sacrifice the critique of anthropocentrism, but to deepen and enrich it."

In "Working with Nature: Reciprocity or Control?" Ariel Salleh documents empirically women's involvement in the environmental movement and argues that it is a "patriachal belief system" that maintains and justifies both the invisibility of both what women do and the continued destruction of the natural environment. According to Salleh, the rationale of the exploitation of women and of nature "has been uncovered by the ecofeminist analysis of patriarchy." What is needed, she argues, is that "the unconscious connection between women and nature needs to be made conscious, and the hierarchical fallacies of the Great Chain of Being acknowledged, before there can be any real growth toward a sane, humane, ecological future." Feminists, environmentalists, and philosophers must see that struggles for equality of women and ecological sustainability are interlinked.

In "The Power and the Promise of Ecological Feminism," Karen J. Warren, like Plumwood, focuses on the conceptual connections between the dominations of women and nature. She argues that because the conceptual connections are located in an oppressive patriarchal conceptual framework characterized by a logic of domination, first, the logic of traditional feminism requires the expansion of feminism to include ecological feminism, and, second, ecological feminism provides a distinctively feminist environmental ethic. Appealing to the argumentative significance of first-person narrative and emerging ecofeminist ethics of care, kinship, and appropriate reciprocity, Warren concludes that any feminism, environmentalism, or environmental philosophy that fails to recognize important woman-nature conenctions is simply inadequate.

THE SIGNIFICANCE OF ECOFEMINISM

The preceding account identifies eight sorts of connections between the domination of women and the domination of nature that have been defended by ecofeminists. It also indicates both generally and specifically (in terms of the four essays included in this section) the nature of the challenges that acceptance of these connections poses for contemporary feminism, environmentalism, and environmental philosophy. But if the power and promise of ecological feminism runs as deep as many ecofeminists suppose, there must be implications of ecofeminism for mainstream philosophy as well. What are some of these?

The historical links suggest that data from the social sciences on women, development, and the environment are important to theoretical undertakings in many areas of philosophy. For instance, in ethics such data raise important issues about anthropocentric and androcentric bias. Can mainstream normative ethical theories generate an environmental ethic that is not male-biased? In epistemology, data on the "indigenous technical knowledge" of women in forestry, water collection, farming and food production (see Warren 1988, 1991a) raise issues about women's "epistemic privilege" and the need for "feminist standpoint epistemologies." In metaphysics, data on the cross-cultural variability of women-nature connections raise issues about the social constructions of conceptions of both women and nature and the human-nature dichotomy of at least dominant Western philosophy (see Warren 1990, this section). In political philosophy, data on the inferior standards of living of women globally raise issues about political theories and theorizing: What roles do unequal distributions of power and privilege play in the maintainance of systems of domination over both women and nature. How do they affect the content of political theories and the methodology of political theorizing? In the history of philosophy, data on the historical inferiorization of what is both female-gender and nature identified raise issues about the andthropocentric and androcentic biases of philosophical theories in any given time period. In philosophy of science, particularly philosophy of biology, such data raise issues about the relationships between feminism and science, particularly ecological science. As Carolyn Merchant asks, "Is there a set of assumptions basic to the science of ecology that also holds implications for the status of women? Is there an ecological ethic that is also a feminist ethic?" (Merchant 1985, 229). Are there important parallels between contemporary ecofeminist ethics and ecosystem ecology that suggest ways in which the two are engaged in mutually supportive projects (see Warren and Cheney 1991)? These are the sorts of questions ecofeminism raises for traditional fields in mainstream philosophy.

Perhaps the most serious challenges to mainstream philosophy are at the level of conceptual analysis and theory. Ecofeminism raises significant issues about the philosophical conceptions of the self, knowledge and the knower, reason and rationality, objectivity, and a host of favored dualisms that form the backbone of philosophical theorizing, even the conception of philosophy itself. These notions will need to be reexamined for possible male-gender bias. The challenge to philosophy is to replace conceptual schemes, theories, and practices that currently feminize nature and naturalize women to the mutual detriment of both with ones that do not. That is what ecofeminists generally, and the authors in this section specifically, argue is needed from feminism, environmentalism, environmental philosophy, and philosophy.

REFERENCES

Adams, Carol J. 1991. Ecofeminism and the eating of animals, *Hypatia* 6: 125–145.
_____. 1990. *The Sexual Politics of Meat: A Feminist-Vegetarian Critical Theory* (New York: Continuum).
American Philosophical Association (APA). *Newsletter on Feminism and Philosophy*, eds. Nancy Tuana and Karen J. Warren. 1989. Special issue on Reason, Rationality, and Gender. 88 (2).
American Philosophical Association (APA). *Newsletter on Feminism and Philosophy*, eds. Nancy Tuana and Karen J. Warren. 1991, 1992. Two-part special issue on Feminism and the Environment (Fall, Winter): forthcoming.
Bell, Barbara Currier. 1988. Cable of blue fire: glimpsing a group identity for humankind, *Studies in the Humanities*. Special Issue on Feminism, Ecology, and the Future of the Humanities, ed. Patrick Murphy. 15(2):90–107.
Cahn, Carol. 1989. Sex and Death in the Rational World of Defense Intellectuals, in *Exposing Nuclear Phallacies*, ed. Russell Diana (New York: Pergamon Press).
Caldecott, Leonie and Stephanie LeLand, eds. 1983. *Reclaim the Earth*. London: The Women's Press.
Cheney, Jim. 1989. Postmodern environmental ethics: ethics as bioregional narrative, *Environmental Ethics* 11(2):117–34.
_____. 1987. Eco-feminism and deep ecology, *Environmental Ethics* 9 (2):115–45.
Collard, Andrée with Joyce Contrucci. 1988. *Rape of the Wild: Man's Violence Against Animals and the Earth* (Bloomington, Ind.: Indiana University Press).
Curtin, Deane. 1991. Toward an ecological ethic of care, *Hypatia*. 6 (1):60–74.
d'Eaubonne, Françoise. 1974. *Le Féminisme ou la Mort*. Paris: Pierre Horay.
Eisler, Riane. 1990. The Gaia Tradition and the Partnership Future, in *Reweaving*

the World: The Emergence of Ecofeminism, eds. Irene Diamond and Gloria Femen Orenstein (San Francisco: Sierra Club Books).

_____. 1988. *The Chalice & The Blade: Our History, Our Future* (San Francisco: Harper and Row).

Gearhart, Sally. 1979. *The Wanderground: Stories of the Hill Women* (Boston: Alyson Publications).

Gray, Elizabeth Dodson. 1981. *Green Paradise Lost* (Wellesley, Mass.: Roundtable Press).

Griffin, Susan. 1981. *Pornography and Silence: Culture's Revenge Against Nature* (New York: Harper and Row).

_____. 1978. *Woman and Nature: The Roaring Inside Her* (San Francisco: Harper and Row).

Griscom, Joan L. 1981. "On healing the nature/history split in feminist thought," *Heresies #13*. Special issue on feminism and ecology. 4:4–9.

Kheel, Marti. 1985. The liberation of nature: A circular affair, *Environmental Ethics* 7 (2):135–49.

King, Ynestra. 1990. Healing the Wounds: Feminism, Ecology, and the Nature/Culture Dualism, in *Reweaving the World: The Emergence of Ecofeminism*, eds. Irene Diamond and Gloria Femen Orenstein (San Francisco: Sierra Club Books).

_____. 1989. The Ecology of Feminism and the Feminism of Ecology, in *Healing the Wounds: The Promise of Ecofeminism*, ed. Judith Plant (Santa Cruz, Calif.: New Society Publishers).

_____. 1983. The Eco-feminist Imperative, in *Reclaim the Earth*, eds. Leonie Caldecott and Stephanie Leland (London: The Women's Press).

_____. 1981. "Feminism and the Revolt of Nature," in *Heresies #13 Feminism and Ecology* 4(1):12–16.

Kolodny, Annette. 1975. *The Lay of the Land: Metaphor as Experience and History in American Life and Letters* (Chapel Hill: University of North Carolina Press).

Lahar, Stephanie. 1991. Ecofeminist theory and grassroots politics, *Hypatia*, 6 (1):28–45.

Merchant, Carolyn. 1985. Feminism and Ecology, in Bill Devall and George Sessions, *Deep Ecology: Living as if Nature Mattered* (Salt Lake City: Peregrine Smith Books).

_____. 1980. *The Death of Nature: Women, Ecology, and the Scientific Revolution* (San Francisco: Harper and Row).

Mies, Maria. 1986. *Patriarchy and Accumulation on a World Scale* (London: Zed Books Ltd).

Mills, Patricia Jagentowicz. 1991. Feminism and ecology: on the domination of nature, *Hypatia*, 6 (1):162–78.

_____. 1987. *Woman, Nature, and Psyche* (New Haven: Yale University Press).

Murphy, Patrick. 1991. Ground, pivot, motion: ecofeminist theory, dialogics, and literary practice, *Hypatia*, 6 (1):146–61.

_____. 1988. Introduction: feminism, ecology, and the future of the humanities, *Studies in the Humanities*. Special issue on feminism, ecology, and the future of the humanities. 15 (2): 85–9.

Ortner, Sherry B. 1974. Is Female to Male as Nature is to Culture? In *Woman, Culture and Society*, eds. Michelle Rosaldo and Louise Lamphere (Stanford: Stanford University Press).

Plant, Judith. 1990. Searching for Common Ground: Ecofeminism and Bioregionalism, in *Reweaving the World: The Emergence of Ecofeminism*, eds. Irene Diamond and Gloria Femen Orenstein (San Francisco: Sierra Club Books).

Plumwood, Val. 1991. Nature, self, and gender: feminism, environmental philosophy and the critique of rationalism, *Hypatia*, 6 (1):3–37.

_____. 1986. Ecofeminism: An overview and discussion of positions and arguments, *Australasian Journal of Philosophy*, Suppl. to Vol. 64:120–37.

Roach, Catherine. 1991. Loving your mother: on the woman-nature relation, *Hypatia*, 6 (1):46–59.

Ruether, Rosemary Radford. 1975. *New Woman/New Earth: Sexist Ideologies and Human Liberation* (New York: The Seabury Press).

Salleh, Ariel Kay. 1990. Living with Nature: Reciprocity or Control? in *Ethics of Environment and Development*, eds. R. and J. Engel (Tucson: University of Arizona Press).

_____. 1988. Epistemology and the metaphors of production: An eco-feminist reading of critical theory, in *Studies in the Humanities*. Special issue on feminism, ecology, and the future of the humanities, ed. Patrick Murphy. 15 (2):130–39.

_____. 1984. Deeper than deep ecology: The eco-feminist connection, *Environmental Ethics* 6 (4):339–45.

Shiva, Vandana. 1988. *Staying Alive: Women, Ecology and Development* (London: Zed Books).

Slicer, Deborah. 1991. Your daughter or your dog? A feminist assessment of animal research issues, *Hypatia*, 6 (1):108–24.

Spretnak, Charlene. 1990. Ecofeminism: Our Roots and Flowering, in *Reweaving the World: The Emergence of Ecofeminism*, eds. Irene Diamond and Gloria Femen Orenstein (San Francisco: Sierra Club Books).

Spretnak, Charlene, ed. 1982. *The Politics of Women's Spirituality* (Garden City, NY: Anchor Press).

Strange, Penny. 1989. It'll Make A Man Out of You: A Feminist View of the Arms Race, in *Exposing Nucelar Phallacies*, ed. Diane Russell (New York: Pergamon Press).

Warren, Karen J. 1991a. Taking Empirical Data Seriously: An Ecofeminist Perspective on Woman-Nature Connections, Working Paper, presented at the North American Society for Social Philosophy (Colorado Springs, Colo.: August 10, 1991).

_____. 1991b. Toward a feminist peace politics, *Journal of Peace and Justice Studies*, 3(1):87–102.

_____. 1990. The power and the promise of ecological feminism, *Environmental Ethics* 12 (2):125–46.

_____. 1989. Water and streams: An ecofeminist perspective, *Imprint* (June):5–7.

_____. 1988. Toward an ecofeminist ethic, *Studies in the Humanities*. Special issue on feminism, ecology, and the future of the humanities, ed. Patrick Murphy. 15(2):140–56.

_____. 1987. Feminism and ecology: making connections, *Environmental Ethics* 9 (1):3–20.

Warren, Karen J. and Jim Cheney. 1991. Ecological feminism and ecosystem ecology, *Hypatia*, 6 (1):179–97.

The Death of Nature

Carolyn Merchant

Carolyn Merchant is a professor of environmental history, philosophy, and ethics in the Department of Conservation and Resource Studies at the University of California at Berkeley. She is the author of numerous publications on feminism and the environment, including The Death of Nature: Women, Ecology and the Scientific Revolution *and* Ecological Revolutions, *and* Radical Ecology: The Search for a Livable World.

INTRODUCTION: WOMEN AS NATURE

Women and nature have an age-old association—an affiliation that has persisted throughout culture, language, and history. Their ancient interconnections have been dramatized by the simultaneity of two recent social movements—women's liberation, symbolized in its controversial infancy by Betty Friedan's *Feminine Mystique* (1963), and the ecology movement, which built up during the 1960s and finally captured national attention on Earth Day, 1970. Common to both is an egalitarian perspective. Women are struggling to free themselves from cultural and economic contraints that have kept them subordinate to men in American society. Environmentalists, warning us of the irreversible consequences of continuing environmental exploitation, are developing an ecological ethic emphasizing the interconnectedness between people and nature. Juxtaposing the goals of the two movements can suggest new values and social structures, based not on the domination of women and nature as resources but on the full expression of both male and female talent and on the maintenance of environmental integrity.

New social concerns generate new intellectual and historical prob-

Excerpted from *The Death of Nature*, originally published by Harper and Row (New York, 1980). Reprinted with permission.

lems. Conversely, new interpretations of the past provide perspectives on the present and hence the power to change it. Today's feminist and ecological consciousness can be used to examine the historical interconnections between women and nature that developed as the modern scientific and economic world took form in the sixteenth and seventeenth centuries—a transformation that shaped and pervades today's mainstream values and perceptions.

The ancient identity of nature as a nurturing mother links women's history with the history of the environment and ecological change. The female earth was central to the organic cosmology that was undermined by the Scientific Revolution and the rise of a market-oriented culture in early modern Europe. The ecology movement has reawakened interest in the values and concepts associated historically with the premodern organic world. The ecological model and its associated ethics make possible a fresh and critical interpretation of the rise of modern science in the crucial period when our cosmos ceased to be viewed as an organism and became instead a machine.

In investigating the roots of our current environmental dilemma and its connections to science, technology, and the economy, we must reexamine the formation of a world view and a science that, by reconceptualizing reality as a machine rather than a living organism, sanctioned the domination of both nature and women.

NATURE AS FEMALE

The world we have lost was organic. From the obscure origins of our species, human beings have lived in daily, immediate, organic relation with the natural order for their sustenance. In 1500, the daily interaction with nature was still structured for most Europeans, as it was for other peoples, by close-knit, cooperative, organic communities.

Thus it is not surprising that for sixteenth-century Europeans the root metaphor binding together the self, society, and the cosmos was that of an organism. As a projection of the way people experienced daily life, organismic theory emphasized interdependence among the parts of the human body, subordination of individual to communal purposes in family, community, and state, and vital life permeating the cosmos to the lowliest stone.

The idea of nature as a living organism had philosophical antecedents in ancient systems of thought, variations of which formed the prevailing ideological framework of the sixteenth century. The organismic metaphor, however, was immensely flexible and adaptable to varying contexts, depending on which of its presuppositions was emphasized. A spectrum of philosophical and political possibilities existed, all of which could be subsumed under the general rubric of *organic*.

Central to the organic theory was the identification of nature, especially the earth, with a nurturing mother: A kindly beneficent female who provided for the needs of mankind in an ordered, planned universe. But another opposing image of nature as female was also prevalent: wild and uncontrollable nature that could render violence, storms, droughts, and general chaos. Both were identified with the female sex and were projections of human perceptions onto the external world. The metaphor of the earth as a nurturing mother was gradually to vanish as a dominant image as the Scientific Revolution proceeded to mechanize and to rationalize the world view. The second image, nature as disorder, called forth an important modern idea, that of power over nature. Two new ideas, those of mechanism and of the domination and mastery of nature, became core concepts of the modern world. An organically oriented mentality in which female principles played an important role was undermined and replaced by a mechanically oriented mentality that either eliminated or used female principles in an exploitative manner. As Western culture became increasingly mechanized in the 1600s, the female earth and virgin earth spirit were subdued by the machine.[1]

The change in controlling imagery was directly related to changes in human attitudes and behavior toward the earth. Whereas the nurturing earth image can be viewed as a cultural constraint restricting the types of socially and morally sanctioned human actions allowable with respect to the earth, the new images of mastery and domination functioned as cultural sanctions for the denudation of nature. Society needed these new images as it continued the processes of commercialism and industrialization, which depended on activities directly altering the earth—mining, drainage, deforestation, and assarting (grubbing up stumps to clear fields). The new activities utilized new technologies—lift and force pumps, cranes, windmills, geared wheels, flap valves, chains, pistons, treadmills, under-and overshot watermills, fulling mills, flywheels, bellows, excavators, bucket chains, rollers, geared and wheeled bridges, cranks, elaborate block and tackle systems, worm, spur, crown, and lantern gears, cams and eccentrics, ratchets, wrenches, presses, and screws in magnificent variation and combination.

These technological and commercial changes did not take place quickly; they developed gradually over the ancient and medieval eras, as did the accompanying environmental deterioration. Slowly over many centuries early Mediterranean and Greek civilization had mined and quarried the mountainsides, altered the forested landscape, and overgrazed the hills. Nevertheless, technologies were low level, people considered themselves parts of a finite cosmos, and animism and fertility cults that treated nature as sacred were numerous. Roman civilization was more pragmatic, secular, and commercial and its environmental impact more intense. Yet Roman writers such as Ovid, Seneca, Pliny, and the Stoic philosophers openly deplored mining as an abuse of their mother, the earth. With the disintegration of feudalism and the expansion of Europeans into new worlds and markets, commercial society began to have an accelerated impact on the natural environment. By the sixteenth and seventeenth centuries, the tension between technological development in the world of action and the controlling organic images in the world of the mind had become too great. The old structures were incompatible with the new activities.

Both the nurturing and domination metaphors had existed in philosophy, religion, and literature. The idea of dominion over the earth existed in Greek philosophy and Christian religion; that of the nurturing earth, in Greek and other pagan philosophies. But, as the economy became modernized and the Scientific Revolution proceeded, the dominion metaphor spread beyond the religious sphere and assumed ascendancy in the social and political spheres as well. These two competing images and their normative associations can be found in sixteenth-century literature, art, philosophy, and science.

The image of the earth as a living organism and nurturing mother had served as a cultural constraint restricting the actions of human beings. One does not readily slay a mother, dig into her entrails for gold or mutilate her body, although commercial mining would soon require that. As long as the earth was considered to be alive and sensitive, it could be considered a breach of human ethical behavior to carry out destructive acts against it. For most traditional cultures, minerals and metals ripened in the uterus of the Earth Mother, mines were compared to her vagina, and metallurgy was the human hastening of the birth of the living metal in the artificial womb of the furnace—an abortion of the metal's natural growth cycle before its time. Miners offered propitiation to the deities of the soil and subterranean world, performed ceremonial sacrifices, and observed strict cleanliness, sexual abstinence, and fasting before violating the sacredness of the living earth by sinking a mine. Smiths assumed an awesome responsibility in precipitating the metal's birth through smelting, fusing, and beating it with hammer and anvil; they were often accorded the status of shaman in tribal rituals and their tools were thought to hold special powers.

The Renaissance image of the nurturing earth still carried with it subtle ethical controls and restraints. Such imagery found in a culture's literature can play a normative role within the culture. Controlling images operate as ethical restraints or as ethical sanctions—as subtle "oughts" or "ought-nots." Thus as the descriptive metaphors and images of nature change, a behavioral restraint can be changed into a sanction. Such a change in the image and description of nature was occurring during the course of the Scientific Revolution.

DOMINION OVER NATURE: FRANCIS BACON'S PHILOSOPHY

Francis Bacon (1561–1626), a celebrated "father of modern science," transformed tendencies already extant in his own society into a total program advocating the control of nature for human benefit. Melding together a new philosophy based on natural magic as a technique for manipulating nature, the technologies of mining and metallurgy, the emerging concept of progress and a patriarchal structure of family and state, Bacon fashioned a new ethic sanctioning the exploitation of nature.

Bacon has been eulogized as the originator of the concept of the modern research institute, a philosopher of industrial science, the inspiration behind the Royal Society (1660), and as the founder of the inductive method by which all people can verify for themselves the truths of science by the reading of nature's book.[2] But from the perspective of nature, women, and the lower orders of society emerges a less favorable image of Bacon and a critique of his program as ultimately benefiting the middle-class male entrepreneur. Bacon, of course, was not responsible for subsequent uses of his philosophy. But, because he was in an extremely influential social position and in touch with the important developments of his time, his language, style, nuance, and metaphor become a mirror reflecting his class perspective.

Sensitive to the same social transformations that had already begun to reduce women to psychic and reproductive resources, Bacon developed the power of language as political instrument in reducing female nature to a resource for economic production. Female imagery became a tool in adapting scientific knowledge and method to a new form of human power over nature. The "controversy over women" and the inquisition of witches—both present in Bacon's social milieu—permeated his description of nature and his metaphorical style and were instrumental in his transformation of the earth as a nurturing mother and womb of life into a source of secrets to be extracted for economic advance.

Much of the imagery Bacon used in delineating his new scientific objectives and methods derives from the courtroom, and, because it treats nature as a female to be tortured through mechanical inventions, strongly suggests the interrogations of the witch trials and the mechanical devices used to torture witches.

The new man of science must not think that the "inquisition of nature is in any part interdicted or forbidden." Nature must be "bound into service" and made a "slave," put "in constraint" and "molded" by the mechanical arts. The "searchers and spies of nature" are to discover her plots and secrets.[3]

This method, so readily applicable when nature is denoted by the female gender, degraded and made possible the exploitation of the natural environment. As woman's womb had symbolically yielded to the forceps, so nature's womb harbored secrets that through technology could be wrested from her grasp for use in the improvement of the human condition:

> There is therefore much ground for hoping that there are still laid up in the womb of nature many secrets of excellent use having no affinity or parallelism with anything that is now known. . .only by the method which we are now treating can they be speedily and suddenly and simultaneously presented and anticipated.[4]

Bacon transformed the magical tradition by calling on the need to dominate nature not for the sole benefit of the individual magician but for the good of the entire human race. Through vivid metaphor, he transformed the magus from nature's servant to its exploiter, and nature from a teacher to a slave. Bacon argued that it was the magician's error to consider art (technology) a mere "assistant to nature having the power to finish what nature has begun" and therefore to despair of ever "changing, transmuting, or fundamentally altering nature."[5]

The natural magician saw himself as operating within the organic order of nature—he was a manipulator of parts within that system, bringing down the heavenly powers to the earthly shrine. Agrippa. . .had begun to explore the possibility of ascending the hierarchy to the point of cohabiting with God. Bacon extended this idea to include the recovery of the power over nature lost when Adam and Eve were expelled from paradise.

Due to the Fall from the Garden of Eden (caused by the temptation of a woman), the human race lost its "dominion over creation." Before the Fall, there was no need for power or dominion, because Adam and Eve had been made sovereign over all other creatures. In this state of dominion, mankind was "like unto God." While some, accepting God's punishment, had obeyed the medieval strictures against searching too deeply into God's secrets, Bacon turned the constraints into sanctions. Only by "digging further and further into the mine of natural knowledge" could mankind recover that lost dominion. In this way, "the narrow limits of man's dominion over the universe" could be stretched "to their promised bounds."[6]

Although a female's inquisitiveness may have caused man's fall from his God-given dominion, the relentless interrogation of another female, nature, could be used to regain it. As he argued in *The Masculine Birth of Time,* "I am come in very truth leading you to nature with all her children to bind her to your service and make her your slave." "We have no right," he asserted, "to expect nature to come to us." Instead, "Nature must be taken by the forelock, being bald behind." Delay and subtle argument "permit one only to clutch at nature, never to lay hold of her and capture her."[7]

Nature existed in three states—at liberty, in error, or in bondage.

> She is either free and follows her ordinary course of development as in the
> heavens, in the animal and vegetable creation, and in the general array of the
> universe; or she is driven out of her ordinary course by the perverseness,
> insolence, and forwardness of matter and violence of impediments, as in the
> case of monsters; or lastly, she is put in constraint, molded, and made as it
> were new by art and the hand of man; as in things artificial.[8]

The first instance was the view of nature as immanent self-development,
the nature naturing herself of the Aristotelians. This was the organic view
of nature as a living, growing, self-actualizing being. The second state was
necessary to explain the malfunctions and monstrosities that frequently
appeared and that could not have been caused by God or another higher
power acting on his instruction. Since monstrosities could not be explained
by the action of form or spirit, they had to be the result of matter acting
perversely. Matter in Plato's *Timaeus* was recalcitrant and had to be
forcefully shaped by the demiurge. Bacon frequently described matter in
female imagery, as a "common harlot." "Matter is not devoid of an appetite
and inclination to dissolve the world and fall back into the old Chaos." It
therefore must be "restrained and kept in order by the prevailing concord
of things." "The vexations of art are certainly as the bonds and handcuffs
of Proteus, which betray the ultimate struggles and efforts of matter."[9]

The third instance was the case of art (techné)—man operating on
nature to create something new and artificial. Here "nature takes orders
from man and works under his authority." Miners and smiths should
become the model for the new class of natural philosophers who would
interrogate and alter nature. They had developed the two most important
methods of wresting nature's secrets from her, "the one searching into the
bowels of nature, the other shaping nature as on an anvil." "Why should
we not divide natural philosophy into two parts, the mine and the furnace?" For "the truth of nature lies hid in certain deep mines and caves,"
within the earth's bosom. Bacon, like some of the practically minded
alchemists, would "advise the studious to sell their books and build
furnaces" and, "forsaking Minerva and the Muses as barren virgins, to rely
upon Vulcan."[10]

The new method of interrogation was not through abstract notions,
but through the instruction of the understanding "that it may in very truth
dissect nature." The instruments of the mind supply suggestions, those of
the hand give motion and aid the work. "By art and the hand of man," nature
can then be "forced out of her natural state and squeezed and molded." In
this way, "human knowledge and human power meet as one."[11]

Here, in bold sexual imagery, is the key feature of the modern experimental method—constraint of nature in the laboratory, dissection by hand
and mind, and the penetration of hidden secrets—language still used today
in praising a scientist's "hard facts," "penetrating mind," or the "thrust of
his argument." The constraints against penetration in Natura's lament over

her torn garments of modesty have been turned into sanctions in language that legitimates the exploitation and "rape" of nature for human good.

Scientific method, combined with mechanical technology, would create a "new organon," a new system of investigation, that unified knowledge with material power. The technological discoveries of printing, gunpowder, and the magnet in the fields of learning, warfare, and navigation "help us to think about the secrets still locked in nature's bosom." "They do not, like the old, merely exert a gentle guidance over nature's course; they have the power to conquer and subdue her, to shake her to her foundations." Under the mechanical arts, "nature betrays her secrets more fully. . .than when in enjoyment of her natural liberty."12

Mechanics, which gave man power over nature, consisted in motion; that is, in "the uniting or disuniting of natural bodies." Most useful were the arts that altered the materials of things—"agriculture, cookery, chemistry, dying, the manufacture of glass, enamel, sugar, gunpowder, artificial fires, paper, and the like." But in performing these operations, one was constrained to operate within the chain of causal connections; nature could "not be commanded except by being obeyed." Only by the study, interpretation, and observation of nature could these possibilities be uncovered; only by acting as the interpreter of nature could knowledge be turned into power. Of the three grades of human ambition, the most wholesome and noble was "to endeavor to establish and extend the power and dominion of the human race itself over the universe." In this way "the human race [could] recover that right over nature which belongs to it by divine bequest."13

The interrogation of witches as a symbol for the interrogation of nature, the courtroom as a model for its inquisition, and torture through mechanical devices as a tool for the subjugation of disorder were fundamental to the scientific method as power. For Bacon. . ., sexual politics helped to structure the nature of the empirical method that would produce a new form of knowledge and a new ideology of objectivity seemingly devoid of cultural and political assumptions.

Human dominion over nature, an integral element of the Baconian program, was to be achieved through the experimental "disclosure of nature's secrets." Seventeenth-century scientists, reinforcing aggressive attitudes toward nature, spoke out in favor of "mastering" and "managing" the earth. Descartes wrote in his *Discourse on Method* (1636) that through knowing the crafts of the artisans and the forces of bodies we could "render ourselves the masters and possessors of nature."14 Joseph Glanvill, the English philosopher who defended the Baconian program in his *Plus Ultra* of 1668, asserted that the objective of natural philosophy was to "enlarge knowledge by observation and experiment. . .so that nature being known, it may be mastered, managed, and used in the services of humane life." To achieve this objective, arts and instruments should be developed for "searching out the beginnings and depths of things and discovering the intrigues of remoter nature."[15] The most useful of the arts were chemistry, anatomy, and mathematics; the best instruments included the microscope, telescope, thermometer, barometer, and air pump.

The new image of nature as a female to be controlled and dissected through experiment legitimated the exploitation of natural resources. Although the image of the nurturing earth popular in the Renaissance did not vanish, it was superseded by new controlling imagery. The constraints against penetration associated with the earth-mother image were transformed into sanctions for denudation. After the Scientific Revolution, *Natura* no longer complains that her garments of modesty are being torn by the wrongful thrusts of man. She is portrayed in statues by the French sculptor Louis-Ernest Barrias (1841–1905) coyly removing her own veil and exposing herself to science. From an active teacher and parent, she has become a mindless, submissive body. Not only did this new image function as a sanction, but the new conceptual framework of the Scientific Revolution—mechanism—carried with it norms quite different from the norms of organicism. The new mechanical order and its associated values of power and control would mandate the death of nature.

THE MECHANICAL ORDER

The fundamental social and intellectual problem for the seventeenth century was the problem of order. The perception of disorder, so important to the Baconian doctrine of dominion over nature, was also crucial to the rise of mechanism as a rational antidote to the disintegration of the organic cosmos. The new mechanical philosophy of the mid-seventeenth century achieved a reunification of the cosmos, society, and the self in terms of a new metaphor—the machine. Developed by the French thinkers Mersenne, Gassendi, and Descartes in the 1620s and 1630s and elaborated by a group of English emigrés to Paris in the 1640s and 1650s, the new mechanical theories emphasized and reinforced elements in human experience developing slowly since the late Middle Ages, but accelerating in the sixteenth century.

New forms of order and power provided a remedy for the disorder perceived to be spreading throughout culture. In the organic world, order meant the function of each part within the larger whole, as determined by its nature, while power was diffused from the top downward through the social or cosmic hierarchies. In the mechanical world, order was redefined to mean the predictable behavior of each part within a rationally determined system of laws, while power derived from active and immediate intervention in a secularized world. Order and power together constituted control. Rational control over nature, society, and the self was achieved by redefining reality itself through the new machine metaphor.

As the unifying model for science and society, the machine has permeated and reconstructed human consciousness so totally that today we scarcely question its validity. Nature, society, and the human body are composed of interchangeable atomized parts that can be repaired or replaced from outside. The "technological fix" mends an ecological malfunction, new human beings replace the old to maintain the smooth functioning of industry and bureaucracy, and interventionist medicine exchanges a fresh heart for worn-out, diseased one.

The mechanical view of nature now taught in most Western schools is accepted without question as our everyday, common sense reality—matter is made up of atoms, colors occur by the reflection of light waves of differing lengths, bodies obey the law of inertia, and the sun is in the center of our solar system. None of this was common sense to our seventeenth-century counterparts. The replacement of the older, "natural" ways of thinking by a new and "unnatural" form of life—seeing, thinking, and behaving—did not occur without struggle. The submergence of the organism by the machine engaged the best minds of the times during a period fraught with anxiety, confusion, and instability in both the intellectual and social spheres.

The removal of animistic, organic assumptions about the cosmos constituted the death of nature—the most far-reaching effect of the Scientific Revolution. Because nature was now viewed as a system of dead, inert particles moved by external, rather than inherent forces, the mechanical framework itself could legitimate the manipulation of nature. Moreover, as a conceptual framework, the mechanical order had associated with it a framework of values based on power, fully compatible with the directions taken by commercial capitalism.

The mechanistic view of nature, developed by the seventeenth-century natural philosophers and based on a Western mathematical tradition going back to Plato, is still dominant in science today. This view assumes that nature can be divided into parts and that the parts can be rearranged to create other species of being. "Facts" or information bits can be extracted from the environmental context and rearranged according to a set of rules based on logical and mathematical operations. The results can then be tested and verified by resubmitting them to nature, the ultimate judge of their validity. Mathematical formalism provides the criterion for rationality and certainty, nature the criterion for empirical validity and acceptance or rejection of the theory.

The work of historians and philosophers of science notwithstanding, it is widely assumed by the scientific community that modern science is objective, value-free, and context-free knowledge of the external world. To the extent to which the sciences can be reduced to this mechanistic mathematical model, the more legitimate they become as sciences. Thus the reductionist hierarchy of the validity of the sciences first proposed in the nineteenth century by French positivist philosopher August Comte is still widely assumed by intellectuals, the most mathematical and highly theoretical sciences occupying the most revered position.

The mechanistic approach to nature is as fundamental to the twentieth-century revolution in physics as it was to classical Newtonian science, culminating in the nineteenth-century unification of mechanics, thermodynamics, and electromagnetic theory. Twentieth-century physics still views the world in terms of fundamental particles—electrons, protons, neutrons, mesons, muons, pions, taus, thetas, sigmas, pis, and so on. The search for the ultimate unifying particle, the quark, continues to engage the efforts of the best theoretical physicists.

Mathematical formalism isolates the elements of a given quantum mechanical problem, places them in a latticelike matrix, and rearranges them through a mathematical function called an *operator*. Systems theory extracts possibly relevant information bits from the environmental context and stores them in a computer memory for later use. But since it cannot store an infinite number of "facts," it must select a finite number of potentially relevant pieces of data according to a theory or set of rules governing the selection process. For any given solution, this mechanistic approach very likely excludes some potentially relevant factors.

Systems theorists claim for themselves a holistic outlook, because they believe that they are taking into account the ways in which all the parts in a given system affect the whole. Yet the formalism of the calculus of probabilities excludes the possibility of mathematizing the gestalt—that is, the ways in which each part at any given instant take their meaning from the whole. The more open, adaptive, organic, and complex the system, the less successful is the formalism. It is most successful when applied to closed, artificial, precisely defined, relatively simple systems. Mechanistic assumptions about nature push us increasingly in the direction of artificial environments, mechanized control over more and more aspects of human life, and a loss of the quality of life itself.

HOLISM

Holism was proposed as a philosophical alternative to mechanism by J. C. Smuts in his book *Holism and Evolution* (1926), in which he attempted to define the essential characteristics of holism and to differentiate it from nineteenth-century mechanism. He attempts to show that

> Taking a plant or animal as a type of whole, we notice the fundamental holistic characters as a unity of parts which is so close and intense as to be more than a sum of its parts; which not only gives a particular conformation or structure

to the parts but so relates and determines them in their synthesis that their functions are altered; the synthesis affects and determines the parts so that they function toward the "whole"; and the whole and the parts therefore reciprocally influence and determine each other and appear more or less to merge their individual characters.[16]

Smuts saw a continuum of relationships among parts from simple physical mixtures and chemical compounds to organisms and minds in which the unity among parts was affected and changed by the synthesis. "Holism is a process of creative synthesis; the resulting wholes are not static, but dynamic, evolutionary, creative....The explanation of nature can therefore not be purely mechanical; and the mechanistic concept of nature has its place and justification only in the wider setting of holism."

The most important example of holism today is provided by the science of ecology. Although ecology is a relatively new science, its philosophy of nature, holism, is not. Historically, holistic presuppositions about nature have been assumed by communities of people who have succeeded in living in equilibrium with their environments. The idea of cyclical processes, of the interconnectedness of all things, and the assumption that nature is active and alive are fundamental to the history of human thought. No element of an interlocking cycle can be removed without the collapse of the cycle. The parts themselves thus take their meaning from the whole. Each particular part is defined by and dependent on the total context. The cycle itself is a dynamic interactive relationship of all its parts, and process is a dialectical relation between parts and whole. Ecology necessarily must consider the complexities and the totality. It cannot isolate the parts into simplified systems that can be studied in a laboratory because such isolation distorts the whole.

External forces and stresses on a balanced ecosystem, whether natural or man made, can make some parts of the cycle act faster than the systems' own natural oscillations. Depending on the strength of the external disturbance, the metabolic and reproductive reaction rates of the slowest parts of the cycle, and the complexity of the system, it may or may not be able to absorb the stresses without collapsing.[17] At various times in history, civilizations which have put too much external stress on their environments have caused long-term or irrevocable alterations.

CONCLUSION

By pointing up the essential role of every part of an ecosystem, that if one part is removed the system is weakened and loses stability, ecology has moved in the direction of the leveling of value hierarchies. Each part contributes equal value to the healthy functioning of the whole. All living things, as integral parts of a viable ecosystem, thus have rights. The necessity of protecting the ecosystem from collapse due to the extinction of vital members was one argument for the passage of the Endangered Species Act of 1973. The movement toward egalitarianism manifested in the democratic revolutions of the eighteenth century, the extension of citizens' rights to blacks, and finally, voting rights to women was thus carried a step further. Endangered species became equal to the Army Corps of Engineers: the snail darter had to have a legal hearing before the Tellico Dam could be approved, the Furbish lousewort could block construction of the Dickey-Lincoln Dam in Maine, the red-cockaded woodpecker must be considered in Texas timber management, and the El Segundo Blue Butterfly in California airport expansion.

The conjunction of conservation and ecology movements with women's rights and liberation has moved in the direction of reversing both the subjugation of nature and women. In the late nineteenth and early twentieth centuries, the strong feminist movement in the United States begun in 1842 pressed for women's suffrage first in the individual states and then in the nation. Women activists also formed conservation committees in the many women's organizations that were part of the Federation of Women's Clubs established in 1890. They supported the preservationist movement for national, state, and city parks and wilderness areas led by John Muir and Frederick Law Olmsted, eventually splitting away from the managerial, utilitarian wing headed by Gifford Pinchot and Theodore Roosevelt.[18]

Today the conjunction of the women's movement with the ecology movement again brings the issue of liberation into focus. Mainstream women's groups such as the League of Women Voters took an early lead in studying and pressing for clean air and water legislation. Socialist-feminist and "science for the people" groups worked toward revolutionizing economic structures in a direction that would equalize female and male work options and reform a capitalist system that creates profits at the expense of nature and working people.

The March 1979 accident at the Three-Mile Island nuclear reactor near Harrisburg, Pennsylvania, epitomized the problems of the "death of nature" that have become apparent since the Scientific Revolution. The manipulation of nuclear processes in an effort to control and harness nature through technology backfired into disaster. The long-range economic interests and public image of the power company and the reactor's designer were set above the immediate safety of the people and the health of the earth. The hidden effects of radioactive emissions, which by concentrating in the food chain could lead to an increase in cancers over the next several years, were initially downplayed by those charged with responsibility for regulating atomic power.

Three-Mile Island is a recent symbol of the earth's sickness caused by radioactive wastes, pesticides, plastics, photochemical smog, and fluoro-carbons. The pollution "of her purest streams" has been supported since the Scientific Revolution by an ideology of "power over nature," an ontology of interchangeable atomic and human parts, and a methodology of "penetration" into her innermost secrets. The sick earth, "yea dead, yea putrified," can probably in the long run be restored to health only by a reversal of mainstream values and a revolution in economic priorities. In this sense, the world must once again be turned upside down.

As natural resources and energy supplies diminish in the future, it will become essential to examine alternatives of all kinds so that, by adopting new social styles, the quality of the environment can be sustained. Decentralization, nonhierarchical forms of organization, recycling of wastes, simpler living styles involving less-polluting "soft" technologies, and labor-intensive rather than capital-intensive economic methods are possibilities only beginning to be explored.[19] The future distribution of energy and resources among communities should be based on the integration of human and natural ecosystems. Such a restructuring of priorities may be crucial if people and nature are to survive.

NOTES

1. On the tensions between technology and the pastoral ideal in American culture, see Leo Marx, *The Machine in the Garden* (New York: Oxford University Press, 1964). On the domination of nature as female, see Annette Kolodny, *The Lay of the Land* (Chapel Hill: University of North Carolina Press, 1975); Rosemary Radford Ruether, "Women, Ecology, and the Domination of Nature," *The Ecumenist* 14 (1975): 1–5; William Leiss, *The Domination of Nature* (New York: Braziller, 1972). On the roots of the ecological crisis, see Donald Hughes, *Ecology in Ancient Civilizations* (Albuquerque: University of New Mexico Press, 1976); Lynn White, Jr., *Medieval Technology and Social Change* (New York: Oxford University Press, 1966); and Lynn White, Jr., "Historical Roots of Our Ecological Crisis," in White, Jr. *Machina ex Deo* (Cambridge, Mass.: M.I.T. Press, 1968), pp. 75–94; Reijer Hooykaas, *Religion and the Rise of Modern Science* (Grand Rapids, Mich.: Eerdmans, 1972); Christopher Derrick, *The Delicate Creation: Towards a Theology of the Environment* (Old Greenwich, Conn.: Devin-Adair, 1972). On traditional rituals in the mining of ores and in metallurgy, see Mircea Eliade, *The Forge and the Crucible*, trans. Stephan Corrin (New York: Harper & Row, 1962), pp. 42, 53–70, 74, 79–96. On the divergence between attitudes and practices toward the environment, see Yi-Fu Tuan, "Our Treatment of the Environment in Ideal and Actuality," *American Scientist* (May-June 1970): 246–49.
2. Treatments of Francis Bacon's contributions to science include Paolo Rossi, *Francis Bacon: From Magic To Science* (London: Routledge & Kegan Paul, 1968); Lisa Jardine, *Francis Bacon: Discovery and the Art of Discourse* (Cambridge, England: Cambridge University Press, 1974); Benjamin Farrington, *Francis Bacon, Philosopher of Industrial Science* (New York:

Schumann, 1949); Margery Purver, *The Royal Society: Concept and Creation* (London: Routledge & Kegan Paul, 1967).

3. Bacon, "The Great Instauration" (written 1620), *Works*, vol. 4, p. 20; "The Masculine Birth of Time," ed. and trans. Benjamin Farrington, in *The Philosophy of Francis Bacon* (Liverpool, England: Liverpool University Press, 1964), p. 62; "De Dignitate," *Works*, vol. 4, pp. 287, 294.

4. Quoted in Moody E. Prior, "Bacon's Man of Science," in Leonard M. Marsak, ed., *The Rise Of Modern Science in Relation to Society* (London: Collier-Macmillan, 1964), p. 45.

5. Rossi, p. 21; Leiss, p. 56; Bacon, *Works*, vol. 4, p. 294; Henry Cornelius Agrippa, *De Occulta Philosophia Libri Tres* (Antwerp, 1531): "No one has such powers but he who has cohabited with the elements, vanquished nature, mounted higher than the heavens, elevating himself above the angels to the archetype itself, with whom he then becomes cooperator and can do all things," as quoted in Frances A. Yates, *Giordano Bruno and the Hermetic Tradition* (New York: Vintage Books, 1964), p. 136.

6. Bacon, "Novum Organum," Part 2, in *Works*, vol. 4, p. 247; "Valerius Terminus," *Works*, vol. 3, pp. 217, 219; "The Masculine Birth of Time," trans. Farrington, p. 62.

7. Bacon, "The Masculine Birth of Time," and "The Refutation of Philosophies," trans. Farrington, pp. 62, 129, 130.

8. Bacon, "De Augmentis," *Works*, vol. 4, p. 294; see also Bacon, "Aphorisms," *Works*, vol. 4.

9. "De Augmentis," *Works*, vol. 4, pp. 320, 325; Plato, "The Timaeus," in *The Dialogues of Plato*, trans. B. Jowett (New York: Random House, 1937), vol. 2, p. 17; Bacon, "Parasceve," *Works*, vol. 4, p. 257.

10. Bacon, "De Augmentis," *Works*, vol. 4, pp. 343, 287, 343, 393.

11. Bacon, "Novum Organum," *Works*, vol. 4, p. 246; "The Great Instauration," *Works*, vol. 4, p. 29; "Novum Organum," Part 2, *Works*, vol. 4, p. 247.

12. Bacon, "Thoughts and Conclusions on the Interpretation of Nature or A Science of Productive Works," trans. Farrington, *The Philosophy of Francis Bacon*, pp. 96, 93, 99.

13. Bacon, "De Augmentis," *Works*, vol. 4, pp. 294; "Parasceve," *Works*, vol. 4, pp. 257; "Plan of the Work," vol. 4, pp. 32; "Novum Organum," *Works*, vol. 4, pp. 114, 115.

14. René Descartes, "Discourse on Method," Part 4, in E. S. Haldane and G. R. T. Ross, eds., *Philosophical Works of Descartes* (New York: Dover, 1955), vol. 1, p. 119.

15. Joseph Glanvill, *Plus Ultra* (Gainesville, Fla.: Scholar's Facsimile Reprints, 1958; first published 1668), quotations on pp. 9, 87, 13, 56, 104, 10.

16. J. C. Smuts, *Holism and Evolution* (New York: Macmillan, 1926), pp. 86, 87. On holism in the biological sciences, see Arthur Koestler, "Beyond Holism and Reductionism: The Concept of the Holon," in *Beyond Reductionism: New Perspectives in the Life Sciences*, ed. A. Koestler and J. R. Smythies (Boston: Beacon Press, 1969).

17. On ecological cycles, see Barry Commoner, *The Closing Circle: Nature, Man, and Technology* (New York; Bantam Books, 1971), Chap. 2.

18. Samuel P. Hays, *Conservation and the Gospel of Efficiency: The Progressive Conservation Movement*, 1890–1920 (Cambridge, Mass.: Harvard University Press, 1959), pp. 142–43.

19. Murray Bookchin, "Ecology and Revolutionary Thought," in *Post-Scarcity Anarchism* (San Francisco: Ramparts Press, 1971), pp. 57–82, and M. Book-

chin, "Toward an Ecological Solution" (Berkeley, Cal.: Ecology Center Reprint, n. d.). See also Victor Ferkiss, *Technological Man* (New York: New American Library, 1969), Chap. 9, pp. 205–11; Theodore Roszak, *Where the Wasteland Ends* (Garden City, N.Y.: Doubleday, 1973), pp. 367–71; Paul Goodman and Percival Goodman, *Communitas,* 2nd ed., rev. (New York: Vintage, 1960); Paul Goodman, *People or Personnel* (New York: Random House, 1965); E. F. Schumacher, *Small Is Beautiful: Economics as if People Mattered* (New York: Harper and Row, 1973); Ernest Callenbach, *Ecotopia* (Berkeley, Cal.: Banyan Tree Books, 1976).

Nature, Self, and Gender: Feminism, Environmental Philosophy, and the Critique of Rationalism

Val Plumwood

Val Plumwood is a forest activist, bushwalker, crocodile survivor, and wombat mother. She has published numerous articles on ecofeminism and environmental philosophy, and has a forthcoming book on ecofeminism, Gender, Ecology, and Identity.

Environmental philosophy has recently been criticized on a number of counts by feminist philosophers. I want to develop further some of this critique and to suggest that much of the issue turns on the failure of environmental philosophy to engage properly with the rationalist tradition, which has been inimical to both women and nature. Damaging assumptions from this tradition have been employed in attempting to formulate a new environmental philosophy that often makes use of or embeds itself within rationalist philosophical frameworks that are not only biased from a gender perspective, but have claimed a negative role for nature as well.

In sections I. through IV. I argue that current mainstream brands of environmental philosophy, both those based in ethics and those based in deep ecology, suffer from this problem, that neither has an adequate historical analysis, and that both continue to rely implicitly upon rationalist-inspired accounts of the self that have been a large part of the

This essay originally appeared in *Hypatia*, VI, No. 1 (Spring, 1991), 3–27. Reprinted with permission.

problem. In sections V. and VI. I show how the critique of rationalism offers an understanding of a range of key broader issues that environmental philosophy has tended to neglect or treat in too narrow a way. Among these issues are those connected with concepts of the human self and with instrumentalism.

I. RATIONALISM AND THE ETHICAL APPROACH

The ethical approach aims to center a new view of nature in ethics, especially universalizing ethics or in some extension of human ethics. This approach has been criticized from a feminist perspective by a number of recent authors (especially Cheney 1987, 1989). I partly agree with and partly disagree with these criticisms; that is, I think that the emphasis on ethics as the central part (or even the whole) of the problem is misplaced, and that although ethics (and especially the ethics of non-instrumental value) has a role, the particular ethical approaches that have been adopted are problematic and unsuitable. I shall illustrate this claim by a brief discussion of two recent books: Paul Taylor's *Respect for Nature* (1986) and Tom Regan's *The Case for Animal Rights* (1986). Both works are significant, and indeed impressive, contributions to their respective areas.

Paul Taylor's book is a detailed working out of an ethical position that rejects the standard and widespread Western treatment of nature as instrumental to human interests and instead takes living things, as teleological centers of life, to be worthy of respect in their own right. Taylor aims to defend a biocentric (life-centered) ethical theory in which a person's true human self includes his or her biological nature (Taylor 1986, 44), but he attempts to embed this within a Kantian ethical framework that makes strong use of the reason/emotion dichotomy. Thus we are assured that the attitude of respect is a moral one because it is universalizing and disinterested, "that is, each moral agent who sincerely has the attitude advocates its universal adoption by all other agents, regardless of whether they are so inclined and regardless of their fondness or lack of fondness for particular individuals" (41). The essential features of morality having been established as distance from emotion and "particular fondness," morality is then seen as the domain of reason and its touchstone, belief. Having carefully distinguished the "valuational, conative, practical and affective dimensions of the attitude of respect," Taylor goes on to pick out the essentially cognitive "valuational" aspect as central and basic to all the others: "It is *because* moral agents look at animals and plants in this way that they are disposed to pursue the aforementioned ends and purposes" (82) and, similarly, to have the relevant emotions and affective attitudes. The latter must be held at an appropriate distance and not allowed to get the upper hand at any point. Taylor claims that actions do not express moral respect unless they are done as a matter of moral principle conceived as ethically obligatory and pursued disinterestedly and not through inclination, solely or even primarily:

> If one seeks that end solely or primarily from inclination, the attitude being expressed is not moral respect but personal affection or love.. . .It is not that respect for nature *precludes* feelings of care and concern for living things. One may, as a matter of simple kindness, not want to harm them. But the fact that one is so motivated does not itself indicate the presence of a moral attitude of respect. Having the desire to preserve or protect the good of wild animals and plants for their sake is neither contrary to, nor evidence of, respect for nature. It is only if the person who has the desire understands that the actions fulfilling it would be obligatory even in the absence of the desire, that the person has genuine respect for nature. (85-86)

There is good reason to reject as self-indulgent the "kindness" approach that reduces respect and morality in the protection of animals to the satisfaction of the carer's own feelings. Respect for others involves treating them as worthy of consideration for their own sake and not just as an instrument for the carer's satisfaction, and there is a sense in which such "kindness" is not genuine care or respect for the other. But Taylor is doing much more than this—he is treating care, viewed as "inclination" or "desire," as irrelevant to morality. Respect for nature on this account becomes an essentially *cognitive* matter (that of a person believing something to have "inherent worth" and then acting from an understanding of ethical principles as universal).

The account draws on the familiar view of reason and emotion as sharply separated and opposed, and of "desire," caring, and love as merely "personal" and "particular" as opposed to the universality and impartiality of understanding, and of "feminine" emotions as essentially unreliable, untrustworthy, and morally irrelevant, an inferior domain to be dominated by a superior, disinterested (and of course masculine) reason. This sort of rationalist account of the place of emotions has come in for a great deal of well-deserved criticism recently, both for its implicit gender bias and its philosophical inadequacy, especially its dualism and its construal of public reason as sharply differentiated from and controlling private emotion (see, for example, Benhabib 1987; Blum 1980; Gilligan 1982, 1987; Lloyd 1983a and 1983b).

A further major problem in its use in this context is the inconsistency of employing, in the service of constructing an allegedly biocentric ethical theory, a framework that has itself played such a major role in creating a dualistic account of the genuine human self as essentially rational and as sharply discontinuous from the merely emotional, the merely bodily, and the merely animal elements. For emotions and the private sphere with which they are associated have been treated as sharply differentiated and inferior, as part of a pattern in which they are seen as linked to the sphere of nature, not the realm of reason.

And it is not only women but also the earth's wild living things that have been denied possession of a reason thus construed along masculine and oppositional lines and which contrasts not only with the "feminine" emotions but also with the physical and the animal. Much of the problem (both for women and nature) lies in rationalist or rationalist-derived conceptions of the self and of what is essential and valuable in the human makeup. It is in the name of such a reason that these other things—the feminine, the emotional, the merely bodily or the merely animal, and the natural world itself—have most often been denied their virtue and been accorded an inferior and merely instrumental position. Thomas Aquinas states this problematic position succinctly: "the intellectual nature is alone requisite for its own sake in the universe, and all others for its sake" (Thomas Aquinas 1976, 56). And it is precisely reason so construed that is usually taken to characterize the authentically human and to create the supposedly sharp separation, cleavage, or discontinuity between all humans and the nonhuman world, and the similar cleavage within the human self. The supremacy accorded an oppositionally construed reason is the key to the anthropocentrism of the Western tradition. The Kantian-rationalist framework, then, is hardly the area in which to search for a solution. Its use, in a way that perpetuates the supremacy of reason and its opposition to contrast areas, in the service of constructing a supposedly biocentric ethic is a matter for astonishment.

Ethical universalization and abstraction are both closely associated with accounts of the self in terms of rational egoism. Universalization is explicitly seen in both the Kantian and the Rawlsian framework as needed to hold in check natural self-interest; it is the moral complement to the account of the self as "disembodied and disembedded," as the autonomous self of liberal theory, the rational egoist of market theory, the falsely differentiated self of object-relations theory (Benhabib 1987; Poole 1984, 1985). In the same vein, the broadening of the scope of moral concern along with the according of rights to the natural world has been seen by influential environmental philosophers (Leopold 1949, 201–2) as the final step in a process of increasing moral abstraction and generalization, part of the move away from the merely particular—*my* self, *my* family, *my* tribe—the discarding of the merely personal and, by implication, the merely selfish. This is viewed as moral progress, increasingly civilized as it moves further away from primitive selfishness. Nature is the last area to be included in this march away from the unbridled natural egoism of the particular and its close ally, the emotional. Moral progress is marked by increasing adherence to moral rules and a movement away from the supposedly natural (in human nature), and the completion of its empire is, paradoxically, the extension of its domain of adherence to abstract moral rules to nature itself.

On such a view, the particular and the emotional are seen as the enemy of the rational, as corrupting, capricious, and self-interested. And if the "moral emotions" are set aside as irrelevant or suspect, as merely subjective or personal, we can only base morality on the rules of abstract reason, on the justice and rights of the impersonal public sphere.

This view of morality as based on a concept of reason as oppositional to the personal, the particular, and the emotional has been assumed in the framework of much recent environmental ethics. But as a number of feminist critics of the masculine model of moral life and of moral abstraction have pointed out (Blum 1980, Nicholson 1983), this increasing abstraction is not necessarily an improvement. The opposition between the care and concern for particular others and generalized moral concern is associated with a sharp division between public (masculine) and private (feminine) realms. Thus it is part of the set of dualistic contrasts in which the problem of the Western treatment of nature is rooted. And the opposition between care for particular others and general moral concern is a false one. There *can* be opposition between particularity and generality of concern, as when concern for particular others is accompanied by *exclusion* of others from care or chauvinistic attitudes toward them (Blum 1980, 80), but this does not automatically happen, and emphasis on oppositional cases obscures the frequent cases where they work together—and in which care for particular others is essential to a more generalized morality. Special relationships, which are treated by universalizing positions as at best morally irrelevant and at worst a positive hindrance to the moral life, are thus mistreated. For as Blum (1980, 78–83) stresses, special relationships form the basis for much of our moral life and concern, and it could hardly be otherwise. With nature, as with the human sphere, the capacity to care, to experience sympathy, understanding, and sensitivity to the situation and fate of particular others, and to take responsibility for others is an index of our moral being. Special relationship with, care for, or empathy with particular aspects of nature as experiences rather than with nature as abstraction are essential to provide a depth and type of concern that is not otherwise possible. Care and responsibility for particular animals, trees, and rivers that are known well, loved, and appropriately connected to the self are an important basis for acquiring a wider, more generalized concern. (As we shall see, this failure to deal adequately with particularity is a problem for deep ecology as well.)

Concern for nature, then, should not be viewed as the completion of a process of (masculine) universalization, moral abstraction, and disconnection, discarding the self, emotions, and special ties (all, of course, associated with the private sphere and femininity). Environmental ethics has for the most part placed itself uncritically in such a framework, although it is one that is extended with particular difficulty to the natural world. Perhaps the kindest thing that can be said about the framework of ethical universalization is that it is seriously incomplete and fails to capture the most important elements of respect, which are not reducible to or based on duty or obligation any more than the most important elements of friendship are, but which are rather an expression of a certain kind of selfhood and a certain kind of relation between self and other.

II. RATIONALISM, RIGHTS, AND ETHICS

An extension to nature of the standard concepts of morality is also the aim of Tom Regan's *The Case for Animal Rights* (1986). This is the most impressive, thorough, and solidly argued book in the area of animal ethics, with excellent chapters on topics such as animal intentionality. But the key concept upon which this account of moral concern for animals is based is that of rights, which requires strong individual separation of rights-holders and is set in a framework of human community and legality. Its extension to the natural world raises a host of problems (Midgley 1983, 61–64). Even in the case of individual higher animals for which Regan uses this concept of rights, the approach is problematic. His concept of rights is based on Mill's notion that, if a being has a right to something not only should he or she (or it) have that thing but others are obliged to intervene to secure it. The application of this concept of rights to individual wild living animals appears to give humans almost limitless obligations to intervene massively in all sorts of far reaching and conflicting ways in natural cycles to secure the rights of a bewildering variety of beings. In the case of the wolf and the sheep, an example discussed by Regan, it is unclear whether humans should intervene to protect the sheep's rights or to avoid doing so in order not to violate the wolf's right to its natural food.

Regan attempts to meet this objection by claiming that since the wolf is not itself a moral agent (although it is a moral patient), it cannot violate the sheep's rights not to suffer a painful and violent death (Regan 1986, 285). But the defense is unconvincing, because even if we concede that the wolf is not a moral agent, it still does not follow that on a rights view we are not obliged to intervene. From the fact that the wolf is not a moral agent it only follows that it is not *responsible* for violating the sheep's rights, not that they are not violated or that others do not have an obligation (according to the rights view) to intervene. If the wolf were attacking a human baby, it would hardly do as a defense in that case to claim that one did not have a duty to intervene because the wolf was not a moral agent. But on Regan's view the baby and the sheep do have something like the same rights. So we do have a duty, it seems, (on the rights view) to intervene to protect the sheep—leaving us where with the wolf?

The concept of rights seems to produce absurd consequences and is impossible to apply in the context of predators in a natural ecosystem, as opposed to a particular human social context in which claimants are part of a reciprocal social community and conflict cases are either few or settleable according to some agreed-on principles. All this seems to me to tell against the concept of rights as the correct one for the general task of dealing with animals in the natural environment (as opposed, of course, to domestic animals in a basically humanized environment).[1]

Rights seem to have acquired an exaggerated importance as part of the prestige of the public sphere and the masculine, and the emphasis on separation and autonomy, on reason and abstraction. A more promising approach for an ethics of nature, and also one much more in line with the current directions in feminism, would be to remove rights from the center of the moral stage and pay more attention to some other, less dualistic, moral concepts such as respect, sympathy, care, concern, compassion, gratitude, friendship, and responsibility (Cook 1977, 118–9). These concepts, because of their dualistic construal as feminine and their consignment to the private sphere as subjective and emotional, have been treated as peripheral and given far less importance than they deserve for several reasons. First, rationalism and the prestige of reason and the public sphere have influenced not only the concept of what morality is (as Taylor explicates it, for example, as essentially a rational and cognitive act of understanding that certain actions are ethically obligatory) but of what is *central* to it or what counts as moral concepts. Second, concepts such as respect, care, concern, and so on are resistant to analysis along lines of a dualistic reason/emotion dichotomy, and their construal along these lines has involved confusion and distortion (Blum 1980). They *are* moral "feelings" but they involve reason, behavior and emotion in ways that do not seem separable. Rationalist-inspired ethical concepts are highly ethnocentric and cannot account adequately for the views of many indigenous peoples, and the attempted application of these rationalist concepts to their positions tends to lead to the view that they lack a real ethical framework (Plumwood 1990). These alternative concepts seem better able to apply to the views of such peoples, whose ethic of respect, care and responsibility for land is often based on special relationships with particular areas of land via links to kin (Neidjie 1985, 1989). Finally these concepts, which allow for particularity and mostly do not require reciprocity, are precisely the sorts of concepts feminist philosophers have argued should have a more significant place in ethics at the expense of abstract, malestream concepts from the public sphere such as rights and justice (Gilligan 1982, 1987, Benhabib 1987). The ethic of care and responsibility they have articulated seems to extend much less problematically to the nonhuman world than do the impersonal concepts which are currently seen as central, and it also seems capable of providing an excellent basis for the noninstrumental treatment of nature many environmental philosophers have now called for. Such an approach treats ethical relations as an expression of self-in-relationship (Gilligan 1987, 24) rather than as the discarding, containment, or generalization of a self viewed as self-interested and non-relational, as in the conventional ethics of universalization.[2] As I argue later, there are important connections between this relational account of the self and the rejection of instrumentalism.

It is not that we need to abandon ethics or dispense with the universalized ethical approach entirely, although we do need to reassess the centrality of ethics in environmental philosophy.[3] What is needed is not so much the abandonment of ethics as a different and richer understanding of it (and, as I argue later, a richer understanding of environmental philosophy generally than is provided by ethics), one that gives an important place to ethical concepts owning to emotionality and particularity and that abandons the exclusive focus on the universal and the abstract associated with the nonrelational self and the dualistic and oppositional accounts of the reason/emotion and universal/particular contrasts as given in rationalist accounts of ethics.

III. THE DISCONTINUITY PROBLEM

The problem is not just one of restriction in ethics but also of restriction *to* ethics. Most mainstream environmental philosophers continue to view environmental philosophy as mainly concerned with ethics. For example, instrumentalism is generally viewed by mainstream environmental philosophers as a problem in ethics, and its solution is seen as setting up some sort of theory of intrinsic value. This neglects a key aspect of the overall problem that is concerned with the definition of the human self as separate from nature, the connection between this and the instrumental view of nature, and broader *political* aspects of the critique of instrumentalism.

One key aspect of the Western view of nature, which the ethical stance neglects completely, is the view of nature as sharply discontinuous or ontologically divided from the human sphere. This leads to a view of humans as apart from or "outside of" nature, usually as masters or external controllers of it. Attempts to reject this view often speak alternatively of humans as "part of nature" but rarely distinguish this position from the obvious claim that human fate is interconnected with that of the biosphere, that humans are subject to natural laws. But on the divided-self theory it is the essentially or authentically human part of the self, and in that sense the human realm proper, that is outside nature, not the human as a physical phenomenon. The view of humans as outside of and alien to nature seems to be especially strongly a Western one, although not confined to the West. There are many other cultures which do not hold it, which stress what connects us to nature as genuinely human virtues, which emphasize continuity and not dissimilarity.[4]

As ecofeminism points out, Western thought has given us a strong human/nature dualism that is part of the set of interrelated dualisms of mind/body, reason/nature, reason/emotion, masculine/feminine and has important interconnected features with these other dualisms.[5] This dualism has been especially stressed in the rationalist tradition. In this dualism what is characteristically and authentically human is defined against or in opposition to what is taken to be natural, nature, or the physical or biological realm. This takes various forms. For example, the characterization of the genuinely, properly, characteristically, or authentically human, or of human virtue, in polarized terms to exclude what is taken to be characteristic of the natural is what John Rodman (1980) has called "the Differential Imperative" in which what is virtuous in the human is taken to be what maximizes distance from the merely natural. The maintenance of sharp dichotomy and polarization is achieved by the rejection and denial of what links humans to the animal. What is taken to be authentically and characteristically human, defining of the human, as well as the ideal for which humans should strive is *not* to be found in what is shared with the natural and animal (e.g., the body, sexuality, reproduction, emotionality, the senses, agency) but in what is thought to separate and distinguish them—especially reason and its off-shoots. Hence humanity is defined not as part of nature (perhaps a special part) but as separate from and in opposition to it. Thus the relation of humans to nature is treated as an oppositional and value dualism.

The process closely parallels the formation of other dualisms, such as masculine/feminine, reason/emotion, and spirit/body criticized in feminist thought (see, for example, Ruether 1975, Griffin 1978, Griscom 1981, King 1981, Lloyd 1983, Jaggar 1983) but this parallel logic is not the only connection between human/nature dualism and masculine/feminine dualism. Moreover, this exclusion of the natural from the concept of the properly human is not the only dualism involved, because what is involved in the construction of this dualistic conception of the human is the rejection of those parts of the human character identified as feminine—also identified as less than fully human—giving the masculine conception of what it is to be human. Masculinity can be linked to this exclusionary and polarized conception of the human, via the desire to exclude and distance from the feminine and the nonhuman. The features that are taken as characteristic of humankind and as where its special virtues lie, are those such as rationality, freedom, and transcendence of nature (all traditionally viewed as masculine), which are viewed as not shared with nature. Humanity is defined oppositionally to both nature and the feminine.

The upshot is a deeply entrenched view of the genuine or ideal human self as not including features shared with nature, and as defined *against* or in *opposition to* the nonhuman realm, so that the human sphere and that of nature cannot significantly overlap. Nature is sharply divided off from the human, is alien and usually hostile and inferior. Furthermore, this kind of human self can only have certain kinds of accidental or contingent connections to the realm of nature. I shall call this the discontinuity problem or thesis and I argue later that it plays a key role with respect to other elements of the problem.

IV. RATIONALISM AND DEEP ECOLOGY

Although the discontinuity problem is generally neglected by the ethical stance, a significant exception to its neglect within environmental philosophy seems to be found in deep ecology, which is also critical of the location of the problem within ethics.[6] Furthermore, deep ecology also seems initially to be more likely to be compatible with a feminist philosophical framework, emphasizing as it does connections with the self, connectedness, and merger. Nevertheless, there are severe tensions between deep ecology and a feminist perspective. Deep ecology has not satisfactorily identified the key elements in the traditional framework or observed their connections to rationalism. As a result, it fails to reject adequately rationalist assumptions and indeed often seems to provide its own versions of universalization, the discarding of particular connections, and rationalist accounts of self.

Deep ecology locates the key problem area in human-nature relations in the separation of humans and nature, and it provides a solution for this in terms of the "identification" of self with nature. "Identification" is usually left deliberately vague, and corresponding accounts of self are various and shifting and not always compatible.[7] There seem to be at least three different accounts of self involved—indistinguishability, expansion of self, and transcendence of self—and practitioners appear to feel free to move among them at will. As I shall show, all are unsatisfactory from both a feminist perpective and from that of obtaining a satisfactory environmental philosophy, and the appeal of deep ecology rests largely on the failure to distinguish them.

A. The Indistinguishability Account

The indistinguishability account rejects boundaries between self and nature. Humans are said to be just one strand in the biotic web, not the source and ground of all value and the discontinuity thesis is, it seems, firmly rejected. Warwick Fox describes the central intuition of deep ecology as follows: "We can make no firm ontological divide in the field of existence. . .there is no bifurcation in reality between the human and nonhuman realms.. . .to the extent that we perceive boundaries, we fall short of deep ecological consciousness" (Fox 1984, 7). But much more is involved here than the rejection of discontinuity, for deep ecology goes on to replace the human-in-environment image by a holistic or gestalt view that "dissolves not only the human-in-environment concept, but every compact-thing-in-milieu concept"—except when talking at a superficial level of communication (Fox 1984, 1). Deep ecology involves a cosmology of "unbroken wholeness which denies the classical idea of the analyzability of the world into separately and independently existing parts." [8] It is strongly attracted to a variety of mystical traditions and to the Perennial Philosophy, in which the self is merged with the other— "the other is none other than yourself." As John Seed puts it: "I am protecting the rain forest" develops into "I am part of the rain forest protecting myself. I am that part of the rain forest recently emerged into thinking" (Seed et al. 1988, 36).

There are severe problems with these claims, arising not so much from the orientation to the concept of self (which seems to me important and correct) or from the mystical character of the insights themselves as from the indistinguishability metaphysics which is proposed as their basis. It is not merely that the identification process of which deep ecologists speak seems to stand in need of much more clarification, but that it does the wrong thing. The problem, in the sort of account I have given, is the discontinuity between humans and nature that emerges as part of the overall set of Western dualisms. Deep ecology proposes to heal this division by a "unifying process," a metaphysics that insists that everything is really part of and indistinguishable from everything else. This is not only to employ overly powerful tools but ones that do the wrong job, for the origins of the particular opposition involved in the human/nature dualism remain unaddressed and unanalyzed. The real basis of the discontinuity lies in the concept of an authentic human being, in what is taken to be valuable in human character, society, and culture, as what is distinct from what is taken to be natural. The sources of and remedies for this remain unaddressed in deep ecology. Deep ecology has confused dualism and atomism and then mistakenly taken indistinguishability to follow from the rejection of atomism. The confusion is clear in Fox, who proceeds immediately from the ambiguous claim that there is no "bifurcation in reality between the human and nonhuman realms" (which could be taken as a rejection of human discontinuity from nature) to the conclusion that what is needed is that we embrace an indistinguishability metaphysics of unbroken wholeness in the whole of reality. But the problem must be addressed in terms of this specific dualism and its connections. Instead deep ecology proposes the obliteration of all distinction.

Thus deep ecology's solution to removing this discontinuity by obliterating *all* division is far too powerful. In its overgenerality it fails to provide a genuine basis for an environmental ethics of the kind sought, for the view of humans as metaphysically unified with the cosmic whole will be equally true whatever relation humans stand in with nature—the situation of exploitation of nature exemplifies such unity equally as well as a conserver situation and the human self is just as indistinguishable from the bulldozer and Coca-Cola bottle as the rocks or the rain forest. What John Seed seems to have in mind here is that once one has realized that one is indistinguishable from the rain forest, its needs would become one's own. But there is nothing to guarantee this—one could equally well take one's own needs for its.

This points to a further problem with the indistinguishability thesis, that we need to recognize not only our human continuity with the natural world but also its distinctness and independence from us and the distinctness of the needs of things in nature from ours. The indistinguishability account does not allow for this, although it is a very important part of respect for nature and of conservation strategy.

The dangers of accounts of the self that involve self-merger appear in feminist contexts as well, where they are sometimes appealed to as the alternative to masculine-defined autonomy as disconnection from others. As Jean Grimshaw writes of the related thesis of the indistinctness of persons (the acceptance of the loss of self-boundaries as a feminine ideal): "It is important not merely because certain forms of symbiosis or 'connection' with others can lead to damaging failures of personal development, but because care for others, understanding of them, are only possible if one can adequately distinguish oneself *from* others. If I see myself as 'indistinct' from you, or you as not having your own being that is not merged with mine, then I cannot preserve a real sense of your well-being as opposed to mine. Care and understanding require the sort of distance that is needed in order not to see the other as a projection of self, or self as a continuation of the other" (Grimshaw 1986, 182–3).

These points seem to me to apply to caring for other species and for the natural world as much as they do to caring for our own species. But just as dualism is confused with atomism, so holistic self-merger is taken to be the only alternative to egoistic accounts of the self as without essential connection to others or to nature. Fortunately, this is a false choice;[9] as I argue below, nonholistic but relational accounts of the self, as developed in some feminist and social philosophy, enable a rejection of dualism, including human/nature dualism, without denying the independence or distinguishability of the other. To the extent that deep ecology is identified with the indistinguishability thesis, it does not provide an adequate basis for a philosophy of nature.

B. The Expanded Self

In fairness to deep ecology it should be noted that it tends to vacillate between mystical indistinguishability and the other accounts of self, between the holistic self and the expanded self. Vacillation occurs often by way of slipperiness as to what is meant by identification of self with the other, a key notion in deep ecology. This slipperiness reflects the confusion of dualism and atomism previously noted but also seems to reflect a desire to retain the mystical appeal of indistinguishability while avoiding its many difficulties. Where "identification" means not "identity" but something more like "empathy," identification with other beings can lead to an expanded self. According to Arne Naess, "The self is as comprehensive as the totality of our identifications.... Our Self is that with which we identify." [10] This larger self (or Self, to deep ecologists) is something for which we should strive "insofar as it is in our power to do so" (Fox 1986, 13-19), and according to Fox we should also strive to make it as large as possible. But this expanded self is not the result of a critique of egoism; rather, it is an enlargement and an extension of egoism. [11] It does not question the structures of possessive egoism and self-interest; rather, it tries to allow for a wider set of interests by an expansion of self. The motivation for the expansion of self is to allow for a wider set of concerns while continuing to allow the self to operate on the fuel of self-interest (or Self-interest). This is apparent from the claim that "in this light. . .ecological resistance is simply another name for self defense" (Fox 1986, 60). Fox quotes with approval John Livingstone's statement: "When I say that the fate of the sea turtle or the tiger or the gibbon is mine, I mean it. All that is in my universe is not merely mine; it is *me*. And I shall defend myself. I shall defend myself not only against overt aggression but also against gratuitous insult" (Fox 1986, 60).

Deep ecology does not question the structures of rational egoism and continues to subscribe to two of the main tenets of the egoist framework— that human nature is egoistic and that the alternative to egoism is self-sacrifice. [12] Given these assumptions about egoism, the obvious way to obtain some sort of human interest in defending nature is through the expanded Self operating in the interests of nature but also along the familiar lines of self-interest. [13] The expanded-self strategy might initially seem to be just another pretentious and obscure way of saying that humans empathize with nature. But the strategy of transferring the structures of egoism is highly problematic, for the widening of interest is obtained at the expense of failing to recognize unambiguously the distinctness and independence of the other. [14] Others are recognized morally only to the extent that they are incorporated into the self, and their difference denied (Warren 1990). And the failure to critique egoism and the disembedded, nonrelational self means a failure to draw connections with other contemporary critiques.

C. The Transcended or Transpersonal Self

To the extent that the expanded Self requires that we detach from the particular concerns of the self (a relinquishment that despite its natural difficulty we should struggle to attain), expansion of self to Self also tends to lead into the third position, the transcendence or overcoming of self. Thus Fox urges us to strive for *impartial* identification with *all* particulars, the cosmos, discarding our identifications with our own particular concerns, personal emotions, and attachments (Fox 1990, 12). Fox presents here the deep ecology version of universalization, with the familiar emphasis on the personal and the particular as corrupting and self-interested—"the cause of possessiveness, war and ecological destruction" (1990, 12).

This treatment of particularity, the devaluation of an identity tied to particular parts of the natural world as opposed to an abstractly conceived whole, the cosmos, reflects the rationalistic preoccupation with the universal and its account of ethical life as oppositional to the particular. The analogy in human terms of impersonal love of the cosmos is the view of morality as based on universal principles or the impersonal and abstract "love of man." Thus Fox (1990, 12) reiterates (as if it were unproblematic) the view of particular attachments as ethically suspect and as oppositional to genuine, impartial "identification," which necessarily falls short with all particulars.

Because this "transpersonal" identification is so indiscriminate and intent on denying particular meanings, it cannot allow for the deep and highly particularistic attachment to place that has motivated both the passion of many modern conservationists and the love of many indigenous peoples for their land (which deep ecology inconsistently tries to treat as a model). This is based not on a vague, bloodless, and abstract cosmological concern but on the formation of identity, social and personal, in relation to particular areas of land, yielding ties often as special and powerful as those to kin, and which are equally expressed in very specific and local responsibilities of care.[15] This emerges clearly in the statements of many indigenous peoples, such as in the moving words of Cecilia Blacktooth explaining why her people would not surrender their land:

> You ask us to think what place we like next best to this place where we always lived. You see the graveyard there? There are our fathers and our grandfathers. You see that Eagle-nest mountain and that Rabbit-hole mountain? When God made them, He gave us this place. We have always lived here. We do not care for any other place. . . .We have always lived here. We would rather die here. Our fathers did. We cannot leave them. Our children were born here—how can we go away? If you give us the best place in the world, it is not so good as this. . . .This is our home. . . .We cannot live any where else. We were born here and our fathers are buried here. . . .We want this place and no other. . . .(McLuhan 1979, 28)

In inferiorizing such particular, emotional, and kinship-based attachments, deep ecology gives us another variant on the superiority of reason and the inferiority of its contrasts, failing to grasp yet again the role of reason and incompletely critiquing its influence. To obtain a more adequate account than that offered by mainstream ethics and deep ecology it seems that we must move toward the sort of ethics feminist theory has suggested, which can allow for both continuity and difference and for ties to nature which are expressive of the rich, caring relationships of kinship and friendship rather than increasing abstraction and detachment from relationship.[16]

V. THE PROBLEM IN TERMS OF THE CRITIQUE OF RATIONALISM

I now show how the problem of the inferiorization of nature appears if it is viewed from the perspective of the critique of rationalism and seen as part of the general problem of revaluing and reintegrating what rationalist culture has split apart, denied, and devalued. Such an account shifts the focus away from the preoccupations of both mainstream ethical approaches and deep ecology, and although it does retain an emphasis on the account of the self as central, it gives a different account from that offered by deep ecology. In section VI. I conclude by arguing that one of the effects of this shift in focus is to make connections with other critiques, especially feminism, central rather than peripheral or accidental, as they are currently viewed by deep ecologists in particular.

First, what is missing from the accounts of both the ethical philosophers and the deep ecologists is an understanding of the problem of discontinuity as created by a dualism linked to a network of related dualisms. Here I believe a good deal can be learned from the critique of dualism feminist philosophy has developed and from the understanding of the mechanisms of dualisms ecofeminists have produced. A dualistically construed dichotomy typically polarizes difference and minimizes shared characteristics, construes difference along lines of superiority/inferiority, and views the inferior side as a means to the higher ends of the superior side (the instrumental thesis). Because its nature is defined oppositionally, the task of the superior side, that in which it realizes itself and expresses its true nature, is to separate from, dominate, and control the lower side. This has happened both with the human/nature division and with other related dualisms such as masculine/feminine, reason/body, and reason/emotion. Challenging these dualisms involves not just a reevaluation of superiority/inferiority and a higher status for the underside of the dualisms (in this case nature) but also a reexamination and reconceptualizing of the dualistically construed categories themselves. So in the case of the human/nature dualism it is not just a question of improving the status of nature, moral or otherwise, while everything else remains the same, but of reexamining and reconceptualizing the concept of the human, and also the concept of the contrasting class of nature. For the concept of the human, of what it is to be fully and authentically human, and of what is genuinely human in the set of characteristics typical humans possess, has been defined oppositionally, by *exclusion* of what is associated with the inferior natural sphere in very much the way that Lloyd (1983), for example, has shown in the case of the categories of masculine and feminine, and of reason and its contrasts. Humans have both biological and mental characteristics, but the mental rather than the biological have been taken to be characteristic of the human and to give what is "fully and authentically" human. The term "human" is, of course, not merely descriptive here but very much an evaluative term setting out an ideal: it is what is essential or worthwhile in the human that excludes the natural. It is not necessarily denied that humans have some material or animal component—rather, it is seen in this framework as alien or inessential to them, not part of their fully or truly human nature. The human essence is often seen as lying in maximizing control over the natural sphere (both within and without) and in qualities such as rationality, freedom, and transcendence of the material sphere. These qualities are also identified as masculine, and hence the *oppositional* model of the human coincides or converges with a masculine model, in which the characteristics attributed are those of the masculine ideal.

Part of a strategy for challenging this human/nature dualism, then, would involve recognition of these excluded qualities—split off, denied, or construed as alien, or comprehended as the sphere of supposedly *inferior* humans such as women and blacks—as equally and fully human. This would provide a basis for the recognition of *continuities* with the natural world. Thus reproductivity, sensuality, emotionality would be taken to be as fully and authentically human qualities as the capacity for abstract planning and calculation. This proceeds from the assumption that one basis for discontinuity and alienation from nature is alienation from·those qualities which provide continuity with nature in ourselves.

This connection between the rationalist account of nature within and nature without has powerful repercussions. So part of what is involved is a challenge to the centrality and dominance of the rational in the account of the human self. Such a challenge would have far-reaching implications for what is valuable in human society and culture, and it connects with the challenge to the cultural legacy of rationalism made by other critiques of rationalism such as feminism, and by critiques of technocracy, bureaucracy, and instrumentalism.

What is involved here is a reconceptualization of the human side of the human/nature dualism, to free it from the legacy of rationalism. Also in need of reconceptualization is the underside of this dualism, the concept of nature, which is construed in polarized terms as bereft of qualities appropriated to the human side, as passive and lacking in agency and teleology, as pure materiality, pure body, or pure mechanism. So what is called for here is the development of alternatives to mechanistic ways of viewing the world, which are also part of the legacy of rationalism.

VI. INSTRUMENTALISM AND THE SELF

There are two parts to the restructuring of the human self in relation to nature—reconceptualizing the human and reconceptualizing the self, and especially its possibilities of relating to nature in other than instrumental ways. Here the critique of the egoistic self of liberal individualism by both feminist and social philosophers, as well as the critique of instrumental reason, offers a rich set of connections and insights on which to draw. In the case of both of these parts what is involved is the rejection of basically masculine models, that is, of humanity and of the self.

Instrumentalism has been identified as a major problem by the ethical approach in environmental philosophy but treated in a rather impoverished way, as simply the problem of establishing the inherent worth of nature.[17] Connection has not been made to the broader account that draws on the critique of instrumental reason. This broader account reveals both its links with the discontinuity problem and its connection with the account of the self. A closer look at this further critique gives an indication of how we might develop an account that enables us to stress continuity without drowning in a sea of indistinguishability.

We might notice first the strong connections between discontinuity (the polarization condition of dualism) and instrumentalism—the view that the excluded sphere is appropriately treated as a means to the ends of the higher sphere or group, that its value lies in its usefulness to the privileged group that is, in contrast, worthwhile or significant in itself. Second, it is important to maintain a strong distinction and maximize distance between the sphere of means and that of ends to avoid breaking down the sharp boundaries required by hierarchy. Third, it helps if the sphere treated instrumentally is seen as lacking ends of its own (as in views of nature and women as passive), for then others can be imposed upon it without problem. There are also major connections that come through the account of the self which accompanies both views.

The self that complements the instrumental treatment of the other is one that stresses sharply defined ego boundaries, distinctness, autonomy, and separation from others—that is defined *against* others, and lacks essential connections to them. This corresponds to object/relations account of the masculine self associated with the work of Nancy Chodorow (1979, 1985) and also to the self-interested individual presupposed in market theory (Poole 1985, 1990).[18] This self uses both other humans and the world generally as a means to its egoistic satisfaction, which is assumed to be the satisfaction of interests in which others play no essential role. If we try to specify these interests they would make no essential reference to the welfare of others, except to the extent that these are useful to serve predetermined ends. Others as means are interchangeable if they produce equivalent satisfactions—anything which conduces to that end is as valuable, other things being equal, as anything else which equally conduces to that end. The interests of such an individual, that of the individual of market theory and of the masculine self as theorized by Chodorow, are defined as essentially independent of or disconnected from those of other people, and his or her transactions with the world at large consist of various attempts to get satisfaction for these predetermined private interests. Others are a "resource," and the interests of others connect with the interests of such autonomous selves only accidentally or contingently. They are not valued for themselves but for their effects in producing gratification. This kind of instrumental picture, so obviously a misdescription in the case of relations to other humans, is precisely still the normal Western model of what our relations to nature should be.

Now this kind of instrumental, disembedded account of the relation of self to others has been extensively criticized in the area of political theory from a variety of quarters, including feminist theory, in the critique of liberalism, and in environmental philosophy (Benhabib 1987; Benhabib and Cornell 1987; Benjamin 1985; Chodorow 1985; Gilligan 1982, 1987; Grimshaw 1986; Jagger 1983; Miller 1978; Plumwood 1980; Poole 1984, 1985, 1990; Warren 1990). It has been objected that this account does not give an accurate picture of the human self—that humans are social and connected in a way such an account does not recognize. People do have interests that make *essential* and not merely accidental or contingent reference to those of others, for example, when a mother wishes for her child's recovery, the child's flourishing is an essential *part* of her flourishing, and similarly with close others and indeed for others more widely ("social others"). But, the objection continues, this gives a misleading picture of the world, one that omits or impoverishes a whole significant dimension of human experience, a dimension which provides important insight into gender difference, without which we cannot give an adequate picture of what it is to be human. Instead we must see human beings and their interests as *essentially* related and interdependent. As Karen Warren notes "Relationships are not something extrinsic to who we are, not an 'add on' feature of human nature; they play an essential role in shaping what it is to be human" (Warren 1990, 143). That people's interests are relational does not imply a holistic view of them—that they are merged or indistinguishable. Although some of the mother's interests entail satisfaction of the child's interests, they are not identical or even necessarily similar. There is overlap, but the relation is one of intentional inclusion (her interest is *that* the child should thrive, that certain of the child's key interests are satisfied) rather than accidental overlap.

This view of self-in-relationship is, I think, a good candidate for the richer account of self deep ecologists have sought and for which they have mistaken holistic accounts. It is an account that avoids atomism but that enables a recognition of interdependence and relationship without falling into the problems of indistinguishability, that acknowledges both continuity and difference, and that breaks the culturally posed false dichotomy of egoism and altruism of interests;[19] it bypasses both masculine "separation" and traditional-feminine "merger" accounts of the self. It can also provide an appropriate foundation for an ethic of connectedness and caring for others, as argued by Gilligan (1982, 1987) and Miller (1978).

Thus it is unnecessary to adopt any of the stratagems of deep ecology—the indistinguishable self, the expanded self, or the transpersonal self—in order to provide an alternative to anthropocentrism or human self-interest. This can be better done through the relational account of self, which clearly recognizes the distinctness of nature but also our relationship and continuity with it. On this relational account, respect for the other results neither from the containment of self nor from a transcendence of self, but is an *expression* of self in relationship, not egoistic self as merged with the other but self as embedded in a network of essential relationships with distinct others.

The relational account of self can usefully be applied to the case of human relations with nature and to place. The standard Western view of the relation of the self to the nonhuman is that it is always *accidentally* related, and hence the nonhuman can be used as a means to the self-contained ends of human beings. Pieces of land are real estate, readily interchangeable as equivalent means to the end of human satisfaction; no place is more than "a stage along life's way, a launching pad for higher flights and wider orbits than your own" (Berman 1982, 327). But, of course, we do not all think this way, and instances of contrary behavior would no doubt be more common if their possibility were not denied and distorted by both theoretical and social construction. But other cultures have recognized such essential connection of self to country clearly enough, and many indigenous voices from the past and present speak of the grief and pain in loss of their land, to which they are as essentially connected as to any human other. When Aboriginal people, for example, speak of the land as part of them, "like brother and mother" (Neidjie 1985, 51; 1989, 4, 146), this is, I think, one of their meanings. If instrumentalism is impoverishing and distorting as an account of our relations to other human beings, it is equally so as a guiding principle in our relations to nature and to place.[20]

But to show that the self can be essentially related to nature is by no means to show that it normally would be, especially in modern Western culture. What is culturally viewed as alien and inferior, as not worthy of respect or respectful knowledge, is not something to which such essential connection can easily be made. Here the three parts of the problem—the conception of the human, the conception of the self, and the conception of nature—connect again. And normally such essential relation would involve particularity, through connection to end friendship for *particular* places, forests, animals, to which one is particularly strongly related or attached and toward which one has specific and meaningful, not merely abstract, responsibilities of care.

One of the effects of viewing the problems as arising especially in the context of rationalism is to provide a rich set of connections with other critiques; it makes the connection between the critique of anthropocentrism and various other critiques that also engage critically with rationalism, such as feminism and critical theory, much more important—indeed essential— to the understanding of each. The problem of the Western account of the human/nature relation is seen in the context of the other related sets of dualisms; they are linked through their definitions as the underside of the various contrasts of reason. Since much of the strength and persistence of these dualisms derives from their connections and their ability to mirror, confirm, and support one another, critiques of anthropocentrism that fail to take account of these connections have missed an essential and not merely additional feature.

Anthropocentrism and androcentrism in particular are linked by the rationalist conception of the human self as masculine and by the account of authentically human characteristics as centered around rationality and the exclusion of its contrasts (especially characteristics regarded as feminine, animal, or natural) as less human. This provides a different and richer account of the notion of anthropocentrism, now conceived by deep ecology (Fox 1990, 5) in terms of the notion of equality, which is both excessively narrow and difficult to articulate in any precise or convincing way in a context where needs are so different. The perception of the connection as at best accidental is a feature of some recent critiques of ecofeminism, for example the discussion of Fox (1990) and Eckersley (1989) on the relation of feminism and environmental philosophy. Fox misses entirely the main thrust of the ecofeminist account of environmental philosophy and the critique of deep ecology which results or which is advanced in the ecofeminist literature, which is that it has failed to observe the way in which anthropocentrism and androcentrism are linked.[21] It is a consequence of my arguments here that this critique needs broadening—deep ecology has failed to observe (and often even goes out of its way to deny) connections with a number of other critiques, not just feminism, for example, but also socialism, especially in the forms that mount a critique of rationalism and of modernity. The failure to observe such connections is the result of an inadequate historical analysis and understanding of the way in which the inferiorization of both women and nature is grounded in rationalism, and the connections of both to the inferiorizing of the body, hierarchical concepts of labor, and disembedded and individualist accounts of the self.

Instead of addressing the real concerns of ecofeminism in terms of connection, Fox takes ecofeminism as aiming to replace concern with anthropocentrism by concern with androcentrism.[22] This would have the effect of making ecofeminism a reductionist position which takes women's oppression as the basic form and attempts to reduce all other forms to it. This position is a straw woman;[23] the effect of ecofeminism is not to absorb or sacrifice the critique of anthropocentrism, but to deepen and enrich it.

NOTES

1. Regan, of course, as part of the animal rights movement, is mainly concerned not with wild animals but with domestic animals as they appear in the context and support of human society and culture, although he does not indicate any qualification in moral treatment. Nevertheless, there may be an important moral boundary here, for natural ecosystems cannot be organized along the lines of justice, fairness and rights, and it would be absurd to try to impose such a social order upon them via intervention in these systems. This does not mean, of course, that humans can do anything in such a situation, just that certain kinds of intervention are not in order. But these kinds of intervention may be in order in the case of human social systems and in the case of animals that have already been brought into these social systems through human intervention, and the concept of rights and of social responsibility may have far more application here. This would mean that the domestic/wild distinction would demarcate an important moral boundary in terms of duties of intervention, although neither Regan (1986) nor Taylor (1986) comes to grips with this problem. In the case of Taylor's "wild living things" rights seem less important than respect for independence and autonomy, and the prima facie obligation may be nonintervention.
2. If the Kantian universalizing perspective is based on self-containment, its major contemporary alternative, that of John Rawls, is based on a "definitional identity" in which the "other" can be considered to the extent that it is not recognized as truly different, as genuinely other (Benhabib 1987, 165).
3. Contra Cheney, who appears to advocate the abandonment of all general ethical concepts and the adoption of a "contextual" ethics based in pure particularity and emotionality. We do need both to reintegrate the personal and particular and reevaluate more positively its role, but overcoming moral dualism will not simply amount to an affirmation of the personal in the moral sphere. To embrace pure particularity and emotionality is implicitly to accept the dualistic construction of these as oppositional to a rationalist ethics and to attempt to reverse value. In general this reactive response is an inadequate way to deal with such dualisms. And rules themselves, as Grimshaw (1986, 209) points out, are not incompatible with recognition of special relationships and responsibility to particular others. Rules themselves are not the problem, and hence it is not necessary to move to a ruleless ethics; rather it is rules that demand the discarding of the personal, the emotional, and the particular and which aim at self-containment.
4. For example, Bill Neidjie's words "This ground and this earth/like brother and mother" (Neidjie 1985, 46) may be interpreted as an affirmation of such kinship or continuity. (See also Neidjie 1985, 53, 61, 62, 77, 81, 82, 88).
5. The logic of dualism and the masculinity of the concept of humanity are discussed in Plumwood (1986, 1988) and Warren (1987, 1989).
6. Nonetheless, deep ecology's approach to ethics is, like much else, doubtfully

consistent, variable and shifting. Thus although Arne Naess (1974, 1984, 1988) calls for recognition of the intrinsic value of nature, he also tends to treat "the maxim of self-realization" as *substituting for* and obviating an ethical account of care and respect for nature (Naess 1988, 20, 86), placing the entire emphasis on phenomenology. In more recent work, however, the emphasis seems to have quietly shifted back again from holistic intuition to a broad and extremely vague "biocentric egalitarianism" which places the center once again in ethics and enjoins an ethic of maximum expansion of Self (Fox 1990).

7. Other critics of deep ecology, such as Sylvan (1985) and Cheney (1987) have also suggested that it shifts between different and incompatible versions. Ecofeminist critics of deep ecology have included Salleh (1984), Kheel (1985), Biehl (1987), and Warren (1990).

8. Arne Naess, quoted in Fox (1982, 3, 10).

9. This is argued in Plumwood (1980), where a relational account of self developed in the context of an anarchist theory is applied to relations with nature. Part of the problem lies in the terminology of "holism" itself, which is used in highly variable and ambiguous ways, sometimes carrying commitment to indistinguishability and sometimes meaning only "nonatomistic."

10. Arne Naess, quoted in Fox (1986, 54).

11. As noted by Cheney (1989, 293-325).

12. Thus John Seed says: "Naess wrote that when most people think about conservation, they think about sacrifice. This is a treacherous basis for conservation, because most people aren't capable of working for anything except their own self-interest. . .Naess argued that we need to find ways to extend our identity into nature. Once that happens, being out in front of bulldozers or whatever becomes no more of a sacrifice than moving your foot if you notice that someone's just about to strike it with an axe" (Seed 1989).

13. This denial of the alterity of the other is also the route taken by J. Baird Callicott, who indeed asserts that "The principle of axiological complementarity posits an essential unity between self and world and establishes the problematic intrinsic value of nature in relation to the axiologically privileged value of self" (1985, 275). Given the impoverishment of Humean theory in the area of relations (and hence its inability to conceive a self-in-relationship whose connections to others are not merely contingent but essential), Callicott has little alternative to this direction of development.

14. Grimshaw (1986, 182). See also the excellent discussion in Warren (1990, 136–38) of the importance of recognition and respect for the other's difference; Blum (1980, 75); and Benhabib (1987, 166).

15. This traditional model of land relationship is closely linked to that of bioregionalism, whose strategy is to engage people in greater knowledge and care for the local areas that have meaning for them and where they can most easily evolve a caring and responsible life-style. The feat of "impartial identification with all particulars" is, beyond the seeking of individual enlightenment, strategically empty. Because it cares "impartially" for everything it can, in practice, care for nothing.

16. Thus some ecofeminists, such as Cheney (1987, 1989) and Warren (1990), have been led to the development of alternative accounts of ethics and ethical theory building and the development of distinctively ecofeminist ethics.

17. Although the emphasis of early work in this area (for example, Plumwood 1975) was mainly directed toward showing that a respectful, noninstrumental view of nature was logically viable since that was widely disputed, it is

certainly well past time to move beyond that. Although there is now wider support for a respectful, noninstrumental position, it remains controversial; see, for example, Thompson (1990) and Plumwood (1991).

18. Poole (1984) has also shown how this kind of self is presupposed in the Kantian moral picture, where desire or inclination is essentially self-directed and is held in check by reason (acting in the interests of universality).

19. In the sense of altruism in which one's own interests are neglected in favor of another's, essentially relational interests are neither egoistic nor altruistic.

20. On rationalism and place see Edward Relph (1976, 1981).

21. Fox (1990, 12), in claiming gender neutrality for cosmologically based identification and treating issues of gender as irrelevant to the issue, ignores the historical scholarship linking conceptions of gender and conceptions of morality via the division between public and private spheres (for example, Lloyd [1984] and Nicholson [1983]). To the extent that the ecofeminist thesis is not an essentialist one linking *sex* to emotionality and particularity or to nature but one linking social and historical conceptions of *gender* to conceptions of morality and rationality, it is not refuted by examples of women who buy a universalizing view or who drive bulldozers, or by Mrs. Thatcher. Fox's argument here involves a sex/gender confusion. On the sex/gender distinction see Plumwood (1989, 2–11).

22. Thus Fox (1990) throughout his discussion, like Zimmerman (1987, 37), takes "the ecofeminist charge against deep ecology" to be that "androcentrism is 'the real root' of ecological destruction" (1990, 14), so that "there is no need to worry about any form of human domination other than androcentrism" (1990, 18). Warren (1990, 144) tellingly discusses Fox's claim that "feminist" is redundant as an addition to a deep ecological ethic.

23. This reductionist position has a few representatives in the literature (perhaps Andrée Collard [1988], and Sally Miller Gearhart [1982]), but cannot be taken as representative of the main body of ecofeminist work. Fox, I believe, is right to resist such a reduction and to insist on the nonliminability of the form of oppression the critique of anthropocentrism is concerned with, but the conclusion that the critiques are unrelated does not follow. Critiques and the different kinds of oppression they correspond to can be distinguishable but, like individuals themselves, still related in essential and not merely accidental ways. The choice between merger (reductive elimination) and disconnection (isolation) of critiques is the same false dichotomy that inspires the false contrasts of holism and atomism, and of self as merged, lacking boundaries, versus self as isolated atom, lacking essential connection to others.

REFERENCES

Benhabib, Seyla. 1987. The generalised and the concrete other. In *Women and moral theory*, 154-77. E. Kittay and D. Meyers, eds. Totowa, N.J.: Rowman and Allenheld.

Benhabib, Seyla and Drucilla Cornell, eds. 1987. *Feminism as critique*. Minneapolis: University of Minnesota Press; Cambridge: Polity Press.

Benjamin, Jessica. 1985. The bonds of love: Rational violence and erotic domination. In *The future of difference*. H. Eisenstein and A. Jardine, eds. New Brunswick: Rutgers University Press.

Berman, Marshall. 1982. *All that is solid melts into air: The experience of modernity.* New York: Simon & Schuster; London: Penguin.

Biehl, Janet. 1987. It's deep, but is it broad? An ecofeminist looks at deep ecology. *Kick It Over* special supplement (Winter).

Blum, Lawrence A. 1980. *Friendship, altruism and morality.* Boston and London: Routledge & Kegan Paul.

Callicott, J. Baird. 1985. Intrinsic value, quantum theory, and environmental ethics. *Environmental Ethics* 7: 261–62.

Cheney, Jim. 1987. Ecofeminism and deep ecology. *Environmental Ethics* 9: 115–145.

———. 1989. The neo-stoicism of radical environmentalism. *Environmental Ethics* 11: 293–325.

Chodorow, Nancy. 1979. *The reproduction of mothering.* Berkeley: University of California Press.

———. 1985. Gender, relation and difference in psychoanalytic perspective. In *The future of difference*, 3–19. H. Eisenstein and A. Jardine, eds. New Brunswick: Rutgers University Press.

Collard, Andrée. 1988. *Rape of the wild: Man's violence against animals and the earth.* Bloomington: Indiana University Press; London: The Woman's Press.

Cook, Francis. 1977. *Hua-Yen Buddhism: The jewel net of Indra.* State College, PA: Pennsylvania State University Press. 118–119.

Eckersley, Robyn. 1989. Divining evolution: The ecological ethics of Murray Bookchin. *Environmental Ethics* 11: 99–116.

Fox, Warwick. 1982. The intuition of deep ecology. Paper presented at Environment, Ethics and Ecology Conference, Canberra. Also published under the title Deep ecology: A new philosophy of our time? *The Ecologist* 14 (1984): 194–200.

———. 1986. Approaching deep ecology: A response to Richard Sylvan's critique of deep ecology. Environmental Studies Occasional Paper 20. Hobart: University of Tasmania Centre for Environmental Studies.

———. 1989. The deep ecology-ecofeminism debate and its parallels. *Environmental Ethics* 11: 5–25.

———. 1990. *Towards a transpersonal ecology: Developing new foundations for environmentalism.* Boston: Shambala.

Gearhart, Sally Miller. 1982. The Future—if there is one—is female. In *Reweaving the web of life*, 266–285. P. McAllister, ed. Philadelphia and Santa Cruz: New Society Publishers.

Gilligan, Carol. 1982. *In a different voice.* Cambridge: Harvard University Press.

———. 1987. Moral orientation and moral development. In *Women and moral theory*, 19–33. E. Kittay and D. Meyers, eds. Totowa, N. J.: Rowman and Allenheld.

Griffin, Susan. 1978. *Woman and nature: The roaring inside her.* New York: Harper and Row.

Grimshaw, Jean. 1986. *Philosophy and feminist thinking.* Minneapolis: University of Minnesota Press. Also published as *Feminist philosophers.* Brighton: Wheatsheaf.

Griscom, Joan L. 1981. On healing the nature/history split in feminist thought. *Heresies* 4(1): 4–9.

Jaggar, Alison. 1983. *Feminist politics and human nature.* Totowa, N.J.: Rowman & Allenheld; Brighton: Harvester.

Kheel, Marti. 1985. The liberation of nature: A circular affair. *Environmental Ethics* 7: 135–49.

King, Ynestra. 1981. Feminism and revolt. *Heresies* 4(1): 12–16.

———. 1989. The ecology of feminism and the feminism of ecology. In *Healing the wounds*. J. Plant, ed., Philadelphia and Santa Cruz: New Society Publishers.

Leopold, Aldo. 1949. *A sand county almanac*, 201–2. Oxford and New York: Oxford University Press.

Lloyd, Genevieve. 1983a. Public reason and private passion. *Metaphilosophy* 14: 308–26.

———. 1983b. Reason, gender and morality in the history of philosophy. *Social Research* 50(3): 490–513.

———. 1984. *The man of reason*. London: Methuen.

McLuhan T. C., ed. 1973. *Touch the earth*. London: Abacus.

Miller, Jean Baker. 1976, 1978. *Toward a new psychology of women*. Boston: Beacon Press; London: Penguin

Midgley, Mary. 1983. *Animals and why they matter*. Athens: University of Georgia Press; London: Penguin.

Naess, Arne. 1973. The shallow and the deep, long-range ecology movement: A summary. *Inquiry* 16: 95–100.

———. 1986. Intrinsic value: Will the defenders of nature please rise. In *Conversation Biology*. M. Soule, ed. Sunderland, MA: Sinauer Associates

———. 1988. *Ecology, community and lifestyle*. Cambridge: University Press.

Neidjie, Bill. 1985. *Kakadu man*. With S. Davis and A. Fox. Canberra: Mybrood P/L.

Neidjie, Bill and Keith Taylor, eds. 1989. *Story about feeling*. Wyndham: Magabala Books.

Nicholson, Linda J. 1983. Women, morality and history. *Social Research* 50(3): 514–36.

Plumwood, Val. 1975. Critical notice of Passmore's *Man's responsibility for nature*. *Australasian Journal of Philosophy* 53(2): 171–85.

———. 1980. Social theories, self-management and environmental problems. IN *Environmental Philosophy*, 217–332. D. Mannison, M. McRobbie, and R. Routley eds. Canberra: ANU Department of Philosophy Monograph Series RSSS.

———. 1986. Ecofeminism: An overview and discussion of positions and arguments. In *Women and philosophy: A radical philosophy reader*. S. Sayers, ed. London: Routledge.

———. 1989. Do we need a sex/gender distinction? *Radical Philosophy* 51: 2–11.

———. 1990. Plato and the bush. *Meanjin* 49(3): 524–36.

———. 1991. Ethics and instrumentalism: A response to Janna Thompson. *Environmental Ethics*. Forthcoming.

Poole, Ross. 1984. Reason, self-interest and "commercial society": the social content of Kantian morality. *Critical Philosophy* 1: 24–46.

———. 1985. Morality, masculinity and the market. *Radical Philosophy* 39: 16–23.

———. 1990. Modernity, rationality and "the masculine." In *Femininity/Masculinity and representation*. T. Threadgold and A. Cranny-Francis, eds. Sydney: George Allen and Unwin, 1990.

Regan, Tom. 1986. *The case for animal rights*. Berkeley: University of California Press.

Relph, Edward. 1976. *Place and placelessness*. London: Pion.

———. 1981. *Rational landscapes and humanistic geography*. London: Croom Helm.

Rodman, John. 1980. Paradigm change in political science. *American Behavioural Scientist* 24(1): 54–55.

Ruether, Rosemary Radford. 1975. *New woman new earth.* Minneapolis: Seabury Press.

Salleh, Ariel. 1984. Deeper than deep ecology. *Environmental Ethics* 6: 339–45.

Seed, John. 1989. Interviewed by Pat Stone. *Mother Earth News* (May/June).

Seed, John, Joanna Macy, Pat Fleming, and Arne Naess. 1988. *Thinking like a mountain: Towards a council of all beings.* Philadelphia and Santa Cruz: New Society Publishers.

Sylvan, Richard. 1985. A critique of deep ecology. *Radical Philosophy* 40 and 41.

Taylor, Paul. 1986. *Respect for nature.* Princeton: Princeton University Press.

Thomas Aquinas. 1976. *Summa contra Gentiles.* Bk. 3, Pt. 2, chap. 62. Quoted in *Animal rights and human obligations*, 56. T. Regan and P. Singer, eds. Englewood Cliffs, N. J.: Prentice Hall.

Thompson Janna. 1990. A refutation of environmental ethics. *Environmental Ethics* 12(2): 147–60.

Warren, Karen J. 1987. Feminism and ecology: Making connections. *Environmental Ethics* 9: 17–18.

_____. 1990. The power and promise of ecological feminism. *Environmental Ethics* 12(2): 121–46.

Zimmerman, Michael E. 1987. Feminism, deep ecology, and environmental ethics. *Environmental Ethics* 9.

Working with Nature: Reciprocity or Control?

Ariel Salleh

Ariel Salleh is an Australian ecofeminist writer and activist. She is currently a visiting scholar in the Environmental Education Program at New York University, where she is completing a book on the relationship between ecofeminism and other radical political movements.

INTRODUCTION

During the 1980s, international agencies acknowledged close connections between women and the natural world. Now the International YWCA's Geneva-based Y's EYES campaigns not only for health and human rights, but also for issues of energy use, water supply, and appropriate technology. The Environment Liaison Centre in Nairobi, an independent non-governmental organization (NGO), runs sessions for women on forestry, sustainable farming, and pollution control, and urges political recognition of women's traditional farming expertise. The Rome/Santiago International Information and Communication Services (ISIS) facilitates women's education in similar areas. The International Women's Tribune Center in New York provides leadership skills and resource material on conservation and development to a vast female network. In Santo Domingo, the United Nation's International Research and Training Institute for the Advancement of Women (INSTRAW), works on water management programmes. In Bangalore, an innovative group called Development Alternatives with Women for a New Era (DAWN), is critical of the imported 'growth' ethic

This essay originally appeared in *Ethics of Environment and Development*, ed. J. Ronald Engel and Joan Gibb Engel (Tucson: The University of Arizona Press, 1990). Reprinted with permission.

and the oppressive gender division this ethic reinforces. World WIDE—Women in Defense of Environment—Washington D.C., is also trying to pre-empt superficial 'development' schemes and 'give voice to the voiceless' in policy.[1]

This recognition of women's involvement in, and concern for, the environment is both essential and rare. For, in the words of Carol Gilligan:

> Though we have listened for centuries to the voices of men and the theories of development that their experience informs, we have come more recently to notice not only the silence of women, but the difficulty of hearing what they say when they speak; yet in the different voice of women lies the truth of an ethic of care, the tie between relationship and responsibility, and the origins of aggression in the failure to connect.[2]

Women could bring to discussions of environmental sustainability 'the truth of an ethic of care'. Yet, their 'different voice' is seldom heard. Ecofeminists are attempting to change that. As a grass-roots political movement which honors the different voices of women across culture and class, ecofeminism points to ways in which women's work, itself, models an alternative environmental ethic and practice.

PATRIARCHAL ECONOMICS

At the celebrated 1985 Nairobi Forum on 'Equality, Development, and Peace', the social and environmental impact of cash-cropping and industrialization were discussed thoroughly, after which the conference resolved to counter harmful development by getting more women into pressure groups, management, and education. The media was asked to promote more constructive images of women, and governments were encouraged to research and modify policies which inhibit women's full participation in community life. These resolutions were adopted by delegates from 157 countries, and later, by the fortieth session of the United Nations General Assembly. The resolutions are to be monitored by the appropriate UN agencies up to the year 2000.[3] Still, the problem remains: just as 'most women's work is invisible, so are our Herculean efforts against [that invisibility], North and South, East and West'.[4]

Some impressive grassroots projects—the Chipko movement among Indian peasants to preserve forests and limestone deposits from the 'formal' economy; the Greenbelt Movement of Kenya women, led by Wangari Maathai, which won an Alternative Nobel Prize; and model farming by the Ação Femínea Democrática Gaucha in the Amazon—are internationally acclaimed. In official accounts of development, however, women's activities are often passed over. While the UN Economic Commission on Africa found that women and their children produce 70 per cent of the continent's food, are responsible for the transport of that food, and work a 14–16-hour day, the UN Food and Agriculture Organization (FAO) describes only 5 per cent of them as employed. Similarly, national statistics on agricultural production in Peru indicate a female contribution of 2.6 per cent, while local estimates put it at 86 per cent. In Egypt, the same cultural phenomenon occurs: official figures show a 3.6 per cent agricultural contribution by women, whereas local opinion has it at 35–50 per cent. Tourist postcards and agency propaganda shots also tend to portray 'rural workers' as male. Further, while 'women grow half the world's food. . .most agricultural advisors are men—who tend to give advice to men'.5 And what kind of advice is that? Famine conditions in Ethiopia have resulted from land being taken out of women's hands by those who would render it profitable in terms defined by an abstract and unpredictable global economy.

Sithembiso Nyoni, coordinator of women's rural progress associations in Zimbabwe, believes that consultants and ministers are too concerned about international hobnobbing to remember that 'we are the basis of their power'. Hence, in the South, the debt crisis gets worse as 'aid programmes' open the way for multinational corporations and an increasing concentration of assets among the wealthy. Meanwhile, the female half of the world's population owns less than 1 per cent of world property. Major breadwinners in the Third World, women receive less than 1 per cent of UN aid. Under the present 'relations of production', their access to land is contingent upon marriage, and other forms of credit are invariably blocked by bureaucratic attitudes. A survey of professional staff in environmental agencies and NGOs by Dutch IUCN administrator Irene Dankelman affirms that women are noticeably few at an advisory level.6 Neither the famous Indian report on the status of women nor India's sixth Five-Year Plan acknowledges problems with water, fuel, and feed. Yet, the daily experience of Third World women gives them an acute knowledge of indigenous species, water holes, drought-resistant seeds, storage methods, and fuel materials.

Beyond this, Hilkka Pietilä, a Finnish ecofeminist, suggests that if women's voices were listened to 'the authentic female approach and value system concerning development [would be] an untapped and fresh resource'.7 The IUCN has now set up a working party on Women, Environment, and Sustainable Development to assess the World Conservation Strategy (WCS). The committee is to draft a supplement considering how the WCS might be 'adapted' to 'incorporate women's issues'. We might well ask, why a 'supplement'? Why is women's central productive role again being marginalized in this way, even by those with the best of intentions?

Why is it that women's work is not counted—that women are not counted—that women 'don't count'? In her booklet, *The Global Kitchen*,

Selma James writes that not only are few women paid for the work they do, but even salaried women receive only two-thirds of what men are paid for the same work. More significantly, most women's labour is left out of that basic government statistic, the gross national product (GNP).[8] A housewife and mother in the 'developed' world completes at least 70 unsalaried hours a week; that is, twice the standard Australian working week of 35 hours. She both *reproduces* the earning labour force, and *produces* use value through cooking, laundry, mending or buying clothes, cleaning, maintenance, and gardening. Then there are the emotional/moral obligations of her open-ended role—helping children, the aged, and sick; sexual relief for the man in her life; and possibly the labour of childbearing consequent to this. Many middle-class women take on a heavy round of voluntary commitments like the Parent-Teacher Association, amnesty work, or resident action. Migrant women use extra energy to absorb the strains put on their families by having continually to rebuild their communities. On top of this, as we have seen, non-metropolitan women in a Two-Thirds world grow the bulk of community food, usually unsupported by men, who are attracted into the urban cash economy. Similarly, in 'advanced' industrialized societies, one family in three is surviving with no male help. North and South, women have more in common than many might think. The general rule is: maximum responsibilities, minimum rights.

The Arusha 1984 United Nations conference on the Advancement of Women in Africa concluded that concrete steps should be taken to quantify the unremunerated contribution of women; to ascertain its exchange value.[9] As Selma James points out, by the logic of the present economy, "the woman who cleans a house is not 'working' but the military man who bombs it, is. However, the work of the same woman, if hired by her husband. . .would pop into the GNP."[10] Interestingly, the compensation of childcare and domestic labour is perceived as a 'gift' from the state, charity, or welfare, but never as 'economic' exchange. James argues that we should allocate domestic hours worked to standard job categories, apply the going wage, then total. Using such a method in the early 1970s, John Kenneth Galbraith estimated that household labour was probably worth 25 per cent of the US GNP. Carnegie, Ford, and Rockefeller Foundation reports in 1985 claimed that housework constituted 33 per cent of the US GNP. No wonder women campaign so vigorously against military involvement; they are defending what they have produced by their labour. Given the predatory structure of the patriarchal economic system, it is not surprising that Norwegian social psychologist, Berit As, should discover that economic growth means more unpaid work being put on women's shoulders.[11] Many examples can be given. The import of tractors to Sri Lanka forces women to pick cotton twice as fast in order to keep wages at the same level. The growing engagement of European women outside the home only locks them into a double shift, for Swedish Central Bureau of Statistics figures show that 70 per cent of men never clean house or cook. According to the sociologist, Ruth Schwartz Cowan, housework in 'advanced' societies takes longer despite new 'labour-saving' gadgets.[12] Home economics and the professionalization of motherhood among educated women has created exacting standards in the quality of care they feel they should give their families. Technology and education may actually reinforce the gender division of labour which restricts women's access to 'economic' work.

The injustice of the global economy also affects women in other ways. Mothers across Europe are picking up the community health costs of nuclear radiation following Chernobyl. In the Third World, female illiteracy rises while a Western middle-class, facing recession, chooses private schooling for its sons. Now the US fast food habit brings deforestation and dispossession to Central American families, where a World Bank-funded enclosure movement subsidizes big cattle ranchers in the hamburger snack business.

Just as the environment is damaged by the growth ethic, so are women's lives. Rural women following men into the cities find themselves in makeshift ghettos, without water, garbage removal, health care, or schools. Lin Nelson, a US occupational health researcher, has documented how those who gain employment in chemical or electronics plants are exposed to toxic contaminants affecting the skin, lungs, and nervous system. Foetal damage, miscarriage, and infant death are frequent among workers in these industries.[13] Elsewhere, women fall victim to dangerous contraceptives. Australian clerical staff suffer an epidemic of neuromuscular repetition strain injury caused by long hours at wordprocessing machines. Female microchip assemblers, employed for their 'dexterity and obedience' in the sweatshops of a rapidly industrializing South Korea, are left blind after two years of intensive production. Finally, in developing countries, an internationally organized tourist trade in sex quietly helps fulfil an urgent need for foreign exchange, while more debt accumulates with the purchase of masculine status symbols, like weapons and oil.

Economic imperialism, not socialism or feminism, is the force most likely to destroy the family. Cecelia Kirkman, who counsels in a battered women's refuge in New York City, describes the neglect of women and children at the apex of the developed world. A marked shift in the tax burden meant that by 1983, the US corporate tax contribution dropped to only 6 per cent of government revenue. Major defence contractors—Boeing, General Dynamics, General Electric, Grumman, and Lockheed—paid no tax at all for a few years in the early 1980s. Yet, in that time, the welfare dollar was severely trimmed. Cuts to social service agencies, schools, hospitals, and day-care centres also badly affected women who work in these major areas of female paid employment. But structural violence is not only economic. To spend the tax dollar on the military is to consent to a dehumanizing brutality. Kirkman has collected statistics which link men's training for war with domestic violence and child abuse.[14] The International Women's Tribune Center is also examining the ties between milita-rism, male sexuality, and violence toward individual women.[15] The deci-mation of family life and concurrent feminization of poverty in the military superstate is exposed in Barbara Ehrenreich's *The Hearts of Men*. Ehrenreich reports that in the USA, 'in the mid-sixties and until the mid-seventies, the number of poor adult males actually declined, while the number of poor women heading households swelled by 100,000 a year'.[16] Money that might have sustained women breadwinners went into arms, foreign investments, six-digit executive salaries, glossy playboy lifestyles, and a paper whirlwind of speculation. For the fact is that men, whether in governments, unions, business, or international agencies, hold almost all authority positions. They make choices and set priorities which are com-fortable to them. North and South, East and West, the flexible, do-it-your-self, cooperative economy of women is daily subsumed by private and public spheres alike; just as the degraded 'resource base' of nature silently absorbs the longer-term costs of what is called 'development'.[17]

ECO-FEMINIST ECONOMICS

Eco-feminist theologians Rosemary Ruether and Elizabeth Dodson-Gray see the patriarchal belief system which justifies all these things as a hierarchy, a 'Great Chain of Being' with God or Allah at the top; next Man, the steward of

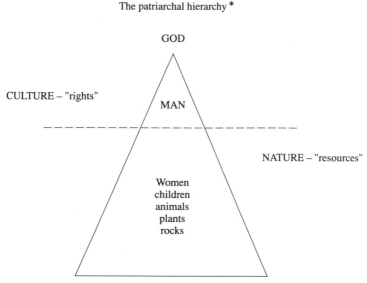

The patriarchal hierarchy *

GOD

CULTURE – "rights"

MAN

NATURE – "resources"

Women
children
animals
plants
rocks

*A modified version of this pyramid by Elizabeth Dodson-Gray was originally published in *Green Paradise Lost*, Roundtable Press, Wellesley, MA, 1981, p. 4.

nature; then women, children, animals, and finally plants and rocks at the base.[18] A deep divide separates the categories of 'Man' and 'Women', and it is this same line which maintains the polarization of 'reality' into the 'truly human' and the 'simply natural'.[19] Traditionally, women, children, animals, and plants have been accorded no rights and have existed solely for the enhancement of God and Man. New modes of industrial production simply extend the underlying logic, as both 'nature' and those who labour with nature are treated as 'resources' without intrinsic value. Modern science, with its devastating tools and techniques, has now absorbed this theology and largely usurped its political function of rationalizing masculine domination.

Why have men chosen to alienate themselves from the rest of life in this way? A growing number of social theorists believe it may have begun with a painful sense of exclusion from the life process, and the realization by men that, while they may 'appropriate' life, they cannot 'produce' it. This hypothesis seems to be substantiated by the work of ecofeminist Maria Mies, who finds the same ancient psychology reappearing in Western economic theory. She notes that the concept of 'labour' is usually reserved for men's work, work that is done with the hands or head. Hands and head are considered 'human' parts of the body, while the womb and breasts are described as 'natural' or 'animal'.[20] Certainly, men's bodily production is not identical with women's. Women may produce in two ways: they may labour with the uterus and/or they may labour with the organs of the head and hands as men do. However, the arbitrary naturalization of women's activities is currently used to foster their exclusion from the paid workforce.

Turning this argument right around to address a future sustainable economy, it is worth noting that not only is there a quantitative difference between men and women's productive contribution, but also a profoundly important qualitative difference. Qualitatively, women's mediation of nature in all its labour forms, is organized around a logic of reciprocity rather than mastery and control. As Mies puts it, women 'are not owners of their own bodies or of the earth, but they cooperate with their bodies and with the earth in order to let grow and to make grow'.[21] This logic of reciprocity is the basis of humankind's first productive economy—invented by women—an informal subsistence economy which is still the mainstay of life for the majority of people on Earth today, despite the superimposition of supposedly more 'efficient' mass-scale modes of production with development.

Under patriarchy then, the things that men do, called 'production' are valued; while the things that women do, especially (re)production, social as well as biological, are not valued. An extract from the Kenya *Standard* illustrates this well:

> As more and more land will be required for food production in order to meet the demand from the population. . .cash crop expansion may stagnate. Given the costs involved in adopting more modern farming *techniques to raise*

*productivity. . .*population growth, if allowed to continue, can only result in more encroachment on vital forest reserves.[22]

The line of reasoning pursued here deflects responsibility away from patriarchal economics and puts the onus for environmental depletion squarely on women. As men see it, women must stop making new life since this is detrimental to economic growth. Investigations by the *New Internationalist* suggest the converse.[23] The reason for Africa's falling food production is not scarcity of land *per se*, nor lack of technology, but the seduction of local men by the formal economy which takes both land and men's labour away from family farming.

The problem of overpopulation is real and needs to be seriously examined. However, given the ethical issues of eugenics/genocide and of a woman's rights over her own body, the targeting of Third World population control by environmentalists has both racist and sexist dimensions. Even as a matter of simple equity, where children provide supplementary farm labour for overworked mothers, it is inappropriate for male elites and their international policy advisors to demand population control. Such programmes originated in a post-World War II middle-class urban desire to protect 'the quality of life'—for which read 'levels of consumerism'. Now the argument for population 'control' is formulated more prudently in terms of protecting Earth's scarce resources. But this injunction as applied to the South exclusively is patently hypocritical. Each infant born into the so-called advanced societies will use about fifteen times more global resources during his or her lifetime than a person born in the Third World.[24] Population restraint may well be called for in the North, hopefully complemented by a scaling back of high-technology excess. On the other hand, subsistence dwellers are producers as much as consumers: As 'prosumers' they are practical examples of human autonomy in a non-exploitative relation to land. To borrow the impoverished language of the dominant materialistic ethos here: in certain circumstances a child born in the South could be seen as an 'asset' rather than a 'liability'. What much of the talk about population 'control' may express is a projection and displacement of the guilt experienced by those who continue to live comfortably off the invisible backs of working women in the Two Thirds World.

Deeper than this, does the constant focus on population control in development debates even reflect a fear of nature or of female power? Fear of that different voice? If not, then why the irrational pursuit by male elites of status in a global economic pecking order and expertise in frankly destructive technologies? Consider this piece from the Kenya *Sunday Nation*:

Only sound social, economic and political policies that favour or promote indigenous scientific and technological potential will help the continent meet its *basic human needs*. . .the minimum target of 1000 scientists and engineers per million inhabitants.[25]

The iniquitous financial transfer from South to North which imported development involves, the predatory consumption of food and energy resources by an industrialized North, lessons from the green revolution— are all glossed over, although they are surely very good arguments for disengagement from the multinational arena and for concentrating on the wealth in one's own back yard. What is overlooked again and again is that the self-reliant, life-affirming, bioregional labours of women, 'the informal or free economy, the world of nurturance and close human relations, is the sphere where basic human needs are anchored and where models for humane alternatives can be found'.[26]

As things stand, women, half the world's population, put in 65 per cent of the world's work, and get back only 10 per cent of all income paid.[27] The rationale for this institutionalized theft, and that of the exploitation of nature, has been uncovered by ecofeminist analyses of patriarchy. But unless the reality of this cultural process is accepted by environmentalists, their handling of the global predicament will fail to make any sense. *Our Common Future*, the 1987 report by the World Commission on Environment and Development, a collection of environmentalists, economists, politicians, scientists, and engineers, is a classic case in point.[28] The wisdom of 'live simply that others may simply live' is lost. Ultimately, its recommendations collapse back into a 'more growth and trickle-down someday' solution to world poverty. Given the metaphysical premises on which economics is currently organized, the costs of growth will again be passed down to women producers and on to nature. Getting more women in advisory positions is only half of the story. The unconscious patriarchal connection between woman and nature needs to be made conscious, and the hierarchical fallacies of the 'Great Chain of Being' acknowledged, before there can be any real growth towards a sane, humane, ecological future. Once this step is made, the way that women work in reciprocity with nature will become visible as a model to learn from. The result would be a fundamental change in the relations of production, a change summarized by ecofeminist Ynestra King, when she says: 'men must stop trying to control nature and join women in identifying with nature'.[29] The personal is indeed political; and struggles for equality and sustainability are closely interlinked.

NOTES

1. *Women and the Environmental Crisis: A Report of Workshop Proceedings at the Nairobi Forum 85: Women in Development* (Philadelphia: New Society Publishers, 1984).
2. Carol Gilligan, *In a Different Voice* (Cambridge, Mass.: Harvard University Press, 1984), 173–74.
3. *Report of the World Conference to Review and Appraise the Achievements of*

the United Nations Decade for Women—Equality, Development, and Peace, Nairobi, 15–16 July 1985 (New York: United Nations, 1986).

4. Selma James, *The Global Kitchen* (London: Housewives in Dialogue Archive, 1985), 25; Marilyn Waring, *Counting for Nothing* (Sydney: Allen & Unwin, 1989).

5. FAO statistics and quotation from *Women and the Environmental Crisis*, 45.

6. Irene Dankelman and Joan Davidson, eds, *Women and Environment in the Third World* (London: Earthscan, 1988), Ch. 7.

7. Hilkka Pietilä, 'Women as an Alternative Culture Here and Now', *Development* 4 (1984), 60.

8. James, *The Global Kitchen*, 1.

9. *Forward Looking Strategies for the Advancement of Women in Africa Beyond the End of the United Nations Decade for Women*, Expert Group Meeting, Arusha, United Republic of Tanzania, 4–6 October, 1984 (New York: United Nations Economic and Social Council, 1984).

10. Ibid., 10–11.

11. Berit As, 'A Five Dimensional Model for Change', *Women's Studies International Quarterly* 4 (1981): 111.

12. Ruth Schwartz Cowan, *More Work for Mother* (New York: Basic Books, 1983).

13. Lin Nelson, 'Feminists Turn to Workplace, Environmental Health', *Women and Global Corporations* 7, 1 and 2 (1986).

14. Cecelia Kirkman, 'The War at Home', *The Non-Violent Activist* 3 (1986): 7.

15. International Women's Tribune Center Team and Anne Walker, 'Peace Is No Violence Against Women', *The Tribune, A Women and Development Quarterly* (3rd Quarter, 1985): 32.

16. Barbara Ehrenreich, *The Hearts of Men* (New York: Anchor, 1983), 172.

17. Hazel Henderson, 'Indicators of No Real Meaning', in Paul Elkins, ed., *The Living Economy: A New Economics in the Making* (London: Routledge and Kegan Paul, 1986), 33.

18. Rosemary Ruether, *New Woman New Earth* (New York: Dove, 1975); Elizabeth Dodson-Gray, *Green Paradise Lost* (Wellesley, Mass: Roundtable Press, 1979).

19. For a more detailed discussion of this hierarchy, see the essay by Hilkka Pietilä in Engel, *op. cit.*

20. Maria Mies, *Patriarchy and Accumulation on a World Scale* (London: Zed Books, 1986).

21. Ibid., 52.

22. 'How Food Production is Hit by Population', *The Standard* (2 October 1987): 14.

23. Debbie Taylor, ed., 'Myth Conceptions', *New Internationalist* (October 1987): 8–9.

24. F.E. Trainer, *Abandon Affluence!* (London: Zed Books, 1985), 1.

25. Otula Owuor, 'Sound Science Policies Called For', *Sunday Nation* (4 October, 1987): 17 (emphasis added).

26. Hilka Pietilä, *Tomorrow Begins Today* (ICDA/ISIS Workshop, Nairobi Forum, 1985), 26.

27. United Nations International Labour Organization (ILO).

28. World Commission on Environment and Development, *Our Common Future* (Oxford: Oxford University Press, 1987).

29. Ynestra King, Address to the international conference on 'Eco-feminist Perspectives—Culture, Nature, Theory', at the University of Southern California, Los Angeles, 1987.

The Power and the Promise of Ecological Feminism

Karen J. Warren

Karen J. Warren is a feminist philosopher who has published essays on ecofeminism and edited several special issues on ecofeminism for Hypatia: A Journal of Feminist Philosophy *and the* American Philosophical Association *Newsletter on Feminism and Philosophy. Warren is completing three books on ecological feminism, one co-authored with Jim Cheney and entitled* Ecological Feminism, *and two anthologies on ecofeminism. Warren also conducts workshops on environmental ethics and critical thinking for elementary and secondary school teachers and students, and is co-creator of an environmental ethics simulation game.*

INTRODUCTION

Ecological feminism (ecofeminism) has begun to receive a fair amount of attention lately as an alternative feminism and environmental ethic.[1] Since Françoise d'Eaubonne introduced the term *l'écoféminisme* in 1974 to bring attention to women's potential for bringing about an ecological revolution,[2] the term has been used in a variety of ways. As I use the term in this paper, ecological feminism is the position that there are important connections—historical, experiential, symbolic, theoretical—between the domination of women and the domination of nature, an understanding of which is crucial to both feminism and environmental ethics. I argue that the promise and

This essay originally appeared in *Environmental Ethics*, Vol. 12, No. 2 (Summer 1990), 125–146. Reprinted with permission.

power of ecological feminism is that *it provides a distinctive framework both for reconceiving feminism and for developing an environmental ethic which takes seriously connections between the domination of women and the domination of nature.* I do so by discussing the nature of a feminist ethic and the ways in which ecofeminism provides a feminist and environmental ethic. I conclude that any feminist theory *and* any environmental ethic which fails to take seriously the twin and interconnected dominations of women and nature is at best incomplete and at worst simply inadequate.

FEMINISM, ECOLOGICAL FEMINISM, AND CONCEPTUAL
FRAMEWORKS

Whatever else it is, feminism is at least the movement to end sexist oppression. It involves the elimination of any and all factors that contribute to the continued and systematic domination or subordination of women. While feminists disagree about the nature of and solutions to the subordination of women, all feminists agree that sexist oppression exists, is wrong, and must be abolished.

A "feminist issue" is any issue that contributes in some way to understanding the oppression of women. Equal rights, comparable pay for comparable work, and food production are feminist issues wherever and whenever an understanding of them contributes to an understanding of the continued exploitation or subjugation of women. Carrying water and searching for firewood are feminist issues wherever and whenever women's primary responsibility for these tasks contributes to their lack of full participation in decision making, income producing, or high status positions engaged in by men. What counts as a feminist issue, then, depends largely on context, particularly the historical and material conditions of women's lives.

Environmental degradation and exploitation are feminist issues because an understanding of them contributes to an understanding of the oppression of women. In India, for example, both deforestation and reforestation through the introduction of a monoculture species tree (e.g., eucalyptus) intended for commercial production are feminist issues because the loss of indigenous forests and multiple species of trees has drastically affected rural Indian women's ability to maintain a subsistence household. Indigenous forests provide a variety of trees for food, fuel, fodder, household utensils, dyes, medicines, and income-generating uses, while monoculture-species forests do not.[3] Although I do not argue for this claim here, a look at the global impact of environmental degradation on women's lives suggests important respects in which environmental degradation is a feminist issue.

Feminist philosophers claim that some of the most important feminist issues are *conceptual* ones: these issues concern how one conceptualizes such mainstay philosophical notions as reason and rationality, ethics, and what it is to be human. Ecofeminists extend this feminist philosophical concern to nature. They argue that, ultimately, some of the most important connections between the domination of women and the domination of nature are conceptual. To see this, consider the nature of conceptual frameworks.

A *conceptual framework* is a set of *basic* beliefs, values, attitudes, and assumptions which shape and reflect how one views oneself and one's world. It is a socially constructed lens through which we perceive ourselves and others. It is affected by such factors as gender, race, class, age, affectional orientation, nationality, and religious background.

Some conceptual frameworks are oppressive. An *oppressive conceptual framework* is one that explains, justifies, and maintains relationships of domination and subordination. When an oppressive conceptual framework is *patriarchal*, it explains, justifies, and maintains the subordination of women by men.

I have argued elsewhere that there are three significant features of oppressive conceptual frameworks: (1) value-hierarchical thinking, i.e., "up-down" thinking which places higher value, status, or prestige on what is "up" rather than on what is "down"; (2) value dualisms, i.e., disjunctive pairs in which the disjuncts are seen as oppositional (rather than as complementary) and exclusive (rather than as inclusive), and which place higher value (status, prestige) on one disjunct rather than the other (e.g., dualisms which give higher value or status to that which has historically been identified as "body," "emotion," and "female"); and (3) logic of domination, i.e., a structure of argumentation which leads to a justification of subordination.[4]

The third feature of oppressive conceptual frameworks is the most significant. A logic of domination is not *just* a logical structure. It also involves a substantive value system, since an ethical premise is needed to permit or sanction the "just" subordination of that which is subordinate. This justification typically is given on grounds of some alleged characteristic (e.g., rationality) which the dominant (e.g., men) have and the subordinate (e.g., women) lack.

Contrary to what many feminists and ecofeminists have said or suggested, there may be nothing *inherently* problematic about "hierarchical thinking" or even "value-hierarchical thinking" in contexts other than contexts of oppression. Hierarchical thinking is important in daily living for classifying data, comparing information, and organizing material. Taxonomies (e.g., plant taxonomies) and biological nomenclature seem to require *some* form of "hierarchical thinking." Even "value-hierarchical thinking" may be quite acceptable in certain contexts. (The same may be said of "value dualisms" in non-oppressive contexts.) For example, suppose it is true that what is unique about humans is our conscious capacity to radically reshape our social environments (or "societies"), as Murray Bookchin suggests.[5] Then one could truthfully say that humans are better equipped to radically reshape their environments than are rocks or plants—a "value-hierarchical" way of speaking.

The problem is not simply *that* value-hierarchial thinking and value dualisms are used, but *the way* in which each has been used in *oppressive conceptual frameworks* to establish inferiority and to justify subordination.[6] It is the logic of domination, *coupled with* value-hierarchical thinking and value dualisms, which "justifies" subordination. What is explanatorily basic, then, about the nature of oppressive conceptual frameworks is the logic of domination.

For ecofeminism, that a logic of domination is explanatorily basic is important for at least three reasons. First, without a logic of domination, a description of similarities and differences would be just that—a description of similarities and differences. Consider the claim, "Humans are different from plants and rocks in that humans can (and plants and rocks cannot) consciously and radically reshape the communities in which they live; humans are similar to plants and rocks in that they are both members of an ecological community." Even if humans are "better" than plants and rocks with respect to the conscious ability of humans to radically transform communities, one does not *thereby* get any *morally* relevant distinction between humans and nonhumans, or an argument for the domination of plants and rocks by humans. To get *those* conclusions one needs to add at least two powerful assumptions, viz., (A2) and (A4) in argument A below:

(A1) Humans do, and plants and rocks do not, have the capacity to consciously and radically change the community in which they live.
(A2) Whatever has the capacity to consciously and radically change the community in which it lives is morally superior to whatever lacks this capacity.
(A3) Thus, humans are morally superior to plants and rocks.
(A4) For any X and Y, if X is morally superior to Y, then X is morally justified in subordinating Y.
(A5) Thus, humans are morally justified in subordinating plants and rocks.

Without the two assumptions that *humans are morally superior* to (at least some) nonhumans, (A2), and that *superiority justifies subordination*, (A4), all one has is some difference between humans and some nonhumans. This is true *even if* that difference is given in terms of superiority. Thus, it is the logic of domination, (A4), which is the bottom line in ecofeminist discussions of oppression.

Second, ecofeminists argue that, at least in Western societies, the oppressive conceptual framework which sanctions the twin dominations of women and nature is a patriarchal one characterized by all three features of an oppressive conceptual framework. Many ecofeminists claim that, historically, within at least the dominant Western culture, a patriarchal conceptual framework has sanctioned the following argument B:

(B1) Women are identified with nature and the realm of the physical; men are identified with the "human" and the realm of the mental.
(B2) Whatever is identified with nature and the realm of the physical is inferior to ("below") whatever is identified with the "human" and the realm of the mental; or, conversely, the latter is superior to ("above") the former.
(B3) Thus, women are inferior to ("below") men; or, conversely, men are superior to ("above") women.
(B4) For any X and Y, if X is superior to Y, then X is justified in subordinating Y.
(B5) Thus, men are justified in subordinating women.

If sound, argument B establishes *patriarchy*, i.e., the conclusion given at (B5) that the systematic domination of women by men is justified. But according to ecofeminists, (B5) is justified by just those three features of an oppressive conceptual framework identified earlier: value-hierarchical thinking, the assumption at (B2); value dualisms, the assumed dualism of the mental and the physical at (B1) and the assumed inferiority of the physical vis-à-vis the mental at (B2); and a logic of domination, the assumption at (B4), the same as the previous premise (A4). Hence, according to ecofeminists, insofar as an oppressive patriarchal conceptual framework has functioned historically (within at least dominant Western culture) to sanction the twin dominations of women and nature (argument B), both argument B and the patriarchal conceptual framework, from whence it comes, ought to be rejected.

Of course, the preceding does not identify which premises of B are false. What is the status of premises (B1) and (B2)? Most, if not all, feminists claim that (B1), and many ecofeminists claim that (B2), have been assumed or asserted within the dominant Western philosophical and intellectual tradition.[7] As such, these feminists assert, as a matter of historical fact, that the dominant Western philosophical tradition has assumed the truth of (B1) and (B2). Ecofeminists, however, either deny (B2) or do not affirm (B2). Furthermore, because some ecofeminists are anxious to deny any ahistorical identification of women with nature, some ecofeminists deny (B1) when (B1) is used to support anything other than a strictly historical claim about what has been asserted or assumed to be true within patriarchal culture— e.g., when (B1) is used to assert that women properly are identified with the realm of nature and the physical.[8] Thus, from an ecofeminist perspective, (B1) and (B2) are properly viewed as problematic though historically sanctioned claims: they are problematic precisely because of the way they have functioned historically in a patriarchal conceptual framework and culture to sanction the dominations of women and nature.

What *all* ecofeminists agree about, then, is the way in which *the logic of domination* has functioned historically within patriarchy to sustain and justify the twin dominations of women and nature.[9] Since *all* feminists (and not just ecofeminists) oppose patriarchy, the conclusion given at (B5), all feminists (including ecofeminists) must oppose at least the logic of domination, premise (B4), on which argument B rests—whatever the truth-value status of (B1) and (B2) *outside of* a patriarchal context.

That *all* feminists must oppose the logic of domination shows the breadth and depth of the ecofeminist critique of B: it is a critique not only of the three assumptions on which this argument for the domination of women and nature rests, viz., the assumptions at (B1), (B2), and (B4); it is also a critique of patriarchal conceptual frameworks generally, i.e., of those oppressive conceptual frameworks which put men "up" and women "down," allege some way in which women are morally inferior to men, and use that alleged difference to justify the subordination of women by men. Therefore, ecofeminism is necessary to *any* feminist critique of patriarchy, and, hence, necessary to feminism (a point I discuss again later).

Third, ecofeminism clarifies why the logic of domination, and any conceptual framework which gives rise to it, must be abolished in order both to make possible a meaningful notion of difference which does not breed domination and to prevent feminism from becoming a "support" movement based primarily on shared experiences. In contemporary society, there is no one "woman's voice," no *woman* (or *human*) *simpliciter*: every woman (or human) is a woman (or human) of some race, class, age, affectional orientation, marital status, regional or national background, and so forth. Because there are no "monolithic experiences" that all women share, feminism must be a "solidarity movement" based on shared beliefs and interests rather than a "unity in sameness" movement based on shared experiences and shared victimization.[10] In the words of Maria Lugones, "Unity—not to be confused with solidarity—is understood as conceptually tied to domination."[11]

Ecofeminists insist that the sort of logic of domination used to justify the domination of humans by gender, racial or ethnic, or class status is also used to justify the domination of nature. Because eliminating a logic of domination is part of a feminist critique—whether a critique of patriarchy, white supremacist culture, or imperialism—ecofeminists insist that *naturism* is properly viewed as an integral part of any feminist solidarity movement to end sexist oppression and the logic of domination which conceptually grounds it.

ECOFEMINISM RECONCEIVES FEMINISM

The discussion so far has focused on some of the oppressive conceptual features of patriarchy. As I use the phrase, the "logic of traditional feminism" refers to the location of the conceptual roots of sexist oppression, at least in Western societies, in an oppressive patriarchal conceptual framework characterized by a logic of domination. Insofar as other systems of oppression (e.g., racism, classism, ageism, heterosexism) are also conceptually maintained by a logic of domination, appeal to the logic of traditional feminism ultimately locates the basic conceptual interconnections among *all* systems of oppression in the logic of domination. It thereby explains at a *conceptual* level why the eradication of sexist oppression requires the eradication of the other forms of oppression.[12] It is by clarifying this conceptual connection between systems of oppression that a movement to end sexist oppression—traditionally the special turf of feminist theory and practice—leads to a reconceiving of feminism as *a movement to end all forms of oppression*.

Suppose one agrees that the logic of traditional feminism requires the expansion of feminism to include other social systems of domination (e.g., racism and classism). What warrants the inclusion of nature in these "social systems of domination"? Why must the logic of traditional feminism include the abolition of "naturism" (i.e., the domination or oppression of nonhuman nature) among the "isms" feminism must confront? The conceptual justification for expanding feminism to include ecofeminism is twofold. One basis has already been suggested: By showing that the conceptual connections between the dual dominations of women and nature are located in an oppressive and, at least in Western societies, patriarchal conceptual framework characterized by a logic of domination, ecofeminism explains how and why feminism, conceived as a movement to end sexist oppression, must be expanded and reconceived as also a movement to end naturism. This is made explicit by the following argument C:

(C1) Feminism is a movement to end sexism.
(C2) But sexism is conceptually linked with naturism (through an oppressive conceptual framework characterized by a logic of domination).
(C3) Thus, feminism is (also) a movement to end naturism.

Because, ultimately, these connections between sexism and naturism are conceptual—embedded in an oppressive conceptual framework—the logic of traditional feminism leads to the embracement of ecological feminism.[13]

The other justification for reconceiving feminism to include ecofeminism has to do with the concepts of gender and nature. Just as conceptions of gender are socially constructed, so are conceptions of nature. Of course, the claim that women and nature are social constructions does not require anyone to deny that there are actual humans and actual trees, rivers, and plants. It simply implies that *how* women and nature are conceived is a matter of historical and social reality. These conceptions vary cross-culturally and by historical time period. As a result, any discussion of the "oppression or domination of nature" involves reference to historically specific forms of social domination of nonhuman nature by humans, just as discussion of the "domination of women" refers to historically specific forms of social domination of women by men. Although I do not argue for it here, an ecofeminist defense of the historical connections between the dominations of women and of nature, claims (B1) and (B2) in argument B, involves showing that within patriarchy the feminization of nature and the naturalization of women have been crucial to the historically successful subordinations of both.[14]

If ecofeminism promises to reconceive traditional feminism in ways which include naturism as a legitimate feminist issue, does ecofeminism also promise to reconceive environmental ethics in ways which are feminist? I think so. This is the subject of the remainder of the paper.

CLIMBING FROM ECOFEMINISM TO ENVIRONMENTAL ETHICS

Many feminists and some environmental ethicists have begun to explore the use of first-person narrative as a way of raising philosophically germane issues in ethics often lost or underplayed in mainstream philosophical ethics. Why is this so? What is it about narrative which makes it a significant resource for theory and practice in feminism and environmental ethics? Even if appeal to first-person narrative is a helpful literary device for describing ineffable experience or a legitimate social science methodology for documenting personal and social history, how is first-person narrative a valuable vehicle of argumentation for ethical decision making and theory building? One fruitful way to begin answering these questions is to ask them of a particular first-person narrative.

Consider the following first-person narrative about rock climbing:

> For my very first rock climbing experience, I chose a somewhat private spot, away from other climbers and on-lookers. After studying "the chimney," I focused all my energy on making it to the top. I climbed with intense determination, using whatever strength and skills I had to accomplish this challenging feat. By midway I was exhausted and anxious. I couldn't see what to do next—where to put my hands or feet. Growing increasingly more weary as I clung somewhat desperately to the rock, I made a move. It didn't work. I fell. There I was, dangling midair above the rocky ground below, frightened but terribly relieved that the belay rope had held me. I knew I was safe. I took a look up at the climb that remained. I was determined to make it to the top. With renewed confidence and concentration, I finished the climb to the top.
>
> On my second day of climbing, I rappelled down about 200 feet from the top of the Palisades at Lake Superior to just a few feet above the water level. I could see no one—not my belayer, not the other climbers, no one. I unhooked slowly from the rappel rope and took a deep cleansing breath. I looked all around me—really looked—and listened. I heard a cacophony of voices—birds, trickles of water on the rock before me, waves lapping against the rocks below. I closed my eyes and began to feel the rock with my hands—the cracks

and crannies, the raised lichen and mosses, the almost imperceptible nubs that might provide a resting place for my fingers and toes when I began to climb. At that moment I was bathed in serenity. I began to talk to the rock in an almost inaudible, child-like way, as if the rock were my friend. I felt an overwhelming sense of gratitude for what it offered me—a chance to know myself and the rock differently, to appreciate unforeseen miracles like the tiny flowers growing in the even tinier cracks in the rock's surface, and to come to know a sense of *being in relationship* with the natural environment. It felt as if the rock and I were silent conversational partners in a longstanding friendship. I realized then that I had come to care about this cliff which was so different from me, so unmovable and invincible, independent and seemingly indifferent to my presence. I wanted to be with the rock as I climbed. Gone was the determination to conquer the rock, to forcefully impose my will on it; I wanted simply to work respectfully with the rock as I climbed. And as I climbed, that is what I felt. I felt myself *caring* for this rock and feeling thankful that climbing provided the opportunity for me to know it and myself in this new way.

There are at least four reasons why use of such a first-person narrative is important to feminism and environmental ethics. First, such a narrative gives voice to a felt sensitivity often lacking in traditional analytical ethical discourse, viz., a sensitivity to conceiving of oneself as fundamentally "in relationship with" others, including the nonhuman environment. It is a modality which *takes relationships themselves seriously*. It thereby stands in contrast to a strictly reductionist modality that takes relationships seriously only or primarily because of the nature of the *relators* or parties to those relationships (e.g., relators conceived as moral agents, right holders, interest carriers, or sentient beings). In the rock-climbing narrative above, it is the climber's relationship with the rock she climbs which takes on special significance—which is itself a locus of value—in addition to whatever moral status or moral considerability she or the rock or any other parties to the relationship may also have.[15]

Second, such a first-person narrative gives expression to a variety of ethical attitudes and behaviors often overlooked or underplayed in mainstream Western ethics, e.g., the difference in attitudes and behaviors toward a rock when one is "making it to the top" and when one thinks of oneself as "friends with" or "caring about" the rock one climbs.[16] These different attitudes and behaviors suggest an ethically germane contrast between two different types of relationship humans or climbers may have toward a rock: An imposed conqueror-type relationship, and an emergent caring-type relationship. This contrast grows out of, and is faithful to, felt, lived experience.

The difference between conquering and caring attitudes and behaviors in relation to the natural environment provides a third reason why the use of first-person narrative is important to feminism and environmental ethics: it provides a way of conceiving of ethics and ethical meaning as *emerging out of* particular situations moral agents find themselves in, rather than as being *imposed on* those situations (e.g., as a derivation or instantiation of some predetermined abstract principle or rule). This emergent feature of narrative centralizes the importance of *voice*. When a multiplicity of cross-cultural *voices* are centralized, narrative is able to give expression to a range of attitudes, values, beliefs, and behaviors which may be overlooked or silenced by imposed ethical meaning and theory. As a reflection on a felt, lived experiences, the use of narrative in ethics provides a stance from which ethical discourse can be held accountable to the historical, material, and social realities in which moral subjects find themselves.

Lastly, and for our purposes perhaps most importantly, the use of narrative has argumentative significance. Jim Cheney calls attention to this feature of narrative when he claims, "To contextualize ethical deliberation is, in some sense, to provide a narrative or story, from which the solution to the ethical dilemma emerges as the fitting conclusion."[17] Narrative has argumentative force by suggesting *what counts* as an appropriate conclusion to an ethical situation. One ethical conclusion suggested by the climbing narrative is that what counts as a proper ethical attitude toward mountains and rocks is an attitude of respect and care (whatever that turns out to be or involve), not one of domination and conquest.

In an essay entitled "In and Out of Harm's Way: Arrogance and Love," feminist philosopher Marilyn Frye distinguishes between "arrogant" and "loving" perception as one way of getting at this difference in the ethical attitudes of care and conquest.[18] Frye writes:

> The loving eye is a contrary of the arrogant eye.
> The loving eye knows the independence of the other. It is the eye of a seer who knows that nature is indifferent. It is the eye of one who knows that to know the seen, one must consult something other than one's own will and interests and fears and imagination. One must look at the thing. One must look and listen and check and question.
> The loving eye is one that pays a certain sort of attention. This attention can require a discipline but *not* a self-denial. The discipline is one of self-knowledge, knowledge of the scope and boundary of the self.. . .In particular, it is a matter of being able to tell one's own interests from those of others and of knowing where one's self leaves off and another begins.. . .
> The loving eye does not make the object of perception into something edible, does not try to assimilate it, does not reduce it to the size of the seer's desire, fear and imagination, and hence does not have to simplify. It knows the complexity of the other as something which will forever present new things to be known. The science of the loving eye would favor The Complexity Theory of Truth [in contrast to The Simplicity Theory of Truth] and presuppose The Endless Interestingness of the Universe.[19]

According to Frye, the loving eye is not an invasive, coercive eye which annexes others to itself, but one which "knows the complexity of the other as something which will forever present new things to be known."

When one climbs a rock as a conqueror, one climbs with an arrogant eye. When one climbs with a loving eye, one constantly "must look and listen and check and question." One recognizes the rock as something very different, something perhaps totally indifferent to one's own presence, and finds in that difference joyous occasion for celebration. One knows "the boundary of the self," where the self—the "I," the climber—leaves off and the rock begins. There is no fusion of two into one, but a complement of two entities *acknowledged* as separate, different, independent, yet *in relationship;* they are in relationship *if only* because the loving eye is perceiving it, responding to it, noticing it, attending to it.

An ecofeminist perspective about both women and nature involves this shift in attitude from "arrogant perception" to "loving perception" of the nonhuman world. Arrogant perception of nonhumans by humans presupposes and maintains *sameness* in such a way that it expands the moral community to those beings who are thought to resemble (be like, similar to, or the same as) humans in some morally significant way. Any environmental movement or ethic based on arrogant perception builds a moral hierarchy of beings and assumes some common denominator of moral considerability in virtue of which like beings deserve similar treatment or moral consideration and unlike beings do not. Such environmental ethics are or generate a "unity in sameness." In contrast, "loving perception" presupposes and maintains *difference*—a distinction between the self and other, between human and at least some nonhumans—in such a way that perception of the other as other *is* an expression of love for one who/which is recognized at the outset as independent, dissimilar, different. As Maria Lugones says, in loving perception, "Love is seen not as fusion and erasure of difference but as incompatible with them."[20] "Unity in sameness" alone is an *erasure of difference*.

"Loving perception" of the nonhuman natural world is an attempt to understand what it means *for humans* to care about the nonhuman world, a world *acknowledged* as being independent, different, perhaps even indifferent to humans. Humans *are* different from rocks in important ways, even if they are also both members of some ecological community. A moral community based on loving perception of oneself *in relationship with* a rock, or with the natural environment as a whole, is one which acknowledges and respects difference, whatever "sameness" also exists.[21] The limits of loving perception are determined only by the limits of one's (e.g., a person's, a community's) ability to respond lovingly (or with appropriate care, trust, or friendship)—whether it is to other humans or to the nonhuman world and elements of it.[22]

If what I have said so far is correct, then there are very different ways to climb a mountain and *how* one climbs it and *how* one narrates the experience of climbing it matter ethically. If one climbs with "arrogant perception," with an attitude of "conquer and control," one keeps intact the very sorts of thinking that characterize a logic of domination and an oppressive conceptual framework. Since the oppressive conceptual framework which sanctions the domination of nature is a patriarchal one, one also thereby keeps intact, even if unwittingly, a patriarchal conceptual framework. Because the dismantling of patriarchal conceptual frameworks is a feminist issue, *how* one climbs a mountain and *how* one narrates—or tells the story—about the experience of climbing also are *feminist issues*. In this way, ecofeminism makes visible why, at a conceptual level, environmental ethics is a feminist issue. I turn now to a consideration of ecofeminism as a distinctively feminist and environmental ethic.

ECOFEMINISM AS A FEMINIST AND ENVIRONMENTAL ETHIC

A feminist ethic involves a twofold commitment to critique male bias in ethics wherever it occurs, and to develop ethics which are not male-biased. Sometimes this involves articulation of values (e.g., values of care, appropriate trust, kinship, friendship) often lost or underplayed in mainstream ethics.[23] Sometimes it involves engaging in theory building by pioneering in new directions or by revamping old theories in gender sensitive ways. What makes the critiques of old theories or conceptualizations of new ones "feminist" is that they emerge out of sex-gender analyses and reflect whatever those analyses reveal about gendered experience and gendered social reality.

As I conceive feminist ethics in the pre-feminist present, it rejects attempts to conceive of ethical theory in terms of necessary and sufficient conditions, because it assumes that there is no essence (in the sense of some transhistorical, universal, absolute abstraction) of feminist ethics. While attempts to formulate joint necessary and sufficient conditions of a feminist ethic are unfruitful, nonetheless, there are some necessary conditions, what I prefer to call "boundary conditions," of a feminist ethic. These boundary conditions clarify some of the minimal conditions of a feminist ethic without suggesting that feminist ethics has some ahistorical essence. They are like the boundaries of a quilt or collage. They delimit the territory of the piece without dictating what the interior, the design, the actual pattern of the piece looks like. Because the actual design of the quilt emerges from the multiplicity of voices of women in a cross-cultural context, the design will change over time. It is not something static.

What are some of the boundary conditions of a feminist ethic? First, nothing can become part of a feminist ethic—can be part of the quilt—that promotes sexism, racism, classism, or any other "isms" of social domination. Of course, people may disagree about what counts as a sexist act, racist attitude, classist behavior. What counts as sexism, racism, or classism may vary cross-culturally. Still, because a feminist ethic aims at eliminating sexism and sexist bias, and (as I have already shown) sexism is intimately connected in conceptualization and in practice to racism, classism, and naturism, a feminist ethic must be anti-sexist, anti-racist, anti-classist, anti-naturist and opposed to any "ism" which presupposes or advances a logic of domination.

Second, a feminist ethic is a *contextualist* ethic. A contextualist ethic is one which sees ethical discourse and practice as emerging from the voices of people located in different historical circumstances. A contextualist ethic is properly viewed as a *collage* or *mosaic*, a *tapestry* of voices that emerges out of felt experiences. Like any collage or mosaic, the point is not to have *one picture* based on a unity of voices, but a *pattern* which emerges out of the very different voices of people located in different circumstances. When a contextualist ethic is *feminist,* it gives central place to the voices of women.

Third, since a feminist ethic gives central significance to the diversity of women's voices, a feminist ethic must be structurally pluralistic rather than unitary or reductionistic. It rejects the assumption that there is "one voice" in terms of which ethical values, beliefs, attitudes, and conduct can be assessed.

Fourth, a feminist ethic reconceives ethical theory as theory in process which will change over time. Like all theory, a feminist ethic is based on some generalizations.[24] Nevertheless, the generalizations associated with it are themselves a pattern of voices within which the different voices emerging out of concrete and alternative descriptions of ethical situations have meaning. The coherence of a feminist theory so conceived is given within a historical and conceptual context, i.e., within a set of historical, socioeconomic circumstances (including circumstances of race, class, age, and affectional orientation) and within a set of basic beliefs, values, attitudes, and assumptions about the world.

Fifth, because a feminist ethic is contextualist, structurally pluralistic, and "in-process," one way to evaluate the claims of a feminist ethic is in terms of their *inclusiveness:* those claims (voices, patterns of voices) are morally and epistemologically favored (preferred, better, less partial, less biased) which are more inclusive of the felt experiences and perspectives of oppressed persons. The condition of inclusiveness requires and ensures that the diverse voices of women (as oppressed persons) will be given legitimacy in ethical theory building. It thereby helps to minimize empirical bias, e.g., bias rising from faulty or false generalizations based on stereotyping, too small a sample size, or a skewed sample. It does so by ensuring that any generalizations which are made about ethics and ethical decision making include—indeed cohere with—the patterned voices of women.[25]

Sixth, a feminist ethic makes no attempt to provide an "objective" point of view, since it assumes that in contemporary culture there really is no such point of view. As such, it does not claim to be "unbiased" in the sense of "value-neutral" or "objective." However, it does assume that whatever bias it has as an ethic centralizing the voices of oppressed persons is a *better bias*—"better" because it is more inclusive and therefore less partial—than those which exclude those voices.[26]

Seventh, a feminist ethic provides a central place for values typically unnoticed, underplayed, or misrepresented in traditional ethics, e.g., values of care, love, friendship, and appropriate trust.[27] Again, it need not do this at the exclusion of considerations of rights, rules, or utility. There may be many contexts in which talk of rights or of utility is useful or appropriate. For instance, in contracts or property relationships, talk of rights may be useful and appropriate. In deciding what is cost-effective or advantageous to the most people, talk of utility may be useful and appropriate. In a feminist *qua* contextualist ethic, whether or not such talk is useful or appropriate depends on the context; *other values* (e.g., values of care, trust, friendship) are *not* viewed as reducible to or captured solely in terms of such talk.[28]

Eighth, a feminist ethic also involves a reconception of what it is to be human and what it is for humans to engage in ethical decision making, since it rejects as either meaningless or currently untenable any gender-free or gender-neutral description of humans, ethics, and ethical decision making. It thereby rejects what Alison Jaggar calls "abstract individualism," i.e., the position that it is possible to identify a human essence or human nature that exists independently of any particular historical context.[29] Humans and human moral conduct are properly understood essentially (and not merely accidentally) in terms of networks or webs of historical and concrete relationships.

All the props are now in place for seeing how ecofeminism provides the framework for a distinctively feminist and environmental ethic. It is a feminism that critiques male bias wherever it occurs in ethics (including environmental ethics) and aims at providing an ethic (including an environmental ethic) which is not male biased—and it does so in a way that satisfies the preliminary boundary conditions of a feminist ethic.

First, ecofeminism is quintessentially anti-naturist. Its anti-naturism consists in the rejection of any way of thinking about or acting toward nonhuman nature that reflects a logic, values, or attitude of domination. Its anti-naturist, anti-sexist, anti-racist, anti-classist (and so forth, for all other "isms" of social domination) stance forms the outer boundary of the quilt: nothing gets on the quilt which is naturist, sexist, racist, classist, and so forth.

Second, ecofeminism is a contextualist ethic. It involves a shift *from* a conception of ethics as primarily a matter of rights, rules, or principles predetermined and applied in specific cases to entities viewed as competitors in the contest of moral standing, *to* a conception of ethics as growing out of what Jim Cheney calls "defining relationships," i.e., relationships conceived in some sense as defining who one is.[30] As a contextualist ethic, it is not that rights, or rules, or principles are *not* relevant or important. Clearly they are in certain contexts and for certain purposes.[31] It is just that what *makes* them relevant or important is that those to whom they apply are entities *in relationship with* others.

Ecofeminism also involves an ethical shift *from* granting moral consideration to nonhumans *exclusively* on the grounds of some similarity they share with humans (e.g., rationality, interests, moral agency, sentiency, right-holder status) *to* "a highly contextual account to see clearly what a human being is and what the nonhuman world might be, morally speaking, *for* human beings."[32] For an ecofeminist, *how* a moral agent is in relationship to another becomes of central significance, not simply *that* a moral agent is a moral agent or is bound by rights, duties, virtue, or utility to act in a certain way.

Third, ecofeminism is structurally pluralistic in that it presupposes and maintains difference—difference among humans as well as between humans and at least some elements of nonhuman nature. Thus, while ecofeminism denies the "nature/culture" split, it affirms that humans are both members of an ecological community (in some respects) and different from it (in other respects). Ecofeminism's attention to relationships and community is not, therefore, an erasure of difference but a respectful acknowledgement of it.

Fourth, ecofeminism reconceives theory as theory in process. It focuses on patterns of meaning which emerge, for instance, from the storytelling and first-person narratives of women (and others) who deplore the twin dominations of women and nature. The use of narrative is one way to ensure that the content of the ethic—the pattern of the quilt—may/will change over time, as the historical and material realities of women's lives change and as more is learned about women-nature connections and the destruction of the nonhuman world.[33]

Fifth, ecofeminism is inclusivist. It emerges from the voices of women who experience the harmful domination of nature and the way that domination is tied to their domination as women. It emerges from listening to the voices of indigenous peoples such as Native Americans who have been dislocated from their land and have witnessed the attendant undermining of such values as appropriate reciprocity, sharing, and kinship that characterize traditional Indian culture. It emerges from listening to voices of those who, like Nathan Hare, critique traditional approaches to environmental ethics as white and bourgeois, and as failing to address issues of "black ecology" and the "ecology" of the inner city and urban spaces.[34] It also emerges out of the voices of Chipko women who see the destruction of "earth, soil, and water" as intimately connected with their own inability to survive economically.[35] With its emphasis on inclusivity and difference, ecofeminism provides a framework for recognizing that what counts as ecology and what counts as appropriate conduct toward both human and nonhuman environments is largely a matter of context.

Sixth, as a feminism, ecofeminism makes no attempt to provide an "objective" point of view. It is a social ecology. It recognizes the twin dominations of women and nature as social problems rooted both in very concrete, historical, socioeconomic circumstances and in oppressive patriarchal conceptual frameworks which maintain and sanction these circumstances.

Seventh, ecofeminism makes a central place for values of care, love, friendship, trust, and appropriate reciprocity—values that presuppose that our relationships to others are central to our understanding of who we are.[36] It thereby gives voice to the sensitivity that in climbing a mountain, one is doing something in relationship with an "other," an "other" whom one can come to care about and treat respectfully.

Lastly, an ecofeminist ethic involves a reconception of what it means to be human, and in what human ethical behavior consists. Ecofeminism denies abstract individualism. Humans are who we are in large part by virtue of the historical and social contexts and the relationships we are in, including our relationships with nonhuman nature. Relationships are not something extrinsic to who we are, not an "add on" feature of human nature; they play an essential role in shaping what it is to be human. Relationships of humans to the nonhuman environment are, in part, constitutive of what it is to be a human.

By making visible the interconnections among the dominations of women and nature, ecofeminism shows that both are feminist issues and that explicit acknowledgement of both is vital to any responsible environmental ethic. Feminism *must* embrace ecological feminism if it is to end the domination of women because the domination of women is tied conceptually and historically to the domination of nature.

A responsible environmental ethic also *must* embrace feminism. Otherwise, even the seemingly most revolutionary, liberational, and holistic ecological ethic will fail to take seriously the interconnected dominations of nature and women that are so much a part of the historical legacy and conceptual framework that sanctions the exploitation of nonhuman nature. Failure to make visible these interconnected, twin dominations results in an inaccurate account of how it is that nature has been and continues to be dominated and exploited and produces an environmental ethic that lacks the depth necessary to be truly *inclusive* of the realities of persons who at least in dominant Western culture have been intimately tied with that exploitation, viz., women. Whatever else can be said in favor of such holistic ethics, a failure to make visible ecofeminist insights into the common denominators of the twin oppressions of women and nature is to perpetuate, rather than overcome, the source of that oppression.

This last point deserves further attention. It may be objected that as long as the end result is "the same"—the development of an environmental ethic which does not emerge out of or reinforce an oppressive conceptual framework—it does not matter whether that ethic (or the ethic endorsed in getting there) is feminist or not. Hence, it simply is *not* the case that any adequate environmental ethic must be feminist. My argument, in contrast, has been that it *does* matter, and for three important reasons. First, there is the scholarly issue of accurately representing historical reality, and that, ecofeminists claim, requires acknowledging the historical feminization of nature and naturalization of women as part of the exploitation of nature. Second, I have shown that the conceptual connections between the domination of women and the domination of nature are located in an oppressive and, at least in Western societies, patriarchal conceptual framework characterized by a logic of domination. Thus, I have shown that failure to notice the nature of this connection leaves at best an incomplete, inaccurate, and partial account of what is required of a conceptually adequate environmental ethic. An ethic which *does not* acknowledge this is simply *not* the same as one that does, whatever else the similarities between them. Third, the claim that, in contemporary culture, one can have an adequate environmental ethic which is *not* feminist assumes that, in contemporary culture, the label *feminist* does not add anything crucial to the nature or description of environmental ethics. I have shown that at least in contemporary culture this is false, for the word *feminist* currently helps to clarify just *how* the domination of nature is conceptually linked to patriarchy and, hence, how the liberation of nature, is conceptually linked to the termination of patriarchy. Thus, because the word 'feminist' has critical bite in contemporary culture, it serves as an important reminder that in contemporary sex-gendered, raced, classed, and naturist culture, an unlabeled position functions as a privileged and "unmarked" position. That is, without the addition of the word *feminist,* one presents environmental ethics as if it has no bias, including male-gender bias, which is just what ecofeminists deny: failure to notice the connections between the twin oppressions of women and nature *is* male-gender bias.

One of the goals of feminism is the eradication of all oppressive sex-gender (and related race, class, age, affectional preference) categories and the creation of a world in which *difference does not breed domination*—say, the world of 4001. If in 4001 an "adequate environmental ethic" is a "feminist environmental ethic," the word *feminist* may then be redundant and unnecessary. However, this is *not* 4001, and in terms of the current historical and conceptual reality the dominations of nature and of women are intimately connected. Failure to notice or make visible that connection in 1990 perpetuates the mistaken (and privileged) view that "environmental ethics" is *not* a feminist issue, and that *feminist* adds nothing to environmental ethics.[37]

CONCLUSION

I have argued in this paper that ecofeminism provides a framework for a distinctively feminist and environmental ethic. Ecofeminism grows out of the felt and theorized about connections between the domination of women and the domination of nature. As a contextualist ethic, ecofeminism refocuses environmental ethics on what nature might mean, morally speaking, *for* humans, and on how the relational attitudes of humans to others—humans as well as nonhumans—sculpt both what it is to be human and the nature and ground of human responsibilities to the nonhuman environment. Part of what this refocusing does is to take seriously the voices of women and other oppressed persons in the construction of that ethic.

A Sioux elder once told me a story about his son. He sent his seven-year-old son to live with the child's grandparents on a Sioux reservation so that he could "learn the Indian ways." Part of what the grandparents taught the son was how to hunt the four leggeds of the forest. As I heard the story, the boy was taught, "to shoot your four-legged brother in his hind area, slowing it down but not killing it. Then, take the four-legged's head in your hands, and look into his eyes. The eyes are where all the suffering is. Look into your brother's eyes and feel his pain. Then, take your knife and cut the four-legged under his chin, here, on his neck, so that he dies quickly. And as you do, ask your brother, the four-legged, for forgiveness for what you do. Offer also a prayer of thanks to your four-legged kin for offering his body to you just now, when you need food to eat and clothing to wear. And promise the four-legged that you will put yourself back into the earth when you die, to become nourishment of the earth, and for the sister flowers, and for the brother deer. It is appropriate that you should offer this blessing for the four-legged and, in due time, reciprocate in turn with your body in this way, as the four-legged gives life to you for your survival." As I reflect upon that story, I am struck by the power of an environmental ethic that grows out of and takes seriously narrative, context, and such values and relational attitudes as care, loving perception, and appropriate reciprocity, and doing what is appropriate in a given situation—however that notion of appropriateness eventually gets filled out. I am also struck by what one is able to see, once one begins to explore some of the historical and conceptual connections between the dominations of women and of nature. A *re-conceiving* and *re-visioning* of both feminism and environmental ethics, is, I think, the power and promise of ecofeminism.

NOTES

1. Explicit ecological feminist literature includes works from a variety of scholarly perspectives and sources. Some of these works are Jim Cheney, "Eco-Feminism and Deep Ecology," *Environmental Ethics* 9 (1987): 115–45; Katherine Davies, "Historical Associations: Women and the Natural World," *Women & Environments* 9, no. 2 (Spring 1987): 4–6; Sharon Doubiago, "Deeper than Deep Ecology: Men Must Become Feminists," in *The New Catalyst Quarterly*, no. 10 (Winter 1987/88): 10–11; Brian Easlea, *Science and Sexual Oppression: Patriarchy's Confrontation with Women and Nature* (London: Weidenfeld & Nicholson, 1981); Ynestra King, "Feminism and the Revolt of Nature," in *Heresies #13: Feminism and Ecology* 4, no. 1 (1981): Greater King 12–16, and "What is Ecofeminism?" *The Nation*, 12 December 1987; Abby Peterson and Carolyn Merchant, "Peace with the Earth: Women and the Environmental Movement in Sweden," *Women's Studies International Forum* 9, no. 5–6. (1986): 465–79; Judith Plant, ed., *Healing Our Wounds: The Power of Ecological Feminism* (Boston: New Society Publishers, 1989); Kirkpatrick Sale, "Ecofeminism—A New Perspective," *The Nation*, 26 September 1987): 302–05; Ariel Kay Salleh, "Deeper than Deep Ecology: The Eco-Feminist Connection," *Environmental Ethics* 6 (1984): 339–45, and "Epistemology and the Metaphors of Production: An Eco-Feminist Reading of Critical Theory," in *Studies in the Humanities* 15 (1988): 130–39; Karen J. Warren, "Feminism and Ecology: Making Connections," *Environmental Ethics* 9 (1987): 3–21; Miriam Wyman, "Explorations of Eco-Feminism," *Women & Environments* (Spring 1987): 6–7; Iris Young, " 'Feminism and Ecology' and 'Women and Life on Earth: Eco-Feminism in the 80's'," *Environmental Ethics* 5 (1983): 173–80.
2. Francoise d'Eaubonne, *Le Feminisme ou la Mort* (Paris: Pierre Horay, 1974), pp. 213–52.
3. I discuss this in my paper, "Toward an Ecofeminist Ethic."
4. The account offered here is a revision of the account given earlier in my paper "Feminism and Ecology: Making Connections." I have changed the account to be about "oppressive" rather than strictly "patriarchal" conceptual frameworks in order to leave open the possibility that there may be some patriarchal conceptual frameworks (e.g., in non-Western cultures) which are *not* properly characterized as based on value dualisms.
5. Murray Bookchin, "Social Ecology versus 'Deep Ecology'," in *Green Perspectives: Newsletter of the Green Program Project*, no. 4–5 (Summer 1987): 9.
6. It may be that in contemporary Western society, which is so thoroughly structured by categories of gender, race, class, age, and affectional orientation, that there simply is no meaningful notion of "value-hierarchical thinking" which does not function in an oppressive context. For purposes of this paper, I leave that question open.
7. Many feminists who argue for the historical point that claims (B1) and (B2) have been asserted or assumed to be true within the dominant Western philosophical tradition do so by discussion of that tradition's conceptions of reason, rationality, and science. For a sampling of the sorts of claims made within that context, see "Reason, Rationality, and Gender," ed. Nancy Tuana and Karen J. Warren, a special issue of the American Philosophical Association's *Newsletter on Feminism and Philosophy* 88, no. 2 (March 1989): 17–71. Ecofeminists who claim that (B2) has been assumed to be true within

the dominant Western philosophical tradition include: Gray, *Green Paradise Lost*; Griffin, *Woman and Nature*; Merchant, *The Death of Nature*; Ruether, *New Woman/New Earth*. For a discussion of some of these ecofeminist historical accounts, see Plumwood, "Ecofeminism." While I agree that the historical connections between the domination of women and the domination of nature is a crucial one, I do not argue for that claim here.

8. Ecofeminists who deny (B1) when (B1) is offered as anything other than a true, descriptive, historical claim about patriarchal culture often do so on grounds that an objectionable sort of biological determinism, or at least harmful female sex-gender stereotypes, underlie (B1). For a discussion of this "split" among those ecofeminists ("nature feminists") who assert and those ecofeminists ("social feminists") who deny (B1) as anything other than a true historical claim about how women are described in patriarchal culture, see Griscom, "On Healing the Nature/History Split."

9. I make no attempt here to defend the historically sanctioned truth of these premises.

10. See, e.g., Bell Hooks, *Feminist Theory: From Margin to Center* (Boston: South End Press, 1984), pp. 51–52.

11. Maria Lugones, "Playfulness, 'World-Travelling,' and Loving Perception," *Hypatia* 2, no. 2 (Summer 1987): 3.

12. At an *experiential* level, some women are "women of color," poor, old, lesbian, Jewish, and physically challenged. Thus, if feminism is going to liberate these women, it also needs to end the racism, classism, heterosexism, anti-Semitism, and discrimination against the handicapped that is constitutive of their oppression as black, or Latina, or poor, or older, or lesbian, or Jewish, or physically challenged women.

13. This same sort of reasoning shows that feminism is also a movement to end racism, classism, age-ism, heterosexism and other "isms," which are based in oppressive conceptual frameworks characterized by a logic of domination. However, there is an important caveat: ecofeminism is *not* compatible with all feminisms and all environmentalisms. For a discussion of this point, see my article, "Feminism and Ecology: Making Connections." What it *is* compatible with is the minimal condition characterization of feminism as a movement to end sexism that is accepted by all contemporary feminisms (liberal, traditional Marxist, radical, socialist, Blacks and non-Western).

14. See, e.g., Gray, *Green Paradise Lost;* Griffin, *Women and Nature;* Merchant, *The Death of Nature;* and Ruether, *New Woman/New Earth.*

15. Suppose, as I think is the case, that a necessary condition for the existence of a moral relationship is that at least one party to the relationship is a moral being (leaving open for our purposes what counts as a "moral being"). If this is so, then the Mona Lisa cannot properly be said to have or stand in a moral relationship with the wall on which she hangs, and a wolf cannot have or properly be said to have or stand in a moral relationship with a moose. Such a necessary-condition account leaves open the question whether *both* parties to the relationship must be moral beings. My point here is simply that however one resolves *that* question, recognition of the relationships themselves as a locus of value is a recognition of a source of value that is different from and not reducible to the values of the "moral beings" in those relationships.

16. It is interesting to note that the image of being friends with the Earth is one which cytogeneticist Barbara McClintock uses when she describes the import-

ance of having "a feeling for the organism," "listening to the material [in this case the corn plant]," in one's work as a scientist. See Evelyn Fox Keller, "Women, Science, and Popular Mythology," in *Machina Ex Dea: Feminist Perspectives on Technology,* ed. Joan Rothschild (New York: Pergamon Press, 1983), and Evelyn Fox Keller. *A Feeling For the Organism: The Life and Work of Barbara McClintock* (San Francisco: W. H. Freeman, 1983).

17. Cheney, "Eco-Feminism and Deep Ecology," 144.
18. Marilyn Frye, "In and Out of Harm's Way: Arrogance and Love," *The Politics of Reality* (Trumansburg, New York: The Crossing Press, 1983), pp. 66–72.
19. Ibid., pp. 75–76.
20. Maria Lugones, "Playfulness," p. 3.
21. Cheney makes a similar point in "Eco-Feminism and Deep Ecology," p. 140.
22. Ibid., p. 138.
23. This account of a feminist ethic draws on my paper "Toward an Ecofeminist Ethic."
24. Marilyn Frye makes this point in her illuminating paper, "The Possibility of Feminist Theory," read at the American Philosophical Association Central Division Meetings in Chicago, 29 April–1 May 1986. My discussion of feminist theory is inspired largely by that paper and by Kathryn Addelson's paper "Moral Revolution," in *Women and Values: Reading in Recent Feminist Philosophy,* ed. Marilyn Pearsall (Belmont, Calif.: Wadsworth Publishing Co., 1986) pp. 291–309.
25. Notice that the standard of inclusiveness does not exclude the voices of men. It is just that those voices must cohere with the voices of women.
26. For a more in-depth discussion of the notions of impartiality and bias, see my paper, "Critical Thinking and Feminism," *Informal Logic* 10, no. 1 (Winter 1988): 31–44.
27. The burgeoning literature on these values is noteworthy. See, e.g., Carol Gilligan, *In a Different Voice: Psychological Theories and Women's Development* (Cambridge: Harvard University Press, 1982); *Mapping the Moral Domain: A Contribution of Women's Thinking to Psychological Theory and Education,* ed. Carol Gilligan, Janie Victoria Ward, and Jill McLean Taylor, with Betty Bardige (Cambridge: Harvard University Press, 1988); Nel Noddings, *Caring: A Feminine Approach to Ethics and Moral Education* (Berkeley: University of California Press, 1984); Maria Lugones and Elizabeth V. Spelman, "Have We Got a Theory for You! Feminist Theory, Cultural Imperialism, and the Women's Voice," *Women's Studies International Forum* 6 (1983): 573–81; Maria Lugones, "Playfulness"; Annette C. Baier, "What Do Women Want In A Moral Theory?" *Nous* 19 (1985): 53–63.
28. Jim Cheney would claim that our fundamental relationships to one another as moral agents are not as moral agents to rights holders, and that whatever rights a person properly may be said to have are relationally defined rights, not rights possessed by atomistic individuals conceived as Robinson Crusoes who do not exist essentially in relation to others. On this view, even rights talk itself is properly conceived as growing out of a relational ethic, not vice versa.
29. Alison Jaggar, *Feminist Politics and Human Nature* (Totowa, N.J.: Rowman and Allanheld, 1980), pp. 42–44.
30. Henry West has pointed out that the expression "defining relations" is ambiguous. According to West, "the "defining" as Cheney uses it is an adjective, not a principle—it is not that ethics defines relationships; it is that

ethics grows out of conceiving of the relationships that one is in as defining what the individual is.

31. For example, in relationships involving contracts or promises, those relationships might be correctly described as that of moral agent to rights holders. In relationships involving mere property, those relationships might be correctly described as that of moral agent to objects having only instrumental value, "relationships of instrumentality." In comments on an earlier draft of this paper, West suggested that possessive individualism, for instance, might be recast in such a way that an individual is defined by his or her property relationships.

32. Cheney, "Eco-Feminism and Deep Ecology," p. 144.

33. One might object that such permission for change opens the door for environmental exploitation. This is not the case. An ecofeminist ethic is anti-naturist. Hence, the unjust domination and exploitation of nature is a "boundary condition" of the ethic; no such actions are sanctioned or justified on ecofeminist grounds. What it *does* leave open is some leeway about what counts as domination and exploitation. This, I think, is a strength of the ethic, not a weakness, since it acknowledges that *that* issue cannot be resolved in any practical way in the abstract, independent of a historical and social context.

34. Nathan Hare, "Black Ecology," in *Environmental Ethics,* ed. K. S. Shrader-Frechette (Pacific Grove, Calif.: Boxwood Press, 1981), pp. 229–36.

35. For an ecofeminist discussion of the Chipko movement, see my "Toward an Ecofeminist Ethic," and Shiva's *Staying Alive.*

36. See Cheney, "Eco-Feminism and Deep Ecology," p. 122.

37. I offer the same sort of reply to critics of ecofeminism such as Warwick Fox who suggest that for the sort of ecofeminism I defend, the word *feminist* does not add anything significant to environmental ethics and, consequently, that an ecofeminist like myself might as well call herself a deep ecologist. He asks: "Why doesn't she just call it [i.e., Warren's vision of a transformative feminism] deep ecology? Why specifically attach the label *feminist* to it. . .?" (Warwick Fox, "The Deep Ecology-Ecofeminism Debate and Its Parallels," *Environmental Ethics* 11, no. 1 [1989]: 14, n. 22). Whatever the important similarities between deep ecology and ecofeminism (or, specifically, my version of ecofeminism)—and, indeed, there are many—it is precisely my point here that the word *feminist* does add something significant to the conception of environmental ethics, and that any environmental ethic (including deep ecology) that fails to make explicit the different kinds of interconnections among the domination of nature and the domination of women will be, from a feminist (and ecofeminist) perspective such as mine, inadequate.

PART FOUR

Social Ecology

Introduction

John Clark

John Clark is professor of philosophy at Loyola University in New Orleans. He is the author of several books, including The Anarchist Moment: Reflections on Culture, Nature and Power, *and is editor of* Renewing the Earth: The Promise of Social Ecology. *He also edits* Mesachabe: The Journal of Surre(gion)alism.

Social ecology, a form of dialectical naturalism, is the most extensively developed ecophilosophy yet to appear.[1] It is dialectical because it sees all of reality as being in a continual process of self-development and self-transformation, and because it interprets phenomena in terms of their mutual determination as inseparable parts of larger wholes. It is a naturalism because it takes reality to be nature, and sees all beings as natural beings. It takes as its ontological and epistemological starting point our perspective as nature knowing itself, or "nature rendered self-conscious."

In affirming such a dialectical naturalism, it rejects both the social divisions and the dualistic ideologies that have been central to the long history of domination of both humanity and nature. In opposition to the dualism of hierarchical society, it proposes a principle of ecological wholeness that sees the entire course of planetary evolution as a process aiming at increasing diversity and the emergence of value. Social ecology thus forms part of a long teleological tradition extending from the ancient Greeks to the most recent organicist and process philosophies. Bookchin (who has brilliantly developed the principles of social ecology in writings spanning the past forty years) avoids the term "teleology" because of its deterministic connotations, and its usual association with a hierarchical worldview. Yet, what is affirmed is that the entire process of development of life and mind has "directiveness," and is a movement toward the greater unfolding of value. There is a tendency (or *nisus*) within substance toward life, consciousness, and self-consciousness.

The evolutionary view presented is above all a *developmental* one. For Bookchin, as for Hegel and other dialectical thinkers before him, there is an important sense in which each phenomenon consists of its own history. Each stage of evolution is seen as "grading" into the next, and each successive level as including within it all that has proceeded it. "Mind" and "body" are thus seen as mutually developing at every level of evolution, so that each human being incorporates within him or herself the entire history of mind and body. For a dialectical naturalism, mind, like all phenomena, must be understood as rooted in nature and in history.

Social ecology takes the major obstacle to social and natural evolution to be the long history of human attempts to dominate others and to conquer even nature itself. One of the most distinctive theories advanced by Bookchin is his view that the human urge to dominate nature (a futile, but nonetheless powerful impulse) results above all from human domination of other humans. He traces the roots of domination to a long history of hierarchy, beginning with the domination of the young by the old, of women by men, and of early communities by military, patriarchal and religious elites. To the Marxist and traditional leftist focus on economic exploitation as the source of all evils, he conterposes a highly elaborated analysis of a complex system of hierarchy and domination. Other social ecologists (including several represented here) have focused more particularly on the importance of such factors as the commodification of reality in an economistic society, the pervasiveness of the historical legacy of patriarchal-authoritarian values, and even the significance of fundamental ontological realities inherent in the human condition.

Some critics have contended that since social ecology often stresses the social roots of the ecological crisis that it should be equated with opposition to social domination. It is thus thought to simplistically claim that "domination of nature" will end when social domination and hierarchy are abolished. Such a critique shows a lack of understanding of the dialectical approach that social ecology (at least when it is consistent) exemplifies. As a dialectical naturalism, it refuses to separate human society from nature. It holds, instead, that we *are* nature, that our interaction with one another is interaction within nature, and that our interaction with the rest of nature is continuous with our interaction with one another. Social ecology focuses on the complex dialectic between these various realms of interaction *within* nature (that is, within these inseparably interrelated natural regions). If and when human society is transformed by ecological consciousness and practice, humanity's interaction with the rest of nature will at the same time be transformed ("immediately," though through numerous social, cultural, imaginary, and spiritual *mediations*). Ecological consciousness and practice requires that humanity think and act as "nature rendered self-conscious." This means that we think as self-conscious energy, self-conscious life, self-conscious animal, self-conscious earth. As we do this, as we re-form ourselves into true members of this "earth household," we begin to abjure our quest for domination of one another and for conquest of nature. It is not that social hierarchy is "prior" to the exploitation of nature, or that ideologies of domination are somehow "prior" to anthropocentrism. This is a false problematic. The roots of ecological crisis are at once institutional and ideological, psychological and cultural. The solution must avoid both one-sided materialist explanations (identifying economic exploitation or other "material conditions" as "the problem") and one-sided idealism (identifying a system of ideas like anthropocentrism as "the problem.")

Bookchin gives us reason to hope for the possibility of such a solution. He counterposes to the long history of domination and hierarchy a submerged and often forgotten "history of freedom" that serves to inspire his utopian vision. He discovers—in the democratic Greek *polis,* in radical heretical and millenarian movements, and in modern revolutionary movements in their most anti-authoritarian moments—the "forms of freedom" that can give direction to a liberatory future. In pursuing such liberation, social ecology proposes the most positive conception of freedom. "Freedom" signifies not the mere "being left alone," of the liberal tradition, but rather *self-determination* in the richest sense. As such, it is found to some degree at all levels of being: from the self-organizing and self-stabilizing tendencies of the atom to the level of the entire universe as a vast sphere of evolutionary development. Latent freedom can be found in the directiveness of all life, and reaches its richest development on this planet in the human potentiality for self-consciousness and self-determination. As nature achieves its most developed self-expression on earth in a free human community in harmony with the rest of the natural world, what was seen as "blind" nature can finally become "free nature."

Social ecology interprets this planetary evolution and unfolding as a holistic process, rather than merely as a mechanism of adaptation. It sees evolution, not simply as a process of adaptation by individual organisms, or even by species, but also as a process that can only be understood by examining the interaction between species and by studying "ecosystems" as complex, developing wholes. Such an examination reveals that the progressive unfolding of the potentiality for freedom (as self-determination and self-directed activity) depends on the existence of symbiotic cooperation at all levels—as Kropotkin pointed out almost a century ago. We can therefore see a striking degree of continuity in nature, so that the free, mutualistic society that is the goal of social ecology is found to be rooted in the most basic levels of being.

Social ecology's holistic, developmental understanding of organic wholes and their evolution has enormous importance for ethics and politics. If the place of humanity in natural evolution and natural processes is understood, we can begin see our own experience of valuing and seeking the good as part of the vast process of the emergence and development of value in nature and human society. Social ecology looks upon the earth as a whole of which all beings are parts, and a community of which all are members. The common planetary good can only be conceptualized in a nonreductionist, holistic, and developmental manner.

A dialectical and holistic theory will go beyond the categories of any atomistic theory of value, yet without dissolving particular beings—and most notably, human beings—into the whole, whether of nature or the biosphere. Rolston's analysis of value is extremely complementary to social ecology here. One of his most important contributions to the development of an ecophilosophy is his challenging of the division of value into the categories of intrinsic and instrumental (or some variation on these terms). When value is generated in a system (or, as social ecology would state it, within a *whole* that is not reduceable to a mere sum of parts), we find that it is not generated in an "instrumental" form, for there is no specific entity or entities for the good of which the value is generated as a means, nor do we find "intrinsic" value in the sense that there is a single coherent, definable good or *telos* for the system. Thus we must posit something like what Rolston calls "systemic value." According to this conception, the value that exists within the system "is not just the sum of the part-values. No part values increase of kinds, but the system promotes such increase. Systemic value is the productive process; its products are intrinsic values woven into instrumental relationships."[2]

This analysis points the way toward the authentically ecological understanding of the value of ecosystems or ecocommunities that is sought by social ecology. For Rolston, the "species-environment complex ought to be preserved because it is the generative context of value."[3] Even this formulation is not fully ecological, since it still seems to rest on the idea of an environment that a species "has." But it points out that the ecosystem (that is, the ecocommunity from which the species cannot be separated and which has shaped its nature) is a value-generating whole. Ultimately, the earth must be comprehended as, for us, the most morally significant value-generating whole. We must fully grasp the conception of a planetary good realizing itself through the simultaneous attainment of good by all the beings that constitute that whole.

A fundamental question is the place of humanity in attaining this good. For social ecology, our ecological responsibility as inhabitants of the earth cannot merely be to reverse the damage we have already done, and to refrain from future damage—as some ecological thinkers would suggest. Rather, humanity's role in nature results from its inextricable interrelationship to the biospheric whole, and from its character as the most richly developed realm of being to emerge thus far in the earth's evolutionary self-realization. We cooperate with natural evolution through our own self-development. In accepting the responsibilities implied by our being "nature rendered self-conscious," we can begin to reverse our presently anti-evolutionary and ecocidal direction, and begin to contribute to the continuation of planetary natural and social evolution.

Success in this endeavor requires that a new ecological sensibility pervade all aspects of our social existence. This sensibility will consist of a nondominating, nonhierarchical outlook toward other beings and toward nature. What Bookchin has called "the epistemology of rule" is thus replaced by a perspective that he has likened to "a new animism." This outlook recognizes a pervasive and ever-developing subjectivity through-out nature that is latent even within matter/energy itself, and which reaches its fully developed form in human intellect and creativity acting on behalf of life and evolution. As we attain such a new ecological sensibility, the mutualism found throughout nature attains its most advanced develop-ment in humanity's mutualistic system of values and perceptions embodied in an ecological society.

Thus, ecological regeneration is inseparable from social regeneration. Consequently, social ecology calls for the creation of ecocommunities and ecotechnologies that establish a creative interaction between humanity and nonhuman nature, and which reverse the present destructive course. Such communities will be a carefully integrated part of their larger natural envi-ronments (which are themselves natural "ecocommunities") and will prac-tice true "economy," the careful attending to and application of "the rules of the household." The extent to which human activity can have a desirable impact on the the earth can only be decided through careful determination of our abilities to act on behalf of nature (including a humbling realization of our vast ignorance in the face of nature's overwhelming complexity), and of the detrimental effects of our disturbances of natural balances.

Social ecology argues that these goals require a radical rethinking of the political. Technobureaucratic state power and capitalist economic power must be replaced by an organic community regulated through common ecological values and a commitment to a common life. The "post-scarcity" society advocated by Bookchin does not transcend the "realm of necessity" through vastly increased production (as Marx advo-cated) or by increased consumption of commodities (as capitalism prom-ises). Rather, future ecocommunities are to achieve abundance through a critical analysis and reshaping of their systems of needs (thus overcoming our present "fetishism of needs"). An ecocommunity can be expected to reject the consumption for its own sake typical of capitalist mass society, while multiplying the true social wealth of the community, in such forms as aesthetically pleasing surroundings, edifying work, creative play, ful-filling interpersonal relationships, and the appreciation of nonhuman nature.

The social forms that will emerge from such a culture will themselves embody the ecological ideal of unity-in-diversity. Bookchin—like Kropot-

kin, Landauer, Buber, and others before him in the libertarian communitarian tradition—proposes as the fundamental social unit in the ecological
society the "commune" or basic community. His approach is authentically
communitarian, in that it sees this level of community, in which humans
can develop fully as social beings, as the most essential social, political,
and, indeed, ethical sphere. While Bookchin's ecological anarchism is a
scathing critique of all conventional politics, it is also a heroic effort to
regain the political in its deepest sense, to re-create an authentic public
space, and to recover our long-obscured nature as *politikon zoon.*

Within an ecocommunity, cooperative institutions in all areas of
social life will begin to emerge. These will include mutualistic associations
for child care and education, for production and distribution, for cultural
creation, for play and enjoyment, for reflection and spiritual renewal.
Organization in an ecocommunity is based, not on the demands of power,
as is inevitable under capitalist and statist institutions, but rather on the
requirements for people's self-realization as free social beings, and for a
nondominating human interaction with the whole of nature. Such a conception of the political requires that institutions be humanly scaled, decentralized, nonhierarchical, and based on face-to-face democracy.

Bookchin argues that a political form that is of crucial importance is
the town or neighborhood assembly. This assembly gives the citizenry an
arena in which to publicly formulate its needs and aspirations. It creates a
sphere in which true citizenship can be developed and exercised in
practice. The community assembly creates a forum through which a highly
valued multiplicity and diversity can be unified and coordinated, and it
thus allows each citizen to conceive vividly of the good of the whole
community. The long-term goal is the replacement of hierarchical capitalist
and statist organization by a confederation of ecological communities—in
short, by true ecological democracy.

Basic to social ecology's vision of a redeemed history and a transformed humanity is the category of *spirit.* While the issue of "spirituality"
is often mentioned in ecological discussions, Kovel is right in directing our
attention to the more fundamental concept of "spirit." Spirit is never far
from the surface in Bookchin's works. World history as it appears in his
classic work *The Ecology of Freedom* follows a familiar theme. Humanity
falls from its primordial unity with nature in "organic society," it suffers
through its long struggle, "the history of freedom," while in bondage during
the "history of domination," finally to regain its lost unity—at a higher
level—with the achievement of "the ecological society." It is a story with
roots far back in Western thought (not to mention its obvious connections
with non-Western myths and philosophies): in the Judeo-Christian story of
the Fall and Redemption, in Hegel's account of Absolute Spirit's self-alien-
ation and self-reconciliation, in Marx's depiction of humanity's enslavement to the realm of necessity and its striving toward the realm of freedom

(a story that I analyze—from the standpoint of social ecology—in "Marx's Inorganic Body," below).

"Spirit" for social ecology signifies our immersion in the movement of reality toward unfolding.[5] Spirit signifies life, growth, development, the striving toward wholeness—realized unity-in-diversity. Though the connection with Hegel's concept of *Geist* is obvious, there are explicit roots in Bookchin's own communitarian anarchist and utopian tradition. For the great communitarian Gustav Landauer, "spirit" was the most fundamental category, and indicated indeed the spirit of creation and growth. "The spirit that impels us," he says, "is a quintessence of life and it creates effective reality."[6] Landauer's word for antithesis of spirit, for the forces of domination, hierarchy, and all the enslaving and destructive impulses is not surprising. "Where spirit is, there is society. Where unspirit is, there is the state. The state is the surrogate for spirit."[7] Landauer was an authentic social ecologist when he argued that "the true society is a multiplicity of real, small affinities that grow out of the binding qualities of individuals, out of the spirit, a structure of communities, and a union."[8]

A necessary condition for the success of this project of social and spiritual regeneration is the liberation of the imagination. Bookchin has rightly said that the creation of an ecological community must be "a work of art." He has also stressed the importance of great visionaries like Fourier, Morris, and the surrealists, who expressed desire and the imagination in their most radical and creative forms. One of the greatest insights of social ecology is its comprehension that the flowering of the human spirit and personality is a continuation of natural evolution. Liberation of the human imagination from the deadening effects of mechanization and commodification is one of the most pressing ecological issues. It is therefore fitting that Kovel nominates William Blake to be the poet of social ecology (though the competition, from Heraclitus and Lao Tzu on, has been stiff!). To quote Landauer again, "we are poets" who desire that "poetic vision, artistically concentrated creativity, enthusiasm, and prophecy will find their place to act, work and build from now on; in life, with human bodies, for the harmonious life, work and solidarity of groups, communities and nations."[9]

Bookchin has often emphasized the fact that liberatory social transformation depends on renewal at the most personal level: that of the self. As he has formulated it, social ecology sees the self as a harmonious synthesis of "reason, passion, and imagination." It affirms an ideal of a many-sided self, in which diverse aspects are not repressed, but rather attain a mutually compatible development. The self is seen as an organic whole, yet as a whole in constant process of self-transformation and self-transcendence. On the one hand, there is a respect for the uniqueness of each person, and a recognition of individuality: the striving of each toward a good that flows from his or her own nature. But self-realization is incomprehensible apart from one's dialectical interaction with other persons, with the community, and with the whole of the natural world. The goal is thus the similtaneous unfolding of both individuality and social being. The replacement of the "hollowed-out" ego of consumer society with such a richly developed selfhood is one of the preeminent goals of social ecology.

Yet inspiring as this goal may be, there remain many areas for development of the social-ecological conception of the self. As Kovel points out, the realm of signification creates an imaginary sphere in which there is a necessary degree of alienation from nature, and even from oneself as nature. A related problem stems from the fact that the "thinglike" aspects of the self—the realm of the preconceptual and of the most primordial layers of desire—can never be fully transcended in either thought or experience. Part of social ecology's project of comprehending "unity-in-diversity" is to adequately theorize this duality and alienation within a nondualistic, naturalistic framework.

In doing so, social ecology will delve more deeply into those inseparable dimensions of body and mind that dualism has so fatefully divided. As we explore such realities as thought, idea, image, sign, symbol, signifier, and language, on the one hand, and feeling, emotion, disposition, instinct, passion, and desire on the other, the interconnection between the two "realms" will become increasingly apparent. Not surprisingly, the poet can once again give direction to our philosophical inquiries. A great contemporary poet of the social and the ecological, Gary Snyder, expresses well the dialectical relationship between the absolutely strange realm of culture and language, and the organic, biological matrix out of which—and within which—it arises. "Language and culture emerge from our biological-social natural existence, animals that we were/are. Language is a mind-body system that coevolved with our needs and nerves. Like imagination and the body, language rises unbidden."[10]

The project of a dialectical naturalism is the investigation of the ways of nature, and, above all, of the ways in which we are nature. While Bookchin has described humanity as "the very knowingness of nature," social ecology also shows that we "know" not only through thought narrowly conceived but through many modes of our being. Bookchin has rightly pointed us toward the "wisdom of the body" and "the wisdom of the cell." Social ecology directs us to a more profound inquiry into the nature of our embodiedness—as thinking, feeling humans, and as thinking, feeling earth. It directs us to the dialectic of being in its many dimensions. To the erotics of reason. To the logic of the passions. To the politics of the imagination.

In doing so, it seeks to regenerate the self, to regenerate human community, and to regenerate the larger community of earth.

The works selected for this section are chosen to reflect the depth and comprehensiveness of social ecology. Bookchin's "What Is Social Ecology?" is an original essay written for this collection, and summarizes the author's extensive work on topics like the place of humanity in nature and evolution, the history of hierarchy and domination, the social roots of the ecological crisis, and the nature of an ecological society. Janet Biehl's "Dialectics in the Ethics of Social Ecology" focuses more specifically on the concept of dialectic and its significance for social ecology's developmental view of human and natural history. It is taken from a larger work showing the relevance of social ecology to feminist thought. My essay "Marx's Inorganic Body" illustrates one aspect of social ecology's relation to the tradition of Western thought. I attempt to show that while an implicit ecological dialectic is found in Marx, he is also a brilliant representative of the tradition of domination that social ecology seeks to overcome. Joel Kovel's "The Marriage of Radical Ecologies" was also written for this volume, and poses certain crucial questions about human nature, transcendence and otherness. Perhaps most important, it raises the issue of the ambiguous human condition of being embedded in nature and at the same time creator of a cultural and symbolic world. Finally, George Bradford, in "Toward a Deep Social Ecology" seeks to find some common ground in the projects of deep ecology and social ecology. However, his major themes are the importance of understanding the social roots of the ecological crisis in specific historical institutions (which he epitomizes as "the Megamachine") and the possibilities for a noneconomistic, noninstrumentalist, and ecological conception of reality.

NOTES

1. Some of the material in this discussion appeared in "What Is Social Ecology?" in John P. Clark, ed., *Renewing the Earth: The Promise of Social Ecology* (London: Green Print, 1990).
2. Holmes Rolston, III, *Environmental Ethics: Duties to and Values in the Natural World* (Philadelphia: Temple University Press, 1988), p. 188.
3. Ibid., p. 154.
4. *The Ecology of Freedom: The Emergence and Dissolution of Hierarchy* (Palo Alto: Cheshire Books, 1982; revised edition, Montreal: Black Rose Books, 1990).
5. For extensive discussion of the idea of spirit and its relevance to all the issues with which social ecology is concerned, see Joel Kovel, *History and Spirit: An Inquiry into the Philosophhy of Liberation* (Boston: Beacon Press, 1991).
6. Gustav Landauer, *For Socialism* (St. Louis: Telos Press, 1978), p. 55.
7. Ibid., p. 42.
8. Ibid., p. 72.
9. Ibid., p. 54
10. Gary Snyder, *The Practice of the Wild* (San Francisco: North Point Press, 1990), p. 17.

What Is Social Ecology?

Murray Bookchin

Murray Bookchin has long been a major figure in anarchist and utopian political theory, theory of technology, urbanism, and the philosophy of nature. He is the cofounder and director emeritus of the Institute for Social Ecology. His many books include Toward an Ecological Society, The Ecology of Freedom, The Rise of Urbanization and the Decline of Citizenship, Remaking Society, *and* The Philosophy of Social Ecology.

What literally defines social ecology as "social" is its recognition of the often overlooked fact that nearly all our present ecological problems arise from deep-seated social problems. Conversely, present ecological problems cannot be clearly understood, much less resolved, without resolutely dealing with problems within society. To make this point more concrete: economic, ethnic, cultural, and gender conflicts, among many others, lie at the core of the most serious ecological dislocations we face today—apart, to be sure, from those that are produced by natural catastrophes.

If this approach seems a bit too "sociological" for those environmentalists who identify ecological problems with the preservation of wildlife, wilderness, or more broadly, with "Gaia" and planetary "Oneness," it might be sobering to consider certain recent facts. The massive oil spill by an Exxon tanker at Prince William Sound, the extensive deforestation of redwood trees by the Maxxam Corporation, and the proposed James Bay hydroelectric project that would flood vast areas of northern Quebec's forests, to cite only a few problems, should remind us that the real battleground on which the ecological future of the planet will be decided is clearly a social one.

Indeed, to separate ecological problems from social problems—or even to play down or give token recognition to this crucial relationship— would be to grossly misconstrue the sources of the growing environmental crisis. The way human beings deal with each other as social beings is crucial to addressing the ecological crisis. Unless we clearly recognize this, we will surely fail to see that the hierarchical mentality and class relationships that so thoroughly permeate society give rise to the very idea of dominating the natural world.

Unless we realize that the present market society, structured around the brutally competitive imperative of "grow or die," is a thoroughly impersonal, self-operating mechanism, we will falsely tend to blame technology as such or population growth as such for environmental problems. We will ignore their root causes, such as trade for profit, industrial expansion, and the identification of "progress" with corporate self-interest. In short, we will tend to focus on the symptoms of a grim social pathology rather than on the pathology itself, and our efforts will be directed toward limited goals whose attainment is more cosmetic than curative.

While some have questioned whether social ecology has dealt adequately with issues of spirituality, it was, in fact, among the earliest of contemporary ecologies to call for a sweeping change in existing spiritual values. Such a change would mean a far-reaching transformation of our prevailing mentality of domination into one of complementarity, in which we would see our role in the natural world as creative, supportive, and deeply appreciative of the needs of nonhuman life. In social ecology, a truly *natural* spirituality centers on the ability of an awakened humanity to function as moral agents in diminishing needless suffering, engaging in ecological restoration, and fostering an aesthetic appreciation of natural evolution in all its fecundity and diversity.

Thus social ecology has never eschewed the need for a radically new spirituality or mentality in its call for a collective effort to change society. Indeed, as early as 1965, the first public statement to advance the ideas of social ecology concluded with the injunction: "The cast of mind that today organizes differences among human and other life-forms along hierarchical lines of 'supremacy' or 'inferiority' will give way to an outlook that deals with diversity in an ecological manner—that is, according to an ethics of complementarity."[1] In such an ethics, human beings would complement nonhuman beings with their own capacities to produce a richer, creative, and developmental whole—not as a "dominant" species but as a supportive one. Although this idea, expressed at times as an appeal for the "respiritization of the natural world," recurs throughout the literature of social ecology, it should not be mistaken for a theology that raises a deity above the natural world or that seeks to discover one within it. The spirituality advanced by social ecology is definitively naturalistic (as one would expect, given its relation to ecology itself, which stems from the biological sciences), rather than supernaturalistic or pantheistic.

To prioritize any form of spirituality over the social factors that actually erode all forms of spirituality, raises serious questions about one's ability to come to grips with reality. At a time when a blind social mechanism, the market, is turning soil into sand, covering fertile land with concrete, poisoning air and water, and producing sweeping climatic and atmospheric changes, we cannot ignore the impact that a hierarchical and class society has on the natural world. We must earnestly deal with the fact that economic growth, gender oppressions, and ethnic domination—not to speak of corporate, state, and bureaucratic interests—are much more capable of shaping the future of the natural world than are privatistic forms of spiritual self-regeneration. These forms of domination must be confronted by collective action and major social movements that challenge the social sources of the ecological crisis, not simply by personalistic forms of consumption and investment that often go under the rubric of "green capitalism." We live in a highly cooptative society that is only too eager to find new areas of commercial aggrandizement and to add ecological verbiage to its advertising and customer relations.

NATURE AND SOCIETY

Let us begin, then, with basics—namely, by asking what we mean by nature and society. Among the many definitions of nature that have been formulated over time, one is rather elusive and often difficult to grasp because it requires a certain way of thinking—one that stands at odds with what we popularly call "linear thinking." This form of "nonlinear" or organic thinking is developmental rather than analytical, or, in more technical terms, dialectical rather than instrumental. Nature, conceived in terms of developmental thinking, is more than the beautiful vistas we see from a mountaintop or in the images that are fixed on the backs of picture postcards. Such vistas and images of nonhuman nature are basically static and immobile. Our attention, to be sure, may be arrested by the soaring flight of a hawk, or the bolting leap of a deer, or the low-slung shadowy loping of a coyote. But what we are really witnessing in such cases are the mere kinetics of physical motion, caught in the frame of an essentially static image of the scene before our eyes. It deceives us into believing in the "eternality" of a single moment in nature.

If we look with some care into nonhuman nature as more than a scenic view, we begin to sense that it is basically an evolving phenomenon, a richly fecund, even dramatic development that is forever changing. I mean to define nonhuman nature precisely as an evolving process, as the *totality*, in fact of its evolution. This encompasses the development from the inorganic into the organic, from the less differentiated and relatively limited world of unicellular organisms into that of multicellular ones equipped with simple, later complex, and presently fairly intelligent neural apparatuses that allow them to make innovative choices. Finally, the acquisition of warm-bloodedness gives to organisms the astonishing flexibility to exist in the most demanding climatic environments.

This vast drama of nonhuman nature is in every respect stunningly wondrous. It is marked by increasing subjectivity and flexibility and by increasing differentiation that makes an organism more adaptable to new environmental challenges and opportunities and renders a living being more equipped to alter its environment to meet its own needs. One may speculate that the potentiality of matter itself—the ceaseless interactivity of atoms in forming new chemical combinations to produce ever more complex molecules, amino acids, proteins, and, under suitable conditions, elementary life-forms—is inherent in inorganic nature. Or one may decide, quite matter-of-factly, that the "struggle for existence" or the "survival of the fittest" (to use popular Darwinian terms) explains why increasingly subjective and more flexible beings are capable of dealing with environmental changes more effectively than are less subjective and flexible beings. But the fact remains that the kind of evolutionary drama I have described did occur, and is carved in stone in the fossil record. That nature is this record, this history, this developmental or evolutionary process, is a very sobering fact.

Conceiving nonhuman nature as its own evolution rather than as a mere vista has profound implications—ethical as well as biological—for ecologically minded people. Human beings embody, at least potentially, attributes of nonhuman development that place them squarely within organic evolution. They are not "natural aliens," to use Neil Evernden's phrase, strange "exotics," phylogenetic "deformities" that, owing to their tool-making capacities, "cannot evolve *with* an ecosystem anywhere."[2] Nor are they "intelligent fleas," to use the language of Gaian theorists who believe that the earth ("Gaia") is one living organism. These untenable disjunctions between humanity and the evolutionary process are as superficial as they are potentially misanthropic. Humans are highly intelligent, indeed, very self-conscious primates, which is to say that they have emerged—not diverged—from a long evolution of vertebrate life-forms into mammalian, and finally, primate life-forms. They are a product of a significant evolutionary trend toward intellectuality, self-awareness, will, intentionality, and expressiveness, be it in oral or body language.

Human beings belong to a natural continuum, no less than their primate ancestors and mammals in general. To depict them as "aliens" that have no place or pedigree in natural evolution, or to see them essentially as an infestation that parasitizes a highly anthropomorphic version of the planet (Gaia) the way fleas parasitize dogs and cats, is bad thinking, not only bad ecology. Lacking any sense of process, this kind of thinking—regrettably so commonplace among ethicists—radically bifurcates the nonhuman from the human. Indeed, to the degree that nonhuman nature is romanticized as "wilderness," and seen presumably as more authentically "natural" than the works of humans, the natural world is frozen into a circumscribed domain in which human innovation, foresight, and creativity have no place and offer no possibilities.

The truth is that human beings not only belong in nature, they are products of a long, natural evolutionary process. Their seemingly "unnatural" activities—like the development of technology and science, the formation of mutable social institutions, of highly symbolic forms of communication, of aesthetic sensibilities, the creation of towns and cities—all would be impossible without the large array of physical attributes that have been eons in the making, be they large brains or the bipedal motion that frees their hands for tool making and carrying food. In many respects, human traits are enlargements of nonhuman traits that have been evolving over the ages. Increasing care for the young, cooperation, the substitution of mentally guided behavior for largely instinctive behavior—all are present more keenly in human behavior. The difference between the development of these traits among nonhuman beings is that among humans they reach a degree of elaboration and integration that yields cultures or, viewed institutionally in terms of families, bands, tribes, hierarchies, economic classes, and the state, highly mutable *societies* for which there is no precedent in the nonhuman world—unless the genetically programmed behavior of insects is to be regarded as "social." In fact, the emergence and development of human society is a shedding of instinctive behavioral traits, a continuing process of clearing a new terrain for potentially rational behavior.

Human beings always remain rooted in their biological evolutionary history, which we may call "first nature," but they produce a characteristically human social nature of their own, which we may call "second nature." And far from being "unnatural," human second nature is eminently a creation of organic evolution's first nature. To write the second nature created hy human beings out of nature as a whole, or indeed, to minimize it, is to ignore the creativity of natural evolution itself and to view it onesidedly. If "true" evolution embodies itself simply in creatures like grizzly bears, wolves, and whales—generally, animals that *people* find aesthetically pleasing or relatively intelligent—then human beings are literally *de*-natured. In such views, whether seen as "aliens" or as "fleas," humans are essentially placed outside the self-organizing thrust of natural evolution toward increasing subjectivity and flexibility. The more enthusiastic proponents of this de-naturing of humanity may see human beings as existing apart from nonhuman evolution, thereby dealing with people as a "freaking," as Paul Shepard puts it, of the evolutionary process. Others simply avoid the problem of humanity's unique place in natural evolution by promiscuously putting human beings on a par with beetles in terms of their "intrinsic worth." In this "either/or" propositional thinking, the social is either separated from the organic, or flippantly reduced to the organic, resulting in an inexplicable dualism at one extreme or a naive reductionism at the other. The dualistic approach, with its quasi-theological premise that the world was "made" for human use is saddled with the name of "anthropocentricity," while the reductionist approach, with its almost meaningless notion of a "biocentric democracy," is saddled with the name of "biocentricity."

The bifurcation of the human from the nonhuman reveals a failure to think organically, and to approach evolutionary phenomena with an evolutionary way of thought. Needless to say, if we are content to regard nature as no more than a scenic vista, mere metaphoric and poetic description of it might suffice to replace systematic thinking about it. But if we regard nature as the history of nature, as an evolutionary process that is going on to one degree or another under our very eyes, we dishonor this process by thinking of it in anything but a processual way. That is to say, we require a way of thinking that recognizes that "what-is" as it seems to lie before our eyes is always developing into "what-it-is-not," that it is engaged in a continual self-organizing process in which past and present, seen as a richly differentiated but shared continuum, give rise to a new potentiality for a future, ever-richer degree of *wholeness*. Accordingly, the human and the nonhuman can be seen as aspects of an evolutionary continuum, and the emergence of the human can be located in the evolution of the nonhuman, without advancing naive claims that one is either "superior to" or "made for" the other.

By the same token, in a processual, organic, and dialectical way of thinking, we would have little difficulty in locating and explaining the emergence of the social out of the biological, of second nature out of first nature. It seems more fashionable these days to deal with ecologically significant social issues like a bookkeeper. One simply juxtaposes two columns—labeled "old paradigm" and "new paradigm"—as though one were dealing with debits and credits. Obviously distasteful terms like "centralization" are placed under "old paradigm," while more appealing ones like "decentralization" are regarded as "new paradigm." The result is an inventory of bumper-sticker slogans whose "bottom line" is patently a form of "absolute good versus absolute evil." All of this may be deliciously synoptic and easy for the eyes, but it is singularly lacking as food for the brain. To truly *know* and be able to give interpretative *meaning* to the social issues so arranged, we should want to know how each idea derived from others and is part of an overall development. What, in fact, do we mean by the notion of "decentralization," and how does it derive from or give rise in the history of human society to "centralization"? Again: processual thinking is needed to deal with processual realities so that we can gain some sense of *direction*—practical as well as theoretical—in dealing with our ecological problems.

Social ecology seems to stand alone, at present, in calling for the use of organic, developmental, and derivative ways of thinking out problems that are basically organic and developmental in character. The very definition of the natural world as a development indicates the need for an organic way of thinking, as does the derivation of human from nonhuman nature—a derivation that has the most far-reaching consequences for an ecological ethics that can offer serious guidelines for the solution of our ecological problems.

Social ecology calls upon us to see that nature and society are interlinked by evolution into one nature that consists of two differentiations: first or biotic nature, and second or human nature. Human nature and biotic nature share an evolutionary potential for greater subjectivity and flexibility. Second nature is the way in which human beings as flexible, highly intelligent primates *inhabit* the natural world. That is to say, people create an environment that is most suitable for their mode of existence. In this respect, second nature is no different from the environment that *every* animal, depending upon its abilities, creates as well as adapts to, the biophysical circumstances—or ecocommunity—in which it must live. On this very simple level, human beings are, in principle, doing nothing that differs from the survival activities of nonhuman beings—be it building beaver dams or gopher holes.

But the environmental changes that human beings produce are significantly different from those produced by nonhuman beings. Humans act upon their environments with considerable technical foresight, however lacking that foresight may be in ecological respects. Their cultures are rich in knowledge, experience, cooperation, and conceptual intellectuality; however, they may be sharply divided against themselves at certain points of their development, through conflicts between groups, classes, nation-states, and even city-states. Nonhuman beings generally live in ecological niches, their behavior guided primarily by instinctive drives and conditioned reflexes. Human societies are "bonded" together by institutions that change radically over centuries. Nonhuman communities are notable for their fixity in general terms or by clearly preset, often genetically imprinted, rhythms. Human communities are guided in part by ideological factors and are subject to changes conditioned by those factors.

Hence human beings, emerging from an organic evolutionary process, initiate, by the sheer force of their biology and survival needs, a social evolutionary development that profoundly involves their organic evolutionary process. Owing to their naturally endowed intelligence, powers of communication, capacity for institutional organization, and relative freedom from instinctive behavior, they refashion their environment—as do nonhuman beings—to the full extent of their biological equipment. This equipment now makes it possible for them to engage in social development. It is not so much that human beings, in principle, behave differently from animals or are inherently more problematical in a strictly ecological sense, but that the social development by which they grade out of their biological development often becomes more problematical for themselves and nonhuman life. How these problems emerge, the ideologies they produce, the extent to which they contribute to biotic evolution or abort it, and the damage they inflict on the planet as a whole lie at the very heart of the modern ecological crisis. Second nature, far from marking the fulfillment of human potentialities, is riddled by contradictions, antagonisms, and conflicting interests that have distorted humanity's unique capacities for development. It contains both the danger of tearing down the biosphere and, given a further development of humanity toward an ecological society, the capacity to provide an entirely new ecological dispensation.

SOCIAL HIERARCHY AND DOMINATION

How, then, did the social—eventually structured around status groups, class formations, and cultural phenomena—emerge from the biological? We have reason to speculate that as biological facts such as lineage, gender distribution, and age differences were slowly institutionalized, their uniquely social dimension was initially quite egalitarian. Later it acquired an oppressive hierarchical and then an exploitative class form. The lineage or blood tie in early prehistory obviously formed the organic basis of the family. Indeed, it joined together groups of families into bands, clans, and tribes, through either intermarriage or fictive forms of descent, thereby forming the earliest social horizon of our ancestors. More than in other mammals, the simple biological facts of human reproduction and protracted maternal care of the infant tended to knit siblings together and produced a strong sense of solidarity and group inwardness. Men, women, and their children were brought into a condition of a fairly stable family life, based on mutual obligation and an expressed sense of affinity that was often sanctified by marital vows of one kind or another.

Outside the family and all its elaborations into bands, clans, tribes and the like, other human beings were regarded as "strangers," who could alternatively be welcomed hospitably or enslaved or put to death. What mores existed were based on an unreflected body of *customs* that seemed to have been inherited from time immemorial. What we call *morality* began as the commandments of a deity, in that they required some kind of supernatural or mystical reinforcement to be accepted by the community. Only later, beginning with the ancient Greeks, did *ethical* behavior emerge, based on rational discourse and reflection. The shift from blind custom to a commanding morality, and finally, to a rational ethics occurred with the rise of cities and urban cosmopolitanism. Humanity, gradually disengaging itself from the biological facts of blood ties, began to admit the "stranger" and increasingly recognize itself as a shared community of human beings rather than an ethnic folk—a community of citizens rather than of kinsmen.

In the primordial and socially formative world that we must still explore, other of humanity's biological traits were to be reworked from the strictly natural to the social. One of these was the fact of age and its distinctions. In the emerging social groups that developed among early humans, the absence of a written language helped to confer on the elderly a high degree of status, for it was they who possessed the traditional wisdom of the community, the kinship lines that prescribed marital ties in obedience to extensive incest taboos, and techniques for survival that had to be acquired by both the young and the mature members of the group. In addition, the biological fact of gender distinctions were to be slowly reworked along social lines into what were initially complementary sororal and fraternal groups. Women formed their own food-gathering and care-taking groups with their own customs, belief systems, and values, while men formed their own hunting and warrior groups with their own behavioral characteristics, mores, and ideologies.

From everything we know about the socialization of the biological facts of kinship, age, and gender groups—their elaboration into early institutions—there is no reason to doubt that people existed in a complementary relationship with one another. Each, in effect, was needed by the other to form a relatively stable whole. No one "dominated" the others or tried to privilege itself in the normal course of things. Yet with the passing of time, even as the biological facts that underpin every human group were further reworked into social institutions, so the social institutions were slowly reworked at various periods and in various degrees, into hierarchical structures based on command and obedience. I speak here of a historical trend, in no way predetermined by any mystical force or deity, a trend that often did not go beyond a very limited development among many preliterate or aboriginal cultures, and even in certain fairly elaborate civilizations. Nor can we foretell how human history might have developed had certain feminine values associated with care and nurture not been overshadowed by masculine values associated with combative and aggressive behavior.

Hierarchy in its earliest forms was probably not marked by the harsh qualities it has acquired over history. Elders, at the very beginnings of gerontocracy, were not only respected for their wisdom but often beloved of the young, and their affection was often reciprocated in kind. We can probably account for the increasing stridency and harshness of later gerontocracies by supposing that the elderly, burdened by their failing powers and dependent upon the community's goodwill, were more vulnerable to abandonment in periods of material want than any other part of the population. In any case, that gerontocracies were the earliest forms of hierarchy is corroborated by their existence in communities as far removed from each other as the Australian Aborigines, tribal societies in East Africa, and Indian communities in the Americas. "Even in simple food-gathering cultures, individuals above fifty, let us say, apparently arrogated to themselves certain powers and privileges which benefitted themselves specifically," observes anthropologist Paul Radin, "and were not necessarily, if at all, dictated by considerations either of the rights of others or the welfare of the community."[3] Many tribal councils throughout the world were really councils of elders, an institution that never completely disappeared (as the word "alderman" suggests), even though they were overlaid by warrior societies, chiefdoms, and kingships.

Patricentricity, in which male values, institutions, and forms of behavior prevail over female ones, seems to have followed gerontocracy. Initially, this shift may have been fairly harmless, inasmuch as preliterate and early aboriginal societies were largely domestic communities in which the authentic center of material life was the home, not the "men's house" so widely present in tribal societies. Male rule, if such it can be strictly called, takes on its most severe and coercive form in patriarchy, an institution in which the eldest male of an extended family or clan has a life-and-death command over all members of the group. Women are by no means the exclusive or even the principal target of the patriarch's domination. The sons, like the daughters, may be ordered how to behave and whom to marry, and may be killed at the whim of the "old man." So far as patricentricity is concerned, however, the authority and prerogative of the male are the product of a slow, often subtly negotiated development in which the male fraternity tends to edge out the female sorority by virtue of the former's growing "civil" responsibilities. Increasing population, marauding bands of outsiders whose migrations may be induced by drought or other unfavorable conditions, and vendettas of one kind or another, to cite common causes of hostility or war, create a new "civil" sphere side by side with woman's domestic sphere, and the former gradually encroaches upon the latter. With the appearance of cattle-drawn plow agriculture, the male begins to invade the horticultural sphere of woman, who had used the simple digging stick, and her earlier economic predominance in the community's life is thereby diluted. Warrior societies and chiefs carry the momentum of male dominance to the level of a new material and cultural constellation. Male dominance becomes extremely active and ultimately yields a world that is managed by male elites who dominate not only women but also other men.

"Why" hierarchy emerges is transparent enough: the infirmities of age, increasing population, natural disasters, certain technological changes that privilege male activities of hunting and caring for animals over the horticultural functions of females, the growth of civil society, the spread of warfare. All serve to enhance the male's responsibilities at the expense of the female's. Marxist theorists tend to single out technological advances and the presumed material surpluses they produce to explain the emergence of elite strata—indeed, of exploiting ruling classes. However, this does not tell us why many societies whose environments were abundantly rich in food never produced such strata. That surpluses are necessary to support elites and classes is obvious, as Aristotle pointed out more than two millennia ago. But too many communities that had such resources at their disposal remained quite egalitarian and never "advanced" to hierarchical or class societies.

It is worth emphasizing that hierarchical domination, however coercive it may be, is not to be confused with class exploitation. Often the role of high-status individuals is very well-meaning, as in the case of commands given by caring parents to their children, of concerned husbands and wives to each other, or of elderly people to younger ones. In tribal societies, even where a considerable measure of authority accrues to a chief—and most chiefs are advisers rather than rulers—he usually must earn the esteem of the community by interacting with the people, and he can easily be ignored or removed from his position by them. Many chiefs earn their prestige, so essential to their authority, by disposing of gifts, and even by a considerable disaccumulation of their personal goods. The respect accorded to many chiefs is earned, not by hoarding surpluses as a means to power but by disposing of them as evidence of generosity.

Classes tend to operate along different lines. Power is usually gained by the acquisition of wealth, not by its disposal; rulership is guaranteed by outright physical coercion, not simply by persuasion; and the state is the ultimate guarantor of authority. That hierarchy is more entrenched than class can perhaps be verified by the fact that that women have been dominated for millennia, despite sweeping changes in class societies. By the same token, the abolition of class rule and economic exploitation offers no guarantee whatever that elaborate hierarchies and systems of domination will disappear.

In nonhierarchical and even some hierarchical societies, certain customs guide human behavior along basically decent lines. Of primary importance in early customs was the "law of the irreducible minimum" (to use Radin's expression), the shared notion that all members of a community are entitled to the means of life, irrespective of the amount of work they perform. To deny anyone food, shelter, and the basic means of life because of infirmities or even frivolous behavior would have been seen as a heinous denial of the very right to live. Nor were the resources and things needed to sustain the community ever completely privately owned: overriding individualistic control was the broader principle of usufruct—the notion that the means of life that were not being used by one group could be used, as need be, by another. Thus unused land, orchards, and even tools and weapons, if left idle, were at the disposition of anyone in the community who needed them. Lastly, custom fostered the practice of mutual aid, the rather sensible cooperative behavior of sharing things and labor, so that an individual or family in fairly good circumstances could expect to be helped by others if their fortunes should change for the worse. Taken as a whole, these customs became so sedimented into society that they persisted long after hierarchy became oppressive and class society became predominant.

THE IDEA OF DOMINATING NATURE

"Nature," in the broad sense of a biotic environment from which humans take the simple things they need for survival, often has no meaning to preliterate peoples. Immersed in nature as the very universe of their lives, it has no special meaning, even when they celebrate animistic rituals and view the world around them as a nexus of life, often imputing their own social institutions to the behavior of various species, as in the case of "beaver lodges" and humanlike spirits. Words that express our conventional notions of nature are not easy to find, if they exist at all, in the languages of aboriginal peoples.

With the rise of hierarchy and human domination, however, the seeds are planted for a belief that nature not only exists as a world apart, but that it is hierarchically organized and can be dominated. The study of magic reveals this shift clearly. Early forms of magic did not view nature as a world apart. Its worldview tended to be such that a practitioner essentially pleaded with the "chief spirit" of the game to coax an animal in the direction of an arrow or a spear. Later, magic becomes almost entirely instrumental; the game is coerced by magical techniques to become the hunter's prey. While the earliest forms of magic may be regarded as the practices of a generally nonhierarchical and egalitarian community, the later forms of animistic beliefs betray a more or less hierarchical view of the natural world and of latent human powers of domination.

We must emphasize, here, that the *idea* of dominating nature has its primary source in the domination of human by human and the structuring of the natural world into a hierarchical Chain of Being (a static conception, incidentally, that has no relationship to the evolution of life into increasingly advanced forms of subjectivity and flexibility). The biblical injunction that gave to Adam and Noah command of the living world was above all an expression of a *social* dispensation. Its idea of dominating nature can be overcome only through the creation of a society without those class and hierarchical structures that make for rule and obedience in private as well as public life. That this new dispensation involves changes in attitudes and values should go without saying. But these attitudes and values remain vaporous if they are not given substance through objective institutions, the ways in which humans concretely interact with each other, and in the realities of everyday life from childrearing to work and play. Until human beings cease to live in societies that are structured around hierarchies as well as economic classes, we shall never be free of domination, however much we try to dispel it with rituals, incantations, ecotheologies, and the adoption of seemingly "natural" ways of life.

The idea of dominating nature has a history that is almost as old as that of hierarchy itself. Already in the Gilgamesh Epic of Mesopotamia, a drama that dates back some 7,000 years, the hero defies the deities and cuts down their sacred trees in his quest for immortality. The *Odyssey* is a vast travelogue of the Greek warrior, albeit a more canny than a heroic one, who essentially dispatches the nature deities that the Hellenic world inherited from its less well-known precursors. That elitist societies devastated much of the Mediterranean basin as well as the hillsides of China provides ample evidence that hierarchical and class societies had begun a sweeping remaking and despoliation of the planet long before the emergence of modern science, "linear" rationality, and "industrial society," to cite causal factors that are invoked so freely in the modern ecology movement. Second nature, to be sure, did not create a Garden of Eden in steadily absorbing and inflicting harm on first nature. More often than not, it despoiled much that was beautiful, creative, and dynamic in the biotic world, just as it ravaged human life itself in murderous wars, genocide, and acts of heartless oppression. Social ecology refuses to ignore the fact that the harm elitist society inflicted on the natural world was more than matched by the harm it inflicted on humanity; nor does it overlook the fact that the destiny of human life goes hand-in-hand with the destiny of the nonhuman world.

But the customs of the irreducible minimum, usufruct, and mutual aid cannot be ignored, however troubling the ills produced by second nature may seem. These customs persisted well into history and surfaced almost explosively in massive popular uprisings, from early revolts in ancient Sumer to the present time. Many of those demanded the recovery of caring and communitarian values when these were under the onslaught of elitist and class oppression. Indeed, despite the armies that roamed the landscape of warring areas, the taxgatherers who plundered ordinary village peoples, and the daily abuses that were inflicted by overseers on workers, community life still persisted and retained many of the cherished values of a more egalitarian past. Neither ancient despots nor feudal lords could fully obliterate them in peasant villages and in the towns with independent craft guilds. In ancient Greece, religions based on austerity and, more significantly, a rational philosophy that rejected the encumbering of thought and political life by extravagant wants, tended to scale down needs and delimit human appetites for material goods. They served to slow the pace of technological innovation to a point where new means of production could be sensitively integrated into a balanced society. Medieval markets were modest, usually local afairs, in which guilds exercised strict control over prices, competition, and the quality of the goods produced by their members.

"GROW OR DIE!"

But just as hierarchies and class structures tend to acquire a momentum of their own and permeate much of society, so too the market began to acquire a life of its own and extended its reach beyond limited regions into the depths of vast continents. Exchange ceased to be primarily a means to provide for modest needs, subverting the limits imposed upon it by guilds or by moral and religious restrictions. Not only did it place a high premium on techniques for increasing production; it also became the procreator of needs, many of which are simply useless, and gave an explosive impetus to consumption and technology. First in northern Italy and the European lowlands, later—and most effectively—in England during the seventeenth and eighteenth centuries, the production of goods exclusively for sale and profit (the capitalistic commodity) rapidly swept aside all cultural and social barriers to market growth.

By the late eighteenth and early nineteenth centuries, the new industrial capitalist class with its factory system and commitment to limitless expansion began to colonize the entire world, and finally, most aspects of personal life. Unlike the feudal nobility, which had its cherished lands and castles, the bourgeoisie had no home but the marketplace and its bank vaults. As a class, they turned more and more of the world into an ever-expanding domain of factories. Entrepreneurs of the ancient and medieval worlds had normally gathered their profits together to invest in land and live like country gentry—given the prejudices of their times against "ill-gotten" gains from trade. On the other hand, the industrial capitalists of the modern world spawned a bitterly competitive marketplace that placed a high premium on industrial expansion and the commercial power it conferred, and functioned as though growth were an end in itself.

It is crucially important, in social ecology, to recognize that industrial growth does not result from a change in a cultural outlook alone—and least of all, from the impact of scientific rationality on society. It stems above all from *harshly objective factors* churned up by the expansion of the market itself, *factors that are largely impervious to moral considerations and efforts at ethical persuasion*. Indeed, despite the close association between capitalist development and technological innovation, the most driving imperative of the capitalist market, given the dehumanizing competition that defines it, is the need to grow, and to avoid dying at the hands of savage rivals. Important as greed or the power conferred by wealth may be, sheer survival requires that an entrepreneur must expand his or her productive apparatus to remain ahead of other entrepreneurs and try, in fact, to devour them. The key to this law of life—to survival—is expansion, and greater profit, to be invested in still further expansion. Indeed, the notion of progress, once identified by our ancestors as a faith in the evolution of greater human cooperation and care, is now identified with economic growth.

The effort by many well-intentioned ecology theorists and their admirers to reduce the ecological crisis to a cultural rather than a social problem can easily become obfuscatory. However ecologically concerned an entrepreneur may be, the harsh fact is that his or her very survival in the marketplace precludes a meaningful ecological orientation. To engage in ecologically sound practices places a morally concerned entrepreneur at a striking, and indeed, fatal disadvantage in a competitive relationship with a rival—notably one who lacks any ecological concerns and thus produces at lower costs and reaps higher profits for further capital expansion.

Indeed, to the extent that environmental movements and ideologies merely moralize about the "wickedness" of our anti-ecological society, and emphasize change in personal life and attitudes, they obscure the need for social action. Corporations are skilled at manipulating this desire to be present as an ecological image. Mercedes-Benz, for example, declaims in a two-page ad, decorated with a bison painting from a Paleolithic cave wall, that "we must work to make more environmentally sustainable progress by including the theme of the environment in the planning of new products."[5] Such deceptive messages are commonplace in Germany, one of western Europe's worst polluters. Advertising is equally self-serving in the United States, where leading polluters piously declare that for them, "Every day is Earth Day."

The point social ecology emphasizes is not that moral and spiritual change is meaningless or unnecessary, but that modern capitalism is *structurally* amoral and hence impervious to any moral appeals. The modern marketplace has imperatives of its own, irrespective of who sits in the driver's seat or grabs on to its handlebars. The direction it follows depends not upon ethical factors but rather on the mindless "laws" of supply and demand, grow or die, eat or be eaten. Maxims like "business is business" explicitly tell us that ethical, religious, psychological, and emotional factors have absolutely no place in the impersonal world of production, profit, and growth. It is grossly misleading to think that we can divest this brutally materialistic, indeed, mechanistic, world of its objective character, that we can vaporize its hard facts rather than transforming it.

A society based on "grow or die" as its all-pervasive imperative must necessarily have a devastating ecological impact. Given the growth imperative generated by market competition, it would mean little or nothing if the present-day population were reduced to a fraction of what it is today. Insofar as entrepreneurs must always expand if they are to survive, the media that have fostered mindless consumption would be mobilized to increase the purchase of goods, irrespective of the need for them. Hence it would become "indispensable" in the public mind to own two or three of every appliance, motor vehicle, electronic gadget, or the like, where one would more than suffice. In addition, the military would continue to demand new, more lethal instruments of death, of which new models would be required annually.

Nor would "softer" technologies produced by a grow-or-die market fail to be used for destructive capitalistic ends. Two centuries ago, the forests of England were hacked into fuel for iron forges with axes that had not changed appreciably since the Bronze Age, and ordinary sails guided ships laden with commodities to all parts of the world well into the nineteenth century. Indeed, much of the United States was "cleared" of its forests, wildlife, soil, and aboriginal inhabitants with tools and weapons that would have been easily recognized, however much they were modified, by Renaissance people who had yet to encounter the Industrial Revolution. What modern technics did was to accelerate a process that was well under way at the close of the Middle Ages. It did not devastate the planet on its own; it abetted a phenomenon, the ever-expanding market system that had its roots in one of history's most fundamental social transformations: the elaboration of hierarchy and class into a system of distribution based on exchange rather than complementarity and mutual aid.

AN ECOLOGICAL SOCIETY

Social ecology is an appeal not only for moral regeneration but also, and above all, for social reconstruction along ecological lines. It emphasizes that an ethical appeal to the powers that be (that embody blind market forces and competitive relationships), taken by itself, is likely to be futile. Indeed, taken by itself, it often obscures the real power relationships that prevail today by making the attainment of an ecological society seem merely a matter of "attitude," of "spiritual change," or of quasi-religious redemption.

Although always mindful of the need for spiritual change, social ecology seeks to redress the ecological abuses that society has inflicted on the natural world by going to the structural as well as the subjective sources of notions like the "domination of nature." That is, it challenges the entire system of domination itself and seeks to eliminate the hierarchical and class edifice that has imposed itself on humanity and defined the relationship between nonhuman and human nature. It advances an ethics of complementarity in which human beings must play a supportive role in perpetuating the integrity of the biosphere, as potentially, at least, the most conscious products of natural evolution. Indeed humans are seen to have a moral responsibility to function creatively in the unfolding of that evolution. Social ecology thus stresses the need for embodying its ethics of complementarity in palpable social institutions that will give active meaning to its goal of wholeness, and of human involvement as conscious and moral agents in the interplay of species. It seeks the enrichment of the evolutionary process by diversification of life-forms. Notwithstanding romantic views, "Mother Nature" does not necessarily "know best." To oppose activities of the corporate world does not mean that one has to become naively romantic and "biocentric." By the same token, to applaud humanity's potential for foresight and rationality, and its technological achievements, does not mean that one is "anthropocentric." The loose usage of such buzzwords, so commonplace in the ecology movement, must be brought to an end by reflective discussion.

Social ecology, in effect, recognizes that—like it or not—the future of life on this planet pivots on the future of society. It contends that evolution, whether in first nature or in second, is not yet complete. Nor are the two realms so separated from each other that we must choose one or the other— either natural evolution with its "biocentric" halo, or social evolution, as we have known it up to now, with its "anthropocentric" halo—as the basis for a creative biosphere. We must go beyond both the natural and the social toward a new synthesis that contains the best of both. Such a synthesis will transcend them in the form of a creative, self-conscious, and therefore "free nature," in which human beings intervene in natural evolution with their best capacities—their moral sense, their unprecedented degree of conceptual thought, and their remarkable powers of communication.

But such a goal remains mere verbiage unless it can be given logistical and social tangibility. How are we to organize a "free nature" that goes beyond the rhetoric so plentiful in the ecology movement? Logistically, "free nature" is unattainable without the decentralization of cities into confederally united communities sensitively tailored to the natural areas in which they are located. It means the use of ecotechnologies, and of solar, wind, methane, and other sources of energy, the use of organic forms of agriculture, the design of humanly scaled, versatile industrial installations to meet regional needs of confederated municipalities. It means, too, an emphasis not only on recycling, but on the production of high-quality goods that can last for generations. It means the substitution of creative work for insensate labor and an emphasis on artful craftspersonship in preference to mechanized production. It means the leisure to be artful and engage in public affairs. One would hope that the sheer availability of goods and the freedom to choose one's material lifestyle would sooner or later influence people to adopt moderation in all aspects of life as a response to the "consumerism" that is promoted by the capitalist market.[6]

But no ethics or vision of an ecological society, however inspired, can be meaningful unless it is embodied in a living politics. By "politics" I do not mean the statecraft practiced by what we call "politicians"—namely, representatives elected or selected to formulate policies as guidelines for social life and to manage public affairs. To social ecology, politics means what it once meant in the democratic *polis* of Athens some two thousand years ago: the formation of policy by popular assemblies and their administration by mandated, carefully supervised boards of coordinators who could easily be recalled if they failed to abide by the decisions of the assembly's citizens. I am very mindful that Athenian politics, even in its most democratic periods, was marred by the existence of slavery, patriarchy, and the exclusion of the stranger from public life. In this respect, it differed very little from most of the Mediterranean civilizations—and Asian ones—of the time. What made Athenian politics unique, however, was that it produced institutions that were extraordinarily democratic—even directly so—by comparison with republican institutions in the so-called "democracies" of the Western world. Either directly or indirectly they inspired later, more all-encompassing democracies, such as certain medieval towns, the little-known "sections" of Paris (which were essentially forty-eight neighborhood assemblies) that propelled the French Revolution in a highly radical direction in 1793, New England town meetings, and more recent attempts at civic self-governance.[7]

Any community, however, risks the danger of becoming parochial, even racist, if it tries to live in isolation and develop a seeming self-sufficiency. Hence, the need to extend ecological politics into confederations of ecocommunities, and to foster a healthy interdependence, rather than an introverted, stultifying independence. Social ecology would embody its ethics in a politics of confederal municipalism, in which municipalities cojointly gain rights to self-governance through networks of confederal councils, to which towns and cities would send their mandated, recallable delegates to adjust differences. All decisions would have to be ratified by a majority of the popular assemblies of the confederated towns and cities. This institutional process could occur in the neighborhoods of giant cities as well as in networks of small towns. In fact, the formation of numerous "town halls" has already repeatedly been proposed in cities as large as New York and Paris, only to be defeated by well-organized elitist groups that sought to centralize power, rather than allow its decentralization.

Power will always belong to elite strata if it is not diffused, in face-to-face democracies, among the people, who are *empowered* as partly autonomous, partly social beings—that is to say, as free individuals, but as individuals responsible to popular institutions. Empowerment of the people in this sense will constitute a challenge to the nation-state—the principal source of nationalism, a regressive ideology, and of statism, the principal source of coercion. Diversity of cultures is obviously a desideratum, the source of cultural creativity, but never can it be celebrated in a nationalistic "apartness" from the general interests of humanity as a whole, without a regression into folkdom and tribalism.

The full reality of citizenship has begun to wane, and its disappearance would mark an irrevocable loss in human development. Citizenship, in the classical sense of the term, meant a lifelong, ethically oriented education to participation in public affairs, not the empty form of national legitimation that it so often indicates today. It meant the cultivation of an affiliation with the interests of the community, one in which the communal interest was placed above personal interest, or, more properly, in which the personal interest was congruent with and realized through the common.

Property, in this ethical constellation, would be shared and, in the best of circumstances, belong to the community as a whole, not to producers ("workers") or owners ("capitalists"). In an ecological society composed of a "Commune of communes," property would belong, ultimately, neither to private producers nor to a nation-state. The Soviet Union gave rise to an overbearing bureaucracy; the anarcho-syndicalist vision to competing "worker-controlled" factories that ultimately had to be knitted together by a labor bureaucracy. From the standpoint of social ecology, property "interests" would become generalized, not reconstituted in different conflicting or unmanageable forms. They would be *municipalized,* rather than nationalized or privatized. Workers, farmers, professionals, and the like would thus deal with municipalized property as citizens, not as members of a vocational or social group. Leaving aside any discussion of such visions as the rotation of work, the citizen who engages in both industrial and agricultural activity, and the professional who also does manual labor, the communal ideas advanced by social ecology would give rise to individuals for whom the collective interest is inseparable from the personal, the public interest from the private, the political interest from the social.

The step-by-step reorganization of municipalities, their confederation into ever-larger networks that form a dual power in opposition to the nation-state, the remaking of the constituents of republican representatives into citizens who participate in a direct democracy—all may take a considerable period of time to achieve. But in the end, they alone can potentially eliminate the domination of human by human and thereby deal with those ecological problems whose growing magnitude threatens the existence of a biosphere than can support advanced forms of life. To ignore the need for these sweeping but eminently practical changes would be to let our ecological problems fester and spread to a point where there would no longer be any opportunity to resolve them. Any attempt to ignore their impact on the biosphere or deal with them singly would be recipe for disaster, a guarantee that the anti-ecological society that prevails in most of the world today would blindly hurtle the biosphere as we know it to certain destruction.

NOTES

1. Murray Bookchin, "Ecology and Revolutionary Thought," initially published in the ecoanarchist journal *New Directions in Libertarian Thought* (Sept., 1964), and collected, together with all my major essays of the sixties in *Post-Scarcity Anarchism* (Berkeley: Ramparts Press, 1972; republished, Mon-

treal: Black Rose Books, 1977). The expression "ethics of complementarity" is from *The Ecology of Freedom* (San Francisco: Cheshire Books, 1982; revised edition, Montreal: Black Rose Books, 1991).

2. Neil Evernden, *The Natural Alien* (Toronto: University of Toronto Press, 1986), p. 109.
3. Paul Radin, *The World of Primitive Man* (New York: Grove Press, 1960), p. 211.
4. Quoted in Alan Wolfe, "Up from Humanism," in *The American Prospect* (Winter, 1991), p. 125.
5. See *Der Spiegel* (Sept. 16, 1991), pp. 144–45.
6. All of these views were spelled out in the essay "Ecology and Revolutionary Thought" by this writer in 1965, and were assimilated over time by subsequent ecology movements. Many of the technological views advanced a year later in "Toward a Liberatory Technology" were also assimilated and renamed "appropriate technology," a rather socially neutral expression in comparison with my original term "ecotechnology." Both of these essays can be found in *Post-Scarcity Anarchism*.
7. See the essay "The Forms of Freedom," in *Post-Scarcity Anarchism*, "The Legacy of Freedom," in *The Ecology of Freedom*, and "Patterns of Civic Freedom" in *The Rise of Urbanization and the Decline of Citizenship* (San Francisco: Sierra Club Books, 1987).

Dialectics in the Ethics of Social Ecology

Janet Biehl

Janet Biehl is a lecturer at the Institute for Social Ecology. She is the author of Rethinking Ecofeminist Politics *and co-editor of* Green Perspectives.

As a dialectical philosophy, social ecology argues that humanity must be understood as the history of humanity, and that nature must be understood as the history of nature. Just so, it also argues that science must be understood as the history of science. It advances the view that there is much to be gained from examining the role that previous cosmologists played in the development of our own in considering the problem of nature and humanity's relationship to each other, and that earlier peoples in Western culture have asked important questions that our present-day science ignores. In particular, earlier cosmologists addressed and tried to explain—to the best of their ability—at least one very important question that modern science, to its detriment, fails to confront.

This is the fact that, on the one hand, there is order in the natural world, and, on the other hand, that human beings have a rational faculty that is capable of comprehending it in varying degrees. Indeed, the human mind sometimes seems as if it were magnificently developed for understanding the order in the natural world. Just as the world is, at least in part, ordered in a certain way, the human mind is so organized as to be able to comprehend it at various levels of adequacy.

This fact must have struck people in early periods of social development as a remarkable "correspondence." For millennia, they explained the "correspondence" between human reason and the intelligible order in nature by an organismic analogy. The rational human mind could under-

This essay originally appeared in *Rethinking Ecofeminist Politics* (Boston: South End Press, 1991). Reprinted with permission.

stand the world because the cosmic macrocosm—like the individual microcosm—had a human kind of mind. The various meanings of the Greek word *logos* encompass both the mind's power of comprehension and the fact of the cosmos' comprehensibility. *Logos* referred both to the immanent intelligibility that is discoverable in nature, as well as to the mind that could discover it. This congruency between the rational mind and the rational cosmos explained how thinking can comprehend the world. Hence, the origin of the word "logic" from *logos*. *Logos* also implied the ability to discuss in a rational way, as in dialogues (from the Greek *dia-logos*), how ideas undergo development. Far from defining reason or *logos* as opposed to nature, Socrates, Plato, and Aristotle studied a mind or *nous* that "was always first and foremost mind *in* nature," writes R. G. Collingwood. For Aristotle, as John Herman Randall, Jr., notes, the fact "that men can know their world [was] not a problem, but the most significant fact, both about us and about the world."[1]

This tradition of *logos* was continued through the ancient and medieval periods. On the one hand, it was transformed into a rigid and immutable natural law by the Stoics and Christians. On the other hand, it was perpetuated in its developmental and dialectical form by mystics. With the emergence of modern science, the order of nature seemed open to the human mind in a new form: mathematics. The cosmos was comprehensible and an open book in mathematical terms. But mathematics preserved *logos* in only its most rigid hypothetico-deductive form. Missing from the mathematical *logos* was any ability to explain Aristotle's "most significant fact," or why it was that the now-mathematical cosmos was intelligible to the human mind. It became a merely "metaphysical" question, and the successors of Descartes "abandoned the attempt to prove this correspondence," as Randall observes. Rather, they simply made the assumption that "the order of men's scientific ideas was, in the nature of things, the same as the order of objects in the world," without attempting to justify it metaphysically, philosophically, or cosmologically, let alone scientifically.[2]

Despite science's efficacy in bringing some understanding of nature's operations, "science, in effect, has been permitted to live a lie," writes Murray Bookchin. Science

> has presupposed, with astonishing success, that nature is orderly, and that this order lends itself to rational interpretation by the human mind, but that reason is exclusively the subjective attribute of the human observer, not of the phenomena observed.. . .Science, in effect, has become a temple built on the foundation of seemingly animistic and metaphysical "ruins," without which it would sink into the watery morass of its own contradictions.[3]

Mind was "erected into a second type of substance that served as a ready dumping-ground for everything in experience which physics did not read in mechanical nature," as Randall observes.[4] The qualities of things, like the wetness of water and the coldness of ice, were shoved into this "dumping-ground." But it was not simply the qualities of things that were so dispensed with. So was the *developmental* causality so typical of organismic life. Self-directiveness and tendency—these too were relegated to the merely subjective, by virtue of their association with the "final causes" of medieval Scholasticism.

Indeed, modern science defined itself most explicitly by its attack on the Scholastics' "final causes," an issue that constituted perhaps the major battleground between science and Scholastic theology. The backlash against Scholasticism was accompanied by a backlash against organicism generally, in "an exaggerated rejection of all organicism."[5] In delivering its "sustained polemic," to use Collingwood's phrase, against the Scholastic theory of final causes with its immutable, predetermined teleological ends, early science eliminated any notion that there was any potentiality or nisus in nature to realize implicit forms that have not been fully actualized. In short, mechanistic science spilled out the baby with the bathwater. In the course of fighting one extreme, Scholasticism, it moved to another extreme, mechanism.

The mind had become a dumping ground of sorts because mechanism established no intelligible place for mind in the very world that it was describing. The mechanistic worldview and its mathematical *logos* could explain everything, it seemed, except the human mind that perceived it, Descartes' *res cogitans.* The human mind in its Newtonian aspect could not explain organisms organismically; developments, developmentally; history, historically; or society in ways appropriate to human social development. In short, with the mathematical *logos,* the human mind and human society could not be explained intelligibly at all, let alone explain the human ability to comprehend mathematical order. The interface between nature and mind, writes Bookchin, was "replaced by an unbridgeable dualism between mentality and the external world."[6]

Despite the social aim of "mastery over nature," human beings had lost their cosmological place in the mechanistic worldview. Human existence in the scheme of things came to be regarded as a brute accident, and it seemed perfectly sensible for Bertrand Russell in the 20th century to conclude that human life and consciousness are a mere accident in the cosmos, a chance spark in a meaningless world.

This epistemological dualism was accompanied by an ultimately futile attempt to subjugate nonhuman nature by economic and technical forces. Even as Western culture engaged in its *vita activa* to "master" nature and industrial capitalism was developing apace, philosophy remained ensconced in this epistemological dualism. The relationship between nonhuman nature and human nature was cast in largely antagonistic terms, and progress was identified as the technical ability to use nonhuman nature to serve the ends of the marketplace. Human destiny was conceived as the redemption of society from a "demonic" natural world.

THE PROBLEM OF INSTRUMENTALISM

When the laws of physics, so suitable for understanding inorganic nature, were applied to human society in various scientistic branches of knowledge, the result was to fuel the rise of an instrumental social ethos. Forces were at work in Western society that stood to make great use of this ethos that explained people in terms of collections of isolated bodies in eternally lawful motion. For one, it perfectly suited the emerging nation-state and its unrelenting centralization, bureaucratization, and domination. If people could be reduced to units, they could be manageable and susceptible to administration. If they could be instrumentalized as workers, they could be administered by gigantic corporate entities. The attempt to standardize, instrumentalize, and homogenize the human being as a worker—whether in the bureaucratic state, in the factory, or in the domestic realm—facilitated massive economic exploitation and political domination, despite the attempts of many people to resist this unsavory dehumanizing process.

The instrumental ethos was particularly suited to the needs of capitalism. Capitalism tried to instrumentalize nonhuman nature as raw materials, even as it tried to instrumentalize people as a mere source of labor. As old ethical systems were eroded, the new *homo oeconomicus* who benefited from the exploitation and domination of others blindly followed an established course of self-interest, according to the new "natural laws" that explained economic competition. No longer were individuals integrated into communities that existed to serve a higher purpose. While individuals were liberated from the oppressive "interconnectedness" of traditional and patricentric society, under capitalism they were obliged either to submit to economic "natural laws" or attempt to master them. This is not merely a matter of ideology; in a market society, it is everyday reality. If the instrumental ethos reduced moral purpose to self-interest in order to survive, capitalism made competition a social imperative. Only mastery of the economic process could assure the self-preservation of the individual capitalist and his enterprise in the all-consuming competitive marketplace.

Ultimately, women in the domestic realm were also to be largely homogenized. As the domestic realm became increasingly reduced to the isolated nuclear family, women's household duties came to be analyzed and prescribed in increasing detail. Despite 19th-century women's cultural "mission" as bearers of morality in the "cult of true womanhood," home economics in the domestic realm was integral to the competitive economics of the marketplace, producing and educating children and administering the household along increasingly rationalized lines. Women's participation in the "caring" professions—of nursing, social work, and others—was necessary to the system for "cleaning up after the men," just as women's childbearing and childrearing were necessary to produce workers for capitalism.

But capitalism did not simply try to transform human and nonhuman nature into raw materials. It also tried to commodify nearly every aspect of human existence, to ensure the dependence of both the public and the domestic spheres on the market. This process ruptured any organic integration between human and nonhuman communities. In this century, everything from transportation and communication, to courtship and reproduction have been subject to commodification. As such, commodification "hollowed out" whatever sense of ethical purpose and meaning of life had been inherited from the past. The recently liberated "individual" became a mere shell of a self.

Most important for the purposes of the present discussion, reason itself fell victim to the very instrumental ethos that it had helped foster. "Gone is the cosmos with whose immanent *Logos* my own can feel kinship, gone the order of the whole in which [humans have their] place," writes Hans Jonas.[7] No longer was the *logos* of the world embedded in an ethical cosmos. No longer addressing ends, reason was reduced to an instrumental means. Neither personal nor social freedom has roots any longer in the objective world, but merely exist in the eyes of the beholder, a function of public opinion rather than objective reality. What we think of as reason today is reason reduced to a mere "skill" or instrument, to a mere means to attain self-interested ends. For instrumental reason, it makes no difference whether its statements are designed to justify women's claims to reproductive freedom or validate racist neo-Nazi claims. Its sole job is to determine whether these claims—or any claim—are logically consistent, not whether they are morally right or wrong. "Rightness" and "wrongness" themselves are merely values or even social constructions that each person may accept or reject, depending upon his or her opinion or needs. In themselves, they have no standing in presumably morally neutral logical operations. It is this kind of thinking that the 1960s counterculture—long before ecofeminists appeared on the scene—regarded as "linear."

Guided by operational standards of logical consistency and pragmatic success, reason was "validated exclusively by its effectiveness in satisfying the ego's pursuits and responsibilities. It makes no appeal to values, ideals, and goals." In politics and ethics, reason was "denatured," as Bookchin has pointed out, "into a mere methodology for calculating sentiments—with the same operational techniques that bankers and industrialists use to administer their enterprises.[8] It became an instrument for advancing personal interests to achieve individual ends—and not for *defining* those ends. Worse, it became an instrument for administering human beings—not for defining and formulating an ethically meaningful existence. Science's

" 'value-free,' presumably ethically 'neutral' methodology" allows instrumentalism to remain ideologically secure. "If we mistrust reason today," writes Bookchin,

> it is because reason has enhanced our technical powers to alter the world drastically without providing us with the goals and values that give these powers direction and meaning. Like Captain Ahab in Melville's *Moby Dick*, we can cry out forlornly: "All my means are sane; my motives and objects mad."[9]

But instrumental reason has been fallaciously criticized as if it constituted reason per se rather than just one form of reason. Here again, the baby is spilled out with the bathwater. As we shall see, there are *other* forms of reason that are not hypothetico-deductive, instrumental, and formalistic in character.

AN EVOLUTIONARY PERSEPCTIVE

Science in the overall reveals a developmental picture, whether it understands itself as doing so or not. For example, a chemist knows that two atoms of hydrogen and one atom of oxygen will always produce water (at least on the terrestrial level). This is an immutable chemical fact. But placed in the context of the development of the inorganic universe, that chemical combination occupies a certain *historical* place. According to the generally accepted big-bang theory, all of the matter and energy in the universe was once concentrated very densely into a tiny volume at a very high temperature. This primeval "fireball" exploded, resulting in an expansion that continues today. Neutrons and protons formed from their quark constituents. In nanoseconds, some of the hydrogen was converted into helium. The expanding universe thinned and cooled enough to condense into individual galaxies and then stars, leading to the present universe. Gravity collapsed the matter into the celestial objects such as we see now. The billions of galaxies in the universe are all receding from each other at speeds comparable to that of light. After a very long time, the solar system, including the earth, was formed. Somewhere in the course of this development, oxygen was formed from "primal" hydrogen and combined with it to form water. Here we see a striking example of a cumulative inorganic evolution: the "natural history of water," as it were. Water was not present in the hot fireball; rather, it is the product of a development in inorganic evolution. Although its chemical formation is subject to natural law, it has a natural history.

When scientists look for alternative explanations to mechanistic natural law, they often turn to randomness. And indeed, to the best of our knowledge, randomness is at work in the universe—although chaos theory has recently been finding mathematical order even in chaos. But when one looks over the course of the development of the universe—from fireball to galaxies to planets to the "nutrient broth" of amino acids to unicellular life to plants, animals, and human society—it is hard to attribute it exclusively to randomness, despite the fact that there were many random events. Its zigs and zags and dead ends notwithstanding, a directionality is apparent in the evolution of the cosmos. Looking back in retrospect, this is simply a fact—not a mere hypothesis—and must be philosophically accounted for. Indeed, both organic and inorganic nature literally develop. The word evolution is correctly applied to both: to inorganic evolution, concerned with the development of the physical universe from unorganized uniformity, as well as to organic evolution, concerned with the development of animals and plants by a process of continuous change and differentiation from previously existing forms.

This is not to say that inorganic or organic evolution *had* to develop in the specific directions they did. Nor is it to say that the history of the cosmos had to lead inevitably from the hot fireball to human society. We do not know if the origination of life in its present forms was inevitable; nor can we say that the organic development that did occur was predetermined. The earth is a microspeck in the infinite universe, and human evolution as we know it may be one form of development among many others in the "tree" of evolution. But a very distinct development *did* take place and has to be *explained*. It cannot be dissolved into mere contingency or fantasies about what might or might not have occurred. Moreover, we must ask not merely *how* it occurred, but *why* it occurred, whether it reveals any rationale or is merely a meaningless flow of random events. When all is said and done, this natural history clearly *reveals* ever greater differentiation of life-forms, increasing subjectivity and flexibility, and finally the emergence of intellectuality, intentionality, and a high order of choice, which forms a precondition for freedom.

To labor over whether this was inevitable is to make a meaningful problem meaningless. We must inquire into the *kind* of development that led to the emergence of existing species, including the human, with its conscious willfulness, enormous powers of conceptual thought, symbolic language, and well-organized but highly mutable social institutions.

One aspect of inorganic and organic evolution that has reflected a remarkable interaction of persistence and change is subjectivity. Subjectivity is not unique to human beings; it too has a natural history of its own. From its most rudimentary forms in unicellular organisms, as mere self-identity and sensitivity, it has expanded throughout natural history. The earliest, simplest organisms that developed had self-identity—even if only as the mere metabolic activity on the part of an amoeba to *actively* persist and reproduce itself in an environment that would otherwise tend to dissolve it. Although it is seemingly unconscious—indeed, perhaps even incapable of consciousness—the very fact that it is busy maintaining itself exhibits the existence of a germinal form of selfhood and a nascent form of subjectivity. Whatever else an amoeba may have, this active self-identity distinguishes it from the nonliving environment in which it is immersed.

> Natural history includes a history of mind as well as of physical structures—a history of mind that develops from the seemingly "passive" interactivity of the inorganic to the highly active cerebral processes of human intellect and volition. This history of what we call "mind" is cumulatively present not only in the human mind but also in our bodies as a whole, which largely recapitulate the expansive development of life-forms at various neurophysical levels of evolution.. . .What we today call "mind" in all its human uniqueness, self-possession, and imaginative possibilities is coterminous with a long evolution of mind.[10]

Mind thus derives as a form of a broad evolution of subjectivity, in the course of the cumulative development of increasingly complex forms. In this sense, human subjectivity is "the very history of natural subjectivity, not merely its product.[11]

DIALECTICAL NATURALISM

Dialectical naturalism is an attempt to grasp nature as a developmental phenomenon, both in its organic and social realms.[12] All organic phenomena change and, even more important, undergo development and differentiation. They form and re-form, while actively maintaining their identity until, barring any accident, they fulfill their potentialities. But since the cosmos, seen in an overview of its evolution, is developmental as well, dialectical naturalism approaches the world as a whole from a developmental perspective. Its various realms—inorganic, organic, and social—are distinct from each other, and yet they grade into one another.

This approach above all focuses on the transitions of a developing phenomenon, which emerge from its potentiality to become fully developed and self-actualized. These transitions, in turn, arise from a process of "contradiction" between a thing as it is, on the one hand, and a thing as it potentially should become, on the other.

As a result of a developmental transition, each new potentiality in a development cumulatively contains all its previous phases, albeit transformed, even as it itself—when it is fully actualized—contains the potentiality to become a new actuality. The emergence of life out of inorganic nature is such a transition. Life emerges from the inorganic and contains the inorganic within itself; yet it is clearly *more* than the inorganic. Together, inorganic and organic nature constitute what social ecology calls "first nature." The emergence of human society out of first nature, in turn, is also such a transition, for society contains the vast evolution of its biological heritage within itself, yet goes beyond biological evolution as such to become what we would rightly call social evolution. This social evolution is thus what social ecology calls "second nature"—a phrase that is meant to emphasize the *natural* continuity between biological and social evolution.

In examining the process of development, dialectical naturalism is especially interested in *form* and the way it is organized in inorganic and organic nature. From formal ensembles, tensions or "contradictions" emerge. Contradiction in dialectical naturalism—as in all dialectical thought—is a dynamic process that impels self-development. But unlike other dialectical approaches, which have regarded contradictions as abstractly logical or as narrowly materialistic, dialectical naturalism "conceives contradiction as distinctly natural."[13]

In an organism, for example, there is a tension between what that organism could potentially be when it is fully actualized, on the one hand, and what it is at any given moment before that development is fulfilled. That which it is *constituted to become or "should be"*—the implicit—causes that which it *is*—its immediate explicit existence at a given moment in its development—to be unstable.

This instability of contradiction propels a being toward self-development, whatever it should become by virtue of the way its potentialities are constituted. Accordingly, impelled by a logic of growth (a process that has its mechanico-chemical aspects, to be sure, in chromosomes and the creation of proteins from nucleic acids), development occurs, yet the old is preserved. This cumulative approach produces a continuum "that contains the entire history of [a beings] development."[14]

Although Western culture—especially in recent centuries—has conceived of mind and body as radically separated from each other, we cannot "heal" this split by reducing the one to the other. A human body without mind can hardly be called conscious. In fact, the mind-body dualism has a basis in an ontological *duality.* Mind does emerge out of body as something distinct, even as it is part of and remains embedded in the body. Indeed, it is a socially conditioned but organic *differentiation* of the body's own development, as the evidence of evolution shows us. A dialectical naturalist approach overcomes mind-body dualism not by rejecting the distinction between the two but by articulating the continuum along which the human mind has evolved. The relationship between mind and body—their distinctness, as well as mind's dependence on and its origins in first nature alike—is a *graded* phenomenon, as Bookchin has argued, not one in which mind and body are rigidly separated.

Development in inorganic nature has not been of precisely the same kind that we find in organic nature. We can explain many biological facts by means of chemistry, Bookchin has pointed out, but we cannot explain chemical facts by means of biology. The history of inorganic nature is a development of reactivity and interactivity, in which increasingly complex forms arise from interactions of elementary particles. The history of organic nature is a fully active development, in which—however nascently—even the simplest unicellular organic forms are busily involved in preventing their self-identity from dissolving into their inorganic environment, even as they absorb from that immediately contiguous environment the substances they need for their self-maintenance. In the evolution of life-forms, nascent self-identity developed into more complex subjectivity and form, and ever-greater self-intentionality emerged in maintaining themselves, in modifying their environment, and in rendering that environment more habitable—an elaboration of the self-identity that distinguishes organic from inorganic development. Yet despite this increasing subjectivity and intentionality of organisms, an evolutionary continuity remains between inorganic and organic nature, and at the roots of the intentionality of complex organisms we find the increasingly complex formal arrangements of inorganic particles and compounds.

Dialectical naturalism, it goes without saying, sees development as immanent in nature itself. First nature alone, in all its wholeness, richness, self-creativity, and marvelousness requires no supernature to explain its processes. Unlike Hegelian dialectics, with its recourse to "Spirit," dialectical naturalism does not posit the presence of a spiritual principle apart from nature's own self-evolving attributes to explain either inorganic or organic existence. Nor does it posit any "Absolute," as Hegelian dialectics did, in which development is completely fulfilled. Rather, in dialectical naturalism, self-directiveness remains a tendency whose fulfillment, while marked by ever-greater degrees of "wholeness," remains open-ended and continually self-formative.

Dialectical reasoning is a form of reasoning that attempts to understand the developmental processes in first and second nature that I have been describing. It clearly differs from instrumental reason, which freezes a phase of a development in order to analyze its components. That physiology and anatomy can satisfactorily analyze a human body only if they regard it as fixed and unchanging should be fairly obvious, even though a living body is continually developing and differentiating. Without operating on this level of fixity, to be sure, we would have none of the knowledge about the structure and functions of the human organism that is indispensable for the details of medical diagnosis and therapy. Analysis, in effect, can indeed provide a great deal of knowledge about things. But instrumental or analytical reason cannot explain the developmental, because developmental processes involve more than simply the rearrangement of component parts into a new arrangement. Development involves a transition from one state of being to another for which mere analysis provides only a woefully incomplete account. Dialectical reasoning, indeed, absorbs analogical and analytical forms of reasoning in its developmental approach but goes far beyond them.

Dialectical reasoning originated in the *logos* concept of the Greeks. Having survived in various forms over the millennia, it blossomed in the 19th-century German Enlightenment and was elaborated most fully in its time by Hegel.[15] For Hegel, dialectical reasoning conceives of basic, seemingly contradictory logical categories—like "being" and "nothing"—as leading to the category of "becoming," a category that dialectical logic takes as its great point of departure and also begins to define becoming for what it really is, namely development. Becoming, with its full wealth of logically educed categories, in Hegel's logical works, is literally the cumulative history of pure thought. Dialectical reasoning describes processes of cumulative change in which the logically prior is partly annulled, incorporated, and transcended by its synthesis as a new category.

In everyday commonsensical thinking, it might seem difficult to believe that a consistent developmental logic could be produced that had the rigor that reason has generally claimed for itself. But despite certain limitations, the logical works of Hegel demonstrate that this can be done with extraordinary brilliance. What Hegel did was to try to systematically understand the nature of becoming, to resolve "the paradox of a 'something' that 'is' and is simultaneously developing into 'what is not.' " He took the vast array of logical categories that had surfaced in Western philosophy, including many of his own, and arranged them from the simplest to the most complex in an order in which each was educed from its own internal logic and incompleteness to its successor, filling out the rich terrain of thought in a cumulative, increasingly differentiated, and ever more adequate approximation of a rational whole.

Hegel referred to the potentiality of a logical category as that which is implicit, or *an sich,* and to the more developed, explicit category emerging from it as the explicit, or *für sich.* He designated the rational fulfillment of a potentiality as its actualization (*an und für sich*). Owing to its incompleteness or "contradictory" nature in the elaboration of the "whole," the implicit strives, in a sense, to fulfill itself by its own developmental logic, the way living forms in nature "strive" to grow and develop by a tension between what they are at any given moment and what they should be in their maturity. The process by which the implicit becomes explicit is rendered in Hegelian terminology by the untranslatable German word *Aufhebung,* sometimes expressed as "transcendence" or "sublation." In an *Aufhebung,* the new category or phase of a development "contradicts" or "negates" the previous one, even as it incorporates it in a more complete condition. It should be emphasized that *contradiction* in dialectical reason does not refer to a contradiction between two arbitrarily chosen statements that have no developmental relationship to each other. Rather, dialectical contradiction involves the fulfillment of a potentiality that negates the previous state, absorbs it, and goes beyond it—not the juxtaposition of ideas or facts that patently have no connection with each other.

Dialectical reasoning uses neither the inductive process of empiricism nor the hypothetico-deductive process of formal reason but a third form of thinking that Bookchin calls *eduction*. Eduction, writes Bookchin, is directed "toward an exploration of [a potentiality's] latent and implicit possibilities." It aims to understand the *inherent logic* of a thing's development—that is, the point from which it started, where it is now, and where by its immanent developmental logic it should go. Eduction attempts to render "the latent possibilities of a phenomenon fully manifest and articulated." Dialectical premises are not random hypotheses but rather potentialities that stem from a distinct continuum, with a past, present, and latent future of their own. From these potentialities is educed a graded differentiation toward wholeness—without dissolving the richly articulated phases that make up the whole into a vague, unarticulated "oneness."

In its Hegelian form, dialectics operates primarily within the realm of thought. Hegel's system invokes an inexplicable cosmic spirit (*Geist*) that culminates in a mystical Absolute. Marxian dialectics, in turn, as developed by Engels, tilts toward the relatively mechanistic science of the 19th century, which dealt more with matter and motion than with a truly organic development. In contrast to both of these, dialectical *naturalism* is completely informed by ecology. Development remains strictly naturalistic, without recourse to Hegel's spirit or to Engels' mechanical kinetics. Nor does the naturalistic dialectics advanced by Bookchin terminate in an Absolute, or any notion of an "end of history." It thus remains more open-ended, fluid, spontaneous, organic, and free from predeterminations than is the dialectical tradition by which it is informed.

In first and second nature, the character of dialectical development varies from the evolution of the inorganic and organic to the evolution of human society. But the very fact of the evolution of the organic out of the inorganic, and of the social out of the organic (each preserving what rationally came before it in a transformed state) dialectically grounds second nature in first nature itself. Dialectical naturalism is thus both a form of reasoning and an ontological form of causality.

As both a form of reasoning and as an account of development in first and second nature, dialectical naturalism offers an explanation for Aristotle's "most significant fact," with which we opened: The fact that the world of nature is comprehensible to the human mind. It is because human beings are a product of the increasing subjectivity in first nature—not created by God, not a microcosm that "corresponds" to an analogical macrocosm—that they can understand the processes of first nature. Human beings and human society evolved out of first nature—even as they remain part of it and are embedded in it. By virtue of the very "physical anthropology" of human mentality, human subjectivity is grounded in first nature, as a product of its emergence, and therefore can comprehend it.

THE ETHICS OF SOCIAL ECOLOGY

A rationality that conceives reality as the actualization of potentialities into ever-differentiating degrees of wholeness has profound ethical implications. Obviously, the ground of an ecological ethics must be ontological: it cannot be grounded in the vagaries of social constructions, public opinion, or tradition, much less in patently absurd myths. In social ecology, nature reenters the philosophical and political sphere of Western culture as an ontological ground for ethics. This ethics is one that is premised on natural evolution and the emergence of second nature out of first nature.

As we have seen, first nature's development is inorganic, then (in our planetary biosphere, at least) biological. Subjectivity increasingly emerges from the most nascent unicellular process of self-maintenance and subjectivity, through the rudimentary choices exercised by highly flexible mammals, to the elementary conceptual thought of advanced primates. Here, as we have seen, is a graded development of subjectivity in the evolution of life.

Yet animal behavior is for the most part determined by biology. Although ethnologists commonly speak of "animal societies," animals do not have the unique type of community structures developed by humans. Their "social arrangements," as Bookchin has argued, such as those of ants, are genetically programmed, even though the role of the genetic is lessened as we approach primate forms of life.

With humanity, natural evolution gives rise to social evolution in the fullest sense of the word. While we are embedded in first nature, we have also evolved from it into something different in very important ways. If "being determines consciousness," so to speak, for animals, it is by no means strictly true for human beings, Marxian theory notwithstanding. Human beings create *institutions* that are often highly mutable, indeed subject to radical and revolutionary changes, a phenomenon that does not appear in animal communities. The evolution of society, which uniquely characterizes humans, gives them the ability to change their social relations in a great variety of ways, potentially toward ever greater self-consciousness and freedom. This represents a development from mere animal community to human society, a crucial advance, however phased it may be, from the world of the biological to the social, from first nature to second nature.

Unlike other animals, human beings can clearly perceive that a society is destroying the biosphere, and they can try to do something about it. Unlike other animals, humans also engage in struggles to make changes in their lives and in their social institutions. With their highly developed nervous systems and brains, they are the only animals with minds that seem capable of sophisticated conceptual reason and a richly symbolic vocabulary that forms the basis for highly intricate modes of thinking and human consociation. And unlike other animals, humans are able to make *moral* choices. They are potentially ethical creatures that can, for example, impart "rights" not only to themselves but even to nonhuman life-forms if they so choose. Second nature thus marks a new evolutionary phase of nature, with its sociality, institutions, intellectuality, language, ethics, and political life.

We know only too well from the history of civilization, however, that human society has not as yet reached its full maturity, rationality, or indeed, its full humanity. Dialectics, by exploring the potentiality and internal logic of a development, educes what society *should be*. This is not an arbitrary endeavor. It must be validated by reason and by real material as well as cultural possibilities. By examining what potentialities humans have as they grade out of first nature, social ecology advances the ethical view that their capacities will not be realized unless they create a rational ecological society based on an ethics of complementarity with first nature. But what society *should be* is vastly different from what it *is*. Where it should be rational and ecological if humanity's potentialities are fulfilled, it is irrational and anti-ecological today. This potentiality, the "should be," becomes in the ethics of social ecology, the overarching standard of actualization and wholeness. Herein lies the *critical* thrust of social ecology's ethics: the fact that by educing the true actualization of humanity's potentialities, it provides a standard by which we may judge the irrationality of the "what is."

There remains still another step, or *Aufhebung*, that must be made in natural and social evolution. This is the step that transforms second nature—with all its marvelous advances and its terrible abuses—into a "synthesis" of first and second nature in the form of a harmonious, conscious, and ecological "free nature." In free nature, both human and nonhuman nature come into their own as a rational, self-conscious, and purposeful unity. Humanity, as a product of natural evolution, brings its consciousness to the service of both first and second nature. It brings its consciousness to the service of first nature by diminishing the impact of natural catastrophes, and promoting the thrust of natural evolution toward diversity and ending needless suffering, thereby fueling the creativity of natural evolution through its technics, science, and rationality. In free nature, we would no longer expect human beings to regard themselves as the lords of creation but as conscious beings, indeed as the products of natural evolution, in the rich ecological mosaic of an ecocommunity. There, human needs and the needs of nonhuman life-forms would be joined in a complementary way so that there is a beneficial, reciprocal relationship between the two. In this truly mutualistic free nature, humanity would cease to be divided against the nonhuman world—and against itself. Indeed, in free nature, human society would be nonhierarchial and cooperative. Society's "completeness" would be based on the "completeness" of humans in their self-fulfillment as rational, free, and self-conscious beings.

Free nature's end is hardly a predetermined "final cause" in a Scholastic sense, nor a predetermined course of social evolution. There is no certainty that society will become free and rational and thereby ecological. The potentiality of society to develop into its fullness is immanent but not inevitable. Today our *conceptions* of freedom have never been so fully elaborated, but it requires a supreme act of consciousness, as Bookchin emphasizes, to achieve a free world. Since we have not attained this free nature, human beings still remain in the perverted development of second nature, and first nature is still being grievously harmed. But we can certainly advance a vision of "free nature" as an ethical "should be" that alone would mark the fruition of nature's and humanity's potentialities, and we can seek to develop an ethics of complementarity, even as we fight to destroy hierarchy in society. It is the end, the telos, so to speak, albeit by no means a predetermined one, toward which we strive to fulfill both ourselves and first nature.16

The ethics of social ecology has particularly profound implications for women. As human beings, women are beings whose lives are no more determined by biology than are men's. Unlike other female animals, the human female is capable of making decisive choices about when and under what circumstances she will reproduce. The distinction between the facile ethical proposals of some ecofeminists and social ecology's ethics should be especially clear on the issue of abortion and reproductive freedom generally. An ethical prescription superficially drawn from first nature which argues that all life is sacred would, if its adherents are to be consistent, oblige us to oppose abortion on the grounds that it is destructive to "life." By contrast, in social ecology's ethics, in which first nature is a realm of increasing subjectivity out of which society emerges, women would have a right to reproductive freedom that is grounded in the emergence of society and natural evolution. As human beings uniquely capable of making ethical choices that increase their freedom in the context of an ecological whole, women's reproductive freedom would be a given.

With an ecological ethics grounded in the potentiality of human beings to consciously and rationally create a free ecological society, we can begin to develop an ecological political movement that challenges the existing order on the grounds that it denies both humans and nonhumans their full actualization. To meet that challenge, we need the best faculties we have—our knowledge of nature, and the understanding of what we should be.

NOTES

1. R.G. Collingwood, *The Idea of Nature* (Oxford: Clarendon Press, 1945, reprinted New York: Oxford University Press, 1978), p. 6; John Herman Randall, Jr., *Aristotle* (New York: Columbia University Press, 1960).
2. John Herman Randall, Jr., *The Making of the Modern Mind* (Boston: Houghton Mifflin, 1926, 1940), p. 269.
3. Bookchin, *Ecology of Freedom*, pp. 234–35.
4. Randall, *Making of the Modern Mind*, p. 269.
5. Bookchin, *Ecology of Freedom*, pp. 285–86.
6. Ibid., p. 238.
7. Jonas, *Gnostic Religion*, p. 323.
8. Bookchin, *Ecology of Freedom*, pp. 270, 165.
9. Ibid., p. 271.
10. Bookchin, *Ecology of Freedom*, pp. 235, 273.
11. Ibid., p. 235.
12. On dialectical naturalism, see Murray Bookchin, *The Philosophy of Social Ecology*, (Montreal: Black Rose Books, 1990). The following discussion is based largely on this book.
13. Ibid., p. 30.
14. Ibid., p. 31.
15. See G. W. F. Hegel, *The Logic*, translated from *The Encyclopaedia of the Philosophical Sciences* by William Wallace, 2d ed., rev. (London: Oxford University Press, 1968).
16. On the ethics of social ecology, see Bookchin, *Ecology of Freedom* and *The Philosophy of Social Ecology*.

Marx's Inorganic Body

John Clark

John Clark is professor of philosophy at Loyola University in New Orleans. He is the author of several books, including The Anarchist Moment: Reflections on Culture, Nature and Power, *and is editor of* Renewing the Earth: The Promise of Social Ecology. *He also edits* Mesachabe: The Journal of Surre(gion)alism.

"Nature is man's inorganic body," according to Marx. But what are we to make of this image? In the view of some recent observers, the conception of nature expressed in this formulation is an ecological one. According to one such commentator, Marx's vision implies that "it is natural for man, the conscious social being, to act rationally and consciously for the good of all species, which is his own long-range good (since nature is his body)."[1] But the same Marx who sees nature as "man's inorganic body" also describes "locomotives, railways, electric telegraphs, self-acting mules, etc." as "organs of the human brain."[2] At best, we seem to be dealing here with a highly distorted body-consciousness.

But perhaps we should not be so hasty in tearing apart the Marxian corpus. As Wordsworth warned us about the impetuously analytical mind, "we murder to dissect." Instead, we should look at the whole of Marx's conception of nature, and its relation to his larger problematic. If we do so, we will find more coherence than these conflicting body-images might suggest, and deeper contradictions than many might suspect.

A longer version of this essay originally appeared in *Environmental Ethics*, Vol. 11, No. 3 (Fall 1989), 243–258. Reprinted with permission.

ECOLOGIZING MARX: PARSONS

The most extensive recent attempt to defend the ecological character of Marx's work is Howard Parsons' 118-page introductory essay to his collection *Marx and Engels on Ecology*. Yet despite numerous references to ecology and environmental problems and valiant attempts to relate these to Marx, he presents little evidence of truly ecological analysis in Marx's own writings, and fails entirely to demonstrate that Marx's predominant perspective toward nature was ecological. Indeed, in spite of himself, Parsons shows that Marx's position on every practical issue reduces to a concern for the more rational exploitation of nature for human ends.

Parsons succeeds in finding abundant evidence of ecological thinking in Marx, but uses a questionable method of interpretation: Automatically putting the most ecologically correct construction on every statement. For example, the famous passage concerning "man's inorganic body" is invoked to show that according to Marx, "man participates organically, i.e., dialectically, in nature."[3] Presumably, we are to focus all our attention on the "organic" term "body." Yet this still leaves us with the rather perplexing and embarrassing fact that the evidence for a reality being "organic" is that it is described as being "inorganic" !

He deals similarly with Marx's contention that to say that "man's physical and spiritual life is linked to nature means simply that nature is linked to itself, for man is a part of nature." He asks rhetorically whether there has ever been "a better, a more succinct, ecological statement of man's place in nature than this."[4] But Marx's statement is evidence of no more than a naturalist or materialist position. Only a detailed analysis of Marx's conception of the "link" between this human "part" and the rest of nature can determine the extent to which such a view is ecological.

Parsons is rather astute in tracing certain implications of a dialectical analysis that lead far from the mechanistic, instrumentalist direction that Marx and most of the Marxist tradition have taken. He argues, quite cogently, that the "logic of man's dialectical relation to nonhuman nature does in fact lead to the conclusion that the ground of values, if not the values themselves, is prior to and independent of man's conscious intervention in and enjoyment of non-human nature."[5] He goes so far as to interpret value not as "an epiphenomenon added to fact," but as "an inherent activity of matter."[6] Evolution can thus be seen to have "a certain directiveness," in which there is a building up of a temporal structure of levels from the simple to the complex."[7] Thus an ecological analysis finds in nature development, emergence, and self-organization.

Significantly, Parsons's discussion of these issues relies very little on Marx himself. Rather, he looks at the implications of a dialectical and ecological perspective, a position which is certainly not identical with Marx's work or the Marxist tradition, which has no patent on dialectics.

Indeed, the most extensive elaboration of such an ecological dialectic has been social ecology, which includes a comprehensive critique of Marxian social theory and philosophy of nature.[8]

Parsons sees only the most noble and theoretically extraneous reasons for the rather glaring failure of Marx and Engels to develop the ecological aspects of their thought. There was, he explains, a more pressing theoretical need for the development of the critique of political economy and greater practical need for amelioration of the suffering of the masses.[9] The possibility of a contradiction between an ecological perspective and the Marxian project of technological development, liberation of productive forces, and political centralization is not considered.

Marx's critique certainly sounds ecological when, as Parsons notes, he condemns capitalism for its "drive towards unlimited extension of production, towards production as an end in itself, towards unconditional development of the social productivity of labour."[10] Parsons concludes that Marx is arguing for the "essential incompatibility" between capitalist production and "the system of nature."[11] But Marx's point is not that this expansionism is in conflict with nature, but rather that capital's quest for surplus value contradicts and limits this development in some ways, to the detriment of humanity. However, an ecological critique would question this very expansionism as being in contradiction with the "system of nature." But the Marxist position, including the version defended by Parsons, holds that after the contradictions between forces and relations of production are resolved, the expansion of production will not be limited, but rather "unfettered."

Of course, there is still to be a limit in the form of rational control of production on behalf of "man's" development. But this does not mean that there would be any limits based on a larger ecological approach, in a non-anthropocentric sense. Parsons seems very naive in claiming that when "essential human needs are secured" people will overcome egocentrism, and that when "there is no need to exploit natural beings," then "exploitation does not occur."[12] For it is quite conceivable that long after all needs that can reasonably be defined as "essential" are fulfilled, human demands on the natural world could still go far beyond ecologically optimal levels.

Parsons, like most Marxists, fails to address the question of productionist ideology. Any political regime which legitimates itself on the basis of fulfilling "human needs" through "development of productive forces" has an enormous incentive to expand and manipulate material consumptionist needs as a means of social control. There is no reason to think that a system of centralized state socialism (or state capitalism, which is, in fact, what orthodox Marxism advocates) would fulfill "real" needs, rather than creating artificial ones, or that it would resolve the contradiction between the industrial and technological system and "the system of nature."

Parsons notes that Marx and Engels accepted the capitalist "stratagem" of "subduing" nature for the sake of "human requirements." He holds that their position is ecologically superior to that of capitalism in holding, first, that the mastery should benefit all people; secondly, that it should "maintain the dialectical balance of natural ecology in harmony with human needs," instead of destroying nature; and finally, that it should include "theoretical understanding and esthetic appreciation" of nature, rather than "contempt."[13] But these stipulations yield, at best, a reformist environmentalism, rather than assuring a radically or even strongly ecological position. For a "mastery" that "maintains" environmental conditions according to the demands of human needs and benefits translates into mere resource management, rather than ecological practice. The acceptance of an understanding and appreciation of nature is compatible with ecologically unenlightened viewpoints (not to mention, the most refined of bourgeois sensibilities).

ECOLOGIZING MARX: LEE

Another notable, though more modest, attempt to salvage Marx as an ecological thinker has been made by Donald C. Lee. It is his position that "both Marxism and capitalism are greedy, violent and destructive of nature" unless they are "ameliorated" by the kind of humanism found in Marx's early works.[14]

Unfortunately, the evidence given in favor of the ecological "early" Marx consists primarily of vague generalities. We are told, for instance, that Marx recognized that "nature was here first,"[15] that "the human being is part of nature,"[16] and that "each of us is identical with each other and with nature."[17] On the basis of such "ecological" propositions, we are urged to conclude from these statements that Marxism strives for an "environmentally unalienated social order."[18]

Yet it is clear from Lee's defense that Marx's analysis is predicated on the very "man-nature dichotomy" that is allegedly absent. Thus, the existence of "ecological difficulties" is attributed to a failure to "master nature" adequately.[19] Alienation from nature is conceived of in a way that it can be overcome by "the extension of human power over nature," and, specifically, "by the social development of machines."[20] As will be shown later, what underlies views such as these is a quite non-ecological humanism. Marx's identification of ecological practice with rational mastery of nature for the good of the human species most definitely preserves the 'dichotomy" that reduces nature to an instrument of human development. His decrying of alienation from nature as "man's" failure to rationally use nature as a means is founded on his affirmation of a deeper alienation from nature.[21]

In his reply to his critics, Lee falls back on the weak claim (similar to that of Parsons) that since Marx's view is dialectical, it *must* be ecological. Thus, we are told that Marx, "for a moment, is clearsighted and sees beyond the myopic view of his age (and ours) to a position in which mankind sees itself as determined by and determinant of nature.. . ."[22] But recognizing such a "mutual determination" on some level does not demonstrate a strongly ecological analysis. The question is begged of the extent to which the actual content of Marx's conception of the relation between humanity and nature is ecological, and, indeed, dialectical. In fact, we are given no evidence that his cosmos was even vaguely as ecological as that "enchanted world" of most traditional peoples on whom he looked back with the most civilized contempt.[23]

DE-ECOLOGIZING MARX: TOLMAN

Charles Tolman's reply to Lee demonstrates ably, if inadvertently, the extent to which Marx's ideas can be plausibly developed in a non-ecological direction. While Tolman sees a certain kind of dialectic at work in history, he does not comprehend this as an ecological dialectic encompassing humanity and the whole of nature in a process of mutual development and unfolding of potentiality. Rather, it remains a human struggle with nature to better utilize the latter as a means for human development. Knowledge of nature is seen as power over nature, in which a "better theoretical understanding of nature" leads to "real mastery of nature."[24]

Of course, the mastery "moves forward fully conscious of the reciprocity and interdependence of nonhuman nature and human needs and aspirations."[25] But this "full consciousness" turns out to be quite limited when one examines the nature of the project. Our opinion of whether a theory is "ecological" must not be based on what the theorist thinks of the theory. Rather, it must rest on how the theory expresses a certain practical relationship between humanity and nature.

In this case, we find an extreme expression of an important aspect of Marx's thought, his productionism. According to Tolman, the central problem of history is (as Marx said in his "preface" to the *Contribution to the Critique of Political Economy*) the liberation of the forces of production. Thus, we find that "environmental problems can only be solved by further advances in the forces of technology."[26] Of course, ecologists often point out that the ecological crisis has been in large part the result of such technological development. Tolman replies, as a good Marxist technological utopian, that the problem has only been the misuse of technology for capitalist purposes, and that socialist technology will cure all ills.

He does not confront the issue of technological rationality and its truly revolutionary effects on modern society, though he does comment, quite revealingly, on the question of consciousness. Rather than forming a barrier to the development of liberatory consciousness, the continuing expansion of the technological system only assures the emergence of critical rationality. This is true because "advance in the forces of production themselves brings with it advance in the consciousness, the motivation and know-how required to bring about the effective transformation of the relations of production."[27] Such a naive and ahistorical faith in technological development is more understandable for Marx's epoch, though some of his contemporaries (particularly those in certain dissident anarchist, utopian, aesthetic, and spiritual traditions) managed to escape it. To perpetuate such an uncritical view of technological development today, despite all evidence against a positive correlation between "advances" in productive forces and growth of critical consciousness (not to mention, ecological consciousness) is astounding.

ECOLOGICAL TENDENCIES IN MARX'S THOUGHT

It is true that there is an implicit ecological dimension to Marx. His philosophy of nature has affinities with ecological thought to the degree to which it maintains the teleological and dialectical perspective that is characteristic of much of his social analysis. Albert Schmidt has argued that Marx's materialist dialectic is non-teleological, in the sense that it contains no doctrine of immanent teleology, but rather only what Hegel calls the "finite-teleological standpoint" arising from the particular ends posited by human beings.[28] Yet Marx retains more of his Aristotelian and Hegelian heritage than this interpretation allows.

This aspect of Marx's thought has been forcefully defended by Scott Meikle in his work, *Essentialism in the Thought of Karl Marx*. He argues that beginning with the emphasis on grasping the "specific nature" of phenomena in the "Critique of Hegel's Doctrine of the State," Marx develops a dialectical methodology in which necessary development determined by the nature or essence of the thing is the focus of analysis.[29] According to this view, a phenomenon cannot be adequately understood according to a static, atomistic analysis; rather, it must be comprehended as a being in process or movement, in which its ergon or peculiar behavior is related to its telos or completed form of development.

Implied in this teleological dialectic is a profoundly organicist dimension, in which the dialectical movement of things is shown to be determined by their place in larger wholes and conditioned by the development of these wholes. These elements of Marx's thought form the basis for what Rader calls the "organic totality" model in Marx's thinking, and for what Ollman discusses as his doctrine of "internal relations."[30] They are exhibited in Marx's assertion that "a being that does not have its nature outside itself is not a natural being,"[31] and in his analysis of the phenomena of history, in which "the whole thing can be shown in its totality (and therefore, too, the reciprocal action of these various sides of one another)."[32]

On the basis of such concepts, the way is opened for the development of a truly ecological dialectic that avoids what Marx aptly diagnoses as "the antithesis of nature and history."[33] In such a dialectic, the entire course of natural history, including the emergence of life, consciousness, and self-consciousness (with all its modes of rationality and symbolization) are seen as aspects of the development of a complex whole. Central to such an analysis is an elaboration of the mutual determination of all forms of life within the biosphere as a unity-in-diversity.

It must be recognized that Marx does on rare occasions move in the direction of such an ecological dialectic. Parsons is able to quote one excellent passage in which Marx presents a social ecological interpretation of the effects of urbanization on agriculture. He perceptively comments that concentration of population under capitalist production prevents "the circulation of matter between man and soil," and has negative effects on both urban health and rural culture.[34] This is one of Marx's most genuinely ecological analyses, in that he integrates the physical, biological, economic, and social aspects of the problem.

Yet Marx himself fails to go very far in developing these rudiments of an ecological dialectic. Quite to the contrary, his thought preserves much of the radically non-ecological dualism that is typical of Western thought, and, indeed, of civilization itself. To develop the submerged ecological dimension of Marx would mean the negation of key aspects of his philosophy of history, his theory of human nature, and his view of social transformation. It would mean the destruction of the productionism and instrumentalism that defenders of Marx like Parsons, Lee, and Tolman still adhere to in varying degrees. The nature of this dominant current in Marx's thought must now be explored.

"MAN'S INORGANIC BODY"

It is understandable that some might feel inclined to credit Marx with a kind of ecological consciousness because of his image of nature in his early works as "man's inorganic body." Indeed, given the tradition of extreme dualism in Western thought, beginning with Plato's condemnation of matter as the prison of spirit and inert receptacle of form, and extending through Descartes' radical dichotomy between thinking and extended substance, such a recognition of the inextricable interdependence between humanity and nature seems a welcome advance. Yet it is important to grasp the precise significance of this image for Marx and to relate it to other images of nature presented in his work.

The discussion of the "inorganic body" in the Paris Manuscripts retains both a dualistic view of humanity and nature and an instrumentalist view of the latter. On the one hand, Marx distinguishes between nature as "organic body," that is, as human body, and nature as "inorganic body," that is, the rest of nature. While a mere distinction between two such realms within material nature is not, obviously, in itself an ontological false step, the valuation underlying the distinction is another question. The "inorganic" quality of "external" nature signifies its instrumental character in relation to an abstracted humanity, which is taken to be the source of all value. Nature is thus valued as a "direct means of life," and as "the material, the object, and the instrument" of the "life activity" of "man."[35] Estrangement from nature is in no way taken to mean non-recognition of intrinsic value throughout nature or of the interrelatedness between human value and the larger unfolding of value over the course of natural history. Rather, it means the failure of "man" to utilize nature self-consciously and collectively in productivity, that is, in "the objectification of man's species-life."[36]

The ecological world view proposes that humanity should see itself as part of a larger organic whole, and that although humanity may indeed be the culmination of the present stage of global evolution, it occupies an inseparable place in a biospheric community of life and mind. Marx's image of the relationship between humanity and nature remains the proprietary one bequeathed to us when the God of ancient Israel gave Adam dominion over the earth. But Marx desires to remain truer to Jehovah's wishes than has civilization thus far. He offers the promise that when private property in land is abolished, "the earth ceases to be an object of huckstering, and through free labor and free enjoyment becomes once more a true personal property of man."[37] Nature, apart from human transformative activity is accorded no value by "man." (Or, perhaps more accurately, it has a significance which must be repressed, both ideologically and through a praxis of negation.) Nature as being-in-itself, or worse, being that is, to no matter how rudimentary a degree, being-for-itself, must be transformed into being for "man." Through his production, "nature appears as his work and his reality," and thus, "he sees himself in a world he has created."[38]

While Marx has been applauded for his conception of "the true resurrection of nature," and there has developed a tradition of mystical and spiritualized Marxism, this tendency has, at best, a shaky foundation in Marx's own speculations. For he states clearly that this "resurrection" consists not in the rising up of that nature done in by such assassins as the Newtonians and the Cartesians, but rather in "man" himself rising up out of the grave of nature. This occurs when private property is abolished and the species collectively appropriates nature, so that the truly human quality of self-creation can be universally achieved for "man." Only at that stage can "his natural existence become his human existence, and nature become man for him."[39] Thus far Marx, prophet not of resurrected nature, but of triumphant enlightenment. *Wo es war, soll Mensch werden!*

It is true that in the Paris Manuscripts Marx rejects a certain kind of opposition between human reality and nature, arguing that "history itself is a real part of natural history."[40] What is more, he even goes so far as to cite approvingly the interpretation of "the formation of the earth, the development of the earth," as "self-generation."[41] Yet rather than taking seriously the idea of human development as part of a larger system of self-unfolding in nature, he quickly reverts to the view of humanity as supreme self-creator. As Jehovah created "man" from formless, lifeless matter, from "the dust of the earth," Marx's "man" creates himself without the assistance of any active, developing nature. For "the entire so-called history of the world is nothing but the creation of man through human labor" so that he has "the visible, irrefutable proof of his own birth through himself."[42] Nature, apart from "man," is therefore necessary only as an instrument in this self-creation. This is not, Marx insists, "utility" in the vulgar sense of the pursuit of individual egoistic satisfaction, but it remains a utilitarian view of nature in a broader, universalistic sense. Thus, "nature has lost its mere utility by use becoming human use."[43]

PROMETHEAN MAN

A similar conception of the relationship between humanity and nature is found in Marx's mature work. It is now placed within the context of a highly developed problematic of human liberation through productivity, technological development, and control of nature. The most detailed discussion of these issues is found in the *Grundrisse.* In that work, Marx repeatedly stresses the theme that historical progress depends on a continual expansion of human domination of nature. The bourgeois epoch is judged progressive for humanity, since despite economic exploitation there has been an enormous expansion of the forces of production. Capitalism, in its ruthless drive toward expansion, has created the preconditions for that many-sided human self-development which is the goal of history; a development that depends on an abundance attainable only through conquest of the forces of nature. For "when the limited bourgeois form is stripped away, what is wealth other than the universality of individual needs, capacities, pleasures, productive forces, etc. created through universal exchange? The full development of human mastery over the forces of nature, those of so-called nature as well as of humanity's own nature?"[44]

Marx waxes eloquent, indeed almost rhapsodic, in his depiction of the ever-expanding power of capital to create new social forms, new human capacities and needs, and new possibilities for human development, for what he earlier called "species-life." This, he says, is "the great civilizing influence of capital; its production of a stage of society in comparison to which all earlier ones appear as mere local developments of humanity and as nature-idolatry."45 Previously, humanity was limited by conceptions of nature which accorded it respect, or even (perish the thought!) reverence. In Marx's view, such attitudes and sensibilities were a product of humanity's inability to master nature. As he had formulated it in *The German Ideology*, early people were "overawed like beasts" by nature's "all-powerful and unassailable force."46 In the *Grundrisse* he speculates that nature mythology was an attempt at illusory domination of nature through the imagination, when actual domination was impossible. Needless to say, "it therefore vanishes with the advent of real mastery."47

Thus, one of the great contributions of capital to human progress is its supposed completion of this process of "disenchantment of the world," owing to its successes in mastering nature. Marx is quite frank in his description of what is left of nature after all "mystical veils" are stripped away—and his vision is far from ecological. "For the first time, nature becomes purely an object for humankind, purely a matter of utility; ceases to be recognized as a power for itself; and the theoretical discovery of its autonomous laws appears merely as a ruse to subjugate it under human needs, whether as an object of consumption or as a means of production."48 Putting aside the narrowness of the bourgeois conception of utility, this result is precisely what is required for the project of human emancipation through expansion of productivity. For it is only "capital's ceaseless striving" that "drives labour beyond the limits of its natural paltriness (*Naturbedürftigkeit*) and thus creates the material elements for the development of. . .rich individuality."49

What Marx finally proposes in the *Grundrisse* as the prerequisite for the emergence of the realm of freedom out of the realm of necessity is a highly automated technological system, in which abundance is ultimately achieved through processes of efficient collective mastery of nature. On the one side stands "man," who, having passed through the "steeling school of labor," has sufficiently subjugated internal nature, armored himself, and transformed himself into a being capable of conquering all foes. On the other side stands nature as the object to be mastered. As the "middle link" there is "the process of nature, transformed into an industrial process,"50 nature turned against itself through the ingenuity of "man." Previously objectified nature becomes the instrument through which living, growing, developing nature is reduced to a lifeless system of objects. Nature becomes its own gravedigger.

Paradoxically, this mechanized nature becomes more "organic" to "man" than the living whole of nature can ever be. Thus, "machines,. . .locomotives, railways, electric telegraphs, self-acting mules, etc." are "natural material transformed into organs of the human will over nature, or of human participation in nature" and "organs of the human brain, created by the human hand," in which "the power of knowledge" is "objectified."[51] Indeed, no organism has ever evolved an organ more suitably adapted to its telos, for in Marx's problematic of human emancipation, the end of humanity, the full unfolding of powers and development of needs, can only be attained through success in the project of the mastery of nature.

Marx's conception of human action on nature perpetuates certain dualisms going back in Western thought to the Greeks. Carol Gould has perceptively commented on the analogy between Marx's view of the nature of form in natural and in made objects and that presented by Aristotle.[52] In the *Grundrisse,* Marx comments that in the made object "there is an indifference on the part of the substance (*Stoff*) towards the form," whereas in the natural object there is an "immanent law of reproduction" that "maintains its form."[53] While this conception fails to recognize the real contribution of nature to the forms of even made objects, it exhibits a recognition of teleology in nature. However, Marx does not develop this teleological conception, which might have enabled him to see in nature emergent subjectivity, developing freedom, and intrinsic value. Instead, what prevails in his thought is another neo-Aristotelian line of analysis which leads in a radically anthropocentric direction.

The prevailing tendency in Marx's analysis is to ignore the significance of form in nature, and to reduce nature to a source of unqualified matter which must be formed and given value through the instrumental activities of "man." It is mere raw material, *materia prima,* lacking actuality, to be given form and value through human techne. "Man" recreates nature in his own image, as an extension of himself. Thus, nature appears as "the pre-existing arsenal of all objects of labor,"[54] "the automatic system of machinery" serves as the means by which to "transmit the worker's activity to the object" or "on to the raw material,"[55] and ultimately, as he had formulated it as early as the Paris Manuscripts, "all objects become for him the objectification of himself, become objects which confirm and realize his individuality, become his objects: that is, man himself becomes the object."[56] The limit of "man's" conquest of nature is therefore his annihilation of it as (to adapt a useful term) a significant Other. It is pure Other, the field for dominating self-assertation, through which human power alone is signified.

OEDIPAL MAN

The necessity that "man" annihilate external nature as a determining force betrays Marx's underlying hostility to nature as a limiting maternal power. In *Capital* he discusses the disastrous effects on "man" of nature as nurturing mother. "Where Nature is too lavish, she 'keeps him in hand, like a child in leading-strings.' She does not impose upon him any necessity to develop himself."[57] Primitive "man" suffers from a "narrowness" in social relationships, because he "has not yet severed the umbilical cord" that ties him to the maternal tribal body and the maternal body of the earth.[58] Primitive "man," in what Marx sees as the infancy of the race (for even the Greeks had only reached "the historic childhood of humanity" !), will remain helplessly dependent until the organic ties with the maternal body are sundered.

In order to achieve independence, "man" must successfully pass through a kind of Oedipal stage in which his infantile maternal attachments are overcome and he attains the power of a self-determining being. But it can never be nature as benevolent, nuturing mother, but only nature as a more demanding, phallic power that can enable "man" to become such an independent and powerful being. Since God the patriarchal father is dead, nature herself must take on the paternal role in the world-historical familial drama.

Fortunately, the stingy, "paltry" nature of certain climes has precisely the correct paternal qualities. Now playing the role of the severe and demanding patriarch, "paltry" nature imposes on "man" the necessity to rely on his own resources, and to develop the capacity to successfully rebel against nature's domination. Indeed, in *Capital* Marx cites in support of his views a passage in which nature is portrayed as the judicious father who grants the adolescent son only the most meager material assistance, so as to force the latter to become independent and self-reliant: "The earth's spontaneous productions being in small quantity, and quite independent of man, appear, as it were, to be furnished by Nature, in the same way as a small sum is given to a young man, in order to put him in a way of industry, and of making his fortune."[59] Nature thus gives "man" the opportunity to prove his manhood, to demonstrate his own powers.

"Man" thus successfully breaks his self-limiting bonds of dependency on maternal nature and takes advantage of the challenges offered him by nature in the guise of surrogate patriarch. Once he has established his independence (or the illusion of independence, which will suffice), the maternal and paternal roles of nature are seemingly surpassed. Nature (and, of course, we are referring always to that "external" nature that "man" confronts in transformative praxis) becomes a pure negative, an Other necessary only as the object through which he develops and expresses his power. The mechanistic and instrumentalist images of nature favored by Marx—nature as "larder" and "tool house," for example—illustrate most adequately his conception of its significance for fully-mature "man."[60]

This is not to say that the nature that is finally "mastered" in the project of technological domination has lost for Marx all aspects of the maternal and the feminine. The significance to Marx of the inevitable return to nature as all-embracing mother is reflected in the extent to which this theme is systematically suppressed in his thought. And nature must retain an underlying femininity, given Marx's traditionalist conceptions of gender. For in achieving maturity and "mastery," "man" has attained what Marx described as his favorite masculine virtue, "strength," while nature comes to manifest emminently his preferred feminine virtue, "weakness."[61] The domination of nature signifies in an important sense the domination of the masculine over the feminine—whatever we are promised regarding the eventual emancipation of woman as worker or even as human being.

CONCLUSION: "THE SIRENS ALL SINK DOWN"

Marx's vision of nature is, then, far from ecological. The ecological world view comprehends nature as a whole, as a unity-in-diversity in which the development of each being is an inseparable part of a larger system of development and unfolding of value.[62] Marx's hopes for an end to the opposition between nature and history, his recognition of the teleological nature of phenomena, and his dialectical methodology, with its emphasis on development, internal relations, and organic wholes point the way toward a truly ecological dialectic.[63] Yet in his anthropocentrism, his instrumentalist view of nature, and in his problematic of liberation through technological domination he failed to overcome the fatal anti-ecological dualisms of the Western tradition. Rather, he succeeded only in founding them more securely in an ideology of humanism, enlightened rationality, and revolutionary transformation that could speak more coherently to the modern age.

Marx's Promethean and Oedipal "man" is a being who is not at home in nature, who does not see the earth as the "household" of ecology. Rather, he is an indomitable spirit who must subjugate nature in his quest for self-realization. The young Marx described such a spirit in an early poem:

> I am caught in endless strife,
> Endless ferment, endless dream;
> I cannot conform to Life,
> Will not travel with the stream.[64]

For such a being, the forces of nature, whether in the form of his own unmastered internal nature or the menacing powers of external nature, must be subdued. He, like Homer's paradigmatic civilized man, Odysseus, must, through repression and domination, vanquish the Sirens. As Marx sums it up in another of his early poetical works:

> The Sirens all sink down
> Before his blazing frown
> In weeping springs of light.
> They seek to follow him.

But ah, the Flood so grim
Engulfs them all from sight."[65]

NOTES

1. Donald C. Lee, "On the Marxian View of the Relationship between Man and Nature," in *Environmental Ethics* 2 (1980), p. 16. The present discussion presupposes a distinction between an anthropocentric, environmentalist view that advocates the regulation of nature for the sake of a real or presumed human good, and an authentically ecological view, which situates the human good in a larger system of goods. In criticizing Marxist environmentalism as inadequately ecological, I develop some of the points made in Val Routley's reply to Lee, "On Karl Marx as Environmental Hero," in *Environmental Ethics* 3 (1981): 237–244.
2. Karl Marx, *Grundrisse: Foundations of the Critique of Political Economy* (New York: Vintage Books, 1973), p. 706.
3. Howard L. Parsons, ed. *Marx and Engels on Ecology* (Westport, Conn.: Greenwood Press, 1977), p. 10.
4. Ibid.
5. Ibid., p. 50.
6. Ibid., p. 52.
7. Ibid., p. 78.
8. See Murray Bookchin, "Marxism as Bourgeois Sociology," in *Toward an Ecological Society* (Montreal: Black Rose Books, 1980). For a discussion of the implications of social ecology for a variety of fields, see John P. Clark, ed. *Renewing the Earth: The Promise of Social Ecology* (London: Green Print, 1990).
9. Parsons, p. 24.
10. Ibid., p. 29.
11. Ibid.
12. Ibid., p.65.
13. Ibid., pp. 67–68.
14. Lee, p. 4.
15. Ibid., p. 5.
16. Ibid., p. 8.
17. Ibid., p. 9.
18. Ibid., p. 11.
19. Ibid., p. 7.
20. Ibid., p. 9.
21. For the sake of space, I will not draw out all the implications of Lee's acceptance of principles such as that " 'overpopulation' is but a function of 'underemployment' " (p. 11). It is true that the concept of "overpopulation" is an ideological one, though today it is used more to legitimate exploitation of the Third World than of the Western proletariat. But the Marxian principle cited, which was once an effective immanent critique of the Malthusian premises of political economy, is less than critical from a social-ecological perspective, even if adapted to the contemporary world economy. The social-ecological view of population deals not only with the relation between humanity and the system of production, but also with the complex interrela-

tionships between human communities and the larger eco-communities of which we are a part.

22. Donald C. Lee, "Toward a Marxian Ecological Ethic: A Response to Two Critics" in *Environmental Ethics* 4 (1982), p. 343.
23. For an incisive critique of the enlightenment views that he shared and a compelling defense of the lost tradition, see Morris Berman, *The Reenchantment of the World* (Ithaca: Cornell University Press, 1981). One should also not neglect Collingwood's classic *The Idea of Nature* (London and New York: Oxford University Press, 1960).
24. Charles Tolman, "Karl Marx, Alienation, and the Mastery of Nature" in *Environmental Ethics 3* (1981), p. 73.
25. Ibid. Presumably, the consciousness will still reside in the "masters" rather than the "mastery"; however, this objectifying language is revealing.
26. Ibid.
27. Ibid., p. 70. This demonstrates well a problem mentioned by Hwa Yol Jung: the Marxian neglect of the metaphysical problem of technology. See "Marxism, Ecology, and Technology" in *Environmental Ethics* 5 (1983): 169–171.
28. Alfred Schmidt, *The Concept of Nature in Marx* (London: New Left Books, 1971), pp. 37–38.
29. Scott Meikle, *Essentialism in the Thought of Karl Marx* (La Salle, Illinois: Open Court, 1985), pp. 42–43.
30. See Melvin Rader, *Marx's Interpretation of History* (New York: Oxford University Press, 1979), Chs. 2 and 3; and Bertell Ollman, *Alienation: Marx's Concept of Man in Capitalist Society* (Cambridge and New York: Cambridge University Press, 1971), Ch. 3.
31. Karl Marx, *Economic and Philosophic Manuscripts of 1844* (Moscow: Progress Publishers, 1974), p. 135.
32. Karl Marx and Frederick Engels, *The German Ideology* (New York: International Publishers, 1947), p. 28.
33. Ibid., p. 30. For an indication of the direction in which such a "Left Aristotelian" position might develop, see John Ely, "Anarchism and Animism" in *Renewing the Earth*, pp. 49–65.
34. Parsons, p. 21.
35. Marx, *Economic and Philosophical Manuscripts*, p. 67.
36. Ibid., p. 69.
37. Ibid., p. 59.
38. Ibid., p. 69.
39. Ibid., p. 92.
40. Ibid., p. 98.
41. Ibid., p. 99. Note also the contrast between the concept of such instrumental activity as "participation," and, for example, the *participation mystique* of animism, described by Norman O. Brown as "symbolical consciousness, the erotic sense of reality." *Love's Body* (New York: Vintage, 1966), p. 254.
42. Ibid., p. 100.
43. Ibid., p. 94.
44. Karl Marx, *Grundrisse*, p. 488.
45. Ibid., pp. 409–410.
46. Marx, *The German Ideology*, p. 19. Marx's term is *imponieren*, literally, "to impress." Since "beasts" in nature, while giving evidence of fear and flight reactions, seem to have little propensity to being "overawed" by superior

forces, perhaps his model was a domesticated European beast "overawed" by a paterfamilias *en colère.*

47. Marx, *Grundrisse,* p. 110.

48. Ibid., p. 410. It is unconvincing and undialectical to interpret this passage as being merely a negative criticism of capitalism. Marx's point is that despite capitalist abuses there is a true *Aufhebung* present in which the disenchantment and objectification will be preserved and developed in higher social formations, rather than being annulled.

49. Ibid., p. 325.

50. Ibid., p. 705.

51. Ibid., p. 706.

52. Carol C. Gould, *Marx's Social Ontology: Individuality and Community in Marx's Theory of Social Reality* (Cambridge: MIT Press, 1978), pp. 44–45.

53. Marx, *Grundrisse,* p. 360.

54. Karl Marx, *Capital: A Critique of Political Economy* (Moscow: Progress Publishers, 1959), Vol. III, p. 825.

55. Marx, *Grundrisse,* p. 692.

56. Marx, *Economic and Philosophical Manuscripts,* p. 95.

57. Karl Marx, *Capital: A Critique of Political Economy* (New York: International Publishers, 1967), Vol. I, p. 513.

58. Ibid., Vol. I, p. 79.

59. Ibid., Vol. I, p. 178.

60. Ibid., Vol. I, p. 179.

61. Karl Marx: *The Essential Writings,* ed. by Frederic Bender (Boulder: Westview Press, 1972), p. vii. These were Marx's answers to questions in a popular game called "Confessions." He also appropriately identified his idea of happiness as "to fight" and of misery as "submission." It is not without grounds that critics like Baudrillard and Axelos have found in this serious revolutionary the absence of a notion of play. Engels' answers to the latter two questions were "Chateau Margaux 1848" and "having to go to the dentist." See "Misery and Philosophy: Marx in his Family" in Jerrold Seigel, *Marx's Fate* (Princeton: Princeton University Press, 1978), Ch. 9, for the context.

62. For a discussion of this issue, see John P. Clark, *The Anarchist Moment: Reflections on Culture, Nature, and Power* (Montréal: Black Rose Books, 1984), especially chapters 8 and 9.

63. See Murray Bookchin, *The Philosophy of Social Ecology: Essays on Dialectical Naturalism* (Montréal: Black Rose Books, 1990), especially the essay "Thinking Ecologically," for the nature of such a dialectic. For the most extensive presentation of the ecological world view, see his book *The Ecology of Freedom* (Palo Alto: Cheshire Books, 1982; revised edition, Montréal: Black Rose Books, 1990).

64. Karl Marx and Frederick Engels, *Collected Works* (New York: International Publishers, 1975–), Vol. I, p. 525.

65. Ibid., p. 545.

The Marriage of Radical Ecologies

Joel Kovel

Joel Kovel is Alger Hiss professor of social studies at Bard College. His many books include White Racism, The Age of Desire, Beyond the State of Nuclear Terror, The Radical Spirit, *and* History and Spirit.

To go beyond reformist environmentalism, to recognize that the social order itself is in some way responsible for the ecological crisis, that the historically constituted way of being human contains within itself the seeds of species destruction—this is the beginning of radical ecological politics. But it is only the beginning. What happens next depends upon our understanding of the social order and its "historically constituted way of being human." It depends also on our understanding of the domination of nature, which is the outcome of this way of being human as well as the society built around it. And this in turn depends upon our understanding of nature and domination.

Our social order is capitalist, and it is undoubtedly true that capitalism, with its insatiable extraction of energy and resources and its relentless production of waste under the imperative of accumulation, is responsible for the ecological crisis. The capitalist must obey the rule of the maximization of profit or disappear, to be replaced by another who obeys; and since profits are made by the exploitation of nature, so must capital exploit nature on an ever-increasing scale. But this, too, is only a beginning. How to proceed next depends upon both a contraction and expansion of insight: Contracting it to examine capitalism concretely—a project we cannot undertake here; and expanding it to consider capitalism beyond a narrowly economic framework, as an entire way of life based upon economization of human reality. The collapse of communism only highlights the importance of this project, for communism, notwithstanding its severe and fatal limits, did stand for the possibility of overcoming capitalism. Its demise lifts a

406

burden from the left, considering how communism had betrayed hopes for emancipation. But it also reinforces the mystique of capitalism and its aura of invincibility. If the heroic socialist revolutions of the twentieth century not only failed to dislodge capitalism but also ended up mimicking it and toadying to it, how can ecological politics hope to achieve more? And yet it must, given the ecocidal nature of the ruling order.

RADICAL ECOLOGIES

Ecological politics is praxis based upon an appropriation of what takes place at the interface between humanity and nature. We might heuristically say that this appropriation takes place in different ways according to the values given its two main terms, humanity and nature. Indeed two of the major branches of radical ecology—social ecology and deep ecology—have defined their differences precisely along this divide.

Social ecology is grounded in the critique of domination, especially the realization that no domination of nature takes place without the domination of humans. Thus it attends primarily to the human world. For social ecologists, the recovery of nature is a vital, indeed essential goal, but it cannot be the primary goal, inasmuch as the natural world has to be approached through a transformation of the human world. Deep ecology, by contrast, proceeds from the critique of anthropocentrism, that which makes man the measure of all things and displaces the rest of nature into the realm of instrumentality. This, to deep ecology, is the "social order" that oppresses nature. From this perspective, the recovery of nature is primarily a matter of decentering the human world. For the deep ecologist, nature must come first, not only in terms of value, but also as the result of an epistemological shift.

It follows that the social-ecological critique of deep ecology accuses it of an indifference to key social distinctions such as class, race, and gender, as well as a romanticization of nature that ominously flirts with reactionary, even fascistic politics. By contrast, the deep-ecological critique of social ecology accuses it of recycling the traditional distancing between humanity and nature, which has characterized all modern politics, whether bourgeois or Marxist. These are of course extreme statements; and in practice there can be considerable convergence between the two tendencies.[1] However, the differences are real, and stem from unresolved issues in the philosophy of nature. It shall be the purpose of this essay to examine some of these issues. I should state at the outset that I see myself on the social-ecological side in the dialogue of radical ecologies. I also, despite everything, remain heavily influenced by Marx, and this is itself a heterodox view within social ecology.[2] This would seem to make me doubly removed from being able to view the claims of deep ecology sympathetically. However, such is not the case. I have serious problems with the political obtuseness and/or reactionary implications of deep ecology. But deep ecology also calls attention to a profound estrangement from nature, which traditional Marxism has tended to reproduce and even social ecology has found difficult to apprehend—an estrangement that raises some fundamental questions about human nature itself.

LANGUAGE AND NATURE

In general, ecological politics has not attended sufficiently to the domain of *language*. And yet language is as close as one can come to describing the specifically human characteristic. Insofar as there is a "human nature," this would include first of all the presence of *a signified field* within human beings. This may be thought of as a dimension of meaning, so long as one regards meaningfulness in its fullest sense, and not as the mere accretion of "information." That is, humans as languaged creatures live in a created universe, a constellation of meaningfulness, mediated by word-symbols, i.e., language, which incorporates and links together all aspects of the human world. Language in this respect is sensuous as well as informational; it is expressive as well as instrumental; it defines the imaginary as well as the real; and it is the stuff of culture. Society as well as the individual in her/his subjectivity would not exist therefore without this signified realm. No other species, the remarkable dolphin notwithstanding, lives this way, for no other species creates its own world. In this sense, what we call the "environment" is a human-made entity—not only created, as it were, by human hands but also constituted as a signified realm.

I would not call this created, signified world, "second nature," for the simple reason that it does not act like nature but has the stamp of humanness on it: the presense of signification. To me, there is a radical distinction between the human and natural worlds, the blurring of which gives rise to illusory expectations that one can be continuously mediated into the other. I do not think such a continuous mediation is possible. This claim challenges a prevalent attitude of social ecologists as well as deep ecologists, which calls for a harmonization of the human and natural worlds. I share this goal. Yet it seems to me that it tends to be rather too facilely postulated, in a way that overlooks the fundamental role played by the signified field. The presence of language, the attachment of the representations of nature to nature itself, means that the path of harmonization between humanity and nature has no endpoint. Nor can it be direct; it must rather traverse the signified field in a dialectical process.

Of this, more later. First, I should like to spin out some of the implications of this signified dimension as it relates to the interface between the human and natural worlds. First of all, "nature" is a word before it is a thing. I have no doubt that the natural world exists independently of human beings, that we are only an infinitesimal corner of the universe that has happened to become conscious of itself, and that should our experiment come to a halt, through ecocide or some other means of annihilation, the universe, i.e., nature, will continue on its way as before. But all of this is beside the point, which is that when I, or any other person, regard nature, I do so through a prism constructed out of language. The only "nature" that is real for any of us is a linguistically constituted field. This may or may not correspond to the natural world that exists independently of human beings. If it does correspond, then we say that our "science" is good, or that our apprehension of nature is true—a desirable state of affairs. But the nature we apprehend—and act upon in ecological politics—is never homologous with nature-in-itself, but always includes the signification of nature. We might say that human beings may asymptotically approach union with nature, but can never achieve this so long as they live. When we die, then our flesh is dedifferentiated and rejoins the universal cycle of matter; until then, we are fated to have a kind of peculiar status, given in the capacity for language—or, what comes to the same thing, consciousness. In this sense language and consciousness are equivalent, as the peculiarity of human consciousness—its self-referentiality—is occupied by the signified dimension. As human beings we differ from the rest of nature in being able to reflect on ourselves and our own existence. Language is both the tool of such reflection and its necessity. We have a biologically programmed capacity for language, such as Chomsky has explored. But this is not the end of our relationship to language. We also have an *ontological* relation with nature—i.e., a relationship where our human being as such unfolds and language concretely appears. We are given to live a basic situation within which the apparatus for language matures and takes form. This situation is defined in the unstructuredness of humans at birth and our absolute need to develop a self through a process of attachment and separation from the source of being. In the psychological frame of reference, this source is needless to say, the parent. Ontologically, however, it becomes thematized as nature itself, the ground of being, the earth mother, and so forth.

Consciousness emerges as languaged in the dense space between self and other, occupying that space with words and making it into the signified field. Since we are not born with developed language but only its precursors, words as such are not the first occupant of ontological space in the developing human being. We must postulate, rather, an original "thing-like" quality to subjectivity, constituting a virtually immediate apprehension of the world—without, however, the benefits of a developed nervous system to give full articulation of that world. In this sense, nature may be regarded as a "thing" before it is a word. However this original, pre-languaged "thingness" belongs to the core or beginning of life, before consciousness as such emerges and becomes surrounded/encrusted with words. Thus from the standpoint of an already developed human being, nature is a word first, which must be gone through to get at the thing.[3]

What we call mystical or meditative experience consists in one degree or another of the appropriation of the primary, unlanguaged relation to nature through stripping away of ordinary consciousness. This is what opens onto the dimension of spirit, in all its myriad manifestations. However, no matter how desirable the mystic or spirit-state, it can never be a full state of being. The value of mystical experience consists precisely in its specialness, its contrast with an everyday consciousness; it depends therefore on the "normal" world of word-significations, on an ordinary consciousness to be stripped away. The state of consciousness is mediated by society, which presents a vast range of possibilities, from the technocratic-egoic form of being which characterizes industrial capitalism and violently repels spiritual experience, to the shamanistic modes which actively seek mystical transport and can still be reclaimed from fragments of the primitive, or state-free worldview. Nonetheless, even the most adept sorcerer or shaman is someone who oscillates—relatively freely, to be sure—between modes of being. Mystical or ecstatic experience is by definition a sort of passage—and where there is passage, there must be some baseline state to be passed from, or transcended, and returned to. The differences between ways of accessibility to radical spirituality are of major historical significance. They may be seen as a distinction between absolutely repressing off the spirit-dimension, and being relatively open to it. We might say it is a matter of splitting or differentiating oneself from an unmediated relation to nature—in other words, a choice between the radical nonrecognition of nature in the self, as against degree of recognition of and participation in nature. But differentiation is still a form of difference; and the most harmoniously achieved kinds of ecological organization—say, for example, the justly admired ways of many native American peoples—are still arrangements worked out by a creature who knows that she or he is not identical to nature, but must still mediate a relation to nature through language and culture. The most differentiated position is not one, therefore, of a static approximation to a vegetative condition, but one of active passage between states of being—a motion that still retains the distinction between those places and therefore never collapses the human and the natural worlds into each other.

I mean for this relationship to be understood as an enrichment of and not a limitation on the possibilities between humans and nature. In order to appreciate this we should learn to live with contradiction, that is, dialectically between contrary states of being. I mean, live with, and not simply intellectually understand, for the contradiction in question is existential. Two kinds of things obtain for us at the same time, in defiance of ordinary logic: we are at one time part of nature, fully participating in natural processes; and at the same time we are radically different from nature, ontologically destined by a dialectic between attachment and separation to define ourselves in a signified field which by its very "nature" negates nature. This contradiction is embedded in social relations, and may, through struggle, develop into an ecological society that lives more organically with nature. But the "organic" relation so sought remains human and signified, hence radically different from other organic processes in its mediation by the dialectic. To accept the contradiction, to accept the dialectic, is to live in a differentiated relation to nature. It seems to me that this should be the ontological foundation of any radical ecological politics.

By contrast, to deny that there is a contradiction, which is to say, to live by splitting, is to engage in the domination of nature. Such a position is one in which the subject does not recognize nature in the self, or the self in nature. It is specific for capitalism inasmuch as the capitalist mode of production requires thoroughgoing objectification and quantification. Here is the ground of that project hinted at above, namely, to see capitalism outside its own economic terms, as a *way of being* anchored in class relations and enforced by the state. This way of being is the economisation of reality,[4] the reduction of everything to relations of exchange, the continual penetration of markets and expansion of value, the ever-expanding power of money and the corresponding decline of the spiritual and sacred. The domination of nature is contained in this process; and when the capitalist economy becomes industrialized, monopolized, and globalized, simple domination turns into the active destruction of nature—ecocide.

In a money economy, nothing can be sacred, since to be sacred means to be nonexchangeable, while a fully developed "market" puts everything on the block. Social movements that seek to restore a sense of the sacred are already undertaking, therefore, a potentially powerful critique of capitalism. No doubt, this is easily co-optable and often squandered. It easily becomes irrational, self-indulgent posturing when not connected with real social critique. It is especially galling to witness the comfortable, empty-headed spectacles of the New Age when one recognizes the emancipatory power inherent in their originating impulse. However, those who only have room for a "real social critique," with no sense of the sacred, no drive, that is, to overcome the ontology of capital as well as its political economy, are certainly no less stunted in their politics, nor can they overcome the domination of nature.

Note, however, that a critique also holds of the other extreme—that deep-ecological fundamentalism that seeks to abolish any sense of specialness from being human, any essential difference from the rest of nature. This also loses the dialectic. The radical attack on "anthropocentrism" becomes another form of splitting when, in seeking to level out all species within nature, it deprives humans of what is in fact our peculiar nature. The dialectic, to be both part of and separate from nature, is in fact human nature, not something which can be set aside in an effort to undo the domination of nature. Aside from the very impossibility and absurdity of this—for what deep ecologist would give up transforming food before it is eaten, or wearing clothing, along with other human peculiarities such as speaking, reading, and making love?—the idea is frankly pernicious, as it denies to people the development of their very human powers. One would hope that the deep ecologist wants to respect the needs of all life on earth. He or she would not want to deprive a dog of the opportunity to sniff at any interesting odor its phenomenal sense of smell discerns, or to deprive a falcon of the chance to fly. Why, then, deny to humans the opportunity to play volleyball or string quartets, or any of the infinite number of practices that entail signification and the productive transformation of nature? The domination of nature inheres in splitting itself, in any effort to flatten out and reduce the dialectic of human being. The fully emancipated ecological society is one that encourages this dialectic to flower. Thus an ecological society is not without conflict, for the basic dialectic is not only preserved but also fully accepted. This confers a sense of respect for nature, indeed, one of wonder and reverence, which logically extends to the care for "wilderness," since wild nature, being nature most fully outside of the net of signification and the least transformed by productive labor, is the most appropriate for the dialectic. But it does not do so outside the framework of otherness. Indeed, it is only because nature must, ultimately, remain other to human beings that we can arrive at the attitude of respect, wonder and reverence.[5] We can add: A differentiated otherness gives rise to this attitude, just as a split otherness makes nature into an object for domination. What differentiated otherness means in this context is that the participation of human being in nature—which is one moment of the dialectic—becomes appropriated within the signified field—which belongs to the other moment of the dialectic, our separateness from nature. Nature therefore does not cease to be an object of transformation, but it is no longer seen as an inert object outside of ourselves, rather as an entity from which we draw our own being and re-create in the act of production. Such an ontological position goes hand-in-hand with the development of "appropriate technology"—technology that, being an extension of the body, is designed for the act of appropriation, that is, a gathering of nature within the net of human signification.

At the same time that part of nature within which our being is subtended—the body—becomes fully invested with meaning. Or to put it another way, the body ceases to be a place of repression, in the two senses of that word: A blockage, a hindrance of flow and energy; and as a denial of full consciousness, a denial of words conjoined with things. The domination of nature begins with the domination of bodies. Indeed, the major forms of social domination, of class, of race and of gender, are each mediated through the domination of nature-as-body. In class domination, the oppressed body of the slave/serf/worker is repressed and converted into a machine for the aggrandizement of the master; in racial domination, sensuousness is lost by the master, who splits off bad parts of the self and invests them in the body of the oppressed; while in patriarchy, female parts of the male self are degraded, repressed and conquered in the body of the woman. It is the myriad interconnections between these zones of otherness and splitting that constitute the fabric of a society alienated from nature—a fabric that social ecology sets itself the task of reweaving.

POESIS AND TRANSFORMATION

> I assert for My self that I do not behold the Outward Creation & that to me it is hindrance & not Action it is as the Dirt upon my feet No part of Me. What it will be Questioned When the Sun rises do you not see a round Disk of fire somewhat like a Guinea O no no I see an Innumerable company of the Heavenly host crying Holy Holy Holy is the Lord God Almighty I question not my Corporeal or Vegetative Eye any more than I would Question a Window concerning a Sight I look thro it & not with it.
>
> —*William Blake, "A Vision of the The Last Judgment"* [6]

Since the warp of the social fabric consists of significations, this task cannot be carried out except through an emancipated relation to language. Indeed, emancipation, whether of human slaves or a dominated nature, begins in the signified field, then spreads dialectically outward. Politics expresses the choices made by the imagination, whether of freedom or repression. Social ecology should begin therefore with the emancipation of the imaginary, signified nature. Thus William Blake, the poet of a transfigured imagination, needs to be appropriated as the poet of social ecology.

The quotation (extracted from his notebooks) offered above is *outré* even by Blakean standards, and is the sort of thing that has led the poet-engraver-artist to be called insane. Yet it is perfectly consistent with the rest of Blake, and is, in its way, perfectly sensible as well, although extremely demanding. The passage, for example, is quite compatible with the astounding question asked in *The Marriage of Heaven and Hell:*

> How do you know but evr'y Bird that cuts the airy way,
> Is an immense world of delight, clos'd by your senses five?[7]

There is nothing insane about Blake, who remains quite aware that there is a fundamental difference between the phenomenal world—Outward Creation—and the inner world of imagination, the signified field. What is radically unusual—and difficult—about him is the insistence on the priority of the inner world, and his willingness to follow it, no matter how eccentric this makes him. We cannot collapse the human and natural worlds one into the other, except as a wishful illusion. We have only the choice as to how nature is to be signified: As an inert other, or as Blake most fully expressed, an entity transfigured with spirit. Blake is talking about how to *behold* nature, as well as about its physical reality—indeed, he claims that the nature of physical reality and how it is beheld are functionally related.[8] He is saying—as we suggested above—that Action, i.e., politics, in this case ecopolitics, must traverse the signified field of nature-as-word before it directly engages the material.

Blake claims that this praxis/choice is a matter of perception: that we can choose to see *with* or *through* the eye. We can first of all look at nature as a mere external given, split off from our being. This is the Newtonian or, as he says in his grammar of the imagination, Urizenic mode of perception, in which the perception of the world is considered homologous with the actual physical nature of the world, so that action seems to be directed against nature as such. Newtonian perception is the commonplace attitude toward nature, reinforced by every fiber of the capitalist system, which functions to strip spirit-qualities from existence in order to prepare the way for commodification. It is certainly the attitude of liberal environmentalism, of all technical-instrumental views of nature that reproduce the domination of the established order. To Blake, this is "single vision."

> Now I a fourfold vision see
> And a fourfold vision is given to me
> Tis fourfold in my supreme delight
> And three fold in soft Beulahs night
> And twofold always. May God us keep
> From Single vision & Newtons sleep[9]

Blake strives for "fourfold vision," the vision afforded by the development of his prophetic narratives with their stupendous array of figures: Los, Albion, Orc, Enitharmon, and their relatives.[10] He strives, that is, for a mythopoesis, the epic/prophetic telling of a story of a people realized in his masterworks *Milton* and *Jerusalem*, written to emancipate humankind from mental slavery and hence corporal slavery—the "mind-forg'd manacles." But this must be built on a foundation of "twofold" vision, a vision that combines the imaginative, signified dimension with the thing signified, that refuses to reduce nature to its physicality, that sees immense worlds of delight in a flying bird and hears heavenly hosts in the sun's disk. This vision is *poesis*, the elemental forging of words into things. So relentless is Blake's pursuit of poesis, so immoderately rejecting of single vision, that it seems at times as if he is guilty of some splitting of his own ("I do not behold the Outward Creation. . .to me it is hindrance & not Action it is as the Dirt upon my feet No part of Me"). But what Blake calls attention to is the immense work needed to overcome the inertia of Newtonian single vision[11] and the constant reinforcement of conventional modes of perception, in short, to the travails of being a radical and revolutionary artist, indeed, the necessity of being thought mad for those who wish to raise "other men into a perception of the infinite."[12]

Blake's success in his mental war against Newtonianism is measured by his merits as a poet, in which pursuit he is able to tack so closely to the interface between language and nature as to raise the dialectic of word and thing into insurpassable heights:

> Hear the voice of the Bard!
> Who Present, Past & Future sees
> Whose ears have heard,
> The Holy Word,
> That walk'd among the ancient trees.[13]

The "simplest" lyrics, written for children, are suffused with this intensity—and with a scream against injustice that Blake never forgets:

> When my mother died I was very young
> And my father sold me while yet my tongue,
> Could scarcely cry weep weep weep weep.
> So your chimneys I sweep & in soot I sleep.[14]

Nor does he forget the link between domination, capitalism, and ecological destruction:

> And did the Countenance Divine,
> Shine forth upon our clouded hills?
> And was Jerusalem builded here,
> Among these dark Satanic Mills?[15]

Poetic mastery is Blake's genius and, for now, not our business, since we are not about to argue that radical ecopolitics requires poetic genius. Nor would we advance the fatuous claim that Blake somehow belongs to social ecology, as a privileged—shall we say, vanguard?—movement with an affinity for this nonpareil of the radical imagination. What we would claim, rather, is that Blake's extraordinary status stems from his fidelity to dialectics, and that a movement faithful to the radical challenge posed by the ecological crisis needs to learn from Blake's vision of the dialectic.[16] If social ecology stands in any privileged capacity here it is insofar as it echoes Blake in refusing to collapse the human into the natural worlds. Social ecology does so when it demands that the radical critique of the domination of nature passes through the domination of humans. But this has to be seen in its full, ontologic status, as the outcome of a creature who lives in two worlds, part of nature yet fated to signify nature, a creature capable of twofold, dialectical vision. Only when we allow our specifically human powers to unfold, poetically or politically, can we truly experience the wonder of natural creation. Thus only a fully humanized creature is capable of protecting and emancipating nature.

> Thou seest the Constellations in the deep & Wondrous Night
> They rise in order and continue their immortal courses
> Upon the mountains & in vales with harp & heavenly song
> With flute & clarion; with cups & measures filld with foaming wine.
> Glittring the streams reflect the Vision of beatitude,
> And the calm Oceans joys beneath & smooths his awful waves!
>
> These are the Sons of Los, & these the Labourers of the Vintage
> Thou seest the gorgeous clothed Flies that dance & sport in summer
> Upon the sunny brooks & meadows: every one the dance
> Knows in its intricate mazes of delight artful to weave:
> Each one to sound his instruments of music in the dance,
> To touch each other & recede; to cross & change & return
> These are the Children of Los; thou seest the Trees on mountains
> The wind blows heavy, loud they thunder thro' the darksom sky
> Uttering prophecies & speaking instructive words to the sons
> Of men: These are the Sons of Los! These the Visions of Eternity
> But we see only as it were the hem of their garments,
> When with our vegetable eyes we view these wond'rous Visions[17]

NOTES

1. *Defending the Earth: A Dialogue Between Murray Bookchin and Dave Foreman* (Boston: South End Press, 1991), provides an example of how two leading exponents of the different tendencies both express their differences and move toward bridging them.

2. Some of my views on Marx (and Freud) and the question of nature were spelled out in "Marx, Freud and the Problem of Materialism," in *The Radical Spirit* (London: Free Association Books, 1988), 306–21; see also "On the Notion of Human Nature," in S. Messer, L. Sass, and R. Woolfolk, eds., *Hermeneutics and Psychological Theory* (New Brunswick: Rutgers University Press, 1988), 370–99; and *History and Spirit* (Boston: Beacon Press, 1991), in which many of the ideas of this essay receive a fuller treatment. This is not the place to develop a Marxist critique of social ecology, but the following may be said: that domination as such, or hierarchy, is not sufficient to account for ecocidal social formations such as what we live under. An example: the Hunza of the mountainous regions of Pakistan live in an extremely hierarchical society in which women are sharply subordinated to men, sexuality is harshly repressed, and everybody bows down to the local prince, who lives off their surplus product. Not an attractive picture for us. Yet these same Hunza are the glory of the health food and holism movements, for their luscious organic produce and salubrious way of life which has induced extraordinary longevity and well-being, most Hunza living to be centenarians. See Jay M. Hoffman, *Hunza* (Valley Center, Calif: Professional Press, 1968 [1985]), a work available in many health-food stores. Clearly, hierarchy in itself does not generate ecocidal degrees of the domination of nature. An engine of exploitation and aggrandizement is required. I cannot imagine a better guide than Marx to the contours of this development.

3. As Freud put it, "word-representations" are added to "thing-representations," and thus provide the ground of consciousness. "The Unconscious," in James Strachey, ed., *The Standard Edition of the Complete Psycholgical Works of Sigmund Freud* (London: Hogarth, 1953–73 [1915]), 159–216; see also Joel Kovel, "Things and Words," in *The Radical Spirit*, 80–115.
4. Therefore, economism in politics is going along with capitalism. If issues are only seen in terms of the workplace, or dollars, the very critique only reproduces capital's elemental gesture. The sensitivity to this point by figures as diverse as Gramsci and Emma Goldmann testifies to their superior status among the adversaries of capitalism.
5. The very term, "wilderness," belongs to the signified realm of one who has to contend with splitting. Native Americans do not have such a word, according to the principle that language arises out of a state of separation from the thing signified. For the history of "wilderness" in our culture, see Roderick Nash, *Wilderness and the American Mind* (New Haven: Yale University Press, 1982).
6. From David Erdman, ed., *The Complete Poetry and Prose of William Blake* (Garden City: Doubleday, 1982), 565–66.
7. Op. cit., 35.
8. We cannot take up the point within the confines of this essay, but Blake's view of the fundamental nature of physical reality itself is remarkably sophisticated and radically differs from that of conventional understanding. He seems to have intuited most of the insights of advanced physics as to the nature of time, space and energy. See Donald Ault, *Visionary Physics: Blake's Response to Newton* (Chicago: University of Chicago Press, 1974).
9. Erdman, 722.
10. The figures are themselves arrayed in configurations of four, organized according to points on the compass, gates to the city, etc. For a compendium of Blake's imaginative universe, see S. Foster Damon, *A Blake Dictionary* (Providence: Brown University Press, 1965).
11. Ault writes: "Many central components of Blake's poetry reveal his struggle to exorcise the consolidating forms of anti-imaginative forces from his own imagination." *Visionary Physics*, 161.
12. Erdman, 39. The words are given to the prophet Ezekiel in *The Marriage of Heaven and Hell,* whom Blake asks "why he eat dung, & lay so long on his right & left side?"
13. Op. cit., 18
14. Op. cit., 10. This discussion cannot begin to be complete unless the other prime manifestation of Blake's vision is comprehended: that of the pictorial artist who published these poems as illuminated manuscripts and was as transfigurative in his painting and engraving as he was in language itself.
15. Op. cit., 95.
16. Of course, it must also extend this notion of the dialectic to the notions of Hegel, Marx, Adorno, etc., a process quite feasible, in my opinion, but beyond present scope. One additional and by no means trivial point: in the Socratic view, dialectic inheres in concrete face-to-face argumentation. It is, in short, a social relation as well as an ontological principle, and can only be realized in a directly democratic society. See Murray Bookchin, *The Rise of Urbanization and the Decline of Citizenship* (San Francisco: Sierra Club Books, 1987).
17. Erdman, 123 (from *Milton*).

Toward a Deep Social Ecology

George Bradford

George Bradford has for many years been an editor and writer for The Fifth Estate *newspaper in Detroit. He is the author of* How Deep is Deep Ecology?

A DEEP SOCIAL ECOLOGY?

The implications of a deep ecological vision as a broad, intuitive sensibility—a refusal of instrumental, commoditized relations with the Earth; the notion of kinship with the land and a land ethic; the understanding that the full realization of the personhood of the human subject and of the planet do not compete with one another but correspond; an affirmation of the primal, animist wisdom that places humanity within the web of life and not at the top of some hierarchy—the rediscovery of this constellation of insights is in my view a fundamental precondition for breaking out of the prison-house of urban-industrial civilization and creating a family of free cultures in harmony with one another and with the Earth.

The same goes for the idea of social ecology, which implies an investigation into the social roots of our permanent crisis in culture, and character, an articulation of the manifold forms of freedom and revolt expressed in and against history, and a radical refusal to be reduced to commodities, resources and machines ourselves. The adjectives accompanying the term "ecology" say enough to be suggestive of a new synthesis of primitive and modern, but they do not say enough to be exact. Turning them into "platforms" undermines their energies and broad promise.

A version of this essay was originally published in *The Fifth Estate*, 4632 Second Ave., Detroit, Michigan 48201.

This essay shares with the perspective of social ecology the idea that our species' deadly conflict with the natural world is rooted in social conflict, though it distinguishes itself from the "platform" elements that came to be expressed by Murray Bookchin during the course of his debates with deep ecologists—in particular, the suggestion in some of his work that technological relations are the consequence of previously determined social relations, and his essentially *irrational* rejection of irrational and intuitive aspects of our reconciliation with nature, aspects which have been admirably explored by some deep ecology writers.[1]

Nevertheless, it is the purpose here to address the problems in deep ecology that stem from its failure to place its discourse on the "nature question" into the broader social context, to see ecological and philosophical questions as rooted in social and historical ones, and to expand the discussion to show how these same problems occur throughout much of current environmental philosophy.[2] Deep ecology and environmental ethics cannot avoid confronting the social question if they hope to realize their promise of laying the groundwork for a culture based on harmonious, rather than sociopathic and suicidal relations with the rest of nature.

What, specifically, is deep ecology's promise and project? Deep ecology philosophers George Sessions and Bill Devall state in their book *Deep Ecology* that it "goes beyond a limited piecemeal shallow approach to environmental problems and attempts to articulate a comprehensive religious and philosophical world view."[3] Sessions has characterized it as one of "the two main post-modern philosophies of the future" (along with, the reader may be surprised to learn, New Age philosophy).[4] Bill Devall argues that deep ecology is "heir to the three great intellectual, perceptual revolutions in the West—Copernicus, Darwin, and ecological (Thoreau, Leopold),"[5] thus locating the perspective within a notion of scientific progress. Such claims are bound to invite criticism, as well they have. When progress and scientific progress are unquestioningly included in a perspective (rather than being seen as historically generated constructs and epistemologies, as they would be by a cautious social ecology), one cannot take entirely seriously the claim of deep ecologists to ask "why" more insistently and consistently than others and to take nothing for granted, as Arne Naess, the founder of deep ecology, urges.[6] Nor can one accept deep ecology's implicit, and, at times even explicit, claim to establish a neutral ground to analyze humanity's relationship to nature (the biocentric or ecocentric starting point). The claim is made, for example, in Alan Drengson's observation that it "applies ecological paradigms not only to plants and animals but also to human culture and its internal and external relationships."[7] It allegedly thinks primarily "in biotic rather than social terms," writes journalist Kirkpatrick Sale in attempting to clarify the differences between deep ecology and its critics.[8]

But, of course, all our terms are social before they are biotic or anything else. Indeed, while deep ecologists claim to take nothing for granted, the terms by which they define their process of inquiry go themselves unquestioned. Assuming—rather than critically examining—the premise that human activities can be explained according to the tenets of ecological science, deep ecologists apply ecological models to everything, from the yearly migrations of birds to the forced migrations of war refugees. Any reference to social causes is met by accusations of "shallowness," since at some level at least, ecological relations do underlie human society. But the real question concerning society isn't whether ecological relations underlie "human culture and its internal and external relationships," the question is whether ecological analysis is sufficient to explain human culture's history and conflicts. And in answering this question at least, deep ecologists have proven to be far shallower than their critics.

Deep ecology has suffered not only from ecological reductionism but from a tendency to graft unexamined, gratuitous political positions onto it as well. This has led to some monstrous conclusions among some activist adherents of the philosophy. This includes, on the one hand, the aberrations of a survivalist catastrophism and misanthropy (found among some deep ecologist members of the group Earth First!), and, on the other hand, an eclectic green liberalism (a variant of the shallow ecology that deep ecologists claim to supersede). While deep ecology philosophers may not be directly responsible for these aberrations, the relationship between them and problems with the philosophical assumptions of deep ecology must be investigated, starting from the recognition that the "biotic terms" of ecology are in some ways as patently inadequate as they are in other ways indispensable. The lack of social critique in deep ecology renders invisible those very forces of domination and alienation that are reducing the planet to a petrochemical Gulag.[9]

This is a problem that the discipline of environmental ethics in general shares with deep ecology. The discourse on the idea of an environmental ethic has become a veritable industry. It may be ironic, but it is certainly no accident, that much of the discussion around establishing a grounding for intrinsic value in nature and a nonanthropocentric ethics is to be found in books and journals outlining the catastrophic mass extinction of species and ecosystems being carried out by the day-to-day operations of the industrial megamachine. Minerva's owl flies, it does indeed appear, only at dusk.

Thus, the legal debate around giving "rights" to wilderness and to other species signals their disappearance. Similarly, the elaboration of highly articulated ethical systems has only accompanied a widening swath of violence and destruction and the armoring of the human personality—such systems are mere pieties as far as capital accumulation is concerned. One would think, reading the literature of deep ecology, animal liberation and environmental ethics, that the rights of human beings have been firmly established, and must now be widened to accommodate a deeper land ethic—this in the age of mass exterminations of people in gas chambers, carpet bombings of whole populations, chemical-biological warfare and the threat of nuclear incineration in increasingly volatile gambles to defend the markets and resources of rival empires.

This was a central element in my original critique of deep ecology: not its poetic identification with the natural world, but its naïveté (and the cynicism of some of its adherents) about power relations—a naïveté (and perhaps a cynicism as well) it inherited from the liberal environmental and conservation movements from which it emerged. One can only shake one's head upon reading how encouraged Arne Naess was after writing numerous "experts" about his deep ecology platform, including "top people in ministries of oil and energy," when "many answered positively in relation to most or all points." According to Naess, we are to be encouraged that "there is a philosophy of the man/nature relationship widely accepted among established experts responsible for environmental decision" which will bring about "substantial change of present politics" to protect the Earth from "shortsighted human interests."[10] This simplistic contrast of nature and human interest, shortsighted or otherwise, leaves Naess blind to the actual organization of power, as well as to the operational characteristics of what is fundamentally an *exterminist* civilization, a global megamachine.

DEEP ECOLOGY AND DUALISM

Another, mostly implicit assumption of deep ecology is its simplistic dualism, which is reflected in its generally unidimensional contrast between nature and an undifferentiated humanity. The dualism occurs simultaneously on two mutually contradictory levels. On the first level, humanity is seen as simply "one" with nature, so that any discussion of humanity's specific problems is seen as "anthropocentric" and an affront to a biospheric egalitarianism that does not investigate history or distinguish between differing levels of complexity. Yet on the second level, humanity is seen at least implicitly as a uniquely negative force and as involved in a polarity with nature. Starting from a legitimate revulsion against the destructiveness of urban-industrial civilization, deep ecology takes for granted an economistic, "zero-sum" picture of the world and nature, in which humanity can thrive only by causing nature to lose. This is essentially the world view of bourgeois civilization, of Adam Smith, Parson Malthus and Thomas Hobbes: "man" struggles against nature, carving progress out of rough, resistant stone. In the deep ecology view, the values or poles are simply reversed; the undifferentiated mass of humanity is compelled to don sackcloth and ashes and make sacrifices in its standard of living to preserve nature. The values themselves are not treated critically as socially and historically generated, as consequences of conditioning within the capitalist commodity system. They are the comforts to which progress itself has mysteriously led, and must be piously given up for the good of a nature that is wholly other. The same dualism is played out in several overlapping polarities. From this ambiguous contrast of biocentrism and anthropocentrism come various other polarities: of intrinsic or inherent value in nature vs. utilitarian or instrumental value (value for human beings); of biospheric egalitarianism and non-interference ("let nature be") vs. "resourcism" or "stewardship" (which is taken to imply a totally administered nature cultivated for the good of some undifferentiated human species' "need"); of "humanism" (seen as a kind of human chauvinism) vs. an ostensibly neutral ecocentrism, along with wilderness.

Yet in his environmental history, *Changes in the Land: Indians, Colonists, and the Ecology of New England*, William Cronon reveals the problems with the kind of dualism characteristic of deep ecology. In social and ecological discourse, he points out, the question is not one of an untouched, "virgin" landscape contrasted with a human one, but between distinct "ways of belonging to an ecosystem." Such a perspective, he argues, would therefore describe precolonial New England not as a virgin landscape of natural harmony but as a landscape whose essential characteristics were kept in equilibrium by the cultural practices of its human community."[11] Cronon quotes Thoreau, who writes in *Walden* that he would like to know "the entire poem" of nature. But this is not possible, Cronon argues. "Human and natural worlds are too entangled for us, and our historical landscape does not allow us to guess what the 'entire poem' of which he spoke might look like. To search for that poem would in fact be a mistake. Our project must be to locate a nature which is within rather than without history, for only by doing so can we find human communities which are inside rather than outside nature."[12] Cronon is speaking to environmental historians, but his advice makes sense for those who would begin to discuss our relationship with the natural world and the present crisis in it.

We must therefore show restraint and some humility in judgments about nature and society. Simply stated, it is one thing to argue that "nature knows best." It is quite another to assume that one philosophical current knows what is best for nature. Such reasoning constitutes a kind of teleology based on assumed omniscience. The resonant remark by Aldo Leopold, "A thing is right when it tends to preserve the integrity, stability and beauty of the biotic community,"[13] provides no answers; it only poses a series of questions.

Such a view, as Peter A. Fritzell writes in a very sensitive essay on the subject, "explains human actions as functions in and of evolving ecosystems only when those actions are *consonant* with the needs of other elements in such systems, where *consonant* means conducive to the continued, healthy existence of all present species—*as defined and deter-*

mined by humans and human science"[14] [my emphasis in latter phrase].
Commenting on Leopold's celebrated passage cited above, Fritzell observes, "Is man to determine when the biotic community is stable and beautiful? Or must man take counsel from other citizens of the community—not only pines, deer, and wolves but cheat grass, gypsy moths and rats? [not to mention women!] Can man take anything other than *human* counsel with the other members of the land community? Can such counsel ever express more than the ecological interests of humans and the species they most closely identify with?"[15] Further on he remarks, "The paradoxes of wilderness preservation are less logical problems than they are communal concerns."[16] And, I would add, concerns which are rooted in a matrix of social conflict and domination.

This is in no way to say that there is nothing to be affirmed in an environmental ethic. It is only to point out the limitations of ecological thinking and the anthropocentrism/biocentrism contrast as a tool of radical critique or as an alternative, new paradigm for thinking. The scientific rationalism on which it rests is extremely contradictory and problematic; it is a knife with no handle. The permanent revolution of the methodological categories and language of science is a reflection of the constant transformations in technological apparatus and the commodity system by which capital itself expands. Science's description of the world is a description of *it's* world; as Goethe knew, "everything factual is already theory."[17]

Regarding this statement by Goethe, Theodore Roszak quotes twentieth-century physicist Werner Heisenberg's comment, "In natural science the object of investigation is not nature as such, but nature exposed to man's mode of inquiry."[18] The violence that the empirical method implies cannot be discerned by Heisenberg's bland statement; one must look to its origins in the scientific revolution and the experimental method, as expressed by Francis Bacon, that "nature exhibits herself more clearly under the trials and vexations of art than when left to herself"[19]—which was to say, when confined and tortured by mechanical devices. For Bacon it was necessary to "hound nature in her wanderings," without scruple "of entering and penetrating into these holes and corners, when the inquisition of truth is man's whole object."[20]

As Carolyn Merchant, quoting from Bacon, explains, nature had to "be bound into 'service' and made a 'slave,' put 'in constraint' and 'molded' by the mechanical arts....The interrogation of witches as symbol for the interrogation of nature, the courtroom as model for its inquisition, and torture through mechanical devices as tool for the subjugation of disorder were fundamental to the scientific method as power."[21] Of course, the actual torture and murder of women as witches were contemporaneous with the rise of scientific method, and both were in fact carried out by the same social class of men—indeed, by many of the same men.

For these men, who not only "vexed nature" but slaughtered midwives and healers with their mechanical arts, "sexual politics helped to structure the nature of the empirical method that would produce a new form of knowledge and a new ideology of objectivity seemingly devoid of cultural and political assumptions,"[22] Merchant writes. Behind this new ideology of science lay the horrors of gynocide—a holocaust against hundreds of thousands, probably millions of women, from the fourteenth to the eighteenth century. The emerging mechanical and industrial technology developed by the rising scientific and economic elites to carry out their "vexations" of nature's body and the bodies of women helped to rapidly extend and consolidate this ideology's power. As Mary Daly has written in her powerful description of the witch burnings, "The escalation of technology and of persecution goosestepped together in the 'march of progress.' "[23] To return to Goethe's remark, the facts which generate this torturous theory were themselves derived from a theory of tortures.

THE PROBLEM OF SCIENTIFIC NATURALISM

The emergence of a new recognition of kinship with nature also has its source in part in that scientific naturalism—in fact one of the traditions of humanism itself—which tore human beings from their traditional metaphysical milieu and redefined them as natural objects. But this "objective" decentering of humanity doesn't stop there; it tends to erode the essentially spiritual intuition of inherent value as soon as it starts to suggest it. Scientific naturalism provides no easy answers to the question raised by Leopold and plagues the contrast between what is anthropocentric and what is biocentric with the same epistemological problem that deep ecology would like to forget: how to establish an ethical ground. Given the corrosiveness of scientific naturalism and the limitations of knowledge, on what ground could deep ecology base its ethical (and consequently, social and political) judgments?

After all, despite the intuition of ecological egalitarianism, from the point of view of scientific naturalism on which ecology rests, there is no egalitarianism. Not only that, organisms—be they viruses decimating seal populations in the North Sea, crown-of-thorns starfish scouring the Great Barrier Reef, zebra mussels colonizing the Great Lakes, or the Purple Martins that chase the bluebirds away from the house we built for them—do not recognize ethics, equality or intrinsic worth. Neither, for that matter, do hurricanes or volcanos. As Hegel put it, animals "do not stand stock still before things of sense as if these were things *per se,* with being in themselves: they despair of this reality altogether, and in complete assurance of the nothingness of things they fall to without more ado and eat them up."[24]

Exploring the problem of intrinsic value and scientific naturalism (which he calls "holistic rationalism"), J. Baird Callicott argues that "if one defends one's intuition that biological impoverishment is objectively wrong by positing organic richness as objectively good, one might well be accused of temporal parochialism and a very subtle form of human arrogance."[25] Callicott cites the periodic mass extinctions of species on earth to support his argument. "Considering our time as but an infinitesimal moment in the three and one-half billion year tenure of life on planet earth (let alone the possibility that earth may be but one of many planets to possess a biota), man's tendency to destroy other species might be viewed quite disinterestedly as a transitional stage in the earth's evolutionary odyssey."[26] Minimally, his observations suggest the tenuousness and inadequacy of ecological science as the sole basis for social critique or ethical action.

Elliot Sober has argued (in an essay in part replying to Callicott) that "to the degree that 'natural' means anything biologically, it means very little ethically. And conversely, to the degree that 'natural' is understood as a normative concept, it has very little to do with biology." From the point of view of science, what is "natural" is ambiguous. Our intuition, Sober writes, tells us that there is a fundamental difference between a mountain and a highway system, "but once we realize that organisms construct their environments in nature, this contrast begins to cloud. Organisms do not passively reside in an environment whose properties are independently determined. Organisms transform their environments by physically interacting with them. An anthill is an artifact just as a highway is."[27]

By such an implacable logic, Sober infers the ultimate indifference to which scientific naturalism can lead. His essay also suggests the problems with an ostensibly omniscient biological egalitarianism that simultaneously sees humanity as "one with nature," "one more species among many," and yet also as a unique source of evil in the biosphere. Any species, after all—from humpback whales to the ecoli bacteria in human feces—is only "one among many," whatever that means. In the case mentioned, do we assign them equal value, meaning, grandeur? If so, why then do deep ecologists complain? As Callicott has suggested, nothing civilization does, not even nuclear war, will destroy life itself, only complex life; what remains would probably follow the tendency to diversify and evolve, as the biota did after other mass extinctions, such as the Permian, when over 90 percent of species disappeared—long before dinosaurs or mammals.[28]

If we are entirely one with nature then we are no different from red tide or viruses or a destructive meteor from space, and nature is doing this strange dance with itself, or is *chaos*. Even the Earth is "one mere planet among many," a speck in the cosmos. In the big picture, extinction is inevitable, since the Earth eventually will be destroyed as the sun expands to a supernova (again, according to the best available scientific theory). In 65 million years (long before that remote end), will we be much more than a layer in the sediment? It is impossible to tell, but I am as fascinated with and as repelled by scientific naturalism as anyone else. It does compel me to withhold final judgment on such matters and to begin where I am: A human being in a world layered with natural, historical, and social inter-relationships, conflicts, affinities and obligations. I don't reject my humanity by identifying with the planet; I am *responding* to it.

BEYOND INTRINSIC VALUE

Environmental philosophers have been unable to reach a conclusive view of the problem of intrinsic worth. Some have argued that human-centered values should not be discarded and can provide a powerful set of motivations for preserving wilderness and protecting the natural world.[29] Even if one avoids the more instrumental character of some arguments of this type (that rain forests contain a wealth of future medicines or food crops, for example), the defense of wilderness as an expression of our own innate biophilia or love of and identification with life, is extremely strong, as when naturalist Edward O. Wilson argues, "We are in the fullest sense a biological species and will find little ultimate meaning apart from the remainder of life."[30] Again, to follow Theodore Roszak's insightful observation, the personhood of the human being is interrelated with and contingent upon the personhood of the planet.[31]

Sober argues that the value of nature and wilderness is ultimately aesthetic, which is not to say frivolous, and he compares the preservation of a majestic cliff to that of the ancient temple which stands on it, seeing them both as important. (For those who may not care for this example, let us substitute that of, say, a magnificent grotto and the paleolithic painting left on its walls.) Indeed, the comparison of natural objects to aesthetic masterpieces is a common motif in all environmental literature, from John Muir's comment during the campaign to save Hetch Hetchy from developers that "everybody needs beauty as well as bread," to Edward Abbey's comparison of the damming of Glen Canyon to the destruction of the Taj Mahal or the cathedral at Chartres, with the distinction that the natural object is alive "and can never be recovered."[32]

Another writer argues that "our duties toward species arise not out of the interests of the species, but are rooted in the general obligation to preserve things of value."[33] And even David Ehrenfeld, who attempts in his provocative if flawed book, *The Arrogance of Humanism*, to explode all the "humanist" shibboleths and along with them this anthropocentric aesthetic criterion, falls into the same reasoning. Ehrenfeld criticizes the humanism in even the land ethic and in related aesthetic criteria as a form of "condescension" that is "not in harmony with the humility-inspiring discoveries of ecology."[34] Instead, he argues for a "Noah principle," stating that natural objects and species "should be conserved because they exist" (a very problematic and ambiguous formulation—everything exists), and because this existence "is itself but the present expression of a continuing historical process of immense antiquity and majesty."[35] Yet concern for antiquity and majesty represents an obviously aesthetic, even classical humanist motivation.

Holmes Rolston considers a distinct intrinsic value impossible, finding "both instrumental and intrinsic values. . .objectively present in ecosystems. The system is a web where loci of intrinsic value are meshed in a network of instrumental value,"[36] since organisms value the rest of nature instrumentally, while valuing themselves intrinsically, in his view. But because neither term is satisfactory "at the level of the holistic ecosystem," he continues, "we need a third term: systemic value." In this way ethics will not be complete "until extended to the land."[37] Rolston's argument confirms what I think must be the insight of a deep social ecology: the necessity to move beyond dualism and even beyond the limitations of science towards an animist mode of kinship, mythopoetic and future-primitive, at the level of the gift, which stands in utter opposition to an economic civilization that reduces the world—including human beings—to resources, to dead units of production and consumption. The presence of agonized philosophical questioning of humanity's relation to nature— while the very fabric of life appears to be coming apart—seems another bitter irony. But it, too, suggests that the emerging ecological ethic may signal more a mythic return, the coming around of a cycle, than the model of advancing progress that one sometimes finds in environmental ethics, in notions of "paradigm change" culled from the concept of scientific revolution, or in some social ecology dialectic.[38]

This idea may seem more valid when we consider the notion of a land community that was already present in the world view of primal peoples. As Callicott has written, not only did Native Americans "regard all features of the environment as enspirited," the social circle and community included nature and other beings (including winds, rivers, stones, and so on) along with human kin.[39]

The original inhabitants of this land knew what Hans Peter Duerr reports in his remarkable book *Dreamtime: Concerning the Boundary Between Wilderness and Civilization*: "To get to the point of origin, to be able, for instance, to 'speak' with plants, a person needs what the Indians call 'reverence.' Humans must become *unimportant* before the other beings of nature: 'When I was still a child, my parents and the old people taught me to treat everything with reverence, even the rocks, the stones and the small crawling insects, for they are all *manitus*,' " Duerr quotes a Native American, and he adds: "To 'become a part' of the *manitu* of all things means to 'speak the common language of all things.' "[40]

A sense of reverence—is this not fundamental to a reawakening of our proper relationship to the planet and to ourselves? And is it not clear that this implies neither a mechanistic imitation of primal society nor the

428   *Social Ecology*

grafting of its insights onto an instrumental science or dualistic model based on competing interest? Where does this reverence come from and how can it be expressed?

Indeed, the current discourse in which deep ecology participates constrains meaning in a language that is already instrumentalized. It not only mechanistically isolates and fragments so-called inherent from instrumental value, but bases itself on a model of necessity and need that reflects the alienated discourse of bourgeois materialism and the capitalist market themselves. When Arne Naess writes that the "vital needs" of human beings must be met, he tries to evade the problems such a formulation suggests by leaving this notion "deliberately vague."[41] But he thus resolves nothing and leaves the entire notion itself unexamined. The dualism of human "need" struggling against natural law—isn't this distorted construct, assuming as it does a polarity between an undifferentiated nature and an equally undifferentiated, simplified "human" need, only an image of *this* society? Ironically, many deep ecologists drink from the same polluted source as the marxists and liberal humanists they vilify: starting from the ideology of natural and historical necessity, they all assume the inevitability of scarcity and its consequent generation of needs. For liberal and marxist alike, increasing needs are a factor of progress; for the deep ecologist, they are the result of increasing numbers—the progress of factors. In these complementary ways, views that are ostensibly opposed diametrically actually share in the mystique produced by the bourgeois civilization that spawned Malthusian scientism, a mechanico-materialist marxism and technocratic liberalism: the ideology of instrumentalism.

But is it possible in nature, as in primal societies, that there is no instrumental value at all, no need, just as there is no economy, no production? Writing about the fundamental differences between objects in western and indigenous contexts, Jamake Highwater observes, "The objects of Indians are expressive and not decorative because they are alive, living in our experience of them. When the Indian potter collects clay, she asks the consent of the river-bed and sings its praises for having made something as beautiful as clay. When she fires her pottery, to this day, she still offers songs to the fire so it will not discolor or burst her wares. And, finally, when she paints her pottery, she imprints it with the images that give it life and power—because for an Indian, pottery is something significant, not just a utility but a 'being' for which there is as much of a natural order as there is for persons or foxes or trees. So reverent is the Indian conception of the 'power' within things, and especially the objects created by traditional craftspeople, that among many Indians, the pottery interred with the dead has a small perforation, a 'kill-hole,' made in the center in order to release the *orenda*—'the spiritual power'—before it is buried."[42]

Again the idea of reverence is raised, and we can see that it is not even a question of refusing to allow what we consider alive by scientific standards to be turned into "dead things," but rather two opposed visions: An ecstatic vision in which everything is alive, and that of capital, within which everything becomes lifeless, dead matter. Intrinsic value has its place on the altar in such a scheme, but instrumental value is the iron hand that rules the world, the iron hand of necessity.

As Jean Baudrillard writes in *The Mirror of Production*, his devastating attack not only on marxism but on all of productivist civilization, necessity is "a Law that takes effect only with the objectification of Nature. The Law takes its definitive form in capitalist political economy; moreover, it is only the philosophical expression of Scarcity."[43] But what is scarcity, this centerpiece of Malthusian ideology? "Scarcity, which itself arises in the market economy, is not a *given* dimension of the economy. Rather, it is what *produces and reproduces* economic exchange."[44] Scarcity, produced by the emergence of economic exchange, becomes the alibi, if you will, for justifying the forces that generated it, and ends in a pre-capitalist mystique of the "tragedy of the commons" and a "life-boat ethic," "the survival of the fittest," "us against them."

Yet neither nature nor primal societies are determined by need, which arises out of this phantasm of scarcity that both fuels and results from capital accumulation; none of this exists, Baudrillard argues, "at the level of reciprocity and symbolic exchange [as in primal society], where the break with nature that leads to. . .the entire becoming of history (the operational violence of man against nature). . .has not occurred."[45] Hence need and social interest are the products of such an economic order, not natural phenomena—and with them, the cleft between intrinsic and instrumental value, between human well-being and the integrity of nature. "The idea of 'natural Necessity,' " writes Baudrillard, "is only a *moral* idea dictated by political economy."[46]

Anthropologist Dorothy Lee puts it another way. She does not claim "that there are no needs; rather, that if there are needs, they are derivative not basic. If, for example, physical survival was held as the ultimate goal in some society, it would probably be found to give rise to those needs which have been stated to be basic to human survival; but I know of no culture where human physical survival has been shown, rather than unquestioningly assumed by social scientists, to be the ultimate goal."[47] To follow the model of deep ecologists, for example, one would assume that "humans" are devouring nature by following a basic species' "need" to maximize food. This ideological image teaches us nothing about the natural history of human beings and even less about the kind of society that maximizes the production of crops even by mining and destroying the very soil on which they depend.

"To the Hopi," on the other hand, writes Lee, "corn is not nutrition; it is a totality, a way of life. Something of this sort is exemplified in the story which Talayesva tells of the Mexican trader who offered to sell salt to the Hopi group who were starting out on a highly ceremonial Salt Expedition. Within its context this offer to relieve the group of the hardships and dangers of the religious journey sounds ridiculous. The Hopi were not just getting salt to season their dishes. To them, the journey was part of the process of growing corn and of maintaining harmonious interrelations with nature and what we call the divine. It was the Hopi Way, containing Hopi value. Yet even an ethnographer, dealing with Hopi culture in terms of basic needs, views the Salt Expedition as the trader did and classifies it under Secondary Economic Activities."[48] The Hopi Way and the mode of life of many primal cultures indicate very clearly to us what the foundations are for the kind of reverence that will bring us back into contact with the planet, but only if we have eyes to see, and enough vision to break through the categories that have been imposed by capital and its thorough instrumentalization and commodification of the world.

"ALL MY RELATIONS"

The sciences have confirmed the animist intuition that we are physically and psychologically continuous with the rest of nature. Geology, astronomy, biology, evolutionary science and genetics all demonstrate that our very bodies are made up of the same elements that existed during the formative period of the Earth and have made their way down to us through time and all the evolutionary changes that have occurred during the last several billion years. The salt of the oceans whence we emerged flows in our veins, and the slow development of our backbones and brains has laid the foundations for our very consciousness. Our first dances and songs moved with the rhythms of the Earth. We are also biological kin to other organisms.[49]

But as I have already noted, none of this scientific reasoning can guarantee that we will develop ethical concern or a proper relation to the biosphere, any more than the knowledge that other human beings are our genetic kin will prevent us from annihilating them in war. Indeed, such generalizations can lead to sociobiological reductionism that suppresses the complex relationship between natural and complex evolution that points to the problematic uniqueness of our troublesome species. Just as Einstein's theory had multiple implications, not the least of which turned out to be nuclearism's war on complex forms of life, so modern ecological theory and its systemic paradigm may usher in a bioengineering age that will culminate in the final conquest of nature as we know it (soon to be followed, obviously, by our extinction). Much of this could flow directly out of an ecological impulse to save the planet from an otherwise inevitable degradation of its biodiversity through the adoption of genetic banks and bioengineering. I am reminded of Marcuse's parallel comment on nuclearism. "Does not the threat of an atomic catastrophe which could wipe out the human race also serve to protect the very forces which perpetuate this danger?" he asked. "The efforts to prevent such a catastrophe overshadow the search for potential causes in contemporary industrial society."[50]

Yet to point to the ambiguities in the ecological vision is not to deny its aspects capable of affirming kinship with and respect and reverence for the land—those elements in evolutionary science capable of confirming the world view of animist native peoples that now stands in such stark contrast to and in condemnation of this instrumental civilization. An ethical element can be derived, in part at least, from evolutionary science. Callicott proposes a "bioempathy" similar to Wilson's notion of biophilia (or perhaps a social aspect of bioempathy standing on the shoulders of biological kinship), rooted in our mammalian evolutionary development. If nature is an "objective, axiologically neutral domain," he asks, "how is it possible to account for the existence of something like morality or ethics among human beings and their prehuman ancestors in a manner consistent with evolutionary theory?"[51]

Drawing on Darwin, he points out that the prolonged parental nurturing of offspring, and the strong emotional bond that accompanies it, would explain such a phenomenon, even suggesting why such groups in which this trait was more pronounced would have increased changes of survivability. Of course the thread that led Kropotkin to write *Mutual Aid* is recognizable here—a work that despite all its illusions about progress and technology and its romantic whimsey (this latter is actually part of its appeal), drew a portrait of evolution stressing cooperation that is now being vindicated by evolutionary theory's deepening understanding of symbiosis and mutualism in nature.[52]

It's possible that there may be a bit too much sociobiology in this description as well, but it does suggest persuasively that an environmental ethic can be rooted in an explicitly human context and need not (and probably cannot) be based on a perspective of neutrality or one-dimensional identification with the otherness of nature. When we anthropomorphize by calling the Earth our Mother, we are reiterating our biological link to the planet and also to our real mothers (and by extension, to our families and communities), just as when Native Americans refer to other species as "all my relations" they are not denying kinship with their human relatives but integrating kinship on both levels.

Such forms of kinship and community are interlocked but not entirely identical. As Rolston notes, "Cultures are a radically different mode" from the ecosystem and thus demand different criteria for judgment and action. "Relations between individual and community have to be analyzed separately in the two communities,"[53] he writes. "To know what a bee is in a beehive is to know what a good (functional) bee is in a bee society, but. . .nothing follows about how citizens function in nation-states or how they ought to."[54]

Accordingly, "It may be proper to let Montana deer starve during a rough winter, following a bonanza summer when the population has edged over the carrying capacity. It would be monstrous to be so callous about African peoples caught in a drought. Even if their problems are ecologically aggravated there are cultural dimensions and duties in any solution that are not considerations in deer management."[55] Ethical considerations aside, the differences in the sources of the two events cannot be forgotten. No one has demonstrated that famine in Africa is any more than the result of social conflicts and capitalist looting. Those sources must be attended to before we can begin to judge the related environmental factors.

Biocentrism cannot therefore replace a social critique or social solidarity. Our recognition of our kinship and community with nature is intertwined with our understanding of the global "planetariat" that we have become since the original rupture in primitive society and the origin of the state megamachines. To turn away from the long, rich traditions of communal revolt and from solidarity with other human communities in their ongoing struggle for freedom would be as violent an error as to deny the biosocial roots of our connections to the land.

SAVING OURSELVES

To save ourselves: to restore the land, to restore ourselves to the land. None of us is absolutely certain how to bring this vision about. And so a sense of humility, in the face of the urgent constellation of challenges that lie before us, is called for. An ethic of respect for the land is emerging as the shadows lengthen over civilization. As Theodore Roszak writes in *Person/Planet*, "We are finally coming to recognize that the natural environment is the exploited proletariat, the downtrodden nigger of everybody's industrial system."[56] But we *are* the land and must renew our connection with it. "For the Earth is not merely a factor of production; she is a living thing that makes an ethical claim upon our loyalty. Our identity is organically woven into her history; she has generated us out of herself, nurtured, shaped and sustained us.. . .And she will be heard."[57] Every scar on the Earth's body, every broken thread in its tapestry, diminishes us, undermines our own evolutionary destiny. To save ourselves we must save the Earth. To save the Earth, we must find a way to create a humane, egalitarian and ecologically sustainable society. If we cannot, we will continue around this vortex created by urban-industrial capitalism down to extinction and poison this planet beyond recognition. It may even be already too late, but there is still life in us, so we keep on.

An environmental philosophy that fails to recognize the interrelatedness of the social and natural crises, and the roots of ecological crisis in class, race, gender and historical conflicts within historically generated societies, will fail to uncover and confront the real sources of the ecological meltdown occurring today. The anthropocentrism that many deep ecologists decry as the source of the ecological crisis is little more than window dressing on this civilization's bloody history of plunder, massacre and devastation. No development scheme, no poisoning of water, no squandering of the soil, no leveling of forests and no mass exodus or slaughter of human populations occurs as a response to "human need" or "human-centeredness" or as the direct consequence of the explosion of human numbers. These phenomena exist, rather, to continue the accumulation of capital and the smooth functioning of a global, imperial work pyramid. To pretend otherwise in the name of ecology is to affirm the very social model that deep ecology wishes to replace. Such a perspective, once it reaches the terrain of social practice, will lead, as it has led, either to a "shallow ecology" form of liberal politics that uses revolutionary rhetoric to lobby for fragile, tenuous environmental reforms that leave the megamachine structurally intact, or to a kind of survivalist catastrophism which is little more than a dangerous pose.

The collapse of the global ecosystem as we know it is not a far-fetched prospect. The Earth's vital signs are showing increased, profound stress, and we have no idea at what point what thresholds will be crossed. We will only inherit the consequences. The possibility that human societies can be transformed in time seems remote, not because we are too many, but because of the social chaos, the entropy that goes in capital's wake.

On the other hand, there is a possibility that we can bring about a revolutionary social-ecological transformation, that our grandchildren or great-great-grandchildren may inherit an Earth which is slowly mending itself, renewing itself. We have a chance, but we must find a way to articulate a dramatic appeal to the people who presently languish under the spiked wheels of the megamachine, who make it go and yet have no stake in it, who have nothing to lose and a world to gain: the oppressed, landless, contaminated, irradiated, and alienated planetariat, the people who will recover the planet and rediscover their own planethood. And if we cannot, the catastrophe will already have occurred, and nature will surely do the rest.

NOTES

1. See, for example, Gary Snyder's lucid and generous book, *The Practice of the Wild* (San Francisco: North Point Press, 1990).
2. For a previous critique and overview of deep ecology, particularly as practiced by its activist adherents, see my *How Deep Is Deep Ecology? With an Essay-Review on Women's Freedom* (Ojai, CA: Times Change Press, 1989); also "Was Malthus Right? An Exchange on Deep Ecology and Population" (with William Catton and others), *Fifth Estate*, Vol. 23, No. 1 (328), Spring 1988; and "Return

of the Son of Deep Ecology: The Ethics of Permanent Crisis and the Permanent Crisis in Ethics," *Fifth Estate*, Vol. 24, No. 1 (331), Spring 1989. This essay is a revised and considerably abridged version of the last article, which also dealt extensively with the question of wilderness, as well as with controversies among radical ecology activists.

3. Bill Devall and George Sessions, *Deep Ecology: Living as if Nature Mattered* (Salt Lake City: Peregrine Smith Books, 1985), p. 65.

4. George Sessions, "Deep Ecology and the New Age," *Earth First! Journal*, Mabon edition, 1987.

5. Bill Devall, personal correspondence, December 7, 1987, unpublished.

6. "Interview with Arne Naess," in Devall and Sessions, *Deep Ecology*, pp. 74–77.

7. Alan Drengson, "Developing Concepts of Environmental Relationships," *Philosophical Enquiry*, Vol. VIII, Nos. 1–2 (Winter-Spring 1986).

8. Kirkpatrick Sale, "Deep Ecology and Its Critics," *The Nation*, May 14, 1989.

9. For a more elaborated discussion of the limitations of both environmentalism and leftism in confronting this crisis, see my "Stopping the Industrial Hydra: Revolution Against the Megamachine," *Fifth Estate*, Vol. 24, No. 3 (333), Winter 1990; and the *Fifth Estate Earth Day Special Edition*, various authors, Spring 1990.

10. Arne Naess, "The Deep Ecology Movement: Some Philosophical Aspects," *Philosophical Enquiry*, Vol VIII, Nos. 1–2 (Winter-Spring 1986), p. 29. For another example of this naïveté, see Fritjof Capra, "Deep Ecology: An New Paradigm," *Earth Island Journal*, Fall 1987.

11. William Cronon, *Changes in the Land: Indians, Colonists, and the Ecology of New England* (New York: Hill and Wang, 1983), p. 12.

12. Ibid., p. 15.

13. Aldo Leopold, *A Sand County Almanac* (New York: Ballantine Books, 1970), p. 262.

14. Peter A. Fritzell, "The Conflicts of Ecological Conscience," in *Companion to A Sand County Almanac*, J. Baird Callicott, ed. (Madison: University of Wisconsin Press, 1987), p. 141.

15. Ibid., p. 144.

16. Ibid.

17. Quoted in Theodore Roszak, *Where the Wasteland Ends: Politics and Transcendence in Postindustrial Society* (New York: Doubleday and Co., 1972), p. 303.

18. Ibid.

19. Carolyn Merchant, *The Death of Nature: Women, Ecology and the Scientific Revolution* (New York: Harper & Row, 1980), p. 169.

20. Ibid., p. 168.

21. Ibid., p. 172.

22. Ibid.

23. Mary Daly, *Gyn/Ecology: The Metaethics of Radical Feminism* (Boston: Beacon Press, 1978), p. 190.

24. G. W. F. Hegel, *The Phenomenology of Mind* (New York: Harper Torchbooks, 1967), p. 159.

25. J. Baird Callicott, "On the Intrinsic Value of Nonhuman Species," in *The Preservation of Species: The Value of Biological Diversity*, Bryan G. Norton, ed. (Princeton: Princeton University Press, 1986), p. 151.

26. Ibid.

27. Elliot Sober, "Philosophical Problems for Environmentalism," in *The Preservation of Species*, pp. 180–188. Many of the categories within biological science are highly problematic in his essay on the current extinction spasm, "Why the Ark is Sinking" in *The Last Extinction*, Les Kaufman and Kenneth Mallory, eds. (Cambridge: MIT Press, 1986), Les Kaufman demonstrates that "our notion of what a species is, or isn't, is largely an artifact of human bias." (p. 9) One can only imagine how such problems are magnified when biology, as current scientific discourse may posit it, invades political discourse. One feminist critic of science, Sandra Harding, suggests that rather than imposing biology on politics, "much of biology should already be conceptualized as social science." See *The Science Question in Feminism* (Ithaca: Cornell University Press, 1986), pp. 43–44.
28. J. Baird Callicott, "On the Intrinsic Vaue of Non-human Species," p. 151.
29. See Edward O. Wilson, *Biophilia* (Cambridge: Harvard University Press, 1984) and Sober, "Philosophical Problems for Environmentalism."
30. Wilson, p. 81.
31. Theodore Roszak, *Person/Planet: The Creative Disintegration of Industrial Society* (New York: Anchor Books, 1975).
32. See Roderick Nash, *Wilderness and the American Mind* (New Haven: Yale University Press, 1982) p. 165; Edward Abbey, *Desert Solitaire* (New York: Ballantine Books, 1968), p. 174.
33. Lily-Marlene Russow, "Why Do Species Matter?" in *People, Penguins and Plastic Trees: Basic Issues in Environmental Ethics.*, ed. Donald VanDeVeer and Christine Pierce (Belmont: Wadsworth Publishing Co., 1986), p. 120.
34. David Ehrenfeld, *The Arrogance of Humanism* (Oxford and New York: Oxford University Press, 1981), p. 207. In the same passage, he attacks as "purely selfish" and condescending even efforts to find aesthetic, non-utilitarian motives for preservation. Yet not only do we *survive* at least partially for "purely selfish reasons" (an observation he himself makes a few pages later), but the sense of awe before the immense beauty of nature is *precisely* what inspires preservationist thinking and an ecological ethic, that refuses, out of a partially "humanist" sensibility, to be reduced to a utilitarian science of energy bits and caloric counts.
35. Ibid., p. 208.
36. Homes Rolston, III, "Duties to Ecosystems," in *A Companion to A Sand County Almanac*, p. 268.
37. Ibid., pp. 269–70.
38. The most complete presentation of Bookchin's ideas is found in *The Ecology of Freedom* (Palo Alto: Cheshire Books, 1982; revised edition, Montréal: Black Rose Books, 1991).
39. J. Baird Callicott, "Traditional American Indian and Western European Attitudes Toward Nature: An Overview," in *In Defense of the Land Ethic: Essays in Environmental Philosophy* (Albany: State University of New York Press, 1989), p. 189. Here Callicott seems to be answering his own question, posed in his essay "On the Intrinsic Value of Nonhuman Species" (printed in both the Ryan Norton anthology and *In Defense of the Land Ethic*), "What are the ethical systems, and more generally, the world views in which claims of the intrinsic value of nonhuman species are embedded?"
40. Hans Peter Duerr, *Dreamtime: Concerning the Boundary Between Wilderness and Civilization* (Oxford and New York: Basil Blackwell, 1985), pp. 110–111.

41. Arne Naess, see note 10 above; also Naess and George Sessions, "Basic Principles of Deep Ecology," in Devall and Sessions, *Deep Ecology*, pp. 69–77.
42. Jamake Highwater, *The Primal Mind: Vision and Reality in Indian America* (New York: Meridian, 1981), pp. 77–78.
43. Jean Baudrillard, *The Mirror of Production* (St. Louis: Telos Press, 1975), p. 59.
44. Ibid.
45. Ibid., p. 61.
46. Ibid., p. 58.
47. Dorothy Lee, *Freedom and Culture* (New York: Prentice Hall/Spectrum, 1959), p. 72
48. Ibid., p. 73. It may be impossible to get entirely beyond this tension between need and necessity and the universe described by Baudrillard and suggested by Lee, Marshall Sahlins (*Stone Age Economics*) and others. On some level, "need" may be said to exist if people go hungry, and people went hungry during certain periods of the seasonal cycle in primal society. For the way in which such periods were integrated into the mythic and gift cycles by one group of native peoples, see the beautiful tales collected and translated by Howard Norman, *Where the Chill Came From: Cree Windigo Tales and Journeys* (San Francisco: North Point Press, 1982). Windigos, usually shown in the form of "a wandering giant with a heart of ice" (p. 4), are the cause of chaos and starvation during lean times. The Windigo is often thought of as the spirit of all those who have ever starved to death. Yet it is also a reflection of a disruption of the gift cycle in the community rather than a simple biological fact. Scarcity—a "law" imposed by bourgeois economic modes of thinking—does not *determine* the activities of the Cree, though it may certainly be argued that scarcity, and hence need, determine human action where the economic reigns. Thus it may be impossible to entirely escape the notion of defending our "interest" or acting to satisfy "need" even as we recognize the problematic, imposed character of these categories. In *Changes in the Land*, Cronon reports that the northern New England natives "accepted as a matter of course that the months of February and March, when the animals they hunted were lean and relatively scarce, would be times of little food." Europeans "had trouble comprehending this Indian willingness to go hungry in the late winter months" and their "apparent refusal to store more than a small amount of the summer's plenty for winter use." The natives replied, "It is all the same to us, we shall stand it well enough; we spend seven and eight days, even ten sometimes, without eating anything, yet we do not die." Ironically, native people "died from starvation much less frequently than did early colonists. . . ." Here we see the refusal of surplus, which is another way of saying the refusal of scarcity (pp. 40–41).
49. See J. Baird Callicott, "The Search for an Environmental Ethic," in *Matters of Life and Death: New Introductory Essays in Moral Philosophy* (New York: Random House, 1986).
50. Herbert Marcuse, *One Dimensional Man* (Boston: Beacon Press, 1966), p. ix.
51. Callicott, "On the Intrinsic Value of Nonhuman Species," p. 156. For Kropotkin, see Graham Purchase, "Kropotkin's Metaphysics of Nature," *Fifth Estate*, Vol. 26, No. 2 (337), Late Summer 1991.
52. Callicot, "On the Intrinsic Value of Non-human Species," pp. 156–58.
53. Rolston, in Callicot, *A Companion to A Sand County Almanac*, p. 264.
54. Ibid.

55. Ibid., pp. 264–65. Here the political terminology, even more than the natural resources terminology, reveals once more the limitations so far of environmental philosophy as radical critique.
56. Roszak, *Person/Planet,* p. 32.
57. Ibid., p. 273.